D1548434

MOVING TO MARKETS IN ENVIRONMENTAL REGULATION

MOVING TO MARKETS IN ENVIRONMENTAL REGULATION

Lessons from Twenty Years of Experience

Edited by
JODY FREEMAN *and* CHARLES D. KOLSTAD

2007

OXFORD
UNIVERSITY PRESS

Oxford University Press, Inc., publishes works that further
Oxford University's objective of excellence
in research, scholarship, and education.

Oxford   New York
Auckland   Cape Town   Dar es Salaam   Hong Kong   Karachi
Kuala Lumpur   Madrid   Melbourne   Mexico City   Nairobi
New Delhi   Shanghai   Taipei   Toronto

With offices in
Argentina   Austria   Brazil   Chile   Czech Republic   France   Greece
Guatemala Hungary   Italy   Japan   Poland   Portugal   Singapore
South Korea   Switzerland   Thailand   Turkey   Ukraine   Vietnam

Published by Oxford University Press, Inc.
198 Madison Avenue, New York, New York, 10016

www.oup.com

Oxford is a registered trademark of Oxford University Press

Library of Congress Cataloging-in-Publication Data

Moving to markets in environmental regulation: lessons from twenty years of experience/
edited by Jody Freeman and Charles D. Kolstad.
    p. cm.
Papers given at a one-day workshop in Santa Barbara, Calif. in 2003.
Includes bibliographical references and index.
ISBN-13 978-0-19-518965-0
ISBN 0-19-518965-5
    1. Environmental policy—Economic aspects.   2. Environmental protection—Economic
aspects.   3. Emissions trading.   4. Environmental impact charges.   5. Wetland mitigation
banking.   6. Environmental law.   I. Freeman, Jody.   II. Kolstad, Charles D.

HC79.E5M684 2006
333.72—dc22   2005049537

9 8 7 6 5 4 3 2 1

Printed in the United States of America
on acid-free paper

Preface

This book had its genesis in conversations that took place over a period of months in 2002, conversations that were helped along by fine Santa Barbara County wine. Our topic was environmental regulation—in particular the long-standing debate over command and control versus market-based environmental regulation—and our discussions made us wonder: How could two scholars—one of us an economist, the other a lawyer—be so concerned about the same problem yet have such different perspectives? The literatures we drew on seemed to have little in common, and our normative frameworks seemed like ships passing in the night. Were we typical? In what ways did economists think about these regulatory design issues differently than legal scholars? Beyond the differences in approach, what did each field actually *know*? Now that we had some experience with market-based regulations, what did the experience tell us? In particular, if we could draw on the most interesting and recent work in both fields, what would it tell us about how well market instruments had performed, relative to prescriptive regulation, to date? To answer these questions, we invited some of the brightest minds concerned with environmental regulation, from both economics and law, to prepare papers and convene for a focused one-day workshop in Santa Barbara in August 2003. Our hope was that the whole emerging from such a dialogue would be much more than the sum of the two disciplinary parts.

The result was quite remarkable. Over the course of the very long day, the intensity never waned. The conversation was relentlessly interesting and truly cross-disciplinary. There were fascinating moments of translation and synergy, agreement and disagreement. The interchange frequently surprised the group and led to questions and issues we had not anticipated. It worked to bring such different perspectives together. Many of us are accustomed to seeing the same friendly faces at conferences and gatherings, and although familiarity has its rewards, what provided energy at the Santa Barbara workshop was the commingling of two groups of scholars, many unknown to each other, who were not accustomed to being on the same bill. We hope we have captured some of the energy of that Santa Barbara meeting in the pages of this volume.

It has taken nearly two years to put together the final versions of the manuscripts prepared for the 2003 workshop. This is because each chapter was subjected to blind refereeing and because most went through several iterations. The result, we believe, is a very strong set of contributions that anyone interested in environmental regulation—from academics to policy makers to practitioners—should find extremely useful and enlightening.

This undertaking was made possible by grants and research support from the UCSB Bren Program in Environmental Law, the UCSB Bren Program in Environmental Economics and Policy, the Ralph and Goldy Lewis Center for Regional Policy Studies at UCLA, Resources for the Future, the Massachusetts Institute of Technology, and the UCSB Bren School of Environmental Science and Management. This book was conceived, and the conference held, while Jody Freeman was a professor at the UCLA School of Law. We thank the Law School for its generous support. Harvard Law School provided research support during the book's completion. Magali Delmas (UCSB) and J. R. DeShazo (UCLA) provided insights as discussants at the workshop. Theresa Benevento and B. J. Danetra deserve thanks for their wonderful help in organizing the Santa Barbara workshop. Andrew Lom provided excellent research assistance.

As always, we thank our partners and families for their good-natured interest and support.

Contents

Part III: Political and Legal Dynamics

Contributors

Jody Freeman
Professor of Law, Harvard University; Director, Harvard Law School Environmental Law Program
Professor Freeman specializes in administrative law, environmental law and policy, natural resources law and policy, regulatory design, and governance.

Charles D. Kolstad
Professor of Economics and Environmental Science and Management, University of California, Santa Barbara; University Fellow, Resources for the Future
A former president of the Association of Environmental and Resource Economists, Professor Kolstad works in the area of environmental regulation, particularly the role of information in environmental decision making and regulation.

David M. Driesen
Angela R. Cooney Professor of Law, Syracuse University
Professor Driesen teaches environmental law, domestic and international, and constitutional law.

A. Denny Ellerman
Senior Lecturer, Sloan School of Management, MIT; Executive Director, MIT Center for Energy and Environmental Policy Research
Professor Ellerman specializes in emissions trading, climate policy, and economics of fuel choice, especially concerning coal and natural gas.

Daniel A. Farber

Sato Sho Professor of Law, University of California, Berkeley; Faculty Director, California Center for Environmental Law and Policy
Professor Farber specializes in environmental law, constitutional law, and legislation.

Hongli Feng

Associate Scientist, Center for Agricultural and Rural Development, University of Iowa
Dr. Feng is an environmental economist who has studied the optimal design of carbon sequestration strategies, emission banking, and carbon markets.

Michael B. Gerrard

Partner and Head of Environmental Practice, Arnold and Porter, LLP, New York
Mr. Gerrard has practiced environmental law in New York since 1979 and has tried numerous cases in federal and state courts and administrative tribunals, and handled the environmental aspects of many transactions and development projects.

Winston Harrington

Senior Fellow, Resources for the Future
Dr. Harrington's research interests include urban transportation, motor vehicles and air quality, and problems of estimating the costs of environmental policy.

Jason Scott Johnston

Robert G. Fuller Jr. Professor of Law; Director, Program on Law and the Environment, University of Pennsylvania Law School
Professor Johnston's fields of expertise include contracts, environmental law, law and economics, and natural resources law and policy.

Nathaniel Keohane

Assistant Professor of Economics, Yale School of Management
Professor Keohane's research focuses on the optimal design and economic performance of environmental regulations and on the political economy of environmental policy.

Catherine Kling

Resource and Environmental Policy Division Head in the Center for Agricultural and Rural Development and Professor of Economics, Iowa State University
Professor Kling's fields of interest include natural resources and environmental economics.

Lyubov Kurkalova

Associate Scientist, Center for Agricultural and Rural Development, University of Iowa
Dr. Kurkalova's current research focuses on energy and agriculture, particularly related to alternative energy production and its environmental impacts.

Peter S. Menell

Professor of Law, University of California, Berkeley; Cofounder and Director, Berkeley Center for Law and Technology

Professor Menell writes in the areas of environmental law, property, and intellectual property, focusing on the interplay of resources, technology, and public policy., regulatory economics, and environmental economics and policy.

Juan-Pablo Montero

Associate Professor of Economics, Pontificia Universidad Católica de Chile; Research Associate, Center for Energy and Environmental Policy Research, MIT

Professor Montero's research interests include applied microeconomics, industrial organizations, regulatory economics, and environmental economics and policy.

Richard D. Morgenstern

Senior Fellow, Resources for the Future

Dr. Morgenstern's research focuses on the economic analysis of environmental issues with an emphasis on the costs, benefits, evaluation, and design of environmental policies, especially economic incentive measures.

Richard G. Newell

Senior Fellow, Resources for the Future

Dr. Newell's research focuses on economic analysis of environmental and resource policy design and performance, with an emphasis on technological change and incentive-based policy.

Kristian Rogers

Research Assistant, Federal Reserve Board

Mr. Rogers works for the Federal Reserve Board's International Finance Division.

J. B. Ruhl

Matthews and Hawkins Professor of Property, Florida State University College of Law

Professor Ruhl is an expert in endangered species protection, wetlands regulation, and ecosystem management. He teaches environmental, land use, and property law.

James Salzman

Professor of Law and Nicholas Institute Professor of Environmental Policy, Duke University

Professor Salzman specializes in environmental law and policy and management of natural resources.

Silvia Secchi

Associate Scientist, Center for Agricultural and Rural Development, University of Iowa

Dr. Secchi's work in environmental and agricultural economics has focused on antibiotic resistance and water quality problems, particularly related to agricultural practices.

Kathleen Segerson

Professor of Economics, University of Connecticut

Professor Segerson's fields of specialization include environmental and natural resource economics, law and economics, and applied microeconomics.

Robert Stavins

Albert Pratt Professor of Business and Government, John F. Kennedy School of Government, Director of the Environmental Economics Program, Harvard University; University Fellow, Resources for the Future

Professor Stavins's research has examined diverse areas of environmental economics and policy and has appeared in a variety of economics, law, and policy journals, plus several books.

Tom Tietenberg

Mitchell Family Professor of Economics, Colby College

A former president of the Association of Environmental and Resource Economists, Professor Tietenberg specializes in the design, implementation, and evaluation of tradable permit markets.

MOVING TO MARKETS IN ENVIRONMENTAL REGULATION

1

Prescriptive Environmental Regulations versus Market-Based Incentives

Jody Freeman & Charles D. Kolstad

When market strategies first emerged on the environmental policy scene over twenty years ago,[1] there was a lively theoretical debate about their perceived advantages over traditional prescriptive regulation. The traditional approach—dubbed by its critics "command-and-control"—was seen as costly, cumbersome, and ineffective. Market approaches, by contrast, would enable government to accomplish its regulatory goals in a more efficient manner. Not only would market instruments be easier and cheaper to administer than prescriptive regulation, they would harness the profit motive in the service of environmental protection and dramatically reduce implementation costs. In addition, it was widely thought, market mechanisms would spur technological innovation, whereas command-and-control would freeze technology in place.

This collection of chapters asks whether, after over twenty years of experience, the promise of market mechanisms has been realized. How, in hindsight, do market-based approaches compare to command-and-control? What have we learned that might help us design the next generation of regulatory instruments for environmental protection? In an effort to provide a balanced discussion of these questions, the contributions are written by scholars from both economics and law, fields that sometimes have different perspectives on the effectiveness of environmental regulations. At the risk of oversimplifying, economists are often concerned with efficiency; legal scholars are often concerned with procedure and equity.

Why does evaluating the performance of market instruments matter, and why do it now? Historically, most of the arguments in favor of market mechanisms have been based on theory. Now that we have some empirical evidence of their performance, it is important to test that theory against experience in practice. Furthermore, a retrospective analysis of both the available empirical evidence and the relevant theoretical arguments is timely in light of recent moves to adopt market tools more often and in new contexts. For example, the U.S. Environmental Protection Agency (EPA) has adopted by rule (and the courts have upheld) an emissions trading program that seeks to reduce the migration of ozone precursors from the upwind states of the Midwest and South to the downwind states of the Northeast.[2] Much of the international community has signed the Kyoto Protocol (the United States and Australia being conspicuous exceptions), a treaty with a number of "flexibility" mechanisms that have a distinctly market flavor. Furthermore, the European Union (EU) has introduced a very significant carbon market as part of its implementation of the Kyoto Protocol.[3] The U.S. Army Corps of Engineers has adopted a wetlands mitigation banking program as a means of achieving its "no net loss" policy when issuing permits to fill wetlands (see chapter 12). And there is no shortage of proposals for adopting still more market-based instruments. In its Clear Skies initiative, the second Bush administration proposed to amend the Clean Air Act to introduce a market trading scheme for a variety of air pollutants, including nitrogen oxides and mercury.[4] There have also been proposals for watershed-based effluent trading to help control the deleterious effects of non–point source runoff into waterways.[5] Although the second Bush administration withdrew from the Kyoto Protocol, if the United States ultimately does pass a domestic statute regulating the greenhouse gases that contribute to global warming, it seems probable that the regime will rely on a market-based approach.[6] In the meantime, state and regional efforts to address greenhouse gas emissions through trading schemes are proliferating.[7]

Lessons gleaned from experience to date might be instructive for these newly adopted and recently proposed applications. What we learn might also point to limitations or disadvantages associated with market instruments—limitations that might have been hard to see initially, before these instruments were deployed. In short, a critical retrospective analysis of how market-based instruments have fared can help us design the next generation of regulatory tools.

Such an analysis might also yield a more accurate picture of command-and-control regulation. Over the past two decades, the superiority of market-based instruments has developed into a virtual orthodoxy. As Denny Ellerman points out in chapter 3, the widespread adoption of the command-and-control moniker represents a semantic triumph for advocates of market mechanisms. Indeed, market-based instruments have gone from being anathema to being "close to politically correct" says Rob Stavins in chapter 2. As a result, defenders of prescriptive regulation have found themselves increasingly on the defensive, even though health-based and technology-based standard setting still dominate the environmental field. Market-based instruments have not only survived claims that they are immoral because they create "rights" to pollute; they have gone on to capture the high ground in policy debates. Indeed, the presumption seems to have shifted toward using market instruments unless one can show they are somehow deficient.

Consider the example of emissions trading—the most common form of market mechanism to have been adopted in environmental regulation thus far. The theory behind emissions trading is that allowing firms to buy and sell pollution rights will achieve a desired level of pollution reduction more efficiently than a prescriptive standard that applies equally to all firms because tradable pollution rights implicitly take account of marginal cost. Trading allows firms for which emissions reductions are relatively inexpensive to cut their emissions and sell their excess credits to firms for which such reductions would be more costly. This presumably achieves the ultimate regulatory target (which government still establishes) at the lowest cost.

In contrast, prescriptive regulation—our preferred terminology instead of command-and-control—is thought to generally prescribe the nature of abatement for firms within an industry. Such an approach, the argument goes, raises costs because of the lack of a mechanism for equalizing marginal costs among sources. Uniform regulation is widely thought to freeze technology because it encourages the adoption of the particular technologies chosen by the regulator to establish the standard, regardless of the peculiarities of different production processes. And firms required to reduce to the same level have no incentive to go further.

Prescriptive regulation also attracts criticism because it can result in substantial implementation costs. First, the administrative apparatus necessary to promulgate, implement, and oversee regulation is cumbersome and costly. For example, the rule-making process for setting air and water standards tends to be slow and conflict-ridden. This makes it difficult to respond to rapid changes in technology or new information. Second, firms can be expected to resist regulation, which makes implementation and enforcement a struggle. Much of the information most relevant to prescriptive regulators is in the hands of industry, which has little incentive for full revelation of control costs and other pertinent data. This adversarial relationship between regulators and regulated entities leads to protracted legal proceedings that are costly for both sides.

This collection of essays takes a critical look at the debate just encapsulated. Are market mechanisms superior to prescriptive regulation? How should we evaluate such a claim, and using which criteria? Are the two approaches really as different as some assume? After more than twenty years of experience, what do we know, and what new questions ought to be studied? What does the evidence tell us?

Many of the chapters in this volume evaluate specific market mechanisms. Some explicitly compare their performance to command-and-control instruments, and others explore legal and political dynamics that are often overlooked in the debate over market and prescriptive tools. The examples in the collection include a broad range of market instruments used in different contexts, including a variety of tradable permit schemes: in air pollution regulation, fisheries management, and wetlands mitigation as well as pay-as-you-throw pricing systems for municipal waste, and information disclosure requirements in hazardous waste regulation. Some of the examples test the boundaries of what has traditionally been considered a market-based instrument, inviting questions about the appropriate scope of the category. For example, chapter 9 examines the relative effectiveness of subsidies to promote agricultural land preservation. Chapter 10 explores the potential of legal liability schemes like the Comprehensive Environmental Response, Compensation, and Liability Act (CERCLA—the federal statute creating retroactive strict, joint, and several liability for hazardous waste contamination) to incentivize hazardous waste cleanups.

Our approach to the question of scope is deliberately inclusive. The chapters span a continuum of measures that are arguably market-based in that they rely primarily on the use of economic incentives to induce compliance with environmental goals while eschewing mandatory pre-defined actions set at the firm level. Yet many of the instruments included here differ significantly from the paradigmatic and familiar example of tradable emissions permits, just as they differ in important respects from each other. Even so, the volume's breadth has its advantages. First, it provides a diverse set of examples across which to make comparisons and from which to draw conclusions. Second, it reflects the recent migration of market mechanisms from the air pollution context into new areas over time and tracks the challenges that this migration poses. Finally, it illustrates how, in practice, regulatory instruments can fail to fit perfectly within either the category of prescriptive regulation or the category of market instrument. Indeed, many instruments are hybrids, and the differences among them seem to be more a matter of difference in degree than in kind.

In conceiving this project we sought to bring together leading economists and legal scholars because, although the two disciplines regularly grapple with matters of regulatory design, they tend to adopt different normative commitments and perspectives. Though there are notable exceptions, economists generally support market mechanisms, whereas lawyers and legal scholars, at least historically, have tended to be somewhat skeptical of them. Generally, too, economists and legal scholars naturally gravitate toward different dimensions of the debate over regulatory tools. For example, economists traditionally focus on the potential for market mechanisms to generate cost savings, whereas legal scholars tend to focus more on procedural regularity and fairness in instrument design, as well as how tool selection might affect the balance of power among the different institutions of government, such as the courts and the executive branch. Economists worry about front-end design issues that affect efficiency, including the point of regulation, the system of allocating entitlements, and the cost of implementation. Lawyers translate these choices into statutes and regulations but traditionally spend most of their energy on the back-end struggles over liability and compliance that frequently lead to legal challenges.

Combining the two perspectives in the same volume has produced some important lessons and strong cross-cutting themes. First, comparisons between market instruments and prescriptive regulation must be fair to be meaningful. Though it seems obvious, this is frequently overlooked. For example, it would be misleading to compare a flawed existing emissions trading regime with an idealized version of a hypothetical prescriptive regime and vice versa. Making fair comparisons is challenging because, among other problems, there has been relatively little ex post evaluation of prescriptive instruments. Even when relevant data exist, studies can suffer from a variety of methodological problems ranging from definitional inconsistencies (in terms of the instruments and variables under study) to the choice of counterfactual or baselines, to questions about whether the examples chosen are representative enough to be useful.

A second lesson is that both market-based instruments and prescriptive regulation suffer from many of the same weaknesses, including a pervasive lack of monitoring and enforcement, which can severely compromise their effectiveness and limit our ability to evaluate their performance. With both kinds of instruments, moreover, policy makers sometimes fail to pay sufficient attention to the details of the context in which the tool will be deployed, leading to significant design flaws. In other words, context affects instrument performance, regardless of the tool selected. As a result, one can find examples of well-designed and effectively implemented market-based regulation just as one can find cases of badly designed and poorly implemented market-based regulation, and the same is true of prescriptive regulation. In short, design matters.

Third, it is important when evaluating market mechanisms to ask not only whether they offer cost savings but also whether and to what extent they accomplish the regulatory purpose for which they are designed. In other words, policy makers ought to pay attention to *benefits* in the form of environmental performance, not just *costs*. Finally, most regulatory contexts involve hybrid approaches in which both kinds of instruments work together. For example, an emissions trading program typically operates against the background of an otherwise highly prescriptive air pollution regime, as with the Clean Air Act's sulfur dioxide trading program. Moreover, these policy instruments can evolve dynamically. It appears common, for example, for prescriptive approaches to develop features of market instruments over time.

Part I of this volume (chapters 2–5) creates a foundation for the other chapters by exploring definitional and methodological questions and by establishing themes that carry through the rest of the collection. In chapter 2, Robert Stavins traces the history of market mechanisms and describes their theoretical advantages over prescriptive regulation. Stavins gives an overview of the lessons learned about market instruments thus far, among them that there is an ongoing need for both flexibility and simplicity and for more effective monitoring and enforcement. He also points out that there remain important limitations to the success of market instruments, including that firms are not yet well equipped to fully utilize them. He concludes with predictions about the conditions under which such instruments are most likely to succeed.

In chapter 3, A. Denny Ellerman explains why cap-and-trade programs (in which government establishes an overall cap on pollution but allows firms to trade allocations beneath the cap) can be both more economically efficient and more environmentally effective than prescriptive regulation. The chapter underscores the importance of measuring effectiveness in ex post evaluations, which Ellerman defines as achieving the proximate goal (i.e., of emissions reduction), rather than the larger goal of solving the underlying problem (i.e., unhealthy air). Ellerman supports his argument in favor of market instruments with data from three emissions trading programs: the SO_2 trading regime in Title IV of the Clean Air Act, the NO_x budget program created by the EPA to address interstate ozone migration, and the RECLAIM program created by the South Coast Air Quality Management District in Southern California. He suggests that market instruments represent a new pragmatism in environmental regulation and that they are part of the maturation of the regulatory process.

In chapter 4, Tom Tietenberg reviews data on tradable permit systems in a variety of different contexts, including air pollution regulation, water supply, fisheries management, grazing rights allocation, water quality, and wetlands preservation. He evaluates these programs against three criteria: implementation feasibility, environmental effectiveness, and economic effectiveness. Tietenberg's analysis makes clear that the particular characteristics of these different regimes affect the evaluation of their performance. Beyond reporting substantive results for each program, the chapter offers insight into the methodological difficulties of ex post evaluations generally. For example, not all studies define economic efficiency or environmental effectiveness in the same way, and studies vary in their choice of comparative benchmark or counterfactual, which can significantly affect results. Ex post evaluations differ as well in terms of both scope (i.e., which outcomes are considered exogenous and which endogenous) and timing (i.e., the point in the life of the program when the evaluation is done). All of these choices can influence the resulting interpretations.

In chapter 5, Winston Harrington and Richard Morgenstern provide a paradigmatic example of the kind of retrospective analysis we had in mind when conceiving this book: the explicit comparison of the actual performance of prescriptive versus market-based regulation for six different environmental problems. The chapter has the added benefit of using examples from both the United States and the European Union. To the extent possible, for each problem the authors studied, they compared a prescriptive approach from one side of the Atlantic with a market instrument from the other side. The chapter echoes Tietenberg's points about the methodological difficulties facing ex ante evaluations by noting that their own study might be faulted for selection bias, small numbers, and the use of exceptional rather than representative examples. The authors test twelve often asserted hypotheses about the comparison between prescriptive regulation and economic instruments, including, among others, that economic instruments are more efficient, require less information, reduce burdens on regulated entities, and have lower administrative costs. Evidence from the case studies suggests that the competition between the two types of instruments ends in a dead heat. Yet because economic instruments tend to bear out what the authors view as the more important hypotheses—about their greater static and dynamic efficiency, their relative effectiveness, and potentially lower regulatory burden—the authors argue that the evidence supports their continued use.

Part II (chapters 6–12) consists of chapters that rely on empirical data, theoretical models, or both, to evaluate a variety of particular instruments, beginning with emissions trading and then moving to other contexts (such as wetlands) and other market instruments (such as subsidies, pricing, liability, and information disclosure). These chapters make clear that a broad range of market instruments are currently in use and that their success depends heavily on both the care with which they are designed and the context in which they are deployed.

In chapter 6, Juan-Pablo Montero evaluates whether tradable emission permits might have advantages over prescriptive emission standards not only for large easily monitored sources but also in cases where monitoring is more difficult and the regulator has incomplete information—cases where one might expect a permit system to result in higher emissions. Montero builds a theoretical model comparing the welfare difference between two optimally designed regulatory systems, one involving tradable permits and one involving prescriptive emission standards. He then applies the model to data from an existing particulate emissions trading program in Santiago, Chile. Although he concludes that in some cases prescriptive regulations actually perform better than market instruments, market-based instruments ought to be the default regulatory tool even in contexts where the regulator has imperfect information on firms' emissions and costs. It may also be desirable, however, to supplement such instruments with some use of prescriptive standards.

In chapter 7, Richard Newell and Kristian Rogers use the case study of the phase-down of lead gasoline in the United States to argue that market-based instruments can be effective in meeting environmental objectives at a lower cost than uniform standards, and can do so more quickly where permit banking is allowed. They assess the performance of the lead phase-down program along several dimensions, including its overall effectiveness, static and dynamic efficiency, revelation of costs, and distributional effects. The authors claim that the program likely saved hundreds of millions of dollars over policies that would not have allowed trading and banking and that it also provided incentives for the development of new technology. The chapter recounts one of the success stories of market-based regulation in the United States, but it also reinforces two lessons— one methodological and one substantive—that appear in earlier chapters. First, a retrospective case study cannot definitively demonstrate the superiority of a market approach because the counterfactual (e.g., of a purely prescriptive lead phasedown program) simply did not occur. Second, the market-based approach in this example worked in tandem with a prescriptive mandate. As the authors point out, the lead phasedown relied on both a tradable permit system and a mandated transition to new vehicle fleets that required cars equipped with catalytic converters to use unleaded fuel.

In chapter 8, Nat Keohane takes a close look at one of the most significant market-based incentives, the sulfur allowance system, adopted in the Clean Air Act amendments of 1990. His starting point is two previous studies, one finding that the allowance system resulted in higher abatement costs than an alternative prescriptive regulation, the other study finding the opposite. Keohane builds a statistical model based on actual utility abatement choice during the first phase of the allowance system. Dividing prescriptive regulations into two classes, performance standards and technology standards, he finds that the allowance system only modestly outperforms performance standards on either cost or abatement criteria (by about 10 percent). However, he also finds that the tradable allowance system very significantly outperforms technology standards. The strength of the analysis is its reliance on actual data on electric utility choice to calculate abatement costs under both the market-based instruments and the counterfactual of prescriptive regulations.

In chapter 9, Hongli Feng, Cathy Kling, Lyubov Kurkalova, and Silvia Secchi compare market-based and prescriptive approaches to agricultural land preservation. The authors treat the Conservation Reserve Program (CRP) administered by the U.S. Department of Agriculture as a market-based instrument because program participants respond to a price signal in the form of payments for retiring land from production. While noting the potential inefficiencies of subsidies as a policy instrument, the authors nevertheless seek to evaluate the CRP relative to the command-and-control alternatives. They compare the CRP as it has been implemented first with an optimal theoretical CRP and then to two kinds of hypothetical prescriptive regimes, one "strict" and one "enlightened." In terms of overall environmental benefits, the data produce no clear winner between the actual CRP and the optimal market instrument. Compared to the strict command-and-control option, the CRP performed less well. Compared to the enlightened prescriptive regime (which seeks to enroll in the program those land parcels with the highest environmental benefits), market instruments perform about the same.

In chapter 10 Kathleen Segerson analyzes the existing empirical literature on the effectiveness of legal liability as an incentive-based instrument for environmental protection. Segerson treats the statutory requirement that certain risks be covered by strict liability (as opposed to negligence) as a policy tool akin to a pricing mechanism because it forces polluters to internalize the cost of pollution. The chapter explains why, in theory, a strict liability regime such as that embodied in CERCLA can provide efficient deterrence incentives under ideal conditions. Even under less than ideal conditions, the data suggest that strict liability may still be better than an alternative regime. The chapter illustrates the challenges of trying to assess the effectiveness of liability schemes: It is difficult to measure empirically their effects on polluter behavior because of so many potentially confounding variables, and hard to directly link a measure of liability to a measure of environmental performance. Nevertheless, the literature suggests that strict liability can function like a market-based incentive and deter polluters from risky behavior under specific conditions, including where liability is prospective rather than retroactive and where damage is known shortly after it occurs. Interestingly, CERCLA itself does not fit these criteria, which suggests that the law as currently drafted may be less than ideal as a deterrent.

In chapter 11, Peter Menell explores the potential for pricing mechanisms to help internalize the costs and benefits of municipal solid waste management. He provides a comprehensive history of the development of variable rate pricing strategies in the United States and explains the challenges involved in moving from conventional municipal solid waste regulation to such pay-as-you-throw systems. After reviewing the empirical studies on the effects of variable rate pricing policies, Menell argues that they have proven to be successful at increasing waste diversion from landfills. Although the net economic impact of variable approaches is still unclear (because of operational costs and adverse impacts), many cities have adopted them and seen their total cost of waste disposal decline.

In chapter 12, James Salzman and J. B. Ruhl evaluate wetlands mitigation banking (WMB) as a tool for accomplishing the policy of no net loss of the nation's wetlands. The history of wetlands protection has evolved from on-site mitigation to banking and off-site mitigation, allowing Salzman and Ruhl to evaluate the shift from a prescriptive to a market approach. The discussion focuses on the three main limitations of WMB design: ensuring meaningful compliance monitoring, currency adequacy, and exchange adequacy. In the watershed context, a trading and banking regime raises problems of incommensurability and nonfungibility because different wetlands may have very different values. This is an excellent example of why, for market instruments, context matters. Salzman and Ruhl also make the useful point that when evaluating regulatory instruments, it is important to distinguish between two kinds of problems: a failure of instrument design and a failure of implementation. One or both types of failure can occur with either market or prescriptive regulation. Salzman and Ruhl also underscore the need to clarify definitions of success when evaluating the performance of market instruments.

Chapters 12–16 (part III) explore how market instruments can affect political and legal dynamics—how, for example, a market trading scheme might alter the typical negotiations between a regulated firm and government agency and how the move to market mechanisms might empower the federal government to regulate even more aggressively than the law currently allows. These political and legal implications are rarely discussed alongside economic implications of market measures. In addition, this section contains a chapter proposing a new market instrument to induce compliance with environmental laws and a chapter challenging the notion that market mechanisms promote technological innovation.

In chapter 13, Jason Scott Johnston pursues an underexplored aspect of the literature on tradable permit regimes by asking which among polluting firms are the likely winners and losers in the shift from a prescriptive approach to a market trading scheme and under which conditions will firms support such a shift? Johnston argues that one of the reasons the literature overlooks such questions is that analysts tend to use an overly simplified and unrealistic notion of command-and-control regulation. As Johnston explains, although in some instances government regulations dictate to firms the particular technologies they must adopt, most prescriptive regulation consists of performance standards that firms may meet any way they choose. So-called command-and-control regulation always relies to some extent on adjustments in light of economic realities, both in the initial phase of level setting when the regulatory agency takes account of industrial processes and capacities in choosing the standard and later, when agencies negotiate particular permits. There is, moreover, considerable flexibility in the enforcement process, when agencies must determine whether firms are out of compliance and what must be done in response. Johnston drives home an important theme in this collection: the legal and bureaucratic realities of implementation must be considered in any evaluation of instrument effectiveness.

Johnston then develops a formal model to discern winners and losers in a hypothetical transition to a tradable permit regime. He compares the equilibrium distribution of firm costs (under various versions of prescriptive regulation, including an ideal version in which firms can minimize their costs of compliance) to firm net costs under a tradable permit regime. The result? Proposals to move to tradable permits may often make both low- and high compliance cost firms better off relative to an ideal version of prescriptive regulation, but such a shift is likely to make high compliance cost firms (i.e., permit buyers) worse off relative to a more realistic version of prescriptive regulation. The analysis also explains why polluters sometimes support tradable permit regimes and why they sometimes do not.

In chapter 14, Daniel Farber suggests that quite apart from the efficiency benefits claimed by economists, market systems may also have unexpected legal benefits. Environmental trading systems may offer opportunities to governments to leverage their constitutional authority in areas where they already possess legal authority and gain influence in areas where they do not. As a result, an indirect benefit of the move to market mechanisms may be their potential to provide a partial antidote to the intensification of constitutional restrictions on the government's regulatory power. For example, the U.S. Supreme Court has made clear that some permit denials to fill wetlands may amount to "takings" of private property, which require compensation. The Court has also held that some wetlands are insufficiently connected to navigable waters to be within the federal government's power to regulate interstate commerce, an issue that was recently litigated in the Supreme Court. Farber explains how market mechanisms might help the government continue to regulate despite these restrictions, which may grow tighter still. For example, the government might allow the banking of isolated wetlands over which it lacks jurisdiction in exchange for granting permits to fill wetlands over which it does have jurisdiction. Similarly, the government could reduce its exposure to constitutional takings liability by demanding mitigation in exchange for granting a permit approving development, or could offer tradable development rights to developers in exchange for prohibiting a proposed use of land. In each situation, with the help of market mechanisms, the government extends its regulatory power to a domain or issue that it otherwise could not reach.

In chapter 15, Michael Gerrard proposes an information disclosure mechanism as a means of encouraging firms to comply with a variety of environmental laws. Gerrard argues that requiring environmental studies at the moment of property transfer could incentivize compliance more than the traditional prescriptive approach. Gerrard treats such disclosure requirements as market-based instruments because they take the characteristics of the property market into account when adjusting incentives, inducing buyers and sellers to move toward compliance when it is in their economic interest to do so, rather than in response to a legal mandate. The chapter provides an overview of CERCLA's liability scheme, noting that it has led to tremendously improved practices for the generation, handling, and cleanup of hazardous waste and that it has also established a precedent for imposing requirements on buyers and sellers at the moment of property transfer. (With his concrete legal perspective, Gerrard provides an interesting contrast to the more theoretical economic discussion of CERCLA and other liability schemes in chapter 10.) Gerrard's proposal to expand the scope of such requirements builds on experience with CERCLA and a number of other laws that have shown that imposing restrictions or liabilities on property transactions can be extremely powerful. Such instruments could have even more beneficial effects on environmental compliance than the direct regulation of hazardous waste management through prescriptive (but ultimately limited) regulatory statutes that have the reduction of hazardous waste as their explicit purpose but that are only incompletely and unevenly enforced.

In the final chapter in the volume, David Driesen challenges the view that market mechanisms spur greater technological innovation than does prescriptive regulation. He argues that the empirical record for such a claim is not persuasive. In fact, he argues, in some cases emissions trading and prescriptive regulation have encouraged innovation, and in some cases they have not. Driesen also provides a theoretical argument for why trading will do a poorer job of encouraging expensive—and especially valuable—innovation than prescriptive regulation.

Some of the chapters in this collection support the argument that market instruments can be both more efficient and more effective than prescriptive regulation. In particular, trading schemes appear to have worked relatively well in the context of air pollution regulation. Other articles suggest that at least some of the criticisms of command-and-control are overstated or miss the mark. Indeed, prescriptive regulation is not as uniform and inflexible as critics often suggest. It is no exaggeration to say that the so-called command-and-control system is infused with negotiation and accommodation.

Other chapters in the collection make clear that both market and prescriptive approaches share some of the same weaknesses. For example, just as prescriptive regulation runs into obstacles in the implementation and enforcement stage, so do market mechanisms. Indeed, the challenge of designing market mechanisms can be just as great (and in some instances greater) than the challenge facing regulators who must establish and implement prescriptive standards. Some of these design problems can be acute. Markets can be too narrowly or too broadly drawn. Political considerations may dominate the initial allocation of entitlements in market trading schemes, which, though often necessary to generate political support for the adoption of the regulatory program, can undermine their purported efficiency.[8]

Trading schemes can falter because of difficulties in both valuing environmental commodities and ensuring that trades involve commensurate goods. For this reason, it may be especially challenging to devise market approaches to natural resource management as compared to pollution control, because natural resources like ecosystems perform functions that may be enormously difficult to value and trade. They raise problems of incommensurability and nonfungibility that may not arise in the context or air or water quality regulation. Markets can also create hot spots of concentrated pollution, which can disproportionately affect subpopulations, leading to claims of distributional inequity.[9] Conceivably market tools can be modified to address some of these problems, but in some instances prescriptive regulation may still be necessary because market mechanisms are too risky or unworkable.

This volume makes a useful start in exploring the available evidence and current thinking about the performance of market instruments, but perhaps its most important lesson is that we still know relatively little about them. Though we have some evidence of significant cost savings in emissions trading regimes, we know much less about how effective (in terms of measurable environmental benefits) and fair (in terms of distributional burdens) they are. And whether market-based instruments will stimulate technological innovation, as is often claimed, remains still, mostly a matter of speculation. We know much less, too, about market-based instruments other than emissions trading. There is little evidence, for example, about how well wetlands mitigation banking has performed, partly because there are almost no incentives for monitoring and record-keeping. As for direct comparisons between market instruments and prescriptive regulation, there is still a relative a dearth of empirical work in this vein. The studies that do exist are laudable and informative, yet their methodological limitations caution against strong conclusions.

Some of the biggest success stories of market-based instruments involve, on closer examination, a mix of prescriptive and market instruments, as with the phasing out of leaded gasoline in the United States. Some success stories—those from Europe, for example—may be due more to aspects of the background regulatory regime or political culture than to instrument choice, as Harrington and Morgenstern point out. Without proper controls then, it may be difficult to conclude that market-based instruments are the real reason for a given policy success.

We hope that this volume begins a new generation of research on a broad range of regulatory instruments—market-based, prescriptive, and hybrid—and that scholars will attempt to overcome some of the lingering methodological and analytic challenges identified in these chapters. As nations look to cap-and-trade instruments to address the most serious global environmental challenge we face—climate change—the need for this research becomes all the more pressing. Whether market mechanisms work well, or well enough relative to prescriptive regulation to displace the latter as the primary tool of environmental regulation depends on a number of factors, some of which are easier to predict and control than others. Some of the determinants of the success of market instruments include the sophistication of the market participants; the size and diversity of the market; the vulnerability of the environmental "good" or "service" to accurate valuation; the vulnerability of the regime to political rigging; legal and bureaucratic obstacles to effective implementation; and the potential for gaming, shirking, and cheating by regulated entities, among other things. More likely, we think, the two approaches will continue to be used in tandem, evolving over time in a dynamic way— sometimes taking on features of each other—and the ongoing challenge will be to carefully design and tailor the right mix of instruments to particular contexts. Meeting this challenge will require economists and legal scholars to continue the dialogue begun here.

NOTES

1. Market incentives for environmental protection were only a theoretical curiosity in the 1960s economics literature. However, the 1970s saw some limited

experiments with incentives in the regulatory process. *See* Robert W. Hahn and Gordon L. Hester, *Marketable Permits: Lessons for Theory and Practice*, 16 Ecology Law Quarterly 361 (1989).

2. *See Appalachian Power v. U.S.*, 249 F.3d 1032, 1036 (D.C. Cir. 2001).

3. Although the Bush administration withdrew from Kyoto in 2001, the treaty went into effect for signatories early in 2005. Despite the lack of U.S. federal action on reducing greenhouse gases, a number of states have been very proactive, including California, which has instituted greenhouse gas emission standards for automobiles produced in 2009 and beyond. *See* Charles D. Kolstad, *Climate Change Policy from the U.S. and the Role of Intensity Targets*, in Emissions Trading for Climate Policy (Bernd Hanjürgens, ed., 2005, Cambridge University Press, New York).

4. Clear Skies Act of 2003, H.R. 999, 108th Cong. § 403 (2003); Clear Skies Act of 2003, S. 485, 108th Cong. § 403 (2003). Though the legislation did not pass, the administration sought to implement much of it through administrative rule making.

5. *See* Office of Water, U.S. Envtl. Protection Agency, Draft Framework for Watershed-Based *Trading* (May 1996), available at www.epa.gov/owow/water shed/framwork.pdf; Office of Water, U.S. Envtl. Protection Agency, Final Water Quality Trading Policy (Jan. 13, 2003), available at www.epa.gov/owow/ watershed/trading/finalpolicy2003.pdf; Andrew M. Wolman, *Effluent Trading in the United States and Australia*, 8 Great Plains Natural Resources Journal 1, 21 (2003) (listing contemporary effluent trading programs in Australia and the United States).

6. *See* Clean Power Act of 2003, S. 366, 108th Cong. (2003) (an alternative bill to Clear Skies, sponsored by Sen. Jeffords, including a cap-and-trade program for carbon). *See also* Climate Stewardship Act of 2003, S. 139, 108th Cong. (2003) (sponsored and cosponsored, respectively, by Sen. Lieberman and Sen. McCain). In 2006, Senate Energy and Natural Resources chair Republican Pete Domenici and ranking Democrat Jeff Bingaman issued a white paper called, "Design Elements of a Mandatory Market-Based Greenhouse Gas Regulatory System," posing questions about how to design a domestic GHG statute and later held hearings to explore the issue. For a summary of the white paper, see www.pewclimate.org/ policy_center/analyses/sec/index.cfm.

7. Under the Regional Greenhouse Gas Initiative (RGGI), as of 2006, eight northeast states signed a memorandum of agreement to reduce greenhouse gas emissions from power plants by 10% from current levels by 2019. The states have pledged to use a cap-and-trade program modeled on the U.S. acid rain program. For a description of RGGI and other subnational climate initiatives, *see* Pew Center on Global Climate Change, Learning from State Action on Climate Change (March 2006 Update), available at www.pewclimate.org/policy_center/policy_reports_ and_analysis/state/index.cfm. The design challenges facing the states are significant, and the potential legal obstacles (including federal pre-emption and constitutional bars under the Commerce Clause) are considerable.

8. Lisa Heinzerling, *Selling Pollution, Forcing Democracy*, 14 Stanford Environmental Law Journal 300 (1995).

9. *See* Stephen M. Johnson, *Economics v. Equity: Do Market-Based Environmental Reforms Exacerbate Environmental Injustice?*, 56 Washington and Lee Law Review 111, 129–30 (1999); Alice Kaswan, *Environmental Justice: Bridging the Gap Between Environmental Laws and "Justice,"* 47 American University Law Review 221, 269 (1997); Richard J. Lazarus, *Pursuing "Environmental Justice": The Distributional Effects of Environmental Protection*, 87 Northwestern University Law Review 787, 848–49 (1992).

Part I

FOUNDATIONS

2

Market-Based Environmental Policies: What Can We Learn from U.S. Experience (and Related Research)?

Robert Stavins

This volume is premised on the notion that market-based instruments have been part of the environmental policy landscape in the United States for twenty years. Although such instruments were first introduced early in the 1970s,[1] and the surge of high-level national interest in this set of policy tools did not commence until late in the 1980s,[2] twenty years is a reasonable reference point to use to reflect on our experiences and search for lessons from this set of experiments with economic-incentive approaches to public policy. In the intervening years, the concept of harnessing market forces to protect the environment seems to have evolved from being almost politically anathema to being close to politically correct.

For purposes of this chapter, I define market-based instruments to be aspects of laws or regulations that encourage behavior through market signals, rather than through explicit directives regarding pollution control levels or methods. These policy instruments, such as tradable permits or pollution charges, can reasonably be described as "harnessing market forces,"[3] because if they are well designed and properly implemented, they encourage firms or individuals to undertake pollution control efforts that are in their own interests and that collectively meet policy goals.

By way of contrast, what may be thought of as conventional approaches to regulating the environment—frequently characterized as command-and-control approaches—allow relatively little flexibility in the means of achieving goals. Such policy instruments tend to force firms to take on similar shares of the pollution control burden, regardless of the cost, sometimes by setting uniform standards for firms, the most prevalent of which are technology- and performance-based standards.

It is well known that holding all sources to the same target can be expensive and, in some circumstances, counterproductive. Although standards may effectively limit emissions of pollutants, they typically exact relatively high costs in the process by forcing some firms to resort to unduly expensive means of controlling pollution. Because the costs of controlling emissions may vary greatly among firms and among sources within firms, the appropriate technology in one situation may not be appropriate (cost-effective) in another.

Control costs can vary enormously due to a firm's production design, physical configuration, age of assets, or other factors. One frequently cited survey of eight empirical studies of air pollution control found that the ratio of actual, aggregate costs of the conventional (command-and-control) approach to the aggregate costs of least-cost benchmarks ranged from 1.07 for sulfate emissions in the Los Angeles area to 22.0 for hydrocarbon emissions at all domestic DuPont plants (Tietenberg 1985). It is important not to misinterpret these numbers, however, because actual command-and-control instruments were essentially contrasted with theoretical benchmarks of cost-effectiveness, that is, what a perfectly functioning market-based instrument would achieve in theory. A more interesting comparison among policy instruments might involve either idealized versions of both market-based systems and alternatives, or—better yet—realistic versions of both (Hahn and Stavins 1992).

In theory, if properly designed and implemented, market-based instruments allow any desired level of pollution cleanup to be realized at the lowest overall cost to society by providing incentives for the greatest reductions in pollution by those firms that can achieve the reductions most cheaply.[4] Rather than equalizing pollution levels among sources (as with uniform emission standards), market-based instruments equalize the incremental amount that sources spend to reduce pollution—their marginal abatement cost (Montgomery 1972; Baumol and Oates 1988; Tietenberg 1995). Command-and-control approaches could—in theory—achieve this cost-effective solution, but this would require that different standards be set for each pollution source, and consequently that policy makers obtain detailed information about the compliance costs each firm faces. Such information is simply not available to government. By contrast, market-based instruments provide for a cost-effective allocation of the pollution control burden among sources without requiring the government to have this information.

In addition, market-based instruments have the potential to bring down abatement costs over time (that is, to be dynamically cost-effective) by providing incentives for companies to adopt cheaper and better pollution control technologies. This is because with market-based instruments, most obviously with emission taxes, it pays firms to clean up a bit more if a sufficiently low-cost method (technology or process) of doing so can be identified and adopted (Downing and White 1986; Malueg 1989; Milliman and Prince 1989; Jaffe and Stavins 1995).

In the next section of the chapter, I briefly summarize a few highlights of the American experience with market-based instruments for environmental protection. Following that, I examine normative lessons that can be learned from these experiences, and then focus on positive political economy lessons. A final section offers some conclusions.

HIGHLIGHTS OF EXPERIENCE

Experiences in the United States with market-based environmental policy instruments have been both numerous and diverse.[5] It is convenient to consider them within four major categories: pollution charges, tradable permits, market friction reductions, and government subsidy reductions.

Charge Systems

Pollution charge systems assess a fee or tax on the amount of pollution that a firm or source generates (Pigou 1920). Consequently, it is worthwhile for the firm to reduce emissions to the point where its marginal abatement cost is equal to the tax rate. A challenge with charge systems is identifying the appropriate tax rate. For social efficiency, it should be set equal to the marginal benefits of cleanup at the efficient level of cleanup, but policy makers are more likely to think in terms of a desired level of cleanup, and they do not know beforehand how firms will respond to a given level of taxation.

An additional problem posed by pollution taxes is associated with their distributional consequences for regulated sources. Despite the fact that such systems minimize aggregate social costs, these systems may be *more* costly than comparable command-and-control instruments *for regulated firms*. This is because with the tax approach, firms pay both their abatement costs *plus* taxes on their residual emissions, whereas for the calculation of aggregate costs in a social benefit-cost or cost-effectiveness analysis, tax payments are simply transfers and so are excluded from the calculations.

The conventional wisdom is that this approach to environmental protection has been ignored in the United States, but this is not really correct. If one defines charge systems broadly, a significant number of applications can be identified. The closest that any U.S. charge system comes to operating as a true Pigovian tax may be the *unit-charge* systems for financing municipal solid waste collection, where households and businesses are charged the incremental costs of collection and disposal. So-called pay-as-you-throw policies, where users pay in proportion to the volume of their waste, are now used in well over 1,000 jurisdictions. The collective experience provides evidence that unit charges have been successful in reducing the volume of household waste generated.[6]

Another important set of charge systems implemented in the United States has been *deposit refund systems*, whereby consumers pay a surcharge when purchasing potentially polluting products and receive a refund when returning the product to an approved center for recycling or proper disposal. A number of states have implemented this approach through "bottle bills" to control litter from beverage containers and to reduce the flow of solid waste to landfills, and the concept has also been applied to lead-acid batteries (Bohm 1981; Menell 1990).

In addition, there has been considerable use of *environmental user charges* in the United States, through which specific environmentally related services are funded. Examples include *insurance premium taxes*, such as those formerly used to fund partially the clean-up of hazardous waste sites through the Superfund program (Barthold 1994).[7] Another set of environmental charges are *sales taxes* on motor fuels, ozone-depleting chemicals, agricultural inputs, and low-mileage motor vehicles. Finally, *tax differentiation* has become part of a considerable number of federal and state attempts to encourage the use of renewable energy sources.

Tradable Permits

Tradable permits—in theory—can achieve the same cost-minimizing allocation of the control burden as a charge system,[8] while avoiding the problems of uncertain responses by firms and the distributional consequences of taxes.[9] Under a tradable permit system, an allowable overall level of pollution is established and allocated among firms in the form of permits. Firms that keep their emission levels below their allotted level may sell their surplus permits to other firms or use them to offset excess emissions in other parts of their operations.[10] If transaction costs are significant, trading volume can be reduced, but even if there is no trading, aggregate abatement costs will be no greater than they would be with an equivalent conventional performance standard.

Applications have included the EPA's emissions trading program (Tietenberg 1985; Hahn 1989)[11]; the leaded gasoline phasedown; water quality permit trading (Hahn 1989; Stephenson et al. 1998); chlorofluorocarbon (CFC) trading (Hahn and McGartland 1989); the sulfur dioxide (SO_2) allowance trading system for acid rain control; the RECLAIM program in the Los Angeles metropolitan region (Harrison 1999); state-level emission reduction credit trading (Swift 2002); and tradable development rights for land use.[12] At least two of these programs—lead trading and the SO_2 allowance system—merit further comment.

The purpose of the lead trading program, developed in the 1980s, was to allow gasoline refiners greater flexibility in meeting emission standards at a time when the lead content of gasoline was reduced to 10 percent of its previous level. In 1982, the EPA authorized interrefinery trading of lead credits, a major purpose of which was to lessen the financial burden on smaller refineries, which were believed to have significantly higher compliance costs. If refiners produced gasoline with a lower lead content than was required, they earned lead credits. In 1985, the EPA initiated a program allowing refineries to bank lead credits, and subsequently firms made extensive use of this option. In each year of the program, more than

60 percent of the lead added to gasoline was associated with traded lead credits (Hahn and Hester 1989a), until the program was terminated at the end of 1987, when the lead phasedown was completed.

The lead program was successful in meeting its environmental targets, although it may have produced some (temporary) geographic shifts in use patterns (Anderson et al. 1990). Although the benefits of the trading scheme are more difficult to assess, the level of trading activity and the rate at which refiners reduced their production of leaded gasoline suggest that the program was relatively cost-effective (Kerr and Maré 1997; Nichols 1997). The high level of trading among firms far surpassed levels observed in earlier environmental markets. The EPA estimated savings from the lead trading program of approximately 20 percent below alternative programs that did not provide for lead banking, a cost savings of about $250 million per year (U.S. EPA, Office of Policy Analysis 1985). Furthermore, the program appears to have provided greater incentives for cost-effective technology diffusion than did a comparable nontradable performance standard (Kerr and Newell 2003).

The most important application made of a market-based instrument for environmental protection has arguably been the SO_2 allowance trading program for acid rain control, established under the Clean Air Act amendments of 1990, and intended to reduce SO_2 emissions by 10 million tons below 1980 levels (Ferrall 1991). A robust market of bilateral SO_2 permit trading gradually emerged, resulting in cost savings on the order of $1 billion annually, compared with costs under likely command-and-control regulatory alternatives. Although the program had low levels of trading in its early years (Burtraw 1996), trading increased significantly over time (Schmalensee et al. 1998; Stavins 1998; Burtraw and Mansur 1999; Ellerman et al. 2000). The degree of cost savings that allowance trading offered is linked with the significant degree of heterogeneity of related abatement costs (Carlson et al. 2000; Newell and Stavins 2003).

Concerns were expressed early on that state regulatory authorities would hamper trading to protect their domestic coal industries, and some research indicates that state public utility commission cost-recovery rules provided poor guidance for compliance activities (Rose 1997; Bohi 1994). Other analysis suggests that this was not a major problem (Bailey 1996). Similarly, in contrast to early assertions that the structure of the EPA's small permit auction market would cause problems (Cason 1995), the evidence now indicates that this had little or no effect on the vastly more important bilateral trading market (Joskow et al. 1998).

The SO_2 reductions required under the 1990 Clean Air Act amendments and achieved via the allowance trading program have had exceptionally positive welfare effects, with benefits being as much as six times greater than costs (Burtraw et al. 1998). The large benefits of the program are due mainly to the positive human health impacts of decreased local SO_2 and particulate concentrations, not the ecological impacts of reduced long-distance transport of acid deposition. This contrasts with what was understood and assumed at the time of the program's enactment in 1990. It appears that Congress did the right thing for the wrong reason.

Market Friction Reduction

Market friction reduction can also serve as a policy instrument for environmental protection. Three types of policies stand out. First, in a number of cases, *markets have been created for inputs or outputs associated with environmental quality*. Examples include measures implemented over the past twenty years that facilitate the voluntary exchange of water rights and thus promote more efficient allocation and use of scarce supplies (Stavins 1983; Howe 1997). Second, *liability rules* have frequently been designed to encourage firms to consider the potential environmental damages of their decisions (Revesz 1997). One important example is the Comprehensive Environmental Response, Compensation, and Liability Act, which established liability for companies that are found responsible for the existence of sites contaminated with hazardous wastes.[13]

Third, because well-functioning markets depend in part on the existence of well-informed producers and consumers, *information programs* can help foster market-oriented solutions to environmental problems.[14] These programs have been of two types. *Product labeling requirements* have been implemented to improve the information set available to consumers. There has been relatively little analysis of the efficacy of such programs, but limited empirical (econometric) evidence suggests that energy-efficiency product labeling has had significant impacts on efficiency improvements, essentially by making consumers and therefore producers more sensitive to energy price changes (Newell et al. 1999).

Another set of information programs has involved *reporting requirements*. A prominent example is the U.S. Toxics Release Inventory (TRI), which was expanded significantly during the past decade and requires firms to make available to the public information on use, storage, and release of specific hazardous chemicals. Such information reporting may increase public awareness of firms' actions, and consequent public scrutiny may encourage firms to alter their behavior, although the evidence is mixed (U.S. General Accounting Office 1992; Hamilton 1995; Bui and Mayer 1997; Konar and Cohen 1997; Ananathanarayanan 1998; and Hamilton and Viscusi 1999).

Government Subsidy Reduction

Government subsidy reduction is the fourth and final category of market-based instruments. Subsidies are the mirror image of taxes and, in theory, can provide incentives to address environmental problems.[15] In practice, however, many subsidies promote economically inefficient and environmentally unsound practices. Unfortunately, assessing the magnitude (let alone the effects), of these subsidies is difficult. For example, because of concerns about global climate change, increased attention has been given to federal subsidies that promote the use of fossil fuels (U.S. Energy

Information Administration 1999, 2000). One EPA study indicated that eliminating these subsidies would have significant effects on reducing carbon dioxide (CO_2) emissions (Shelby et al. 1997), but a substantial share of these subsidies were enacted during previous oil crises to encourage the development of domestic energy sources and reduce reliance on imported petroleum.

NORMATIVE LESSONS

Although there has been considerable experience in the United States with market-based instruments for environmental protection, this relatively new set of policy approaches has not replaced or come anywhere close to replacing conventional command-and-control policies. When and where these approaches have been used in their purest form and with some success, they have not always performed as anticipated. Therefore, I ask what lessons can be learned from our experiences. I consider normative lessons for design and implementation of market-based instruments, analysis of prospective and adopted systems, and identification of new applications.

Normative Lessons for Design and Implementation

The performance to date of market-based instruments for environmental protection provides evidence that these approaches can achieve cost savings while accomplishing their environmental objectives. The performance of these systems also offers lessons about the importance of flexibility, simplicity, the role of monitoring and enforcement, and the capabilities of the private sector to make markets of this sort work.

Regarding flexibility, it is important that market-based instruments should be designed to allow for a broad set of compliance alternatives, in terms of both timing and technological options. For example, allowing flexible timing and intertemporal trading of permits—that is, banking allowances for future use—played a very important role in the SO_2 allowance trading program's performance (Ellerman et al. 1997), much as it did in the U.S. lead rights trading program a decade earlier (Kerr and Maré 1997). One of the most significant benefits of using market-based instruments may simply be that technology standards are thereby avoided. Less flexible systems would not have led to the technological change that may have been induced by market-based instruments (Burtraw 1996; Ellerman and Montero 1998; Bohi and Burtraw 1997; Keohane 2001), nor the induced process innovations that have resulted (Doucet and Strauss 1994).

In regard to simplicity, transparent formulae—whether for permit allocation or tax computation—are difficult to contest or manipulate. Rules should be clearly defined up front, without ambiguity. For example, requiring prior government approval of individual trades may increase uncertainty and transaction costs, thereby discouraging trading; these negative effects should be balanced against any anticipated benefits due to requiring prior government approval. Such requirements hampered the EPA's Emissions Trading Program in the 1970s, and the lack of such requirements was an important factor in the success of lead trading (Hahn and Hester 1989b). In the case of SO_2 trading, the absence of requirements for prior approval reduced uncertainty for utilities and administrative costs for government and contributed to low transactions costs (Rico 1995).

Although some problematic program design elements reflect miscalculations of market reactions, others were known to be problematic at the time the programs were enacted, but nevertheless were incorporated into programs to ensure adoption by the political process. One striking example is the 20 percent rule under the EPA's Emission Trading Program. This rule, adopted at the insistence of the environmental advocacy community, stipulates that each time a permit is traded, the amount of pollution authorized thereunder must be reduced by 20 percent. Because permits that are not traded retain their full quantity value, this regulation discourages permit trading and thereby increases regulatory costs (Hahn 1990).

Experience also argues for using absolute baselines, not relative ones, as the point of departure for credit programs. The problem is that without a specified baseline, reductions must be credited relative to an unobservable hypothetical—what the source would have emitted in the absence of the regulation. A combined system—where a cap-and-trade program is combined with voluntary opt-in provisions—creates the possibility for paper trades, where a regulated source is credited for an emissions reduction (by an unregulated source) that would have taken place in any event (Montero 1999). The result is a decrease in aggregate costs among regulated sources, but this is partly due to an unintentional increase in the total emissions cap. As was experienced with the EPA's Emissions Trading Program, relative baselines create significant transaction costs by essentially requiring prior approval of trades as the authority investigates the claimed counterfactual from which reductions are calculated and credits generated (Nichols et al. 1996).

Experiences with market-based instruments also provide powerful reminders of the importance of monitoring and enforcement. These instruments, whether price or quantity based, do not eliminate the need for such activities, although they may change their character. In the programs where monitoring or enforcement have been deficient, the results have been ineffective policies. One counterexample is provided by the U.S. SO_2 allowance trading program, which includes (costly) continuous emissions monitoring of all sources. On the enforcement side, the act's stiff penalties (much greater than the marginal cost of abatement) have provided sufficient incentives for the very high degree of compliance that has been achieved (Stavins 1998).

In nearly every case of implemented cap-and-trade programs, permits have been allocated without charge to participants. The same characteristic that makes such allocation attractive in positive political economy terms—the conveyance of scarcity rents to the private sector—makes allocation without charge problematic in normative, efficiency terms (Fullerton and Metcalf 1997). It has been estimated that the costs of SO_2 allowance trading would be 25 percent lower if permits were auctioned rather than allocated without charge, because revenues can be used to finance reductions in preexisting distortionary taxes (Goulder et al. 1997). Furthermore, in the presence of some forms of transaction costs, the post-trading equilibrium—and hence aggregate abatement costs—are sensitive to the initial permit allocation (Stavins 1995). For both reasons, a successful attempt to establish a politically viable program through a specific initial permit allocation can result in a program that is significantly more costly than anticipated.[16]

Improvements in instrument design will not solve all problems. One potentially important cause of the mixed performance of implemented market-based instruments is that many firms are simply not well equipped to make the decisions necessary to fully utilize these instruments. Because market-based instruments have been used on a limited basis only, and firms are not certain that these instruments will be a lasting component on the regulatory landscape, it is not surprising that most companies have not reorganized their internal structure to fully exploit the cost savings these instruments offer (Reinhardt 2000). Instead, most firms continue to have organizations that are experienced in minimizing the costs of complying with command-and-control regulations, not in making the strategic decisions allowed by market-based instruments.[17]

The focus of environmental, health, and safety departments in private firms has been primarily on problem avoidance and risk management, rather than on the creation of opportunities made possible by market-based instruments. This focus has developed because of the strict rules companies have faced under command-and-control regulation, in response to which companies have built skills and developed processes that comply with regulations but may not help them benefit competitively from environmental decisions (Reinhardt 2000). Absent significant changes in structure and personnel, the full potential of market-based instruments will probably not be realized.

Normative Lessons for Analysis

When assessing market-based environmental programs, economists need to employ some measure by which the gains of moving from conventional standards to an economic incentive scheme can be estimated. When comparing policies with the same anticipated environmental outcomes, aggregate cost savings may be the best yardstick for measuring success of individual instruments. The challenge for analysts is to make fair comparisons among policy instruments: either idealized versions of both market-based systems and likely alternatives or realistic versions of both (Hahn and Stavins 1992).

It is not enough to analyze static cost savings. For example, the savings due to banking allowances should also be modeled (unless this is not permitted in practice). It can likewise be important to allow for the effects of alternative instruments on technology innovation and diffusion (Milliman and Prince 1989; Jaffe and Stavins 1995; Doucet and Strauss 1994), especially when programs impose significant costs over long time horizons (Newell et al. 1999). More generally, it is important to consider the effects of the preexisting regulatory environment. For example, the level of preexisting factor taxes can affect the total costs of regulation (Goulder et al. 1997), as already indicated. Most broadly, changes in relative prices—whether exogenous or policy-induced—can drive technological change and thereby differentially affect the performance of alternative policy instruments (Snyder et al. 2003).

Normative Lessons for Identifying New Applications

Market-based policy instruments are considered today for nearly every environmental problem that is raised, ranging from endangered species preservation to what may be the greatest of environmental problems, global climate change.[18] Experiences with market-based instruments offer some guidance to the conditions under which such approaches are likely to work well and when they may face greater difficulties.

First, where the cost of abating pollution differs widely among sources, a market-based system is likely to have greater gains, relative to conventional, command-and-control regulations (Newell and Stavins 2003). For example, it was clear early on that SO_2 abatement cost heterogeneity was great because of differences in ages of plants and their proximity to sources of low-sulfur coal (Carlson et al. 2000). But where abatement costs are more uniform across sources, the political costs of enacting an allowance trading approach are less likely to be justifiable.

Second, the greater the degree of mixing of pollutants in the receiving airshed or watershed, the more attractive a market-based system will be, relative to a conventional uniform standard. This is because taxes or tradable permits, for example, can lead to localized hot spots with relatively high levels of ambient pollution. This is a significant distributional issue, and it can also become an efficiency issue if damages are nonlinearly related to pollutant concentrations. In cases where this is a reasonable concern, the problem can be addressed, in theory, through the use of ambient permits or through charge systems that are keyed to changes in ambient conditions at specified locations (Revesz 1996). But despite the extensive theoretical literature on such ambient systems going back to Montgomery (1972), they have never been implemented, with the partial exception of a two-zone trading system under Los Angeles's RECLAIM program.

Third, the efficiency of price-based (tax) systems compared with quantity-based (tradable permit) systems depends on the pattern of costs and benefits. If uncertainty about marginal abatement costs is significant, and if these costs are quite flat and marginal benefits of abatement fall relatively quickly, then a quantity instrument will be more efficient than a price instrument (Weitzman 1974). Furthermore, when there is also uncertainty about marginal benefits, and these benefits are positively correlated with marginal costs (which, it turns out, is not uncommon), then there is an additional argument in favor of the relative efficiency of quantity instruments (Stavins 1996). Likewise, when incomplete enforcement occurs in the presence of benefit and cost uncertainty, quantity instruments are anticipated to perform relatively better than equivalent price instruments (Montero 2002). On the other hand, the regulation of stock pollutants will often favor price instruments when the optimal stock level rises over time (Newell and Pizer 2003). It should also be recognized that despite the theoretical efficiency advantages of hybrid systems—nonlinear taxes or quotas combined with taxes—in the presence of uncertainty (Roberts and Spence 1976; Kaplow and Shavell 1997),[19] no hybrid systems have yet been adopted.

Fourth, the long-term cost-effectiveness of taxes versus tradable permit systems is affected by their relative responsiveness to change. This arises in at least three dimensions. In the presence of rapid rates of economic growth, a fixed tax leads to an increase in aggregate emissions, whereas with a fixed supply of permits there is no change in aggregate emissions (but an increase in permit prices). In the context of general price inflation, a unit (but not an ad valorem) tax decreases in real terms, so emissions levels increase; whereas with a permit system, there is no change in aggregate emissions. In the presence of exogenous technological change in pollution abatement, a tax system leads to an increase in control levels, that is, a decrease in aggregate emissions, whereas a permit system maintains emissions, with a fall in permit prices (Stavins and Whitehead 1992).

Fifth, tradable permits will work best when transaction costs are low, and experience demonstrates that if properly designed, private markets will tend to render transaction costs minimal.

Sixth, a potential advantage of tradable permit systems in which allocation is without charge, relative to other policy instruments, is associated with the incentive thereby provided for pollution sources to identify themselves and report their emissions (to claim their permits).[20]

Seventh, it is important to keep in mind that in the absence of decreasing marginal transactions costs (essentially volume discounts), the equilibrium allocation and hence aggregate abatement costs of a tradable permit system are independent of initial allocations (Stavins 1995). Hence, an important attribute of a tradable permit system is that the allocation decision can be left to politicians, with limited normative concerns about the potential effects of the chosen allocation on overall cost-effectiveness. In other words, cost-effectiveness or efficiency can be achieved, and distributional equity is simultaneously addressed with the same policy instrument. This is one of the reasons why an international tradable permit mechanism is particularly attractive in the context of concerns about global climate change. Allocation mechanisms can be developed that address legitimate equity concerns of developing countries and thus increase the political base for support, without jeopardizing the overall cost-effectiveness of the system.[21]

Eighth and finally, considerations of political feasibility point to the wisdom (more likely success) of proposing market-based instruments when they can be used to facilitate cost-effective, aggregate emissions reductions (as in the case of the SO_2 allowance trading program in 1990), as opposed to cost-effective reallocations of the status quo burden.

POSITIVE POLITICAL ECONOMY LESSONS

I now turn to a set of positive political economy questions that are raised by the increasing use of market-based instruments for environmental protection. First, why was there so little use of market-based instruments in the United States relative to command-and-control instruments, over the thirty-year period of major environmental regulation that began in 1970, despite the apparent advantages these instruments offer? Second, when market-based instruments have been adopted, why has there been such great reliance on tradable permits allocated without charge, despite the availability of a much broader set of incentive-based instruments? Third, why has the political attention given to market-based environmental policy instruments increased dramatically in recent years? To address these questions, it is useful to consider the demand for environmental policy instruments by individuals, firms, and interest groups and their supply by the legislature and regulatory agencies.[22]

Why Have Command-and-Control Instruments Dominated?

The short answer is that command-and-control instruments have predominated because all of the main parties involved had reasons to favor them: affected firms, environmental advocacy groups, organized labor, legislators, and bureaucrats.

On the regulatory demand side, affected firms and their trade associations have tended to prefer command-and-control instruments because standards can improve a firm's competitive position while often costing a firm less than pollution taxes or (auctioned) tradable permits. Command-and-control standards are inevitably set up with extensive input from existing industry and trade associations, which frequently obtain more stringent requirements for new sources and other advantages for existing firms. In contrast, auctioned permits and pollution taxes require firms to pay not only abatement costs to reduce pollution to some level but also regulatory costs associated with emissions beyond that level in the form either of permit purchases or tax payments. Because market-based instruments focus on the quantity of pollution, not who generates it or the methods used to reduce it, these instruments can make the lobbying role of trade associations less important.

For a long time, most environmental advocacy groups were actively hostile toward market-based instruments. One reason was philosophical:

Environmentalists frequently perceived pollution taxes and tradable permits as licenses to pollute. Although such ethical objections to the use of market-based environmental strategies have greatly diminished, they have not disappeared completely (Sandel 1997). A second concern was that damages from pollution—to human health and ecological well-being—were difficult or impossible to quantify and monetize and thus could not be summed up in a marginal damage function or captured by a Pigovian tax rate (Kelman 1981). Third, environmental organizations have opposed market-based schemes out of a fear that permit levels and tax rates—once implemented—would be more difficult to tighten over time than command-and-control standards. If permits are given the status of property rights, then any subsequent attempt by government to reduce pollution levels further could meet with demands for compensation.[23] Similarly, increasing pollution tax rates may be unlikely because raising tax rates is always politically difficult. A related strategic issue is that moving to tax-based environmental regulation would shift authority from environment committees in Congress, frequently dominated by pro-environment legislators, to tax-writing committees, which are generally more conservative (Kelman 1981).[24] Finally, environmental organizations have objected to decentralized instruments on the grounds that even if emission taxes or tradable permits reduce overall levels of emissions, they can—in theory—lead to localized hot spots with relatively high levels of ambient pollution.

Organized labor has also been active in some environmental policy debates. In the case of restrictions on clean air, organized labor has taken the side of the United Mine Workers, whose members are heavily concentrated in Eastern mines that produce higher-sulfur coal, and had therefore opposed pollution-control measures that would increase incentives for using low-sulfur coal from the largely nonunionized (and less labor-intensive) mines in Wyoming's and Montana's Powder River Basin. Thus, in the 1977 debates over amendments to the Clean Air Act, organized labor fought to include a command-and-control standard that effectively required scrubbing, thereby seeking to discourage switching to cleaner Western coal (Ackerman and Hassler 1981). Likewise, the United Mine Workers opposed the SO_2 allowance trading system in 1990 because of a fear that it would encourage a shift to Western low-sulfur coal from nonunionized mines.

Turning to the supply side of environmental regulation, legislators have had a number of reasons to find command-and-control standards attractive. First, many legislators and their staffs are trained in law, which may predispose them to favor legalistic regulatory approaches. Second, standards tend to help hide the costs of pollution control (McCubbins and Sullivan 1984), while market-based instruments generally impose those costs more directly, and deliberately make them explicit. Compare, for example, the nature and tone of public debates associated with proposed increases in gasoline taxes with those regarding commensurate increases in the stringency of the Corporate Average Fuel Economy (CAFE) standards for motor vehicles.

Third, standards offer greater opportunities for symbolic politics, because strict standards—strong statements of support for environmental protection—can readily be combined with less visible exemptions or with lax enforcement measures. Congress has frequently prescribed administrative rules and procedures to protect intended beneficiaries of legislation by constraining the scope of executive intervention (McCubbins et al. 1987). Such stacking of the deck is more likely to be successful in the context of command-and-control legislation, because market-based instruments leave the allocation of costs and benefits up to the market. Of course, the underlying reason symbolic politics works is that voters have limited information and so respond to gestures while remaining relatively unaware of details.

Fourth, if politicians are risk-averse, they will prefer instruments that involve more certain effects.[25] The flexibility inherent in market-based instruments creates uncertainty about distributional impacts and local levels of environmental quality. Typically, legislators in a representative democracy are more concerned with the geographic distribution of costs and benefits than with comparisons of total benefits and costs. Hence, aggregate cost-effectiveness—the major advantage of market-based instruments—is likely to play a less significant role in the legislative calculus than whether a politician is getting a good deal for his or her constituents (Shepsle and Weingast 1984).

Finally, legislators are wary of enacting programs that are likely to be undermined by bureaucrats in their implementation. And bureaucrats are less likely to undermine legislative decisions if their own preferences over policy instruments are accommodated. Bureaucratic preferences—at least in the past—were not supportive of market-based instruments on several grounds: Bureaucrats were familiar with command-and-control approaches, market-based instruments do not require the same kinds of technical expertise that agencies have developed under command-and-control regulation, and market-based instruments can imply a scaled-down role for the agency by shifting decision making from the bureaucracy to the private sector. In other words, government bureaucrats—like their counterparts in environmental advocacy groups and trade associations—might be expected to oppose market-based instruments to prevent their expertise from becoming obsolete, that is, to preserve their human capital.[26]

Why Has There Been So Much Focus on Tradable Permits Allocated without Charge?

Economic theory suggests that the choice between tradable permits and pollution taxes should be based on case-specific factors, but when significant market-based instruments have been adopted in the United States, they have nearly always taken the form of tradable permits rather than emission taxes. Moreover, the initial allocation of such permits has always been through initial distribution without charge, rather than through auctions,[27] despite the apparent economic superiority of the latter mechanism in terms of economic efficiency (Spulber 1985; Stavins 1995; Goulder et al. 1997; Fullerton and Metcalf 1997).

Again, many actors in the system have reasons to favor tradable permits allocated without charge over other market-based instruments. On the regulatory demand side, existing firms favor tradable permits allocated without charge because they convey rents to them. Moreover, like stringent command-and-control standards for new sources, but unlike auctioned permits or taxes, permits allocated without charge give rise to entry barriers, because new entrants must purchase permits from existing holders. Thus, the rents conveyed to the private sector by tradable permits allocated without charge are, in effect, sustainable.

Environmental advocacy groups have generally supported command-and-control approaches, but given the choice between tradable permits and emission taxes, these groups strongly prefer the former. Environmental advocates have a strong incentive to avoid policy instruments that make the costs of environmental protection highly visible to consumers and voters; taxes make those costs more explicit than permits. Also, environmental advocates prefer permit schemes because they specify the quantity of pollution reduction that will be achieved, in contrast with the indirect effect of pollution taxes. Overall, some environmental groups have come to endorse the tradable permits approach because it promises the cost savings of pollution taxes but without the drawbacks that environmentalists associate with tax instruments.

Tradable permits allocated without charge are easier for legislators to supply than taxes or auctioned permits, again because the costs imposed on industry are less visible and less burdensome, because no money is exchanged at the time of the initial permit allocation. Also, permits allocated without charge offer a much greater degree of political control over the distributional effects of regulation, facilitating the formation of majority coalitions. Joskow and Schmalensee (1998) examined the political process of allocating SO_2 allowances in the 1990 amendments and found that allocating permits on the basis of prior emissions can produce fairly clear winners and losers among firms and states. An auction allows no such political maneuvering.[28]

Why Has the Attention Given to Market-Based Instruments Increased?

Given the historical lack of receptiveness by the political process to market-based approaches to environmental protection, why has there been a recent rise in the use of these approaches? It would be gratifying to believe that increased understanding of market-based instruments had played a large part in fostering their increased political acceptance, but how important has this really been? In 1981, Steven Kelman surveyed congressional staff members and found that support and opposition to market-based environmental policy instruments was based largely on

ideological grounds: Republicans, who supported the concept of economic incentive approaches, offered as a reason the assertion that "the free
market works," or "less government intervention" is desirable, without any real awareness or understanding of the economic arguments for
market-based programs. Likewise, Democratic opposition was based
largely on ideological factors, with little or no apparent understanding of
the real advantages or disadvantages of the various instruments (Kelman
1981). What would happen if we were to replicate Kelman's survey today? My refutable hypothesis is that we would find increased support
from Republicans, greatly increased support from Democrats, but insufficient improvements in understanding to explain these changes.[29] So
what else has mattered?

First, one factor has surely been increased pollution control costs,
which have led to greater demand for cost-effective instruments. By the
late 1980s, even political liberals and environmentalists were beginning to
question whether conventional regulations could produce further gains
in environmental quality. During the previous twenty years, pollution
abatement costs had continually increased, as stricter standards moved
the private sector up the marginal abatement-cost function. By 1990, U.S.
pollution control costs had reached $125 billion annually, nearly a 300
percent increase in real terms from 1972 levels (U.S. Environmental Protection Agency 1990; Jaffe et al. 1995).

Second, a factor that became important in the late 1980s was strong and
vocal support from some segments of the environmental community.[30] By
supporting tradable permits for acid rain control, the Environmental Defense Fund (EDF) seized a market niche in the environmental movement
and successfully distinguished itself from other groups.[31] Related to this,
a third factor was that the SO_2 allowance trading program, the leaded
gasoline phasedown, and the CFC phaseout were all designed to *reduce*
emissions, not simply *reallocate* them cost-effectively among sources.
Market-based instruments are most likely to be politically acceptable when
proposed to achieve environmental improvements that would not otherwise be feasible (politically or economically).

Fourth, deliberations regarding the SO_2 allowance system, the lead
system, and CFC trading differed from previous attempts by economists
to influence environmental policy in an important way: the separation of
ends from means, that is, the separation of consideration of goals and
targets from the policy instruments used to achieve those targets. By
accepting—implicitly or otherwise—the politically identified (and potentially inefficient) goal, the ten-million-ton reduction of SO_2 emissions, for
example, economists were able to focus successfully on the importance of
adopting a cost-effective means of achieving that goal. The risk, of course,
was "designing a fast train to the wrong station."

Fifth, acid rain was an unregulated problem until the SO_2 allowance
trading program of 1990; the same can be said for leaded gasoline and
CFCs. Hence, there were no existing constituencies—in the private sector,

the environmental advocacy community, or government—for the status quo approach, because there was no status quo approach. One should be more optimistic about introducing market-based instruments for "new" problems, such as global climate change, than for existing, highly regulated problems, such as abandoned hazardous waste sites.

Sixth, by the late 1980s, there had already been a perceptible shift of the political center toward a more favorable view of using markets to solve social problems. The George H. W. Bush administration, which proposed the SO_2 allowance trading program and then championed it through an initially resistant Democratic Congress, was (at least in its first two years) moderate Republican; phrases such as "fiscally responsible environmental protection" and "harnessing market forces to protect the environment" do have the sound of quintessential moderate Republican issues.[32] But beyond this, support for market-oriented solutions to various social problems had been increasing across the political spectrum for the previous fifteen years, as was evidenced by deliberations on deregulation of the airline, telecommunications, trucking, railroad, and banking industries. Indeed, by the mid-1990s, the concept (or at least the phrase) *market-based environmental policy* had evolved from being politically problematic to politically attractive.

Seventh and finally, the adoption of the SO_2 allowance trading program for acid rain control—like any major innovation in public policy—can partly be attributed to a healthy dose of chance that placed specific persons in key positions, in this case at the White House, the EPA, Congress, and environmental organizations.[33]

CONCLUSIONS

Some eighty years ago, economists first proposed the use of corrective taxes to internalize environmental (and other) externalities. But it was a little more than a decade ago that the portfolio of potential economic-incentive instruments was expanded to include quantity-based mechanisms—tradable permits—and these incentive-based approaches to environmental protection began to emerge as prominent features of the policy landscape.

Given that most experience with market-based instruments has been generated quite recently, one should be cautious about drawing conclusions from these experiences. Important questions remain. For example, relatively little is known empirically about the impact of these instruments on technological change. Also, much more empirical research is needed on how the preexisting regulatory environment affects performance, including costs. Moreover, the great successes with tradable permits have involved air pollution: acid rain, leaded gasoline, and CFCs. Experience (and success) with water pollution is much more limited, and in other areas, there has been no experience at all. Even for air pollution problems, the differences between SO_2 and acid rain, on one hand, and the combustion of fossil fuels and global climate change, on the other hand, suggest that a rush to judgment regarding global climate policy instruments is unwarranted.

There are sound reasons why the political world has been slow to embrace the use of market-based instruments for environmental protection, including the ways economists have packaged and promoted their ideas in the past: failing to separate means (cost-effective instruments) from ends (efficiency) and treating environmental problems as little more than "externalities calling for corrective taxes." Much of the resistance has also been due, of course, to the very nature of the political process and the incentives it provides to both politicians and interest groups to favor command-and-control methods instead of market-based approaches.

But despite this history, market-based instruments have moved to center stage, and policy debates today look very different from those twenty years ago, when these ideas were characterized as licenses to pollute or dismissed as completely impractical. Market-based instruments are considered seriously for each and every environmental problem that is tackled, ranging from endangered species preservation to regional smog to global climate change. It is reasonable to anticipate that market-based instruments will enjoy increasing acceptance in the years ahead. But no particular form of government intervention, no individual policy instrument—whether market-based or conventional—is appropriate for all environmental problems. Which instrument is best in any given situation depends on characteristics of the environmental problem and the social, political, and economic context in which it is being regulated.

ACKNOWLEDGMENTS This chapter draws in part on Stavins (2000, 2002, 2003). Helpful comments on a previous version were provided by Juan-Pablo Montero, Richard Newell, Sheila Olmstead, and an anonymous referee. The author alone is responsible for any errors.

NOTES

1. Beginning in 1974, the U.S. Environmental Protection Agency (EPA) experimented with emissions trading as part of the Clean Air Act's program for improving local air quality through the control of volatile organic compounds (VOCs), carbon monoxide (CO), sulfur dioxide (SO_2), particulates, and nitrogen oxides (NO_x). The EPA later codified this diverse set of initiatives (bubbles, netting, offsets, and banking) in its Emissions Trading Program in 1986. *See* Tietenberg 1985; Hahn 1989; Foster and Hahn 1995.

2. Among other developments during the late 1980s, U.S. Senators Timothy Wirth and John Heinz launched what they called "Project 88: Harnessing Market Forces to Protect our Environment—Initiatives for the New President." In a series of reports, conferences, and briefings of White House officials and congressional members and staff, Project 88 put forward a diverse set of market-based policy instruments for environmental protection and resource management (Stavins 1988, 1991). Of equal importance, the Environmental Defense Fund split from the

rest of the environmental advocacy community and lent its enthusiastic support to the Bush White House's development of what subsequently became the SO_2 allowance trading program in the Clean Air Act amendments of 1990. *See* Hahn 2000.

3. *See* Organisation for Economic Co-operation and Development (1989, 1991, 1998) and U.S. Environmental Protection Agency (1991, 1992, 2001). Another strain of literature—known as free market environmentalism—focuses on the role of private property rights in achieving environmental protection (Anderson and Leal 1991).

4. This chapter focuses on policy instruments in the environmental realm, chiefly those instruments that reduce emissions or concentrations of pollution, as opposed to those that operate in the natural resources realm. This means, for example, that tradable development rights, wetlands mitigation banking, and tradable permit systems used to govern the allocation of fishing rights are not discussed. The distinction between environmental and natural resource policies is somewhat arbitrary, and some policy instruments that bridge the environmental and natural resource realms, such as removing barriers to water markets, are considered.

5. For a detailed review of both U.S. and international experiences, *see* Stavins (2003).

6. *See* McFarland 1972; Wertz 1976; Stevens 1978; Efaw and Lanen 1979; Skumatz 1990; Lave and Gruenspecht 1991; Repetto et al. 1992; Miranda et al. 1994; and Fullerton and Kinnaman 1996.

7. The taxes that previously supported the Superfund trust fund—primarily excise taxes on petroleum and specified chemical feedstocks and a corporate environmental income tax—expired in 1995 and have not been reinstated.

8. Over thirty years ago, Crocker (1966) and Dales (1968) independently developed the idea of using transferable discharge permits to allocate the pollution control burden among sources. Montgomery (1972) provided the first rigorous proof that such a system could provide a cost-effective policy instrument. A sizable body of literature has followed, much of it stemming from Hahn and Noll (1982). Early surveys were provided by Tietenberg (1980, 1985). Much of the literature may be traced to Coase's (1960) treatment of negotiated solutions to externality problems.

9. This assumes that the allocation is made without charge, but it could also be through sale or auction, in which case the distributional implications of a comparable tradable permit program are similar to the emission tax previously described. Likewise, a revenue-neutral emissions tax, in which revenues are refunded to regulated firms (but not in proportion to their emissions levels), can resemble—in distributional terms—a comparable tradable permit program in which the permits are allocated without charge. The simple tradable permit program described is acap-and-trade system, but some systems operate as credit programs, where permits or credits are assigned only when a source reduces emissions below what is required by source-specific limits.

10. Furthermore, if command-and-control instruments take the form of technology standards or emission rate standards, they are likely to provide less certainly regarding the achievement of an aggregate emissions (or ambient concentration) target than a cap-and-trade program, because the former do not control for product output.

11. *See* Stavins (2000, 2002, 2003).

12. In addition, the Energy Policy and Conservation Act of 1975 established Corporate Average Fuel Economy (CAFE) standards for automobiles and light trucks, requiring manufacturers to meet minimum sales-weighted average fuel efficiency for their fleets sold in the United States. A penalty is charged per car sold per unit of average fuel efficiency below the standard. The program operates like an intrafirm tradable permit system, because manufacturers can undertake efficiency improvements wherever they are cheapest within their fleets. For reviews of the program's costs relative to equivalent gasoline taxes, see Crandall et al. 1986; Goldberg 1997; and National Research Council 2002. Light trucks, which are defined by the federal government to include sport utility vehicles, face weaker CAFE standards.

13. Retroactive liability provisions can of course provide incentive effects only for future actions that might be subject to liability rules. For economic analyses of the Superfund program, *see*, for example, Hamilton 1993; Gupta et al. 1996; and Hamilton and Viscusi 1999.

14. For a comprehensive review of information programs and their apparent efficacy, *see* Tietenberg 1997. The International Standards Organization's (ISO) benchmark, ISO 14001, provides standards for environmental management systems. To obtain certification, firms must commit to environmental performance targets. More than 8,000 plants worldwide obtained certification through 1999 (Wheeler et al. 2000).

15. Although subsidies can advance environmental quality (*see*, for example, Jaffe and Stavins 1995), it is also true that subsidies, in general, have important and well-known disadvantages relatives to taxes (Baumol and Oates 1988); hence, I do not consider them as a distinct category of market-based instruments in this chapter.

16. Also, for these same two reasons, auctioning of permits—rather than allocation without charge—is particularly desirable on economic grounds in some situations.

17. There are, of course, exceptions. *See* Hockenstein et al. 1997.

18. *See*, for example, Goldstein 1991 and Bean 1997 on species protection; and Fisher et al. 1996, Hahn and Stavins 1995, Schmalensee 1996, and Stavins 1997 on applications to global climate change. More broadly, *see* Ayres 2000.

19. In addition to the efficiency advantages of noninear taxes, they also have the attribute of reducing the total (but not the marginal) tax burden of the regulated sector, relative to an ordinary linear tax, which is potentially important in a political economy context.

20. Although my focus is on U.S. experience, it is worth noting that such self-reporting incentives were empirically validated in a market-based program for particulate control in Santiago, Chile (Montero and Sanchez 2002).

21. *See*, for example, the proposal for growth targets by Frankel (1999).

22. This political market framework was developed by Keohane et al. (1998), and these sections of the chapter draw on that work and on Hahn and Stavins (1991) and Stavins (1998).

23. This concern was alleviated in the SO_2 provisions of the Clean Air Act amendments of 1990 by an explicit statutory provision that permits do not represent property rights.

24. These strategic arguments refer, for the most part, to pollution taxes, not to market-based instruments in general. Indeed, as I discuss later, one reason some environmental groups have come to endorse the tradable permits approach is that

it promises the cost savings of taxes, without the drawbacks that environmentalists associate with tax instruments.

25. Legislators tend to behave as if they are risk-averse if their constituents punish unpredictable policy choices or their reelection probability is very high (McCubbins et al. 1989, p. 22).

26. Subsequently, this same incentive led EPA staff involved in the acid rain program to become strong proponents of trading for a variety of other pollution problems.

27. The EPA does have an annual auction of SO_2 allowances, but this represents less than 2 percent of the total allocation (Bailey 1996). Although the EPA auctions may have helped in establishing the market for SO_2 allowances, they are a trivial part of the overall program (Joskow et al. 1998).

28. Given the strong (positive) political preference for tradable permits relative to pollution taxes combined with the significant normative advantages of tax instruments, researchers have begun to ask whether flexible quantity-based instruments can be designed to mimic some of the more desirable features of price-based policies but without the financial transfers that such policies normally entail (Newell et al. 2003).

29. But there has been some increased understanding of market-based approaches among policy makers. This has partly been due to increased understanding by their staffs, a function—to some degree—of the economics training that is now common in law schools, and the proliferation of schools of public policy (Hahn and Stavins 1991).

30. But the environmental advocacy community is by no means unanimous in its support for market-based instruments. *See*, for example, Seligman 1994.

31. When the memberships (and financial resources) of other environmental advocacy groups subsequently declined with the election of the environmentally friendly Clinton-Gore administration, the EDF continued to prosper and grow (Lowry 1993). In 2003, the World Resources Institute was alone among environmental advocacy groups to support the George W. Bush administration's water quality trading policy.

32. The Reagan administration enthusiastically embraced a market-oriented ideology but demonstrated little interest in employing actual market-based policies in the environmental area. From the Bush administration through the Clinton administration, interest and activity regarding market-based instruments— particularly tradable permit systems—continued to increase, although the pace of activity in terms of newly implemented programs declined during the Clinton years, when a considerable part of the related focus was on global climate policy (Hahn et al. 2003).

33. Within the White House, among the most active and influential enthusiasts of market-based environmental instruments were Counsel Boyden Gray and his deputy, John Schmitz; Domestic Policy Adviser Roger Porter; Council of Economic Advisers (CEA) Member Richard Schmalensee; CEA Senior Staff Economist Robert Hahn; and Office of Management and Budget Associate Director Robert Grady. At the EPA, administrator William Reilly—a "card-carrying environmentalist"— enjoyed valuable credibility with environmental advocacy groups; and deputy administrator Henry Habicht and assistant administrator for Air and Radiation William Rosenberg were key early supporters of market-based instruments. In Congress, Senators Timothy Wirth and John Heinz provided high-profile, bipartisan support for the SO_2 allowance trading system and, more broadly, for a wide

variety of market-based instruments for environmental problems through their Project 88 (Stavins 1988). Finally, in the environmental community, EDF executive director Fred Krupp, senior economist Daniel Dudek, and staff attorney Joseph Goffman worked closely with the White House to develop the initial allowance trading proposal.

REFERENCES

Ackerman, B.A., and W.T. Hassler (1981), *Clean Coal/Dirty Air* (Yale University Press, New Haven).

Ananathanarayanan, A. (1998), "Is There a Green Link? A Panel Data Value Event Study of the Relationship between Capital Markets and Toxic Releases," Rutgers University Working Paper.

Anderson, R.C., L.A. Hofmann, and M. Rusin (1990), *The Use of Economic Incentive Mechanisms in Environmental Management*, Research Paper 51 (American Petroleum Institute, Washington, DC).

Anderson, T., & D. Leal (1991), *Free Market Environmentalism* (Pacific Research Institute for Public Policy, San Francisco).

Ayres R.E. (2000), "Expanding the Use of Environmental Trading Programs into New Areas of Environmental Regulation," *Pace Environmental Law Review* 18(1):87–118.

Bailey, E.M. (1996), "Allowance Trading Activity and State Regulatory Rulings: Evidence from the U.S. Acid Rain Program," MIT-CEEPR 96–002 WP, Center for Energy and Environmental Policy Research, Massachusetts Institute of Technology.

Barthold, T.A. (1994), "Issues in the Design of Environmental Excise Taxes," *Journal of Economic Perspectives* 8(1):133–51.

Baumol, W.J., and W.E. Oates (1988), *The Theory of Environmental Policy*, 2nd edition (Cambridge University Press, New York).

Bean, M.J. (1997), "Shelter from the Storm: Endangered Species and Landowners Alike Deserve a Safe Harbor," *New Democrat* (March/April):20–21.

Bohi, D. (1994), "Utilities and State Regulators Are Failing to Take Advantage of Emissions Allowance Trading," *Electricity Journal* 7:20–27.

Bohi, D., and D. Burtraw (1997), "SO$_2$ Allowance Trading: How Do Expectations and Experience Measure Up?" *Electricity Journal*: 67–75.

Bohm, P. (1981), *Deposit-Refund Systems: Theory and Applications to Environmental, Conservation, and Consumer Policy* (Resources for the Future, Johns Hopkins University Press, Baltimore, MD).

Bui, L.T.M., and C.J. Mayer (1997), "Public Disclosure of Private Information as a Means of Regulation: Evidence from the Toxic Release Inventory in Massachusetts," mimeo.

Burtraw, D. (1996), "The SO$_2$ Emissions Trading Program: Cost Savings without Allowance Trades," *Contemporary Economic Policy* 14:79–94.

Burtraw, D., A.J. Krupnick, E. Mansur, D. Austin, and D. Farrell (1998), "The Costs and Benefits of Reducing Air Pollution Related to Acid Rain," *Contemporary Economic Policy* 16:379–400.

Burtraw, D., and E. Mansur (1999), "The Environmental Effects of SO$_2$ Trading and Banking," *Environmental Science and Technology* 33(20):3489–94.

Carlson, C., D. Burtraw, M. Cropper, and K.L. Palmer (2000), "Sulfur Dioxide Control by Electric Utilities: What Are the Gains from Trade?" *Journal of Political Economy* 108:1292–326.

Cason, T.N. (1995), "An Experimental Investigation of the Seller Incentives in EPA's Emission Trading Auction," *American Economic Review* 85:905–22.

Coase, R. (1960), "The Problem of Social Cost," *Journal of Law and Economics* 3:1–44.

Crandall, R.W., H.K. Gruenspecht, T.E. Keeler, and L.B. Lave (1986), *Regulating the Automobile* (Brookings Institution, Washington, DC).

Crocker, T.D. (1966), "The Structuring of Atmospheric Pollution Control Systems," in: H. Wolozin, ed., *The Economics of Air Pollution* (Norton, New York).

Dales, J. (1968), *Pollution, Property and Prices* (University of Toronto Press, Toronto).

Doucet, J., and T. Strauss (1994), "On the Bundling of Coal and Sulphur Dioxide Emissions Allowances," *Energy Policy* 22(9):764–70.

Downing, P.B., and L.J. White (1986), "Innovation in Pollution Control," *Journal of Environmental Economics and Management* 13:18–27.

Efaw, F., and W.N. Lanen (1979), "Impact of User Charges on Management of Household Solid Waste," Report prepared for the U.S. Environmental Protection Agency under Contract No. 68–3-2634 (Mathtech, Princeton, NJ).

Ellerman, D., P. Joskow, R. Schmalensee, J. Montero, and E. Bailey (2000), *Markets for Clean Air: The U.S. Acid Rain Program* (Cambridge University Press, New York).

Ellerman, D., and J. Montero (1998), "The Declining Trend in Sulfur Dioxide Emissions: Implications for Allowance Prices," *Journal of Environmental Economics and Management* 36:26–45.

Ellerman, D., R. Schmalensee, P. Joskow, J. Montero, and E. Bailey (1997), *Emissions Trading under the U.S. Acid Rain Program: Evaluation of Compliance Costs and Allowance Market Performance* (MIT Center for Energy and Environmental Policy Research, Cambridge, MA).

Ferrall, B.L. (1991), "The Clean Air Act Amendments of 1990 and the Use of Market Forces to Control Sulfur Dioxide Emissions," *Harvard Journal on Legislation* 28:235–52.

Fisher, B., S. Barrett, P. Bohm, M. Kuroda, J. Mubazi, A. Shah, and R. Stavins (1996), "Policy Instruments to Combat Climate Change," in: J.P. Bruce, H. Lee, and E.F. Haites, eds., *Climate Change 1995: Economic and Social Dimensions of Climate Change* (Cambridge University Press, New York), 397–439.

Foster, V., and R.W. Hahn (1995), "Designing More Efficient Markets: Lessons from Los Angeles Smog Control," *Journal of Law and Economics* 38:19–48.

Frankel, J.A. (1999), *Greenhouse Gas Emissions*. Policy Brief #52, June (Brookings Institution, Washington, DC).

Fullerton, D., and T.C. Kinnaman (1996), "Household Responses to Pricing Garbage by the Bag," *American Economic Review* 86:971–84.

Fullerton, D., and G. Metcalf (1997), "Environmental Controls, Scarcity Rents, and Pre-Existing Distortions," NBER Working Paper 6091 (National Bureau of Economic Research, Cambridge, MA).

Goldberg, P.K. (1997), "The Effects of the Corporate Average Fuel Efficiency Standards," Working Paper, Department of Economics, Princeton University.

Goldstein, J.B. (1991), "The Prospects for Using Market Incentives to Conserve Biological Diversity," *Environmental Law* 21.

Goulder, L., I. Parry, and D. Burtraw (1997), "Revenue-Raising vs. Other Approaches to Environmental Protection: The Critical Significance of Pre-Existing Tax Distortions," *RAND Journal of Economics*.

Gupta, S., G. Van Houtven, and M. Cropper (1996), "Paying for Permanence: An Economic Analysis of EPA's Cleanup Decisions at Superfund Sites," *RAND Journal of Economics* 27(3):563–82.

Hahn, R.W. (1989), "Economic Prescriptions for Environmental Problems: How the Patient Followed the Doctor's Orders," *Journal of Economic Perspectives* 3:95–114.

Hahn, R.W. (1990), "Regulatory Constraints on Environmental Markets," *Journal of Public Economics* 42:149–75.

Hahn, R.W. (2000), "The Impact of Economics on Environmental Policy," *Journal of Environmental Economics and Management* 39:375–99.

Hahn, R.W., and G.L. Hester (1989a), "Marketable Permits: Lessons for Theory and Practice," *Ecology Law Quarterly* 16:361–406.

Hahn, R.W., and G.L. Hester (1989b) "Where Did All the Markets Go? An Analysis of EPA's Emissions Trading Program," *Yale Journal of Regulation* 6:109–53.

Hahn, R.W., and A.M. McGartland (1989), "Political Economy of Instrumental Choice: An Examination of the U.S. Role in Implementing the Montreal Protocol," *Northwestern University Law Review* 83:592–611.

Hahn, R., and R. Noll (1982), "Designing a Market for Tradeable Permits," in: W. Magat, ed., *Reform of Environmental Regulation* (Ballinger, Cambridge, MA).

Hahn, R.W., S.M. Olmstead, and R.N. Stavins (2003), "Environmental Regulation During the 1990s: A Retrospective Analysis." *Harvard Environmental Law Review* 27(1).

Hahn, R.W., and R.N. Stavins (1991), "Incentive-Based Environmental Regulation: A New Era from an Old Idea?" *Ecology Law Quarterly* 18:1–42.

Hahn, R.W., and R.N. Stavins (1992), "Economic Incentives for Environmental Protection: Integrating Theory and Practice," *American Economic Review* 82(May):464–68.

Hahn, R.W., and R.N. Stavins (1995), "Trading in Greenhouse Permits: A Critical Examination of Design and Implementation Issues," in: H. Lee, ed., *Shaping National Responses to Climate Change: A Post-Rio Policy Guide* (Island Press, Cambridge, MA), 177–217.

Hamilton, J.T. (1993), "Politics and Social Costs: Estimating the Impact of Collective Action on Hazardous Waste Facilities," *RAND Journal of Economics* 24:101–25.

Hamilton, J. (1995), "Pollution as News: Media and Stock Market Reactions to the Toxics Release Inventory Data," *Journal of Environmental Economics and Management* 28:98–113.

Hamilton, J., and K. Viscusi (1999), *Calculating Risks? The Spatial and Political Dimensions of Hazardous Waste Policy* (MIT Press, Cambridge, MA).

Harrison, D. Jr. (1999), "Turning Theory into Practice for Emissions Trading in the Los Angeles Air Basin," in: S. Sorrell and J. Skea, eds., *Pollution for Sale: Emissions Trading and Joint Implementation* (Edward Elgar, London).

Hockenstein, J.B., R.N. Stavins, and B.W. Whitehead (1997), "Creating the Next Generation of Market-Based Environmental Tools," *Environment* 39(4):12–20, 30–33.

Howe, C.W. (1997), "Increasing Efficiency in Water Markets: Examples from the Western United States," in: Terry L. Anderson and Peter J. Hill, eds., *Water Marketing—The Next Generation* (Rowman and Littlefield, Lanham, MD), 79–99.

Jaffe, A.B., S.R. Peterson, P.R. Portney, and R.N. Stavins (1995), "Environmental Regulation and the Competitiveness of U.S. Manufacturing: What Does the Evidence Tell Us?" *Journal of Economic Literature* 33:132–63.

Jaffe, A.B., and R.N. Stavins (1995), "Dynamic Incentives of Environmental Regulation: The Effects of Alternative Policy Instruments on Technology Diffusion," *Journal of Environmental Economics and Management* 29:S43–63.

Joskow, P.L., and R. Schmalensee (1998), "The Political Economy of Market-Based Environmental Policy: The U.S. Acid Rain Program," *Journal of Law and Economics* 41:81–135.

Joskow, P.L., R. Schmalensee, and E.M. Bailey (1998), "Auction Design and the Market for Sulfur Dioxide Emissions," *American Economic Review.*

Kaplow, L., and S. Shavell (1997), "On the Superiority of Corrective Taxes to Quantity Regulation," NBER Working Paper 6251 (National Bureau of Economic Research, Cambridge, MA).

Kelman, S. (1981), *What Price Incentives?: Economists and the Environment* (Auburn House, Boston).

Keohane, N.O. (2001), "Essays in the Economics of Environmental Policy," unpublished Ph.D. diss., Harvard University.

Keohane, N.O., R.L. Revesz, and R.N. Stavins (1998), "The Choice of Regulatory Instruments in Environmental Policy," *Harvard Environmental Law Review* 22:313–67.

Kerr, S., and D. Maré (1997), "Efficient Regulation through Tradeable Permit Markets: The United States Lead Phasedown," Department of Agricultural and Resource Economics, University of Maryland, College Park, Working Paper 96–06 (January).

Kerr, S., and R.G. Newell (2003), "Policy-Induced Technology Adoption: Evidence from the U.S. Lead Phasedown," *Journal of Industrial Economics* 51:317–431.

Konar, S., and M.A. Cohen (1997), "Information as Regulation: The Effect of Community Right to Know Laws on Toxic Emissions," *Journal of Environmental Economics and Management* 32:109–24.

Lave, L., and H. Gruenspecht (1991), "Increasing the Efficiency and Effectiveness of Environmental Decisions: Benefit-Cost Analysis and Effluent Fees," *Journal of Air and Waste Management* 41:680–90.

Lowry, R.C. (1993), "The Political Economy of Environmental Citizen Groups," Unpublished Ph.D. diss., Harvard University.

Malueg, D.A. (1989), "Emission Credit Trading and the Incentive to Adopt New Pollution Abatement Technology," *Journal of Environmental Economics, and Management* 16:52–57.

McCubbins, M.D., R.G. Noll, and B.R. Weingast (1987), "Administrative Procedures as Instruments of Political Control," *Journal of Law, Economics, and Organization* 3:243–77.

McCubbins, M.D., R.G. Noll, and B.R. Weingast (1989), "Structure and Process, Politics and Policy: Administrative Arrangements and the Political Control of Agencies," *Virginia Law Review* 75:431–82.

McCubbins, M.D., and T. Sullivan (1984), "Constituency Influences on Legislative Policy Choice," *Quality and Quantity* 18:299–319.

McFarland, J.M. (1972), "Economics of Solid Waste Management," in: Sanitary Engineering Research Laboratory, College of Engineering and School of Public Health, University of California, Berkeley, *Comprehensive Studies of Solid Waste Management, Final Report*, Report no. 72(3):41–106.

Menell, P. (1990), "Beyond the Throwaway Society: An Incentive Approach to Regulating Municipal Solid Waste," *Ecology Law Quarterly* 17:655–739.

Milliman, S.R., and R. Prince (1989), "Firm Incentives to Promote Technological Change in Pollution Control," *Journal of Environmental Economics and Management* 17:247–65.

Miranda, M.L., J.W. Everett, D. Blume, and B.A. Roy Jr. (1994), "Market-Based Incentives and Residential Municipal Solid Waste," *Journal of Policy Analysis and Management* 13:681–98.

Montero, J.P. (1999), "Voluntary Compliance with Market-Based Environmental Policy: Evidence from the U.S. Acid Rain Program," *Journal of Political Economy* 107:998–1033.

Montero, J.P. (2002), "Prices versus Quantities with Incomplete Enforcement," *Journal of Public Economics* 85:435–54.

Montero, J.P., and J.M. Sanchez (2002), "A Market-Based Environmental Policy Experiment in Chile," *Journal of Law and Economics* 45:267–87.

Montgomery, D. (1972), "Markets in Licenses and Efficient Pollution Control Programs," *Journal of Economic Theory* 5:395–418.

National Research Council (2002), *Effectiveness and Impact of Corporate Average Fuel Economy (CAFE) Standards.* Committee on the Effectiveness and Impact of Corporate Average Fuel Economy (CAFE) Standards, Board on Energy and Environmental Systems, Transportation Research Board. (National Academies Press, Washington, DC).

Newell, R.G., A.B. Jaffe, and R.N. Stavins (1999), "The Induced Innovation Hypothesis and Energy-Saving Technological Change," *Quarterly Journal of Economics* 114(3):941–75.

Newell, R.G., and W. Pizer (2003), "Regulating Stock Externalities under Uncertainty," *Journal of Environmental Economics and Management* 45:416–32.

Newell, R.G., W.A. Pizer, and J. Zhang (2003), "Managing Permit Markets to Stabilize Prices," Resources for the Future Discussion Paper 03–34, Washington, DC.

Newell, R., and R.N. Stavins (2003), "Cost Heterogeneity and the Potential Savings from Market-Based Policies," *Journal of Regulatory Economics* 23(1):43–59.

Nichols, A.L (1997), "Lead in Gasoline," in: R.D. Morgenstern, ed., *Economic Analyses at EPA: Assessing Regulatory Impact* (Resources for the Future, Washington, DC), 49–86.

Nichols, A., J. Farr, and G. Hester (1996), "Trading and the Timing of Emissions: Evidence from the Ozone Transport Region," National Economic Research Associates, Cambridge, MA.

Organisation for Economic Co-operation and Development (1989), *Economic Instruments for Environmental Protection* (OECD, Paris).

Organisation for Economic Co-operation and Development (1991), *Environmental Policy: How to Apply Economic Instruments* (OECD, Paris).

Organisation for Economic Co-operation and Development (1998), *Applying Market-Based Instruments to Environmental Policies in China and OECD Countries* (OECD, Paris).

Pigou, A.C. (1920), *The Economics of Welfare* (Macmillan, London).

Reinhardt, F.L. (2000), *Down to Earth: Applying Business Principles to Environmental Management* (Harvard Business School Press, Boston).

Repetto, R., R. Dower, R. Jenkins, and J. Geoghegan (1992), *Green Fees: How a Tax Shift Can Work for the Environment and the Economy* (World Resources Institute, Washington, DC).

Revesz, R.L. (1996), "Federalism and Interstate Environmental Externalities," *University of Pennsylvania Law Review* 144:2341.

Revesz, R.L. (1997), *Foundations in Environmental Law and Policy* (Oxford University Press, New York).

Rico, R. (1995), "The U.S. Allowance Trading System for Sulfur Dioxide: An Update of Market Experience," *Environmental and Resource Economics*, 5(2):115–29.

Roberts, M.J., and M. Spence (1976), "Effluent Charges and Licenses under Uncertainty," *Journal of Public Economics* 5(3–4):193–208.

Rose, K. (1997), "Implementing an Emissions Trading Program in an Economically Regulated Industry: Lessons from the SO_2 Trading Program," in: R.F. Kosobud and J.M. Zimmerman, eds., *Market Based Approaches to Environmental Policy: Regulatory Innovations to the Fore* (Van Nostrand Reinhold, New York).

Sandel, M.J. (1997), "It's Immoral to Buy the Right to Pollute," *New York Times*, December 15, p. A29.

Schmalensee, R. (1996), *Greenhouse Policy Architecture and Institutions*, paper prepared for National Bureau of Economic Research conference, Economics and Policy Issues in Global Warming: An Assessment of the Intergovernmental Panel Report, Snowmass, CO (July 23–24).

Schmalensee, R., P.L. Joskow, A.D. Ellerman, J.P. Montero, and E.M. Bailey (1998), "An Interim Evaluation of Sulfur Dioxide Emissions Trading," *Journal of Economic Perspectives* 12(3):53–68.

Seligman, D.A. (1994), *Air Pollution Emissions Trading: Opportunity or Scam? A Guide for Activists* (Sierra Club, San Francisco).

Shelby, M., R. Shackleton, M. Shealy, and A. Cristofaro (1997), *The Climate Change Implications of Eliminating U.S. Energy (and Related) Subsidies* (U.S. Environmental Protection Agency, Washington, DC).

Shepsle, K.A., and B.R. Weingast (1984), "Political Solutions to Market Problems," *American Political Science Review* 78:417–34.

Skumatz, L.A. (1990), "Volume-Based Rates in Solid Waste: Seattle's Experience," Report for the Seattle Solid Waste Utility (Seattle Solid Waste Utility, Seattle, WA).

Snyder, L.H., N.D. Miller, and R.N. Stavins (2003), "The Effects of Environmental Regulation on Technology Diffusion: The Case of Chlorine Manufacturing." *American Economic Review* 93:431–35.

Spulber, D.F. (1985), "Effluent Regulation and Long Run Optimality," *Journal of Environmental Economics and Management* 12:103–16.

Stavins, R.N. (1983), *Trading Conservation Investments for Water* (Environmental Defense Fund, Berkeley, CA).

Stavins, R.N., ed. (1988), *Project 88: Harnessing Market Forces to Protect Our Environment*, sponsored by Senator Timothy E. Wirth, Colorado, and Senator John Heinz, Pennsylvania, Washington, DC.

Stavins, R.N., ed. (1991), *Project 88—Round II Incentives for Action: Designing Market-Based Environmental Strategies*, sponsored by Senator Timothy E. Wirth, Colorado, and Senator John Heinz, Pennsylvania, Washington, DC.

Stavins, R.N. (1995),"Transaction Costs and Tradable Permits," *Journal of Environmental Economics and Management* 29:133–48.

Stavins, R.N. (1996), "Correlated Uncertainty and Policy Instrument Choice," *Journal of Environmental Economics and Management* 30:218–32.

Stavins, R.N. (1997), "Policy Instruments for Climate Change: How Can National Governments Address a Global Problem?" *University of Chicago Legal Forum*: 293–329.

Stavins, R.N. (1998), "What Have We Learned from the Grand Policy Experiment: Lessons from SO_2 Allowance Trading," *Journal of Economic Perspectives* 12(3):69–88.

Stavins, R.N. (2000), "Market-Based Environmental Policies," in: P.R. Portney and R.N. Stavins, eds., *Public Policies for Environmental Protection* (Resources for the Future, Washington, DC).

Stavins, R.N. (2002), "Lessons from the American Experiment with Market-Based Environmental Policies," in: J.D. Donahue and J.S. Nye Jr., eds., *Market-Based Governance: Supply Side, Demand Side, Upside, and Downside*(Brookings Institution, Washington, DC).

Stavins, R.N. (2003), "Experience with Market-Based Environmental Policy Instruments," in: K.-G. Mäler and J. Vincent, eds., *Handbook of Environmental Economics*, volume 1 (Elsevier Science, Amsterdam), 355–435.

Stavins, R.N., and B.W. Whitehead (1992), "Pollution Charges for Environmental Protection: A Policy Link Between Energy and Environment," *Annual Review of Energy and the Environment* 17:187–210.

Stephenson, K., P. Norris, and L. Shabman (1998), "Watershed-Based Effluent Trading: The Nonpoint Source Challenge," *Contemporary Economic Policy* 16: 412–21.

Stevens, B.J. (1978), "Scale, Market Structure, and the Cost of Refuse Collection," *Review of Economics and Statistics* 40:438–48.

Swift, B. (2002), "Emission Reduction Credit Trading Systems: An Overview of Recent Results and an Assessment of Best Practices" (Environmental Law Institute, Washington, DC).

Tietenberg, T. (1980), "Transferable Discharge Permits and the Control of Stationary Source Air Pollution: A Survey and Synthesis," *Land Economics* 56:391–416.

Tietenberg, T. (1985), *Emissions Trading: An Exercise in Reforming Pollution Policy* (Resources for the Future, Washington, DC).

Tietenberg, T. (1995), "Tradeable Permits for Pollution Control When Emission Location Matters: What Have We Learned?" *Environmental and Resource Economics* 5:95–113.

Tietenberg, T. (1997), "Information Strategies for Pollution Control," paper presented at the Eighth Annual Conference, European Association of Environmental and Resource Economists, Tilburg, The Netherlands (June 26–28).

U.S. Energy Information Administration (1999), *Federal Financial Interventions and Subsidies in Energy Markets: Primary Energy* (U.S. Department of Energy, Washington, DC).

U.S. Energy Information Administration (2000), *Federal Financial Interventions and Subsidies in Energy Markets: Energy Transformation and End Use* (U.S. Department of Energy, Washington, DC).

U.S. Environmental Protection Agency (1990), *Environmental Investments: The Cost of a Clean Environment*, report of the administrator to Congress (U.S. EPA, Washington, DC).

U.S. Environmental Protection Agency (1991), *Economic Incentives, Options for Environmental Protection*, Document P-2001 (EPA, Washington, DC).

U.S. Environmental Protection Agency (1992), *The United States Experience with Economic Incentives to Control Environmental Pollution*, EPA-230-R-92–001 (EPA, Washington, DC).

U.S. Environmental Protection Agency (2001), *The United States Experience with Economic Incentives for Protecting the Environment*, EPA-240-R-01–001 (EPA, Washington, DC).

U.S. Environmental Protection Agency, Office of Policy Analysis (1985), *Costs and Benefits of Reducing Lead in Gasoline, Final Regulatory Impact Analysis* (EPA, Washington, DC).

U.S. General Accounting Office (1992), *Toxic Chemicals: EPA's Toxics Release Inventory Is Useful but Could be Improved* (U.S. GAO, Washington, DC).

Weitzman, M. (1974),"Prices vs. Quantities," *Review of Economic Studies* 41:477–91.

Wertz, K.L. (1976), "Economic Factors Influencing Households' Production of Refuse," *Journal of Environmental Economics and Management* 2:263–72.

Wheeler, D., et al. (2000), *Greening Industry: New Roles for Communities, Markets and Governments* (Oxford University Press for the World Bank, New York).

3

Are Cap-and-Trade Programs More Environmentally Effective than Conventional Regulation?

A. Denny Ellerman

INTRODUCTION

Like other market-based instruments (MBIs), cap-and-trade programs have been advocated because of the theoretical prediction that they could achieve an environmental objective at less cost than conventional regulatory instruments (Crocker 1966; Dales 1968; Montgomery 1972; Tietenberg 1985). Experience with cap-and-trade systems in the United States over the past decade has confirmed the theoretically predicted economic advantages (Ellerman et al. 2000, 2003; Carlson et al, 2000) and failed to find a degradation of environmental performance (Burtraw and Mansur 1999; Swift 2000). As a result, MBIs, especially cap-and-trade systems, have become widely accepted in the policy community. Recognizing this circumstance, opponents of the use of MBIs tend to attack the assumption that the environmental performance is equal (Clear the Air 2002; Moore 2002). Their argument is that although the economic performance may be better, the environmental performance is worse, and the increased environmental damages outweigh the savings in abatement cost.

This chapter makes the contrary argument that the experience with the cap-and-trade programs suggests that at least this form of MBI may be more environmentally effective than the usual command-and-control alternatives, in addition to being more economically efficient. The evidence rests mainly on the SO_2 cap-and-trade system created by Title IV of the 1990 Clean Air Act amendments (also known as the Acid Rain Program), but corroborating evidence emerges from the Northeastern NO_x Budget Program and the RECLAIM programs for trading NO_x and SO_2 emissions in the Los Angeles basin. Despite the small sample, the reasons for the observed better performance appear to be capable of more general application.

Two definitional issues must be discussed first. The alternative to a cap-and-trade program is commonly described as command-and-control regulation. If ever economists have managed a semantic triumph, it is with command and control, for it is hard to imagine a less appealing term for the latter part of the twentieth century and the beginning of the twenty-first century. *Command and control* is also not a very precise term for identifying the essential difference between the contending instruments because the requirement to surrender allowances can be seen as a command that will control aggregate emissions. The important distinction is that the command does not extend to the production decisions of individual firms and applies only to the aggregate level of emissions. The instruction given to each individual firm, namely, to surrender an allowance, is equivalent to the practical requirement to pay for any other input into production. More specifically, the firm is not faced with a regulatory prescription concerning how much to emit or what control equipment to use, only a requirement to pay for emissions whatever their level. As pointed out by Shabman, Stevenson, and Shobe (2002), the essential distinction concerns who makes the abatement decision, the regulator or the firm, not whether some command exists. Accordingly, I have adopted the less value-laden and more accurate term *prescriptive regulation* to describe the conventional alternative to cap-and-trade systems and more generally MBIs.

The second definitional clarification concerns environmental effectiveness. By this phrase, I mean the proximate environmental goal, which is often the reduction of emissions, not the underlying environmental problem, which may be nondangerous ambient concentrations of known pollutants or acidification of certain regions. The relation between proximate goal and underlying environmental problem is a matter of program design, and it is common to both prescriptive regulatory programs and MBIs. As emphasized by MacAvoy (1979) generally with respect to health, environmental, and safety regulation and specifically with reference to the Clean Air Act (MacAvoy 1987), the realities of implementation and administration led to more or less uniform design specifications and equipment product standards, which were only indirectly related to the underlying environmental objectives that typically required some differentiation to account for differences in air quality and different causative circumstances. Setting aside the many issues of program design and the inevitable compromises involved therein, the common feature of both prescriptive regulation and MBIs is that these measures are presumed to reduce emissions. Accordingly, for the purposes of this chapter, environmental effectiveness is defined relative to emissions, for which the intended reduction is assumed to be well chosen for the underlying environmental objective.

THE TITLE IV STORY

Four Environmentally Advantageous Features

Four features describe the environmental performance of the Acid Rain Program.[1] First, a large reduction of emissions was accomplished relatively quickly—in the fifth year following passage of the enabling legislation. Second, the schedule of emission reduction was accelerated significantly as a result of banking. Third, no exemptions, exceptions, or relaxations from the program's requirements were granted. Four, the hot spots that were feared to result from emissions trading have not appeared.

The first two features are illustrated in figure 3.1, which shows the relationship between the cap, actual emissions, and several estimates of what emissions would have been absent Title IV for those units required to be subject to Title IV beginning in 1995—the "big dirties," as they are sometimes called.

The program caused a significant reduction of SO_2 emissions in the fifth year following enactment of the 1990 Clean Air Act amendments and the first year in which the program was effective. Moreover, most of the reduction observed in 1995 was due to banking, which was not mandated but a form of voluntary, early action on the part of program participants. Banking implies that the early "overcompliance" will be followed by later "undercompliance," as can be observed in the first three years after the cap was lowered to its Phase II level; however, if a positive discount rate is attached to the timing of the benefits of emission reduction, this

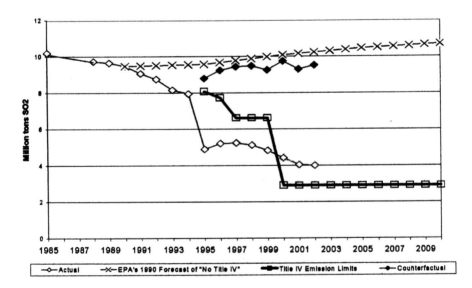

Figure 3.1. Title IV in Historical Perspective: Phase 1 Units

Source: Ellerman et al. (2000) as amended with data for more recent years based on the EPA's annual compliance reports.

behavior will usually lead to a net environmental gain.[2] During the five years of Phase I, emissions were reduced by twice as much as was required to meet the Phase I cap. On a yearly basis, the annual emission reduction has increased steadily from 3.9 million tons in the first year, 1995, to 4.4 million tons in 1999, the last year of Phase I, and to 6.9 million tons in 2002, a 77 percent increase in abatement by the eighth year.

The Environmental Protection Agency (EPA) often notes that Title IV has achieved 100 percent compliance.[3] This curious statement requires some interpretation because U.S. environmental regulation is not characterized by widespread legal violations of statute or regulation. What is meant is that the program was implemented without the granting of the exemptions, exceptions, or relaxations of the regulatory requirement that are typically issued to avoid the undue hardship that can result when a more or less uniform mandate is imposed on sources exhibiting cost heterogeneity. To return to the early critique in MacAvoy (1979), "postponements and waivers were granted, based on economic hardship to the company or community, or on the ability of the agency to handle only a limited number of cases.... Whatever the reasons, numerous exceptions and variances in issuing permits rendered the uniform standards process less than completely effective."[4]

The notable feature of these prescriptive programs is that the deviations are all in one direction because the owners of sources incurring less onerous costs never step forward to request more stringent regulation, and the regulator does not have the information or will to impose a compensating tightening of the standard on these units. The Acid Rain Program avoided this loosening bias through the trading mechanism, which provided the means by which compensating reductions could be made. More important, the emergence of a market in allowances made the purchase of these compensating reductions cheaper than seeking some form of regulatory relaxation.

The term *hot spots* refers to the possibility that emissions trading might allow the sources contributing the most to environmental damage to avoid making emission reductions. A well-designed trading program would make hot spots impossible, but the practical requirements of program design and implementation will often allow this possibility. In the Acid Rain Program, the fear was that the required emission reductions would not be made in the Midwest, which was the source of the emissions most responsible for acidification in the Northeast, but in other areas, such as the Southeast. As it turned out, most of the emission reductions did take place in the Midwest. Sources in Ohio, Indiana, Illinois, Kentucky, Tennessee, Missouri, Pennsylvania, and West Virginia have provided about 80 percent of the nationwide emission reduction achieved by Title IV while accounting for about 50 percent of current emissions and about 60 percent of what emissions would have been absent Title IV.

It is hard to imagine a prescriptive regulatory program that would have had equal environmental performance, even assuming that such a program could have achieved the legislative consensus accorded to Title IV after nearly a decade of stalemated proposals that would have mandated scrubbers and other prescriptive standards. Although there is surprisingly little ex post evaluation of the performance of conventional prescriptive regulations,[5] they are typically not characterized by quick implementation with significant emission reductions relatively soon after enactment, nor by voluntary actions that have the effect of accelerating required emission reductions. More often, implementation occurs only after a long period of regulatory rule making, administrative proceedings, and litigation as participants seek to shape the rules and gain some form of relaxation and competitive advantage over other firms.

Reasons for Better Environmental Effectiveness

Only one of the four aspects of environmental performance noted can be attributed to a specific design feature of the Acid Rain Program: the acceleration of the required emission reduction, which is clearly due to the two-phased implementation of the cap on SO_2 emissions and banking provisions of Title IV (Ellerman and Montero 2002). The remaining environmental features—quick implementation, 100 percent compliance, and the absence of hot spots—reflect more fundamental characteristics of the program.

Quick implementation occurred because there was comparatively little for the EPA to do in the way of regulatory implementation once the statute was enacted.[6] More typically, the EPA must translate general congressional intent into specific, concrete, and enforceable objectives that can be applied to specific sources. In the case of the SO_2 allowance trading program, all the EPA needed to do (after Congress had established a system of freely tradable emission rights and distributed those rights) was to set up the reporting and accounting system needed to ensure adequate enforcement. Although very important, this task is much less demanding and time-consuming than translating general intent into specific and enforceable prescription. More important, the prior distribution of allowances, which were effectively entitlements to the rents created by the restriction on SO_2 emissions, greatly reduced firms' interest in the EPA's administrative proceedings. Because regulatory implementation did not involve prescribing the abatement and the cost individual sources would incur, the economic interest of affected firms was much less engaged, and there was consequently much less administrative involvement, political intervention, and litigation than normally characterizes the implementation of Congress's intent in environmental matters. The issue that had the most impact on individual firms' profits, the allocation of allowances, had been decided, and the rest depended on an impersonal and inscrutable market and how well the firm used the allowances it had been allocated.

Another factor leading to quicker implementation in the case of Title IV is that parties unhappy with the allocation and the concomitant distribution of rents cannot sue Congress, whereas suing the EPA administrator for alleged arbitrary and capricious action in effectively doing the same thing is not only possible but frequently done. It is revealing that the most significant litigation in the implementation of Title IV concerned the one area in which the EPA had some discretion in allocating allowances: those for units that were voluntarily brought into the program in Phase I as substitution and compensation units.

What the EPA calls 100 percent compliance reflects another little noticed feature of the explicit property rights system that Congress established with Title IV. Compliance became cheaper than seeking the various forms of relaxation that characterize conventional regulatory programs. Firms facing relatively high costs of compliance in prescriptive programs can reduce those costs only by petitioning for and receiving some type of dispensation. This involves nonnegligible transaction costs and a less than 100 percent probability of success. Consequently, the decision to seek some form of relaxation depends on a comparison of the abatement cost savings from a successful petition, its likelihood, and the cost of obtaining that dispensation. This calculation of expected cost and cost savings confronts the regulator in a conventional regulatory program with an unenviable choice. Lower transaction costs reduce the inequities involved in applying the rule, but they also encourage more petitions and less compliance with the original mandate. Conversely, higher transaction costs result in greater compliance, but also a more inequitable incidence of the regulatory requirement and greater political resistance.

Cap-and-trade systems avoid this dilemma entirely. Where a market can be assumed, which has proven to be the case for the cap-and-trade systems in the United States, firms facing relatively high costs of abatement incur very low transaction costs in purchasing abatement by others. Thus it becomes cheaper for these firms to comply than to seek some relaxation of the standard. Moreover, the existence of a market removes the primary reason for seeking relaxation: unique hardship due to the application of a uniform rule to inappropriate source-specific circumstances. No one is uniquely disadvantaged in a market with many buyers, and the highest cost is that of a permit.

The happy result is a regulatory system in which compliance has been made cheaper than seeking some type of relaxation. Although much is made of the ability of emissions trading to provide cheaper abatement options to firms facing relatively higher abatement costs, this compliance-enhancing, environmentally beneficial feature of cap-and-trade systems has been rarely noticed.

The lack of hot spots in the Acid Rain Program might be seen as accidental in that the cheapest sources of abatement were also the sources of the most damaging emissions, but there is more to this correspondence than happenstance. It reflects the circumstance that the cheapest abatement is typically found where the largest sources are located, and these sources are usually the greatest contributors to the underlying environmental problem. Most deep abatement technology, like scrubbing, is capital intensive and the per-ton cost depends on how many tons are removed per MW of capacity. Higher utilization of the source and higher sulfur content of the combusted coal mean more tons of abatement over which the fixed capital cost can be spread and lower total abatement cost per ton. Thus where capital-intensive, deep-abatement technology is an option, market systems will direct abatement to relatively larger and more heavily utilized sources with relatively high emission intensities. If these sources are the most damaging from an environmental standpoint, the experience with Title IV suggests they will abate first. A further implication of this result is that broader markets can be formed where reason exists to believe that the pollution problem is caused mostly by the larger and more polluting sources.

IS TITLE IV AN EXCEPTION?

Title IV's SO_2 emissions trading program is widely recognized as successful, and perhaps exceptional, so that the relevant question is always whether the results from this program can be generalized. Neither of the two other major cap-and-trade programs in the United States, the Northeastern NO_x Budget Program and the RECLAIM programs in the Los Angeles basin, has been studied as extensively as the Acid Rain Program. Nevertheless, they do provide support for the argument that cap-and-trade programs are more effective environmentally than alternative prescriptive programs. They also provide clearer evidence of a tendency that can be seen in the adoption of Title IV after years of stalemated legislative proposals to reduce SO_2 emissions by more conventional means, namely, for cap-and-trade approaches to supplant conventional prescriptive regulation. This tendency is the more remarkable in that unlike the Acid Rain Program where congressional action was required to impose the environmental constraint, these cap-and-trade programs were implemented through administrative action by regulatory bodies that possessed the legal authority to impose prescriptive measures with equivalent environmental effect.

The NO_x Budget Program

The NO_x Budget Program is a multistate, regional program that was formed for the purpose of attaining the National Ambient Air Quality Standard (NAAQS) for ground-level ozone in the Northeastern United States.[7] The 1990 Clean Air Act amendments mandated a prescriptive standard of reasonably available control technology (RACT) for all sources located in nonattainment areas beginning in 1995, and it also authorized an Ozone Transport Commission (OTC) to coordinate action among the thirteen Northeastern and mid-Atlantic states and the District of Columbia to end the persistent nonattainment along the Northeastern corridor. Negotiations among these states led to a Memorandum of Understanding in 1994 that established a three-phase program of control of NO_x emissions from electric utility and large industrial boilers. Phase 1 was a relabeling of the RACT standard that took effect in 1995, but it was recognized that additional NO_x emission reductions would be required to achieve attainment. Phases 2 and 3, beginning in 1999 and 2003, consist of a progressively more stringent cap-and-trade program encompassing eleven of the fourteen jurisdictions during the ozone season (May through September) when the formation of ground-level ozone occurs.[8] Beginning in 2004, the third phase was extended to cover most of the states east of the Mississippi River in what is known as the NO_x SIP Call.

Although the trading phases of the Northeastern NO_x Budget Program differ in important aspects from the Acid Rain Program—for instance, in placing limits on the use of banked allowances—Phases 2 and 3 have reduced NO_x emissions in the Northeast. EPA compliance reports frequently note that ozone-season NO_x emissions are 60 percent below 1990 baseline levels, but two-thirds of this reduction was accomplished in the first phase under the prescriptive RACT standard that did not involve emissions trading. A more accurate statement for the purpose of this chapter is that the second phase cap has reduced summer emissions by about 30 percent over the level achieved by the earlier RACT requirement and that the third and final phase, begun in 2003, will effect another 35 percent reduction. Thus, the trading phases of the Northeastern NO_x cap-and-trade program will have reduced emissions by about 50 percent from what had been achieved under the prescriptive RACT standard. As was the case with the Acid Rain Program, these reductions occurred in the first year of each phase of the program without any delays or exceptions. Although limits were placed on the use of banked allowances, banking of allowances still occurred but not in the same magnitude as in the Acid Rain Program. Similarly, concerns about hot spots, called "wrong-way trades," in this program proved to be unfounded (Farrell 2000).

The interesting question about this program is why a cap-and-trade mechanism was chosen for the later, more stringent phases instead of simply prescribing a more demanding, source-specific emission rate limit, which would have been more in keeping with well-established regulatory practice in the United States. This question is the more intriguing in that NO_x emission rates, representing modified RACT and best available control technology, provided the basis, when applied against 1990 baseline emissions from all sources, for determining the level of the caps and allocating the available regional emission budget to the states for further distribution of allowances to sources.

One explanation might be that environmental regulators were swept up with the enthusiasm for MBIs that characterized the 1990s, but this is a group that is generally not suspected of such sentiment. A more likely explanation is that regulators had come to recognize the limits of the conventional prescriptive approach for controlling air emissions and that they turned to the most practicable alternative to achieve the desired reductions in sources of pollution. They may also have concluded that the costs of a conventional program would be too high to be politically acceptable and were honest enough to admit that they did not possess the information to impose an efficient command-and-control program.

An additional factor influencing the choice of cap-and-trade programs may have been a greater willingness on the part of the owners of affected sources to accept this type of market-based instrument when the allowances are distributed to them for free. As noted presciently by Buchanan and Tulloch (1975), "decisions on the alternative policy instruments in democratic governments are surely influenced by the preferences of those who are subjected to them." Any form of MBI would have provided the flexibility to achieve the environmental goal at least cost, but only grandfathered permits—unlike environmental charges or auctioned permits—would provide incumbents with the scarcity rents they would receive under conventional regulatory programs. The new rights have the advantage of being more secure than the contingent rights embodied in conventional programs, and they are separable from the facilities to which they are granted.[9]

The RECLAIM Programs

The RECLAIM NO_x and SO_2 programs provide additional evidence of the tendency to supplant existing regulation with a cap-and-trade approach to achieve further increments of emission reduction.[10] Like the NO_x Budget Program, the RECLAIM programs are aimed at bringing a particular region, the Los Angeles basin, into attainment with the NAAQS. In this case, however, an explicit prescriptive regulatory program to achieve this environmental objective by 2010—the 1989 Air Quality Management Plan—had already been developed, but its implementation, which would involve 130 specific control measures, would have been costly and slow. Three years of negotiation between regulators and the regulated eventuated in agreement in late 1993 on two separate, phased-in cap-and-trade programs, one for NO_x and the other for SO_2, that would achieve the desired level of aggregate emissions in ten years, or by 2003, seven years sooner than the goal in the 1989 plan. Facilities participating in these programs were then exempt from the prescriptive requirements contained in the 1989 plan as concerns NO_x and SO_2 emissions.

As was the case with the Northeastern NO_x Budget Program, regulators seem to have realized that proceeding in the conventional manner would impose too high a cost to be politically practicable and they lacked the information to devise an efficient prescriptive program. At the same time, RTCs, or RECLAIM trading credits as allowances were called in these programs, were granted to incumbent firms in perpetuity. The long and sometimes difficult negotiations concerning the allocation of these allowances indicates that firms were aware of the value being conveyed. It is reasonable to assume that this feature made them more willing to agree to the measures being proposed.

The environmental effectiveness of the RECLAIM programs has been comparable to those of the other cap-and-trade programs. Despite significant disruptions to the NO_x program as a result of the electricity market problems in early 2001, both NO_x and SO_2 emissions have been reduced by about 40 percent since the program's start in 1994. In 2003, when fully phased in, the emission reduction from preprogram levels will be 50%.[11] The RECLAIM SO_2 cap has been met in each of the years since the program started. The NO_x cap was exceeded in 2000 by 3,294 tons (16 percent) and in 2001 by 28 tons (0.25 percent) as a result of the electricity market problems in California in these years. The limited amount of banking and borrowing allowed through the use of overlapping cycles reduced the exceedences in 2000 by two-thirds (to 1,089 tons) and those without sufficient RTCs on an individual facility basis paid a $15,000/ton mitigation fee to fund off-system emission reductions and had an equivalent number of RTCs deducted from future allowance allocations.

This exceedence of the NO_x cap is unfortunate, but it must be placed in context. The events of 2000–2001 in California's electricity market led to an extraordinary call on old generating plants in the Los Angeles basin that were not equipped with NO_x emission control devices because heretofore they have been dispatched for only a few hours a year to meet peak demand (Joskow 2001). The unanticipated call on these units to meet electricity demand increased the demand for RTCs to cover the resulting NO_x emissions beyond what could be provided within the temporally constrained time period within which the credits are valid (one year with some banking and borrowing possible because of overlapping compliance cycles). The result was (1) unprecedented high prices (up to $90,000/ton); (2) the establishment of the $15,000/ton mitigation fee; (3) the temporary removal of electric utility units from the cap-and-trade system through at least December 31, 2003; and (4) the imposition of mandates on those units to retrofit NO_x emission control devices.[12]

The relevant question in assessing this performance is how the prescriptive regulatory program that RECLAIM supplanted would have fared under the same circumstances. For one thing, the exceedences would not have been recognized (much less compensated) because the conventional program regulated emission rates, not total emissions, and lacked any mechanism for determining "excess" emissions. The only argument for better environmental performance by an alternative prescriptive system is that it would have succeeded in having NO_x abatement equipment installed, prior to summer 2000, on the generating units that were the source of the problem, thereby avoiding the large spike in emissions. This circumstance alone raises a question about the purported effectiveness of prescriptive regulations; however, the likely reason is that the prior low utilization of these units and the high cost of capital-intensive retrofits would have made such actions prohibitively expensive. Also, given the high price of NO_x allowances since summer 2000, it is hard to imagine that owners of these units would have resisted retrofitting them, unless they expected the units to return to the earlier level of low utilization. Accordingly, mandating the retrofit of these generating units has had the effect either of prescribing what would have been done anyway in response to the higher prices and expected higher utilization, or of providing very high-cost protection against future allowance price spikes.

CONCLUDING OBSERVATIONS AND QUALIFICATIONS

Critics of the use of market-based approaches will argue that the adoption of cap-and-trade programs reflects a public policy fad or, at least, public policy experimentation in an inappropriate domain. If so, then the decisions to adopt these programs were fortunate in revealing instruments that are not only less costly but also more environmentally effective. However, another explanation, less dependent on serendipity, is that conditions have changed. Today's environmental problems are not as obvious as before, and further increments of emissions reduction are more costly even when efficiently accomplished. Results-oriented environmental regulators have recognized that the familiar blunt instruments do not work as well in these new circumstances and that they do not have the information needed to design and administer conventional programs efficiently. Moreover, changes in information technology have helped in making data-intensive monitoring and reporting of emissions and the tracking of allowances cheaper and feasible over a broader range of environmental applications (Kruger et al. 2000).[13] Finally, the political requirements for gaining meaningful agreement by all relevant parties, whether for congressional enactment or administrative implementation, make cap-and-trade programs with initially grandfathered allowances an obvious choice among the array of MBIs. All in all, the experience with these programs indicates a new pragmatism in which regulators have come to recognize the political and economic limits of their ability to prescribe source-specific emission reductions and affected firms have come to accept the costs involved in making emission reductions conditional on the receipt of improved rights to allowed emissions.

It is not surprising that this new pragmatism should lead to the emergence of an explicit property rights approach. By giving legal recognition to the right to emit that is conveyed by conventional prescriptive regulation and in making that right separable from the regulated asset, legislators and regulators have enabled the emergence of markets that provide the incentive for recipients of these rights to comply and to use the information available to each to make efficient abatement choices. Whether or not they recognize it, legislators and regulators have adopted the simple rule, suggested over a decade ago by Laffont and Tirole (1993), that these programs not place impossibly high informational demands on regulators and provide the incentive and flexibility for firms to do the right thing.

The argument presented here is not that the extensive body of environmental regulation that has been developed and administered in the

United States over the past three decades has been ineffective. By most measures, it has been. The issue is one of relative environmental effectiveness, just as the case for MBIs is one of relative economic efficiency. If the experience with the admittedly small sample of cap-and-trade programs can be generalized more broadly, the policy implications for choice of tradable permits is even stronger than is commonly assumed.

ACKNOWLEDGMENTS Funding from CEEPR and the EPA for the research leading to the argument presented in this chapter is gratefully acknowledged. I am also indebted to an anonymous referee, Paul Joskow, Nathaniel Keohane, and participants of the UCSB/UCLA Seminar at which this chapter was first presented for encouragement and helpful comments. All errors remain my own.

NOTES

1. The most comprehensive evaluation of the Acid Rain Program is Ellerman et al. (2000). For a more recent assessment, *see* Ellerman (2004).

2. A net gain might not occur if demographic changes, such as aging or migration, led to increased or more serious exposure in later periods.

3. *See* any of the annual compliance reports for 1995 through 1999 (for instance U.S. EPA 2000). In both 2000 and 2001, very small amounts of emissions were out of compliance: 54 tons in 2000 and 11 tons in 2001 out of more than 10 million tons. Fines were assessed, and an equivalent number of the next vintage allowances were deducted from the unit accounts of these noncomplying units. For all practical purposes, the compliance rate has been 100 percent for all years.

4. In his later study, MacAvoy (1987) notes that the process of adjusting stringent, health-based federal standards to local political and economic realities eventuated in a requirement whereby "emissions equipment... was not so costly that the plant would have to shut down in the process of conforming to the plan. The rule of thumb was that ninety percent of sources... must be able financially to comply."

5. The available literature tends to focus on three separate issues: (1) the disconnect between environmental goal and the prescriptive regulations as implemented, (2) the effects of differential regulation between new and existing sources, and (3) whether observed aggregate emission reductions can be attributed to regulatory programs having this objective. MacAvoy (1979, 1987) provides the best discussion of the first point and also finds that observed emission reductions are generally due to other causes. This latter conclusion has been contested by others (Gollop and Roberts 1983; Fuller 1987; Ringquist 1993) who have found that regulation has reduced emissions, although none address whether the underlying environmental objective was being met. Greenstone (2004) and Chay and Greenstone (2004) examine the issue of environmental effectiveness from the standpoint of ambient concentrations; they find weak evidence of the effectiveness of regulations affecting SO_2 emissions and total suspended particulates, respectively. Dubroeucq (2004) relates trends in ambient concentrations with emissions reductions for SO_2 at the state level and finds weak evidence for the effectiveness of the prescriptive regulatory system only during 1980–85. The second issue in this literature, the effects of differential regulation on emissions from stationary sources, is addressed in Nelson et al. (1993). None of these studies provide what

could be considered a complete ex post evaluation of a specific, discrete program. Typically, some subset of affected sources is examined and the results generalized.

6. Nat Keohane makes the valid and interesting point that the issue is when the clock starts. It could be argued that the highly visible scrap over rents that accompanies the allocation of grandfathered allowances takes longer than the enactment of legislation that simply states intent and leaves the rest to the EPA. If so, then the choice is between quick adoption with slow implementation or slow adoption with quick implementation. However, it is not obvious that rent-seeking behavior is more prevalent in the adoption of cap-and-trade programs than in the adoption of prescriptive regulation. Moreover, it can be argued that providing a ready currency to make the politically required pay-offs leads to faster adoption than concocting and agreeing on special regulatory provisions to achieve the same ends. Although other factors were also operative, the Acid Rain Program offers an example. The legislation that ultimately gained legislative consensus required nineteen months from the initial proposal by the Bush administration in April 1989 to final enactment in November 1990. A number of legislative proposals submitted between 1980 and 1989 to effect comparable reductions by prescriptive regulation all failed to generate a consensus.

7. U.S. EPA-OTC (2003) provides a convenient summary of this program.

8. Virginia did not sign the Memorandum of Understanding, and Maine and Vermont did not participate in the later phases because the few sources in these two states had already achieved the required emission levels with the RACT standard and other state rules.

9. Much of the regulatory intervention and litigation surrounding the implementation of prescriptive regulation can be seen as jockeying for the competitive advantage and associated rents created by these programs.

10. The material in this section is drawn largely from Harrison (2004) and SCAQMD (2003).

11. The reduction in the number of RTCs distributed annually from 1994 through 2003 declined by 70 percent for NO_x and 60 percent for SO_2, but in both cases the annual caps were set intentionally to be initially nonbinding. Because banking is not allowed, the early excess RTCs had no effect on eventual compliance.

12. As of August 2004, power-producing facilities have not been reintegrated into the program. The current proposal is that their reentry be delayed until 2007 and that the allocations to these units be reduced by about 25 percent. The further lowering of the cap is being proposed to avoid a surplus of RTCs coming onto the market because the mandated NO_x controls have reduced emissions from power-producing facilities below the post-2003 RTC allocations to these units (SCAQMD 2004; Unger 2004).

13. Rosenzweig and Varilek (2003) provide an insightful description of the problems of handling the required data for one of the first experiments in emissions trading, the lead in gasoline trading program.

REFERENCES

Buchanan, James M., and Gordon Tullock (1975). "Polluters' Profits and Political Response: Direct Controls versus Taxes," *American Economic Review* 65(1): 139–47.

Burtraw, Dallas, and Erin Mansur (1999). "The Environmental Effects of SO_2 Trading and Banking," *Environmental Science and Technology* 33(20): 3489–94.

Carlson, Curtis P., Dallas Burtraw, Maureen Cropper, and Karen Palmer (2000). "SO$_2$ Control by Electric Utilities: What Are the Gains from Trade?" *Journal of Political Economy* 108(6): 1292–326.

Chay, Kenneth Y., and Michael Greenstone (2004). *Air Quality, Infant Mortality and the Clean Air Act of 1970.* MIT-CEEPR Working Paper available online at web.mit.edu/ceepr/www/2004–006.pdf.

Clear the Air: National Campaign against Dirty Power (2002). "Darkening Skies: Trends toward Increasing Power Plant Emissions," Washington, DC. Available online at cta.policy.net/fact/darkening_skies.

Crocker, Thomas D. (1966). "The Structuring of Atmospheric Pollution Control Systems," in *The Economics of Air Pollution,* ed. Harold Wolozin. New York: Norton.

Dales, J. H. (1968). *Pollution, Property and Prices: An Essay in Policy-Making and Economics.* Toronto: University of Toronto Press.

Dubroeucq, Florence (2004). *Effectiveness of the Clean Air Act on SO$_2$ Emissions from U.S. Electric Utilities: A Detailed Analysis of the Influence of Attainment Status and Unit-Level Characteristics on the Reduction of SO$_2$ Emissions from 1976 to 2002.* Master's thesis in Technology and Science, MIT, Cambridge, MA.

Ellerman, A. Denny (2004). "The U.S. SO$_2$ Cap-and-Trade Program," in *Tradeable Permits: Policy Evaluation, Design and Reform.* Paris: OECD, pp. 71–97. Also available as MIT/CEEPR Working Paper online at web.mit.edu/ceepr/www/2003–003.pdf.

Ellerman, A. Denny, and Juan-Pablo Montero (2002). *The Temporal Efficiency of SO$_2$ Emissions Trading.* MIT-CEEPR Working Paper 02–003 (September).

Ellerman, A. Denny, Paul L. Joskow, and David Harrison (2003). *Emissions Trading: Experience, Lessons, and Considerations for Greenhouse Gases.* Washington, D.C.: Pew Center for Global Climate Change.

Ellerman, A. Denny, Paul L. Joskow, Richard Schmalensee, Juan-Pablo Montero, and Elizabeth Bailey (2000). *Markets for Clean Air: The U.S. Acid Rain Program.* Cambridge: Cambridge University Press.

Farrell, Alex (2000). "The NO$_x$ Budget: A Look at the First Year." *Electricity Journal* March: 83–92.

Fuller, Dan A. (1987). "Compliance, Avoidance, and Evasion: Emissions Control under Imperfect Enforcement in Steam-Electric Generation," *RAND Journal of Economics* 18(1): 124–37.

Gollop, Frank M., and Mark J. Roberts (1983). "Environmental Regulations and Productivity Growth: The Case of Fossil-Fueled Electric Power Generation" *Journal of Political Economy* 91(4): 654–74.

Greenstone, Michael (2004). *Did the Clean Air Act Cause the Remarkable Decline in Sulfur Dioxide Concentrations?* MIT-CEEPR Working Paper 2004–007, available online at web.mit.edu/ceepr/www/2004–007.pdf.

Harrison, David Jr. (2004). "Ex Post Evaluation of the RECLAIM Emissions Trading Programmes for the Los Angeles Air Basin," in *Tradeable Permits: Policy Evaluation, Design and Reform.* Paris: OECD, pp. 45–69.

Joskow, Paul L. (2001). "California's Electricity Crisis," *Oxford Review of Economic Policy* 17(3): 365–88.

Kruger, Joseph A., Brian J. McLean, and Rayenne Chen (2000). "A Tale of Two Revolutions: Administration of the SO$_2$ Trading Program," in *Emissions Trading: Environmental Policy's New Approach,* ed. Richard Kosobud. New York: Wiley.

Laffont, Jean-Jacques, and Jean Tirole (1993). *A Theory of Incentives in Procurement and Regulation.* Cambridge, MA: MIT Press.

MacAvoy, Paul W. (1979). *The Regulated Industries and the Economy.* New York: Norton.

MacAvoy, Paul W. (1987). "The Record of the Environmental Protection Agency in Controlling Industrial Air Pollution," in *Energy: Markets and Regulation, Essays in Honor of M. A. Adelman,* eds. Richard L. Gordon, Henry D. Jacoby, and Martin B. Zimmerman, Cambridge, MA: MIT Press, pp. 107–36.

Montgomery, W. David (1972). "Markets in Licenses and Efficient Pollution Control Programs," *Journal of Economic Theory* 5:395–418.

Moore, Curtis A. (2002). *Marketing Failure: The Experience with Air Pollution Trading in the United States.* Unpublished study.

Nelson, Randy A., Tom Tietenberg, and Michael R. Donihue (1993). "Differential Environmental Regulation: Effects on Electric Utility Capital Turnover and Emissions," *Review of Economics and Statistics* 75(2): 368–73.

Ringquist, Evan J. (1993). "Does Regulation matter? Evaluating the Effects of State Air Pollution Control Programs," *Journal of Politics* 55(4): 1022–45.

Rosenzweig, Richard, and Matthew Varilek (2003). *Key Issues to Be Considered in the Development of Rate-Based Emissions Trading Programs: Lessons Learned from Past Programs.* Final discussion draft for EPRI Workshop in Vancouver, BC, Canada, April 29.

Shabman, Leonard, Kurt Stephenson, and William Shobe (2002). "Trading Programs for Environmental Management: Reflections on the Air and Water Experiences," *Environmental Practice* 4(3): 153–62.

South Coast Air Quality Management District (SCAQMD) (2003). *Annual RECLAIM Audit Report for the 2001 Compliance Year.* Available online at www .aqmd.gov/hb/030336a.html.

South Coast Air Quality Management District (SCAQMD) (2004). *Draft White Paper: Key Issues Relative to Proposed Amendments to Regulation XX—Regional Clean Air Incentives Market (RECLAIM).* Available online at www.aqmd.gov/ RECLAIM/docs/White%20Paper%20August%202004%20DRAFT.pdf.

Swift, Byron (2000). "Allowance Trading and SO_2 Hot Spots: Good News from the Acid Rain Program," *Environment Reporter* 31(19)L 954–59.

Tietenberg, Tom H. (1985). *Emissions Trading: An Exercise in Reforming Pollution Policy.* Washington, DC: Resources for the Future.

Unger, Samantha (2004). *RECLAIM Poised for Major Changes.* Evolution Markets LLC Executive Brief no. 25, available online at www.evomarkets.com/assets/ evobriefs/nw_1093900761.pdf.

U.S. Environmental Protection Agency (EPA) (2000). *1999 Compliance Report: Acid Rain Program.* EPA-430-R000–007. Available online at www.epa.gov/airmarkets/ cmprpt/arp99/arpcomprpt99.pdf.

U.S. Environmental Protection Agency and the Ozone Transport Commission (EPA-OTC) (2003). *NO_x Budget Program: 1999–2002 Progress Report.* Available online at www.epa.gov/airmarkets/otc.

4

Tradable Permits in Principle and Practice

Tom Tietenberg

INTRODUCTION

Background

One of most prominent approaches for coping with the problem of rationing access to the commons involves the use of tradable permits. Applications of this approach have spread to many different types of resources and many different countries. A recent survey found nine applications in air pollution control, seventy-five applications in fisheries, three applications in managing water resources, five applications in controlling water pollution, and five applications in land use control (OECD 1999, Appendix 1, pp. 18–19). And that survey failed to include many current applications, including those that have sprung up in response to the Kyoto Protocol.

The Kyoto Protocol authorizes three cooperative implementation mechanisms that involve tradable permits: emission trading, joint implementation, and the Clean Development Mechanism. These programs have, in turn, spawned others. The European Parliament passed a bill capping European industry's carbon dioxide output and letting firms trade the allowed emissions. Beginning in January 2005, many plants in the oil refining, smelting, steel, cement, ceramics, glass, and paper sectors need special permits to emit carbon dioxide (CO_2). Individual countries such as the United Kingdom (Hartridge 2003) and Denmark (Pederson 2003) have created their own national trading programs. Individual companies are even involved. BP, an energy company, has established company-wide goals and a trading program to help individual units to meet those goals. Despite the fact that the

United States has not signed the Kyoto Protocol, American companies, states, and municipalities have accepted voluntary caps on CO_2 and methane emissions and are using trading to facilitate meeting those goals. A new institution, the Chicago Climate Exchange,[1] has been set up to facilitate these trades. The unprecedented scope of these programs breaks new ground in terms of geographic coverage, the number of participants, and the types of polluting gases covered.

Overview

In this chapter I review the experience with three main applications of tradable permit systems—air pollution control, water supply, and fisheries management—as well as some unique programs, such as the U.S. program to mitigate the loss of wetlands (Shabman 2004), the program in the Netherlands to control the damage to water pollution from manure spreading (Wossink 2004), and the U.S. program to allocate grazing rights on federal land (Raymond 2003).[2] The purpose of this review is to exploit the large variation in implementation experience to isolate the lessons about the design and applicability of tradable permit systems that can be gleaned from this rich variety of applications.

At the most general level, the major conclusion of this review is that context does matter. The various resources being controlled by tradable permits have different characteristics, and those characteristics affect program evaluation, design, and effectiveness. Our sense of what has been accomplished by these programs is also quite dependent not only on the details of the ex post evaluation process (such as its scope, the evaluation criteria, and definition of the comparative baseline) but also on the implementation details of the programs being evaluated (such as the initial allocation, the legal nature of the entitlement, and transferability rules).

The review proceeds in several steps. First, because what we know depends on the methods of analysis used to derive the conclusions, I examine how ex post evaluation is currently practiced as revealed in the published literature. This section not only points out how decisions about the structure of the analysis affects findings but also provides a basis for discerning what lessons can be derived for improving the ex post analysis process itself. Second, I examine the substantive results from these studies using three specific criteria: implementation feasibility, environmental effectiveness, and economic effectiveness. This section lays the groundwork not only for isolating what seems to work and not work but also for isolating the implications of these results for how design characteristics affect success. Finally, in the last section I draw together the lessons that can be extracted from this review. The three subsections in this part of the chapter focus on lessons for the design of effective programs, the design of ex post evaluation systems that are useful both for improving and evaluating the implemented systems, and finally how expectations from theory might be modified in the light of this wealth of experience with implemented programs.

EX POST EVALUATION: PROBLEMS AND PROSPECTS

In principle, establishing how well a program has worked in actual application seems a simple matter. In practice it is more complicated. As a result, reasonable people viewing the same experience can come to different conclusions. Therefore before delving into the evidence provided from ex post evaluations, it seems reasonable to take a close look at the ex post evaluation process itself.

Defining the Evaluation Criterion

Variants of the Efficiency Criterion

Ex post studies examining economic efficiency typically rely on some or all of three rather different concepts: pareto optimality, cost-effectiveness, or market effectiveness. Because these are in fact quite different concepts, studies relying on them could come to very different conclusions, even if they are examining the same program.

Pareto optimality, or its typical operational formulation, maximizing net benefits, examines whether the policy derives all the net benefits from the resource use that are possible. Naturally this requires a comparison of the costs of the program with all the benefits achieved, including the value of reduced pollution or conserved resources. (Burtraw et al. 1998) Conducting this kind of evaluation is time and information intensive and, in my experience with tradable permit systems, rather rare.[3] An alternative form, which is somewhat less rare, is simply to compare the present value of net benefits for the program with the net benefits from some predefined alternative.

A more common evaluation approach, particularly for ex ante studies, relies on cost-effectiveness (Farrell et al. 1999). This approach typically takes a predefined environmental target as given (such as an emissions cap or a total allowable catch) and examines whether the program minimizes the cost of reaching that target.[4] Another form is to compare the cost of reaching the target with the program to the cost of reaching the target with the next most likely alternative. This approach, of course, compares the program not to an optimal benchmark but to a pragmatic benchmark.[5]

Finally, a number of evaluations focus on whether the market structure is effective. In the absence of an initial allocation that happens to mimic the cost-effective allocation, transactions costs and market power can inhibit trade and prevent a market from achieving the target at minimum cost.[6] A number of studies (Ellerman 2004; Wossink 2004, Young 2004; Harrison 2004) examine market effectiveness.[7] They use both qualitative and quantitative assessments.[8]

Counterfactuals and Baselines

Because many ex post evaluations compare the environmental policy to an alternative pragmatic benchmark, defining the appropriate benchmark is crucial. It is also difficult.

Tradable permits of course are not usually implemented in a vacuum. They frequently complement other policies. For example the U.S. sulfur allowance program operates within the more general framework of sulfur oxide regulation established by the National Ambient Air Quality Standards. The RECLAIM program in California operates within the context of a rather dramatic electric deregulation program. The Dutch Nutrient Quota Program operates within the framework of the European Union's Common Agricultural Policy. The interdependence of these programs makes it difficult to disentangle the unique effects of a tradable permit policy and to draw implications for how the policy might work in a rather different policy environment.

Ellerman (2004), for example, points out that the comprehensive analysis of the sulfur allowance program conducted at MIT is based on the assumption that the heat input observed at affected units in each year would not change from the pre–Title IV rates. As he also notes, this counterfactual assumption has the effect of making the baseline emissions insensitive to changes in demand, either at individual units or in the aggregate. To the extent that other environmental regulations or changes in relative fuel prices would have caused the emission rate at affected units to fall during the period of evaluation, the effect of the SO_2 program would be overestimated.

Developing counterfactuals about costs is necessarily more subjective because relative costs depend directly on the degree of inefficiency assumed in the imagined alternative regime. Because that regulatory regime doesn't exist, it is not always easy to figure out what it might have been.

Finally, using the easy counterfactual by simply extrapolating past trends might prove quite misleading. Young (2004) points out that the recent preliminary assessment of the costs and benefits of environmental flow enhancement for the Murray River was built on a baseline scenario of increasing river salinity and hence declining regional income. This was a very different counterfactual than would have been produced by simply extrapolating historic trends. The simpler baseline would have been physically impossible and, hence, its use would be quite misleading.

The Scope of the Evaluation

It is important to note that evaluation difficulties arise not only from specifying what policies to include in (or omit from) the counterfactual but also in isolating the degree to which changes in observed outcomes are endogenous or exogenous to the policy change. To the extent that the introduction of the program influences outcomes that are normally considered outside of the scope of the analysis, important aspects may be missed. And, as will be elaborated, several circumstances can be identified where the apparent effects of the program do transcend normal evaluation boundaries.

Clearly the outcome of the sulfur allowance program has been heavily influenced by rather dramatic changes in scrubber technology and in the markedly enhanced rail availability of low sulfur coals from the Western United States. Would these events have occurred in the absence of the sulfur allowance program (and therefore should be in the counterfactual) or were they the result of the program (and therefore should not be in the counterfactual)? Definitive conclusions about the effectiveness of this program depend on the answers to those questions.

As described shortly in the section dealing with substantive results, environmental outcomes, which cost-effectiveness evaluations may normally assume to be the same under alternative policy regimes, may not be the same at all. One example of such a source of variability involves both the degree and cost of monitoring and enforcement.

Do monitoring and enforcement costs rise under tradable permit programs? The answer depends both on the level of required enforcement activity (greater levels of enforcement effort obviously cost more) and on the degree to which existing enforcement resources are used more or less efficiently. Even higher enforcement costs may not by themselves be definitive because they can be financed from the enhanced profitability promoted by the tradable permit system.[9]

One other difficulty posed for ex post evaluation is that monitoring and enforcement technologies can change, sometimes dramatically, during (and even as a result of) tradable permit programs. Take the U.S. sulfur allowance system, for example. (Kruger et al. 1999) Both the collection and dissemination of the information derived from the continuous emissions monitors is now handled via the Web. Special software has been developed to take individual inputs and to generate information both for the public and for EPA enforcement activities. According to Kruger et al. (1999), the development of this technology has increased administrative efficiency, lowered transaction costs, and provided greater environmental accountability. To the extent that these changes in monitoring technology are endogenous, ex post evaluation schemes that treat them as exogenous will be biased.

Evaluations of tradable permit programs must have a sufficiently large scope as to take "external" effects into account. Resources controlled by the permit program are frequently not the only resources affected.

- In water, one significant problem has been the protection of "in-stream" uses of water (Young 2004). Evaluations that focus only on withdrawals will miss this crucial aspect.
- In air pollution control, several effects transcend the normal boundaries of the program. In the climate change program, for example, it is widely recognized (Hartridge 2003; Ekins 1996) that

the control of greenhouse gases will result in substantial reductions of other pollutants as a side effect.
- Other, more detrimental effects include the clustering of emissions either in space or time. For some (but not all) pollutants the location of the emissions or resource use can matter (Tietenberg 1995). Any cost-effectiveness analysis that doesn't account for the actual spatial or temporal heterogeneity in emissions may be defining effectiveness incorrectly.
- In fisheries, two main effects on nontargeted species have been the discard of fish for which no quota is held (bycatch discards) and habitat destruction. Focusing the evaluation solely on effects on the targeted species would miss these potentially important effects on the ecosystem as a whole (National Research Council Committee to Review Individual Fishing Quotas 1999).

The Timing of the Evaluation

Evaluations can be conducted at any time during the life of the program, but when they are conducted will affect what they find and how useful they are. Most of these programs evolve considerably over their lifetime. Apparently not only do participants and administrators experience a considerable amount of "learning by doing" as the program matures, but design parameters are frequently altered in light of the early experience.

Consider some specific examples. The nature of the harvesting right was changed in the New Zealand fishery (Kerr 2004), banking was added to the lead banking program (Nussbaum 1992), and an additional 10 percent reduction in swine was added to the Dutch nutrient quota system (Wossink 2004). In addition in the sulfur allowance program, firms looked first to internal trades and process adjustments rather than to external trades. Thus in the early stages of this program the equalization of marginal costs, the focus of the theory, proved to be less important than the opportunity to exploit technological flexibility within the firm (Bohi and Burtraw 1997).

Because evolution is so common for tradable permit programs, a strong case can be made for thinking of midcourse corrections as routine. The mirror image of this insight is that early evaluations may well not provide much insight about the ultimate success or failure of the program because dramatic change is so common.

The Role of Administrative Costs

Although a complete ex post evaluation would examine how policy choice affects administrative costs as well as abatement cost, most don't. Although most published case studies don't shed much light on administrative costs, some case studies do. As will be demonstrated, they demonstrate that the amount and nature of public administration tasks can change with the adoption of a tradable permits approach. Therefore ex post studies that fail to consider administrative cost omit by design a potentially important comparative element.

A complete ex post evaluation must also confront the effect of the choice of policy instrument on the regulatory structure itself. Ex post evaluation also has begun to reveal how tradable permits, particularly cap-and-trade systems, change the fundamental nature of regulation (Ellerman 2004; Harrison 2004; McLean 2003). With tradable permits bureaucrats are no longer in charge of defining the appropriate way to meet the goal. Instead, they are in charge of assuring that the user meets the goal.

A REVIEW OF EX POST EVALUATIONS OF TRADABLE PERMIT SYSTEMS

This assessment of the outcomes of these systems focuses on three major categories of effects. The first is implementation feasibility. A proposed policy regime cannot perform its function if it cannot be implemented or if its main protective mechanisms are so weakened by the implementation process that it is rendered ineffective. What matters to policy makers is not how a policy regime works in principle but how it works in practice. The second category seeks to answer the question, "How much environmental protection did it offer not only to the targeted resource but to other resources that might have been affected either positively or negatively by its implementation?" Finally, what were the economic effects on those who either directly or indirectly use the resource?

Implementation Feasibility

Until recently the historic record on tradable permits seemed to indicate that resorting to this approach usually only occurred after other, more familiar approaches had been tried and had failed. In essence the adjustment costs of implementing a new system with which policy administrators have little personal experience are typically perceived as so large that they can only be justified when the benefits have risen sufficiently to justify the transition (Libecap 1990).

This review finds some support for that view, particularly in the earlier years. Most fisheries that have turned to these policies have done so only after a host of alternative input and output controls have failed to stem the destructive pressure being placed on the fishery (National Research Council Committee to Review Individual Fishing Quotas 1999). A similar story can be told for air pollution control. The offset air pollution control policy, introduced in the United States during the 1970s, owes its birth to an inability to find any other policy to reconcile the desire to allow economic growth with the desire to improve the quality of the air (Tietenberg 2001).

It is also clear from the historical record that not every attempt to introduce a tradable permit approach has been successful. In air pollution control, attempts to establish transferable permit approaches have failed in Poland (Zylicz 1999) and Germany (Scharer 1999). The initial attempts to introduce an SO_2 trading system also failed in the United Kingdom (Sorrell 1999), although recent attempts to establish a CO_2 program in that country have succeeded. Programs in water pollution control have historically not been very successful (Hahn and Hester 1989).

On the other hand, it does appear that the introduction of new tradable permit programs becomes easier with familiarity. In the United States following the very successful lead phaseout program, new supporters appeared and made it possible to pass the sulfur allowance program. The introduction of the various flexibility mechanisms into the Kyoto Protocol was facilitated by the successful experience with the U.S. sulfur allowance program, among others. And the recent introduction of tradable permits systems in several European countries and the European Union itself was precipitated by the opportunities provided by the Kyoto Protocol.

It also seems quite clear that to date at least, using a free distribution approach to the initial allocation has been a necessary ingredient in building the political support necessary to implement the approach (Raymond 2003). Existing users frequently have the power to block implementation, but potential future users do not. This has made it politically expedient to allocate a substantial part of the economic rent that these resources offer to existing users as the price of securing their support. Although this strategy reduces the adjustment costs to existing users, it generally raises them for new users.

One tendency that seems to arise in some new applications of this concept is placing severe restrictions on its operation as a way to quell administrative fears about undesirable, unforeseen outcomes. As Shabman (2004) points out, this is precisely the case with the U.S. wetlands credit program. In some cases, and the wetlands program may well be an example, these restrictions are so severe that they cripple the program, thereby preventing its ultimate evolution to a smoothly operating system. Although with increased familiarity (and comfort) initially imposed restrictions tend to disappear over time, they can severely diminish the early accomplishments of the program.

Environmental Effects

One common belief about tradable permit programs is that their environmental effects are determined purely by the imposition of the aggregate limit, an act that is considered to lie outside the system. Hence, it is believed, the main purpose of the system is to protect the economic value of the resource, not the resource itself.

That is an oversimplification for several reasons. First, whether it is politically possible to set an aggregate limit at all may be a function of the policy intended to achieve it. Second, both the magnitude of that limit and its evolution over time may be related to the policy. Third, the choice of policy regime may affect the level of monitoring and enforcement and noncompliance can undermine the achievements of the limit. Fourth, the policy may trigger environmental effects that are not covered by the limit.

The Stringency of the Limit

In general the evidence seems to suggest that by lowering compliance costs, tradable permit programs facilitate the setting of more stringent caps. In air trading programs the lower costs offered by trading were used in initial negotiations to secure more stringent pollution control targets (Acid Rain Program, lead phaseout, and RECLAIM) or earlier deadlines (lead phaseout program). The air quality effects from more stringent limits were reinforced by the use of adjusted offset ratios for trades in non-attainment areas. (Offset rations were required to be greater than 1.0, implying that a portion of each acquisition would go for improved air quality.) In addition, environmental groups have been allowed to purchase and retire allowances (Acid Rain Program). Retired allowances represent pollution that is authorized but not emitted.

In fisheries the institution of individual transferable quotas (ITQs) has sometimes (but not always) resulted in lower (more protective) total allowable catches (TACs). In the Netherlands, for example, the plaice quota was cut in half over time (and prices rose to cushion the income shock; Davidse 1999).

Meeting and Enforcing the Limit

In theory, the flexibility offered by tradable permit programs makes it easier to reach the limit, suggesting the possibility that the limit may be met more often under these systems than under those that preceded it. In most fisheries this expectation seems to have been borne out. For example, while exceeding the TAC was common before the imposition of an ITQ system in the Alaskan halibut and sablefish fisheries, the frequency of exceedances dropped significantly after the introduction of the ITQ (National Research Council Committee to Review Individual Fishing Quotas 1999).

Regardless of how well any tradable permit system is designed, noncompliance can prevent the attainment of its economic, social, and environmental objectives.[10] Although it is true that any management regime faces monitoring and enforcement issues, tradable permit regimes raise some special issues. One of the most desirable aspects of tradable permits for resource users, their ability to raise income levels for participants, is a double-edged sword because it also raises incentives for noncompliance. In the absence of an effective enforcement system, higher profitability could promote illegal activity. Insufficient monitoring and enforcement could also result in failure to keep a tradable permit system within its environmental limit.[11]

One increasingly important aspect associated with transferable permit systems involves their ability to raise revenue for both enforcement and administration. In many permit systems, enforcement costs are now routinely financed from the enhanced profitability promoted by the tradable permit system. Not only has the recovery of monitoring and enforcement costs from users become standard practice in some fisheries (New Zealand, for example), but funding at least some monitoring and enforcement activity out of rents generated by the fishery has already been included as a provision in the most recent amendments to the U.S. Magnuson-Stevens Act. This concept is beginning to affect air pollution control as well. In the sulfur allowance program, for example, the environmental community demanded (and received) a requirement that continuous emission monitoring be installed (and financed) by every covered utility. Coupling this with the rather stringent penalty system has meant almost 100 percent compliance. In the Danish system (Pederson 2003), which does not rely on continuous emission monitoring, the electricity producers pay an administration fee of 0.079 DKK per ton of CO_2 allowance to the DEA to cover the administration costs (verification of CO_2 emissions, control, hearing and distribution of allowances, operating the registry, monitoring of trading, development of the scheme, etc.).

A successful enforcement program also requires a carefully constructed set of sanctions for noncompliance. In the sulfur allowance program, generally considered the most successful tradable permit program, those found in noncompliance must not only pay a substantial financial penalty for noncompliance but also forfeit a sufficient number of future allowances to compensate for the overage. Any egregious violations can lead to forfeiture of the right to participate in the program.

Direct Effects on the Resource

Air pollution programs have typically had a very positive effect on reducing emissions. The U.S. programs to phase out lead (Nussbaum 1992) and reduce ozone-depleting gases (Hahn and McGartland 1989) were designed to eliminate (not merely reduce) pollutants. Both the U.S. program to control sulfur (Burtraw and Mansur 1999) and RECLAIM (Harrison 2004) involve substantial reductions in emissions over time.

What have been the effects on biomass in fisheries? The evidence on the overall effect on fisheries has been mixed. In the Chilean squat lobster fishery, the exploitable biomass rebounded from a low of about 15,500 tons (prior to ITQs) to a level in 1998 of between 80,000 and 100,000 tons (Bernal and Aliaga 1999). The herring fishery in Iceland experienced a similar rebound (Runolfsson 1999).

How typical are these examples? One review of thirty-seven ITQ or individual quota (IQ) fisheries found that twenty-four experienced at least some temporary declines in stocks after instituting the programs. These were largely attributed to a combination of inadequate information on which to set conservative TACs and illegal fishing activity resulting from ineffective enforcement. Interestingly twenty of the twenty-four fisheries experiencing declines had superimposed additional command-and-control regulations, such as closed areas, size/selectivity regulations, trip limits, vessel restrictions, and so on, on top to the tradable permits system (OECD 1997, 82). These additional regulations were apparently also in-effective in protecting the resource; the problems plaguing ITQs plague more traditional approaches as well.

Effects on Other Resources

The resource controlled by the permit program is frequently not the only resource affected. In water applications, one significant problem has been the protection of nonconsumptive uses of water (Young 2004). In the United States some states only protected private entitlements to water if water was diverted from the stream and consumed. The entitlements for water left in the stream to promote recreational uses could be confiscated by authorities, because "unused" rights did not meet the definition of a beneficial use. Recent changes in policy and some legal determinations have afforded more protections to these environmental uses of water.

According to Shabman (2004) the wetlands permitting program has failed to stem the degradation of wetlands and therefore the degradation of all ecosystems dependent on those wetlands. His review suggests that the ecological functions, especially for wildlife and habitat, of avoided wetlands and on-site wetlands offsets have become compromised by polluted runoff and adverse changes in hydrologic regimes. In some cases, ecological failure resulted from poor construction techniques. In other cases, a promised offsetting restoration project may not have been undertaken at all. In general the failure to prevent these compromises to the program can apparently be traced back to limited agency enforcement resources.

Leakage provides another possible source of external effects. Leakage occurs when pressure on the regulated resource is diverted to an unreg-ulated or lesser regulated resource, such as when fishermen move their boats to another fishery or polluters move their factory to a country with lower environmental standards.

In some cases leakage can intensify the positive effects of a program, as is the case when the control of greenhouse gases results in substantial reductions of other air pollutants associated with the combustion of fossil fuels (Ekins 1996). But in others the effects on other resources can be quite detrimental.

In fisheries the possibilities for detrimental effects on nontargeted species are particularly large. Two examples of these effects are bycatch and habitat destruction. Bycatch, the harvesting of nontargeted species (perhaps due to the nonspecificity of the harvesting gear) is a problem in many fisheries, regardless of the means of control. Harvested fish for which no quota is held are likely to be discarded before reaching shore. For many species, these discards die rather than recover. No clear pattern emerges from the literature about how the introduction of ITQs affects bycatch. Two reviews found that bycatch may either increase or decrease in ITQ fisheries, depending on the fishery (OECD 1997, 83; National Research Council Committee to Review Individual Fishing Quotas 1999, 177).

Habitat damage occurs when the fishing gear causes damage to the seabed or geological formations that provide habitat for species dwelling on or near the ocean floor. Tradable permits could in principle increase or decrease the amount of habitat damage by affecting both the type of gear used and the timing and location of its use. Evidence about tradable permits intensifies or limits this problem is extremely limited (National Research Council Committee to Review Individual Fishing Quotas 1999).

Economic Effects

Though the evidence on environmental consequences is mixed (especially for fisheries), the evidence on economic consequences is clearer. In the presence of adequate enforcement, tradable permits do appear to increase the value of the resource (in the case of water and fisheries) or lower the cost of compliance (in the case of emissions reduction).

In air pollution control, considerable savings in meeting the pollution control targets have been found (Ellerman 2004; Harrison 2004; Hahn and Hester 1989; Tietenberg 1990). For water the increase in value brought about by transferring the resources from lower valued to higher valued uses has typically been quite large (Young 2004; Easter et al. 1998). In fisheries a substantial income increase not only results from more appropriately scaled capital investments (resulting from the reduction in overcapitalization) but also from the fact that ITQs frequently make it possible to sell a more valuable product at higher prices (fresh fish rather than frozen fish; National Research Council Committee to Review Individual Fishing Quotas 1999). One review of twenty-two fisheries found that the introduction of ITQs increased wealth in all of them (OECD 1997, 83).

In both water and air pollution, the regulatory transition following the introduction of transferable permits was not from an open-access resource to tradable permits, but from a less flexible control regime to a more flexible one. The transition has apparently been accomplished with few adverse employment consequences, though sufficient data to do a comprehensive evaluation on that particular question do not exist (Berman and Bui 2001; Goodstein 1996).

The employment consequences for fisheries have been more severe. The introduction of ITQs has usually been accompanied by a considerable reduction in the amount of fishing effort. Normally this means not only fewer boats but also less employment. The evidence also suggests, however, that the workers who remain in the industry work more hours during the year and earn more money (National Research Council Committee to Review Individual Fishing Quotas 1999, 101).

The introduction of ITQs in fisheries has also had implications for crew, processors, and communities. Traditionally in many fisheries crew have been coventurers in the fishing enterprise, sharing in both the risk and reward. In some cases the shift to ITQs has shifted the risk and ultimately shifted the compensation system from a profit-sharing to a wage system. Though this has not generally lowered incomes, it has changed the culture of fishing (McCay et al. 1989; McCay and Creed 1990).

Secondary industries can be affected by the introduction of tradable permits in a number of ways. Consider, for example, the effects on fish processors. First the processing sector is typically as overcapitalized as the harvesting sector. Because the introduction of ITQs typically extends the fishing season and spreads out the processing needs of the industry, less processing capacity is needed. In addition the more leisurely pace of harvesting reduces the bargaining power of processors versus fishers. In some remote areas such as Alaska, a considerable amount of this processing capital may lose value due to its immobility (Matulich et al. 1996; Matulich and Sever 1999).

Communities can be (and in some cases have been) adversely affected when quota held by local resource users is transferred to resource users who operate out of other communities. As described later in the design lessons section of the chapter, techniques developed to mitigate these effects, however, seem to have been at least moderately successful (National Research Council Committee to Review Individual Fishing Quotas 1999, 206).

Generally market power has not been a significant issue in most permit markets despite some tendencies toward the concentration of quota. In part this is due to accumulation limits that have been placed on quota holders and the fact that these are typically not markets in which accumulation of quota yields significant monopoly-type powers. In fisheries some concern has been expressed (Palsson 1998) that the introduction of ITQs will mean the demise of the smaller fishers as they are bought out by larger operations. The evidence does not seem support this concern (National Research Council Committee to Review Individual Fishing Quotas 1999, 84).

Although hard evidence on the point is scarce, a substantial amount of anecdotal evidence is emerging about how tradable permit programs can change the way environmental risk is treated within polluting firms (Hartridge 2003; McLean 2003). This evidence suggests that environmental management used to be relegated to the tail end of the decision-making process. Historically the environmental risk manager was not involved in the most fundamental decisions about product design, production processes, selection of inputs, and so on. Rather he or she was simply confronted with the decisions already made and told to keep the firm out of trouble. This particular organizational assignment of responsibilities inhibits the exploitation of one potentially important avenue of risk reduction—pollution prevention.

Because tradable permits put both a cap and a price on environmental risks, it tends to get corporate financial people involved. Furthermore, as the costs of compliance rise in general, environmental costs become worthy of more general scrutiny. Reducing environmental risk can become an important component of the bottom line. Given its anecdotal nature, the evidence on the extent of organizational changes that might be initiated by tradable permits should be treated more as a hypothesis to be tested than a firm result, but its potential importance is large.

Economic theory treats markets as if they emerge spontaneously and universally as needed. In practice the applications examined in this review point out that participants frequently require some experience with the program before they fully understand (and behave effectively) in the market for permits. This finding seems potentially important for the implementation of the Kyoto Protocol's Clean Development Mechanism, which involves the creation of transferable credits in developing countries.

The type of tradable permits system seems to affect administrative costs. Credit-based programs (such as the Emissions Trading System [ETS] designed in the United Kingdom; [Hartridge 2003]) keep a large element of the previous administrative work in place. Programs with regulatory preapproval (i.e., wetlands credits and water trading) do so to an even greater extent. In addition, other specific design features (such as the opt-in in the sulfur allowance program [Ellerman 2004] and the use of relative targets in the U.K. ETS [Hartridge 2003]) also add considerably to administration costs. Because the design features vary so much from program type to program type, it is difficult to generalize insights about administrative costs across programs.

Two general themes that emerge are that the administration of tradable permit systems involves fewer administrative person-hours (McLean 2003) and that the bureaucratic functions performed are quite different (McLean 2003; Harrison 2004). These changing administrative functions have implications for the nature of the skills required by administrators. Those who can monitor and enforce compliance replace engineers who seek to identify the correct control strategies for sources and negotiate permit exemptions.

One rather unexpected point that emerges from ex post evaluation of tradable permit systems is the degree to which the number of errors in preexisting emission registries are brought to light by the need to create accurate registries for TP schemes. (Wossink 2004; Pedersen 2003; Montero 2002; Hartridge 2003). Although inadequate inventories plague all quantity-based approaches, tradable permits seem particularly effective at bringing them to light and getting them corrected.

LESSONS

The evaluation of operating systems has implications for the way one evaluates these systems, the way one designs these systems, and the way one interprets the outcomes. I now turn to those lessons.

Lessons about Ex Post Evaluation

The form of the evaluation matters. Efficiency studies, for example, that consider the programmatic effects on other markets, particularly in the presence of distortionary taxes, find a marked advantage for auctions (due to the ability to recycle revenue) over initial allocations based on free distribution. Cost-effectiveness studies, which are unable to consider this aspect, find no such advantage.

As noted earlier, evaluation is made more difficult by the interdependence between tradable permit programs and mandatory constraints or other policy measures with which they may coincide. Many permit programs arise against the backdrop of prescriptive requirements. This is true, for example, of the sulfur dioxide trading program in the U.S. Clean Air Act, which operates in the context of a statute that requires the EPA to set mandatory national ambient standards for pollutants—effectively creating a ceiling under which the trading scheme operates. Disentangling the effects of a trading program from the regulatory context in which it arises can be challenging. But if they fail to do so, researchers might mistakenly attribute advantages to the trading program that are more accurately attributable to an interaction among coexisting policies.

Failure to recognize either nonhomogeneity or endogeneity in the evaluation process can lead to biased evaluations. Treating systems that have ex ante identical emission reductions or withdrawal as equivalent may miss important temporal or spatial impact on the targeted resources as well as external effects on nontargeted resources. Considering aspects such as the feasibility of the system, the level of the target, the likelihood of reaching the target, and the effectiveness of monitoring and enforcement as outside the scope of analysis can miss important consequences of instrument choice.

Failure to recognize the evolutionary nature of the system may result in conclusions drawn from an analysis of a transitory stage being mistakenly interpreted as reflecting what would have been found at a later stage. It may also underestimate of the importance of early evaluations in shaping the speed and form of the evolution.

Lessons for Program Design

The Baseline Issue

In general, tradable permit programs fit into one of two categories: credit programs or cap-and-trade programs. Air pollution control systems and water have examples of both types. Fisheries tradable permit programs are all of the cap-and-trade variety.

Credit trading, the approach taken in the U.S. Emissions Trading Program (the earliest program), allows emission reductions above and beyond baseline legal requirements to be certified as tradable credits (Tietenberg 1985). The baseline for credits in that program was provided by traditional technology-based standards.

In a cap-and-trade program, a total resource access limit (the cap) is defined and then allocated among users. Compliance is established by simply comparing actual use with the assigned firm-specific cap as adjusted by any acquired or sold permits.

Establishing the baseline for credit programs in the absence of an existing permitting system can be very difficult. For example, the basic requirement in the Clean Development Mechanism component of the Kyoto Protocol is "additionality." In other words, the traded reductions must be surplus to what would have been done otherwise. Deciding whether created entitlements are surplus requires the existence of a baseline against which the reductions can be measured. When emissions are reduced below this baseline, the amount of the reduction that is additional can be certified as surplus.

Defining procedures that assure that the baselines don't allow unjustified credits is no small task. A pilot program for Activities Implemented Jointly, which was established at the first Conference of the Parties in 1995, is useful for demonstrating the difficulties of ensuring additionality. Results under this program indicate that requiring a showing of additionality can impose very high transaction costs as well as introduce considerable ex ante uncertainty about the actual reductions that could be achieved (Rentz 1996, 1998; Jepma 2003).

Many credit-based programs keep a large element of the previous regulatory structure in place. For example, some programs require regulatory preapproval for all transfers (i.e., wetlands credits and water trading). In addition, other specific design features (such as the opt-in in the sulfur allowance program [Ellerman 2003] and the use of relative targets in the U.K. ETS [Hartridge 2003]) also add administrative complexity.

Theory would lead us to believe that *allowance* systems would be much more likely to achieve the efficiency and environmental goals than *credit* programs and the evidence emerging from ex post evaluations seems to support that conclusion (Shabman et al. 2002). This is of considerable potential importance in climate change policy because only one of the three Kyoto programs (Emissions Trading) is a cap-and-trade program.

The Legal Nature of the Entitlement

Although the popular literature frequently refers to the tradable permit approach as "privatizing the resource" (Spulber and Sabbaghi 1993; Anderson 1995), in most cases it doesn't actually do that. Instead it privatizes the right to access the resource to a prespecified degree.

Economists have consistently argued that tradable permits should be treated as secure property rights to protect the incentive to invest in the resource. Confiscation of rights or simply insecure rights could undermine the entire process.

The environmental community, on the other hand, has just as consistently argued that the air, water, and fish belong to the people, and as a matter of ethics, they should not become private property (Kelman 1981). In this view, no end could justify the transfer of a community right into a private one (McCay 1998).

The practical resolution of this conflict in most U.S. tradable permit settings has been to attempt to give "adequate" (as opposed to complete) security to the permit holders, while making it clear that permits are not property rights.[12] For example, according to the title of the U.S. Clean Air Act dealing with the sulfur allowance program: "An allowance under this title is a limited authorization to emit sulfur dioxide.... Such allowance does not constitute a property right" (104 Stat 2591).

In practice this means that although administrators are expected to refrain from arbitrarily confiscating rights (as sometimes happened with banked credits in the early U.S. Emissions Trading program), they do not give up their ability to adopt a more stringent cap as the need arises. In particular they would not be required to pay compensation for withdrawing a portion of the authorization to emit as they would if allowances were accorded full property right status. It is a somewhat uneasy compromise, but it seems to have worked.

Adaptive Management

One of the initial fears about tradable permit systems was that they would be excessively rigid, particularly in the light of the need to provide adequate security to permit holders. Policy rigidity was seen as possibly preventing the system from responding either to changes in the resource base or to better information. This rigidity could be particularly damaging in biological systems by undermining their resilience. Resilient systems are those that can adapt to changing circumstances (Hollings 1978).

Existing tradable permit systems have responded to this challenge in different ways depending on the type of resource being covered. In air pollution control the need for adaptive management is typically less immediate, and the right is typically defined in terms of tons of emissions. In biological systems, such as fisheries, the rights are typically defined as a share of the TAC. In this way the resource managers can change the TAC in response to changing biological conditions without triggering legal recourse by the right holder. Some fisheries and water allocation systems actually have defined two related rights (Young 1999, 2004). The first conveys the share of the cap, whereas the second conveys the right to withdraw a specified amount in a particular year. Separating the two rights allows a user to sell the current access right (perhaps due to an illness or malfunctioning equipment) without giving up the right of future access embodied in the share right. Though share rights have not been used in air pollution control, they have been proposed (Muller 1994).

Water has a different kind of adaptive management need. Considerable uncertainty among users is created by the fact that the amount of water can vary significantly from year to year, implying that caps are likely to vary from year to year. Because different users have quite different capacities for responding to shortfalls, the system for allocating this water needs to be flexible enough to respond to this variability or the water could be seriously misallocated.

These needs have been met by a combination of technological solutions (principally water storage) and building some flexibility into the rights system. In the American West, the appropriation doctrine that originated in the mining camps created a system of priorities based on the date of first use. The more senior rights then have a higher priority of claim on the available water in any particular year and consequently could be expected to claim the highest price (Howe and Lee 1983; Livingston 1998).[13] Other systems, most notably in Australia, use a system of proportionality that resembles the share system in fisheries (Livingston 1998).

Caps and Safety Valves

Even if the apparent schedule of targets is equivalent to those under direct regulation—in the face of "shocks" a cap may be binding in a way that is not the case for other policies such as environmental taxation. This has been particularly true in RECLAIM (Harrison 2004),[14] the Australian water case (Young 2004),[15] and New Zealand fisheries (Kerr 2004).[16]

The experience with the price shocks in the RECLAIM case shows how to handle unexpected and sometimes rather large changes in circumstances that can cause the cost of achieving the cap to skyrocket. The general prescription is to allow a safety valve in the form of a predefined penalty that can be imposed on all emissions over the cap in lieu of meeting the cap. This penalty can be different from the normal sanction imposed for noncompliance during more normal situations. In effect this penalty would set a maximum price that would be incurred in pursuit of environmental goals in unusually trying times (Roberts and Spence 1976; Harrison 2004; Pizer 1999). RECLAIM rules specified that if permit prices went over some threshold, the program would be suspended until they figured out what to do. An alternative (substantial) fee per ton was imposed in the interim with the revenue used to subsidize additional alternative emission reductions (Harrison 2004).

Initial Allocation Method

The initial allocation of entitlements is perhaps the most controversial aspect of a tradable permits system (Raymond 2003). Four possible methods for allocating initial entitlements are:

- Random access (lotteries);
- First come, first served;
- Administrative rules based on eligibility criteria; and
- Auctions.

All four of these have been used in one context or another. Both lotteries and auctions are frequently used in allocating hunting permits for big game. Lotteries are more common in allocating permits among residents, whereas auctions are more common for allocating permits to nonresidents. First come, first served was historically common for water, especially when it was abundant.

Though an infinite number of possible distribution rules exist, rules that pay some attention to prior use tend to predominate. Under virtually all implemented tradable permit programs discussed in this chapter, existing sources get free allocations of rights rather than having to pay for them as in an auction. They only have to purchase any additional permits they may need over and above the initial allocation (as opposed to purchasing *all* permits in an auction market).

Free distribution has its advantages and disadvantages. Recent work examining how the presence of preexisting distortions in the tax system affects the efficiency of the chosen instrument suggests that the ability to recycle the revenue from the sale of these permits (rather than give it to users) can enhance the efficiency of the system by a large amount. That work, of course, supports the use of taxes or auctioned permits rather than free distribution (Goulder et al. 1999).

How revenues are distributed, however, also affects the attractiveness of alternative approaches to environmental protection from the point of view of the various stakeholders.

To the extent that stakeholders can influence policy choice, using free distribution in general and prior use in particular as allocation criteria may have increased the feasibility of implementation of transferable permit systems (Svendsen 1999; Raymond 2003). Interestingly the empirical evidence suggests that the amount of the revenue needed to hold users harmless during the change is only a fraction of the total revenue available from auctioning, not the whole amount (Bovenberg et al. 2000). Allocating all permits free of charge is therefore not inevitable in principle, even if political feasibility considerations affect the design.

Although reserving some free permits for new firms is possible, this option is rarely exercised in practice. As a result, under the free distribution scheme new firms typically have to purchase all permits, and existing firms get an initial allocation free. Thus the free distribution system imposes a bias against new users in the sense that their financial burden is greater than that of an otherwise identical existing user. In air pollution control this new user bias has retarded the introduction of new facilities and new technologies by reducing the cost advantage of building new facilities that embody the latest innovations (Maloney and Brady 1988).[17]

Basing the initial allocation on prior use may promote inefficient strategic behavior. When the initial allocation is based on historic use and users are aware of this aspect in advance, an incentive to inflate historic use (to qualify for a larger initial allocation) is created (Berland et al. 2001).

This strategic behavior can intensify the degradation of the resource before the control mechanism is set in place.

Finally, Raymond's (2003) detailed review of the initial allocation processes for three major tradable permit programs concludes, convincingly in my opinion, not only that equity norms play a large role in crafting the initial allocation in these three cases but also that applying these norms is much more complicated than simply relying on prior use. His analysis suggests that in terms of prevailing equity norms, auctions may have a tough time gaining a foothold in initial allocations despite their attractiveness from an efficiency point of view.

Compromises designed to gain the political feasibility of the system may also affect the level of the cap, at least initially. Some tendency to over allocate quota in the initial years has been evident.

- The evaluation of the Dutch phosphate quota program, for example, shows that initial quota was overallocated 10 to 25 percent (Wossink 2004).
- Initial allocations were also inflated in the initial years of the RECLAIM program (Harrison 2004).

In the climate change case, a primary concern has been about hot air (den Elzen and deMoor 2002). (Hot air is the part of an Annex I country's assigned amount that is likely to be surplus to its needs without any additional efforts to reduce emissions.) Hot air resulted from the initial allocation under the Kyoto Protocol because assigned amounts are defined in terms of 1990 emission levels, and for some countries (most notably Russia and the Ukraine), economic contraction has resulted in substantially lower emissions levels. Hence these countries would have surplus permits to sell, resulting in the need for less emission reduction from new sources.

Other initial allocation issues involve determining both the eligibility to receive permits and the governance process for deciding the proper allocation. In fisheries, for example, the decision to allocate permits to boat owners has triggered harsh reactions among both crew and processors.

Finally some systems allow agents other than those included in the initial allocation to participate through an opt-in procedure. This is a prominent feature of the sulfur allowance program, but it can be plagued by adverse selection problems (Montero 1999, 2000).

Traditional theory suggests that tradable permits offer a costless trade-off between efficiency and equity, because, regardless of the initial allocation, the ability to trade ensures that permits flow to their highest valued uses. This implies that the initial allocation can be used to pursue fairness goals without lowering the value of the resource.

In practice, implementation considerations must deal with a host of competing demands, including fairness, political feasibility, strategic considerations, and concern over allowing the entrance of new firms. The failure of initial allocations to completely respond to equity concerns has caused the introduction of other means to protect equity considerations (such as restrictions of transfers). These additional restrictions tend to raise transactions cost and to limit the cost-effectiveness of the program.

Transferability Rules

Though the largest source of controversy about tradable permits seems to attach to the manner in the permits are initially allocated, another significant source of controversy is attached to the rules that govern transferability. According to supporters, transferability not only serves to ensure that rights flow to their highest valued use but also provides a user-financed form of compensation for those who voluntarily decide to no longer use the resource. Therefore restrictions on transferability only serve to reduce the efficiency of the system. According to critics, allowing the rights to be transferable produces a number of socially unacceptable outcomes, including the concentration of rights, destruction of community interests, and degradation of the environment.

Making the rights transferable does allow the opportunity for some groups to accumulate permits. The concentration of permits in the hands of a few could either reduce the efficiency of the tradable permits system (Hahn 1984; Anderson 1991; Van Egteren and Weber 1996), or it could be used as leverage to gain economic power in other markets (Misiolek and Elder 1989; Sartzetakis 1997). Although it has not played much of a role in air pollution control, concentration has been a concern (if not a major issue) in fisheries (Palsson and Helgason 1995).

Typically the problem in fisheries is *not* that the concentration is so high that it triggers antitrust concerns (Adelaja et al. 1998) but that it allows small fishing enterprises to be bought out by larger fishing enterprises. Smaller fishing enterprises are seen by some observers as having a special value to society that should be protected (Palsson 1998).

Protections against "unreasonable" concentrations of quota are now common. One typical strategy involves putting a limit on the amount of quota that can be accumulated by any one holder. In New Zealand fisheries, for example, these range from 20 percent to 35 percent depending on the species (National Research Council Committee to Review Individual Fishing Quotas 1999, pp. 90–91), whereas in Iceland the limits are 10 percent for cod and 20 percent for other species (National Research Council Committee to Review Individual Fishing Quotas 1999, 102).

Another coping strategy, one that attempts to resolve market power problems without restricting transfers, focuses on trying to mitigate the potential anticompetitive effects of hoarding. The U.S. sulfur allowance does this in two main ways. First it sets aside a supply of allowances that could be sold at a predetermined (high) price if hoarders refused to sell to new entrants.[18] Second, it introduced a zero-revenue auction that among its other features, requires permit holders to put approximately 3 percent of its allowances up for sale in a public auction once a year. The revenue is returned to the sellers rather than retained by the government. Hence the name zero-revenue auction (Svendsen and Christensen 1999).

Another, quite different approach involves directly restricting transfers that are perceived to violate the public interest. In the Alaskan halibut and sablefish ITQ program, for example, several size categories of vessels were defined. The initial allocation was based on the catch record within each vessel class and transfer of quota between catcher vessel classes was prohibited (National Research Council Committee to Review Individual Fishing Quotas 1999, 310). Further restrictions required the owner of the quota to be on board when the catch was landed. This represented an attempt to prevent the transfer of ownership of the harvest rights to absentee landlords.

A rather different transferability concern relates to the potentially adverse economic impacts of permit transfers on some communities. Those holders who transfer permits will not necessarily consider the interests of communities that have depended on their commerce in the past. For example in fisheries a transfer from one quota holder to another might well cause the fish to be landed in a different community. In air pollution control, owners of a factory might shut down its operation in one community and rebuild in another community, taking their permits with them.

One common response to this problem in fisheries involves allocating quota directly to communities. The 1992 Bering Sea Community Development Quota Program, which was designed to benefit remote villages containing significant native populations in Alaska, allocated 7.5 percent of the walleye pollock quota to these communities (Ginter 1995). In New Zealand the Treaty of Waitangi (Fisheries Claims) Settlement Act of 1992 effectively transferred ownership of almost 40 percent of the New Zealand ITQ to the Maori people (Annala 1996). For these allocations the community retains control over the transfers, and this control gives it the power to protect community interests. In Iceland this kind of control is gained through a provision that if a quota is to be leased or sold to a vessel operating in a different place, the assent of the municipal government and the local fishermen's union must be acquired (National Research Council Committee to Review Individual Fishing Quotas 1999, 83).

A final concern with transferability relates to possible external effects of the transfer. The theory presumes that the commodity being traded is homogenous. With homogeneity, transfers increase net benefits by allowing permits to flow to their highest valued use. In practice, without homogeneity, transfers can confer external benefits or costs on third parties, resulting in allocations that do not maximize net benefits.

When the location of the resource use matters, spatial issues can arise because the transfer could alter the location of use (Tietenberg 1995). Spatial issues can be dealt with within the tradable permit scheme, but those choices typically make transfers more difficult. Both the RECLAIM

(Harrison 2004) and the Nutrient Quota in the Netherlands (Wossink 2004) programs place restrictions on the spatial area within which the permits may be traded. The U.S. wetlands program requires regulatory preapproval of trades in part to control potentially harmful spatial aspects of trades. In the sulfur allowance program (Ellerman 2004), no regulatory restrictions are placed on permit trades, but permit users do have to ensure that any permit use does not result in a violation of the National Ambient Air Quality Standards.

The Temporal Dimension

Standard cost-effectiveness theory suggests that a cost-minimizing tradable permit system must have full temporal fungibility, implying that allowances can be both borrowed and banked (Rubin 1996; Kling and Rubin 1997). Banking allows a user to store its permits for future use. Borrowing allows a permit holder to use permits earlier than their stipulated date.

Tradable permit schemes differ considerably in how they treat banking or the role of forward markets. No existing system that I am aware of is fully temporally fungible. Older pollution control programs have had a more limited approach. The Emissions Trading Program allowed banking, but not borrowing. The lead phaseout program originally allowed neither, but partway through the program it allowed banking. The sulfur allowance program has banking, but not borrowing, and RECLAIM has an overlapping time frame for compliance that is equivalent to a highly restricted banking and borrowing system.

How important is temporal flexibility? The message that emerges from this review is that this temporal flexibility can be quite important. Ellerman (2004) discusses the considerable role that both banking and forward markets have played in the U.S. sulfur allowance program. Harrison (2004) reports that during the tremendous pressure placed on the market by the power problems in California, even the limited temporal flexibility in RECLAIM allowed the excess emissions to be reduced by more than a factor of three—from about 19 percent to 6 percent. Pedersen (2003) also notes the importance of temporal flexibility for investment in the Danish greenhouse gas program.

Design Preconditions?

This discussion of design lessons also raises the question of when tradable permits might be appropriate policy instruments and how effective permit systems might be implemented. The evidence is very persuasive that tradable permit systems have worked extremely well in many circumstances, but it is equally clear that the success of tradable permit system seems to rest on certain preconditions.

Some preconditions suggested by this review include:

- Either the absence of significant externalities or an ability to deal with them in system design.
- A reasonable ability to monitor resource use (emissions or withdrawal) and an acceptable capability to enforce compliance.
- A sufficient level of information to set a politically acceptable cap.
- Permit holders who are sufficiently knowledgeable about the system and the menu of choices to use it effectively.
- A sufficient number of participants to make an active market.

The degree to which each of these preconditions is met is, of course, a continuous variable. Nonetheless isolating these conditions sets the stage for thinking about defining the appropriate niche for tradable permit systems.

Lessons about Program Effectiveness

How well have tradable permits performed? The evidence has been mixed. In certain applications, such as the sulfur allowance program and several of the fisheries, tradable permits have lived up to the high expectations of the theory. They have produced both lower costs and better environmental quality. In order areas, such as wetlands banking, they have neither lowered costs nor provided improved environmental quality.

The air pollution programs, on balance, seem to be the most successful in achieving both economic and environmental objectives. In part this seems to be due to the presence of fewer (though certainly not zero) externalities in these programs. Fisheries must cope with potentially severe bycatch problems in multispecies fisheries. Water control authorities must cope with the consequences of trades on downstream users. Small-scale, complex resources with multiple externalities may be better managed by cooperative arrangements than by tradable permits.

The academic community has emphasized the importance of comanagement of environmental resources with users having a substantial role (Ostrom et al. 2002). Although tradable permit systems in principle allow a variety of governance systems, only in fisheries and water is there any evidence of an evolution in this direction. The current predominant form in both air pollution control and fisheries seems to be a system of shared management with users playing a smaller role than envisioned by most comanagement proposals. For those resource regimes located in the United States it is common for the goals to be set at the national level and considerable top-down management to be in evidence. The management of water resources seems closest to user-controlled comanagement schemes. And in those systems the rights markets tend to be at the informal end of the spectrum.

It should not be surprising that although tradable permit systems potentially allow for a considerable role for users, a nontrivial comanagement role exists only in fisheries and water. The pollution and natural resource cases exhibit an important asymmetry. For air pollution control, the benefits from resource protection fall on the victims of air pollution, not on the polluters who use the resource. From a purely self-interest point of view, resource users (polluters) would be quite happy to pollute the air if they could get away with it. On the other hand, water users and fishers can both benefit from protection of the resource. Their collective self-interest is compatible with resource protection. This suggests that the incentives for collective action should be quite different in these two cases, and this difference could well explain the lower propensity for collective self-governance in the air pollution case.

A main element of controversy in tradable permits systems involves both the processes for deciding the initial allocation and the initial allocation itself. These problems seem least intense for air pollution and most intense for fisheries. Though a rich set of management and initial allocation options exists, current experience seems not to have been very creative in their use.

Tradable permit programs are sometimes held to be a relatively rigid approach to resource management. This expectation is based on the belief that once they are instituted, property rights become institutionalized and therefore impervious to change. In fact implemented tradable permit programs have exhibited a considerable amount of flexibility and evolution over time. A variety of new design features (such as zero revenue auctions [Svendsen and Christensen 1999], bycatch quotas [National Research Council Committee to Review Individual Fishing Quotas 1999, pp. 123–24], and drop-through mechanisms [Young 1999]) have emerged that are tailored to the characteristics of particular resources.

Lessons for Theory-Based Expectations

Theory creates expectations, and in the case of tradable permits the expectations have been high, sometimes unreasonably high. Several assumptions behind the theory may be violated in practice.

One case in point is the assumption that the tradable commodity is homogenous. In many applications the tradable commodity is clearly not homogenous. The location or timing of permit use may matter as might the extraction or emission methods used by the permit holder. The impact of the nonhomogeneity is intensified when the associated environmental benefits or damage are external to the users. In this case, permit holders who use or trade permits cannot be expected to maximize society's net benefits when they maximize their own.

Another aspect of tradable permit systems that seems to have been under appreciated is endogeneity. The choice of a policy instrument can affect aspects of implementation that are frequently considered exogenous, but that in fact are not. These include the targeted degree of control, the feasibility of implementation, the likelihood of compliance, the form and intensity of monitoring and enforcement, as well as the degree of technical change.

The role equity plays in the design of operating tradable permit systems has been more important than typically believed (Tietenberg 1998; Raymond 2003). Analysis that assumes that fairness is either completely handled by the initial allocation or has no analytical importance may miss a comparative aspect of policy instrument choice that seems to matter. Theory tells us that a cost-effective allocation will ultimately be achieved regardless of the initial allocation of permits. In principle this allows equity goals to be pursued via the initial allocation and cost-effectiveness goals to be handled by transfers. In practice initial allocations are frequently either used to improve feasibility (thereby reducing or eliminating their ability to address fairness issues) or they prove inadequate in addressing equity concerns (especially when the equity concerns arise from transfers). Responding to fairness concerns about transfers frequently involves placing restrictions on transfers, restrictions that reduce the cost-effectiveness of the system.

Historically tradable permit systems have tended to evolve considerably over time. Regulators have had to become comfortable with the flexibility these systems afford. Users have had to become comfortable with the fact that defining the means of control is now up to them. Initial tradable permit markets may bear only a remote resemblance to the goods or asset markets with which we are more familiar.

Permit markets certainly have achieved a large and growing niche in the collection of favored policies to control access to the commons. This reading of the evidence suggests that is appropriate, but it also suggests that the resource context and program design not only matter, they matter a lot.

ACKNOWLEDGMENTS This chapter draws on previous studies completed for the National Research Council in the United States (Tietenberg 2002) and the OECD in Paris (OECD 2004) as well as a previous article (Tietenberg 2004) published in the *Oxford Review of Economic Policy*. Though the Oxford article focuses on a different subject (climate change), it does depend on the same analysis of the experience with implemented systems that forms the foundation for this chapter. The author is grateful for helpful comments from participants at the Santa Barbara workshop and from Eban Goodstein.

NOTES

1. For more information on this institution *see* www.chicagoclimatex.com.

2. For a previous survey that also examines tradable permit systems across resource settings *see* Colby (2000).

3. None of the studies from the recent OECD Workshop on Ex Post Evaluation (2004) attempt this type of evaluation.

4. The demonstration that the traditional regulatory policy was not cost-minimizing has two mirror-image implications. It either implies that the same environmental goals could be achieved at lower cost or that better environmental quality could be achieved at the same cost. In air pollution control, although the earlier programs were designed to exploit the first implication, later programs attempted to produce better air quality *and* lower cost.

5. One difficulty that did emerge from the workshop was that cost-effectiveness typically treats the environmental target as predetermined and exogenous. In fact, several of the studies seem to indicate that the target may be affected by the choice of the policy instrument (*see* Ellerman 2004; Kerr 2004). To the extent this is true, the target become endogenous rather than exogenous, and this makes the typical cost-effectiveness study more difficult. I elaborate this point later.

6. For a theoretical treatment of the role of transactions costs in permit markets *see* Stavins (1995).

7. Interestingly, the ex post empirical studies have rather more to say about transaction costs than they do on market power. Though many ex ante studies have traditionally focused on market power, the ex post studies cast more light on transaction costs. The long history of modeling market power combined with the fact that suggestive data are available ex ante (i.e., number of players, market share, etc.) may bias the ex ante agenda toward the analysis of market power, whereas the theory about transaction costs is relatively less rich and the evidence of it usually only emerges once the market commences operation.

8. Both Wossink (2004) and Young (2004) reveal information of an "anecdotal" nature about transaction costs. Wossink (2004) shows how the nutrient program in the Netherlands explicitly provided support to help participants understand the nature of the market, based on anecdotal evidence that small farmers were having trouble functioning in the market.

9. Not only has the recovery of monitoring and enforcement costs from users become standard practice in some fisheries (New Zealand, for example), but funding at least some monitoring and enforcement activity out of rents generated by the fishery has already been included as a provision in amendments to the U.S. Magnuson-Stevens Act. In addition the sulfur allowance program mandates continuous emissions monitoring financed by the emitting sources.

10. Noncompliance not only makes it more difficult to reach stated goals, it sometimes makes it more difficult to know whether the goals are being met In fisheries, for example, stock assessments sometimes depend on the size and composition of the catch. If the composition of the landed harvest is unrepresentative of the actual harvest due to illegal discards, this can bias the stock assessment and the total allowable catch that depends on it. Not only would true mortality rates be much higher than apparent mortality rates, but the age and size distribution of landed catch would be different from the size distribution of the initial harvest (prior to discards). This is known in fisheries as data fouling.

11. Prior to 1988, the expected positive effects of ITQs did not materialize in the Dutch cutter fisheries due to inadequate enforcement. Fleet capacity increased further, the race for fish continued, and the quotas had to be supplemented by input controls, such as a limit on days at sea (National Research Council Committee to Review Individual Fishing Quotas 1999, 176).

12. One prominent exception is the New Zealand ITQ system. It grants full property rights in perpetuity (National Research Council Committee to Review Individual Fishing Quotas 1999, 97).

13. In the western United States, the number of rights expected to be fulfilled in any given year is determined by snowpack measurements and satellite monitoring of streamflows (Livingston 1998).

14. RECLAIM participants experienced a very large unanticipated demand for power that could only be accommodated by older, more polluting plants. Permit prices soared in a way that was never anticipated.

15. In the Australian water case, excessive withdrawal would trigger substantial increases in salinity.

16. In the New Zealand fisheries case, a lack of understanding of the biology of the orange roughy led to a cap that permitted unsustainable harvests.

17. The new source bias is, of course, not unique to tradable permit systems. It applies to any system of regulation that imposes more stringent requirements on new sources than existing ones.

18. This set-aside has not been used because sufficient allowances have been available through normal channels. That doesn't necessarily mean the set-aside was not useful, however, because it may have alleviated concerns that could have otherwise blocked the implementation of the program.

REFERENCES

Adelaja, A., J. Menzo, et al. (1998). "Market Power, Industrial Organization and Tradeable Quotas." *Review of Industrial Organization* 13(5): 589–601.

Anderson, L. G. (1991). "A Note on Market Power in ITQ Fisheries." *Journal of Environmental Economics and Management* 21(2): 291–96.

Anderson, L. G. (1995). "Privatizing Open Access Fisheries: Individual Transferable Quotas." In *The Handbook of Environmental Economics*, ed. D. W. Bromley. Oxford, Blackwell: 453–74.

Annala, J. H. (1996). "New Zealand's ITQ System: Have the First Eight Years Been a Success or a Failure?" *Reviews in Fish Biology and Fisheries* 6: 43–62.

Berland, H., D. J. Clark, and P. A. Pederson (2001), "Rent Seeking and the Regulation of a Natural Resource." *Marine Resource Economics* 16: 219–33.

Berman, E., and L. T. M. Bui (2001). "Environmental Regulation and Labor Demand: Evidence from the South Coast Air Basin." *Journal of Public Economics* 79(2): 265–95.

Bernal, P., and B. Aliaga (1999). "ITQ's in Chilean Fisheries." In *The Definition and Allocation of Use Rights in European Fisheries: Proceedings of the Second Workshop Held in Brest, France, 5–7 May 1999*, ed. A. Hatcher and K. Robinson. Portsmouth, UK, Centre for the Economics and Management of Aquatic Resources.

Bohi, D. R., and D. Burtraw (1997). "Trading Expectations and Experience." *Electricity Journal* 10(7): 67–75.

Bovenberg, A. L., and L. H. Goulder (2000). "Neutralizing Adverse Impacts of 2000 CO_2 Abatement Policies: What Does it Cost?" In *Behavioral and Distributional Effects of Environmental Policy*, ed. C. E. Carraro and G. E. Metcalf. Chicago, University of Chicago Press.

Burtraw, D., et al. (1998). "Costs and Benefits of Reducing Air Pollutants Related to Acid Rain." *Contempory Economic Policy* 16(4): 379–400.

Burtraw, D. and E. Mansur (1999). "Environmental Effects of SO_2 Trading and Banking." *Environmental Science and Technology* 33(20): 3489–94.

Colby, B. G. (2000). "Cap and Trade Challenges: A Tale of Three Markets." *Land Economics* 76 (4): 638–58.

Davidse, W. (1999). "Lessons from Twenty Years of Experience with Property Rights in the Dutch Fishery." In *The Definition and Allocation of Use Rights in European Fisheries: Proceedings of the Second Workshop Held in Brest, France, 5–7 May 1999*, eds. A. Hatcher and K. Robinson. Portsmouth, UK, Centre for the Economics and Management of Aquatic Resources: 153–63.

Den Elzen, M. G. J., and A. P. G. deMoor (2002). "Analyzing the Kyoto Protocol under the Marrakesh Accords: Economic Efficiency and Environmental Effectiveness." *Ecological Economics* 43(2–3): 141–158.

Easter, K. W., A. Dinar, et al. (1998). "Water Markets: Transactions Costs and Institutional Options." In *Markets for Water: Potential and Performance*, eds. K. W. Easter, A. Dinar, and M. W. Rosegrant. Boston, Kluwer Academic Publishers: 1–18.

Ekins, P. (1996). "The Secondary Benefits of CO_2 Abatement: How Much Emission Reduction Do They Justify?" *Ecological Economics* 16(1): 13–24.

Ellerman, A. D. (2004) "The U.S. SO_2 Cap-and-Trade Programme." In Organisation for Economic Co-operation and Development, *Tradable Permits: Policy Evaluation, Design and Reform*. Paris, OECD: 71–97.

Farrell, A., R. Carter, and R. Raufer (1999). "The NO_x Budget: Market-Based Control of Tropospheric Ozone in the Northeastern United States." *Resource and Energy Economics* 21(2): 103–24.

Ginter, J. J. C. (1995). "The Alaska Community Development Quota Fisheries Management Program." *Ocean and Coastal Management* 28(1–3): 147–63.

Goodstein, E. (1996). "Jobs and the Environment—An Overview." *Environmental Management* 20(3): 313–21.

Goulder, L. H., et al. (1999). "The Cost-Effectiveness of Alternative Instruments for Environmental Protection in a Second-Best Setting." *Journal of Public Economics* 72(3): 329–60.

Hahn, R. W. (1984). "Market Power and Transferable Property Rights." *Quarterly Journal of Economics* 99(4): 753–65.

Hahn, R. W., and G. L. Hester (1989). "Marketable Permits: Lessons from Theory and Practice." *Ecology Law Quarterly* 16: 361–406.

Hahn, R. W., and A. M. McGartland (1989). "The Political Economy of Instrument Choice: An Examination of the U.S. Role in Implementing the Montreal Protocol." *Northwestern University Law Review* 83(3): 592–611.

Harrison, D. Jr. (2004). "Ex Post Evaluation of the RECLAIM Emissions Trading Programmes for the Los Angeles Air Basin." In Organisation for Economic Co-operation and Development, *Tradable Permits: Policy Evaluation, Design and Reform*. Paris, OECD: 45–69.

Hartridge, O. (2003). "The UK Emissions Trading Scheme: A Progress Report." In *Proceedings of the OECD Workshop on Ex Post Evaluation of Tradable Permits: Methodological and Policy Issues*. Paris, OECD.

Hollings, C. S. (1978). *Adaptive Environmental Assessment and Management*. New York, Wiley.

Howe, C. W., and D. R. Lee (1983). "Priority Pollution Rights: Adapting Pollution Control to a Variable Environment." *Land Economics* 59(2): 141–49.

Jepma, C. J. (2003). "The EU Emissions Trading Scheme (ETS): How Linked to JI/CDM?" *Climate Policy* 3(1): 89–94.

Kelman, S. (1981). *What Price Incentives? Economists and the Environment* Westport, CT, Greenwood.

Kerr, S. (2004). "Evaluation of the Cost Effectiveness of the New Zealand Individual Transferable Quota Fisheries Market." In *Tradable Permits: Policy Evaluation, Design and Reform*. Paris, OECD: 121–34.

Kling, C., and J. Rubin (1997). "Bankable Permits for the Control of Environmental Pollution." *Journal of Public Economics* 64(1): 99–113.

Kruger, J. A., B. McLean, et al. (1999). *A Tale of Two Revolutions: Administration of the SO₂ Trading Program. Draft Report.* Washington, DC, U.S. Environmental Protection Agency.

Libecap, G. D. (1990). *Contracting for Property Rights.* Cambridge, Cambridge University Press.

Livingston, M. L. (1998). "Institutional Requisites for Efficient Water Markets." In *Markets of Water: Potential and Performance,* ed. K. W. Easter, M. W. Rosengrant, and A. Dinar. Boston, Kluwer Academic Publishers: 19–33.

Maloney, M., and G. L. Brady (1988). "Capital Turnover and Marketable Property Rights." *Journal of Law and Economics* 31(1): 203–26.

Matulich, S. C., and M. Sever (1999). "Reconsidering the Initial Allocation of ITQs: The Search for a Pareto-Safe Allocation between Fishing and Processing Sectors." *Land Economics* 75(2): 203–19.

Matulich, S. C., R. C. Mittelhammer, et al. (1996). "Toward a More Complete Model of Individual Transferable Fishing Quotas: Implications of Incorporating the Processing Sector." *Journal of Environmental Economics and Management* 31(1): 112–28.

McCay, B. J. (1998). *Oyster Wars and the Public Trust: Property, Law and Ecology in New Jersey History.* Tucson, University of Arizona Press.

McCay, B. J., and C. F. Creed (1990). "Social Structure and Debates on Fisheries Management in the Mid-Atlantic Surf Clam Fishery." *Ocean and Shoreline Management* 13: 199–229.

McCay, B. J., J. B. Gatewood, et al. (1989). "Labor and the Labor Process in a Limited Entry Fishery." *Marine Resource Economics* 6: 311–30.

McLean, Brian (2003). "Ex Post Evaluation of the US Sulphur Allowance Programme." In *Proceedings of the OECD Workshop on Ex Post Evaluation of Tradable Permits: Methodological and Policy Issues.* Paris, OECD.

Misiolek, W. S., and H. W. Elder (1989). "Exclusionary Manipulation of Markets for Pollution Rights." *Journal of Environmental Economics and Management* 16(2): 156–66.

Montero, J. P. (1999). "Voluntary Compliance with Market-Based Environmental Policy: Evidence from the U.S. Acid Rain Program." *Journal of Political Economy* 107(5): 998–1033.

Montero, J. P. (2000). "A Market-Based Environmental Policy Experiment in Chile." Working Paper of the Center for Energy and Environmental Policy Research, MIT-CEEPR 2000–005 WP.

Montero, J. P. (2002). "Permits, Standards, and Technology Innovation." *Journal of Environmental Economics and Management* 44(1): 23–44.

Muller, R. A. (1994). "Emissions Trading with Shares and Coupons—A Laboratory Experiment." *Energy Journal* 15(2): 185–211.

National Research Council Committee to Review Individual Fishing Quotas (1999). *Sharing the Fish: Toward a National Policy on Fishing Quotas.* Washington, DC, National Academy Press.

Nussbaum, B. D. (1992). "Phasing Down Lead in Gasoline in the U.S.: Mandates, Incentives, Trading and Banking." In *Climate Change: Designing a Tradeable Permit System,* ed. T. Jones and J. Corfee-Morlot. Paris, OECD: 21–34.

Organisation for Economic Co-Operation and Development (OECD) (1997). *Towards Sustainable Fisheries: Economic Aspects of the Management of Living Marine Resources.* Paris, OECD.

OECD (1999). *Implementing Domestic Tradable Permits for Environmental Protection.* Paris, OECD.

OECD (2004). *Tradable Permits: Policy Evaluation, Design and Reform.* Paris, OECD).

Ostrom, E., T. Dietz, et al., eds. (2002). *The Drama of the Commons.* Washington, DC, National Academy Press.

Palsson, G. (1998). "The Virtual Aquarium: Commodity Fiction and Cod Fishing." *Ecological Economics* 24(2–3): 275–88.

Palsson, G., and A. Helgason (1995). "Figuring Fish and Measuring Men: The Individual Transferable Quota System in Icelandic Cod Fishery." *Ocean and Coastal Management* 28(1–3): 117–46.

Pederson, S. L. (2003). "Experience Gained with CO_2 Cap and Trade in Denmark." *Proceedings of the OECD Workshop on Ex post Evaluation of Tradable Permits: Methodological and Policy Issues.* Paris, OECD.

Pizer, W. (1999). *Choosing Price or Quantity Controls for Greenhouse Gases.* Resources for the Future, Climate Issues Brief 17, Washington, DC.

Raymond, L. (2003). *Private Rights in Public Resources: Equity and Property Allocation in Market-Based Environmental Policy.* Washington, DC, Resources for the Future.

Rentz, H. (1996). "From Joint Implementation to a System of Tradeable CO_2 Emission Entitlements." *International Environmental Affairs* 8(3): 267–76.

Rentz, H. (1998). "Joint Implementation and the Question of 'Additionality'—A Proposal for a Pragmatic Approach to Identify Possible Joint Implementation Projects." *Energy Policy* 26(4): 275–79.

Roberts, M. J., and M. Spence (1976). "Effluent Charges and Licenses under Uncertainty." *Journal of Public Economics* 5 (3–4): 193–208.

Rubin, J. D. (1996). "A Model of Intertemporal Emission Trading, Banking, and Borrowing." *Journal of Environmental Economics and Management* 31(3): 269–86.

Runolfsson, B. (1999). "ITQs in Icelandic Fisheries: A Rights-based Approach to Fisheries Management." In *The Definition and Allocation of Use Rights in European Fisheries: Proceedings of the Second Workshop Held in Brest, France, 5–7 May 1999,* eds. A. Hatcher and K. Robinson. Portsmouth, UK, Centre for the Economics and Management of Aquatic Resources: 164–93.

Sartzetakis, E. S. (1997). "Raising Rivals' Costs Strategies via Emission Permits Markets." *Review of Industrial Organization* 12(5–6): 751–65.

Scharer, B. (1999). "Tradable Emission Permits in German Clean Air Policy: Considerations on the Efficiency of Environmental Policy Instruments." In *Pollution for Sale: Emissions Trading and Joint Implementation,* eds. S. Sorrell and J. Skea. Cheltenham, UK, Edward Elgar: 141–53.

Shabman, L. (2004). "Compensation for the Impacts of Wetland Fill: The US Experience with Credit Sales." In Organisation for Economic Co-operation and Development, *Tradable Permits: Policy Evaluation, Design and Reform.* Paris, OECD: 155–71.

Shabman, L., K. Stephenson, and W. Shobe (2002). "Trading Programs for Environmental Management: Reflections on the Air and Water Experiences." *Environmental Practice* 4: 153–62.

Sorrell, S. (1999). "Why Sulfur Trading Failed in the UK." In *Pollution for Sale: Emissions Trading and Joint Implementation,* ed. S. Sorrell and J. Skea. Cheltenham, UK, Edward Elgar: 170–210.

Spulber, N., and A. Sabbaghi (1993). *Economics of Water Resources: From Regulation to Privatization.* Hingham, MA, Kluwer Academic.

Stavins, R. N. (1995). "Transaction Costs and Tradeable Permits." *Journal of Environmental Economics and Management* 29(2): 133–148.

Svendsen, G. T. (1999). "Interest Groups Prefer Emission Trading: A New Perspective." *Public Choice* 101(1–2): 109–28.

Svendsen, G. T., and J. L. Christensen (1999). "The US SO_2 Auction: Analysis and Generalization." *Energy Economics* 21(5): 403–16.

Tietenberg, T. H. (1985). *Emissions Trading: An Exercise in Reforming Pollution Policy.* Washington, DC, Resources for the Future.

Tietenberg, T. H. (1990). "Economic Instruments for Environmental Regulation." *Oxford Review of Economic Policy* 6(1): 17–33.

Tietenberg, T. H. (1995). "Tradable Permits for Pollution Control When Emission Location Matters: What Have We Learned?" *Environmental and Resource Economics* 5(2): 95–113.

Tietenberg, T. H. (1998). "Ethical Influences on the Evolution of the US Tradeable Permit Approach to Pollution Control." *Ecological Economics* 24(2,3): 241–25.

Tietenberg, T. H. (2001). "Introduction." In *Emissions Trading Programs Volume I: Implementation and Evolution,* ed. T. Tietenberg. Aldershot, UK, Ashgate Publishing: xi–xxvii.

Tietenberg, T. H. (2002). "The Tradable Permits Approach to Protecting the Commons: What Have We Learned?" In *The Drama of the Commons,* ed. E. Ostrom et al. Washington, DC, National Academy Press: 197–232.

Tietenberg, T. H. (2004). "The Tradable Permits Approach to Protecting the Commons: Lessons for Climate Change." *Oxford Review of Economic Policy* 19(3): 400–419.

Van Egteren, H., and M. Weber (1996). "Marketable Permits, Market Power and Cheating." *Journal of Environmental Economics and Management* 30(2): 161–73.

Wossink, Ada (2004). "The Dutch Nutrient Quota System: Past Experience and Lessons for the Future." In Organisation for Economic Co-operation and Development, *Tradable Permits: Policy Evaluation, Design and Reform.* Paris, OECD: 99–120.

Young, M. D. (1999). "The Design of Fishing-Right Systems—The NSW Experience." *Ecological Economics* 31(2): 305–16.

Young, Michael D. (2004) "Learning from the Market: *Ex Post* Water Entitlement and Allocation Trading Assessment Experience in Australia." In Organisation for Economic Co-operation and Development, *Tradable Permits: Policy Evaluation, Design and Reform.* Paris, OECD: 135–53.

Zylicz, T. (1999). "Obstacles to Implementing Tradable Pollution Permits: the Case of Poland." In *Implementing Domestic Tradable Permits for Environmental Protection.* Paris, OECD: 147–65.

5

International Experience with Competing Approaches to Environmental Policy: Results from Six Paired Cases

Winston Harrington & Richard D. Morgenstern

I. INTRODUCTION

This chapter reports on the results of an international effort[1] to compare the actual outcomes of pollution control policies using economic incentive (EI) instruments with those using direct regulation or "command and control" (CAC).[2] For six environmental problems, we compare the policies used by the federal government in the United States with the policies of one or more Western European countries. To the extent possible the problems and the policies were chosen so that a CAC policy on one side of the Atlantic is paired with an EI policy on the other.

The six problems are: (1) SO_2 emissions from utility and industrial boilers, (2) NO_x emissions from utility and industrial boilers, (3) point-source industrial water pollution, (4) phaseout of leaded gasoline, (5) phaseout of chlorofluorocarbons (CFCs) and other ozone-depleting substances (ODSs), and (6) chlorinated solvents. We identified researchers who had previously worked on these policies and commissioned them to update previous work and in a few instances prepare new case studies.

At the outset we define what we mean by EI and CAC. In a strict (and perhaps trivial) sense, all environmental policies are both regulations and economic instruments. They are regulations in that they involve coercion, and they provide economic incentives because the coercion generally takes the form of economic penalties. The key difference is that in a CAC regime the quantity of pollutant discharge is specified in the regulation or by the regulatory authority. In an EI regime, each firm has discretion over its pollutant discharge, but at a cost. The authority directly or indirectly controls the aggregate emissions, rather than the emissions of each firm.

Only recently has it been possible to find enough EI policies to carry out a project such as this. Until about fifteen years ago, environmental policies consisted almost exclusively of CAC approaches. In the United States, the 1970s saw a great volume of new federal regulation to promote environmental quality, none of which could be characterized as economic incentives. Beginning around 1980, however, there has been a remarkable surge of interest in EI approaches in environmental policy. Since 1990, whenever new environmental policies are proposed, it is almost inevitable that economic incentive instruments will be considered and will receive a respectful hearing.

The reasons for the newfound popularity of EI policies are unclear. Perhaps it is due to the growth in awareness of economic incentive approaches among policy makers and policy analysts in the years between 1970 and 1990. In the 1970s these approaches were generally unfamiliar to those outside the economics profession. Another possibility is the emergence of tradable emission permits in the late 1970s. Before then, the main EI alternative to the regulatory policies being implemented was the effluent fee. As we will discuss further, effluent fees could only encourage pollution sources to reduce pollution; they could not offer assurances that the sources would actually do so. By the 1980s the policy community was generally aware of a "quantity-based" EI alternative—tradable emission permits—that seemed to provide the same assurances of the achievement of environmental goals that were offered by CAC approaches.

A third possible cause is the widespread disappointment with outcomes of the CAC regulations adopted in the 1970s. The U.S. experience between 1970 and 1990 repeatedly raised questions about the presumed effectiveness of CAC approaches. Even though Congress had passed air and water pollution statutes requiring stringent regulations on pollutant sources and tight timetables for implementation, it proved to be very difficult for the Environmental Protection Agency (EPA) to put such programs into effect. The regulations that were promulgated were typically complex to administer, cumbersome, and often rigid. These characteristics, together with the natural reluctance of firms to comply with costly regulations, spawned a raft of legal challenges. As Melnick (1983) demonstrates for air quality regulations, courts frequently excused firms from compliance with the new requirements.

In other words, much of the enthusiasm for EI could be attributed to disenchantment with CAC. Whatever the cause of this turnabout, it is clear that systematic comparison of the actual performance of CAC and EI policy interventions did not play a major role. That is our goal here: the explicit comparison of EI and CAC policies and outcomes in real-world application. To provide structure for this comparison, we have compiled a list of assertions or arguments, mostly made about these instruments during the 1970s when Western countries were for the first time forming comprehensive policies for controlling environmental pollution. We compare these ex ante expectations with after-the-fact or ex post outcomes along a number of dimensions.

Our study is grounded in the belief that the examination of these six pairs of cases will yield insights into the performance of EI and CAC instruments. Nonetheless we are also acutely aware of the limitations of examining a small number of cases, nonrandomly selected. As discussed further later, our European cases are representative not of the EU as a whole but of the economically advanced countries of Northern Europe. In contrast, our American cases are national policies that represent the entire United States. In addition, perhaps the nature of the environmental problem and the information available have affected the choice of instrument. For some environmental problems there may be practical or political barriers to the use of economic instruments. Regulation of acute toxic wastes may fall into this category. If so, then any conclusions we draw would be limited to problems of a nature similar to the ones represented among our cases.

The next section describes six of the environmental problems examined on both sides of the Atlantic. Section III examines some of the major differences between U.S. and European regulations. Section IV lays out the bare-bones elements of the assertions or hypotheses used to structure the case studies. Section V reports the results in terms of the individual hypotheses. The final section offers some overall conclusions about the competing approaches to environmental policy.

II. THE SIX ENVIRONMENTAL PROBLEMS

This section describes the six environmental problems examined, along with the comparative case studies conducted on both sides of the Atlantic. For each problem background information is provided on the general issues, as well as on the nature of the policies adopted in the different countries.

SO$_2$ Emissions from Utility Boilers: Permit Market (U.S.) versus Sulfur Emission Standards (Germany)

U.S. SO$_2$ Trading Program

Title IV of the 1990 U.S. Clean Air Act Amendments (CAAAs) regulates emissions of sulfur dioxide (SO$_2$) from electric generating facilities under an emission trading program that is designed to encourage the electricity industry to minimize the cost of reducing emissions.[3] The industry is allocated a fixed number of allowances and firms are required to surrender one allowance for each ton of sulfur dioxide they emit.[4] Firms are permitted to transfer allowances among facilities or to other firms or to bank them for use in future years. The annual cap on average aggregate emissions by electric generators was set at about one-half of the amount emitted in 1980.

The case study provides an overview of the origins, design and performance of the U.S. Acid Rain Program. The study emphasizes innovation, including changes in technology, the organization of markets, and incremental improvements made after experimentation at individual boilers, most of which arguably would not have occurred under a more prescriptive approach. By 2000 actual emission reductions exceeded the scheduled reductions, at considerably lower costs than predicted.

Emission Reductions at Large Combustion Boilers in Germany

One of the most serious environmental problems in recent German history has been the decline of forest vegetation caused by air pollution, a process that came to be known as *waldsterben* (forest death).[5] Arousing great public attention, it coincided with (and may have accelerated) the emergence of the Green Party in Germany. *Waldsterben* created enormous pressure on politicians and industry to reduce SO_2 emissions believed to be responsible for much of the environmental damage. Because large combustion plants in the electricity sector were by far the largest source of SO_2 emissions, a strong consensus emerged that emissions from these sources had to be reduced significantly if the environmental situation was to be alleviated.

Consequently, a stringent regulatory regime entitled the *Großfeuerungsanlagen-Verordnung* (GFA-VO, Ordinance on Large Combustion Plants) was put in place in July 1983. Following the enactment of the prescriptive, CAC-oriented GFA-VO, the electricity supply industry embarked on a major (and expensive) reduction program that led to a sharp decline in SO_2 emissions. Between 1983 and 1993 annual emissions of SO_2 declined from 2.9 million to 0.7 million tons. The case study examines a number of key questions, including the rationale and performance of the GFA-VO, the implications of the regulation for technical progress in the electricity sector, and related issues.

NO_x Emissions from Utility Boilers: Emission Taxes (Sweden and France) versus NO_x New Source Performance Standards (U.S.)

NO_x Reductions from Coal-Fired Utility Boilers in the United States

Emissions of nitrogen oxides (NO_x) contribute to formation of particulate matter and ozone, and also to acidification of the environment.[6] The electricity sector is an important focus of NO_x policies in the United States for two reasons. First, it contributes about 20 percent of NO_x emissions. Second, these emissions are often emitted through tall stacks at high velocity, causing wide dispersion and contributing to regional pollution problems. Although NO_x is listed as one of the six criteria air pollutants in the Clean Air Act due to its ubiquitous nature, it was not stringently regulated through the 1970s and 1980s, especially insofar as emissions from stationary sources are concerned. NO_x is the only criteria pollutant that has experienced an emissions increase nationally since 1970 (U.S. EPA 2001).

The case study surveys the important NO_x programs affecting the electricity sector. These programs have followed a path beginning with traditional command and control regulations leading to expanded use of flexible market-based approaches. Today both approaches play an important role. The case study focuses on those coal-fired boilers subject to Title IV of the 1990 CAAAs. In 2000, these units represent about 85 percent of total NO_x emissions from the electricity sector.[7]

NO_x Taxes on Utility Boilers in Sweden and France

Both Sweden and France have special charges as supplementary instruments to CAC to limit emissions of NO_x from the energy sector and from industry boilers.[8] The revenues from the relatively high Swedish charge (which dates back to 1992) are automatically recycled through payments to industry based on energy output. France has a tax, which in some respects is similar, applied to four different categories of air pollution, but at a much lower level and with a much more individual form of refunding of the tax revenues. The origin of the French tax system goes back to the mid-1980s and the debate on acid rain. The Swedish tax was also due primarily to concern over acid rain and introduced as a specific policy tool to accelerate the reduction of NO_x emissions from the industry sector. Both systems build on preexisting CAC regulation, and they aim, at least in the French case, to complement rather than substitute for this regulation. The case study compares the similarities and differences between these two European countries that have used charges or taxes to deal with NO_x emissions.

Industrial Water Pollution: Effluent Fees (Netherlands) versus Effluent Guidelines and NPDES Permits (U.S.)

Dutch Effluent Fee

The Dutch fees on water pollution came into existence as a side effect of the Surface Water Pollution Act of 1970.[9] This act aimed at improving the greatly deteriorated quality of surface water. The law permitted responsible authorities to introduce fees to cover the substantial costs of cleaning up sewage water from households and industry. The fees were meant as a mechanism to raise resources to finance sewage water treatment, not so much to influence the behavior of households and businesses. The law delegated the task of water quality management to the provincial authorities and through these authorities to district water boards.

Within a few years almost every water board had raised its rates to a level that encouraged businesses to reduce their wastewater discharges into the sewage system. Degradable organic pollution, for instance, was taxed with a hefty charge per unit of pollution, more than twice as much as in a comparable German program. Meanwhile, almost all district water boards also established fees on heavy metals in the wastewater. By 1990 effluent discharges had dropped by almost 75 percent even though industrial production increased over the period. The case study presents evidence on the effectiveness of Dutch effluent fees in the period 1986–95 and compares it with earlier findings from 1975–80. The focus is on the reduction of the waste load, not the improvement of the surface water quality. The analysis focuses on the effectiveness of the program, the static and dynamic efficiency of fees, and related topics.

U.S. Effluent Guidelines

Water quality became a mainly federal responsibility in the United States in 1972, with the passage of the Clean Water Act.[10] Prior to 1972, water quality was primarily a state and local concern, and the federal government's role was limited to providing grants to municipalities for wastewater treatment as well as information and planning assistance to the states. The Clean Water Act relied primarily on two tools to achieve its goals: First, the Construction Grants Program would provide massive federal support to publicly owned treatment works (POTWs)—wastewater treatment plants owned and operated by municipalities and local sewer districts.[11] Second, a system of technology-based regulations was introduced to control the discharge of water pollution from point sources. These point sources included both POTWs and two classes of industrial facilities: *direct dischargers*, which discharge effluent directly into receiving waters, and *indirect dischargers*, which discharge effluent into a sewer, where it is carried to a POTW. The industrial standards are the focus of this case study. Of particular concern is how the regulatory structure may have affected the incentives governing the behavior of industrial dischargers, municipal waste treatment plant operators, and regulators. Surprisingly, the case study finds some evidence that the Clean Water Act, because it impacts industrial point sources, may be evolving into an effluent fee policy, or at least a mixed policy, despite the fact that it was originally established as a strict CAC system.

Leaded Gasoline: Marketable Permits for Leaded Fuel Production (U.S.) versus Mandatory Lead Phaseouts Plus Differential Taxes to Prevent Misfueling (Most European Countries)

U.S. Leaded Gasoline Phaseout

Refiners in the United States and Europe started adding lead compounds to gasoline in the 1920s to boost octane levels and improve engine performance by reducing engine knock and allowing higher engine compression.[12] Lead was used because it was inexpensive relative to other fuel additives for boosting octane (i.e., ethanol and other alcohol-based additives), and because people were generally ignorant of the dangers of lead emissions, which include mental retardation and hypertension. The reduction in lead in gasoline in the United States came in response to two main factors: (1) the mandatory use of unleaded gasoline to protect catalytic converters in all cars starting with the 1975 model year, and (2) increased awareness of the negative human health effects of lead, leading to the phasedown of lead in leaded gasoline in the 1980s. Beginning in 1974 and coincidental with the introduction of catalyst-equipped vehicles, manufacturers were required to offer unleaded gasoline for sale. The United States has had a complex policy that began as a CAC policy, was switched to an EI policy in 1981, and switched back to CAC in 1988. In 1995, leaded gasoline was banned for use in all vehicles.

Phaseout of Leaded Gasoline in Europe

The combination of the increased attention to the negative health effects of lead and the development of catalytic converters in the United States was the starting point for the phaseout of leaded gasoline in the European Union.[13] However, with the exception of Germany, the phaseout did not start until the early 1980s. As the case study describes, most European countries ultimately relied on a policy specifying a date after which sale of leaded fuel would be illegal, coupled with a differential tax to ensure the price of leaded fuel exceeded that of unleaded to prevent misfueling. Most EU nations completed the phaseout of lead from gasoline by the mid-1990s, although as recently as 2000 as much as 20 percent of the gasoline pool still contained lead in some EU countries.

CFC Permit Market (U.S.) versus Mandatory Phaseouts (Other Industrial Countries)

The first commercially important CFCs were developed in the 1930s for use as the working fluid in refrigeration systems.[14] These compounds are chemically stable, nonflammable, and nontoxic. By the 1970s, CFCs were widely used in a variety of industrial and consumer applications. In addition to their use in building, home, and automobile air conditioning and refrigeration systems, CFCs were used as aerosol propellants for personal care and other products, as blowing agents in manufacturing rigid foams (for insulation and packaging) and flexible foams (for cushioning), and as solvents in the manufacture of electronic and other components. Closely related compounds were also used as solvents (e.g., methyl chloroform) and in fire-extinguishing systems (e.g., halons). CFCs and related compounds were released to the environment either during use (e.g., aerosols) or through leakage or product disposal (refrigeration, closed-cell foams). In 1974, Molina and Rowland published a paper suggesting that environmental release of CFCs might deplete stratospheric ozone. With less ozone, more UV light penetrates to ground level, where it causes damage to human health (e.g., skin cancer and cataracts), ecosystems (e.g., destruction of phytoplankton), certain crops, and some materials (e.g., plastics). The Montreal Protocol, which mandated the initial phase down of CFCs was adopted in 1987 and subsequently strengthened via various amendments.

A single case study describes the American and European policy responses to the threat that CFCs would deplete stratospheric ozone. The United States used a tradable permit policy to phase out production of CFCs. The EU allocated emission caps to each European nation and gave each the responsibility to use specific regulations to phase out the production and use of CFCs. The case study highlights several characteristics of the CFC–stratospheric ozone issue that are important from a policy perspective. First, there was significant uncertainty about whether CFCs would in fact reduce the concentrations of stratospheric ozone, by how much, and how serious the consequences of ozone depletion would be for human health and the environment. Second, because the stratosphere is well mixed, the effects of CFC releases are independent of the location of release. It is not possible for any country to protect itself solely by reducing its own CFC emissions. Third, because of their chemical stability, CFCs survive in the atmosphere for long periods—for many of the compounds, approximately a century. As a result, with emissions increasing, even if CFC emissions were eliminated, the amount of ozone depletion would continue to increase for years, and the protective effects of reducing CFC emissions would lag well behind the costs of emission reductions.

Chlorinated Solvents: Source Regulation (U.S.) versus Three Distinct Policy Approaches in Europe

Chlorinated Solvent Regulation in the United States

Halogenated or chlorinated solvents—including methylene chloride, perchloroethylene, 1,1,1-trichloroethane, and trichloroethylene (TCE)—are widely used for metal cleaning, chemical manufacturing, and as components of paints and other substances.[15] Health impacts include skin irritation, neurological effects, as well as liver and kidney damage. There is also evidence for carcinogenicity. In the United States, chlorinated solvents are regulated under at least four federal statutes plus numerous state laws. This case study examines the regulation of TCE in degreaser cleaning, which accounted for about 90 percent of TCE use in 1992. A notable feature of the governing statute, Section 112 of the U.S. Clean Air Act, is the focus on design or performance-based National Emission Standards for Hazardous Air Pollutants, established for relevant source categories of hazardous air pollutants (HAPs) based on the maximum achievable control technology (MACT).

The approach adopted for regulating TCE under section 112 involves a combination of design and performance-based standards complemented by certain market-based elements. Although the regulation does not involve emission trading or other commonly considered market-based instruments, it does allow limited within-facility averaging among specified HAPs, a type of "emissions bubble." An early reduction provision contained in the statute provides an additional market-based mechanism.

Specifically, a firm is granted an extension of six years beyond the established compliance date to meet the standard if it can demonstrate that
it has achieved at least a 90 percent reduction in emissions of HAPs below
a baseline level prior to the date the MACT is proposed. This early reductions provision introduces at least some financial incentives into the
firm's decision on how to meet the stipulated environmental goal. Conceptually, the early reductions provision can be seen as a form of facility-
specific intertemporal emissions trading. A particularly interesting aspect
of the rule is that in the ex ante analysis the EPA estimated *net savings*
rather than the more common *net costs* associated with most environmental regulations. Overall, as the case study demonstrates, the potential
for the use of the economic incentive measures was not realized. Either
because the compliance costs of the command and control rules were so
low, or because of various constraints on the use of the economic incentives, few firms adopted the incentive measures.

Chlorinated Solvent Regulation in Germany, Sweden, and Norway

Similar to the United States, in Europe chlorinated solvents such as TCE
are used for degreasing and related activities.[16] Because the solvents are
hazardous to human health, more or less strict regulations are in place in
most countries, and there is a drive to find less harmful substitutes. Some
countries have gone further and tried to eliminate or reduce TCE use quite
drastically. In Sweden, for example, use of TCE was prohibited by Parliament. This case study compares the efficiency of the Swedish ban to the
approaches adopted in neighboring countries such as Norway and Denmark, which used environmental taxes, and Germany, which created a
system of detailed technology-based regulations. The results show that
the prohibition was only partially effective and in all likelihood not very
efficient compared to a tax.

Table 5–1 lists the various components of these twelve policies, separated by whether those components might reasonably be characterized as
EI or CAC. As shown, ten of the twelve policies under review here
actually contained a mix of EI and CAC instruments. The German SO_2
ordinance was a "pure" CAC policy, and the TCE policies in the various European countries were pure policies (though different from each
other).

Some of the policy mixes are predominantly CAC but containing traces
of EI (such as U.S. TCE); for others the opposite pattern applies (such as
Swedish NO_x). In the U.S. leaded fuel case, we find CAC and EI instruments applied sequentially. In U.S. industrial water pollution, a few experiments with marketable permits have taken place within an overall
CAC framework, and the waste surcharges imposed on POTWs may be
taking on the incentive properties of effluent fees. In the U.S. acid rain
case, an EI policy was imposed on top of an existing CAC structure, much
of which remained in place. Note that there are few cases where the same

Table 5.1 Comparison of Policy Instruments in the Case Studies

Case	EI elements	CAC elements
U.S. Acid Rain: 1990 Clean Air Act, Title IV	Marketable permits distributed to existing power plants (1990)	BACT for new power plants (1977) RACT for existing plants (1977) New source review (1977)
EU Acid Rain German Large Boiler SO$_2$ Ordinance		Stringent technology-based standards for utility boilers
U.S. NO$_x$ Emissions 1990 Clean Air Act, Title IV	NO$_x$ SIP call institutes trading program (2000)	Technology-based standards for existing utility boilers (1990 Clean Air Act Title IV)
EU NO$_x$ emissions FR and SE NO$_x$ emission fee	NO$_x$ emission fees, automatically recycled to industry based on output FR: $40/metric ton SE: $3,000/metric ton	FR and SE: emission permits required for all sources
U.S. Lead in motorfuel:	Supply side: Trading and banking of permits through interrefinery averaging (1982–87)	Supply side: Introduction of catalysts in new vehicles (1975) Refiners required to make unleaded fuel available (1974) Lead-content standards for all refiners (79–82) Demand side: Prohibition of leaded fuel in catalyst-equipped vehicles, enforced by inlet restrictors
EU Lead in motorfuel	Demand side: Differential fuel taxation, making leaded fuel more expensive than unleaded (1985 SE, AT, all EU countries by 1990)	Supply side: Introduction of catalysts in new vehicles (1986 Mandated availability of unleaded fuel (1984 DE, SE, 1989 EU) Prohibition of leaded fuel in catalyst-equipped vehicles, enforced by inlet restrictors (1985–90)

U.S. Industrial water pollution Effluent guidelines	Direct dischargers (1972): State tradable permit programs in water quality-limited river basins (e.g. Fox River, WI; Neuse River, NC) Indirect dischargers (1972) Tradable rights to POTW capacity (NJ) Sewer surcharge fees on BOD, TSS, various measurements of nitrogen—applied by most POTWs	Direct dischargers: NPDES permits based on Technology-based effluent guidelines (in effluent-limited streams) More stringent standards in water quality-limited streams Indirect dischargers Federal pretreatment standards for some industries and pollutants Local limits for other industries
EU Industrial water pollution NL Surface Water Pollution Act	Pollutant discharge fees primarily for oxygen-demanding substances	Discharge permits issued by district water boards
U.S. TCE NESHAPS, Clean Air Act	Within-facility emissions bubble Early adoption incentives	MACT standards for hazardous pollutants
EU TCE DE: Emission standards NO and DK: Emission tax SE: Product ban	Production tax (NO, DK)	Technology-based standards (DE) Production (SE)
U.S. Ozone-depleting substances	Response to Montreal Protocol (1987): Tradable permits for production and consumption of ODS Excise tax on ODS	Pre–Montreal Protocol Prohibitions in specific applications (e.g., aerosols and foams) (1979–87) Labeling requirements in individual states (1975) Response to Montreal Protocol (1987): Prohibition of small-quantity sales SNAP rules (governing replacement of ODSs)

(*continued*)

Table 5.1 continued

Case	EI elements	CAC elements

EU Ozone-depleting substances	Response to Montreal Protocol (1987):
	Tradable production or import permits
	  By firms within EU member states
	  Between member states
	Individual country actions:
	  AT: deposit-refund system for refrigerants
	  DK: tax on ODS
	  SE: fee on successful applications for exemptions
		Pre–Montreal Protocol
		Aerosol bans in NO and SE (1979)
		Response to Montreal Protocol
		Comprehensive controls in AT, DK, FI,
		  DE, IT, NL, SE
		No comprehensive legislation in FR, GR,
		  IR, PO, SP, UK

source is subject to both types of instruments at the same time. Even in those cases where a source is subject to two constraints on behavior, at any particular point in time only one will be active for a particular source. (For example, if an emission fee is imposed on top of an existing emission standard, the fee will be the binding constraint for low-marginal-cost dischargers and the standard for high-marginal-cost dischargers.) In principle at least, it is possible to observe the various instruments at work. In practice, the mix of instruments may make it more difficult to determine the effects of each, but it does not preclude an examination of the performance of different types of regulatory instruments.

III. EUROPEAN VERSUS AMERICAN ENVIRONMENTAL REGULATION

Before turning to instrument choice, we make a few observations about differences between European and American regulation, at least as revealed in these cases.

One versus Many

Our six case study pairs illustrate that American and European regulators have to deal with similar environmental problems, but they often deal with them in different ways. The most obvious difference is that the European Union consists of many countries, whereas the United States is only one. It is one, moreover, that has allocated principal responsibility for environmental rule making to the federal government, even though most environmental problems are local. This centralization of environmental policy making is primarily the result of a series of landmark statutes that were passed between 1969 and 1980.[17] It is not obvious that these centralizing moves were part of a grand plan; rather they appear to have been prompted by more ad hoc concerns. First, there *were* some environmental problems that crossed state lines. More important, there was an atmosphere of crisis at the time, a concern that environmental problems had to be dealt with right away or there wouldn't be any environment left to protect. Most of the states had, in the minds of many, demonstrated that they could not act quickly enough or forcefully enough to deal with the multitude of environmental problems facing the country. The federal government was thought to be powerful enough to stand up to the large corporations that were presumably the primary source of environmental degradation. Federal authority over environmental policy also avoided the much-feared race to the bottom—polluters' shopping around for lenient states willing to sacrifice environmental quality for new jobs and economic growth.

Unlike the United States, the environmental tide in Europe reached flood stage at different times in different countries, beginning in the late 1960s in the wealthiest nations of Western Europe, especially the Nordic countries, and sweeping south and east to reach the countries of the former Soviet Union by 1990 or so. Each country adopted its own policies according to its own timetable. But more recently the gathering momentum of economic, social and political integration in the EU has also provided a centralizing impulse to all kinds of policies, not least environmental policy.

Our European cases reflect this mix of country-specific and EU-wide policy initiatives. For example, the TCE case study concentrates on Sweden's ban but also refers to Norway's tax and to Germany's stringent regulation (albeit short of a ban). The mix of country-specific and EU-wide policies is seen in the leaded gasoline case. Individual countries had their own policies on introducing vehicles with catalytic converters. But if any countries required catalytic converters, possible intercountry travel would require *all* countries to introduce unleaded fuel, a measure that was to be fully implemented in the EU by 1989. The EU also implemented regulations in 1981 specifying the maximum and minimum content of lead in leaded fuel and in 1998 specified a complete switchover to unleaded fuel by 2005. However, the heterogeneity among European countries on this issue (as on other issues) is noticeable.

Moreover, selection bias is clearly an issue for the cases examined. This bias occurs in the regulations selected for study and in the particular nations chosen to represent Europe. In fact, in most instances the European cases were chosen because an innovative policy had been adopted in a particular jurisdiction. Thus, most of the European regulations selected represent the *exceptional* European action, whereas the U.S. regulations are, by their very nature, national in scope. In that respect the U.S. actions can be thought of as representing the *average* rather than the exceptional policy.

Furthermore, these regulatory comparisons completely ignore the issues of timing or preexisting environmental conditions. Certainly, earlier reductions are more valuable than those undertaken at a later date. Thus, the observation that the U.S. and European nations both phased out (covered) CFCs ignores the fact that the United States began the CFC phaseout almost a decade earlier than the Europeans. Similarly, although a few Northern European nations actually started phasing out lead from gasoline earlier than the United States, most finished later—in some cases by a decade or more. Furthermore, neither the preexisting pollution levels nor the difficulty of achieving particular reductions are fully considered in the case studies. Overall, as appealing as it might be to draw implications about the relative stringency of the environmental programs across the shores of the Atlantic, we do not believe that our selection of case studies provide sufficient information to make credible assertions on this issue. About the most that can be said is that European environmental regulation tends to be much more heterogeneous than corresponding regulation in the United States.

Ex Ante Analysis

Our case studies also suggest that European and American regulations differed substantially in the amount and nature of ex ante analysis. This difference is largely attributable to the long-standing requirement imposed on U.S. government agencies to carry out a Regulatory Impact Analysis to project the economic consequences of regulatory proposals and make it possible to compare the direct effects of the regulation with the cost.[18] For each regulatory alternative to control pollution, analysts at the EPA had to estimate the environmental effects, the abatement costs, any other indirect costs, and often any economic dislocations (such as plant closures or unemployment) likely to result from the regulation.

There was no European counterpart to this requirement. Very likely, regulators, regulatees, and other parties in Europe were just as concerned about the benefits and costs of regulations as they were in the United States. But without a formal requirement to produce a public report, there was no paper trail available to researchers. Although our case study authors were in most cases able to reconstruct or infer estimates of the environmental consequences of the regulations in question, in only two cases were they able to find an ex ante estimate of anticipated costs. In three other cases, ex ante estimates of environmental effects were easy to produce because the policy in question was a ban on discharge of a particular substance, and the anticipated change equaled the current discharge.

Perhaps coincidentally, it is interesting that both cases in which emission reductions exceeded expectations involved market-based approaches, whereas both cases where actual performance fell short of expectations relied on traditional CAC measures. A similar result is discussed in more detail in Harrington et al. (2000).

Regulatory Ambition

A third potential point of comparison between European and American case studies lies in the stringency and effectiveness of the corresponding regulations. In light of recent transatlantic environmental controversies such as the U.S. refusal to sign the Kyoto Protocol on global climate change or the fight over genetically modified food, it would be easy for the casual observer to conclude that Europeans are much more concerned about environmental quality than Americans are. On this question it is useful to separate ex ante stringency from ex post regulatory performance.

Overall, these cases do not support the notion that European environmental objectives have been generally more ambitious than American ones. These cases suggest American environmental regulation often precedes that of most European countries by several years, and the American environmental statutes enacted in the early 1970s were nothing if not ambitious. U.S. air and water pollution policy, which is represented in our set by the industrial water pollution regulations and the NO_x emission regulations prior to 1990, fits this pattern. In both cases ambitious goals were to be achieved within seven years (for air) or thirteen years (for water) of implementation. The objective of the 1972 water pollution statute—zero discharge of pollutants by 1985—is so extraordinary that there is some question whether this goal was ever taken literally by the members of Congress voting on it, and if so whether they fully understood the ramifications of zero discharge. The objective of the 1970 Clean Air Act, which was to achieve by 1977 air quality so clean that it protected the health of the most sensitive members of the population, is also quite stringent, and there can be little doubt that this objective is meant to be taken seriously. Although the primary ambient standards for ozone and fine particles still have not been achieved in many urban areas, they remain the main drivers of clean air policy in the United States. Moreover, those standards were just revised, and some were made even more stringent to reflect recent health-effects research.[19]

Regulatory Performance

Although the United States has adopted ambitious environmental policies, a few European countries have had comparable or even greater success in implementation of such policies. As noted by case study authors Wätzold and Hansjürgens, Germany adopted a very stringent acid rain regulation requiring in excess of 90 percent abatement of SO_2 in flue gas from utility boilers. This is much more stringent than the celebrated U.S. acid rain trading program. Sweden adopted a NO_x regulation for large industrial and utility sources that imposed marginal costs of $3,000/ton of emitted NO_x, a level comparable to permit prices in American NO_x permit markets (such as the RECLAIM program in southern California).[20] In both these cases, the authorities could point to severe environmental problems resulting from acid deposition, causing dramatic and visible ecological damage to forests and lakes. Although comparable in outcome, the U.S. accomplishments seem to have required more effort.

One reason frequently given for the apparent differences in effort is American litigiousness. It is a rare U.S. environmental regulation that does not end up in court. Proposed rules are challenged in regulatory proceedings and, after promulgation, in federal district courts. These district court decisions are frequently appealed to the circuit courts, and even further appeals to the U.S. Supreme Court are not uncommon. Every one of the U.S. policies in our sample of cases provoked courtroom challenges, and some, such as the effluent guidelines, provoked hundreds of such challenges. In the European TCE case, author Sterner reports that the Swedish ban was challenged by the Swedish chemical industry and then comments on how unusual this is for Europe.

Litigation by industry has had two effects on regulatory productivity in the United States. First, it has delayed promulgation of rules. Numerous lawsuits have prevented implementation of the Clean Water Act "best available technology" (BAT) rules, for example, and tied up EPA resources in revising the remanded rules. Arguably, the litigation over the BAT rules has also resulted in rules that are less stringent. On the other hand, these effects have to some extent been limited by litigation initiated by environmental groups. For example, an Natural Resources Defense Council lawsuit over the missed BAT deadlines resulted in a court-determined timetable for the issuance of new rules in the early 1990s. Sometimes environmental groups have also intervened successfully to prevent watering down of rules.

Product Bans

Product bans, the polar case of regulatory stringency, are well represented in our sample of cases on both the European and the American side. Several regulations fall into this category: both leaded fuel cases, both CFCs, and TCE in Sweden. Some might add industrial water pollution in the United States, because it established a goal of zero discharge. However, this "ban" is much larger in scale and scope than the others mentioned, and it is possible that some in Congress regarded the goal as aspirational or rhetorical.

Of these, the leaded fuel and CFC bans were ultimately successful. Swedish TCE failed to achieve 100 percent emission reductions, although it did achieve reductions of 65 percent—roughly the same reductions achieved in the United States (which did not include a ban). U.S. industrial water also failed to achieve zero discharge of pollutants, as required by the statute, but it can be seen as a special case.

If the bans were successful, then the postregulation pollution level is zero. It is often easier to determine whether a ban has been effectively implemented than to estimate the effects of a policy that does not attempt to eliminate the pollutant entirely. Ordinarily the technology implementing a ban is the substitution of a new process or product, which is easier to observe.

Use of Economic Incentives

In the main we found little difference between the countries of Europe and the United States in the predilection for using economic incentives. However, we did find a dramatic difference in the type of instruments used. Among our cases, nearly all EI policies in the EU are emission taxes, whereas nearly all EI policies in the United States are marketable permits.[21] Why is this?

Europe's lack of interest in marketable permits may reflect the limits of national boundaries. As long as environmental policies are still being set at the national level rather than the EU level, it will be difficult to trade permits across frontiers, keeping permit markets thin and limiting the efficiency advantages of trading.

European countries also have different attitudes toward taxes. European tax rates are generally higher than in the United States and are structured differently, with more reliance on commodity taxes and less on income taxes. Europeans are accustomed to extremely high tax rates on some products, such as motor fuel, where taxes can make up over 80 percent of the total price of the product. Europeans are also more comfortable with the notion of using taxes to achieve other policy goals besides revenue raising.

One possible explanation for American preference for permit trading is that U.S. environmental policies are more likely to have ambient objectives supported by specific targets and timetables for emission reductions. As noted in the discussion of hypotheses that follow, one characteristic of emission fees is that setting the level of the fee determines the final marginal cost of abatement, not the pollution abatement target. Europeans perhaps are more apt to be motivated by the "polluter pays" principle than the need to set some prespecified ambient (or emissions) target.

An additional element pushing the United States toward marketable permits was the fact that the EPA does not have authority to levy new taxes. That power belongs to and is jealously guarded by congressional tax-writing committees.

The preference for tradable permit systems in the United States dates back to 1976, when it became clear that a number of cities would not meet the 1977 deadline for attainment of the National Ambient Air Quality Standard, especially for ozone and particulates. Under the Clean Air Act, nonattainment meant no new air pollution sources or expansion of existing sources in the affected area. However, the EPA allowed new or expanding sources to proceed with their plans as long as they could find offsetting emission reductions among existing sources. Thus were the bubble and offset policies born.

Equity

In recent years, questions about the fairness or equity of environmental regulation have arisen on both sides of the Atlantic. The most common question arising in public discussions is whether different income or racial groups have been disproportionately affected by either the uncontrolled risks or the costs associated with the regulations. Accordingly, we asked the case study authors to pay particular attention to this issue. The results are somewhat surprising.

When the question is posed as a potential impact on the general population, only the U.S. case of lead in gasoline seemed to involve significant public debate on equity issues.[22] However, equity issues were frequently mentioned in an entirely different context: the potential burdens of the regulation on one or more segments of industry—mostly on small business. Six of the cases identified small business impacts as significant (U.S. TCE, France NO_x, U.S. water, U.S. lead, Sweden lead). In each of these instances the governments explicitly addressed the equity issue in the design of the regulation. The most common regulatory response was to exempt at least some categories of small business from the regulation. In the case of U.S. TCE, for example, most small gasoline station/repair facilities were exempted.

An additional response to equity concerns can be seen in the differential timeframes that particular nations adopted for new regulatory requirements. This is particularly true in Europe where EU directives generally permit a good deal of flexibility at the country level. The authors of the European case on lead phasedown highlight this issue. Specifically, they argue that despite the relatively high exposure to airborne lead among low-income groups—and thus the obvious gains to this group from rapid adoption of the lead phasedown program—a number of European nations, particularly low-income nations, have been slow to adopt the program. Though part of this response may be explained by the differences in perceived benefits, the case study authors suggest that this differential timing in adopting the regulation is based, in part, on cross-national equity concerns.[23]

IV. THE HYPOTHESES

The last couple of decades have seen a good deal of speculation and disputation over the differences between EI and CAC instruments in practice, leading to the development of a fairly long list of assertions or hypotheses about these differences. Unfortunately, if you ask ten knowledgeable people, the ten lists you get will differ—probably dramatically so. That's because some of the characteristics of these policies can vary depending on policy details or may be true only under some circumstances. Different observers may have different policies or circumstances in mind. On other characteristics, the advocates and skeptics may agree. Where they may disagree is on the importance of the criterion. We do our best to be clear about what our assumptions are.

Policy details can also be altered to accommodate criticisms implicit in these hypotheses. For example, CAC policies can be made more or less cost-effective depending on how much effort is put into setting abatement requirements for individual polluters at optimal levels.

In this section we simply list the hypotheses. In the next section, we provide a rationale and review what the case study outcomes reveal about them.

1. *Static efficiency.* EI instruments are more efficient than CAC instruments.
2. *Information requirements.* Generally, EI instruments require less information than CAC instruments to achieve emission reductions cost-effectively.
3. *Dynamic efficiency.* The real advantages of EI instruments over CAC are only realized over time, because unlike CAC policies they provide a continual incentive to reduce emissions, thus promoting new technology, and they permit a maximum of flexibility in the means of achieving emission reductions.
4. *Effectiveness.* CAC policies achieve their objectives quicker and with greater certainty than EI policies.
5. *Regulatee burden.* Regulated firms are more likely to oppose EI regulations than CAC because they fear that they will face higher costs, despite the greater efficiency of EI instruments.
6. *Administrative burden.* CAC policies have higher administrative costs.

7. *Hot spots and spikes.* The performance of all pollution-abatement instruments is seriously compromised for pollutants with highly differentiated spatial or temporal effects, but more so for EI than for CAC instruments.

8. *Monitoring requirements.* The monitoring requirements of EI policies are more demanding than those of CAC policies because they require credible and quantitative emission estimates, whereas CAC policies only require evidence of excess emissions or the absence of abatement technology.

9. *Tax interaction effects.* Adverse tax interaction effects are likely to be larger with EI instruments than CAC instruments achieving the same emission reductions.

10. *Effects on altruism.* Economic incentives encourage the notion that the environment is "just another commodity" and reduce the willingness of firms and citizens to provide environmental public goods voluntarily.

11. *Adaptability.* Compared to CAC instruments, EI instruments can be changed more quickly and easily in response to changing environmental or economic conditions.

12. *Cost revelation.* With EI instruments, it is easier to observe the cost of environmental regulation. Theory tells us that for a firm subject to an emission fee, the marginal cost is the same as the fee rate; in a tradable permit regime, the marginal cost is the market price of the permits. With CAC instruments, a firm must clean up to a prespecified quantity; there are no fees or permit prices to which marginal costs can be equated.

V. PERFORMANCE OF EI AND CAC INSTRUMENTS

The selection of individual case studies was governed in large part by a desire to compare performance of different environmental instruments in at least a partially controlled environment. The control is the common environmental problem addressed in two or more different jurisdictions. Fixing the environmental problem to be addressed makes meaningful some comparisons that would not be clear if we simply studied different instruments in arbitrary applications, including stringency, abatement cost, technologies employed, introduction of new technology, and speed of implementation. These comparisons yield the most insights about the hypotheses.

However, there are also some important limits of our approach. First, we suffer from the common problem of all case study research—a small number of observations, nonrandomly selected. Second, these cases differ in many aspects besides the policy instrument chosen—for example, political institutions, history, and preexisting environmental quality. These differences can affect the outcomes we observe as much as the difference in instrument can. The complexity of the regulatory history or the varying structure of regulation in most cases made it difficult to make straight-up comparisons of a U.S. case with its European counterpart regarding certain hypotheses. Accordingly, we make tentative judgments about some of the hypotheses by examining only one case out of a pair. Sometimes such comparisons are facilitated by the application of both types of instruments at different times, such as U.S. leaded fuel.

Third, as Table 5–1 made clear, our instrument comparisons are rarely as clean as we would like. For each hypothesis, what we would like is to measure the quantitative difference in a response between the EI instrument and the CAC instrument. For example, the first hypothesis on efficiency would be supported if we conclude that the unit cost of abatement is less for the EI instrument than for the corresponding CAC instrument. But sometimes those differences cannot be observed quantitatively, because one case study is unable to report anything of relevance on the variable in question, or because differences in another variable hinder the ability to make comparisons. To continue with the efficiency example, a difference in unit costs between the two policies could be due to a difference in overall stringency, which would have no particular implications for the efficiency hypothesis.

Notwithstanding these limitations, the richness of the case studies means that we can often arrive at a tentative judgment about a hypothesis even if we have results from only one of a pair of studies. For example, the finding of high administrative costs in the U.S. water pollution case (CAC) is based on the extremely large number of regulations that had to be written and on the extensive delays. This observation required no close comparison with the Dutch opposite number, which incurred no similar delays. However, when we observe that the administrative costs of the German SO_2 policy (also CAC) were relatively low compared to the U.S. acid rain policy, then it raises the question of whether it is the instrument chosen that is driving administrative costs or American litigiousness.

Static Efficiency
EI instruments are more efficient than CAC instruments.

Rationale

Under textbook assumptions, EI instruments are more cost-effective than CAC instruments at achieving a given emission reduction, because they allow polluting firms to choose their pollutant discharge rate so that the marginal abatement cost equals the emission fee (or the permit price). To get from cost-effectiveness to efficiency additionally requires the standard assumptions of perfect competition, in particular price-taking firms and complete information. It also requires the emissions to be "uniformly mixed," that is, their effects are not location-specific, and abatement cost functions are convex. Finally, in an emission fee system the fee has to be set to equal the marginal social damage caused to the emissions.

In a world of perfect information, a CAC instrument can be designed to be efficient as well. The regulator just has to choose the emission standard for each source so that the marginal costs of abatement equal the marginal social costs of pollutant damage. Emission fees do have a long-run theoretical advantage, however. Spulber (1985) shows that in principle, the firm producing a good X should pay a fee on the use of environmental services associated with production of X, just as it has to pay for all other inputs. Without it, in the long run too much X will be produced. In a transferable permit system this advantage can be met by auctioning the permits rather than distributing them gratis among the firms producing X.

Performance

Although not all of the cases made explicit comparisons between the two instruments, those that did were uniform in their findings of efficiency advantages for economic incentive measures. Some of the larger gains from such measures are found in the U.S. SO_2 and lead phasedown programs. As SO_2 case study authors Burtraw and Palmer argue, after accounting for exogenous changes in fuel markets in a consistent manner, realized costs are only about one-half the predicted levels based on information available to legislators in 1990 and perhaps a quarter of the cost of a linear rollback CAC technology standard.

Lead case study authors Newell and Rogers report that the banking program itself, by allowing for a more cost-effective allocation of new investment within the industry, saved over $225 million when compared to an inflexible CAC approach. The whole program, including trading, is estimated to have saved considerably more.

In the Dutch water case, study authors Bressers and Lulofs note that the degree of pollution reductions in the early years corresponded well to the production cost incentives created by the fees, which indicates that discharges were reduced fairly efficiently. In contrast, in the United States, the ex ante estimates of marginal abatement costs varied by a factor of thirty across a sample of industry categories. Thus, even though no additional information was available ex post, case study author Harrington suggests it was not very likely that cost-effective reductions were achieved.

German SO_2 case study authors Watzold and Hansjergens note that there can be limits to the static efficiency advantages of economic incentives. In cases where the regulations are extremely stringent and everyone has to do all that is technically feasible to meet the emissions goal—as in the case of the German SO_2 regulations—the gains from trade are very limited. In that case economic incentives are not likely to yield significant savings without jeopardizing achievement of the stringent quantity objectives.

In contrast, there is solid evidence that economic incentives achieved substantial cost savings when used to orchestrate the elimination of CFCs and lead in gasoline. Presumably EIs worked in these cases of maximal stringency because there were cost heterogeneities that could be exploited during the phasedown period. In the German SO_2 case, the similarity of the power plants and the abatement technologies available suggest relative uniformity of costs, thereby reducing the potential advantage for economic incentives.

Overall, it appears that these cases at least lend support to the textbook proposition that EIs are more cost-effective than CAC approaches to pollution control.

Information Requirements

Generally, EI instruments require less information than CAC instruments to achieve emission reductions cost-effectively.

Rationale

The claim of smaller information requirements for EIs clearly refers to the burdens placed on the regulator as opposed to the regulated entity. To set cost-effective standards using a CAC instrument, a regulator needs to know the marginal costs of all the regulated sources. In contrast, for EI instruments, the regulator does not require the same detailed cost data to ensure that the emission reductions made by each discharger are achieved at minimum cost. Instead, the cost data can remain with the regulated entities who in turn will have obvious incentives to develop accurate, facility-specific data that they might not otherwise be motivated to collect or share with regulators. (See the discussion on the cost revelation hypothesis.) We should note, however, that with a price-based EI instrument it cannot be guaranteed that an aggregate emission target will be met, whereas with a quantity-based EI instrument it can.

However, there are several other kinds of information needed to make successful environmental policy, including the enforceability and environmental effects of regulations. In these areas, EI instruments have no obvious information-economizing advantages over CAC instruments. Because we treat these types of information specifically shortly (when we consider the hot spot and monitoring issues), we focus here only on the cost information.

Performance

With this proviso, the hypothesis appears to be reasonably well supported by the case studies. To implement the EI instruments in Europe, the authorities did not have to acquire a great deal of information about plant-level costs. Indeed, in the Netherlands water pollution case, what was intended to be a revenue fee turned out to have substantial incentive properties and resulted in cost-effective effluent reduction without any information collection. In the United States, it is unlikely that cost information was *required* to implement EI instruments, but the information was collected just the same. Because of the emphasis on ex ante studies in the United States, some information about costs for leaded gasoline and flue gas desulfurization had to be collected prior to implementation of these EI instruments (or had already been collected to implement earlier CAC rules). Moreover, the novelty of EIs, together with the need to meet emission reduction targets specified in legislation, required careful analysis of regulatory proposals prior to issuance to raise the confidence of all parties that the new regime was going to work as anticipated.

When we turn to CAC rules we find substantial information requirements even when no attempt is made to write cost-effective regulations. For technology-based standards, it was originally thought that the main task of information collection was to identify a standard and a technology that would meet that standard, and that such a task could be accomplished by considering broad classes of industries, with no need for more detailed data collection. For the EPA's Effluent Guidelines, for example, case study author Harrington reports that considerations of cost impact, not cost-effectiveness, created substantial demands for information. For one thing, the sheer heterogeneity of industry and industrial processes was staggering. The information requirements of technology-based standards turned out to be formidable, because of the multiplicity of industries (and technological processes) and often the need to set several standards for each process. Although the same abatement technologies could be designated for several different industries, the EPA nonetheless had to provide evidence that the designated technology was a feasible choice for that industry. Furthermore, equity considerations–both substantive and procedural—placed additional information collection burdens on the EPA. Typically, the EPA has been besieged with claims that great harm to petitioning firms would follow from the regulations, often supported by extensive documentation that, in turn, placed additional burdens on the agency to respond. Under the terms of the Administrative Procedures Act, the EPA had to take these claims seriously, often requiring further analysis and sometimes collection of new data.

Dynamic Efficiency

The real advantages of EI instruments over CAC are only realized over time, because unlike CAC policies they provide a continual incentive to reduce emissions, thus promoting new technology, and they permit a maximum of flexibility in the means of achieving emission reductions.

Rationale

The effects of CAC regulation on technology are potentially complex. On one hand, costly regulations provide a continual spur to find less costly ways of achieving compliance. Furthermore, new source performance standards, which are a common feature of CAC regulations, were intended to encourage dissemination of advanced abatement technology as old plants retired and were replaced by new plants with current technology. On the other hand, the very requirement to install new technology conceivably discourages research in new abatement methods by pollutant dischargers, because discovering ways to reduce emissions can become the basis of even more stringent standards. This phenomenon has been called the regulatory ratchet. (It would not discourage innovation by the pollution abatement industry, of course.) New source performance standards have the stated objective of promoting new technology, which they may do, but they could also have the pernicious effects of postponing retirements of older, dirtier plants and increasing barriers to entry by outside firms.

Performance

The evidence from the case studies on dynamic efficiency provides general, although not universal, support for the traditional textbook view that EI provide a greater incentives than CAC for continuing innovation over time. Certainly, the U.S. lead and SO_2 cases, as well as the Swedish NO_x case, provide strong support for this hypothesis.

In the case of the U.S. lead phasedown program, the authors note that the pattern of technology adoption was consistent with an economic response to market incentives and plant characteristics. Specifically, they found a significant divergence in the pattern of technology adoption among refineries with low versus high compliance costs: low-cost refineries (i.e., expected permit sellers) significantly increased their likelihood of adoption relative to the high-cost facilities (expected permit buyers) under market-based lead regulation compared to under individually binding performance standards. Interestingly, in the case of the U.S. SO_2 program, the authors note that innovation has occurred principally through changes in organizational technology, the organization of markets, and through experimentation at individual boilers rather than through more traditional measures, for example, patentable discoveries. They argue that under a prescriptive regulatory approach the incentives would not have existed for some of these discoveries, such as fuel blending or performance improvements at scrubbers.

As Swedish/French NO_x case study authors Sterner and Millock report, the Swedish NO_x charge created strong incentives for fuel switching, modifications to combustion engineering, and the installation of specific abatement equipment, such as catalytic converters and selective non-catalytic reduction. Equally important, the use of a fee created incentives to *use* the equipment, to fine-tune combustion and other processes in such a way as to minimize emissions. The Swedish experience suggests a strong connection between the monitoring requirements and the observed emission reductions via fine-tuning. The monitoring, in turn, only became a reality due to the high charges that had to be based on accurate emission figures.

In the Dutch water case, although much of the initial responses represented little more than good housekeeping measures, subsequently more advanced, so-called process-integrated measures were also taken. Furthermore, the Netherlands became a world leader in the development of new water purification technologies, for example, nitrate bacteria, membranes. Also, a number of engineering consulting firms sprung up in the country subsequent to the development of the new policies. Overall, it is estimated that on average the unit abatement costs for organic pollutants dropped by half between 1986 and 1995.

CAC approaches can also create incentives for innovation. For example, authors Wätzold and Hansjürgens find that the German SO_2 ordinance (GFA-VO) was truly technology-forcing. The required stringency put the regulation at or beyond the technological frontier for flue gas desulfurization, and utility officials were very concerned whether advances in technology would enable the regulation to be met. However, the pollution abatement industry was able to rise to this challenge. Indeed, Wätzold and Hansjürgens observe that the regulatory ratchet—the incentive for firms to avoid innovation if it simply means that they are subject to more stringent future regulation—does not apply to vendors of pollution abatement equipment, who have strong incentives to demonstrate advanced technology, regardless of policy instrument.

Similarly, U.S. NO_x case study authors Burtraw and Evans report that some experimentation with innovative postcombustion controls occurred for compliance with Phase I Ozone Transport Region (OTR) RACT standards even though the abatement policy in the region was relatively inflexible. They also note that those plants that engaged in experimentation in the OTR region were often treated differently by regulators and some received subsidies from the Department of Energy. Thus, innovation incentives in CAC regimes often come about through administrative procedures or exceptions that are supplemental to the regulation.

A similar finding of possible innovation under CAC is also found in the U.S. water case. As case study author Harrington notes, if the adoption of process changes instead of end-of-pipe treatment is taken as the measure of innovation, then one can clearly observe a significant increase in the use of innovative technologies during the period of the CAC regulations. Although it is impossible to say what use of process change would have been employed in an economics incentives regime, the results do suggest that CAC is not without effect in encouraging out-of-the-box thinking in abatement. At the same time, Harrington also reports anecdotal evidence that a set of technical documents prepared by the EPA in 1975–80 describing wastewater treatment technologies is still considered a pretty accurate description of the current technology, at least for some industries.

Overall, the evidence suggests that innovation occurs under both CAC and EI regimes, but the pattern of innovative behavior is different. In an EI regime, the technology adoption decision is an economic decision, made jointly with decisions about plant operations and remaining life. For example, older plants with high costs and relatively short remaining lives are less likely to adopt new technology in response to EI. Afterward their cost disadvantage relative to newer plants tends to deteriorate, so that their operating rates decline and their retirements tend to be advanced. It is difficult to approximate the full set of these choices with a CAC instrument. For example, it is common among CAC instruments to apply more stringent standards to newer plants, a pattern that may have prolonged the lives of industrial plants in some industries.

Effectiveness

CAC policies achieve their objectives quicker and with greater certainty than EI policies.

Rationale

In the early 1970s, CAC looked like a straightforward application of the government's police power. Disinterested experts would develop emission standards for each point source industry based on the technology criteria established by Congress. This approach might not find the least costly abatement opportunities, but at least it would establish clear rules and identify specific ways of complying with those rules, thus expediting compliance.

Concerns about effectiveness were probably the main reason for the reluctance to adopt EI instruments early on. Emission fees bore especially heavy criticism in this respect, deriving from the uncertainty about the emission reductions that would result from a particular fee. For the earliest emission offset policies there was also a concern about the possibility of "paper trades" or fanciful estimates of emission credits. During the early offset programs there did seem to be some cases of bogus trades (Liroff 1986). Eventually, concerns about the authenticity of emission reductions led to tighter restrictions on trade, which of course reduced the number of trades and the potential efficiency of the instrument.

With marketable permits, there is a cap on aggregate emissions, so presumably effectiveness is high. However, it is still likely that if we compare a nontradable permit (i.e., CAC) policy to a tradable policy with the same aggregate emission rate, we will find lower overall emissions with the CAC policy. Under a CAC policy, plants routinely overcomply with emission permits. If these permits can be traded, then this emission gap suddenly has value and will likely be traded to a source that will use them (Oates et al. 1989 describe a similar mechanism for ambient standard setting).

Performance

The evidence on the comparative effectiveness of the different instruments is quite mixed. In both TCE cases—which focus on CAC approaches—there is evidence that substantial emission reductions were achieved in a short period of time. The dramatic character of the prohibition in Sweden appears to have speeded up research into alternatives and likely benefited users even outside Sweden. However, the Swedish ban was ultimately unsuccessful, achieving an emission reduction of only about two-thirds. In a direct comparison to the high tax rate on chlorinated solvents in neighboring Norway, case study author Sterner found the economic incentive policy to be more cost-effective and at least as effective. Sterner also suggests that a lower but broader tax on many chlorinated solvents, as was used successfully in Denmark, would very likely have reduced toxic exposure by at least the same amount as the existing Swedish ban at much lower cost. Case study authors Loh and Morgenstern report that in the United States the observed emission reductions—roughly the same percentage as achieved in Sweden—were based almost entirely on CAC mechanisms. Apparently, the early reduction program developed by the EPA was not sufficiently attractive to industry to encourage widespread participation.

In the case of lead phasedown in Europe, the case study authors argue that the use of a tax differential without also mandating the use of catalytic converters and the maximum lead content of fuels would have slowed the phasedown significantly. Similarly, the authors of the German SO_2 case study highlight the rapid reductions achieved under the CAC system. Specifically, they note that large emission reductions were required within five years for plants installing scrubbers and within two years for plants that switched fuels—clearly a faster pace than in the market-based U.S. system. They also note that at least in the early years of the program there was a good deal of overcompliance, as firms tended to operate with significant safety margins to avoid both the mandated compliance penalties and the adverse publicity associated with violations.[24] Although there has been considerable overcompliance in the U.S. system as well, the fact that the excess reductions could be used at a later date has very different environmental implications than in the German case.

Contrary to the stated hypothesis, considerable support can also be gleaned for the view that incentive-based policies achieve emission reductions no less rapidly than CAC approaches. In the Dutch water case, an effluent fee kept actual emissions well below the source-specific effluent limits imposed at the same time. In the U.S. SO_2 and lead cases, the general concerns about the lack of effectiveness of EI were not borne out.

In the U.S. SO_2 case, the authors argue that the almost perfect compliance record established under Title IV makes a strong case that market-based instruments can be effective. Of course, the German case study demonstrates the same for CAC. Because continuous emission monitors (CEMs) were required in both systems, there was (presumably) a high degree of reporting accuracy in Germany as well as in the United States. In the Dutch water case, the authors argue that the influence of effluent fees on organic waste load reductions was prompt and extremely large. In the U.S. lead phasedown, the authors argue that the incentive-based phasedown program, combined with the requirements that cars install catalytic converters, achieved in 1981 what the fee turnover alone would not have achieved for an additional six years.

Interestingly, at least two of the cases point to significant environmental gains from both approaches, albeit with some undesirable side effects over the longer term. For example, the prescriptive approaches adopted to reduce U.S. NO_x emissions led to emission reductions of about 17 percent from coal-fired power plants, if measured under somewhat fictional assumptions that their influence did not affect other operational and investment decisions. However, it is widely believed that the CAA's New Source Performance Standards (NSPS) provided an incentive to extend the life of existing plants to avoid costs associated with pollution control at new plants. This perverse incentive is likely to have undermined the accomplishments of NSPS to some degree. At the same time, the authors argue that in the Title IV NO_x program, the absence of an aggregate cap may be responsible for the observed (net) increases in emissions from coal-fired boilers during the 1990s. In the U.S. water case, the authors point out the difficulty of making highly prescriptive environmental regulations as stringent in practice as they appeared at the time they were debated in Congress. Thus, they note that for many industries covered by the Effluent Guidelines program, the BAT (CAC) regulations were mired in so many details that they were delayed for more than a decade past their statutory deadlines.

Finally, in the Swedish TCE case study, Sterner suggests that unsuccessful CAC policies may have broader implications for the credibility of environmental institutions. In response to the regulation, Swedish users of TCE were able to act in a concerted manner to persuade the public and the environmental authorities that complete implementation of the ban would cause undue harm. The authorities allowed numerous waivers and exceptions to the ban. These successes may have undermined the authority of the Swedish EPA, emboldened firms to oppose other regulations, and demoralized those firms that did comply with the regulation, perhaps giving them reason to think twice about cooperation with the environmental authority in the future. It is doubtful whether a similar problem would arise with EI instruments. After all, the firm's cost is capped by an emission fee or the price of an emission permit. The fee or permit price, moreover, is known to the regulator, which pretty much eliminates the possibility of bluffing by the firm. Even if it decides not to abate, it can do so by paying the fee rather than challenging the authorities.

Taken as a whole, the cases offer little evidence of systematic problems with effectiveness among economic incentives.

Regulatee Burden

Regulated firms are more likely to oppose EI regulations than CAC because they fear that they will face higher costs, despite the greater efficiency of EI instruments.

Rationale

The assertion of greater cost-effectiveness of EI instruments refers to *social* costs, the sum of costs to all members of society. When it comes to the *private* costs imposed on regulated firms, the burden of EI will often be greater than that of CAC.

Under CAC, a polluting firm pays the cost of pollution abatement. Under an emission fee policy, the firm pays the cost of abatement plus a fee for remaining pollution discharged. The firm is better off only if the abatement cost is lower by an amount at least as great as the fee payments. Buchanan and Tullock (1975) point out that this could account for much of the opposition of the business community to effluent fees during the 1970s.

Under some circumstances it will be possible to use the fee revenues to overcome such opposition, by revenue recycling—redistributing fee revenues to pollution sources. To preserve the incentive effects, the redistribution has to be made not proportional to emissions but on some other basis. With tradable permits, such concerns can be overcome by distributing permits gratis to emitters rather than auctioning them off. However, such reimbursements subsidize the use of environmental resources in production and in the long run encourage overproduction of output.

Performance

Experience on both sides of the Atlantic suggests that no government ever put this hypothesis to the test, which, in a way, is strong support for it. Although recent legislative proposals in the United States have called for partial auctioning of allowances, historically permits have been allocated gratis. That is, the grandfathering of permits has so far been a politically essential element of market trading programs.

In Europe, regulatory burdens were reduced in the French and Swedish NO_x cases by returning the collected emission fees to the industries from which it had been collected. In Sweden the fees were returned directly on the basis of energy produced. In France the revenues were used to subsidize abatement investments by the firms contributing the fees. In France the burden was small in any case because the tax rate itself was so low. Its primary purpose was to give firms an additional incentive to comply with CAC emission limits.

Authors Hammar and Löfgren of the European lead phasedown case argue that the use of a tax differential—with a lower tax rate on unleaded—tended to reduce the overall burden of gasoline taxation on the refinery sector. Although via a different logic, the authors of the U.S. lead phasedown case also conclude that the regulatory burden of the regulation was reduced by the use of a rate-based program *cum* banking. On both sides of the Atlantic the refiners were able to pass most of the additional costs forward to consumers.

In the first phase of Title IV of the U.S. SO_2 program, the case study authors argue that the regulatory burden associated with permit costs was not an important factor for either producers or consumers. This is because most of the U.S. electricity sector was regulated according to cost of service, and prices reflected allowance costs at the original cost to the firm. Because allowances were distributed for free, they typically were not reflected in electricity prices. This approach is politically appealing but, as the authors note, may create costs in the form of a misallocation of resources in the general economy.

In the Dutch case, the fee collections were used to support the construction of treatment facilities; the incentive effects were unanticipated. They were hardly a burden because the contribution to collective treatment replaced much of the firms' private abatement costs. Instead, the fee system served as a device to distribute treatment costs fairly on the basis of the polluter-pays principle. Against this yardstick, no extra direct costs are imposed on industry as a result of the tax.

In all cases where economic incentive measures were used, explicit efforts were made to recycle tax revenues or otherwise limit the burden on existing sources, for example, by grandfathering allowances. Especially in the cases where the firms were able to pass the costs forward to consumers, it is likely that the regulatory burden was significantly reduced—possibly even completely offset. In contrast, under a CAC system, where no revenues are generated, there is no obvious means of offsetting regulatory costs.

Administrative Burden

CAC policies have higher administrative costs.

Rationale

Administrative burden is closely related to information costs and hence to policy objectives. Beyond information, administrative costs are determined by the amount of interaction between the regulator and the regulated sources. There are several reasons to think these costs might be greater under a CAC than, for example, under an emission fee. During the preimplementation phase, establishing a CAC policy requires the setting of specific requirements for each regulated source, whereas only one (or at most a small number of) fee rates need to be set, applicable to all sources.

The multiplicity of individual standards, and the possibility of changing them, might encourage more lobbying and negotiation by affected sources as well. After implementation, CAC policies have higher administrative costs because violations quickly pass from the administrative system to the legal system. Fee collections, on the other hand, are another case of tax collections, for which the authorities usually have an administrative system established and which leads to legal difficulties only in exceptional cases.

One final administrative advantage of EI instruments concerns the incentives they offer to regulated sources to contest the policy. By their very nature, fee collections for increased emissions tend to rise gradually, whereas with CAC there is a bright line that separates compliance from violation, which in principle means that there is a step discontinuity in the penalty function. The potentially high incremental cost at the point of violation gives sources an incentive to defend themselves legally rather than accept sanctions.

Of all the hypotheses we examine this is one of the most informal and ad hoc. However, we think most observers who have spent time dealing with bureaucracies have an intuitive idea of what administrative costs are, and therefore it makes sense to ask whether some policy instruments impose more costs than others.

Performance

Although it is clear that implementation of the CAC oriented Effluent Guidelines program—one of the key elements of the U.S. water case— imposed high administrative costs on the EPA, a number of the other cases carry more mixed messages. In the case of the U.S. lead phasedown, the authors argue that the complexity and flexibility of the program increased the likelihood of both intentional and unintentional violations, especially by smaller refiners and inexperienced fuel blenders. This, in turn, increased the monitoring and enforcement costs of the EPA. The authors argue that much of this problem is attributable to the fact that the program relied on a ratio of lead use to total output, rather than an overall cap on lead usage.[25]

The U.S. SO_2 cap-and-trade program has gained a reputation for low administrative costs, a feature that has made it popular with both the EPA and industry. At the same time, the authors of the German SO_2 reduction program argue that there is no evidence that the administrative costs of designing and implementing their CAC type program were higher than for a comparable incentive-based program.

In the case of the U.S. NO_x program, the authors argue that the CAC-based Phase I of OTC was probably more difficult to develop than the Phase II trading program, but only slightly so. They note that gratis pollution allocations present a regulator with rent-seeking behavior on behalf of market participants, thereby forcing the regulator to establish rules for allocation and, subsequently, for verifying claims for allocations. In addition, regulators are still faced with the burden of demonstrating that incentive-based polices are feasible. In the case of the NO_x SIP Call program, this required the identification of available abatement controls, their applicability to U.S. facilities and coal types, and electricity market modeling.

In Europe, the costs of administering the incentive-based (tax) measures used to regulate NO_x emissions are thought to be quite low. In France, administration costs were allocated a fixed percentage rate of total tax revenues (6 percent). In Sweden, the EPA estimates the central administrative costs to be approximately 0.6 percent of total yearly tax revenues. Monitoring requirements are an order of magnitude higher. In the French case, however, monitoring relies to a large extent on existing regulatory structures for control of standards-based regulation. A fair amount of flexibility was granted to the individual firms so they could choose whether to use direct measures or apply emission coefficients set by the regulatory agency.

The authors of the Dutch water study generally support the view that CAC approaches have higher administrative costs, although they note that the permit-granting and enforcement activities associated with the fee program have been substantial. In the same vein, the authors of the U.S. TCE case note that a General Accounting Office report identified the complexity and cost of establishing a facility-specific baseline—a prerequisite to participating in the early reductions program—as an important barrier to the success of that program.

Overall, the evidence on this hypothesis is quite mixed. Although there is some evidence that administrative burdens associated with CAC rules are higher than for EI-based rules, there are also a number of counterexamples. The extent of the burden depends on the context and nature of the policy action.

Hot Spots and Spikes

The performance of all pollution abatement instruments is seriously compromised for pollutants with highly differentiated spatial or temporal effects, but more so for EI than for CAC instruments.

Rationale

As noted, one of the regulators' chief concerns with EI instruments is the limited source-specific control that can be exercised over discharges at individual facilities. In a CAC system it is easier to require more stringent emission reductions at those plants where the emissions cause greater damage. If there were a few sources with high marginal damages, a CAC instrument that targets those sources directly would very likely be superior to an EI instrument (Rose-Ackerman 1973). Likewise, during unusual weather conditions that make ordinary emission discharges hazardous, a short-term CAC instrument is likely to be more effective than an economic instrument.

There have been attempts to design EI instruments to address this problem, such as spatially or temporally varying emissions fees, so-called ambient permit markets (separate permit markets for each receptor, with each source required to hold a portfolio of permits for each receptor), or zoned permit markets (where sources are only allowed to trade within their zone). Some of these schemes have been analyzed by Montgomery (1972), Oates et al. (1983), and Kneese and Bower (1968). Examples include the southern California RECLAIM program for controlling NO_x emissions, wetlands mitigations programs, and some fisheries. Local congestion and transport fees imposed in Singapore and more recently in London are also to be interesting examples.

Performance

It is certainly true that EI approaches offer the clearest advantages for controlling pollutants for which location does not matter, such as stratospheric ozone depleters, greenhouse gases, and lead. Though lead has high spatial differentiation, U.S. lead authors Newell and Rogers point out that environmental hot spots are not a significant concern because the pollution is created through gasoline consumption, not production, and there is likely little or no relationship between the location of refineries and automobile exhaust across the country.

In principle, a prescriptive approach to regulation could do a better job than incentive-based measures in targeting specific areas or time periods. In both TCE cases, for example, the pollutant is a potential workplace hazard where micro/local aspects are dominant. On its face, this would tend to support prescriptive regulation in which regulators have the authority to prescribe more stringent controls where necessary to preserve environmental quality. Although an incentive-based approach could also be designed to protect specific areas or time periods, this often requires a relatively complex design.

In practice, however, the situation is not so clear: Incentive-based measures may work to the detriment or to the benefit of any particular area. Evidence presented about the U.S. SO_2 program suggests that emissions trading has (serendipitously) benefited geographic areas that contain a disproportionate number of sensitive ecosystems and has led to aggregate health benefits in addition to those that would have resulted absent trading. However, this has not prevented state environmental authorities and public utility commissioners from trying to interfere with specific emission trades that would have the effect of increasing emissions in their state. Recently, moreover, some concerns about environmental justice have arisen with respect to the SO_2 trading program, although the evidence thus far presented suggests that the effects are at most fairly small.

Ironically, in the one EI case study where a hot spot issue arose, the problem was that the emission fee was deeply discounted, not that it was insufficient to achieve environmental quality. Specifically, in the northern Netherlands, a financially distressed industry (potato starch) was for some time allowed to pay much lower emission fees than other industries, significantly delaying the achievement of acceptable water quality in the region. But this hardly counts as a mark against EI instruments, because similar exceptions are routinely granted in CAC regimes.

Ultimately, if hot spot problems do develop with EI regimes, there are potential remedies. The authors of the U.S. NO$_x$ case note that a hybrid approach may be a useful way of addressing them. They observe that although the OTC trading program confers considerable flexibility in achieving abatement requirements beyond RACT, the RACT standards are still in place during the trading season. In effect there is a limit to the concentration of pollution that can be released from any source, so the potential for emissions hot spots is reduced. In addition, correction of hot spots is a potential use of the revenues collected from fees and permit auctions, as those revenues could be used to subsidize the construction of abatement equipment in particular locations.

Monitoring Requirements

The monitoring requirements of EI policies are more demanding than those of CAC policies because they require credible and quantitative emission estimates, whereas CAC policies at most require evidence of excess emissions.

Rationale

This assertion is often made, but it seems to assume that what is being measured to enforce a CAC policy is always simpler than what is being measured for an EI instrument. Certainly, it is easier to detect compliance for a CAC standard that only requires use of a designated technology than for an EI instrument that requires a fee payment or permit per unit discharged. (However, compared to an EI instrument that provides a tax penalty for failure to adopt the designated technology, the monitoring requirements are identical.) As for performance standards, many of the monitoring methods that have been used to determine compliance in CAC regimes cannot be used for EI policies, because they don't measure mass emissions that are typically required for determining compliance with EI instruments. Examples include opacity tests, property line measurements, and inferences drawn from equipment malfunctions. However, with the long-term decline of the cost of monitoring in the past two decades, an increasing number of sources of pollution are now required to have continuous monitoring or frequent emission sampling, so that the significance of this issue may have lessened over time.[26] One should also note that making firms pay real cash for emissions raises interest in emission figures, thereby making monitoring and emission data more visible to management.

Performance

Although only a limited number of cases report information on monitoring requirements, the results do not generally support the notion that incentive-based approaches are more demanding then CAC policies. In the case of SO_2, it appears that both the German and U.S. programs adopted CEMs, although the U.S. authors claim that other techniques, for example, coal sampling and engineering formulas, could have been used to estimate SO_2 emissions at less cost and nearly as accurately. Expensive monitors (CEMS), they argue, were necessary to achieve a political consensus. Similarly, in the U.S. NO_x case Title IV required CEMs (at least for major sources), so the monitoring requirements were the same under all the programs after 1990. Previously, NSPS did not require CEMs.

A particularly interesting story emerges in the case of European NO_x controls. Here, the authors argue, the high fees made emissions more visible to both management and the regulators. The perceived importance of accuracy in emission measurement increased, as significant monetary payments were based on these emission numbers. In fact, one of the principal discoveries of the Swedish program was that emissions were very sensitive to small changes in plant operations. Detailed monitoring is the only way plant engineers themselves could determine the effects of small changes in temperature and other combustion conditions on the overall operation and particularly the cost-effectiveness of the facility.

The U.S. lead case generally supports the notion that the difficulties of monitoring are not significantly different under the alternative regulatory approaches. Specifically, the EPA delegated the responsibilities of data collection and assimilation to the refiners themselves, which then reported their figures to the agency. Figures on lead usage were easily checked against sales figures of additive suppliers. Gasoline volume was not as easily monitored as lead, however, and more enforcement cases involved misreported output than misreported lead use. In the view of the authors, although it may be true that the marketable permit program required monitoring a greater quantity and variety of information than a CAC policy would have, the collection of this information was fairly straightforward and inexpensive.

Overall, based on our limited sample, there is not strong and consistent evidence that incentive-based policies pose more onerous monitoring requirements than prescriptive ones. New programs of both types— operating on both sides of the Atlantic—increasingly require similar high-tech methods for measuring emissions, ensuring compliance, and the like. As noted, in at least one case (Swedish NO_x), the stringent monitoring requirements helped firms achieve certain operational efficiencies by fine-tuning the temperature and other combustion conditions in their boilers.

Tax Interaction Effects

Adverse tax interaction effects are likely to be larger with EI instruments than CAC instruments achieving the same emission reductions.

Rationale

The theoretical literature suggests that interaction of environmental regulations with preexisting regulations or taxes causes the social cost of new regulations to be higher than would be measured in partial equilibrium analysis. One important type of hidden cost stems from the interaction of the program with the preexisting tax system, such as the labor income tax, which imposes a difference between the before-tax wage (or the value of the marginal product of labor to firms) and the after-tax wage (or the opportunity cost of labor from the worker's perspective).

Any regulation that raises product prices potentially imposes a hidden cost on the economy by lowering the real wage of workers. This can be viewed as a virtual tax magnifying the significance of previous taxes, with losses in productivity as a consequence.

Economic instruments allow for more efficient allocation of emissions reductions among regulated firms than prescriptive approaches. However, economic instruments are likely to impose a greater cost through the tax interaction effect, particularly if these efficiency savings are not great. The reason is that they drive up a firm's marginal production costs not only by the abatement costs but also by the cost of the emissions embodied in another unit of output. The corresponding price increase serves to erode the real wage even further. This tax interaction effect can be at least partially offset if abatement costs under the EI mechanism are lower than under the CAC, or if the environmental policy raises revenue that can be used to reduce reliance on distortionary taxes, or at least to mitigate the price impact of the regulation.

Performance

Though this hypothesis is not empirically testable directly, researchers have examined these tax interactions in computable general equilibrium models and found the importance of preexisting tax distortions to depend strongly on the details of particular policies. Because an environmental policy has to have major effects in the broader economy before the tax interaction effects become noticeable, it is of special interest in the debate over global climate change policy.

Among the EI cases we examine, none used the revenues to reduce other tax rates. In both of the relevant cap and trade cases (U.S. SO_2 and NO_x), permits were grandfathered. In the U.S. SO_2 case, Burtraw and Palmer suggest that the difference in the tax distortion may have made the policy almost as costly as the CAC program. In the Dutch water case, the fee revenues were returned to industry to support new investments. In the

Swedish NO_x case, revenues were rebated back to firms based on generation output. Theoretical analyses have shown that this tax rebate mechanism is approximately equivalent to a tradable performance standard (Fischer 2001); both encourage abatement but relieve firms of the additional cost, on average, of the emissions embodied in output. Consequently, one would expect a lesser tax interaction with this mechanism. On the other hand, the weaker price increase also sends less of a signal to encourage conservation as a means of reducing emissions, so these allocation mechanisms are still less efficient than optimal revenue recycling. However, in all these cases the authors argue that it would not have been politically acceptable to use the revenues to offset other (distortionary) taxes.

Goulder et al. (1997) investigated the magnitude of the tax interaction effect in the context of the SO_2 program and found that it adds an additional 70 percent to their estimated compliance costs for the program, under the assumption that electricity prices are set in the market rather than by regulators, which is increasingly the case. However, if prices are set by regulators based on the cost of service, then the regulatory burden is much lower because allowances under Title IV were distributed at zero original cost. If the government were to auction the SO_2 allowances and use the revenue from the auction to reduce preexisting distortionary taxes, the additional cost falls to 29 percent of estimated compliance costs.

Effects on Altruism

Economic incentives encourage the notion that the environment is "just another commodity" and reduces willingness of firms and citizens to provide environmental public goods voluntarily. CAC policies are consistent with a norm that requires every discharger to "do his best" and thus provide a better basis for a change in social and personal attitudes about one's responsibility to the environment (Kelman 1981).

Rationale

In a regulatory context, altruism is easy enough to define: voluntary limitation of emission discharges to rates lower than the unconstrained level or than what the regulation allows. It can also be readily observed, for one can usually observe both the emission standard and the actual emission rate. Although there may be several other reasons why plants overcontrol emissions (such as indivisibilities in abatement equipment or concern about excess emissions during process upsets), but whether this is truly altruism is less important than the fact that emissions are lower than expected.

In an EI context, the definition of altruism is also straightforward: lower emissions than what is economically justified based on the emission fee or the permit price. Furthermore, when this is observed it almost certainly represents voluntary emission reductions, because in an EI regime the other justifications for emission reductions are not present. However, it is more difficult to observe, because determining whether the emissions are "economically justified" requires the observer to know the marginal abatement costs. But the usual way marginal abatement costs are estimated is to equate them to the observed price. In other words, in an EI regime the only way to conclude that the firm is behaving altruistically is to assert that marginal abatement costs are higher than the emission fee or permit price, but it is not clear what the basis of such an assertion would be.

Perhaps this is another reason for skepticism about the presence of altruism in EI regimes. Presumably a firm engages in altruistic behavior to gain other, nonmonetary benefits, such as a reputation for public-spiritedness. If the good behavior cannot be conclusively observed, how can the firm earn this reputation? It would be better off choosing another venue for altruism.

Performance

As expected, there were few signs of voluntary behavior among the economic incentive cases. In the Dutch water quality case study, authors Bressers and Lulofs noted that among the employees at many firms there was a genuine desire to cut pollution, and the fees may have reduced the conflicts within the business between doing the right thing for the shareholders and for the environment. However, a CAC policy would very likely have had the same effect.

For the CAC instruments, there is mixed evidence that the companies were operating in an altruistic manner. In the U.S. water pollution case, industries fought fiercely against the establishment of the Effluent Guidelines. The EPA had to litigate virtually every rule and every important issue raised. During the 1970s and early 1980s there was little evidence that firms or trade associations were willing to meet the agency halfway in responding to the guidelines. Something similar appears to have happened in the TCE cases, where the stringent regulation provoked an almost "antigreen" reaction among some companies. On the other hand, there was evidence from several case studies that pollution abatement typically exceeded the regulatory requirements. In the German SO_2 study, the average emission rate (in mg/L) achieved by 1995 was only 38.5 percent of the emission standard. Even for the Effluent Guidelines some well-known national firms made it a practice to exceed performance requirements with a substantial margin, so that there would never be questions raised about compliance. Also significant is the case of the Swedish firm SKF, which after the TCE ban in its home country, decided to phase out TCE all over the world and not just in their Swedish plants.

Adaptability

Compared to CAC instruments, EI instruments can be changed more quickly and easily in response to changing environmental or economic conditions.

Rationale

Changing any policy that regulated sources and others have adapted to is likely to provoke considerable resistance, whether it is to make the policy more or less stringent, but it is likely to be particularly difficult for CAC systems. Behind this hypothesis is the observation that EI instruments are defined by a small number of parameters. To change the stringency of an emission fee system, just raise or lower the emission fee or the number of tradable permits. With permits, one would have to be careful not to confiscate permits held by firms or destroy their value by issuing new permits.

Because CAC systems tend to be tailored to individual sources or categories of sources, changing the regulation could require changing many regulations instead of, say, just one tax rate. This is more difficult administratively and probably also politically, as the multiplicity of separate regulatory actions gives the opposition plenty of opportunities to fight the change.

Performance

A review of the actual cases indicates that incentive-based and prescriptive approaches can be quite similar in their inability to adapt to new information. For example, a well-known flaw of Title IV of the Clean Air Act was that as new information became available about the relative benefits and costs of SO_2 reductions, there was no ability to change the cap short of an act of Congress.[27] A more prescriptive approach, such as the NO_x provisions of Title IV, shares this attribute.

The French NO_x tax was notably slow to change, as its levels were fixed (too low) for five years. However, the authors argue, an advantage of the French tax was that it allowed for government and regulatory agencies to collect and improve information on emission levels and abatement actions undertaken by firms in different industry sectors. In this sense, it yielded a distinct advantage compared to the existing CAC regulation. In the Dutch water case it was noted that the provincial authorities—which must approve fee increases by the water boards—tend to be more reluctant to grant increases during recessions than during periods of a booming economy.

An alternative to a firm cap would be one that adjusted in response to new information. Others have suggested similar trigger mechanisms on emission caps to provide economic relief if costs are greater than expected (Pizer 2002), but as the SO_2 case study authors argue, such an approach might be more politically acceptable if coupled with a mechanism that provided additional environmental improvement when costs are less than expected. A safety valve that relaxes the cap when allowance prices hit a specified level, or lowers the cap when allowance prices are below a floor, acts like a tax system in this regard by incorporating new information about costs.

Perhaps the most interesting situation involving adaptability can be found in the Effluent Guidelines program, which appears to be changing in ways that no one anticipated when it began back in 1972. At that time the focus of the program was on the technology-based standards for direct dischargers. In recent years, direct dischargers, though still important in some industries, have gradually become fewer in number and less important in environmental terms. Furthermore, among indirect dischargers it is likely that waste surcharges are having increasingly larger incentive effects as rates are being raised by local POTWs for revenue purposes. Thus, as author Harrington notes, this quintessential regulatory program may be gradually evolving into a hybrid program with important EI elements.

Cost Revelation

With EI instruments, it is easier to observe the cost of environmental regulation.

Rationale

Theory tells us that for a firm subject to an emission fee, the marginal cost is the same as the fee rate; in a tradable permit regime, the marginal cost is the market price of the permits. Under a CAC instrument, a firm must clean up to a prespecified quantity; there are no fees or permit prices to which marginal costs can be equated.

Performance

Generally speaking, this hypothesis is supported by the case studies, where we have much more ex post information on costs for EI instruments than for CAC instruments. But there are qualifications.

To begin, we are reminded by the authors of the Dutch case study that the equating of marginal costs of abatement to the effluent tax rate or to the price of permits is a theoretical result, not an empirical observation. Based on their research, Bressers and Lulofs argue that firms do not generally know what portion of their costs are driven by abatement concerns. However, they also point out that at least the firms have to make a calculation of how much to abate, just as they have to calculate how much of other inputs they use. The choice of abatement level has to be based on something, and it is almost certainly closer to the point equating price and marginal cost than would be obtained in a CAC regime.

Clearly, the economic incentive instruments in our sample elicited considerable information about the cost of abatement, but there were also complicating factors in several cases. Probably the most successful case in this respect was the U.S. Acid Rain Program. The cap-and-trade program provided a way to observe marginal costs and infer total costs. However, originally this information was not widely disseminated, because allowance prices do not need to be reported to the EPA. Independent allowance trading firms have developed indices to make such information more readily available. Also the EPA allowance auction can reveal important information about prices, and the first EPA auction in 1993 was particularly important in this regard. Such information is not available with a prescriptive regulation. At the same time, even actual price information can be misleading and require careful interpretation. During the first few years of the program, the price of allowance price fell to less than $100 per ton, which according to most observers is far below the long-run marginal cost of abatement. Apparently, a number of utilities made major investments in flue gas desulfurization, creating a glut that caused prices to crash. Since the mid-1990s they have recovered to $150–175 per ton.

In hybrid CAC/EI systems the information revealed by the economic instrument depends on whether that instrument is binding. At $40 per metric ton, the French NO_x tax is probably too low to have incentive effects (which are provided by the emission standard in force), but the Swedish NO_x tax is something else entirely. Its rate of $4,000 per metric ton is almost certainly the binding constraint, so the level of the tax clearly reveals something about marginal abatement costs.

In the U.S. leaded gasoline case, Hahn and Hester estimate from anecdotal evidence that the price of lead removal to be under $0.01 per gram prior to banking, and from $0.02 to $0.05 during the banking phase when standards were becoming increasingly stringent (Hahn and Hester 1989). However, this was a system based on lead concentrations, not on total lead in fuel, which meant that some assumptions were required to get to total lead. Were the program designed more in the spirit of the SO_2 trading program, with clearly specified lead allowances rather than the lead averaging scheme, an even clearer market price would likely have emerged as it has in the SO_2 market.

The one instance where EI instruments do not reveal costs, even in principle, occurs when there is a so-called corner solution in an effluent fee regime. Consider, for example, the use by several European countries of a tax differential policy to ensure that the price of leaded fuel remained above the price of unleaded. That is, the countries involved were *seeking* a corner solution, at least after about 1995 when valve seat recession in older engines ceased to be an issue. As case study authors Hammar and Löfgren report, the tax differential—together with the fact that it was successful—does reveal an upper bound of the cost of removing lead from gasoline. Not surprisingly, that differential was much larger than the imputed cost of lead removal in the United States, where the tradable permit program did elicit cost information from the refinery industry. However, the U.S. lead permit trading program did not reveal the cost of eliminating lead from gasoline, because the program switched back to a CAC program by the time of the final phaseout.

VI. CONCLUSION

Simple and dramatic conclusions, the staple of newspaper headlines, rarely emerge from collections of detailed studies such as those discussed here. Yet at the risk of oversimplifying, we start with the most basic observation of all: Based on a dozen cases drawn from Europe and the United States, it appears that environmental regulation of pollutants has worked, in the sense that the discharge rates of many targeted pollutants today is much lower than it was in 1970. Although this comes as no shock to policy experts, it remains surprisingly common to hear complaints, emanating largely from the business community, that environmental regulations are not very effective in achieving results.

These case studies document significant environmental results. Averaged across all the cases, emissions fell by about two-thirds when compared to baseline estimates. Though any comparison with an estimated baseline is hypothetical by its very nature, the fact that the authors were able to document the credibility of the baseline assumptions as well as the actual emission reductions supports the basic observation that regulations can be quite effective in achieving environmental results.

Also interesting is the fact that the case study authors were able to find or re-create ex ante estimates of expected emission reductions in all of the U.S. cases and four of the European cases. Comparison of the ex ante with ex post observations suggests a reasonable degree of accuracy in the estimates. Not surprisingly, the cases where emission reductions were greater than expected involved EI instruments. The cases where reductions fell short of expectations involved CAC approaches. This finding, consistent with other literature, suggests that regulators may be unduly pessimistic about the performance of EI instruments or unduly optimistic about the performance of CAC approaches.[28]

A further set of observations concerns the actual categorization of rules. As noted earlier, in all cases examined in this project except the German SO_2 ordinance, the policies consisted of a mix of CAC and EI instruments. How did this come about? As far as we are aware, none of these policies were hybrids to begin with, and there were no cases where we observed what was initially an EI policy that took on CAC elements. Rather, they began as CAC instruments and over time had EI components added. For some—the ones we consider EI—the preexisting CAC policy was superseded but not abandoned and remains to set a minimum level of performance. This minimum level is the binding constraint for few (if any) sources, however. Perhaps these CAC relics persist because of a reluctance among regulators to trust the market completely, or maybe their repeal would have the appearance of a retreat, so they are retained for cosmetic reasons. The policies we characterize as CAC also began life as CAC policies, with EI elements added later. It is reasonable to suppose that they are on a transition path themselves but aren't far enough along yet to be characterized as incentive policies (and it is certainly not inevitable that any will complete the journey).

The continued growth in popularity of EI instruments is due in part to the actual and perceived success of existing examples, of which the ones considered in this book are among the most prominent. This growing interest is consistent with the results of our case studies, which, we would say, generally support the continued use of market-based instruments. This can be seen in Table 5–2, which summarizes our discussion of the hypotheses. In the table we have sorted the hypotheses so that the ones favoring EI appear first, followed by the ones favoring CAC. In each group, there are six hypotheses, and in each three are supported and three are not. This arrangement makes it appear as though the competition between EI and CAC instruments ended in a dead heat.

However, we would argue that these hypotheses are not all of equal importance. In our view, the most important are efficiency, both static and dynamic, effectiveness, and regulatory burden. Of the remaining hypotheses (e.g., monitoring requirements, hot spots, administrative burden), many are special cases of these two and are of secondary importance. In addition, questions of effectiveness and efficiency were at the core of the controversy over the initial selection of policy instruments in the 1970s and 1980s. As advertised by their proponents, EI instruments do appear to produce cost savings in pollution abatement, as well as a steady stream of innovations that reduce cost of abatement. At the same time, the main concern of opponents of EI instruments—that they would not work—is not borne out in these case studies. In the cases presented in this chapter, they worked quite well.

The finding of economic efficiency of EI instruments is tempered by one other strong finding from these comparisons. As discussed in the preceding section, the regulatory burden hypothesis—the idea that polluters prefer CAC to EI because of the tax payment or purchase of permits required by EI policies in addition to abatement expenditures—received strong support. Indeed, for all but one of the EI instruments examined, the actual or potential revenue raised by EI instruments has been reimbursed to users, either by explicit tax distributions (as in the Swedish NO_x tax) or by grandfathering emission permits. The only exception was the Dutch effluent fees, which were used to finance wastewater treatment facilities. (In fact, that was their design use; their incentive properties didn't emerge until later.)

Using revenues in this way, of course, means they cannot be used for other purposes, thus short-circuiting one of the chief advantages of economic incentives, namely, that they generate a source of revenue to (potentially) overcome the problems raised by regulation. For example, they could be used to correct a preexisting tax distortion exacerbated by the instrument, overcome a hot spot problem by subsidizing additional abatement, or correct a perceived or actual inequity in their application. In almost all real-world cases, those opportunities have been foreclosed by

Table 5.2 Summary of Outcomes

Hypothesis	Supported?	Comments/Exceptions
Favorable to EI		
1. *Static efficiency.* EI instruments are more efficient than CAC instruments.	Yes	If the emission standard is stringent enough, as in the German SO_2 ordinance, then there is no EI advantage.
2. *Information requirements.* Generally, EI instruments require less information than CAC instruments to achieve emission reductions cost-effectively.	No	All policies turned out to require much information.
3. *Dynamic efficiency.* The real advantages of EI instruments over CAC are only realized over time, because unlike CAC policies they provide a continual incentive to reduce emissions, thus promoting new technology, and they permit a maximum of flexibility in the means of achieving emission reductions.	Yes	This often shows up not in patentable innovations but in site-specific changes to equipment and operating practices.
6. *Administrative burden.* CAC policies have higher administrative costs. During the preimplementation phase, greater information is required to prepare emission standards.	No	
11. *Adaptability.* Compared to CAC instruments, EI instruments can be changed more quickly and easily in response to changing environmental or economic conditions.	No	Many primarily CAC policies show adaptability by adopting EI instruments.
12. *Cost revelation.* With EI instruments, it is easier to observe the cost of environmental regulation.	Yes	

(continued)

Table 5.2 continued

Hypothesis	Supported?	Comments/Exceptions
Favorable to CAC		
4. *Effectiveness.* CAC policies achieve their objectives quicker and with greater certainty than EI policies.	No	
5. *Regulatory burden.* Regulated sources will tend to prefer CAC instruments to EI instruments, because of the strong possibility that they have to pay more under EI even though the social costs may be less.	Yes	The only major EI instruments that have been adopted have overcome this problem by designing instruments to be revenue-neutral (i.e., grandfathered tradable permit systems or recycling of effluent tax revenues)
7. *Hot spots and spikes.* The performance of all pollution-abatement instruments is seriously compromised for pollutants with highly differentiated spatial or temporal effects, but more so for EI than for CAC instruments.	Yes	
8. *Monitoring requirements.* The monitoring requirements of EI policies are more demanding than those of CAC policies because they require credible and quantitative emission estimates.	No	Monitoring requirements of both instruments have been exacting.
9. *Tax interaction effects.* Adverse tax interaction effects are likely to be larger with EI instruments than CAC instruments achieving the same emission reductions.	Yes	
10. *Effects on altruism.* Economic incentives encourage the notion that the environment is "just another commodity" and reduce the willingness of firms and citizens to provide environmental public goods voluntarily.	No	

the need to gain political support by easing the regulatory burden imposed on polluting firms. This apparent inability in practice to use the revenues generated by EI instruments to address hot spots or other regulatory problems may be particularly important vis-à-vis adverse tax interactions. In fact, as Burtraw and Palmer note, the failure to auction off SO_2 emission permits almost completely nullified the efficiency advantage of the SO_2 Trading Program over the most plausible CAC alternative.

ACKNOWLEDGMENTS We are grateful to David Driessen, J. Clarence Davies, and Thomas Sterner for helpful comments on an earlier draft, but they are not implicated in any errors that remain.

NOTES

1. The project resulted in publication of a book (Harrington et al. 2004), containing the case studies and introductory and concluding chapters by the coeditors.

2. This terminology was introduced by Kneese and Schultze (1975).

3. *See* Dallas Burtraw and Karen Palmer, "SO_2 Cap and Trade Program in the United States: A "Living Legend" of Market Effectiveness," in Harrington et al. (2004).

4. Allowances are allocated to individual facilities in proportion to fuel consumption during the 1985–87 period multiplied by an emission factor. About 2.8 percent of the annual allowance allocations are withheld by the EPA and distributed to buyers through an annual auction run by the Chicago Board of Trade. The revenues are returned to the utilities that were the original owners of the allowances.

5. *See* Frank Wätzold and Bernd Hansjürgens, "SO_2 Emissions in Germany: Regulations to Fight Waldsterben," in Harrington et al. (2004)

6. *See* Dallas Burtraw and David Evans, "NO_x Emissions in the United States: A Potpourri of Policies," in Harrington et al. (2004).

7. NOx SIP Call initiated a market in NOx emissions in 1999, but the period examined in this case study is 1990–99.

8. *See* Thomas Sterner and Katrin Millock, "NOx Emissions in France and Sweden: Advanced Fee Schemes versus Regulation," in Harrington et al. (2004).

9. *See* J. T. A. Bressers and K. R. D. Lulofs, "Industrial Water Pollution in the Netherlands: A Fee-Based Approach," in Harrington et al. (2004).

10. Winston Harrington, "Industrial Water Pollution in the United States: Direct Regulation or Market Incentive?" in Harrington et al. (2004).

11. In addition to these federal funds, several states contributed matching funds to the capital costs of municipal wastewater treatment plants. Maryland, for example, contributed an additional 5 percent.

12. Richard Newell and Kristian Rogers, "Leaded Gasoline in the United States: The Breakthrough of Permit Trading," in Harrington et al. (2004). Octane is a characteristic of fuel components that improves the performance of engines by preventing fuel from combusting prematurely in the engine. The availability of high-octane fuel allows more powerful engines to be built. Cars will not operate efficiently with a lower octane fuel than that for which they were designed. In addition, some older cars need more than a minimum level of lead (less than 0.1 grams of lead per gallon) to prevent a problem called valve seat recession.

13. Henrik Hammar and Åsa Lofgren, "Leaded Gasoline in Europe: Differences in Timing and Taxes," in Harrington et al. (2004).

14. A single case study covered both the United States and the European Union: James K. Hammit, "Regulation of Stratospheric-Ozone-Depleting Substances," in Harrington et al. (2004).

15. Miranda Loh and Richard D. Morgenstern, "Trichloroethylene in the United States: Embracing Market-Based Approaches?" in Harrington et al. (2004).

16. Thomas Sterner, "Trichloroethylene in Europe: Ban versus Tax," in Harrington et al. (2004).

17. Including the National Environmental Policy Act (1969), the Clean Air Act of 1970, and the Federal Water Pollution Control Act Amendments of 1972.

18. Executive Order 12291, reinforced by Executive Order 12866.

19. PM2.5 and 8 hr 03 stds.

20. NO_x prices averaged about $4,200 per ton in the RECLAIM market in 1999, before increased demand for electric power caused prices to climb rapidly in 2000, peaking at over $80,000 per ton in October 2000. *Environmental Finance*, November 2000 (available online at www.environmental-finance.com/2000/newsnov2.htm; accessed July 11, 2003).

21. The only exceptions are found in the policies for ODS, where a supplementary emission tax was used in the United States and a tradable permit system was used in the EU.

22. In the United States, measurements of increased blood levels among urban children—where minorities were disproportionately represented—were widely discussed in the press and in policy circles.

23. The United States focused on the toxic aspects of lead in gasoline, whereas the Europeans emphasized the air quality issues.

24. For the same reason they argue that it is also not so important that suppliers of abatement equipment provide such strict guarantees of abatement performance. Interestingly, they note that this reported overcompliance was reduced once the liberalization of the energy market took place.

25. This particular type of cap created an incentive to increase output, particularly by fuel blenders.

26. Note that this need not apply to all industries because there may be an opposite trend toward increasing product and process complexity.

27. A related concern is that tradable permits may instill a property right that would be difficult to change. This was forestalled in the design of Title IV by explicitly stating that allowances did not constitute a property right.

28. In six of the cases, the authors judged the estimates to be reasonably accurate predictions of actual outcomes. In two of the cases the authors found that actual emission reductions were larger than predicted ex ante (U.S. NO_x and Sweden lead phasedown). In the other two cases they found that actual reductions fell short of the predicted levels (Sweden TCE, U.S. water). *See* Harrington et al. (2000) for other ex ante/ex post findings.

REFERENCES

Buchanan, James, and Gordon Tullock. 1975. "Polluters' Profits and Political Response: Direct Controls versus Taxes." *American Economic Review* 65 (1).

Fischer, Carolyn. 2001. "Rebating Environmental Policy Revenues: Output-Based Allocations and Tradable Performance Standards." RFF Discussion Paper 01–22.

Goulder, Lawrence H., Ian W. H. Parry, and Dallas Burtraw. 1997. "Revenue-Raising vs. Other Approaches to Environmental Protection: The Critical Significance of Pre-Existing Tax Distortions." *RAND Journal of Economics* 28 (4): 708–31.

Hahn, Robert, and Gordon Hester. 1989. "Where Did All the Markets Go? An Analysis of EPA's Emissions Trading Program." *Yale Journal on Regulation* 6(1): 109–53.

Harrington, Winston, Richard D. Morgenstern, and Peter Nelson. 2000. "On the Accuracy of Regulatory Cost Estimates." *Journal of Policy Analysis and Management*19(2): 297–322.

Harrington, Winston, Richard D. Morgenstern, and Thomas Sterner, eds. 2004. *Choosing Environmental Policy: Comparing Instruments and Outcomes in the United States and Europe.* Washington, DC: RFF Press.

Kelman, Steven. 1981. *What Price Incentives? Economists and the Environment.* Dover, MA: Auburn House.

Kneese, Allen, and Blair Bower. 1968. *Managing Water Quality: Economics, Technology, Institutions.* Baltimore: Johns Hopkins University Press for Resources for the Future.

Kneese, Allen, and Charles Schultze. 1975. *Pollution, Prices and Public Policy.* Washington, DC: Brookings Institution.

Liroff, Richard A. 1986. *Reforming Air Pollution Regulation: The Toil and Trouble of EPA's Bubble.* Washington, DC: Conservation Foundation.

Melnick, R. Shep. 1983. *Regulation and the Courts: The Case of the Clean Air Act.* Washington, DC: Brookings Institution.

Molina, M. J., and F. S. Rowland. 1974. "Stratospheric Sink for Chlorofluouromethanes: Chlorine Atom-Catalysed Destruction of Ozone." *Nature* 249: 810–12.

Montgomery, W. David. 1972. "Markets in Licenses and Efficient Pollution Control Programs." *Journal of Economic Theory* 5: 395–418.

Oates, Wallace E., Alan J. Krupnick, and E. Van De Verg. 1983. "On Marketable Air-Pollution Permits: The Case for a System of Pollution Offsets." *Journal of Environmental Economics and Management* 10: 233–37.

Oates, Wallace E., Paul Portney. and Albert McGartland. 1989. "The Net Benefits of Incentive-Based Regulation: A Case Study of Environmental Standard-Setting," *American Economic Review* 79: 1233–42.

Pizer, W. A. 2002. "Combining Price and Quantity Controls to Mitigate Global Climate Change." *Journal of Public Economics* 85(3): 409–34.

Rose-Ackerman, Susan. 1973. "Effluent Charges: A Critique." *Canadian Journal of Economics* 6 (4).

Spulber, Daniel F. 1985. "Effluent Regulation and Long Run Optimality." *Journal of Environmental Economics and Management* 12: 103–16.

U.S. EPA. 2001. *The United States Experience with Economic Incentives for Protecting the Environment.* Washington, DC: EPA.

Part II

EMPIRICAL AND THEORETICAL EVIDENCE

6

Tradable Permits with Incomplete Monitoring: Evidence from Santiago's Particulate Permits Program

Juan-Pablo Montero

INTRODUCTION

Attention to tradable emission permits (or emissions trading) as an alternative to the traditional command-and-control (CAC) approach of setting uniform emission and technology standards has significantly increased in the past decade or so. A notable example is the 1990 U.S. Acid Rain Program that implemented a nationwide market for electric utilities' sulfur dioxide (SO_2) emissions (Schmalensee et al. 1998; Ellerman et al. 2000). To have a precise estimate of the SO_2 emissions that are going to the atmosphere, the Acid Rain Program requires each affected electric utility unit to install costly equipment that can continuously monitor emissions. Another example with similar monitoring requirements is the southern California RECLAIM program that implemented separated markets for nitrogen oxide (NO_x) and SO_2 emissions from power plants, refineries, and other large stationary sources.[1]

These and other market experiences, which are also documented by Stavins and Tietenberg elsewhere in this book, suggest that conventional tradable permits programs are likely to be implemented in those cases where emissions can be closely monitored, which almost exclusively occurs in large stationary sources like electric power plants and refineries. At least this is consistent with the evidence that environmental authorities continue relying on CAC instruments to regulate emissions from smaller sources for which continuous monitoring is prohibitively costly (or technically unfeasible). In such cases, compliance with CAC instruments only requires the authority to ensure that the regulated source has installed the required abatement technology or that its emissions per unit of output are equal or lower than a certain emissions rate standard.

These observations raise the question as to why the flexibility of permit trading cannot be extended to the regulation of sources whose emissions can only be imperfectly measured through the observation of their abatement technologies or emission rates, as would be done under CAC regulation.[2] Under such a (second-best) permit scheme sources would not be trading emissions but some proxy for emissions, so one may conjecture that actual emissions can be higher or lower than under an alternative CAC regulation. One can argue, for example, that emissions are likely to be higher if the trading pattern is such that lower output firms sell permits to higher output firms.

In looking for an answer to the question, it is interesting to observe that despite its limited information on each source's actual emissions (and costs), the Santiago, Chile, environmental agency has already implemented a market to control total suspended particulate (TSP) emissions from a group of about 600 stationary sources (Montero et al. 2002).[3] Based on estimates from annual inspections for technology parameters such as source's size and fuel type, Santiago's environmental regulator approximates each source's actual emissions by the maximum amount of emissions that the source could potentially emit in a given year. In particular, the observable firm's emission rate (mg/m^3) is multiplied by its maximum possible output ($m^3/year$) to infer its maximum emissions ($mg/year$) for which the firm must buy permits.[4]

Because most of the literature on environmental regulation under asymmetric information deals with the case in which firms' costs are privately known but emissions are publicly observed (see Lewis 1996 for a survey), a closer examination of Santiago's TSP permits program represents a unique case study of issues of instrument choice and design that can arise in the practical implementation of permits markets under imperfect monitoring of emissions (e.g., air pollution in large cities).[5] Although there is some literature looking at the latter (e.g., Segerson 1988; Fullerton and West 2002; Cremer and Gahvari 2002),[6] only Montero (2004) focus specifically on the effect of imperfect information about emissions and costs on the design and performance of a permits market.

In comparing permits versus standards, Montero (2004) identifies a trade-off between cost savings and possible higher emissions.[7] On one hand, the permits policy retains the well-known cost-effectiveness property of conventional permits schemes (i.e., those based on actual emissions), that is, that permit trading allows heterogenous firms to reduce their abatement and production costs. On the other hand, the permits policy can sometimes provide firms with incentives to choose combinations of output and abatement technology that may lead to higher aggregate emissions than under standards (i.e., CAC regulation). Thus when (abatement and production) cost heterogeneity across firms is large, the permits policy is likely to work better. In contrast, as heterogeneity disappears, the advantage of permits reduces, and standards might work better provided that they lead to lower emissions.

In this chapter I extend the theoretical model of Montero (2004) and then apply it to the TSP program with the purpose of comparing the actual performance of this program with that of a hypothetically equivalent standards policy. In doing so, I first recover production and abatement cost characteristics of affected sources and the regulator's perception about environmental damages. Based on these estimates, I find that permits have provided large cost savings but also lead to higher emissions; about 6 percent higher than what would have been observed under an equivalent standards policy. However, the welfare loss from higher emissions is only 8 percent of the welfare gain from lower abatement and production costs.

The theoretical and empirical results of this chapter make a strong case for the wider use of pollution permits even in those situations in which emissions are imperfectly observed. Furthermore, because permits are always less costly than standards and may or may not lead to higher emissions, I would also indicate that permits should be adopted as a default, unless the available cost and pollution damage information indicates the opposite. In other words, the burden of proof should lie with the CAC policy and not with the permits policy. Nevertheless, in many cases it may be welfare improving to combine permits with some optimally chosen standard rather than just use permits (Montero 2004).[8]

The rest of the chapter is organized as follows. In the next section I present the model. I consider a competitive market for an homogeneous good supplied by a continuum of firms whose pollution is going to be regulated by either permits or a uniform emission rate standard. Then I derive the optimal design for these two regulations and compare the welfare difference between the two optimal designs. After that, I apply the theoretical model to data from the Santiago's TSP permits program. Concluding remarks follow in the final section.

THE MODEL

Consider a geographic area with a large number of firms where each firm produces output into a competitive market and emissions of a uniform flow pollutant. Output is denoted by q and emissions by e. In my particular case, q represents a firm's boiler utilization level, that is, the number of hours the boiler operates during the year. As already discussed in the introduction, the regulator observes neither q nor e. During an inspection visit, however, the regulator can correctly measure the firm's emissions rate, which is the level of pollution per unit of output (or utilization). I denote the firm's emission rate by r. And because the emissions rate is assumed to be the same throughout the year, the emissions rate is $r = e/q$.

To simplify notation, I assume that when the firm does not utilize any pollution abatement device emissions are equal to $e = (1 + \alpha)q$, where α is a parameter that varies across firms, so $1 + \alpha$ is the firm's emissions rate in the absence of regulation. I can assume that the regulator knows the value of α of each firm, although it is not needed for the results.

A firm can abate pollution at a positive cost by installing some abatement technology. The level of abatement chosen by the firm is denoted by the variable x, which measures the level of reduction in the emissions rate; that is, if the firms install x of abatement technology, its emissions will reduce from $(1 + \alpha)q$ to $(1 + \alpha - x)q$. Or alternatively, that the firm's emission rate will reduce from $1 + \alpha$ to $1 + \alpha - x$. Thus, the firm's decision variables are output q and abatement level x. The firm will choose these variables to maximize its profits.

As in any industry, firms are not homogeneous but vary in terms of their costs of production and abatement. To capture this heterogeneity, I work with a cost function of the form $C(q, x, \beta, \gamma)$, where β and γ are a firm's cost parameters. We will see that the higher β and γ the more costly is for the firm to produce q and install x. As commonly seen in the practice of regulation, the values of β and γ are firm's private information, which is unavailable to the regulator.

To keep the model mathematically tractable, I assume that the cost function has the following quadratic form in the relevant output-abatement range

(1) $$C(q, x, \beta, \gamma) = \frac{c}{2}q^2 + \beta q + \frac{k}{2}x^2 + \gamma x + vxq,$$

where c, k, and v are publicly known parameters common to all firms and $c > 0$, $k > 0$ and $v \gtrless 0$.[9] A firm with lower β will have relatively lower production costs, so it will produce relatively more (or its boiler will be run more often) than a firm with higher β, all else equal. Similarly, a firm with lower γ will have relatively lower abatement costs, so it will tend to install more abatement technology, all else equal. Note that although α does not directly enter into the cost function, it can be indirectly related to costs through its correlation with β and γ, capturing, for example, that a firm with high counterfactual emissions (i.e., high α) is likely to find it cheaper to reduce emissions (i.e., low γ).

Although the regulator does not observe firms' individual values of α, β, and γ (but observes the emissions rate r), I assume that she knows that they are distributed according to the cumulative joint distribution $F(\alpha, \beta, \gamma)$ on $\alpha \in [\underline{\alpha}, \overline{\alpha}]$, $\beta \in [\underline{\beta}, \overline{\beta}]$ and $\gamma \in [\underline{\gamma}, \overline{\gamma}]$.[10] To simplify notation further and without any loss of generality I let $\text{Exp}[\alpha] = \text{Exp}[\beta] = \text{Exp}[\gamma] = 0$, where $\text{Exp}[\cdot]$ is the expected value operator.[11]

Function (1) incorporates two key cost parameters that are essential to understand firms' behavior under permits and standards regulation. One of these cost parameters is the correlation between β and γ (that I shall denote by $\rho_{\beta\gamma}$), which captures whether firms with higher output ex ante (i.e., before the regulation) are more or less likely to install more abatement x. If, for example, the cost of structure of the group of affected sources is such that there is a positive correlation between β and γ, it is likely that the firms with higher utilization will be the ones installing more abatement technologies. The implication for the functioning of a tradable permit system, where firms have the flexibility of choosing both q and x, is that firms more heavily utilized will tend to be the sellers of permits, dissipating any concern that emissions could be higher under permits.

The other cost parameter that is essential for the understanding the differences between permits and standards regulation is the interaction parameter v, which captures the effect of abatement on output ex post (note that I have constrained v to be the same for all firms, thus, a negative value of v would indicate that on average, the larger the x the larger the increase in q ex post). If v is negative, for example, firms installing more abatement technologies will also reduce their production costs so they will tend to produce relatively more ex post. As before, the implication for the functioning of a tradable permit system is that firms installing more abatement technologies are likely to increase their utilization relative to those firms doing less abatement. An example may help. Suppose there is a clean and cheap fuel available. Switching to this new fuel, however, requires such a large up-front investment for adapting the boiler to the new fuel that no firm will ever switch to it unless there is an environmental constraint. But those firms that decide to switch will also face a reduction in their variable production costs from the fact that are now burning a cheaper fuel, a cost advantage that will allow the switching firms to increase their share in the output market.[12]

Although the value of the cost parameters v (the interaction parameter) and $\rho_{\beta\gamma}$ (the correlation parameter) is ultimately an empirical question, I will show that these parameters play a fundamental role in the design and choice of policy instruments when emissions are not closely monitored.

Market (inverse) demand is totally elastic and given by $P(Q) = P$, where Q is total output. This is equivalent to assuming that the price P is cleared in an international market. Total damage from pollution is a linear function given by $D(E) = hE$, where E are total emissions and $h > v$. Functions $P(Q)$ and $D(E)$ are known to the regulator.

Firms behave competitively, taking the output clearing price P as given. Hence, in the absence of any environmental regulation, each firm will produce to the point where its marginal production cost equals the product price (i.e., $C_q[q, x, \beta, \gamma] = P$), and install no abatement technology (i.e., $x = 0$). Because production involves some pollution, this market equilibrium is not socially optimal.

The regulator's problem is then to design a regulation that maximizes social welfare. I let the benevolent regulator's social welfare function be

$$W = CS - TC - D(E),$$

where CS is consumer surplus, TC is total production and abatement costs, and $D(E)$ is total damages from pollution. In this welfare function, the regulator does not differentiate between consumer and producer surplus, and transfers from or to firms are lump-sum transfers between consumers and firms with no welfare effects.[13]

Under my notation, the social welfare function becomes

$$\text{(2)} \qquad W = PQ - \int_{\alpha\beta\gamma} C(q, x, \beta, \gamma) dF_{\gamma\beta\alpha} - hE$$

where $Q = \int_{\alpha\beta\gamma} q(\beta, \gamma) dF_{\gamma\beta\alpha}$ is total output and $E = \int_{\alpha\beta\gamma} r(\alpha, \beta, \gamma) q(\beta, \gamma) dF_{\gamma\beta\alpha}$ is total emissions with $r(\alpha, \beta, \gamma) = 1 + \alpha - x(\beta, \gamma)$. Note that because of the form of the cost function both production q and abatement technology x will vary across firms according to β and γ, but the emission rate r will also depend on α.

The regulator's problem then becomes to maximize (2) subject to different information constraints and to the restriction that she can use one of two regulatory instruments: standards or permits.[14] It should be mentioned that I focus on these two simpler policies and not on more optimal ones not only because the latter include the use of nonlinear instruments and transfers to firms which, as documented in other chapters of this book, has not been used in practice,[15] but more important, because I want to specifically explore whether permits can still provide an important welfare advantage over traditional CAC regulation when emissions are imperfectly monitored.

INSTRUMENT DESIGN AND CHOICE

The regulator faces a sequential instrument design and choice problem. Given the information that he has at hand, he must first derive the optimal designs for standards and permits and then determine which of the two optimal designs lead to higher welfare W. Proceeding in this same order, this section develops the solution to the regulator's overall problem. Throughout, I assume that there is full compliance with either regulatory instrument.

The Optimal Standards Design

The regulator's problem here is to find the emission rate standard r_s to be required of all firms that maximizes social welfare (subscript s denotes standards policy). This is a uniform policy in that it requires all firms to comply with the exact same standard or abatement technology.

The regulator knows that for any given r_s, a firm which individual characteristics are given by the triple (α, β, γ) will maximize its profit function $\pi(q, x_s, \alpha, \beta, \gamma) = Pq - C(q, x_s, \beta, \gamma)$ subject to $r = 1 + \alpha - x \leq r_s$. Because abatement is costly, we know that no firm will reduce emissions beyond the standard r_s, so each firm will just install abatement technology to comply with the standard, that is

$$\text{(3)} \qquad x_s(r_s) \equiv x_s = 1 + \alpha - r_s.$$

In turn, the firm's output decision will solve the first-order condition

$$\frac{\partial \pi}{\partial q} = P - cq - \beta - vx_s = 0,$$

which provides the regulator with firm's output q as a function of the standard r_s,

(4) $$q_s(r_s) \equiv q_s = \frac{P - \beta - v \cdot (1 + \alpha - r_s)}{c}.$$

The regulator knows that if he establishes a standard r_s, a firm with production parameter β will produce according to expression (4).

Anticipating firms' response to a standard r_s, the regulator's problems is then to choose the value of r_s that maximizes social welfare. Using the welfare function (2), the regulator's problem can be more precisely written as

$$\max_{r_s} \int_{\alpha\beta\gamma} [Pq_s(r_s) - C(q_s(r_s), x_s(r_s)) - r_s q_s(r_s)h]\, dF_{\gamma\beta\alpha},$$

where $x_s(\cdot)$ and $q_s(\cdot)$ are given by (3) and (4), respectively. By the envelope theorem, the regulator's first-order condition is

(5) $$\int_{\alpha\beta\gamma} \left[(-kx_s - \gamma - vq_s)\frac{\partial x_s}{\partial r_s} - r_s h \frac{\partial q_s}{\partial r_s} - q_s h \right] dF_{\gamma\beta\alpha} = 0.$$

By replacing $\partial x_s/\partial r_s = -1$, (4) and $\partial q_s/\partial r_s = v/c$ into (5), the first-order condition (5) reduces to

$$ck \cdot (1 - r_s) + v \cdot (P - v + vr_s) - hr_s v - h \cdot (P - v + vr_s) = 0,$$

which leads to the optimal standard[16]

(6) $$r_s^* = \frac{\Lambda + hv - P \cdot (h - v)}{\Lambda + 2hv} = 1 - \frac{P \cdot (h - v) + hv}{\Lambda + 2hv} < 1 + \underline{\alpha},$$

where $\Lambda \equiv ck - v^2$ is a positive constant. Note that we are assuming that the optimal standard r_s^* is that even the firm with the lowest counterfactual emission rate, that is, $1 + \underline{\alpha}$, is asked to reduce emissions.

Comparative statics (i.e., how the optimal standard varies to changes in parameters values) can be easily illustrated for the case in which $v = 0$. In this case, the optimal standard is $r_s^* = 1 - Ph/ck$. As expected, the optimal standard becomes tighter (i.e., lower) as marginal damages increase (i.e., higher h) and less stringent as marginal (production and abatement) costs shift up (i.e., higher c and k). It is perhaps less obvious that the optimal standard decreases with the output price P. The reason is that an increase in P stimulates more output and higher emissions, which makes it optimal to tighten the standard all else equal.

Permits Design

Because the regulator only observes the firm's emissions rate r, the permits scheme is not based on actual emissions e but on some proxy for emissions that I denote by $\tilde{e}$. The regulator's problem is then to find the total number permits $\tilde{e}_0$ to be distributed among firms that maximizes social welfare. Let R denote the equilibrium price of permits, which will be determined shortly.[17] The regulator knows that a firm (α, β, γ) will take R as given and solve

$$\max_{q,x} \pi(q, x, \beta, \gamma) = Pq - C(q, x, \beta, \gamma) - R \cdot (\tilde{e} - \tilde{e}_0),$$

where $\tilde{e} = (1 + \alpha - x)\tilde{q}$ are firm's proxied emissions and $\tilde{q}$ is some arbitrarily output or utilization level that is common to all firms. For example, $\tilde{q}$ could be set, as in the TSP program in Santiago, equal to the maximum possible output that could ever be observed (i.e., 100 percent utilization throughout the year). As I will show later, the exact value of $\tilde{q}$ turns out to be irrelevant because it simply works as a scaling factor. Note that if $\tilde{e} < \tilde{e}_0$ the firm will be a seller of permits.

From firms' first-order conditions (now firms are free to choose x)

(7) $$\frac{\partial \pi}{\partial x} = -kx - \gamma - vq + R\tilde{q} = 0$$

(8) $$\frac{\partial \pi}{\partial q} = P - cq - \beta - vx = 0,$$

I have that for a firm with characteristics (α, β, γ), the optimal abatement and output responses to R and $\tilde{q}$ (or, more precisely, to $R\tilde{q}$) are

(9) $$x_p = \frac{R\tilde{q}c - \gamma c - (P - \beta)v}{\Lambda}$$

(10) $$q_p = \frac{P - \beta - vx_p}{c},$$

where the subscript p denotes permits policy (recall that the firm's rate will be $r_p = 1 + \alpha - x_p$).

I can now solve the regulator's problem of finding the optimal $\tilde{e}_0$. Because the market clearing condition is (total emissions equal to the total number of permits distributed)

(11) $$\int_{\alpha\beta\gamma} \tilde{e}dF_{\gamma\beta\alpha} = \int_{\alpha\beta\gamma} (1 + \alpha - x_p)\tilde{q}dF_{\gamma\beta\alpha} = \tilde{e}_0$$

and x_p is a function of $R\tilde{q}$ as indicated by (9), it is irrelevant whether I solve for $R\tilde{q}$ or $\tilde{e}_0/\tilde{q}$. Hence, I let the regulator to find $R\tilde{q}$ to maximize (permits purchases and sales are transfers with no net welfare effects)

$$\int_{\alpha\beta\gamma} [Pq_p(x_p(R\tilde{q})) - C(q_p(x_p(R\tilde{q})), x_p(R\tilde{q}))$$

$$- (1 + \alpha - x_p(R\tilde{q}))q_p(x_p(R\tilde{q}))h]dF_{\gamma\beta\alpha}.$$

By the envelope theorem, the first-order condition is

(12) $$\int_{\alpha\beta\gamma}\left[-(1+\alpha-x_p)h\frac{\partial q_p}{\partial(R\widetilde{q})}+q_ph\frac{\partial x_p}{\partial(R\widetilde{q})}-R\widetilde{q}\frac{\partial x_p}{\partial(R\widetilde{q})}\right]dF_{\gamma\beta\alpha}=0.$$

By plugging $\partial q_p/\partial(R\widetilde{q})=[\partial q_p/\partial x_p][\partial x_p/\partial(R\widetilde{q})]$, $\partial q_p/\partial x_p=-v/c$, (9) and (10) into (12), the first-order condition can be rearranged to obtain the optimal permits price

(13) $$R^*\widetilde{q}=\frac{Ph(kc+v^2)+hv\Lambda}{(\Lambda+2hv)c},$$

which in turn allows me to obtain the optimal permits allocation $\widetilde{e}_0^*/\widetilde{q}$ by simply replacing (13) in (9) and that in (11).

I can now replace $R^*\widetilde{q}$ in (9) and (10) to obtain expressions for x_p, r_p, and q_p that are more readily comparable to x_s, r_s, and q_s (see equations [4] and [6]). After some algebra, the following expressions are obtained

(14) $$x_p=1-r_s^*+\frac{v\beta-c\gamma}{\Lambda}=x_s-\alpha+\frac{v\beta-c\gamma}{\Lambda}$$

(15) $$r_p=r_s^*+\alpha-\frac{v\beta-c\gamma}{\Lambda}$$

(16) $$q_p=\frac{P-v\cdot(1-r_s)}{c}-\frac{k\beta-v\gamma}{\Lambda}=q_s+\frac{v\alpha}{c}-\frac{v^2\beta-cv\gamma}{c\Lambda},$$

where r_s^* is the (uniform) optimal standard defined by (6).

Expressions (14)–(16) present a good summary where one can grasp a first comparison between firms' responses to the two policies. If firms are homogenous in all respects (i.e., $\alpha=\beta=\gamma=0$ for all firms), it is not surprising that both regulations prompt the exact same response among firms, that is $x_p=x_s$, $r_p=r_s$ and $q_p=q_s$. If firms are equal in all respects there is no reason for firms to install different abatement technologies, even under a permits program where they have the flexibility not to do so. Because responses are identical, it also holds that under perfect homogeneity both regulations provide the same welfare.

As firms become heterogeneous (i.e., differ in their values of α, β, and γ), however, their responses are no longer the same. It is not difficult to see that x, r, and q can move in different magnitude and sometimes direction depending on the policy choice, which will ultimately affect the welfare comparison between the two policies. Suppose, for example, that $v>0$. As firms differ on their abatement costs γ, emission rates r increase with γ under the permits regulation while they remain constant under CAC regulation. Thus permits appear more efficient in accommodating abatement cost heterogeneity to abatement decisions because it allows firms with higher abatement costs (higher γ) to do less abatement (less x or more r).

It is not easy to extend this comparison in other dimensions and at the same time obtain welfare implications. In the next section, I present a more formal welfare comparison of the two policy instruments.

The Choice between Permits and Standards

For a regulator that is limited to use permits or standards, the difference in the social welfare between implementing an optimal permits policy and implementing an optimal standards policy is

$$(17) \qquad \Delta_{ps} = W_p(\tilde{e}_0^*/\tilde{q}) - W_s(r_s^*),$$

where $\tilde{e}_0^*$ is the optimal number of permits normalized by some $\tilde{q}$ and r_s^* is the optimal standard. The normative implication of (17) is that if $\Delta_{ps} > 0$, the regulator should implement the permits policy because it provides higher welfare.

To explore under which conditions this is the case, I write (17) as

$$(18) \quad \Delta_{ps} = \int_{\alpha\beta\gamma} [Pq_p - C(q_p, x_p) - r_p q_p h - Pq_s + C(q_s, x_s) + r_s q_s h]\, dF_{\gamma\beta\alpha},$$

where q_p, x_p (or r_p), q_s and x_s (or r_s) can be expressed according to (14)–(16). Because both policies lead to the same amount of total output, that is $Q_p = Q_s = (P - v(1 - r_s))/c$, equation (18) can be simply rewritten as

$$(19) \qquad \Delta_{ps} = \int_{\alpha\beta\gamma} [\{C(q_s, x_s) - C(q_p, x_p)\} + \{r_s q_s - r_p q_p\} h]\, dF_{\gamma\beta\alpha}.$$

Recalling that $e = rq$, the first curly bracketed expression of the right-hand side of (19) is the difference in costs between the two policies, whereas the second expression in curly brackets is the difference in emissions that multiplied by h gives the difference in pollution damages.

If I plug (14)–(16) into (19), after some algebra, (19) becomes

$$(20) \quad \Delta_{ps} = \frac{\Lambda^2\sigma_\alpha^2 + v^2\sigma_\beta^2 + c^2\sigma_\gamma^2 - 2v\Lambda\rho_{\alpha\beta}\sigma_\alpha\sigma_\beta + 2c\Lambda\rho_{\alpha\gamma}\sigma_\alpha\sigma_\gamma - 2cv\rho_{\beta\gamma}\sigma_\beta\sigma_\gamma}{2c\Lambda}$$
$$- h \cdot \frac{ckv\sigma_\beta^2 + cv\sigma_\gamma^2 - \Lambda v^2\rho_{\alpha\beta}\sigma_\alpha\sigma_\beta + vc\Lambda\rho_{\alpha\gamma}\sigma_\alpha\sigma_\gamma - (kc + v^2)cp_{\beta\gamma}\sigma_\beta\sigma_\gamma}{c\Lambda^2},$$

where σ_i^2 is the variance of $i (= \alpha, \beta, \gamma)$ and $\rho_{ij}\sigma_i\sigma_j$ is the covariance between i and j. The variance measures how different are firms along some particular parameter. For example, if for some reason firms do not differ in their counterfactual emission rates (i.e., all have the same α) then the variance of α will be $\sigma_\alpha^2 = 0$. On the other hand, the covariance between two parameters, say, between α and β, measures whether a firm with a high (or low) α is more (or less) likely to have a high β.

Equation (20) is a long expression whose sign is not readily seen. Fortunately, there is an equivalent and simplified version for it. From (15), the variance of firms' emission rates under permits, $r_p(\alpha, \beta, \gamma)$, is

$$\text{Var}[r_p] = \frac{1}{\Lambda^2}(\Lambda^2\sigma_\alpha^2 + v^2\sigma_\beta^2 + c^2\sigma_\gamma^2 - 2v\Lambda\rho_{\alpha\beta}\sigma_\alpha\sigma_\beta$$

(21)
$$+ 2c\Lambda\rho_{\alpha\gamma}\sigma_\alpha\sigma_\gamma - 2cv\rho_{\beta\gamma}\sigma_\beta\sigma_\gamma),$$

which one can see that is very similar to the first term of (20). Recalling that the variance under standards is zero because all firms are required to comply with the same standards r_s, the variance $\text{Var}[r_p]$ is a measure of how different are emissions rates across firms under the permits policy. As long as there is some heterogeneity across firms (different values of α, β, and γ), the permits policy will lead firms to choosing different levels of abatement.

On the other hand, I can use (15) and (16) to obtain that the covariance between firms' output and emission rates under permits, $q_p(\alpha,\beta,\gamma)$ and $r_p(\alpha,\beta,\gamma)$, is

$$\text{Cov}[q_p, r_p] \equiv \text{Exp}[q_p r_p] - \text{Exp}[q_p]\text{Exp}[r_p]$$

$$= \frac{1}{c\Lambda^2}(ckv\sigma_\beta^2 + cv\sigma_\gamma^2 - \Lambda v^2\rho_{\alpha\beta}\sigma_\alpha\sigma_\beta + vc\Lambda\rho_{\alpha\gamma}\sigma_\alpha\sigma_\gamma$$

(22)
$$- (kc + v^2)c\rho_{\beta\gamma}\sigma_\beta\sigma_\gamma),$$

which one can see that is very similar to the second term of (20). Recalling that the covariance between output and emissions rate under standards is zero because all firms are required to comply with the same standards r_s, the covariance $\text{Cov}[q_p, r_p]$ tells us whether under permits firms with high output q_p are, on average, more or less likely to do more abatement (i.e., to have lower r). This covariance will certainly depend on the correlation between β and γ and on the interaction parameter v.

Now I can use (21) and (22), to conveniently rewrite the welfare difference between permits and standards as

(23)
$$\Delta_{ps} = \frac{\Lambda}{2c}\text{Var}[r_p] - h\text{Cov}[q_p, r_p].$$

As in (20), the first term in (23) is the difference in total costs between standards and permits, and the second term is the difference in environmental damages. More precisely, $\text{Cov}[q_p, r_p]$ is the difference in aggregate emissions between the two policies (i.e., $\text{Cov}[q_p, r_p] = E_p - E_s$), which multiplied by h gives us the difference is environmental damages. As I shall show in the next section, expression (23) greatly simplifies the empirical comparison of the two policies because this comparison can be just based on data from an existing permits policy with no need for an explicit construction of a counterfactual of the standards policy.

Expression (23) also facilitates understanding of the conditions under which the permits policy dominates the standards policy. Unlike a standards policy, a permits policy allows emission rates r_p to vary across firms. Because of this flexibility, firms will always find it cheaper to comply with permits than with standards. This flexibility cannot leave firms worse off because if it were cheaper for firms to comply with a uniform technology firms will do so under permits as well. Depending on the degree of heterogeneity across firms (i.e., differences along α, β, and γ), this flexibility can result in substantial (production and abatement) cost savings, as indicated by the first term of (23).

The second term of (23) shows, on the other hand, that the same flexibility that allows firms to save on production and abatement costs can sometimes provide these firms with incentives to choose combinations of output and abatement levels that may lead to higher aggregate emissions than under standards. This is so when the cost structure of firms is such that the permits policy prompts a positive correlation between output q_p and emission rates r_p. Because actual emissions are the product of q_p and r_p, a positive correlation will indicate that more utilized firms are on average those with higher emission rates, that is, doing less abatement. In other words, permits are flowing from low-utilized firms to more highly utilized firms.

These results suggest that when the cost heterogeneity across firms is large (such that emission rates r_p vary greatly across firms), the permits policy is likely to work better than the standards policy. In contrast, as heterogeneity disappears, the advantage of permits reduces, and standards might work better provided that they lead to lower emissions. The possibility that permits can result in higher emissions depends to a large extent on the values of two parameters of the cost function: $\rho_{\beta\gamma}$ (the correlation between production costs and abatement costs) and v (the interaction between production and abatement).

In fact, if $v = \rho_{\beta\gamma} = 0$, the second term in (20) vanishes, that is, aggregate emissions are the same under either instrument. Provided that firms' output are, on average, the same under either policy (see equation [16]), when there is neither correlation nor interaction between production and abatement, any given firm is equally likely to emit as much as under permits than under standards. Conversely, if $v = 0$ but $\rho_{\beta\gamma} \neq 0$, the second term in (20) reduces to $h\rho_{\beta\gamma}\sigma_\beta\sigma_\gamma$. In particular, when there is a negative correlation between production and abatement costs (i.e., $\rho_{\beta\gamma} < 0$), aggregate emissions are higher under permits because permits induce primarily low-output firms to install abatement technologies, while standards force all firms to invest in abatement more or less equally.

Similarly, if $\rho_{\beta\gamma} = 0$ but $v \neq 0$, the second term in (20) is likely to be different from zero. In particular, if $\rho_{\alpha\beta} = \rho_{\alpha\gamma} = \rho_{\beta\gamma} = 0$ and $v > 0$, emissions will be larger under permits. In this case, when firms doing more abatement find it optimal to reduce output ex post (i.e., $v > 0$), the permits policy has the disadvantage of reducing the output of firms doing more abatement relative to the output of those doing less abatement. This problem is less significant under standards because all firms are required to install similar abatement technologies.

Because the different parameters values are likely to vary from case to case, there will be cases in which standards are the correct policy choice and others in which permits are the correct choice.[18] It could be argued, however, that because permits are always less costly than standards and may or may not lead to higher emissions, permits should be adopted as a default, unless the available cost and pollution damage information indicates the opposite. In other words, the burden of proof should lie with the CAC policy and not with the permits policy.

AN EMPIRICAL EVALUATION

The theoretical analysis indicates that whether permits welfare dominate standards when emissions are imperfectly observed is ultimately an empirical question. In this section, I use the experience from Santiago's TSP permits program to evaluate the advantages, if any, of using permits for regulating the emissions of the sources affected by the program. Because firms are not required to provide the regulator with information on production and abatement costs, I apply the theoretical framework previously developed to infer the cost structure of the firms affected by the TSP program and other parameters. These estimates are then used to compare the actual performance of the TSP permits program with the performance of a hypothetically equivalent standards policy.

The empirical evaluation is carried out under several assumptions that deserve explanation. First, I retain the exact structure of the theoretical model that includes, among other things, constant output prices P and constant marginal pollution damages h. Although the TSP program is relatively small to affect output prices and total emissions, I retain these assumptions because otherwise I would not be able to estimate the parameters of the model in a relatively simple way. In other words, I use the model as a useful interpretive guide of the data, but this does not exclude other alternative interpretations of the data. Second, in recovering key parameters of the model such as P and h and comparing policies, I impose some consistency in the regulator's behavior in that the equivalent standards policy is constructed under the assumption that if the regulator had to introduce a standard he will do it optimally using the same value of h (together with the other parameters) that he implicitly used in implementing the permits policy.[19] This does not imply, however, that the regulator is necessarily implementing a policy based on a value of h supported by scientific evidence.

The TSP Permits Program

The city of Santiago has constantly presented air pollution problems since the early 1980s. The TSP trading program, established in March 1992, was designed to curb TSP emissions from the largest stationary sources in Santiago (industrial boilers, industrial ovens, and large residential and commercial heaters) whose emissions are discharged through a duct or stack at a flow rate greater than or equal to $1,000 \, m^3/hr$. Because sources were too small to require sophisticated monitoring procedures, the authority did not design the program based on sources' actual emissions but on a proxy variable equal to the maximum emissions that a source could emit in a given period of time if it operates without interruption.

The proxy for emissions (expressed in kg of TSP per day) used by the authority in this particular program was defined as the product of emissions concentration (in mg/m^3) and flow rate (in m^3/hr) of the gas exiting the source's stack (multiplied by 24 hr and 10^{-6} kg/mg to obtain kg/day).[20] Although the regulatory authority monitors each affected source's concentration and flow rate once a year,[21] emissions $\tilde{e}$ and permits $\tilde{e}_0$ are expressed in daily terms to be compatible with the daily TSP air quality standards. Thus, a source that holds one permit has the right to emit a maximum of 1 kg of TSP per day indefinitely over the lifetime of the program.

Sources registered and operating by March 1992 were designated as existing sources and received grandfathered permits equal to the product of an emissions rate of 56 mg/m^3 and their flow rate at the moment of registration. New sources, on the other hand, receive no permits, so must cover all their emissions with permits bought from existing sources. The total number of permits distributed (i.e., the emissions cap) was 64 percent of aggregate (proxied) emissions from existing sources prior to the program. After each annual inspection, the authority proceeds to reconcile the estimated emissions with the number of permits held by each source (all permits are traded at a 1:1 ratio). Note that despite the fact that permits are expressed in daily terms, the monitoring frequency restricts sources to trade permits only on an annual or permanent basis.[22]

The Data

The data for the study were obtained from PROCEFF's databases for the years 1993 through 1999.[23] Each database includes information on the number of sources and their dates of registration, flow rates, fuel types, emission rates, and utilization (i.e., days and hours of operation during the year). Information on flow rates, fuel types, and emission rates is directly obtained by the authority during its annual inspections, and information on utilization is obtained from firms' voluntary reports.[24] The 1993 database contains all the information, including the flow rate used to calculate each source's allocation of permits, before the program became effective in 1994. Table 6.1 presents a summary of the data. The first two rows show the proportion of existing and new sources.[25]

The next rows of table 6.1 provide information on the evolution of flow rates, emission rates, and utilization. The large standard deviations indicate that these three variables vary widely across sources in all years.[26] To comply with the TSP trading program, affected sources can hold permits, reduce emissions, or do both. They can reduce emissions either by decreasing their size (i.e., flow rate) or by decreasing their emission rates. The latter can be done through either fuel switching (for example, from wood, coal, or heavy oil to light oil, liquid gas, or natural gas) or the installation of end-of-pipe technology (e.g., filters, electrostatic precipitators, cyclones, and scrubbers).[27] Sources do not gain anything, in terms of emissions reduction, by changing their utilization level (i.e., days and hours of operation), because by definition it is assumed to be at 100 percent. Given that the authority controls for the size of the source (i.e., flow rate) at the moment of permits allocation and monitoring, emission rates and utilization are captured, respectively, by r_p and q_p in the theoretical model.

The last two rows of table 6.1 show data on total emissions and permits.[28] Although 1994 was in principle the first year of compliance with the program, trading activity did not occur until 1996 when compliance was more effectively enforced (Montero et al., 2002). The emissions goal of

Table 6.1 Summary Statistics for All Affected Sources: 1993–99

Variable	1993	1995	1996	1997	1998	1999
No. of sources						
Existing	635	578	504	430	365	365
New	45	112	127	146	221	208
Total affected	680	690	631	576	566	573
Flow rate (m³/h)						
Average	4,910.7	4,784.1	4,612.6	4,062.1	4,213.9	4,146.6
SD	15,058.8	14,908.0	15,490.9	9,498.6	13,091.0	11,793.5
Max.	261,383.9	261,304.7	261,304.7	182,843.0	207,110.6	183,739.5
Min.	499.2	204.3	204.3	493.3	216.9	165.6
Emission rate (mg/m³)						
Average	94.9	83.1	78.5	54.7	31.1	27.8
SD	88.1	77.8	76.8	43.0	21.1	18.5
Max.	702.0	698.2	674.0	330.7	110.0	108.2
Min.	1.5	1.5	3.4	3.6	2.9	4.6
Utilization (%)*						
Average	39.4	48.0	47.1	49.2	51.7	53.7
SD	30.3	31.5	31.7	31.8	32.0	32.3
Max.	100	100	100	100	100	100
Min.	0	0	0	0	0	0
No. of observations	278	463	457	499	543	542
Total emissions (kg/day)	7,051.9	6,320.9	5,094.4	3,535.0	1,975.3	1,665.0
Total permits (kg/day)	4,604.1	4,604.1	4,604.1	4,087.5	4,087.5	4,087.5

Source: Elaborated from PROCEFF's databases.
* An utilization of 100 percent corresponds to 24 hrs of operation during 365 days a year. As indicated by the no. of observations, utilization figures are not based on all sources (recall that information on utilization is not required for monitoring and enforcement purposes).

the TSP program was only achieved by 1997 (total emissions below to-tal permits).[29] This is the year after which natural gas became available from Argentina at unexpectedly attractive prices, such that many affected sources switched to this cleaner fuel, leaving the cap of 4,087.5 permits largely nonbinding.[30] Consequently, the empirical evaluation that follows is mainly based on the 1997 data and to a lesser extent on the 1998 data.

Estimation of Parameters and Δ_{ps}

Based on (23), the sign of Δ_{ps} can be first explored by looking at the covariance matrix for the emission rate (r_p) and utilization (q_p). Using the flow rate as a weight to control for size differences across sources, the weighted statistics for the 1997 data (499 observations) are $\text{Var}[q_p] = 0.112$, $\text{Var}[r_p] = 0.211$, and $\text{Cov}[r_p, q_p] = 0.026$ (to work with dimensionless variables hereafter, emission rates are divided by their 1993 mean value of $94.9 \, \text{mg/m}^3$)[31] and for the 1998 data (543 observations) the weighted statistics are, respectively, 0.111, 0.056, and 0.005. Although these figures do not allows me to sign Δ_{ps} yet, they indicate that emissions have been somewhat larger than what would have been under an equivalent standards policy. Because $E_p = \text{Exp}[r_p q_p]$ and the weighted value of $\text{Exp}[r_p q_p]$ in 1997 is 0.445, emissions would have been 0.419 under the equivalent standard of 0.663 (the latter is the weighted value of $\text{Exp}[r_p]$ in 1997).

The 1997 figures also show that $\text{Var}[r_p]$ is more than eight times larger than $\text{Cov}[r_p, q_p]$, raising the possibility that the higher emissions may be more than offset by cost savings. To test for this possibility, however, more information on various parameters is required.

A more precise estimate of Δ_{ps} requires then values of v, c, k, h, and P. This information is to be recovered from the data described in table 6.1 (no detailed information on production and abatement costs is available elsewhere; at least to my knowledge). I start with the estimation of v. Based on first-order conditions (7) and (8), v is obtained by estimating the following simultaneous-equation system

(24)
$$REDUC_i = a_0 + a_1 UTIL_i + a_2 FLOW93_i + a_3 EMRTE93_i$$
$$+ a_4 ENDPIPE_i + a_5 INDUST_i + a_6 STATE_i + \varepsilon_i$$

(25)
$$UTIL_i = b_0 + b_1 REDUC_i + b_2 UTIL93_i + b_3 FLOW93_i$$
$$+ b_4 INDUST_i + b_5 STATE_i + u_i,$$

where i indexes sources, ε^i and u^i are error terms whose characteristics will be discussed shortly, and the different variables relate to those in (7)–(8) as follows. $REDUC$ corresponds to x_p, that is, the level of reduction under the permits policy. $REDUC$ is calculated as the difference between the source's counterfactual emission rate $(1 + \alpha)$ and its actual emission rate (r_p).[32] I use the 1993 as the counterfactual year,[33] so $EMRTE93$ is the counterfactual emissions rate.

The variable $UTIL$ corresponds to q_p, that is, the level of utilization or output. As in the theoretical model, the TSP program's authority does not observe $UTIL$, and therefore he cannot use it for monitoring and enforcement purposes. To put it differently, because the regulator only observes a source's flow rate and emissions rate, he only has control over changes in emissions due to changes in the source's size (i.e., flow rate) and emission rates but not over changes in emissions due to changes in utilization.

The variables $FLOW93$, $EMRTE93$, $ENDPIPE$, $INDUST$, and $STATE$ included in (24) are intended to capture differences in abatement costs across sources (i.e., γ).[34] $FLOW93$ is the source's flow rate in 1993. If there are any scale economies associated with pollution abatement, then one should expect more abatement from bigger sources (i.e., larger $FLOW93$), other things equal (I also use $FLOW93^2$ and ln $FLOW93$).[35] Similarly, I expect a source with a high emissions rate before the TSP program (i.e., high $EMRTE93$) to face more abatement possibilities and hence lower costs. Conversely, I expect a source already equipped with some end-of-pipe abatement technology required by previous (and source-specific) regulation to be less likely to reduce emissions. Hence, I introduce the dummy variable $ENDPIPE$ that equals 1 if the source has any type of end-of-pipe abatement technology by 1993. I also introduce the dummy variables $INDUST$ and $STATE$ to see whether there is any difference in abatement costs (or abatement behavior) between industrial sources ($INDUST = 1$) and residential/commercial sources, or between state- or municipality-owned sources ($STATE = 1$) and privately owned sources.[36]

The variables $UTIL93$, $FLOWRTE93$, $INDUST$, and $STATE$ included in (25) are intended to capture differences in production costs across sources (i.e., β).[37] $UTIL93$ is the source's utilization in 1993 and serves as a proxy for the level of utilization that would have been observed in the absence of the TSP program and of changes in exogenous factors (e.g., input prices, demand, etc.).[38] Because on average, utilization has been increasing over time, $FLOW93$ should capture whether expansion in larger units is relatively cheaper than in smaller units. For the same reason, I also include $INDUST$ and $STATE$.

An estimate of the sign (and relative value) of v can then be inferred from either $a_1 = -v/k$ or $b_1 = -v/c$. Because $UTIL$ and $REDUC$ enter as endogenous variables in (24)–(25), however, their correlations with the error terms ε_i and u_i would produce biased ordinary least squares estimators. Therefore, I employ a two-stage least squares (2SLS) estimation procedure to obtain unbiased estimates. 2SLS results for equations (24) and (25) are presented in table 6.2 (first-stage results are omitted).

The first three columns of table 6.2 show the results for the 1997 data. Results in column (1) indicate that the coefficients of $UTIL$ and $REDUC$ (i.e., a_1 and b_1, respectively), although positive, are not significantly different from zero. Because the theoretical model assumes that all firms are expected to produce, on average, the same amount of output

Table 6.2 2SLS Estimates for the Reduction and Utilization Equations

Independent Variables	(1)	(2)	(3)	(4)	(5)	(6)
Reduction equation						
UTIL	0.078	0.137	0.087	0.256*	0.539*	0.308
	(0.153)	(0.175)	(0.175)	(0.132)	(0.309)	(0.322)
FLOW93	−0.789**	−0.788***		−0.937***	−1.090***	
	(0.330)	(0.275)		(0.345)	(0.422)	
FLOW93^2	0.270**	0.271**		0.346***	0.373**	
	(0.131)	(0.111)		(0.129)	(0.151)	
ln(FLOW93)			−0.088***			−0.093***
			(0.032)			(0.031)
EMRTE93	0.741***	0.717***	0.698***	0.987***	0.944***	0.940***
	(0.094)	(0.115)	(0.116)	(0.019)	(0.039)	(0.035)
ENDPIPE	−0.058	−0.191	−0.027	−0.128	−0.032	0.182
	(0.198)	(0.251)	(0.140)	(0.083)	(0.100)	(0.129)
INDUST	−0.008	0.079	0.120	0.014	−0.031	0.023
	(0.077)	(0.149)	(0.153)	(0.042)	(0.061)	(0.056)
STATE	−0.137	−0.193**	−0.193**	−0.105**	−0.083	−0.118
	(0.106)	(0.084)	(0.082)	(0.050)	(0.077)	(0.074)
Constant	−0.390***	−0.474***	0.217	−0.420***	−0.512***	0.272
	(0.075)	(0.116)	(0.201)	(0.050)	(0.115)	(0.211)
Utilization equation						
REDUC	−0.003	0.005	−0.017	0.012	0.063*	0.054
	(0.030)	(0.032)	(0.039)	(0.029)	(0.035)	(0.039)
UTIL93	0.560***	0.567***	0.532***	0.364***	0.313***	0.275***
	(0.055)	(0.064)	(0.061)	(0.064)	(0.093)	(0.089)
FLOW93	0.401***	0.384***		0.416	0.417***	
	(0.130)	(0.096)		(0.267)	(0.129)	
FLOW93^2	−0.095**	−0.087***		−0.101	−0.098**	
	(0.048)	(0.033)		(0.101)	(0.045)	
ln(FLOW93)			0.078***			0.090***
			(0.012)			(0.011)
INDUST	0.069*	0.038	0.022	0.141***	0.077	0.044
	(0.037)	(0.045)	(0.049)	(0.044)	(0.057)	(0.057)
STATE	−0.077*	−0.042	−0.038	−0.039	−0.117**	−0.098*
	(0.045)	(0.045)	(0.043)	(0.058)	(0.051)	(0.055)
Constant	0.158***	0.182***	−0.407***	0.221***	0.293***	−0.376***
	(0.034)	(0.045)	(0.100)	(0.042)	(0.057)	(0.090)
No. observations	344	344	344	288	288	288

Notes: First-stage results are omitted. White-corrected SEs are in parenthesis. Columns (2), (3), (5), and (6) present weighted estimates (the 1997 flow rate is the weight in (2) and (3) and the 1998 flow rate in (5) and (6)).

*Significant at 10%, ** significant at 5%, *** significant at 1%.

$(\text{Exp}[q_p] = [P - vx_s]/c)$, however, one can argue that these coefficients may provide a biased estimation of v by not taking into account the fact that firms have different sizes. One could further argue that the true value of v may even be of different sign, because the coefficients of $FLOW93$ and $FLOW93^2$ in the reduction equation indicate that the amount of re-duction decreases with size throughout the relevant range. To control for such possibility, I run a weighted 2SLS regression using the 1997 flow rate as weight. The new estimates, which are reported in columns (2) and (3), are not very different from the unweighted estimates, confirming that the interaction term v in equation (1) is not statistically different from zero.

The last three columns of table 6.2 show the 2SLS results for the 1998 data (weighted estimates are in columns 5 and 6). In particular, I observe that the coefficients of $UTIL$ and $REDUC$ in column (5) are positive and significantly different from zero at the 10 percent level. This negative value of v can be attributed in large part to the arrival of natural gas at relatively low prices by the end of 1997.[39] Although the 1998 results must be carefully interpreted because of the apparently slack cap, they are useful to illustrate the estimation of Δ_{ps} when v is different from zero, as I shall show next.

I can finally use the estimated value of v to obtain an estimate for the remaining parameters of the model, and hence, for Δ_{ps}. Following the 1997 econometric results, I first consider the case in which $v = 0$. When this is the case, I have that $h = c\tilde{R}\tilde{q}/P$ from (13), $\tilde{R}\tilde{q} = k\text{Exp}[x_p]$ from (9), and $P = c\,\text{Exp}[q_p]$ from (10). Replacing the 1997 (weighted) statistics for $\text{Exp}[x_p] = 0.203$ and $\text{Exp}[q_p] = 0.631$ in the expression for h, (23) reduces to

$$\Delta_{ps}\big|_{97,\,v\,=\,0} = \frac{k}{2}\,\text{Var}[r_p] - \frac{k\,\text{Exp}[x_p]}{\text{Exp}[q_p]}\,\text{Cov}[r_p, q_p]$$

$$= (0.1055 - 0.0084)k = 0.097k > 0.$$

These numbers not only indicate that the permits policy is welfare su-perior to an equivalent standards policy but, more important, that the welfare loss from higher emissions is only 8 percent of the welfare gain from cost savings.

Based on the 1998 results contained in column (5) of table 6.2, I now consider the case in which $v < 0$. From the coefficients of $UTIL$ and $RE-DUC$ I obtain, respectively, $k = -1.86v$ and $c = -15.87v$ (which in turn, yields $\Lambda = 28.52v^2$). In addition, by simultaneously solving (9) and (10) for P and $\tilde{R}\tilde{q}$ with $\text{Exp}[x_p] = 0.466$ and $\text{Exp}[q_p] = 0.669$, I get $P = -10.15v$ and $\tilde{R}\tilde{q} = -0.20v$ that replaced into (13) gives $h = -0.31v$. Plugging these numbers and the corresponding statistics into (23), I finally obtain $\Delta_{ps}\big|_{98,\,v\,<\,0} = (0.0503 - 0.0016)(-v) = -0.049v > 0$. This result, though qualitatively similar to the 1997 result, shows an even smaller welfare loss from higher emissions—only 3 percent of the welfare gain from cost savings.

FINAL REMARKS

I have developed a model to study the design and performance of pollution markets (i.e., tradable permits) when the regulator has imperfect information on firms' emissions and costs. A salient example is the control of air pollution in large cities where emissions come from many small (stationary and mobile) sources for which continuous monitoring is prohibitively costly. In such a case the well-known superiority of permits over the traditional CAC approach of setting technology and emission standards is no longer evident. Because the regulator only observes a firm's abatement technology but neither its emissions nor its output (utilization), permits could result in higher emissions if firms doing more abatement are at the same time reducing output relative to other firms and/or if more highly utilized firms find it optimal to abate relatively less. I then used emissions and output data from Santiago TSP permits program to explore the implications of the theoretical model. I found that the production and abatement cost characteristics of the sources affected by the TSP program are such that the permits policy is welfare superior. The estimated cost savings are only partially offset (about 8 percent) by a moderate increase in emissions relative to what would have been observed under an equivalent standards policy.

Because sources under the TSP program are currently responsible for less than 5 percent of total TSP emissions in Santiago, the model developed here can be used to study how to expand the TSP program to other sources of TSP that today are subject to CAC regulation. A good candidate would be powered-diesel buses, which are responsible for 36.7 percent of total TSP emissions. According to Cifuentes (1999), buses that abate emissions by switching to natural gas are likely to reduce utilization relative to buses that stay on diesel and that older, less-utilized buses are more likely to switch to natural gas. Because switching to natural gas is a major abatement alternative, both of these observations would suggest that the optimal way to integrate buses into the TSP program is by imposing, in addition to the allocation of permits, an emission standard specific to buses. It may also be optimal to use different utilization factors ($\bar{q}$) for each type of source (see Falk 2003). These and related design issues deserve further research.

ACKNOWLEDGMENTS I wish to thank J. R. DeShazo, Charlie Kolstad (the editor), two anonymous referees, and participants at the UC-Santa Barbara Workshop on Economic Instruments for numerous comments.

NOTES

1. It is worth noting that RECLAIM did not include a market for volatile organic compounds (VOCs) in large part because of the difficulties with monitoring actual emissions from smaller and heterogeneous sources (Harrison 1999).

2. It is also assumed that the firm's output or utilization is not observed by the regulator, so actual emissions cannot be indirectly inferred.

3. These 600 sources affected by the TSP program are responsible for only 5 percent of 2000 TSP emissions in Santiago. Remaining TSP sources are controlled through CAC regulation.

4. As we shall see later, using the source's maximum emissions as a proxy does not prevent any adverse effects that the use of permits (instead of CAC regulation) could eventually have on aggregate emissions. The choice of proxy is an arbitrary matter because the number of permits being allocated can always be adjusted accordingly with no efficiency effects.

5. Varios of the permit trading programs documented in U.S. EPA (2001) face similar issues because these are programs that are not based on actual emissions (e.g., the averaging programs for mobile sources, the fireplace permit trading in Colorado, etc.).

6. Segerson (1988) studies the control of emissions from (few) nonpoint sources using a "moral hazard in teams" approach. Fullerton and West (2002) consider the control of vehicle emissions using a combination of taxes on cars and gasoline as an alternative to an (unavailable) tax on emissions. Cremer and Gahvari (2002) look at output and emission taxation under costly (rather than imperfect) monitoring.

7. The instrument choice problem studied by the Montero (2004) publication is similar in spirit and approach to the instrument choice dilemma considered by Weitzman (1974). There are, however, important differences. Weitzman (1974) compares the relative advantage of a price instrument (taxes) over a quantity instrument (permits) when the regulator has imperfect information about the aggregate abatement cost curve (and possibly about the damage curve as well). Thus, cost heterogeneity across firms plays no role in Weitzman's analysis. Instead, Montero (2004) compares the performance of two quantity instruments and focuses on the effect of cost heterogeneity on instrument performance.

8. There are very few cases, which are unlikely to hold in practice, in which it may be optimal to just rely on standards and totally abstract from permits. *See* Montero (2004) for more.

9. The parameter v can be negative, for example, if switching to a cleaner fuel saves on fuel costs but involves such a large retrofitting cost (i.e., high k) that no firm switches to the cleaner and cheaper fuel unless regulated.

10. Note that one can easily add aggregate uncertainty to this formulation by simply letting $\beta^i = \beta^i + \theta$ and $\gamma^i = \gamma^i + \eta$, where θ and η are random variables common to all firms.

11. Note that because β and γ are negative for some firms, one can argue that marginal costs can take negative values. This possibility is eliminated by assuming parameter values (including those in the demand and damage functions) that lead to interior solutions for q and x in which $\partial C/\partial q > 0$ and $\partial C/\partial x > 0$ for all β and γ. Furthermore, because these interior solution are assumed to fall within the range in which (1) is valid, what happens beyond this range is not relevant for the analysis of instrument design and choice that follows. Alternatively, one can let $\beta \in [0, \bar{\beta}]$ and $\gamma \in [0, \bar{\gamma}]$ with some further notation in the optimal designs but no change in the welfare comparisons.

12. This same ex post increase in output was observed among the power plants that installed scrubbers in the SO_2 trading program (Ellerman et al. 2000).

13. The model can be generalized by allowing the regulator to consider a weight $\mu \neq 1$ for firm profits and a shadow cost $\lambda > 0$ for public funds. However, this would not add much to the discussion.

14. Montero (2004) derives the optimal hybrid policy that optimally combines permits and standards. In many cases, this optimal hybrid policy converges to the permits-alone policy and in others, although very few, to the standards-alone policy.

15. *See also* Stavins (2003) and Hahn et al. (2003).

16. Note that the second-order condition imposes $-ck + v^2 - 2hv < 0$.

17. Note that under a tax policy, the optimal price R will be the tax. If we add aggregate uncertainty to the model, the two policies will not be equivalent from an efficiency standpoint (Weitzman 1974).

18. Yet in other cases the correct choice is to optimally combine permits and standards (Montero 2004).

19. Allowing for a regulator with objective functions and parameter values that depend on the instrument under consideration introduces new elements to the policy analysis that go beyond the scope of this chapter.

20. In terms of the model, this is equivalent as to make $\tilde{q}$ equal to the maximum possible output, which in this case is $(P - \beta)/c$. But note that the program would have worked equally well with an either higher or lower $\tilde{q}$. The use of a different $\tilde{q}$ only requires to adjust the number of quasi-permits $\tilde{e}_0$ to be distributed such that $R\tilde{q}$ remains at its optimal level.

21. There are also random inspections to enforce compliance throughout the year.

22. In addition, the authority introduced an emission rate standard of 112 mg/ m^3 for all stationary sources. It seems, however, that this either was only enforced by 1998 or became nonbinding after the arrival of natural gas.

23. PROCEFF is the government office responsible for enforcing the TSP program.

24. Because utilization has no effect at all on the source's compliance status, there is no reason to beleive that firms have incentives to misreport their true utilization. For the same reason, this information is available for most but not all sources.

25. It is interesting to point out that by 1999, 36 percent of the affected sources were new sources despite the fact they did not receive any permits.

26. It may seem strange to observe some flow rates below the 1,000 (m^3/hr) mark. In general, these are existing sources for which flow rates were wrongly estimated to be above 1,000 (m^3/hr) at the time of registration. Nevertheless, these sources chose to remain in the program to keep the permits they had already received.

27. Note that for most sources, flow rates do not change over time.

28. A few permits were retired from the market in 1997 as the authority revised the eligibility of some sources to receiving permits (Montero et al. 2002).

29. The fact that total emissions in 1997 are somewhat below the cap should not be interpreted as either overcompliance or nonbinding regulation. One explanation is that firms tend to hold a few extra permits as an insurance against some measurement uncertainty (inherent to a monitoring precedure of this sort). A second explanation is the uncertainty associated with revision of the initial allocation of permits carried out by the authority after the beginning of the program. The 1997 allocation drop is, in fact, the result of such a revision.

30. This is consistent with the fact that interfirm trading activity stopped by mid-1998. Obviously, intrafirm trading activity has continued as new sources come into operation.

31. The unweighted statistics are, respectively, 0.101, 0.221, and 0.004.

32. Recall that emission rates are normalized by the 1993 mean.

33. Results do not qualitatively change when I use 1995 as the counterfactual year (the year in which I have a few more data points).

34. Because sources' emissions were unregulated by 1993 (except for a very few sources that were required to install end-of-pipe abatement technology before 1993), there is no reason to believe that a sources' utilization in the absence of emission control ($UTIL93$) could tell anything about how easy or difficult is for the source to reduce emissions.

35. I use the 1993 flow rate instead of the actual flow rate to control for possible endogeneity problems. However, results are virtually the same when I use the actual flow rate. This is in part because the firm's flow rate barely change over time (the drop in average flow rates shown in table 6.1 is mainly due to changes in one particular large firm).

36. For example, $INDUST = 0$ and $STATE = 1$ for the boiler of the central heating system of a public hospital.

37. Note that the variables $EMRTE93$ and $ENDPIPE$ are excluded from the utilization regression. There is nothing particular about $ENPIPE$ and $EMRTE93$ that can affect utilization beyond its effect, if any, in 1993, which is already captured by $UTIL93$.

38. To work with a larger data set I use the 1995 utilization for sixty-six sources. This should not baised the results in any particular way because the TSP program was not effectively enforced until 1996 (*see* table 6.1).

39. In fact, 112 of the 144 affected sources that switched to natural gas in 1998 increased or maintained their utilization relative to 1997.

REFERENCES

Cifuentes, L. (1999), "Costos y beneficios de introducir gas natural en el transporte público en Santiago," mimeo, Catholic University of Chile.

Cremer, H., and F. Gahvari (2002), "Imperfect observability of emissions and second-best emission and output taxes," *Journal of Public Economics* 85, 385–407.

Ellerman, A.D., P. Joskow, R. Schmalensee, J.-P. Montero, and E.M. Bailey (2000), *Markets for Clean Air: The U.S. Acid Rain Program*, Cambridge University Press, Cambridge.

Falk, D. (2003), *Permisos Transable con Monitoreo Imperfecto*, Master's thesis, Economics Department, Catholic University of Chile.

Fullerton, D., and S.E. West (2002), "Can taxes on cars and on gasoline mimic an unavailable tax on emissions?," *Journal of Environmental Economics and Management* 43, 135–57.

Hahn, R.W., S.M. Olmstead, and R.N. Stavins (2003), "Environmental regulation in the 1990s: A retrospective analysis," *Harvard Environmental Law Review* 27, 377–415.

Harrison, David Jr. (1999), "Turning theory into practice for emissions trading in the Los Angeles air basin," in Steve Sorrell and Jim Skea (eds.), *Pollution for Sale: Emissions Trading and Joint Implementation*, Edward Elgar, Cheltenham, UK.

Lewis, T. (1996), "Protecting the environment when costs and benefits are privately known," *RAND Journal of Economics* 27, 819–47.

Montero, J.-P. (2004), "Pollution markets with imperfectly observed emissions," *RAND Journal of Economics*.

Montero, J.-P., J.M. Sánchez, and R. Katz (2002), "A market-based environmental policy experiment in Chile," *Journal of Law and Economics* 45, 267–87.

Schmalensee, R., P. Joskow, D. Ellerman, J.P. Montero, and E. Bailey (1998), "An interim evaluation of sulfur dioxide emissions trading," *Journal of Economic Perspectives* 12, 53–68.

Segerson, K. (1988), "Uncertainty and incentives for nonpoint pollution control," *Journal of Environmental Economics and Management* 15, 87–98.

Stavins, R. (2003), "Experience with market-based environmental policy instruments," in Karl-Göran Mäler and Jeffrey Vincent (eds.), *Handbook of Environmental Economics*, Elsevier Science, Amsterdam.

U.S. Environmental Protection Agency (USEPA, 2001), *The United States Experience with Economic Incentives for Protecting the Environment*, EPA-20-R-01-001, Washington, D.C.

Weitzman, M. (1974), "Prices vs quantities," *Review of Economic Studies* 41, 477–91.

7

The Market-Based Lead Phasedown

Richard G. Newell & Kristian Rogers

INTRODUCTION

One of the great successes during the modern era of environmental policy was the phasedown of lead in gasoline, which took place in the United States principally during the decade of the 1980s. The phasedown was accomplished in part through a tradable permit system among refineries, whereby lead credits could be exchanged or banked for later use. The lead trading program represents the first large-scale implementation of a tradable permit program for the environment, predating the well-known sulfur dioxide trading program by more than a decade.

Unlike sulfur in coal, however, lead does not occur naturally in petroleum. Refiners in the United States started adding lead compounds to gasoline in the 1920s to boost octane levels and improve engine performance by reducing engine knock and allowing higher engine compression.[1] Lead was used because it was inexpensive for boosting octane relative to other fuel additives (i.e., ethanol and other alcohol-based additives) and because people were ignorant of the dangers of lead emissions, including mental retardation and hypertension. In the early 1970s, before legal requirements for reducing lead came into force, lead levels in gasoline were a little over 2 grams of lead per gallon of gasoline, amounting to about 200,000 metric tons of lead in total. The reduction in lead in gasoline in the United States came in response to two main factors: (1) the mandatory use of unleaded gasoline to protect catalytic converters in all cars starting with the 1975 model year, and (2) increased awareness of the negative human health effects of lead.

Unleaded Fuel Cars Starting with Model Year 1975

The phasedown of lead in gasoline began in 1974, when, under the authority of the Clean Air Act amendments of 1970, the U.S. Environmental Protection Agency (EPA) introduced rules requiring the use of unleaded gasoline in new cars equipped with catalytic converters. (See a summary of the phasedown in table 7.1.) The introduction of catalytic converters for control of hydrocarbons (HCs), nitrogen oxides (NO_x), and carbon monoxide (CO) emissions required that motorists use unleaded gasoline, because lead destroys the emissions control capacity of catalytic converters. The eventual phasedown of lead in gasoline is largely attributable to the decreasing share of leaded gasoline that resulted from the transition to a new car fleet. This transition is shown in figure 7.1. To help promote the supply of unleaded gasoline and avoid misfueling, the EPA also mandated that unleaded cars have specially designed fuel inlets that fit only unleaded gasoline nozzles and that gasoline retailers offer unleaded gasoline for sale.

Phasedown of Lead in Gasoline

To further promote the production of unleaded gasoline, the EPA also scheduled performance standards requiring refineries to decrease the average lead content of all gasoline (leaded and unleaded pooled) beginning in 1975, but these were postponed until 1979 through a series of regulatory adjustments. By then, studies had provided increasing evidence of the adverse effects of atmospheric lead on the IQ of children and on blood pressure in adults (U.S. EPA 1985a).[2] Although lead use would have eventually dwindled as the last pre-1975 cars were retired, the growing evidence of health impacts prompted an accelerated phaseout of lead in gasoline.

The EPA established individual facility performance standards for refineries and a series of deadlines for compliance that took effect over several years, beginning in October 1979. Before these regulations came into effect, refiners were adding about 1.8 grams of lead per gallon of leaded gasoline. The standards varied according to the size of the facility. Large refiners (those with production capacity over 50,000 barrels per day [bpd] and/or those owned or controlled by a refiner having total capacity over 137,500 bpd) were to produce a quarterly average of no more than 0.8 gram per gallon (gpg) for the first year and 0.5 gpg in the next two years. Small refiners (with capacity of up to 50,000 bpd) faced a scale of five different standards, ranging from 2.65 gpg for the smallest of the group to 0.8 gpg for the largest. It was up to the individual refiner to meet these standards in the time allotted. About 60 percent of refineries were small according to the definition. The average refinery had a capacity of about 67,000 bpd, with individual refineries ranging in size from 50 bpd to 640,000 bpd.

It is important to note that the early regulation set an average lead concentration for total gasoline output, both leaded and unleaded. This

Table 7.1 Federal Standards for Lead Phasedown

Deadline	Standard	Exceptions
July 4, 1974	Gasoline retailers must offer unleaded gasoline and design fuel nozzles so that cars with catalytic converters can accept only unleaded gasoline.	Small retailers that sell less than 200,000 gallons annually and have fewer than six retail outlets are exempt.
July 4, 1974	Car manufacturers must design tank filler inlets to accept only unleaded gasoline and must apply "Unleaded Gasoline Only" labels.	The standard applies only to cars with catalytic converters, which became mandatory for model year 1975.
October 1, 1979	Refineries must not produce gasoline averaging more than 0.5 gpg per quarter, pooled (leaded and unleaded).	The standard is relaxed to 0.8 gpg until October 1, 1980, if a refinery increases unleaded gasoline production by 6 percent over prior-year quarter. Small refineries are subject to a less stringent standard. See table 7.2.
November 1, 1982	Refineries must meet a leaded gas standard of 1.1. Interrefinery averaging of lead rights is permitted among large refineries and among small refineries, but not between refineries of different sizes.	Very small refineries are subject to a less stringent pooled standard. See table 7.2.
July 1, 1983	Very small refineries are also subject to a standard of 1.1 (leaded). Averaging is permitted among all refineries.	
January 1, 1985	During 1985 only, refineries are permitted to bank excess lead rights for use in a subsequent quarter.	
July 1, 1985	The standard is reduced to 0.5 (leaded).	
January 1, 1986	The standard is reduced to 0.1 (leaded).	
January 1, 1988	Interrefinery averaging and withdrawal of banked lead usage rights are no longer permitted. Each refinery must comply with the 0.1 standard.	
January 1, 1996	Lead additives in motor vehicle gasoline are prohibited.	

Source: U.S. Code of Federal Regulations, 1996.
Note: gpg = grams of lead per gallon.

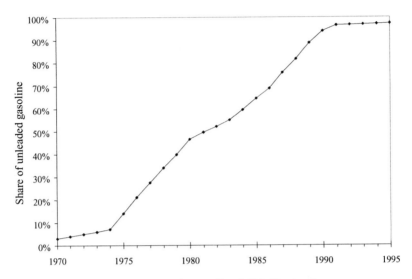

Figure 7.1. Share of Unleaded Gasoline in Total U.S. Production

Source: Petroleum Marketing Monthly, Statistical Abstracts, and other sources. See Kerr and Newell (2003).

averaging method deliberately provided refiners with the incentive to increase unleaded production while not necessarily removing lead from their leaded gasoline—in fact, the regulation actually allowed refiners to increase lead concentration levels, provided they sufficiently raised unleaded gasoline output. Nonetheless, these regulations still prompted a decrease in total lead usage because car owners were retiring their pre-catalyst automobiles and replacing them with new cars that required unleaded fuel.

As illustrated in figure 7.2, by the early 1980s gasoline lead levels had declined about 80 percent as a result of both the regulations and the fleet turnover. As part of President Reagan's Task Force on Regulatory Relief, the EPA considered deferring the deadlines and relaxing the standards in response to growing complaints from lead additive manufacturers (who contended that the lead regulations were unnecessary because lead was on its way out anyway) and small refiners who were having difficulty complying on time. Due to mounting evidence on the negative health effects of lead, however, this consideration met very strong opposition, both from within the agency and from environmental groups and public health officials. The agency subsequently withdrew its consideration and instead decided to tighten the standards. The 1982 regulations narrowed the definition of a small refinery, phased out special provisions for such refineries by mid-1983, and recalculated lead limits as an average of lead in leaded gas only (because unleaded fuel was by then a well-established product). Small refineries challenged the new regulations but gained only a slight extension in some of their compliance deadlines.[3] The new rules

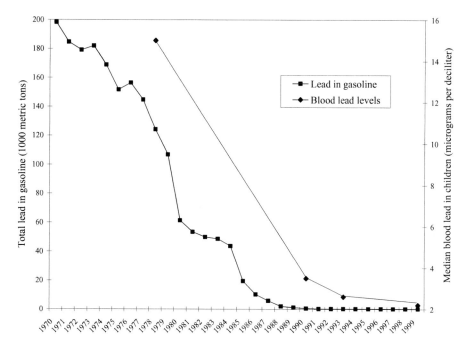

Figure 7.2. Total Lead in Gasoline and Blood Lead Levels over Time
Source: Total lead usage based on *Trends in Petroleum Fuels* (U.S. Department of Energy 1996), U.S. EPA lead program reports, and *Petroleum Marketing Monthly*. Blood lead levels from *America's Children and the Environment* (U.S. Environmental Protection Agency 2003).

changed the basis of the lead regulations to a standard that specifically limited the allowable content of lead in leaded gasoline to a quarterly average of 1.1 grams per leaded gallon (gplg). Very small refineries faced less stringent standards for a short time until 1983.

From 1983 to 1985, the EPA conducted an extensive cost-benefit analysis of a dramatic reduction in the lead standard to 0.1 gplg by 1988. The decision to consider tightening the lead standard so dramatically came in light of new scientific studies that linked two sorts of health problems directly to the ingestion of lead from fuel emissions. The first negative effect associated with lead, identified by the Centers for Disease Control and other health agencies, was mental retardation and in some cases death, especially in the case of young children. The second negative effect linked lead to elevated blood pressure, at least in middle-aged adults. Even without factoring in the blood pressure effects of lead, cost-benefit analysis unambiguously suggested the desirability of a substantial tightening of the standards. Later we cover the particulars of this analysis. Figure 7.2 illustrates the strong connection between gasoline lead and lead levels in children's blood.

The analysis suggested not only that a goal of 0.1 gplg by 1988 was feasible but that an even tighter standard might be achieved, partly because large refiners had already acquired the technology to reduce lead below the standards (Nichols 1997). In August 1984, the agency proposed a reduction of lead to 0.1 gplg by January 1, 1986. However, it was understood that some refineries might not be able to achieve this so quickly, so the agency also considered a more gradual phasedown, involving banking, that would reach 0.1 gplg by January 1, 1988. The proposal also hinted that the agency was considering a total ban on lead, but only in the long run. Thus, during 1985, the standard was reduced to 0.5 gplg, and beginning in 1986, the allowable content of lead in leaded gasoline was reduced to 0.1 gplg.

The phasedown received widespread support from the public as well as from environmentalists, the medical community, and the Office of Management and Budget, which had to review the regulations before they could be enacted. By this time, even the refiners, for the most part, accepted the reasons for removing lead from gas, though some obviously expressed reservations about the proposed timeline. Only the lead additive manufacturers and small refineries remained opposed.

To ease the transition for refineries, the 1982 regulations also permitted both trading and banking of lead permits through a system of "inter-refinery averaging." Trading of lead credits among refineries was allowed from late 1982 through the end of 1987. Banking was allowed during 1985–87. Beginning in 1988, the EPA reimposed a performance standard of 0.1 gplg on individual refineries. Lead was banned as a fuel additive in the United States beginning in 1996. Figure 7.3 shows the decline over time in the lead content of leaded gasoline in the United States. Refer to

Figure 7.3. Lead Content in Leaded Gasoline (U.S. Average)

Source: Trends in Petroleum Fuels (U.S. Department of Energy 1996), and U.S. EPA lead program reports. See Kerr and Newell (2003).

Table 7.2 Small Refinery Standards for Lead Phasedown

Deadline	Standard (gpg)	Gasoline Production in Prior Year (bpd)	Definition of Small Refinery
October 1, 1979	2.65 (pooled)	Up to 5,000	50,000 bpd or less crude oil throughput capacity and owned by a company with 137,500 bpd or less total capacity
	2.15 (pooled)	5,001 to 10,000	
	1.65 (pooled)	10,001 to 15,000	
	1.30 (pooled)	15,001 to 20,000	
	0.80 (pooled)	20,001 and over	
November 1, 1982	2.65 (pooled)	Up to 5,000	10,000 bpd or less gasoline production and owned by a company with 70,000 bpd or less total gasoline production
	2.15 (pooled)	5,001 to 10,000	
July 1, 1983 and after	Same as other refineries		

Source: U.S. Code of Federal Regulations, 1996.
Note: gpg = grams of lead per gallon; bpd = barrels per day.

table 7.1 for a summary of the phasedown timeline and table 7.2 for standards for small refineries.

Constraints on the amount of lead that could be used to boost octane increased the demand for more expensive substitute sources of octane. There are two basic approaches to reducing the need for lead. One is the use of other octane-enhancing additives, such as MTBE (methyl tertiary-butyl ether). These are more expensive than lead and provide only a part of the long-term solution. Additives including MTBE provided about one-third of the octane lost due to the removal of lead in the final phasedown. Another approach is to increase refineries' ability to produce high-octane gasoline components through process changes (primarily reforming and isomerization). In the short run, existing equipment can be run more intensively to increase octane production, but eventually new investment is required. Isomerization provided around 40 percent of additional octane requirements, and alkylation, catalytic cracking, and reforming together provided most of the remaining 30 percent of lost octane. A refinery can also adjust somewhat by altering the type of crude oil it purchases, by buying intermediate products with higher octane content, or by changing its output mix to one requiring less octane.

The Mechanics of Lead Trading and Banking

Until 1982, the EPA took a prescriptive approach to regulating lead, based on technology standards and individually binding refinery performance standards for lead content. However, the agency realized by the early 1980s that this policy was causing small refiners substantial difficulty in meeting the standards on time. Smaller refineries faced higher costs of complying with the lead phasedown because they typically lacked the more sophisticated processing equipment needed to replace lost octane (e.g., reformers, alkylation). The lack of such equipment also increased the costs of installing new technologies, such as isomerization. As mentioned, small refineries were concurrently facing the loss of favorable treatment under the petroleum allocation program, which increased their cries for regulatory relief.

At the same time, several large firms had already succeeded in implementing technology that could remove more lead from their gasoline than required by the regulations, at a cost lower than that faced by small refineries. Although the vast majority of the refining industry was initially united in its support of rescinding the lead regulations, several of the larger firms realized—given they were already making compliance investments—that it was in their competitive interest to keep the regulations and remove the exemptions for small refineries.

With the release of dramatic new health evidence on the health risks of lead by the Centers for Disease Control in 1982, the Reagan administration and the EPA found they needed to quickly find an alternative to their plan for rescission. The lead trading program, which had been floated earlier by EPA analysts but had met with little support, became the instrument for reconciling this political dilemma. Lead was controlled, refineries with excess octane capacity were provided a means by which they could sell excess lead credits, small refineries were provided with significant flexibility relative to uniform standards, and the administration was able to save some face by promoting a policy that was in keeping with the market-based perspective of the Task Force on Regulatory Relief.

Also, the fact that the EPA planned to keep lowering the standards over time compounded the refiners' problem of high abatement costs, because the cost of removing an increment of lead from gasoline increased as more lead was removed, also raising issues of optimal timing of abatement investments. The solution to this issue was the banking program. The banking option was introduced at the beginning of 1985 and ended with the trading rights program at the end of 1986, although refiners were able to use their banked rights through 1987.

The new marketable permit system allowed for interrefinery lead averaging, whereby some refiners could produce higher concentrations than others, as long as the average across refineries met the agency's standard. This system alleviated at least some of the financial burden on many small firms. It also allowed the entire refining industry a measure of flexibility in allocating the reduction among its firms and in allocating investments over time, resulting in a more cost-effective reduction. The underlying premise was that the EPA should involve itself as little as possible in the trading and instead allow the marketplace itself to develop the system.

The regulations presented this scheme as interrefinery averaging and left the logistics of trading up to the refineries. Interrefinery averaging allowed all gasoline refineries and importers, whether owned by the same refiner or not, to average lead usage over a calendar quarter through a process called constructive allocation. Constructive allocation allowed refiners to comply with the applicable lead content standard by allocating actual lead usage "in any manner agreed upon by the refiners"—so long as average lead usage over the quarter did not surpass the applicable standard (e.g., 1.1, 0.5, or 0.1 gplg). Refineries or importers engaging in interrefinery averaging were free to carry out constructive allocation through whatever means they saw fit, including trades and negotiations, both monetary and otherwise. Because interrefinery averaging was offered as an alternative to individual refinery compliance, only those refineries that found this alternative beneficial would use it.

Under the basic lead content regulations, refineries were required to report quarterly on the quantity of leaded and unleaded gasoline they produced and quantities of lead used. Specifically, refineries engaging in interrefinery averaging needed to provide the following information:

- Total grams of lead that the reporting refinery allocated (sold) to other refineries, and the names and addresses of such other refineries (A);
- Total grams of lead that the reporting refinery was allocated (bought) from other refineries, and the names and addresses of such other refineries (B);
- Total grams of lead "constructively used" by reporting refinery (C = actual lead usage—A + B);
- "Constructive average" lead content of each gallon of leaded gasoline produced by the reporting refinery during the compliance period (C / total gallons produced); and
- If compliance was demonstrated through averaging with more than one other refiner, supporting documentation showing that all parties agreed to the constructive allocation.

One implication of this averaging approach, highlighted by the last bullet and discussed further shortly, is that the documentation necessary to demonstrate and monitor compliance becomes very complex as the number of parties engaged in transactions with one another increases.

The second market-based component of the lead phasedown was a banking scheme introduced in 1985 that was intended to offer a buffer for refineries facing the significant lead content decreases slated for 1986. This modification provided temporal flexibility to refiners in addition to the interrefinery trading flexibility established in 1982. Under the banking mechanism, refiners who used less than 0.5 gplg but more than 0.1 gplg of lead in leaded gas in 1985 were permitted to use this same amount of lead in gasoline between 1985 and 1988, in addition to the lead permits issued and bought during that time period. Production of leaded gas with less than 0.1 gplg did not generate additional credits. Thus, the banking regulations extended a refinery's time frame for compliance with the 0.1 gplg standard.

The 1985 regulations also eliminated the interrefinery averaging provisions of the 1982 regulations as of January 1, 1986, although refiners were permitted to buy credits from other refiners' banks until the end of 1987. The EPA was concerned that the interrefinery trading provisions encouraged the production of leaded gasoline with only trace amounts of lead. The agency believed that engines designed to use leaded gas required at least 0.1 gplg to operate properly and wanted to eliminate any incentive to generate lead credits by producing leaded gas with concentrations below this threshold. Thus, with the end of the banking regulation in 1988, the lead trading program was completed.

The next section presents information on projected estimates of the effects of the program prior to its implementation. Then we present ex post evidence on the efficiency and effectiveness of the program measured after the policy had run its course. We draw overall conclusions and lessons for future policy in the final section.

PROJECTED EFFECTS OF THE MARKET-BASED LEAD PHASEDOWN

Ex ante estimates of the effects of the lead trading program were derived primarily from an EPA regulatory-impact analysis (RIA) performed between 1984 and 1985, which predicted the costs and benefits of bringing the lead standard down to 0.1 gplg by the beginning of 1986.[4] Refer to table 7.3 for physical measures of the proposal's benefits and table 7.4 for its monetized costs and benefits.

Projected Benefits

The benefits associated with the proposed rule fall into four categories: children's health, health and environmental effects from nonlead pollutants, vehicle maintenance and fuel economy effects, and blood pressure effects (Nichols 1997). The first benefit, children's health effects related to lead, was quantified in monetary terms as the avoided costs of medical treatment and remedial education that would be incurred if existing (1982) standards (1.1 gplg) remained in effect. The avoided medical costs were estimated at $900 (in 1983$) per child with blood-lead levels above 25 micrograms per deciliter (μg/dl). The estimates for compensatory education averaged about $2,600 per child with blood levels above the same threshold. The total benefits in this category ranged from about $600 million in 1986 to $350 million in 1992 (U.S. EPA 1985a). (Note that all monetary figures are in 1983 dollars.) The benefits tend to fall over time because the baseline against which the regulatory impact is measured

Table 7.3 Physical Measures of Estimated Benefits of Final Lead Phasedown Rule

Estimated Effects	Year			
	1985	1986	1987	1988
Reductions in children above 25 micrograms/dl blood lead (1,000s)	64	171	156	149
Reduced emissions of conventional pollutants (1,000s ton)				
HC	0	244	242	242
NO$_x$	0	75	95	95
CO	0	1,692	1,691	1,698
Reduced blood-pressure effects in males age 40–59				
Hypertension (1000s)	547	1,796	1,718	1,641
Myocardial infarctions	1,550	5,323	5,126	4,926
Strokes	324	1,109	1,068	1,026
Deaths	1,497	5,134	4,492	4,750

Source: Nichols (1985, table 1) and (U.S. EPA 1985a).

Table 7.4 Estimated Monetized Costs and Benefits of Final Lead Phasedown Rule (in millions $1983)

Estimated Effects	Year			
	1985	1986	1987	1988
Monetized benefits				
Lead-related effects in children	223	600	547	502
Blood pressure–related (males, 40–59)	1,725	5,897	5,675	5,447
Conventional pollutants	0	222	222	224
Maintenance and fuel economy	137	1,101	1,029	931
Total monetized benefits	2,084	7,821	7,474	7,105
Costs				
Increased refining costs	96	608	558	532
Net benefits				
Including blood pressure	1,988	7,213	6,916	6,573
Excluding blood pressure	264	1,316	1,241	1,125

Source: U.S. EPA 1985a, Table VIII-7c.

includes the transition to an unleaded car fleet. Thus, there are fewer cars using leaded gasoline over time, which lessens the impact of a reduction in the lead content of leaded fuel.

The second benefit, health and environmental effects related to other pollutants, were quantified in two different ways. The first method was a direct valuation: The EPA estimated the physiological responses to various doses and estimated and assigned dollar values to health and welfare endpoints. However, these values were deemed to be highly uncertain and did not include any values for some potentially important impacts (Nichols 1997). For example, the study considered only the effects of reductions in HC and NO_x, and omitted CO as a factor. Internal EPA offices had argued those effects were too uncertain to include in the analysis. The second method was an implicit valuation of the reductions, in which the EPA used the forgone expenses of repairing damaged catalytic converters to indicate a minimum value of preventing the pollution. Catalytic converters faced damage when individuals misfueled unleaded cars with leaded gas. The final estimates were based on an average of the two methods and totaled $222 million in 1986 (U.S. EPA 1985a).

The EPA also estimated benefits in the form of reduced maintenance costs and increased fuel economy. It estimated the maintenance benefits at about $0.0017 per vehicle mile, or an aggregate of about $900 million in 1986, along with additional fuel economy benefits of about $200 million per year (U.S. EPA 1985a).

Finally, the EPA included limited estimates of the proposal's effects on blood pressure. The RIA predicted that the policy would reduce the number of middle-aged men with hypertension by about 1.8 million in 1986 at a value of $220 per year per case of hypertension avoided (U.S. EPA 1985a). Also, the reduced hypertension would mitigate the likelihood of other cardiovascular afflictions. Based on a number of epidemiological studies, the estimates yielded benefits of $60,000 per heart attack and $40,000 per stroke avoided. Added to the benefits of reduced mortality rates, these figures result in total blood pressure–related benefits of over $5 billion each year from 1986 to 1988.

Projected Costs

The estimated costs of the rule include the cost to refiners of additional processing or the use of other additives to replace the fuel octane previously supplied by lead plus the lost consumer surplus due to higher gasoline prices. The results took into account the costs saved through the banking program. The additional processing costs (primarily from reforming or isomerization) totaled less than $100 million for the second half of 1985, under the 0.5 gplg standard (U.S. EPA 1985a). Under the 0.1 gplg rule, the projected costs fell over time from $608 million in 1986 to $441 million in 1992 due to projected declines in the demand for leaded gasoline in the absence of the new rule (Nichols 1997).

The RIA further predicted that refiners would achieve substantial cost savings through the innovative banking program. It estimated that refiners would together bank between 7.0 and 9.1 billion grams of lead in 1985, which would reduce the present value costs of the 0.1 gplg rule by between $173 and $226 million, or about 16 to 20 percent, depending on when refiners began banking (U.S. EPA 1985a). In actuality, refineries began banking immediately on being permitted to do so, in line with the higher cost-saving estimate. The RIA did not estimate the cost savings from allowing trading relative to a more prescriptive, uniform standards alternative.

At the time of the RIA, the average retail price of unleaded was about $0.07 per gallon higher than that of leaded. However, all other measures of the marginal value of lead in gasoline (i.e., wholesale prices, lead permit prices, and lead shadow prices) indicated the significantly narrower differential of less than $0.02 per gallon. The EPA believed the $0.07 figure was mainly a result of marketing strategies and that the $0.02 figure was more representative of real resource costs (Nichols 1997).

As an addendum to the RIA, the EPA also estimated the benefits and costs of a complete ban on lead in 1988—that is, moving from 0.1 gplg to no leaded fuel. A ban on leaded gasoline, the agency reported, would further reduce the number of children with toxic blood-lead levels by about 7,000 in 1988, prevent up to 100,000 more cases of hypertension among middle-aged men, and reduce heart-related fatalities by about 400 (U.S. EPA 1985b). The incremental cost to refiners of a complete ban was predicted to be $149 million, and the incremental benefits were placed between $193 million and $635 million (U.S. EPA 1985b). These results clearly provided justification for a ban on gasoline, but the EPA chose to wait to minimize the risk of damage to older engines (Nichols 1997). A ban was enacted in 1996, but by then virtually all lead had already been eliminated.

EX POST EVALUATION OF THE PHASEDOWN

In this section, we assess the performance of the lead trading system along several dimensions, including its overall effectiveness, static and dynamic efficiency, revelation of costs, and distributional effects that include environmental hot spots, regulatory and administrative burden, and monitoring requirements. We have made use of all information on program impacts that was available to us, although in some cases that information is admittedly incomplete.

Overall Effectiveness

Probably the most useful measure of the phasedown's effectiveness is the extent to which the regulations accelerated the reductions in lead consumption that were already being made thanks to the fleet turnover. The phasedown program, along with the turnover effects, achieved in 1981 what the fleet turnover alone would not have achieved until around 1987. From the start of the phasedown in 1979 to the completion of the marketable permit program in 1988, the regulations imposed on the refineries accounted for about 36 percent of the total gasoline lead reduction during that time, amounting to over half a million tons of lead that would otherwise have been emitted (Holley and Anderson 1989). The use of banking in the program further accelerated the lead reductions relative to what they would have been in the absence of banking.[5] Figure 7.2

illustrates the decline in total gasoline lead from 1970 onward, along with the concurrent decline in lead levels in the blood of children. The decline in blood lead levels is due largely to the phasing out of lead in gasoline between 1973 and 1995, but also to the reduction in the number of homes with lead-based paint (U.S. EPA 2003).

Static Efficiency

The static efficiency of the marketable lead permit program can be measured by the cost savings it achieved—that is, the difference in the costs to abate the same amount of lead under uniform standards versus the tradable permit policy. Unfortunately, the EPA collected no comprehensive data on permit prices, so this amount can only be estimated. Anecdotal evidence suggests that prebanking permit prices (i.e., under the 1.1 gplg standard) were typically under $0.01 per gram, and then rose significantly to $0.02–$0.05 per gram after the regulations were tightened in 1985 (Hahn and Hester 1989). Based on these figures, Hahn and Hester (1989) estimate that the marketable permit program saved hundreds of millions of dollars in abatement costs. Unfortunately, there are no other available estimates of the ex post cost savings from the program.

There are other indications that the tradable permit program allowed for lower costs than comparable uniform standards, most notably the fact that permits were traded at all. Assuming that refineries were not systematically shooting themselves in the foot, it follows logically that they traded permits because doing so saved money. Low-cost firms were able to abate a portion of their lead and sell the corresponding permits to high-cost refineries, realizing a net gain in revenues in the process. The high-cost refineries that bought the permits did so because the permit price was less than the cost for them to reduce the corresponding lead, allowing them to save money. Indeed, the lead rights market was very active in terms of volume of permits traded, and this activity increased as the trading program matured. Lead rights traded as a percent of all lead produced increased from around 7 percent in the third quarter of 1983 to over 50 percent in the second quarter of 1987 (Hahn and Hester 1989).

In addition, the mechanics of the marketable permit policy were such that transaction costs appear to have done little to inhibit permit trading (Kerr and Maré 1997). These costs could arise from firms having to establish their marginal value of lead, collect information on permit prices and find trading partners, collect information on the validity of the permits to be traded, negotiate permit quantities or prices (or both), and having to release potentially sensitive business information in the process of trading. Selling permits also meant parting with their option value, which would be important in the event of abatement cost shocks (Kerr and Maré 1997). This may imply that transaction costs are likely to be more burdensome for small refiners, as they lack the scale and resources that would keep these costs relatively low. Using econometric methods, Kerr and Maré (1997) estimate that more than 80 percent (and probably closer to 90 percent) of efficiency was achieved in the lead trading program—that is, close to 90 percent of trades that would have occurred absent any transaction costs still did occur with those costs, all else being equal. They find an efficiency loss of only 10 percent, owing to a failure to trade as a result of transaction costs.

Dynamic Efficiency

The banking program offered additional cost savings to participating refiners. This program allowed refiners to lower their overall costs of abatement by "smoothing out" their emissions over time. This was an important component for many firms, as their marginal cost schedules increased rapidly with increasing lead restrictions. This situation is evidenced by the fact that both large and small refiners produced lead in concentrations below the standards early in 1985, the year banking was introduced, implying that they were banking the difference. Both groups then exceeded the tighter standards in 1986 and 1987, when they used the saved permits to ease their transition to tighter standards. The EPA's ex ante projection that banking would save upward of $226 million probably turned out to be an underestimate, as the agency's figures assumed that 9.1 billion grams of lead would be banked, whereas 10.6 billion grams were actually banked, starting at the earliest possible date (Hahn and Hester 1989). There seems no doubt that the banking program saved hundreds of millions of dollars.

Kerr and Newell (2003) address dynamic efficiency in the context of the U.S. lead phasedown through their analysis of octane-enhancing technology (i.e., isomerization) adoption to replace lead. They investigated the influence of refinery characteristics (i.e., size of refineries or firms, technological sophistication), technology costs, and most important, regulatory variables, including regulatory stringency and form (e.g., tradable permits versus individually binding performance standards). They found a large positive response of lead-reducing technology adoption to increased regulatory stringency, indicating that the regulations were effective in providing incentives for dynamic changes in technology. In addition, they found a pattern of technology adoption across firms that is consistent with an economic response to market incentives, plant characteristics, and alternative policies.

Economic theory suggests that tradable permit programs create an incentive for more efficient technology adoption than uniform performance or technology standards—that is, they provide greater incentives for reducing abatement costs, including dynamically over time. Intuitively, the tradable permit system encourages all plants to take action until their marginal costs equal the permit price. Taking the price of permits as given, plants that have marginal costs below the market permit price (sellers) can capture even greater profits under the permit system (compared to a uniform standard) by adopting new technology that further reduces costs. This is in contrast to plants that have marginal costs above the permit price (buyers), for whom buying permits is a less costly option than installing the new technology. The incentives to adopt would thus be lower for buyers under the permit system than under uniform standards, because they could buy permits rather than being forced to self-comply with relatively expensive reductions (Malueg 1989).

Thus the tradable permit system provides incentives for more efficient adoption, but it can lower adoption incentives for some plants with high compliance costs.[6] Under a nontradable performance standard, such opportunities for flexibility do not exist to the same degree. If plants face individually binding standards, they will be forced to take individual action—such as technology adoption—regardless of the cost, with the resultant inefficiency reflected in a divergence across plants in the marginal costs of pollution control.

As suggested by theory, Kerr and Newell found a significant divergence in the adoption behavior of refineries with low versus high compliance costs under the tradable permit program. The positive differential in the adoption propensity of expected permit sellers (i.e., low-cost refineries) relative to expected permit buyers (i.e., high-cost refineries) was significantly greater under market-based lead regulation compared to under individually binding performance standards. Overall, their results are consistent with the finding that the tradable permit system provided more efficient incentives for technology adoption decisions.

To be clear, however, that research did not explore whether the market-based program resulted in *greater* technology adoption overall or greater incentives for new innovations. It is entirely possible, for instance, that a rigid uniform standard could lead to greater technology adoption because it forces all firms to individually comply. From the perspective of economic efficiency, however, the goal is not more technology adoption and innovations per se but minimization of the total costs over time of achieving a desired set of environmental and other objectives. From that perspective, the lead phasedown seems to have performed quite well.

Distributional Effects

Many very small refineries, with the highest cost structures, were inevitably eliminated from the market by the phasedown and other economic and regulatory forces, and the ones that did survive were more likely to become permit buyers than sellers. Empirical evidence, in fact, shows this to be true. Hahn and Hester (1989) report that net transfers of lead rights tended to be from large refiners to small ones (large refiners tending to have lower abatement costs than small ones). Small refiners had to purchase permits from large ones, incurring a transfer of private revenue from small refiners to large ones. Nevertheless, relative to a uniform performance standard, small refineries were better off under the tradable permit policy.

Environmental hot spots and spikes were not a significant concern in the case of lead emissions from automobile exhaust. The pollution is created through gasoline consumption, not production, and there is little relationship between the location of refineries and automobile exhaust across the country. Even if there existed a case where a local region was predominantly served by small refineries producing gasoline with relatively high lead content, it is not clear that a comparable standards-based policy would not have granted exemptions to small refineries, as they had done in the past. Thus prescriptive instruments had no clear advantage over market-based incentives with respect to hot spots and spikes of atmospheric lead from gasoline.

Monitoring and Administrative Burden

The EPA delegated the responsibilities of data collection and assimilation to the refiners themselves, which then reported their figures to the agency. The agency set up a computer system, which processed refinery reports to detect inconsistencies and probable inaccuracies. Participating refiners had to report their quarterly lead rights transactions, including trade volumes and the names of trading partners; refiners who used the banking option were also required to report deposits and withdrawals. All of the information required by the reports was readily available to the refiners, so the added costs of monitoring were relatively low (Holley and Anderson 1989). Figures on lead usage were checked against sales figures of additive suppliers. Gasoline volume was not as easily monitored as lead, however, and more enforcement cases involved misreported output than misreported lead use. Although the marketable permit program may have required monitoring a greater quantity and variety of information than a prescriptive policy would have, the collection of this information was fairly straightforward and inexpensive. The actual design of the rule was fairly simple: The agency had only to establish the desired lead concentration and review refiners' reports regarding their lead usage, gasoline production, and any averaging.

Nonetheless, the administrative burden of the lead permit program on the EPA was considerable relative to what it might have been if the system had been based on the allocation and trading of discrete emission units (e.g., grams of lead), such as in the U.S. SO_2 permit system. Rather, the system was based on averaging among refineries of lead content per unit of output, which meant that lead credits could in effect be created by producing gasoline. Had the system been based on the allocation of discrete emission units (e.g., grams of lead), there would not have been an ability to create lead credits by increasing gasoline production. This also might not have been a significant issue if the EPA had more narrowly or more carefully drawn the boundaries on participants in the program. But it did not, which gave rise to the entry of a large number of unexpected small entities who were primarily in the business of creating lead credits.

In the end, the output-based averaging basis of the marketable permit system created substantial monitoring and enforcement problems for the EPA (Holley and Anderson 1989).

The most significant problem was related to the unexpected creation of a quasi-industry of alcohol blenders, which were mainly large service stations that added alcohol to leaded fuel. In doing so, these blenders lowered the average lead content of the aggregate volume of fuel, thereby generating lead credits that could be sold in the permit market to other refineries. This approach to compliance was made possible by the fact that the lead performance standard was measured as a ratio to output, and there were few restrictions on who could participate in lead trading.[7] By the beginning of 1985, there were 300 blenders reporting permit trades, and within a year that figure had doubled. This was a significant increase on top of the expected reports from about 250 traditional refineries. The EPA's rules considered the blenders to be in effect refineries, and the agency's enforcement and monitoring mechanisms treated them as such. Thus, the unexpected inflow of 600 additional lead production/trading reports significantly slowed the monitoring and enforcement processes.[8] Although it was the output-based nature of the program that gave rise to incentives for these participants to enter, the problem might have been controlled by limiting the universe of potential participants, as with the Title IV NO_x program, which also includes an averaging provision but is limited to a clear set of electricity generation units.

To make matters worse, the reporting blenders were relatively disorganized, and their reports to the EPA were replete with errors, causing problems with the agency's report-processing system. During the time that the reports were being manually processed, invalid permits might have been sold or even resold, and financially unstable market participants might have disappeared before their violations were ever detected (Holley and Anderson 1989).

Detection of such problems is likely to have been inhibited by the documentation necessitated by the averaging approach, because demonstrating and monitoring compliance becomes increasingly complex as the number of parties engaged in transactions with one another increases. That is, if two refineries average only with one another, it is reasonably straightforward to demonstrate that the average standard is met. But if either or both of these refineries averages with other refineries as well, the lead input and gasoline output of all the refineries is necessary to demonstrate compliance of any of the parties. And if any of these elements is found to be incorrect, the compliance of all parties is potentially called into question, and it may not be exactly clear who has legitimate versus illegitimate lead credits. Layer on top of this the ability to bank and it quickly becomes clear that problems could emerge, especially if some parties are short-lived or are careless in their reporting. Individually binding refinery standards would likely not have experienced many of these enforcement problems.

Independent of the blender problem, the lead permit program gave rise to a number of other administrative and enforcement issues. The most common violations were:

- Self-reported excess lead usage;
- Failure to report regulated activities as required;
- Incorrect report indicating compliance, but where the average lead usage per gallon is actually above the standard due to using more lead or producing less gasoline than was reported (either of these raises lead content per gallon);
- Failure to include shipments of imported gasoline in reports;
- Falsifying banked rights;
- Changes in accounting systems resulting in the disappearance of lead that should have been accounted for; and
- Claiming lead rights based on fictitious production.

Because lead credits were fully fungible, and because false credits could be traded several times before being discovered by the EPA, tracing invalid rights to their source proved very difficult (Holley and Anderson 1989). The EPA had expected most of the violations to be committed by a small number of large refiners and planned its enforcement policies accordingly. But it turned out that most of the violations were in fact committed by a fairly large number of small refiners with small amounts of lead rights to which the existing enforcement mechanics were less easily applied.

In 1985, with the increased stringency of the standard and the introduction of the banking program, the EPA therefore began to perform audits of suspect refineries. Up to this point, the agency had detected violations through inconsistencies and inaccuracies in refinery reports, resulting in seventy-one notices of violation with proposed penalties totaling $17.8 million through 1986 (Holley and Anderson 1989). After the agency started auditing, it issued seventeen notices of violation in 1987 alone, with proposed penalties topping $54 million. In some settlement cases, refiners were presented with the option of retiring a portion of their lead rights instead of paying direct financial penalties. Refiners who chose this option relinquished some 150 million grams of lead pollution rights (assuming those permits would have been used), representing an estimated value of about $40 million in 1983 dollars (Holley and Anderson 1989).

Holley and Anderson suggest that the relatively high level of enforcement activity through audits brought about a reduction in noncompliance. They point to the trend that as the EPA devoted an increasing amount of resources to audits and as the number of audits performed increased, the number of noncompliance cases decreased. But despite the agency's success in detecting many violations through audits, it was partly the flexible nature of the agency's marketable permit approach that increased the likelihood of administrative difficulties and violations. It is possible much of this could have been avoided, however, by establishing a trading system with fixed rather than output-based allocations, or by simply limiting the universe of market participants to traditional refiners. On the other hand, such restrictions can limit the potential for unforeseen opportunities for low-cost mitigation. In addition, one of the reasons the definition of a refinery was written so broadly was apparently to prevent loopholes.

LESSONS LEARNED FROM THE LEAD PHASEDOWN

One can draw several lessons from the U.S. experience with phasing the lead out of gasoline. Most important, the program demonstrated that a tradable permit system could be effective in meeting its environmental objectives. The phasedown from 1979 to 1988 accelerated the virtual elimination of lead in gasoline by at least a few years, reducing by 1988 an additional half-million tons over what the fleet turnover would have achieved. The banking component further demonstrated that environmental objectives can be met more quickly under a permit system with banking than if banking is not allowed.

The marketable lead permit system also established that a given environmental target could be met more cost-effectively through trading and banking, saving hundreds of millions of dollars relative to comparable uniform standards not allowing trading or banking. The banking program itself saved over $225 million because it allowed for a more cost-effective allocation of technology investment within the refining industry. The lead phasedown experience also showed that transaction costs do not necessarily cripple tradable permit programs, with estimates suggesting that transaction costs brought about only a modest reduction in the efficiency of the market-based program.

Evidence also suggests that the market-based nature of the lead permit program provided incentives for more efficient adoption of new lead-removing technology, relative to a uniform standard. The pattern of technology adoption under this program was consistent with an economic response to market incentives and plant characteristics. As theory contends, there was a significant divergence in the adoption behavior of refineries with low versus high compliance costs. Expected permit sellers (i.e., low-cost refineries) significantly increased their adoption of new technology relative to expected permit buyers (i.e., high-cost refineries) under market-based lead regulation compared to under individually binding performance standards.

Distributional effects are always high in political importance, with the lead phasedown demonstrating that the use of market-based instruments can be consistent with addressing distributional concerns. It is likely that the lead permit program was actually more responsive to the high costs of small refiners than comparable uniform standards would have been. Another key worry about tradable permit programs, environmental hot spots, was shown not to be a significant concern in this case, although it certainly could be with some localized pollutants.

Unfortunately, basing the lead program on a system of averaging lead per unit output, without sufficient constraints on program participation, increased the incidence of both intentional and unintentional violations, especially on the part of smaller refiners and fuel blenders. This added an unexpected administrative burden to the EPA's existing monitoring and enforcement costs and in some cases was associated with outright fraud. Individually binding performance standards would likely not have had these problems, although the problem could likely have been avoided by basing the program on the allocation of discrete emission units or by more carefully restricting the ability of entities to participate in the program. On the other hand, there was likely to have been efficiency advantages to the participation of unexpected program participants, which serves as a reminder that one of the advantages of flexible, incentive-based programs is that they provide opportunities and incentives for unanticipated means of cost-effective compliance. In the end, the introduction of an effective audit and enforcement programs was crucial.

Overall, the benefits of the U.S. lead phasedown are likely to have outweighed its costs ten to one, with lead trading and banking significantly lowering those costs. But the lead phasedown did not involve only a tradable permit system. It also relied heavily on the transition to a new unleaded car fleet, mandated by the requirement to use unleaded fuel in cars with catalytic converters. A similar story can probably be told for most major environmental problems, where technology standards, performance standards, and other approaches are used in tandem with economic incentives.

ACKNOWLEDGMENTS The authors thank Dan Balzer, Denny Ellerman, and Winston Harrington for assistance on earlier drafts of this chapter.

NOTES

1. Octane is a characteristic of fuel components that improves the performance of engines by preventing fuel from combusting prematurely in the engine. The availability of high-octane fuel allows more powerful engines to be built. Cars will not operate efficiently with a lower octane fuel than that for which they were designed. In addition, some older cars may need more than a minimum level of lead (less than 0.1 grams of lead per gallon) to prevent a problem called valve seat recession.

2. As described in Nichols (1997), lead emissions from gasoline are linked to elevated blood-lead levels, which are associated with significant health effects, especially in the case of young children. In sufficiently high doses, lead can cause severe retardation and sometimes even death. Moderate to high blood-lead levels are sufficient to negatively effect cognitive performance in children, though the magnitude of cognitive effects due to low-level lead exposure are still disputed. In addition, studies have suggested that elevated blood-lead levels are associated with increased blood pressure and hypertension rates in middle-aged adults. Lead

in gasoline can also raise maintenance costs by causing salt corrosion in an automobile's engine and exhaust system, causing damage to the muffler, spark plugs, and other components.

3. It is relevant to note that this coincides in time with the removal by the Reagan administration in 1981 of remaining petroleum price and allocation controls, which had originally been established during the 1970s in response to the Arab oil embargo. Small refineries had received favorable treatment under these programs and in response the number of refineries had swelled from 268 in 1973 to 324 in 1981, with the bulk of these refineries being small (U.S. EIA 1990). With removal of the allocation controls, the number of refineries fell back to pre-embargo levels within two years.

4. After an initial analysis of achieving the standard by 1988, in which the benefits easily outweighed the costs, the EPA proposed the even closer deadline of January 1, 1986. The following presents estimates from the RIA for the later proposal.

5. Although it is true that one could imagine a traditional regulatory standard that simply forced reductions earlier to coincide with the pattern of reductions under the banking provisions, this is not the appropriate counterfactual in this case. When the proposed regulations for accelerating the phasedown were issued, the banking provision was treated as an independent option, treated separately from the averaging scheme and the phasedown schedule. The final banking rule was in fact issued as a separate regulation.

6. Whether any of these policies provide incentives for fully efficient technology adoption depends on a comparison with the social benefits of technology adoption and the usual weighing of marginal social costs and benefits.

7. *See* Helfand (1991) for an assessment of the incentives given by alternative designs of regulatory standards.

8. On the other hand, there was likely to have been efficiency advantages to the participation of blenders in lead compliance, because they apparently offered a cost-effective means to reducing lead content. This serves as a reminder that one of the advantages of flexible, incentive-based programs is that they provide opportunities and incentives for unanticipated means of cost-effective compliance.

REFERENCES

Hahn, Robert W., and Gordon L. Hester. 1989. "Marketable Permits: Lessons for Theory and Practice." *Ecology Law Quarterly* 16: 380–91.

Helfand, Gloria E. 1991. "Standards versus Standards: The Effects of Different Pollution Restrictions." *American Economic Review* 81(3): 622–34.

Holley, John, and Phyllis Anderson. 1989. *Lead Phasedown—Managing Compliance.* Draft Internal Report, Appendix A. Field Operations and Support Division, Office of Mobile Sources, U.S. EPA.

Kerr, Suzi, and David Maré. 1997. *Transaction Costs and Tradable Permit Markets: The United States Lead Phasedown.* College Park: University of Maryland.

Kerr, Suzi, and Richard G. Newell. 2003. "Policy-Induced Technology Adoption: Evidence from the U.S. Lead Phasedown." *Journal of Industrial Economics* 51(3): 317–43.

Malueg, D. A. 1989. "Emission Credit Trading and the Incentive to Adopt New Pollution Abatement Technology." *Journal of Environmental Economics and Management* 16(1): 52–57.

Nichols, Albert L. 1997. "Lead in Gasoline." In *Economic Analyses at EPA: Assessing Regulatory Impact*, edited by Richard D. Morgenstern. Washington, DC: Resources for the Future, pp. 49–86.

U.S. EIA (Energy Information Administration). 1990. *The U.S. Petroleum Refining Industry in the 1980s.* DOE/EIA-0536. Washington, DC: EIA.

U.S. EPA (Environmental Protection Agency). 1985a. *Costs and Benefits of Reducing Lead in Gasoline: Final Regulatory Impact Analysis.* EPA-230–05–85–006. February. Washington, DC: EPA Office of Policy Analysis.

U.S. EPA. 1985b. *Supplementary Preliminary Regulatory Impact Analysis of a Ban on Lead in Gasoline.* February. Washington, DC: EPA Office of Policy, Planning and Evaluation.

U.S. EPA. 2003. *America's Children and the Environment.* Washington, DC: EPA.

8

Cost Savings from Allowance Trading in the 1990 Clean Air Act: Estimates from a Choice-Based Model

Nathaniel O. Keohane

INTRODUCTION

Title IV of the Clean Air Act of 1990 represented a major innovation in environmental policy in the United States. Before 1990, clean air regulations for electric power plants in the United States were exclusively prescriptive in nature—requiring individual units to meet strict performance standards or even install particular abatement technologies. Title IV took a much different tack: It instituted a market for sulfur dioxide (SO_2) emissions. Utilities affected by the regulation were allocated a certain number of allowances, with each allowance representing one ton of SO_2 emissions. Utilities that reduced their emissions could sell their excess allowances to other utilities or bank them for future use.

Economists have long asserted the virtues of such market-based environmental policies over traditional prescriptive or command-and-control regulation, such as performance or technology standards. In theory, market-based instruments are *cost-effective*: That is, they can achieve a given level of abatement for the least possible total cost.[1] Title IV offers the first major test of how a market-based instrument can perform in practice.

Overall, this grand policy experiment (Stavins 1999) has been overwhelmingly successful to date. After a slow start, allowance trading has been vigorous. The utilities' ability to bank allowances, meanwhile, led to deeper than expected cuts in emissions during Phase I with concomitant environmental benefits.[2] Surprisingly, however, a consensus has yet to emerge on the actual cost savings realized from the allowance market. Expectations of cost savings certainly ran high before the program began. Studies done in the early 1990s by the General Accounting Office and by the Environmental Protection Agency (EPA) anticipated cost savings between \$250 and \$470 million annually during Phase I (cited in table 10.8 of Ellerman et al. 2000). The two major ex post analyses of cost savings from allowance trading, however, have reached opposite conclusions. Carlson, Burtraw, Cropper, and Palmer (2000; henceforth *CBCP*) find that the costs of abatement during Phase I were *higher* than they would have been under prescriptive regulation. On the other hand, a study by Ellerman, Joskow, Schmalensee, Montero, and Bailey (2000; henceforth *MCA* after the title of their volume, *Markets for Clean Air*) estimates that the use of allowance trading led to savings of hundreds of millions of dollars per year.

This chapter offers a comprehensive assessment of the cost savings over the first five years of the allowance trading program. The current study has two methodological advantages over the previous ones. The first is the completeness of the data used. Like the two previous studies, this study estimates scrubber costs from costs reported in survey data, although the current study is able to use cost data from the full five years of Phase I. The data on coal prices used here are much more detailed than that in the other two studies, allowing for plant-level estimates of sulfur premia and counterfactual sulfur content.

The second and more significant advantage of the current study is methodological. I employ an econometric model of the abatement choices actually made by utilities to simulate the decisions that *would have been* made under prescriptive regulation. Thus abatement costs under counterfactual policies are estimated on the basis of observed behavior under actual policy regimes, rather than on the basis of engineering estimates or least-cost algorithms.

Using observed behavior to estimate costs is critical for two reasons. First, it allows for a warts-and-all comparison of policies as they would have been implemented, rather than comparing an actual outcome with an idealized counterfactual. Indeed, because I can estimate the idealized outcomes as well, the model demonstrates the importance of taking compliance behavior into account in estimating the consequences of policy choice.

Second, this approach incorporates differences in the incentives provided by policy regimes for the adoption of abatement technologies. Market-based instruments in theory offer regulated firms greater incentives to install technologies with low marginal costs (Downing and White 1986; Milliman and Prince 1989; Kerr and Newell 2003). In the context of sulfur dioxide regulation, this effect implies that the decisions made by utilities whether to install scrubbers should differ systematically by policy regime (Keohane 2004). Thus an explicit model of decision making under different policy instruments also accounts for differences in how those policy regimes reward the adoption of low-marginal-cost methods of pollution control.[3]

As a starting point, I use the econometric choice model to generate a baseline scenario corresponding to predicted outcomes under the actual policy. I focus on the set of units that were required to participate in the allowance market—the Table A units, named after the table that listed them in the legislation. Aggregate abatement at Table A units under the baseline scenario is 4.2 million tons annually, and abatement costs total $747 million per year. These model predictions accord closely with estimates of abatement and cost based on actual choices.

The richness of my data and the flexibility of the econometric model allow me to compare the actual policy with a wide range of counterfactual scenarios. My central comparison is between the baseline scenario and a counterfactual uniform emissions rate standard that would have achieved the same total amount of abatement among all units that were required to participate in the trading program. I estimate that under such an emissions standard the aggregate costs of compliance would have been $153 million greater during each year of Phase I—an increase of 20 percent over the model's baseline prediction. This estimate corresponds to cost *savings* of 17 percent. I estimate a similar percentage increase in costs for a more stringent emissions standard calibrated to the abatement actually achieved among all Phase I units, including voluntary participants.

Other plausible prescriptive policies would have been even costlier. I estimate that costs would have been 25 percent higher under source-specific emissions limits pegged to the allowance allocations under Title IV (and scaled to achieve the same 4.2 million tons of abatement as under the baseline scenario). Because this scenario mimics actual allowance allocations without allowing trading, it represents an alternative pure measure of the gains from trade.

Costs would have been astronomically high under a technology-forcing policy requiring utilities to install scrubbers—soaring by $1.8 billion per year. The enormous increase in estimated cost under a technology standard relative to a performance standard underscores the importance of giving polluters flexibility in how to reduce emissions.

As a final assessment of alternative real-world policies, I estimate the additional abatement attributable to the allowance market, relative to a performance standard with the same aggregate cost. Computing the pollution savings in this way involves the obverse of the cost savings question usually asked; in some ways it is more relevant to policy debates. It is also a novel contribution of this study, because it requires a model that can predict abatement costs and choices under a variety of counterfactual scenarios. I estimate that the trading program achieved 10 percent more abatement during Phase I than could have been realized by a uniform standard with the same total cost.

My econometric model relies on observed abatement choices to predict what would have happened under alternative policy regimes. Alternatively, one can assess the performance of the allowance trading system against two theoretical benchmarks that assume least-cost compliance at every unit. First, I estimate the theoretical minimum cost of abating 4.2 million tons to be $315 million/year. The wide gap between this figure and the baseline cost estimate suggests that the choices actually made by managers did not minimize costs, at least over the span of Phase I. Thus although the allowance market achieved considerable cost savings over alternative policies, it appears—not surprisingly, perhaps—to have fallen short of its theoretical potential.

In its examination of pollution control decisions and its comparison of market-based policies with conventional prescriptive regulation, this chapter is heir to a line of comparative studies that thrived in the 1970s and early 1980s (e.g., Atkinson and Lewis 1974; Seskin et al. 1983; Kolstad 1986; Krupnick 1986). These studies compared actual or imminent prescriptive air pollution regulation with hypothetical market-based regimes. The Title IV allowance trading program, along with two decades of prescriptive regulations involving the same pollutant from the same types of sources, allows a comparison of marked-based and prescriptive policy instruments that is grounded in actual experience with both.

Note that this chapter focuses exclusively on the costs of abatement, rather than net benefits. Estimates of overall net benefits from the Title IV program have been overwhelmingly positive (e.g., Burtraw et al. 1998). Burtraw and Mansur (1999) and Shadbegian et al. (2004) study the net benefits of trading relative to a counterfactual command-and-control alternative, taking into account the distribution of emissions reductions and resulting environmental benefits.

The next section briefly reviews the regulatory context for the current study. Then I describe the econometric analysis used to generate the baseline scenario representing the performance of the actual tradable permits regime. The fourth section compares the baseline scenario with the range of alternative outcomes. Then I compare the results from this study with the findings in *CBCP* and *MCA*. The sixth section concludes.

REGULATION OF SULFUR DIOXIDE EMISSIONS

Emissions regulations apply at the level of the generating unit—that is, an individual electric turbine, powered by steam produced by an associated boiler burning coal or another fuel. A typical power plant will have more than one unit—usually two or three and sometimes a half-dozen or more, often built at different times and thus subject to regulations of different form and stringency. The primary means of reducing sulfur dioxide emissions are installing end-of-pipe devices called flue-gas desulfurization units (better known as scrubbers) and switching to fuel with lower sulfur content.

Federal regulation of SO_2 emissions from power plants began under the Clean Air Act amendments (CAAA) of 1970. Generating units built after August 17, 1971, were subject to New Source Performance Standards (NSPS), which imposed a maximum allowable emissions rate of 1.2 pounds of SO_2 per million Btus. In response to concerns from coal interests and environmentalists, Congress strengthened these regulations in the Clean Air Act amendments of 1977.[4] Starting in September 1978, new generating units were required not only to meet the existing emissions rate of 1.2 lbs/mmBtus but also to do so by removing a certain percentage of SO_2 from the flue gases—a de facto scrubbing requirement.

By the late 1980s, growing concern over acid rain (to which SO_2 emissions are a major contributor) led Congress to consider imposing regulations on the power plants built before 1971, which had been grandfathered out of the earlier federal regulations. The result was the allowance trading program provision of Title IV. Phase I of the program lasted from 1995 to 1999. It applied directly to the 263 largest, dirtiest existing generating units, listed on Table A of the legislation. In addition, utilities that owned Table A units could voluntarily enroll other generating units in the allowance market during Phase I. This "substitution and compensation" provision, however, invited adverse selection: Units that chose to enroll would almost certainly have reduced their emissions anyway (Montero 1999). Phase II of the program started in 2000 and extended the allowance market to every fossil-fired power plant greater than 25 MW in generating capacity.

Alongside this federal regulatory structure exists a patchwork of emissions standards imposed by state governments, who must comply with federal National Ambient Air Quality Standards (NAAQS). Because power plants are a prominent source of air pollution, they are natural targets of state regulation. These state-level regulations are always prescriptive in nature; for the most part, they specify unit-level maximum allowable emissions rates.[5]

This chapter seeks to use observed behavior to generate counterfactual estimates of what abatement and cost at Table A plants would have been under alternative policies. By definition, all of the Table A units were built decades before the allowance market took effect. Similarly, nearly all units regulated at the state level were built before the passage of air pollution laws. For all these units, therefore, scrubbers had to be retrofitted onto the existing boilers. Retrofitting a unit is more costly than building the scrubber and boiler simultaneously. Moreover, the decision whether to retrofit an old boiler is likely to differ in fundamental ways from the decision whether to build a scrubber at a newly constructed unit. Hence I restrict attention to retrofitted units only, and leave the NSPS units out of the analysis entirely.[6]

THE MODEL OF TECHNIQUE CHOICE AND THE BASELINE SCENARIO

The Choice of Abatement Technique

Econometric Model

The simulation of counterfactual policies is based on the econometric model of technique choice under different policy regimes presented in

Keohane (2004). The model has two stages. In the first stage, scrubbing costs are estimated with a maximum-likelihood Heckman model (Heckman 1974). This approach controls for potential selection bias by estimating a model of scrubber choice simultaneously with scrubber costs. This approach provides consistent estimates of what scrubber costs would have been at units that did not install them. In the second stage, these predicted scrubbing costs are entered into a probit model of the scrubbing decision, along with predicted price premia for low-sulfur coal and a number of other explanatory variables.

My interest in the choice estimation here is purely instrumental: The goal is to predict the choices that utilities would have made under counterfactual policies. Accordingly, I simply summarize how the costs were estimated and then briefly report the results from the probit choice model. The reader interested in the full choice model is referred to Keohane (2004).

In that analysis, average scrubbing cost (in dollars per ton of SO_2 abated) is modeled as a log-linear function of the nameplate capacity of the unit (MW of electricity at maximum output); the capacity factor, or percent utilization of the unit; the sulfur content of the coal used (expressed for convenience in the emissions rate that would result from burning the coal unabated); annual heat input (in millions of British thermal units, or Btus);[7] a dummy variable for units that share a stack, along with interactions between that dummy and measures of generating capacity and heat consumption on the common stack; the vintage of the scrubber; a dummy variable for the boiler type (specifically, whether the boiler has a wet bottom); and a dummy variable for the north Atlantic region, where anecdotal evidence suggests that construction and even operating costs are systematically high. Finally, the model interacts the log of sulfur content with the log of vintage and nameplate capacity. The average cost of scrubbing is estimated simultaneously with the decision to have a scrubber (described in the next paragraph), and the estimated coefficients employed to predict scrubbing cost at all units.

The scrubber decision is then estimated by probit, as a function of the estimated cost of scrubbing relative to the cost of switching to low-sulfur coals, taking into account a range of other factors. The decision of whether to install a scrubber is modeled as taking place at a particular point in time, corresponding to the year in which the scrubber would have first operated.[8] The primary measure of the cost of switching to low-sulfur coal is the estimated price premium for low-sulfur coal relative to the cheapest available coal at a given unit. Because transportation costs make up a large fraction of the delivered price of coal, the premium for low-sulfur coal varies widely among power plants. Units that lack a viable source of low-sulfur coal are accounted for by an indicator variable, as are units that were already burning low-sulfur coal at the time of the scrubber decision.[9]

I also include a range of other factors: applicable state-level emissions regulations; a dummy variable for units that were already burning low-sulfur coal at the time of the scrubber decisions; a dummy variable for plants located adjacent to a coal mine; a dummy variable for plants larger than the median plant; a dummy for Table A units located in states that enacted rules to encourage scrubbing, as determined by Lile and Burtraw (1998); and (for Table A units) the number of other Phase I units under common ownership, which reflects the scope of interutility trading. For Table A units, I also include the expected sulfur content in five years' time and the extent of long-term contracts, as reported by the power plants five years before the beginning of Phase I. Finally, to account for the differences in policy regimes, I also include a dummy for Table A status and interact it with several of the variables in the choice equation. In particular, I allow the scrubbing cost, low-sulfur coal premium, performance standard, and plant size variables to vary with the policy regime.

Data

Data for the estimation are discussed in more detail in Keohane (2004). They are drawn from two primary sources. Form EIA-767, an annual survey of electric power plants administered by the Energy Information Administration (EIA) of the Department of Energy (DOE), provides data on unit-level operation, including the costs and operating performance of scrubbers, the amounts and characteristics of coal burned, and applicable state and federal emissions regulations. I use these data to estimate emissions and abatement at the unit level.[10]

The second principal data source is FERC Form 423, a survey of fuel purchases at power plants conducted by the Federal Energy Regulatory Commission. I supplement these coal delivery data with plant-level information on transportation options and actual rail and barge distances to coal districts. By regressing coal prices on rail and barge distances and plant characteristics, I am able to estimate coal prices at every plant in the data for a variety of coals, and thus can estimate price premia for low-sulfur coal even at plants that purchase only one type of coal. The low-sulfur coal premium used in the choice model represents the difference between the predicted price of the cheapest available coal and that of the most attractive low-sulfur coal. Moreover, the estimated prices of low-sulfur coal take into account the costs of adjusting existing boilers to burn coal with lower sulfur.[11]

The entire data set includes observations on 846 units, of which 247 were listed on Table A and thus subject to the tradeable permits regime. Table 8.1 gives summary statistics. In these data, average scrubbing costs are actual costs for units with scrubbers. For units without scrubbers, I use the *predicted* scrubbing costs from the first-stage Heckman model. Finally, for the handful of units with scrubbers that lack cost data, I use the predicted scrubbing cost, conditional on having a scrubber.

Table 8.1 Summary Statistics for Scrubber Choice Estimation

Variable	Mean	SD	Minimum	Maximum
State-regulated units				
(599 units, 41 scrubbed)				
Est. avg. scrubbing cost ($/ton)	2166.62	8171.79	77.95	159753.9
Price premium for low-sulfur				
coal (cents/mmBtus)	12.72	12.59	0	97.90
Low-S coal infeasible	0.03	0.18	0	1
Minemouth location	0.03	0.17	0	1
Already burning low-sulfur coal	0.10	0.30	0	1
SO_2 emissions standard				
(lbs/mmBtus)	2.87	1.81	0.1	9.5
Large plant	0.53	0.49	0	1
Table A units				
(247 units, 27 scrubbed)				
Est. avg. scrubbing cost ($/ton)	729.94	923.70	173.60	8156.07
Price premium for low-sulfur				
coal (cents/mmBtus)	16.81	16.16	0	96.40
Low-S coal infeasible	0	0	0	0
Minemouth location	0.09	0.29	0	1
Already burning low-sulfur coal	0.03	0.18	0	1
SO_2 emissions standard				
(lbs/mmBtus)	4.95	1.84	1.2	12
Large plant	0.52	0.50	0	1
Large Table A plant	0.41	0.49	0	1
Expected sulfur content in 5 yrs	1.29	1.02	0	4.1
Pct. of coal under long-term contract	0.28	0.39	0	1.84
Capital-intensive statutory bias	0.57	0.49	0	1
Number of commonly owned				
Phase I units	19.29	16.31	1	59

Results

Table 8.2 presents the estimated coefficients from the choice model.[12] Overall, units were significantly less likely to install scrubbers when scrubbing was relatively expensive. Moreover, variation in average scrubbing cost had a much greater effect for units governed by the tradable permits regime. As discussed in Keohane (2004), this finding is consistent with the theoretical literature on the incentives for technology adoption under various policy instruments. For Table A units, the probability of scrubbing also rises with the cost of low-sulfur coal, although the effect is weak. The estimates suggest that state-regulated units, however, are more likely to have a scrubber when low-sulfur coal is inexpensive—a perverse effect, albeit a weak one. Other measures of sulfur content and low-sulfur coal availability have the expected effects. A lack of feasible sources of low-sulfur coal increases the likelihood of scrubbing significantly, as does

Table 8.2 Results from Probit Estimation of Scrubber Choice

Dependent variable: Equals 1 if unit has scrubber

ln(Avg. scrubbing cost)	−0.705 ***
	(0.233)
ln(Avg. scrubbing cost) × Table A	−2.007 ***
	(0.627)
ln(Low-S price premium)	−0.228 *
	(0.135)
ln(Low-S price premium) × Table A	0.535
	(0.312)
Low-sulfur coal infeasible	3.489 ***
	(1.068)
Minemouth location	1.659 ***
	(0.478)
Already burning low-sulfur coal	−0.641
	(0.392)
ln(SO_2 performance standard)	−3.144 ***
	(0.469)
ln(So_2 performance standard) × Table A	3.067 ***
	(0.623)
Large plant	−0.157
	(0.264)
Table A unit	8.289 **
	(3.738)
Expected sulfur content in 5 yrs	0.682 ***
	(0.191)
Pct. of coal under long-term contract	−0.044
	(0.436)
Capital-intensive statutory bias	0.189
	(0.379)
Large Table A plant	−1.887 ***
	(0.609)
No. of commonly owned Phase I units	−0.027 *
	(0.015)
Constant	5.016 ***
	(1.754)
Number of units	846
Number of scrubbed units	68
Log likelihood	−81
Wald statistic χ^2 (16)	310
	($p < 0.001$)

Notes: * denotes significance at 10% level ** at 5% level *** at 1% level minemouth location. The expected sulfur content of coal is also a significant predictor of scrubbing, implying that units with readily available high-sulfur coal were more likely to scrub.

For units regulated by prescriptive regulation, scrubbing is much more likely when regulation is more stringent (thus the negative sign on $\ln(SO_2$ PERFORMANCE STANDARD$_i$)). The effect of performance standards vanishes for Table A units. This accords with expectations: Although Table A units remained subject to state-level emissions standards, those standards became less salient in the scrubbing decision than the allowance market was. Surprisingly, state biases toward capital-intensive compliance with Title IV have no discernible effect.[13] Finally, scrubbing is more likely at Table A units, all else equal, although this effect diminishes at larger plants.

Estimating Costs and Abatement under the Baseline Scenario

Methodology

I use the results from the choice estimation to predict scrubber choices under the allowance regime (see table 8.3). Predicted scrubbers are those for which the probit model assigns a probability of scrubbing greater than a certain cutoff. I used a cut point of 0.35, which maximizes the percentage of correct predictions among all units. This cut point also results in the

Table 8.3 Actual Scrubber Choices vs. Baseline Predictions

Panel A: Table A units

Baseline	Counterfactual		Total
	No	Yes	
No	213	7	220
Yes	7	20	27
Total	220	227	247

Panel B: State-regulated retrofitted units

Baseline	Counterfactual		Total
	No	Yes	
No	556	2	558
Yes	7	34	41
Total	563	36	599

Panel A compares actual scrubbers with scrubbers predicted by the baseline model at Table A units. For example, the cell in the "Yes" row and "Yes" column gives the number of units (20) that both actually have a scrubber and are predicted to have one in the baseline scenario. Panel B presents the same comparison for retrofitted units governed by state-level emissions standards.

same number of predicted scrubbers as actual scrubbers, among the 247 Table A units included in the choice model. The model correctly predicts 823 out of 846 choices (97 percent).[14] I shall refer to this set of predictions as the baseline scenario. Using the baseline scenario as the basis of comparison with other policies, rather than the actual choices, ensures internal consistency in my estimates.

For units whose predicted and actual choices coincided, baseline emissions are set equal to actual emissions. For units that actually installed scrubbers but are not predicted to have done so by the model, baseline emissions are equated to unconstrained (i.e., gross) emissions. For units that were predicted to have scrubbers but did not actually install them, baseline emissions were computed using the average operating removal rate among Table A units, which was 91 percent.[15]

To estimate the *abatement* attributable to Title IV requires an estimate of what emissions would been in the absence of any federal regulation on Table A units—that is, the business-as-usual (BAU) outcome. BAU emissions are computed by multiplying an estimate of each unit's unconstrained emissions rate by a counterfactual estimate of the unit's heat input, absent Title IV. As an estimate of the unconstrained emissions rate for scrubbed units, I simply use the sulfur content of the coal actually burned, because that is presumably the cheapest coal available. For unscrubbed units, the sulfur content of the cheapest available coal (as determined by the same coal price regressions used to estimate low-sulfur coal premia, as already discussed) is taken as a benchmark rate in determining a unit's unconstrained emissions. I use the emissions rate in 1992 (i.e., just in advance of any changes made in anticipation of Title IV) when that rate is less than the benchmark rate *and* the state emissions standard is nonbinding (meaning that the estimated cheapest available coal would satisfy it). Finally, I use the observed average emissions rate during Phase I, when that is greater than the benchmark rate. Thus my approach relies on actual choices to the extent possible.

As demonstrated in *MCA*, heat input rose at Table A units that installed scrubbers as well as those that were close to the Powder River basin (PRB); meanwhile, it fell at other Table A units (relative to non–Table A units). To account for these effects of regime, scrubbers, and location, I estimate a fixed-effects regression on panel data for 1985–99 for 820 units, regressing annual heat input on unit-level fixed effects, year effects, dummies for each Phase I year, total state electricity demand in each year, scrubber status (by itself as well as interacted with a dummy for the Phase I period and another for Table A units during Phase I), and a dummy variable indicating that coal from the PRB is estimated to be the cheapest available coal (again, entering by itself as well as interacted with Table A status).[16] The predicted BAU heat input is computed from these coefficients by setting the scrubber dummy and all the Table A variables equal to 0. Multiplying this heat input by the corresponding BAU emissions rate results in total BAU emissions of 8.56 million tons.

Predicted emissions at the unit level account for the effects of scrubbing on heat input, using the fixed-effects regression just described. For example, predicted heat input exceeds actual heat input at units that are predicted to have scrubbers but did not actually install them. Predicted abatement is then the difference between BAU and predicted emissions.

The estimated cost at units without predicted scrubbers is simply the low-sulfur coal premium used in the choice model, expressed per ton of SO_2, multiplied by predicted abatement conditional on not having a scrubber. Estimating abatement cost at units predicted to have scrubbers requires two further adjustments. First, for units with binding state regulations, the abatement cost due to Title IV is estimated as the total cost of scrubbing minus the cost of meeting the state regulation by burning low-sulfur coal. Doing so accounts for the abatement costs that units would have incurred in the absence of Title IV, while recognizing that scrubbers would not have been used simply to meet existing state standards. Second, I add the estimated cost of "parasitic power loss"—that is, the electricity used by the scrubber. Parasitic power loss accounts for roughly 5 percent of total average scrubbing costs. It is computed by multiplying reported electricity usage by the average wholesale electricity price for the parent utility. For units without scrubbers, I use the average percentage of parasitic power loss among scrubbed units and then use the units' own electricity prices.

Baseline Estimates

Table 8.4 summarizes aggregate outcomes predicted by the model, along with estimates based on actual choices. The set of units includes the 247 units in the choice model, plus one more: Yates Y1BR, which is excluded from the choice model because it was a demonstration unit partially funded by the DOE and designed to test a scrubber on a unit burning relatively low-sulfur coal.

Total emissions among the 248 Table A units in the baseline scenario are 4.33 million tons per year (see the third entry of the first row of the table). Aggregate abatement under the baseline scenario is 4.23 million tons. The estimated cost of this abatement is $747 million annually, in constant 1995 dollars. As table 8.2 shows, the baseline estimates corresponding to predicted scrubbing choices agree well with estimates based on actual choices, presented in column (2). The model slightly understates emissions and overstates abatement, but the difference is less than 1 percent. Baseline abatement cost is even closer to estimated cost.

The table also compares the baseline and actual emissions estimates to emissions as measured by Continuous Emissions Monitoring Systems (CEMS) that utilities were required to install on their stacks under Title IV. Column (1) of table 8.4 shows the average annual emissions based on the CEMS data for 1996–99. Measured emissions are nearly 200,000 tons (4 percent) higher than my estimates, which are based on mass-balance

Table 8.4 Comparison of Key Outcomes: Actual Estimates versus Baseline Scenario

Variable	(1) Actual (Measured)	(2) Actual (Estimated)	(3) Baseline (Predicted)	(4) Difference (3)–(2)	(5) Percentage Difference
Average annual aggregate emissions (000 tons)	4513	4302	4331	−29	−0.7%
Average annual aggregate abatement (000 tons)	—	4260	4231	29	0.7%
Average annual aggregate Abatement cost (1995 $ millions)	—	751	747	−4	−0.5%

Notes: Column (1) presents actual measurements of emissions (for years 1996–99). Columns (2) and (3) both present *estimates.* "Actual" refers to the scrubber choices.) Column (4) shows the difference between the actual estimates and the baseline predictions, and column (5) shows that difference in percentage terms (relative to the actual estimates). All comparisons are among the 248 Table A units only (247 in probit estimation + Yates Y1BR, which was omitted from the probit for reasons explained in the text).

calculations (as explained in note 8). At the unit level, the correlation between the CEMS data and my estimates is 0.97.

Figure 8.1 illustrates the close correspondence between the baseline prediction and the estimates based on actual choices. Each curve represents what might be called a quasi-marginal-abatement-cost (quasi-MAC) curve. Each step corresponds to a single Table A unit: The height represents the average cost of abatement (given the actual or predicted scrubber choice), and the width of the step represents abatement. With the Table A units arranged in order of average abatement cost, the resulting graph shows how aggregate abatement cost increases with the amount of abatement done.[17] These are not true marginal cost curves; they are *conditional* on the set of actual or predicted choices (which may not have been cost-minimizing), and they end at total abatement (4.2 million tons) by construction. They are best seen as descriptions of the distribution of abatement costs among units: The flatter the curve, the more similar are per ton abatement costs across a range of units.

THE COST SAVINGS FROM TITLE IV

In this section I estimate the cost savings from Title IV, relative to a range of alternative plausible policies. I start by comparing the predictions in the baseline scenario to a uniform performance standard that would have achieved the same aggregate emissions and abatement among Table A units. This comparison measures the savings due to trading alone, because the performance standard would have allowed individual units flexibility in determining *how* to abate. In other words, it estimates of the

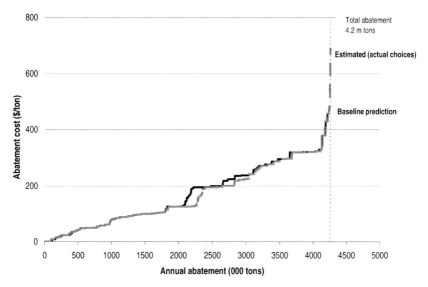

Figure 8.1. Baseline and Estimated Quasi-Mac Curves

gains from a market-based policy, relative to what some observers (such as *CBCP*) call enlightened command-and-control.

Following this central comparison, I estimate abatement costs under a range of other counterfactual scenarios. The first three alternatives represent plausible prescriptive policies that could have been enacted in place of the allowance market: a uniform standard tied to total Phase I abatement (including that by units that participated voluntarily), a set of source-specific standards tied to Table A allowance allocations, and a technology standard requiring most firms to install a scrubber. I also estimate the abatement achieved by a uniform performance standard with the same cost as the baseline, to derive an alternative measure of the gains from trading. Finally, I estimate the costs of two theoretical benchmarks—the cost-effective outcome and the minimum cost of meeting a uniform emissions standard. These scenarios provide an alternative yardstick with which to measure the performance of the actual policy.

Comparisons with Performance-Based Standards

Uniform Emissions Rate Standard: Table A Abatement

The counterfactual uniform standard is chosen so that the aggregate abatement predicted by the counterfactual scenario for all Table A units equals the aggregate abatement among the same units under the baseline scenario. I assume that such a federal standard—like actual standards—would not have superseded more stringent state regulations where they exist. Thus under the counterfactual uniform emissions rate scenario, each Table A unit is assigned an emissions rate standard equal to the minimum of its actual state-imposed regulation and 2.3 lbs/mmBtus. This particular standard yielded the closest fit with predicted baseline abatement, among the set of all emissions rate standards in increments of 0.01 lbs/mmBtus. By comparison, the benchmark emissions rate under Title IV, embodied in the basic allowance allocation rule, was 2.5 lbs/mmBtus; and even this was more stringent than the eventual reality, because the benchmark rate did not incorporate the numerous bonus allowances granted during Phase I. More abatement was done than was required to meet the cap, largely due to the effect of banking, as has been documented in detail in *MCA* and elsewhere.

The coefficients from the probit estimation of scrubber choice (table 8.2) were then used to generate predicted choice probabilities, conditional on the counterfactual regime. The actual emissions standard for each unit was replaced with the counterfactual emissions standard; coefficient estimates for state-regulated units were used for scrubbing and switching costs and for the emissions standard (i.e., the interaction terms with Table A status were dropped); and the coefficients on Table A status, Table A plant size, and capital-intensive bias were dropped.[18] The premium for low-sulfur coal was also reestimated, taking the counterfactual standard into account; thus low-sulfur coals with sulfur content above the standard (which might profitably have been burned under Title IV) were dropped from each unit's choice set. A unit was predicted to have a scrubber under the counterfactual if its predicted choice probability exceeded the cut point of 0.35.

Importantly, my model allows units with scrubbers to overcomply with the uniform standard, just as they actually do (Oates et al. 1989). Each unit without a scrubber was assigned a predicted removal rate based on observed behavior at actual scrubbed units subject to state regulations.[19] An alternative would be to assume that units governed by a prescriptive regulation meet it exactly. Estimating removal efficiencies as a function of observed characteristics is attractive not only because it more faithfully mimics observed behavior but also because it better matches the econometric estimates of scrubber cost, which are based on actual patterns of scrubber utilization.

Table 8.5 provides an overview of the scrubber choice predictions from the simulation. The number of units predicted to install scrubbers decreases slightly under the emissions standard, falling from twenty-seven under the baseline scenario to twenty-four under the counterfactual. Of the twenty-four counterfactual scrubbers, fifteen have scrubbers under the baseline (of which fourteen actually have scrubbers).

Table 8.6 compares the model predictions for aggregate abatement and cost under this counterfactual policy with the estimates from the baseline scenario. By construction, emissions and abatement are nearly identical under the two scenarios. The predicted annual aggregate abatement cost is considerably greater under the uniform emissions rate standard, however. The estimated increase in cost is $153 million per year—an increase

Table 8.5 Predicted Scrubber Choices under Baseline
           Scenario and Uniform (Table A) Emissions
           Standard

	Counterfactual		
Baseline	No	Yes	Total
No	212	9	221
Yes	12	15	27
Total	224	24	248

of 20 percent over the baseline scenario. Equivalently, the tradable allowances regime resulted in cost savings of 17 percent relative to a uniform emissions rate standard.

Figure 8.2 compares the quasi-MAC curves under the baseline and
counterfactual scenarios. The same caveats apply as in figure 8.1. Recall
that these curves are drawn conditional on a particular set of choices and
thus on a particular policy. In particular, unlike a true marginal cost
curve, they do *not* provide a direct estimate of what marginal or total costs
would have been at a lower level of abatement (such as 3 million tons).
For the same reason, the prescriptive regulation curve does not necessarily
lie everywhere below the baseline cost curve. (On the other hand, the total
areas under the curve do correspond to the total costs of abatement.)

Nonetheless, the curves are informative. At the low end of abatement
costs, the distribution of units is similar in the two policy scenarios. Units
that would find it relatively inexpensive to meet a standard would, by the
same token, find it attractive to abate under the tradable allowances regime. As costs increase, however, the distributions of abatement costs

Table 8.6 Comparison of Key Outcomes: Baseline versus PR Counterfactual

	(1)	(2)	(3)	(4)
	Baseline	PR Counterfactual	Difference	Percentage
Variable	(Predicted)	(Predicted)	(PR–Baseline)	Difference
Average annual aggregate emissions (000 tons)	4331	4332	1	0.0%
Average annual aggregate abatement (000 tons)	4231	4230	−1	−0.0%
Average annual aggregate abatement cost ($millions)	747	900	153	20%

Notes: This table compares aggregate outcomes predicted by the baseline scenario with outcomes
under the prescriptive regulation (PR) counterfactual with a Table A abatement target. All
comparisons are among Table A units only.

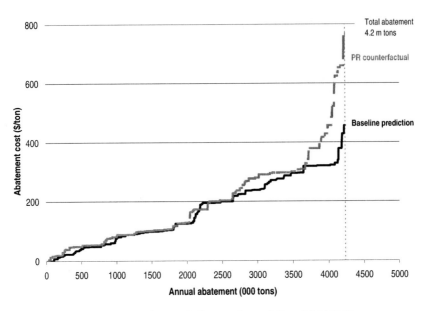

Figure 8.2. Baseline and Counterfactual Quasi-MAC Curves

diverge. Units with high unconstrained emissions and relatively high costs of abatement can opt to buy allowances under the tradable allowances system and would choose to do so once abatement costs rose above the allowance price. At the same time, units that do abate under the tradable allowances system have incentive to abate more than under the standard. Thus per ton abatement costs are driven much higher under the emissions standard as cumulative abatement increases, driving up the total cost of abatement.

A More Stringent Counterfactual: Matching Phase I Abatement

The assumption of an abatement target tied to reductions at Table A units is conservative, because it excludes abatement that was achieved by units that opted into Phase I voluntarily. To assess the sensitivity of my results to the abatement target, I reestimate the model using a Phase I abatement target that requires predicted abatement among Table A units to equal the estimated abatement achieved among *all* Phase I units. This Phase I uniform standard of 2.21 lbs/mmBtus accounts for emissions reductions that were accomplished by voluntary units as well as those directly subject to the regulation.

Table 8.7 summarizes the key results. The total annual abatement cost under the counterfactual is now estimated to be $162 million higher than under the baseline. Of course, the baseline cost has also risen, because it now represents the total abatement cost among all Phase I units. Hence in percentage terms, the difference is similar to that for the Table A abatement

Table 8.7 Comparison of Key Outcomes: Baseline versus PR Counterfactual
(Phase I Abatement Target)

Variable	(1) Baseline (Predicted)	(2) PR Counterfactual (Predicted)	(3) Difference (PR–Baseline)	(4) Percentage Difference
Average annual aggregate Abatement (000 tons)	4417	4413	−4	−0.1%
Average annual aggregate abatement cost ($millions)	779	941	162	21%

Notes: This table compares aggregate outcomes under the baseline scenario and the alternative prescriptive regulation counterfactual, in which abatement is scaled to total Phase I abatement. Thus the baseline estimate aggregates abatement and abatement cost across all 312 Phase I units in the sample. The PR counterfactual, in contrast, sums over Table A units only.

target. The cost increase is 21 percent of the baseline (Phase I) costs, corresponding to cost savings of 17 percent.

Unit-Specific Emissions Standards

An alternative counterfactual policy is a set of source-specific emissions limitations. Although prescriptive regulation at the federal level has generally taken the form of uniform standards, state-level regulation commonly involves source-specific standards. Moreover, allowance allocations varied widely among units, so that the application of the actual policy was far from uniform.

The simplest approach would limit emissions at each Table A unit to that unit's allowance allocation under Table A.[20] The estimated costs of such an approach turn out to be 3 percent *less* than in the baseline scenario. However, this cost savings arises only because abatement falls by 600,000 tons, or 14 percent. This drop in abatement, of course, reflects the substantial permit banking that took place during Phase I. Had Table A units used up their full allocations, abatement would have been considerably less during Phase I than it actually was.

A more useful counterfactual for comparison with the actual policy is a set of standards that achieves the same estimated level of abatement as under the baseline. Accordingly, I scale the Table A allocations by a uniform factor (= 0.89) to achieve 4.2 million tons of abatement. In some respects, this scenario affords a purer measure of the gains from allowance trading. By controlling for the different abatement responsibilities assigned to different units, these source-specific standards isolate the cost savings that were due to trading, conditional on the initial assignment of abatement responsibility. Under this scenario, total estimated abatement costs are $930 million—an increase of $183 (25 percent). The cost savings from the allowance market, relative to this no-trading scenario, amounted to 20 percent. These results are summarized in table 8.8.

Note that total abatement cost under this counterfactual is $30 million *greater* than the total cost under a uniform standard. This is surprising at first blush: To the extent that nonuniform standards take into account (marginal) abatement costs, they should result in lower total costs than a uniform standard. The disparity demonstrates the extent to which the allowance allocations were motivated by distributional politics rather than efficiency. Allowance allocations under Title IV were determined not by a cost-minimizing regulator but by an explicitly political process, as detailed by Joskow and Schmalensee (1998). The higher estimates of compliance costs suggest that the political process resulted in a negative correlation between abatement cost and allowance allocations: Units that could abate more cheaply tended to receive more allowances. Of course, one of the well-known attractions of tradable allowances as a policy instrument is that the equilibrium outcome—and thus the aggregate abatement cost—is robust to the initial allocation, as long as transactions costs are low.[21] Thus the allowance allocations might well have been different (since their distributional implications would have been so) if a different policy instrument had been chosen.

Comparison with a Technology-Based Counterfactual

Next, I contemplate a technology standard achieving the same aggregate abatement as the baseline scenario. This comparison provides a direct estimate of the cost savings from a market-based policy relative to what might be termed *unenlightened* command-and-control. Consider a policy requiring units with unconstrained emissions above 2.5 lbs/mmBtus to

Table 8.8. Comparison of Key Outcomes: Baseline versus Source-Specific Standards

Variable	(1) Baseline (Predicted)	(2) PR Counter-factual (Predicted)	(3) Difference (PR–Baseline)	(4) Percentage Difference
Average annual aggregate emissions (000 tons)	4331	4334	3	0.1%
Average annual aggregate abatement (000 tons)	4231	4228	−3	−0.1%
Average annual aggregate abatement cost ($millions)	747	930	183	25%

Notes: This table compares aggregate outcomes predicted by the baseline scenario with outcomes under the prescriptive regulation counterfactual with source-specific standards pegged to Table A allowance allocations and scaled to a Table A abatement target. All comparisons are among Table A units only.

install scrubbers. (Under this counterfactual policy, units whose cheapest available coal would meet or beat the 2.5 lbs/mmBtus emissions rate standard would not be required to install a scrubber or indeed even to abate at all.) I then apply a uniform percentage-removal requirement to these units, chosen to yield the aggregate abatement target. This counterfactual policy is modeled on the actual NSPS in the 1977 CAAA. Because it exempts units with unconstrained emissions below 2.5 lbs/mmBtus, it represents a relatively low-cost technology standard. Moreover, note that (unlike the 1977 NSPS) this technology standard is constructed to achieve the same amount of abatement as under the baseline scenario. I estimate that such a technology requirement would have cost $2.6 billion annually—an increase of $1.8 billion over than the baseline scenario. This represents a more than threefold increase in abatement cost. Judged against this alternative, the tradable allowances system yielded cost savings of 71 percent.

Of perhaps equal interest is the comparison between this technology standard and the uniform performance standard discussed. Both achieve the same aggregate abatement, and both represent prescriptive regulation imposed at the unit level. The crucial difference is that the performance standard allows units the choice of how to comply. The estimated savings from increased flexibility are enormous: $1.7 billion per year, or 65 percent of the costs under the scrubbing requirement.

This comparison—between enlightened and unenlightened command-and-control regulations—underscores the relative importance of regulatory flexibility versus trading per se. Though the allowance market yielded sizable gains relative to a uniform performance standard, those gains are less than one-tenth the size of the estimated gains from regulating emissions rather than technology. In other words, allowing intraunit flexibility in compliance was much more significant than allowing interunit flexibility, although both yielded substantial cost savings. In this respect, my findings accord with arguments made early in the allowance trading program by Burtraw (1996).

"Pollution Savings" as an Alternative Measure of Gains from Trade

Thus far I have equated aggregate abatement and compared the resulting costs. Next, I return to the uniform performance standard counterfactual—but rather than matching aggregate abatement with the baseline predictions, I match aggregate abatement *cost*. Doing so provides an alternative measure of the gains from a market-based policy: namely, the increased abatement made possible by the allowance trading system, relative to an equally costly prescriptive regulation.

This measure of pollution savings (rather than cost savings) may be more relevant from a political perspective, because increasing environmental protection may be more rhetorically compelling than reducing cost. Certainly this is the more salient strategic question for environmental advocacy groups. Hahn and Stavins (1991), for example, describe the role of the Environmental Defense Fund (EDF) in proposing and supporting the use of tradable allowances in Title IV. Such market-based environmental policies had previously been anathema to environmentalists. The EDF, however, argued that the cost savings from such an approach would make possible greater cuts in emissions. In essence, the EDF supported the Bush administration's favored market-based proposal in return for a more ambitious target for SO_2 abatement than the administration would have otherwise contemplated.

My model suggests that a uniform performance standard of 2.47 lbs/mmBtus would have matched the cost of the actual outcome. I estimate that such an equal-cost policy would have resulted in 3.8 million tons of abatement—400,000 tons less than the baseline scenario. Thus the use of the market-based instrument resulted in an increase in abatement of roughly 10 percent.

Interestingly, this pollution savings based on equal-cost outcomes is considerably smaller, in percentage terms, than the cost savings estimated on the basis of scenarios with equal abatement. Though the current model provides only a single instance, there is reason to believe that this asymmetry is general. It results from the different effects of an increase in abatement on total costs under different policy instruments. At lax levels of a standard, many regulated units can comply by burning low-sulfur coal of varying sulfur content. As the stringency of a standard increases, some sources of low-sulfur coal no longer satisfy the standard, forcing units that would otherwise burn low-sulfur coal to install scrubbers instead. This effect intensifies as the standard tightens further, so that total costs rise more than proportionally with abatement. Under a market-based instrument, on the other hand, much of an increase in abatement can be achieved by units with relatively low costs. Though tightening the overall cap drives permit prices up, this results in a smoothly increasing incentive to install a scrubber, rather than the kind of threshold effect created by a performance standard that requires all units to reduce emissions. As a result, costs rise less steeply with abatement, relative to the case of prescriptive regulation.

Hence the relative cost savings of a market-based instrument are higher, the more stringent the abatement target. A direct implication is the asymmetry found: The percentage increase in abatement achieved by a market-based instrument, relative to a performance standard with equal cost, will be less than the percentage increase in cost under a performance standard relative to a market-based instrument with equal abatement.

Theoretical Benchmarks

Thus far, I have assessed the allowance market against plausible alternative policies. I can also ask: How well did the tradable allowances program perform relative to what theory would predict? Two natural benchmarks stand out for comparison. The first is the cost-effective outcome. With the considerable benefit of hindsight, what is the minimum total cost for which baseline level of abatement could have been achieved?

I estimate the cost-effective outcome to be $315 million annually—less than half the baseline cost. This suggests that the allowance market fell far short of what theory predicts. Of course, there are a range of explanations for why units may not appear to have minimized abatement costs during Phase I. For example, abatement decisions in the first few years of the program may have been made with an eye toward Phase II, when allowance allocations were ratcheted down. In particular, some investment in scrubbers may have been motivated by longer time horizons. Pessimistic expectations about market liquidity could also have given rise to scrubbing decisions that turned out not to be optimal.[22]

Indeed, ample evidence suggesting that utilities overinvested in scrubbers during Phase I. Ellerman and Montero (1998) argue that an abundance of scrubbers (due partly to inflated expectations about allowance prices) contributed to the downward pressure on allowance prices during Phase I, along with lower than expected prices of low-sulfur coal from Wyoming. In the data set used in the present study, average total costs of scrubbing at Table A units with scrubbers are clustered between $200 and $450 per ton—higher than actual Phase I allowance prices but lower than published forecasts of allowance prices. These data suggest that scrubbing decisions may have been individually rational given ex ante expectations; but because those expectations turned out to be wrong, the scrubbers that were installed did not minimize costs ex post.

Whatever the reason for the failure of utilities to behave as perfect cost minimizers during Phase I, it is evident in the disparity between the theoretical least-cost outcome and the baseline estimate. Even allowing for considerable uncertainty in the least-cost estimate, the magnitude of the gap suggests that the actual market fell well short of theoretical cost-effectiveness. From a methodological point of view, this result underscores the importance of taking actual behavior into account, rather than assuming perfect foresight and cost minimization by unit managers.

The second theoretical benchmark is an ideal prescriptive regulation scenario, in which predicted abatement decisions at the unit level are made to minimize abatement costs, subject to compliance with a uniform standard.[23] This scenario is no more realistic than the cost-effective outcome, because it assumes perfectly rational (and foresighted) utility managers. Nonetheless, it remains useful as the appropriate behavioral analog to the theoretical least-cost scenario. The estimated cost under this scenario is $546 million annually.

The difference in costs between the ideal prescriptive regulation scenario and the least-cost outcome provides a second measure of the gains from trade—one based on theoretical cost-minimizing behavior, rather than on predictions of what would have occurred under alternative policies. Figure 8.3 illustrates the comparison. The top curve, corresponding to the ideal prescriptive regulation, is conditional on the choice of

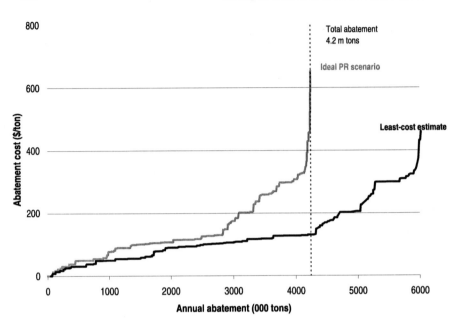

Figure 8.3. Theoretical MAC Curve and Ideal CAC Quasi-MAC Curve

emissions standard. The least-cost estimate (the lower curve) is now a true marginal cost curve, because it assumes cost minimization; thus it extends beyond actual total abatement. The area between the two curves, up to the total abatement of 4.2 million tons, represents the theoretical cost savings from trading—$231 million annually, or 42 percent of the costs under the ideal prescriptive regulation.

Table 8.9 summarizes the abatement cost estimates under six of the scenarios just discussed, relative to the baseline prediction. The central comparison with the counterfactual corresponding to a uniform emissions standard and a Table A abatement target is in bold.

COMPARISONS ACROSS STUDIES

The bottom three rows of table 8.7 present the cost savings from Title IV estimated by the two major prior studies, MCA and CBCP.[24] A glance at the table shows considerable agreement among the three studies with respect to the baseline cost estimates. The estimated cost *savings*, however, are strikingly different among the three studies. The MCA study estimates cost savings of $358 million to $626 million annually, and CBCP estimate that compliance costs under the actual policy were 10 percent *greater* than they would have been under a performance standard.

Two differences are worth noting about the data used in the present study. First, I have restricted attention to Table A units, on the grounds that because those were the units directly identified by Congress for

Table 8.9 Summary of Estimated Cost Differences Due to the Policy Regime

Scenario	(1) Baseline Scenario ($ millions)	(2) Counter-factual ($ millions)	(3) Cost Difference (2)–(1)	(4) Cost Increase (3)/(1)	(5) Cost Savings (3)/(2)
This study					
Theoretical cost-effective outcome	747	315	−426	−57%	−135%
Least−cost compliance with PR standards	747	546	−201	−27%	−37%
Uniform emissions rate standards	**747**	**900**	**153**	**20%**	**17%**
Uniform standards (Phase I target)	779	941	162	21%	17%
Unit−specific emissions standards	747	930	183	25%	20%
Technology standards (forced scrubbing)	747	2555	1808	242%	71%
Prior studies					
CBCP[a]	871	790	−81	−9%	−10%
MCA (Phase I actual abatement)[b]	735	1361	626	85%	46%
MCA (Phase I req. abatement)[c]	167	525	358	214%	68%

Notes: All costs are expressed in millions of 1995 dollars per year.
[a]Average estimates for 1995–96 in table 3 of *CBCP*, p. 1318.
[b]Estimates for cost savings from spatial trading *plus* banking, per Phase I year (*MCA*, p. 281).
[c]Estimates computed from areas underneath Phase I MAC and CACC curves in figure 10.5 of *MCA*, p. 278.

regulation, they are the natural group to perform on which to counter factual analysis. Both the *MCA* and *CBCP* analyses, in contrast, comprise all affected units—that is, voluntary Phase I participants as well as Table A units. Second, this study draws on data from all five years of Phase I. *CBCP* used only the first two years, and *MCA* used actual data for 1995–97 and extrapolated to the remaining two years in estimating Phase I averages. This is relevant because the number of voluntary participants declined during each year of Phase I; thus the sets of units used by *CBCP* and *MCA* are both larger than the set of Phase I units that participated throughout the program.[25] This change in the number of units affected also argues in favor of focusing on the Table A units, which were required to participate throughout the program.

The difference in the units considered, however, does not explain the large differences in estimated cost savings. The difference in approach is reflected in the counterfactual estimates as well as in the baseline scenario. Moreover, I have already shown that in percentage terms the choice of baseline has little effect on the estimated cost savings. And the greatest divergence is between the *MCA* and *CBCP* estimates, which rely on the same set of units (and nearly the same years of data).

In the remainder of this section, I examine the *CBCP* and *MCA* estimates more closely. The sources of the differences are varied, but two stand out. First, the two studies compare the actual policy to counterfactual scenarios that differ in subtle but crucial respects from each other and from that used here. Second, the *MCA* group—lacking a direct means of estimating the costs of prescriptive regulation—employs a short cut that appears benign but in fact leads them to overstate the cost savings from Phase I by nearly a factor of two.

Comparison with *CBCP*

The striking result in *CBCP* is that costs were higher during the first few years Phase I than they would have been under an equivalent command-and-control scenario. The authors cast their finding in strong terms: "The fact that our estimate of actual compliance costs exceeds our estimate of the cost of command and control suggests that the uniform performance standard would have been no less efficient than the actual pattern of emissions chosen by utilities" (p. 1318). Their finding has been similarly interpreted by other analysts, such as Ellerman (2003). *CBCP* attribute their surprising finding in part to their focus on the first two years of the program, when the allowance market was just getting under way. Their key argument, however, concerns the behavior of utilities under the allowance market. They write: "Adjustment costs associated with changing fuel contracts and capital expenditures as well as regulatory policies may make it appear that firms have failed to minimize costs when they have actually done so" (p. 1318).

A simpler explanation is that *CBCP* compare the actual policy to an idealized version of command-and-control. As in the present study, *CBCP* specify as their counterfactual a uniform emissions rate standard chosen to achieve an equivalent level of emissions as under the actual outcome. However, they assume cost-minimizing behavior by the utilities. The appropriate comparison with my estimates, therefore, is to my ideal prescriptive regulation scenario. Like *CBCP*, I estimate that the costs under such a scenario would have been lower than they were under the actual policy. Indeed, my estimate of costs under such a scenario is even lower (relative to actual costs) than the *CBCP* estimate.[26]

The importance of assumed behavior can also be seen in *CBCP*'s estimates of the long-run cost savings from trading. *CBCP* estimate gains from trade of $780 million in the final year of Phase II (2010), relative to estimated costs under prescriptive regulation of $1.8 billion. In making this long-run comparison, of course, *CBCP* assume cost-minimizing behavior under *both* policy regimes. Note that their estimated long-run cost savings amount to 43 percent of the costs under the counterfactual policy. This is virtually identical (in percentage terms) to the difference between the ideal prescriptive regulation and cost-effective scenarios I considered earlier, which incorporate the same assumption about decision making.

CBCP adopt the assumption of cost-minimizing behavior because it is theoretically and practically attractive: It accords with economic reasoning, and it can easily be implemented by a least-cost algorithm. But the assumption of cost minimization skews their results, because they end up comparing an idealized version of one policy with the actual implementation of another. There is considerable irony in CBCP's assertion that the allowance market was more costly (in the short run) than prescriptive regulation would have been. When the early articles in this line of literature were written, prescriptive regulation was the norm, and the counterfactual policies were market-based. In that context, it was the cost savings from trading programs that were inevitably overstated.

In summary, my data confirm CBCP's finding that abatement costs under the allowance market were higher than they would have been under a uniform standard with cost-minimizing behavior. But that is not really the right benchmark for comparison. Using actual behavior by electric utilities under other policy regimes as a guide, a prescriptive approach would also have ended up costing much more in practice than one would predict on the basis of cost-minimizing behavior. A consistent approach compares the costs under the actual program with the costs that a performance standard would actually have entailed.

Comparison with MCA

Of the three studies, MCA calculates the largest cost savings from the allowance market—estimating that trading saved $358 million per year of Phase I. The dramatically higher cost savings are not due to differences in abatement or baseline cost estimates. MCA estimates actual abatement to have been 4.2 million tons, identical to the estimate in this study, and the estimated baseline abatement cost of $735 million is very close to my estimate. Rather, these high cost savings can be attributed to how the MCA group calculates costs under the command-and-control counterfactual.

To understand this point, it helps to consider their methodology. An important contribution of the MCA study is its conceptualization of the cost savings attributable to trading. MCA partitions cost savings into the gains from spatial trading and those from intertemporal trading. The gains from spatial trading represent the reduced costs of achieving *required* (rather than actual) abatement through the allowance market, relative to a counterfactual prescriptive regulation. Gains from intertemporal trading result from overcompliance in early years, with the extra abatement banked for Phase II. Indeed, the $358 million figure represents only the first of these types of savings. If the intertemporal savings from Phase I abatement are credited to the first phase of the program as well, the MCA estimate of total cost savings rises to $626 million annually.

In contrast, the approach taken in the body of this chapter (as well as by CBCP) compares the costs of *actual* abatement with the estimated costs of reaching the same level of abatement under a counterfactual scenario. The appeal of this latter approach is that it can be estimated on the basis of actual data, rather than requiring extrapolation about future costs (i.e., costs under either policy regime in Phase II). The strength of the *MCA* approach, on the other hand, is that it explicitly addresses the dynamic nature of the allowance program. The drawback is that to do so it must rely on conjectures about costs during Phase II.

To identify the cost savings from spatial trading, *MCA* first estimates the abatement that was effectively required by Phase I of the program— that is, the difference between the total number of allowances and what emissions would have been in the absence of regulation. *MCA* estimates required abatement for all Phase I units together to be 2 million tons annually. Using actual data, *MCA* then estimates a linear quasi-MAC curve corresponding to the tradable allowances regime.

The actual policy is compared to a particular counterfactual scenario: a set of source-specific standards based on actual allowance allocations and summing to required abatement. To estimate costs under this counter-factual, the *MCA* group assume that actual behavior under the allowance market was cost-minimizing, allowing them to infer that costs under the counterfactual would have been at least as high. Under the additional assumption of a linear relationship between cumulative abatement and average cost at the marginal unit, they posit a linear command-and-control cost curve (with much the same interpretation as the quasi-MAC curves drawn in figures 8.1–3). The area between the posited command-and-control cost (CACC) curve and the quasi-MAC curve under the actual policy corresponds to the estimated cost savings from spatial trading of $358 million.

The derivation of the CACC curve turns out to be the source of the very high estimate of cost savings. To demonstrate this, I first use my model to estimate the costs of achieving required abatement among Table A units via a set of source-specific standards based on Table A allocations. That required abatement was 2.25 million tons annually.[27] The increase in required abatement relative to the *MCA* estimate stems from the fact that I focus on Table A units only, rather than all Phase I units. Although it might seem paradoxical at first, the abatement required of Table A units *exceeded* the abatement required of the larger set of all Phase I units. The reason is simple: In the absence of Title IV, emissions at units that partici-pated in Phase I voluntarily would have been less than the allowances those units were allocated. This gap, between required abatement at Table A units and that at all Phase I units, neatly demonstrates the adverse selection problem (and the resulting loosening of the cap) created by the opt-in program (Montero 1999).

I estimate the total costs of exactly meeting the 2.25 million tons requirement to be $346 million annually. The cost of achieving the same amount of abatement under the baseline was $165 million. Thus the estimated cost savings of achieving required abatement under the allowance market, on the basis of my model, was $181 million—just half of the $358 million estimated in *MCA*.[28] Figure 8.4 plots the Phase I CACC and MAC curves used in *MCA* along with the quasi-MAC curves corresponding to my estimates of the costs under the baseline scenario and under the required-abatement counterfactual.[29]

For the actual policy, the linear approximation used by *MCA* coincides reasonably well with my estimated quasi-MAC curve. Thus, as the *MCA* group point out, the linearity assumption has only a small effect on estimated costs under the baseline. Their CACC curve, however, diverges significantly from my econometrically based estimate. In figure 8.4, the area under the linear CACC curve (up to 2.25 million tons) is $664 million—much greater than the $346 million represented by the area under the curve estimated by my model. Far from being linear, the actual curve is rather flat at first and then turns sharply up. This shape is not accidental: It is driven by the wide variation in abatement costs under prescriptive regulation. As argued, the quasi-MAC curve is best thought of as representing the distribution of abatement costs under a particular policy. Because units must comply with a performance standard even if it is very costly, the highest cost units under such a policy are likely to have very high costs indeed, even while costs at the low end of the distribution may correspond closely with costs under the tradable allowances regime.

Of course, a linear approximation to the actual quasi-MAC curve exists that will preserve the area below it. One might alternatively identify the

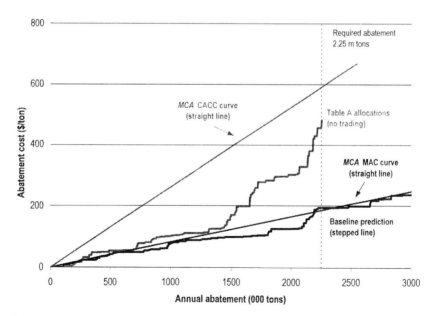

Figure 8.4. Quasi-MAC Curves under the Baseline and Required Abatement Scenarios, along with a Comparison with the Curves in *MCA*

particular linear approximation selected by *MCA* as the source of the inflated estimate of cost savings. Regardless of how I frame the argument, figure 8.4 makes clear that the curve they posit has a dramatic (and unappreciated) effect.

The strength of the *MCA* approach is that it takes into account the intertemporal equilibrium. To preserve this strength while correcting for their ad hoc estimate of costs under prescriptive regulation, I replicate their analysis drawing on the data used here. Figure 8.5 presents the same four curves as in figure 10.3 of *MCA*, drawn to match the data here. The stepped Phase I curves correspond to my model estimates; the straight lines correspond to linear approximations that preserve the area underneath the curves.[30] As the *MCA* group points out, if one assumes that observed Phase I abatement reflected optimal intertemporal behavior by utilities, then the cost of the last ton of abatement during Phase I should equal the abatement cost at the margin during Phase II. Accordingly, as in *MCA*, I have drawn the Phase II MAC curve as a straight line from the end of the Phase I curve down to a right-hand origin. The horizontal distance equals the total allowances available during Phase II, averaged over the five years of Phase I (yielding 15.04 million tons, as in *MCA*).[31] Finally, continuing to follow the approach taken by *MCA*, the Phase II CACC (line O_2D) in figure 8.5 is drawn so that the ratio of its slope to that of the Phase II MAC equals the ratio of the slopes of the linear approximations to the corresponding Phase I curves (1.64). This embodies an assumption that the ratio of prescriptive regulation costs to costs under the trading regime is constant over time.

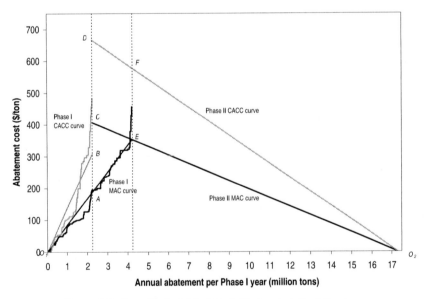

Figure 8.5. Two-Period Model of Abatement Cost Savings

I can now compute the various types of cost savings. Annual cost savings from spatial trading during Phase I—the area between the Phase I curves to 2.25 million tons—amount to $181 million, as already discussed. Annual cost savings from banking correspond to the area below the Phase II quasi-MAC and above the Phase I quasi-MAC, computed over the 1.98 million ton difference between required and actual abatement. This gain is $169 million for each year of Phase I. Alternatively, using the straight-line approximations to the Phase I curves yields estimated cost savings of $134 million for spatial trading (area O_1AB) and $216 for banking (area ACE). The effect of the straight-line approximations is to increase the cost savings from spatial trading by $47 million and reduce the cost savings from banking by the same amount. This smoothing results because the linear approximation lies above the cost curve at low levels of abatement and below it at higher levels.

These estimated cost savings from abatement during Phase I are well below the corresponding figures in *MCA*. The $169 million in gains from banking, for example, is nearly $100 million less than *MCA*'s estimate of $268 million per Phase I year. Overall, the combined estimated cost savings from spatial and intertemporal trading during Phase I equals $350 million—somewhat over half the corresponding *MCA* estimate of $626 million.

Following *MCA*, I can also use figure 8.5 to estimate cost savings during Phase II. In particular, the area of triangle O_2CD corresponds to the spatial trading gains during Phase II. This area is $2.0 billion per Phase I year. Assuming (with *MCA*) that the allowance bank will be exhausted in 2007, this estimate represents an annual cost savings of $1.2 billion for each of those eight years—far below the *MCA* estimate of $2.1 billion.

In fairness, any estimate of cost savings must rely on a particular choice of counterfactual. What the comparison in this section highlights is the importance of that choice. Indeed, in a thorough sensitivity analysis, *MCA* shows that their estimates of the gains from trading are most sensitive to the assumed costs under prescriptive regulation (*MCA*, p. 290). For example, their lower-bound estimate of cost savings during Phase II, based on an alternative assumption that prescriptive regulation would be less costly relative to the trading regime during Phase II, is $1.1 billion annually—much closer to my estimate.

Although the cost savings estimated in *MCA* appear to have been inflated, their analysis provides a useful alternative framework for thinking about cost savings. Because the drawback of their approach is its reliance on conjectures about Phase II, it will be even more attractive when direct estimates of Phase II costs can be made from actual data. The apparent overestimates in *MCA* also illuminate the usefulness of paying more careful and direct attention to modeling the actual behavior of utilities under various policy regimes.

CONCLUSION

This chapter has used an econometric model of decisions made by utilities to estimate total costs of abatement under the Title IV program as well as a range of counterfactual prescriptive regulations. The allowance trading program resulted in estimated annual cost savings of $150 million (17 percent) during Phase I, relative to a uniform performance standard that would have achieved the same aggregate abatement. Holding estimated abatement costs constant, the allowance market achieved roughly 10 percent more abatement than would have been possible under a uniform standard.

Estimated cost savings are somewhat higher—$180 million—relative to a counterfactual policy of source-specific standards based on Table A allowance allocations. The cost of a technology standard, meanwhile, would have been astronomically high—nearly three and a half times the cost of the actual policy. The wide gap between the technology standard and the performance standard illustrates that allowing flexibility in compliance *within* regulated units (by regulating emissions rather than technology) is even more consequential than allowing flexibility *among* regulated units through trading.

The results of this study demonstrate the usefulness of estimating abatement costs on the basis of actual behavior. Previous studies were dependent on assumptions of cost minimization or relatively ad hoc estimates of costs under command-and-control. In contrast, the current study incorporates information about decisions made by utilities under varying forms of environmental regulation. This approach both allows for systematic deviations between actual decisions and those that would appear to minimize costs and incorporates the differences among policy regimes in the incentives for installing pollution control technologies.

ACKNOWLEDGMENTS An earlier version of a portion of the work here appeared in a 2003 working paper titled "What Did the Market Buy?: Cost Savings under the U.S. Tradeable Permits Program for Sulfur Dioxide." I am grateful to many for helpful comments, including Denny Ellerman, Erin Mansur, Robert Mendelsohn, Juan-Pablo Montero, Sheila Olmstead, Chris Timmins, seminar participants at the University of California Energy Institute, participants at the conference on Twenty Years of Market-Based Instruments for Environmental Protection at UC-Santa Barbara, and an anonymous referee. All remaining errors, of course, are my own.

NOTES

1. For a comprehensive discussion of the economics of environmental policy, *see* Baumol and Oates (1988).

2. For broader assessments of the performance of Title IV and associated lessons for policy, *see* Ellerman et al. (2000) and Stavins (1999).

3. In addition to affecting adoption incentives, the policy regime may also affect technological innovation and thus the costs of scrubbing (see Bellas 1998 and

Lange and Bellas 2004 for discussions of technological change in scrubbing as a result of sulfur dioxide regulation). Those innovation effects are not explicitly addressed in this chapter; to the extent they were present in Phase I, therefore, this work understates the cost savings associated with the use of a market-based instrument.

4. Ackerman and Hassler (1981) provide a fascinating account of the politics behind the 1977 CAAA.

5. *See* Keohane and Lee (2004) for an analysis of state-level regulation of SO_2 emissions from power plants.

6. A handful of state-regulated plants were required to install scrubbers; these are dropped from the analysis. Note that an earlier version of this chapter included NSPS-D units as well; acquisition of data on retrofitted state-regulated units made those unnecessary.

7. Ellerman and colleagues demonstrate in *MCA* that heat input rose sharply among Table A units with scrubbers (*MCA*, chap. 5). Units with scrubbers have lower variable costs (inclusive of abatement costs) than units that buy more expensive low-sulfur coal, and hence are utilized more. To overcome this endogeneity problem, I use 1990 heat input and utilization factors for all Table A units in estimating scrubbing cost.

8. For Table A units I use 1995, the year the allowance market took effect. For retrofitted units regulated by the states, I use the year in which state-level regulations were tightened (if such a year exists) or else 1985 (which is the first year for which I have scrubber operation data). *See* the discussion in Keohane (2004).

9. For state-regulated units that installed scrubbers before 1985 (the first year of the data), I set this indicator variable equal to 1 for units where low-sulfur coal is the cheapest available coal.

10. Emissions estimates at the unit level were computed on a mass-balance basis. I employed the estimation formulae used by the Energy Information Administration, taking into account the design of the boiler and the sulfur content of the coal used; for scrubbed units, I incorporated information on hours of scrubber operation and removal efficiency. The mass-balance calculations were used because the data include a range of units that began operation well before the advent of CEMS in place since 1996, which measure emissions in real time. For the years available, however, my computed emissions estimated agree very well with these data. At the unit level, the correlation between the emissions measures is 0.97; I present aggregate comparisons shortly.

11. I use different capital costs for adjustment to bituminous and to subbituminous (i.e., Powder River basin) coals. I use the estimated adjustment costs reported in *MCA*. Again, details can be found in Keohane (2004).

12. Standard errors are not corrected for the use of econometrically estimated regressors. The *t*-statistics on the variables of greatest interest are sufficiently large, however, that one might reasonably expect them to remain significant even accounting for the generation of the regressors. Note, too, that the correct standard errors need not be larger than the ones presented here: The bias can go in either direction. *See* Murphy and Topel (1985).

13. Bailey (1998) reached a similar conclusion in a more detailed analysis of state regulations.

14. Given the low frequency of scrubbers in the data set, a natural point of comparison is the percentage of correct predictions from the simple rule $Pr(\text{scrub})$ = 0. This rule would result in 783 correct predictions (92.5 percent).

15. This mean removal efficiency takes into account the fraction of hours that the scrubber was in operation. As an alternative, the removal efficiency could be predicted from data. For the Table A units, however, such a prediction yields virtually no improvement over the mean. Moreover, a Heckman estimation of removal efficiencies yielded no evidence of selection.

16. *MCA* estimates a similar regression on emissions (see chap. 5 in that volume), and I follow their lead in choosing the right-hand-side variables for the regression. Likewise, I follow them in using as my sample generating units from all states east of the Mississippi River, not including North or South Carolina, along with Kansas, Missouri, Iowa, and Minnesota. One difference is that my more detailed data on coal prices allow me to use a direct measure of the attractiveness of PRB coal (namely, whether it was the cheapest available coal), rather than relying on the cruder measure of distance from the PRB. Moreover, my data include only coal-fired units, so I cannot estimate (as they do) the shift from oil- and gas-fired units to coal-fired units, although I can identify changes that affected Table A units differently than other coal-fired units.

17. The very end of each quasi-MAC curve is truncated to maintain a useful scale. In particular, the Yates Y1BR unit has average scrubbing costs of nearly $2,500 per ton and is left off of the plot. In the same way, I truncate the plotted quasi-MAC curves under prescriptive regulation. In all cases, the truncation applies only to the graph: these high-cost units (including Yates) are included in the estimates of aggregate abatement and cost.

18. The coefficients on expected sulfur content and coal under long-term contract were retained, however, because the same expectations and contracts would have been in place regardless of regime.

19. The predicted removal rates were generated using coefficients from an ordinary least squares regression of the operating removal rate on sulfur content, emissions regulations, nameplate capacity, and scrubber vintage. The sample for the regression comprised the thirty-eight state-regulated scrubbers; the regression R^2 was 0.73, and all the variables were significant at at least the 5 percent level.

20. Actual allowance allocations diverged from those listed on Table A: nearly 1 million bonus and extension allowances were handed out each year for the first two years, as a result of political horse trading or as an incentive for adopting scrubbers (*MCA*, p. 41). These were awarded on the basis of provisions written in general terms in the act itself but specifically administered by the EPA. Because I lack the data on the actual allocations that resulted, however, I use the figures from Table A.

21. Of course, when transactions costs exist in the permit market, the initial allocation may well distort the final outcome. *See* Stavins (1995) for a discussion of transactions costs in permits markets.

22. I thank an anonymous referee for suggesting these explanations.

23. The counterfactual emissions standard (achieving the same level of abatement as under the baseline) is now 2.02 lbs/mmBtus. It is lower than the uniform standard used earlier because fewer scrubbers are installed in the cost-minimizing case for any given standard and because units are now assumed to meet abatement requirements exactly (rather than overcomplying).

24. A third study of cost savings, in a working paper by Burtraw and Mansur (1999), found cost savings of $97 million (relative to an estimate of Phase I costs of $650 million) from trading during Phase I. In percentage terms, that estimate (13 percent cost savings) is quite close to the preferred estimate presented here,

despite being based on a state-level model employing engineering estimates of abatement cost and a least-cost choice algorithm.

25. As explained in *MCA*, an important incentive for units to participate voluntarily in Phase I was to receive exemption from subsequent NO_x emissions regulations. To receive this exemption, a unit had to opt into the program in 1995—but did not have to remain in subsequent years. *See MCA*, chap. 8.

26. *CBCP* use estimates of actual emissions that accord well with those in *MCA* and in this study. To calculate what emissions would have been absent Title IV, they multiply actual emissions rates in 1993 by electricity generation in 1995 and 1996. For Table A units, this method yields unconstrained emissions of 7.5 million tons—well below my estimate of 8.6 million tons. Thus their estimates appear to significantly *underestimate* actual abatement—a fact that helps explain why their estimated counterfactual cost is relatively close to their estimated cost of the actual program.

27. Table 5.2 of *MCA* reports that an average of 6.31 million total allowances per year allocated to Table A plants during Phase I (using the 1997 figure for years 1998 and 1999). I estimate unconstrained emissions as 8.56 million tons per year. The difference is my estimate of required abatement.

28. This figure of $181 million is not directly comparable to the cost savings estimates derived earlier on the basis of actual abatement, for two reasons. The estimate of counterfactual costs is high, because it entails source-specific standards. On the other hand, the estimated cost of meeting required abatement under the allowance market (computed by finding the area under the baseline quasi-MAC curve up to 2.25 million tons of abatement) is low, because estimated marginal cost under the baseline is relatively flat at low levels of abatement and rises more steeply at higher levels.

29. The *MCA* MAC curve is a ray from the origin through the point (4.2,$350); the *MCA* CACC curve passes from the origin through the point (2.0,$525).

30. Thus the dashed line O_1B in figure 8.6 runs from the origin to the point (2.25,$308), encompassing an area equal to that under the quasi-MAC curve corresponding to the required abatement scenario with no trading. Similarly, the ray from the origin to the point labeled E, (4.23,$353), is a linear approximation of the baseline prediction—drawn so that the area underneath equals the estimated $747 aggregate cost of Phase I abatement.

31. Of course, one might be more concerned about the assumption of optimal intertemporal behavior given the evidence already presented that utility decisions did not minimize costs during Phase I.

REFERENCES

Ackerman, Bruce A., and William T. Hassler. 1981. *Clean Coal/Dirty Air.* New Haven, CT: Yale University Press.

Atkinson, Scott E., and David H. Lewis. 1974. "A Cost-Effectiveness Analysis of Alternative Air Quality Control Strategies." *Journal of Environmental Economics and Management* 1: 237–50.

Bailey, Elizabeth M. 1998. "Allowance Trading Activity and State Regulatory Rulings: Evidence from the U.S. Acid Rain Program." MIT-CEEPR Working Paper 98–005 WP (March).

Baumol, William J., and Wallace E. Oates. 1988. *The Theory of Environmental Policy*, 2nd ed. (New York: Cambridge University Press).

Bellas, Allen. 1998. "Empirical Advances in Scrubbing Technology." *Resource and Energy Economics* 20: 327–43.

Burtraw, Dallas. 1996. "The SO_2 Emissions Trading Program: Cost Savings without Allowance Trades." *Contemporary Economic Policy* 14: 79–94.

Burtraw, Dallas, Alan J. Krupnick, Erin Mansur, David Austin, and Deirdre Farrell. 1998. "The Costs and Benefits of Reducing Air Pollutants Related to Acid Rain." *Contemporary Economic Policy* 16: 379–400.

Burtraw, Dallas, and Erin Mansur. 1999. "The Effects of Trading and Banking in the SO_2 Allowance Market." Resources for the Future Discussion Paper 99–25.

Carlson, Curtis, Dallas Burtraw, Maureen Cropper, and Karen L. Palmer. 2000. "Sulfur Dioxide Control by Electric Utilities: What Are the Gains from Trade?" *Journal of Political Economy* 108: 1292–326.

Downing, P. B., and L. J. White. 1986. "Innovation in Pollution Control." *Journal of Environmental Economics and Management* 13: 18–29.

Ellerman, A. Denny. 2003. "Ex Post Evaluation of Tradeable Permits: The U.S. Cap-and-Trade Program." Paper prepared for the National Policies Division of the Environmental Directorate of the OECD.

Ellerman, A. Denny, Paul L. Joskow, Richard M. Schmalensee, Juan-Pablo Montero, and Elizabeth M. Bailey. 2000. *Markets for Clean Air.* Cambridge: Cambridge University Press.

Ellerman, A. Denny, and Juan-Pablo Montero. 1998. "The Declining Trend in Sulfur Dioxide Emissions: Implications for Allowance Prices." *Journal of Environmental Economics and Management* 36: 26–45.

Hahn, Robert W., and Robert N. Stavins. 1991. "Incentive-Based Environmental Regulation: A New Era from an Old Idea." *Ecology Law Quarterly* 1: 24.

Heckman, James J. 1974. "Shadow Prices, Market Wages, and Labor Supply." *Econometrica* 42(4): 679–94.

Joskow, Paul L., and Richard Schmalensee. 1998. "The Political Economy of Market-Based Environmental Policy: The U.S. Acid Rain Program." *Journal of Law and Economics* 41: 37–83.

Keohane, Nathaniel O. 2004. "Environmental Policy and the Choice of Abatement Technique: Evidence from Coal-Fired Power Plants." Working paper, Yale University, available online at www.som.yale.edu/faculty/nok4.

Keohane, Nathaniel O., and Christine T. Lee. 2004. "How Responsive Is Environmental Regulation to Costs and Benefits? Evidence from State Regulation of Sulfur Dioxide Emissions." Working paper, Yale University, available online at www.som.yale.edu/faculty/nok4.

Kerr, Suzi, and Richard G. Newell. 2003. "Policy-Induced Technology Adoption: Evidence from the U.S. Lead Phasedown." *Journal of Industrial Economics* 51: 317–43.

Kolstad, Charles D. 1986. "Empirical Properties of Economic Incentives and Command-and-Control Regulations for Air Pollution Control." *Land Economics* 62: 250–68.

Krupnick, A. J. 1986. "Costs of Alternative Policies for the Control of Nitrogen Dioxide in Baltimore." *Journal of Environmental Economics and Management* 13: 189–97.

Lange, Ian, and Allen Bellas. 2004. "Secondary Benefits of Market-Based Regulation: The Case of Scrubbers." Working paper, University of Washington, available online at students.washington.edu/ilange1/-adobes/lange_paper1.pdf.

Lile, Ron, and Dallas Burtraw. 1998. "State-Level Policies and Regulatory Guidance for Compliance in the Early Years of the SO_2 Emission Allowance Trading Program." RFF Discussion Paper 98–35 (May). Washington, DC: Resources for the Future.

Milliman, S. R., and R. Prince. 1989. "Firm Incentives to Promote Technological Change in Pollution Control." *Journal of Environmental Economics and Management* 17: 247–65.

Montero, Juan-Pablo. 1999. "Voluntary Compliance with Market-Based Environmental Policy: Evidence from the U.S. Acid Rain Program." *Journal of Political Economy* 107: 998–1033.

Murphy, Kevin M., and Robert H. Topel. 1985. "Estimation and Inference in Two-Step Econometric Models." *Journal of Business and Economic Statistics* 3(4): 370–79.

Oates, Wallace E., Paul R. Portney, and Albert M. McGartland. 1989. "The Net Benefits of Incentive-Based Regulation: A Case Study of Environmental Standard Setting." *American Economic Review* 79: 1233–42.

Seskin, E. P., Anderson, R. J. Jr., and R. O. Reid. 1983. "An Empirical Analysis of Economic Strategies for Controlling Air Pollution." *Journal of Environmental Economics and Management* 10: 112–24.

Shadbegian, Ronald J., Wayne Gray, and Cynthia Morgan. 2004. "The 1990 Clean Air Act Amendments: Who Got Cleaner Air—And Who Paid for It?" Working paper (July). Available online at www.clarku.edu/faculty/wgray/personalwebpage/currentpapers/whopaid04.pdf.

Stavins, Robert N. 1995. "Transactions Costs and Tradeable Permits." *Journal of Environmental Economics and Management* 29: 133–48.

Stavins, Robert N. 1999. "What Can We Learn from the Grand Policy Experiment? Lessons from SO_2 Trading." *Journal of Economic Perspectives* 12: 69–88.

9

Subsidies! The Other Incentive-Based Instrument: The Case of the Conservation Reserve Program

Hongli Feng, Catherine Kling,
Lyubov Kurkalova, & Silvia Secchi

INTRODUCTION

Environmental economists have produced numerous studies of the potential efficiency gains associated with the flexibility allowed to firms from market-like or incentive-based regulatory approaches.[1] Although much has been learned from these explorations, they are primarily ex ante and designed to address questions about the potential efficiency gains that could accrue from the implementation of a well-functioning incentive-based system relative to a command-and-control (CAC) policy that has actually been in place. In contrast, there has been relatively little study of the efficiency of actual incentive-based programs, relative to a hypothetical CAC strategy.[2]

Although the efficacy of the SO_2 trading program is being increasingly studied (Carlson et al. 2000; Schmalensee et al. 1998; Arimura 2002), there is in general a paucity of ex post studies of the effectiveness of incentive-based mechanisms. This omission has been credited largely to the sparse existence of such programs. In fact, however, incentive-based instruments for environmental control are not particularly rare in one large sector: agriculture. Rather, environmental programs in agriculture have a long history of implementing incentive-based instruments, albeit with a notable twist: Instead of charging fees or constructing tradable quotas, agricultural programs have generally paid farmers in the form of cost-sharing or subsidies to retire land or adopt environmentally friendly practices.

Table 9.1 provides a summary, adapted from Claassen et al. (2001), of some of the key programs that have been implemented by the U.S. Department of Agriculture (USDA) over the past century related to environmental performance of agricultural land and practices. These programs

Table 9.1 Summary of Major USDA Conservation Programs Related to Agriculture

Title	Duration	Program Summary
Agricultural Conservation Program	1936–96	Annual expenditures of over $175 million during 1980s and 1990s. Cost-share provided for conservation practices on agricultural land
Conservation Compliance, Sodbuster and Swampbuster	1985–	Requires farmers with highly erodible land to implement a soil conservation plan or lose eligibility for federal support programs
Conservation Reserve Program	1985–	Farmers retire land for 10–15 years from production in exchange for per acre payment
Conservation Reserve Enhancement Program	1996–	Same as the CRP except that farmers can sign up any time of the year, and it emphasizes federal and state partnership
Emergency Wetlands Reserve Program	1993–	Paid farmers to convert flood-damaged cropland to permanent wetlands. About 90,000 acres enrolled through 1997
Environmental Quality Incentives Program	1996–	Provides education, technical assistance, and funding to farmers to adopt practices for 5–10 years to reduce environmental problems. Payments capped at $10,000 per person
Wildlife Habitat Incentives Program	1996–	Provides cost sharing for development of habitat for wildlife. Cost share payments of up to 75 percent for 5- to 10-year commitments
Water Quality Incentive Projects	1990–96	Incentive payments provided for eligible producers to undertake 3- to 5-year agreements to implement approved management practices. Over 800,000 acres enrolled in 1995
Wetlands Reserve Program	1990–	Easement payment and restoration costs for land permanently converted to wetlands. As of 2000, 915,000 acres enrolled.
Conservation Security Program (CSP)	2002–	Green payments to provide farmers incentive to adopt various environmentally friendly practices, details still being determined

Notes: Summarized from chapter text and appendix 1 of Claassen et al. (2001), with additional information provided on the CSP. The CSP was established in the 2002 farm bill and is yet to be implemented.

rely on voluntary participation and direct payments. Hence, these programs can be categorized as environmental subsidies: payments for undertaking activities that benefit the environment, although they are imperfectly Pigovian in the sense that the payments are not directly linked to environmental effluent or performance.[3]

In this chapter, we study a very large and important example of an environmental subsidy program—the Conservation Reserve Program (CRP). The CRP was introduced in 1985. Prior to 1990, all acreage classified as highly erodible land (HEL) was eligible for enrollment in the program. From this set of land, administrators chose willing landowners to enroll acreage in the program when their offer prices were less than region-specific predetermined rental prices. There was a minimum goal of 5 million acres to be enrolled in 1986 and at least 10 million acres each year for 1987–89. These targets were met.

The CRP is of substantial magnitude, both in terms of its budget and the environmental benefits credited to it, which include erosion control, water quality, wildlife habitat, and drinking water supplies. For example, over the period 1982–97, total erosion on U.S. cropland declined by about 49 percent; much of this reduction is attributed to the presence of the CRP. Feather et al. (1999) estimate that the annual surplus from freshwater recreation, pheasant hunting, and wildlife viewing directly associated with the CRP totals almost half a billion dollars. By almost any standard, the CRP's budget outlay is enormous: over $15 billion was spent from 1989 through 2000 in payments to keep up to 36 million acres out of production (Claassen et al. 2001), representing about 10 percent of total cropland. In contrast, for the SO_2 trading program, the total (annualized) cost of reducing emissions by 3.9 million tons in 1995 was estimated to have been about $726 million (Schmalensee et al. 1998). To achieve the SO_2 cap of 8.95 million tons in 2010, the minimum cost is estimated to be about $1.04 billion, and an "enlightened" CAC policy would cost $1.82 billion (Carlson et al. 2000).

Though the CRP can be interpreted as a market-based incentive (MBI) program in the sense that program participants are faced with a price signal in the form of payments for retiring land from production, it is important to note that there are several efficiency problems with a subsidy as a policy instrument. First, whereas per unit subsidies have the same short-run efficiency properties as a corresponding tax, they may generate inefficiencies in the long run due to excessive entry (Bramhall and Mills 1966; Baumol and Oates 1988). In essence, the subsidy may make it profitable for firms to remain in an industry or for new firms to enter, when in its absence fewer firms would be present. However, an important exception for this inefficiency result occurs when there is a fixed factor associated with production of the externality-generating industry. In that case, the value of the subsidy can be expected to be capitalized into the price of the fixed factor, preventing excessive entry.[4] Given that there is a fixed stock of HEL from which CRP contracts could have been drawn, there is ample opportunity for capitalization of the subsidy into the price of land to occur, and therefore, long-run inefficiency associated with excessive entry may not be a significant problem.

Another potential difficulty with a subsidy program is that forward-looking firms may increase their emission levels prior to the imposition of a subsidy so that they can receive higher subsidy payments to abate (Kamien et al. 1966 appear to be the first to have raised this concern). Probably most troublesome for the case of the CRP is the potential deadweight loss associated with the social opportunity cost of funds. This argument notes that when the revenue used to pay subsidies comes from a distortionary tax system, a dollar of program expenditure represents an opportunity cost of more than a dollar (Wu and Babcock 1999). Large subsidy payments, such as those associated with a program as big as the CRP, can then have potentially very high efficiency costs, depending on the magnitude of the distortionary tax system. The estimates we provide in this chapter do not account for this second-best nature of the tax system or other distortionary programs and thus may be unduly favorable toward a subsidy system relative to a CAC alternative that does not transfer revenue from the government to individual agents.

Several previous empirical studies have considered the performance of the CRP (Osborne 1993; Reichelderfer and Boggess 1988; Babcock et al. 1996; Goodwin and Smith 2003). For example, Reichelderfer and Boggess (1988) noted that land enrolled in the CRP results in reduced commodity program spending as well as savings in other conservation expenditures. They estimated these cost savings associated with the actual CRP implemented in the first year of the program and the cost savings that might have accrued had alternate selection criteria been employed in selecting parcels for enrollment.

Babcock et al. (1996) focused on environmental targeting and investigated the proportion of gains achieved by the actual CRP relative to the environmental benefits achieved under targeting. Wu (2000) studied the magnitude of the slippage of land that had not previously been cropped into cropped land due to the price and substitution effects of the CRP. Finally, Goodwin and Smith (2003) evaluated how much the CRP erosion reduction benefits have been offset by increased erosion resulting from other government programs.

In this chapter, we ask a fundamentally different question from the previous empirical studies; specifically, we investigate how much less efficient, if any, a CAC form of regulation would have been. That is, we seek to assess the policy as implemented relative to a fundamentally different form of regulation—CAC. We then study the ex post performance of this incentive-based instrument. In so doing, we provide information on the degree to which MBI programs, as they have actually been implemented, have or have not lived up to the original optimism with which economists viewed such instruments. In this vein, we follow the work of Carlson et al. (2000), who undertook an ex post assessment of the efficacy of the SO_2 trading program in its early years, and Kolstad (1986) who studied the ex post performance of a variety of incentive-based instruments. Like Oates et al. (1989), we study the degree to which well-conceived CAC policies can be efficient alternatives to incentive-based measures. We also investigate a particularly understudied form of MBI: the subsidy.

We begin by discussing the key features of the CRP as it has been implemented and how the program has evolved over time. Next we study the optimal ex ante CRP as an incentive-based instrument by providing a simple model to describe its optimal implementation in its early years. Using the same analytical framework, we describe two general types of CAC policies that might reasonably have been implemented in lieu of the actual MBI subsidy: one we call a "strict" CAC policy and a second "enlightened" policy that allows more flexibility in attaining environmental improvements. To make appropriate comparisons with these CAC policy scenarios, we also study an improved MBI policy that seeks to maximize environmental benefit for a given budget.

The second part of the chapter discusses the program cost and environmental consequences of counterfactual MBI and CAC policies, the ex ante optimal CRP as outlined in the theory section, and the actually implemented (ex post) CRP land allocations. Comparison between the incentive-based and CAC policies are done under two different baselines: (1) one in which the total amount of land acreage put into CRP is held constant between the MBI and the CAC policies, and (2) one in which the total cost of the program is the same under the MBI and each CAC policy. The second baseline is particularly useful for assessing the efficiency of the policies, whereas the first is interesting because much of the (especially early) focus of the CRP was to assure a significant amount of land retirement from agricultural production.

INCENTIVE-BASED INSTRUMENTS

The CRP was initially managed to retire the most acres from production allowed by the budget authorization within the class of HELs (Smith 1995; Reichelderfer and Boggess 1988; Goodwin and Smith 2003).[5] Thus, it functioned both as an environmental program and an income support plan. It was an environmental program in that it targeted land that was particularly susceptible to soil and water erosion, but only in a rough (and thereby potentially inefficient) way because the category of HEL contains land that differs in many important environmental characteristics. The program was also implemented with income support and production control goals, as minimum requirements on the number of acres to be enrolled were met each year and limits on the number of acres per county were also required. These acreage requirements assured that a large number of farmers were included in the program and that the funds were spread widely across the United States.[6]

This program focus changed in 1990 when the Environmental Benefits Index (EBI) was initiated and used to identify land most desirable for retirement. Six environmental factors were used in constructing the EBI: wildlife, water quality, erosion, enduring benefits, air quality, and whether the acreage is located within a Conservation Priority Area. In Signup 15, the first major signup using the EBI, the first three factors could earn up to 100 points in the index, with 25–50 points possible for the remaining three environmental factors.[7] The cost of enrolling a parcel is a seventh factor in the index. Though the weights for some factors or sub-factors were adjusted for different signups, the relative magnitudes of weights have stayed largely the same.

We now turn to studying the optimal ex ante CRP policy as an incentive-based instrument.

MBI Policy 1: The Ex Ante Optimal CRP with an Acreage Maximization Objective

Suppose there are N parcels, each with a size of $\bar{x}_n$. The cost of converting a parcel to CRP is b_i. As described, in the pre-1990 CRP, land was chosen for enrollment from among the bids offered primarily to maximize the amount of land enrolled. A regulator interested in maximizing acres en-rolled from among the eligible land would solve the following[8]

$$(1) \qquad Max \sum_i x_i \ \text{ such that } x_i \geq 0, \text{ and } \sum_i b_i x_i \leq B, \ x_i \in X^{HEL}.$$

where the total budget, B, for the CRP is the total program expenditure, x_i is the amount of parcel ith land to be enrolled, and X^{HEL} is the set of all land classed as highly erodible.[9] The first-order conditions to this problem are simply

$$
\begin{aligned}
x_i^* &= \bar{x}_i, && \text{if } b_i - \lambda^* < 0; \\
x_i^* &= 0, && \text{if } b_i - \lambda^* > 0; \\
(2) \qquad x_i^* &= X - \sum_{\{i:\, b_i - \lambda^* < 0\}} x_i^*, && \text{if } b_i - \lambda^* = 0.
\end{aligned}
$$

where λ^* is the optimized value of the Lagrange multiplier from the budget constraint.[10] A heuristic solution to this problem can be obtained simply by ranking each piece of land from lowest to highest in terms of its bid price and then accepting land into the program starting at the top until the budget is expended.

Once the accepted acres are identified, the environmental benefits of the program can be computed as $\sum_i x_i^* e_i$, where the environmental improvement on parcel i is represented by $e_i = \sum_k \theta^k e_i^k$. The vector $(e_i^1, e_i^2, \dots, e_i^m)$ measures the various environmental benefits associated with CRP enrollment, such as reduction in soil erosion, reduction in nu-trient runoff/leaching, improvement in wildlife habitat, carbon seques-tration, and so on, and the weight placed on attribute e_i^k is θ^k. Thus, e_i can be interpreted as an environmental index for each parcel. The EBI of the post-1990 CRP is an example of one such index, but others are possible. Alternatively, e_i could be a measure of a single environmental amenity, such as the contribution of that parcel of land to improved water quality. This is equivalent to setting θ^k for all other factors to zero.

If landowners bid their opportunity cost then the budgetary outlay (B) represents the social cost of the program as well as the program costs.[11] In the ex ante optimal policy, farmers with low cost land should offer it for bid and the regulator should choose the cheapest land to put into the program.

Whether the actual CRP parcels correspond to the ex ante optimal ones depends on whether the lowest cost landowners enter low-cost bids that then get selected. Although we would predict that outcome in a full information market setting with no transaction costs, there may be a number of reasons in practice the actual CRP land allocations do not match this optimal one. Carlson et al. (2000) ask whether the SO_2 program as implemented actually solved the trading problem efficiently—that is, did the "right" firms trade so that all the gains from trade were truly exhausted? In the same way, we compare the optimal acreage-maximizing solution to the actual CRP policy. We refer to the actual CRP land allocation as the ex post or actual policy.

In addition to assessing whether the CRP policy as actually implemented prior to 1990 achieved the greatest acreage at least cost, we are also keenly interested in the environmental efficacy of the program. Thus, we next examine an MBI policy that maximizes environmental benefits for a given budget outlay.

MBI Policy 2: An Improved MBI CRP Policy with an Objective to Maximize Environmental Benefit

A regulator interested in maximizing environmental benefits from among the eligible land would solve the following[12]

$$(3) \qquad Max \sum_i e_i x_i \quad such\ that \quad x_i \geq 0, \quad and \quad \sum_i b_i x_i \leq B, \; x_i \in X^{HEL}.$$

where the objective function now is to maximize environmental gain from the program.

The first-order conditions to this problem are

$$x_i^* = \bar{x}_i, \quad if \; e_i/b_i - \lambda^* > 0;$$
$$x_i^* = 0, \quad if \; e_i/b_i - \lambda^* < 0;$$

$$(4) \qquad x_i^* = \left(B - \sum_{\{i:\, e_i/b_i - \lambda^* > 0\}} b_i x_i^* \right) / b_i, \quad if \; e_i/b_i - \lambda^* = 0,$$

where λ^* is again the optimized value of the Lagrange multiplier. Ranking parcels from highest to lowest based on their environmental contribution per cost and choosing those parcels to enroll until the budget is exhausted will yield an optimal solution. This, of course, corresponds to the efficient solution. Again, once the accepted acres are identified, the environmental benefits of the program can be computed.

CAC ALTERNATIVES

In considering the CRP as an MBI and comparing its efficiency to a CAC policy that might have been implemented in its stead, we define two types of CAC regimes, employing the terminology of Carlson et al. (2000). A strict CAC regime is one that treats all sources of environmental damage (or benefit) the same, regardless of (1) the costs of compliance or provision of the environmental service, and (2) the benefits associated with compliance or provision. In such a policy, each firm or farm faces the same standard, technology requirement or other obligation. In contrast, an enlightened CAC regime treats all sources the same in one of the two dimensions, costs or benefits, but makes allowance for variation in the sources' costs of environmental compliance *or* the heterogeneity in benefits, but not both. Clearly, a super-enlightened CAC regime that took account of both would be on par with a well-functioning MBI from an efficiency perspective. We consider counterfactual policies of both CAC types beginning with a strict CAC approach.

CAC Policy 1: Strict CAC, Equal Percentage Reduction in HEL

In its purest form, this policy would require that all farms with HEL retire a fixed percentage of HEL from active production. This approach would clearly be in the spirit of CAC because all farms are treated the same, regardless of the opportunity cost of retiring land or the erosion benefits from doing so. This policy could be implemented on a farm scale (its purest form), a county scale (equal percentage reduction required of all counties), or possibly a state scale.

CAC Policy 2: Enlightened CAC Policy, Erosion Index Ranking

In this case, the policy will target land for enrollment based on a measure of environmental performance. We choose the erodibility index as a likely candidate because during the 1980s erosion control was a primary environmental concern for agricultural land.

The policy maker's problem is to maximize environmental benefit by deciding which land to enroll subject to an acreage or program outlay cap. The optimization could occur at the entire state level or within a specific county; in either case, the policy maker wants to choose the parcels to enroll based on a specific environmental index (e_i) to maximize erosion benefits, thus his or her objective is to maximize $\sum_i x_i e_i$. In this case, e_i is a scalar measure of erosion benefits. A comparison between this policy and an incentive-based policy can be accomplished in two different ways. First, the total amount of land in the state enrolled in the program can be held constant at the level achieved by the incentive-based program so that the regulator faces the constraint that $\sum_i x_i = X$. The first-order conditions for this problem are

$$x_i^* = \bar{x}_i, \quad if \ e_i - \lambda^* > 0;$$
$$x_i^* = 0, \quad if \ e_i - \lambda^* < 0;$$

(5)
$$x_i^* = X - \sum_{\{i: \ e_i - \lambda^* > 0\}} x_i^*, \quad if \ e_i - \lambda^* = 0.$$

The conditions indicate that the optimal policy is to enroll land into the program until the total acreage cap X is reached. Denote $\bar{e}$ as the erosion benefit of the parcel where $e_i = \lambda^*$. Then, another way to interpret the first-order conditions is that parcel i should be enrolled in CRP if and only if $e_i \geq \bar{e}$. Heuristically, the solution can be found by ranking the parcels from highest to lowest in terms of the value of their environmental index. Parcels would then be accepted into the program until the acreage constraint is satisfied. A second way to compare this policy to the incentive-based approach is to hold the total program cost constant. In this case, parcels are accepted into the program until the budget is exhausted.[13]

DATA

The data for simulations comes from the National Resource Inventory (NRI). The NRI sample design ensures statistical reliability for state and multicounty analysis of nonfederal land (Nusser and Goebel 1997). Because the bulk of Iowa private land is in agricultural use, the NRI sample is ideally suited to represent Iowa agricultural land. In the simulations, we regard each NRI point as representing one producer with a farm homogenous in management and in natural conditions. The size of the farm is assumed equal to the number of acres represented by the point (the NRI expansion factor).

The 1997 NRI data are based on surveys conducted at five-year intervals since 1982. The data provide information on land use and natural resource characteristics of the land in the survey years. In addition, land-use information is available for the three years preceding the survey years. For the NRI points in the CRP, the information on conservation practices established and the year of CRP signup is provided. For the NRI points in crop production, information on the crop grown and conservation practices is available. A site-specific erodibility index, $e_i^1 = EI_i$ is provided in the NRI.

A site-specific per acre opportunity cost of converting a parcel to CRP, b_i, was estimated using a CRP rental rate function. The rental rate function, fitted on the census of Iowa 1987 CRP contracts, relates the CRP rental rate to the parcel location and its suitability for agricultural use. Details on the rental rate function estimation are provided in the appendix.[14]

RESULTS

Because the 1997 NRI contains resource information in five-year intervals since 1982 and the CRP was initiated in 1986, we had three possible years to choose from: 1987, 1992, or 1997. We chose CRP land enrolled in 1987 as our baseline because the other NRI years are less suitable for our study. Compared to 1987, there was little CRP enrollment in 1992, and for 1997 the NRI does not have site-specific enrollment information for land enrolled. A CRP parcel's enrollment year is important because we need to choose CAC points in the same year as the actual CRP points' enrollment year to make valid comparisons.

Table 9.2 gives a list of the policy scenarios studied, along with their total CRP acreage, average erodibility indexes (EIs) of enrolled land, and total EI gained by each program. For the CRP as implemented, 800 NRI points in Iowa were enrolled in 1987 with a total of 1,095,800 acres at an annual cost of $90,519,251. The total acreage or the annual program cost is used to ensure that alternative policy scenarios have comparable scales. Because the pre-1990 CRP is more consistent with targeting HEL acreage rather than maximizing an environmental benefits index, we analyzed the ex ante optimal MBI designed to maximize the amount of HEL in the program.

In line with this focus, the only strict CAC policy evaluated is the one for which the total acreage enrolled equals the acreage for the CRP as implemented. In the case of enlightened CRP, the CAC policy enrolls land

Table 9.2 Summary of CRP Policies Studied

Policies	Total Acres	Average EI	Total EI
MBI policy 0: the actual CRP	1,095,800	20.1	22,025,580
MBI policy 1: the ex ante optimal CRP	1,288,641	24.4	31,442,840
MBI policy 2: the improved MBI–equal acres	1,095,800	56.6	60,946,556
MBI policy 2: the improved MBI–equal costs	1,188,402	53.9	64,112,202
CAC policy 1: the strict CAC CRP	1,095,800	53.9	59,063,620
CAC policy 2: the enlightened CAC–equal acres	1,095,800	56.4	61,803,120
CAC policy 2: the enlightened CAC–equal costs	1,174,300	55.0	64,586,500

Note: By construction, MBI policy 2, CAC policy 1, and CAC policy 2 have the total acres equal to those for the actual CRP (MBI policy 0).

into CRP with the highest EIs until the total acreage is reached or until the total program cost is exhausted.[15] When the total acreage is used as a cap, we call the CAC policy based on EI the equal acreage enlightened CAC. When the total cost is used as a cap, we call the CAC policy equal cost enlightened CAC. We also use EI as an indicator to see how these CAC scenarios compare to the MBI policy scenarios that maximize the EIs of enrolled land for a given budget. Similar to the enlightened CAC policies, we consider two versions of the improved MBI scenarios: one with the total acreage as a cap, and the other in which land is enrolled in the program until the total program budget is exhausted. We refer to the MBI scenarios as the improved MBI–equal acres and the improved MBI–equal costs, respectively.

Because the ex ante optimal CRP policy enrolls land with the lowest costs, it is able to enroll the most land into CRP. The acreage enrolled is 1,288,641 acres, 17.6 percent more than the acreage of the actual CRP.

Land enrolled in the actual CRP accounted for about 15.8 percent of cropland with an EI greater than 8 (i.e., HEL) in Iowa. This percentage number is used as a basis for the strict CAC policy. More specifically, each county enrolls the same percentage, 15.8 percent of its HEL into the CRP, which implies that the total enrolled land under the strict CAC is equal to the total acreage of the actual CRP.

The average EI of the actual CRP (20.1) is much lower than the average EI of the CAC policies (above 50 for all three CAC scenarios). The equal acreage enlightened CAC has an annual cost of about $84.6 million, which is lower than that of the actual CRP. Conversely, the equal cost enlightened CAC is able to enroll more land (a total of 1,174,300 acres). This is because land with a higher EI tends to have lower values than land with a lower EI. Although the average EI is highest under the enlightened CAC with equal acreage constraint, the total EI is higher under the enlightened CAC with equal costs.

As illustrated by tables 9.2–3 and figures 9.1 and 9.2, the enlightened CAC scenarios are strikingly similar to the improved MBI scenarios: for equal costs, they enroll about the same total acres of land, and for equal acreage, the total costs are about the same. Given that the CAC is based on the environmental benefit (parcels with the highest EIs are chosen) and the MBI is based on environmental benefit per dollar (parcels with the highest EI per dollar are chosen), this is surprising. The explanation lies in the relationship between the parcels' EIs and their rental costs. As figure 9.3 illustrates, relative to the differences in EIs, the rental rates of the parcels are very flat. Thus, the ranking of the parcels based on their EIs divided by the rental rates is quite similar to the ranking based only on EIs. Consequently, a policy based on the ranking of EIs (e.g., the enlightened CAC scenarios) would choose similar parcels as a policy based on the ranking of EIs per dollar (e.g., the improved MBI scenarios).

Table 9.3 Common Land Enrolled Both by the Counterfactual
CRP and by the Actual CRP

Policies	Acres	% (of the Total Actual CRP acres)
The ex ante optimal CRP	35,100	3.2
The strict CAC CRP	12,100	1.1
The improved MBI CRP–equal acres	11,000	1.0
The improved MBI CRP–equal costs	11,000	1.0
The enlightened CRP–equal acres	8,500	0.78
The enlightened CRP–equal costs	9,600	0.88

The distribution of CRP land under the different policies, as shown in figures 9.1–9.6, is another way to illustrate their different implications. Figure 9.4 indicates that land enrolled in the actual CRP is fairly evenly distributed around the state. By construction, land enrolled in the strict CAC program is also evenly scattered in the state. However, the ex ante optimal CRP would enroll land predominantly in southern Iowa and a few counties along the Missouri River, where land generally is cheaper than in other parts of the state. The CRP land under the two enlightened CAC and the two improved MBI policies comes mainly from counties in the south and along the Mississippi and Missouri Rivers on the state

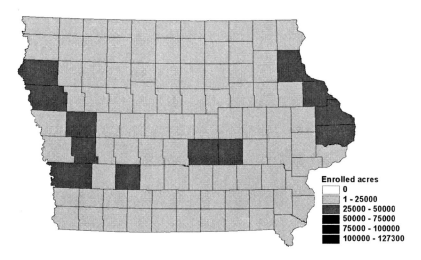

Figure 9.1. The Distribution of CRP Acres: The Strict CAC

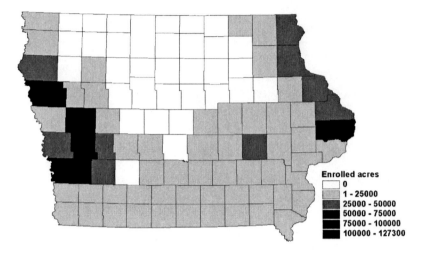

Figure 9.2. The Distribution of CRP Acres: The Improved MBI–Equal Costs

boundary. The equal-cost and equal-acre policies have similar CRP land distributions because they have the same criterion for enrollment, and the only difference lies in how the total CRP acreage is set. Thus, only the distributions for one of them—equal-cost scenarios—are illustrated in the maps.

It is interesting that both the ex ante optimal CRP and the two enlightened policies move land away from a uniform distribution across the state to more acreage enrolled in the south and along the two rivers. At

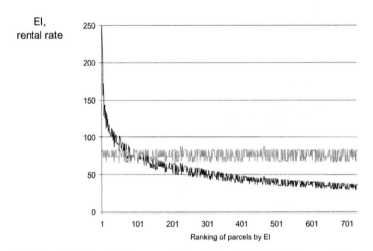

Figure 9.3. The Relationship between EI and Rental Rate for Some of the Top-Ranked Parcels

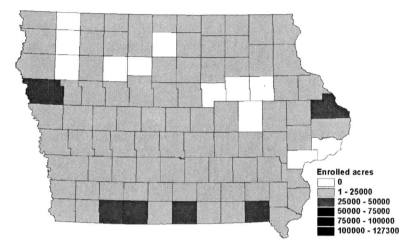

Figure 9.4. The Distribution of CRP Acres: The Actual CRP

first blush, this is surprising given that the criteria used to identify the plots of land enrolled are different: costs in the cases of the ex ante CRP and the erodibility index in the case of the CAC policies. But as Babcock et al. (1997) note, this result is expected when there is a strong negative correlation between an environmental amenity (EI in this case) and the cost of the land.[16]

Another way to illustrate the difference between the actual CRP and a counterfactual policy alternative is to identify which parcels would be enrolled in a CRP whether the parcel selection was made as it actually was (the actual CRP) or had it been made using the decision criteria of

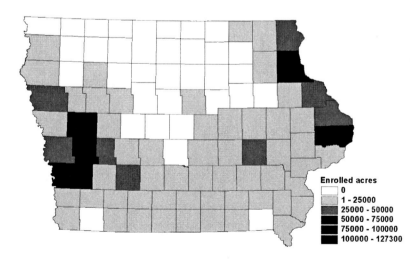

Figure 9.5. The Distribution of CRP Acres: The Enlightened CAC–Equal Costs

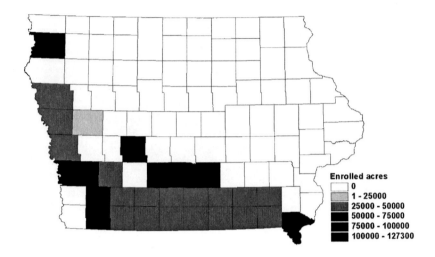

Figure 9.6. The Distribution of CRP Acres: The Ex Ante Optimal

a counterfactual policy. Table 9.3 lists such overlapping acres between the actual CRP and the counterfactual polices examined in this chapter. It is clear that the extent of overlap is quite small in all cases; thus, the alternative decision criteria may have significant environmental consequences.

The different location of CRP points under the different policies also implies that different people may benefit from the CRP policies. For example, the benefit of improved soil productivity from reduced erosion is mainly enjoyed by local landowners. On the other hand, some environmental benefits are more regional, for example, the reduction of nutrient runoff in Iowa may help relieve the hypoxia situation in the Gulf of Mexico. In this case, the different CRP land distributions may be less significant, although the spatial location of the CRP points may have significant regional consequences as well. In any case, it is important to know the relative magnitude of each dimension of environmental benefits to assess the overall implication of CRP. It would be an interesting topic for future research to investigate how the use of EBI changes the distribution of CRP acres.

DISCUSSION AND CONCLUSION

In terms of overall environmental benefits from the program, as represented by the EI, there is no clear winner between the ex ante optimal MBI and the actual CRP. Our results show that more HEL acreage with a higher average EI could have been enrolled in the subsidy program, with the same goal as manifested by the actual implementation of the CRP, than actually was, implying that the MBI could have achieved greater efficiency. This is consistent with the findings of Smith (1995).

Compared to a CAC alternative, the MBI of CRP as actually implemented yielded less enrolled HEL acreage for a given budget outlay. When the acreage totals are held constant, the budget outlay is lower and the average EI is higher with the CAC alternatives. Interestingly, because the rental costs do not vary that much relative to the EI for parcels with the highest EIs, the MBI policy that seeks to maximize EI enrolls similar parcels as the enlightened CAC policy. This indicates that using EI as an indicator, these CAC and MBI CRPs will perform about the same.

There are many CAC policy alternatives. In our study of the CRP, the EI forms the basis for all of the CAC policies. Our results concerning the efficiency of CAC relative to the MBI are undoubtedly highly influenced by this choice: With a different method for implementing the CAC, the policy would be more or less attractive relative to the MBI. The use of the EI to form the basis for the CAC policy is intuitive and consistent with a long history of agricultural conservation policy, making it a natural choice for study. Alternative choices, for example, the EBI, could be interesting for future study.

APPENDIX: ESTIMATION OF CRP RENTAL RATE FUNCTION

To estimate the function relating the per-acre CRP rental rate to the parcel location and its suitability for agricultural use, we used the data on all the actual CRP contracts enrolled in the program in Iowa in 1987 (USDA/FSA 2003). Out of the 15,270 records available, 15,221 were complete and used in estimation.

The rental rate function model is described as

$$(A1) \qquad rent_i = \alpha_0 + \sum_{j=1}^{98} \alpha_j \delta_{ji} + \beta class_i + \varepsilon_i.$$

Here the subscript i refers to the ith contract ($i = 1, \ldots, 15, 221$), subscript j refers to the jth Iowa county, $rent_i$ is the CRP rental rate in dollars per acre, δ_{ji} is the county indicator, that is, $\delta_{ji} = 1$ if parcel i is located in county j and zero otherwise, and $class_i$ is the land-use capability classification of the parcel. The land-use capability classification system evaluates land according to its limitations for agricultural use with the land of classes 1 to 3 suitable for cultivation, land of class 4 suitable for limited cultivation, and land of classes higher than 4 not suitable for cultivation (Troeh and Thompson 1993). The ε_i is an error term, and the α's and β are the parameters of interest. Summary statistics for the data are presented in Table 9,A1.

Estimation of model (A1) on the data resulted in good fit ($R^2 = 0.852$). As expected, the estimate of β is negative and statistically significant, meaning that land better suited for agricultural production requires higher CRP rental rate. For the sake of brevity, the estimates of the

Table 9.A1 Summary Statistics for the Data Used in Estimation of CRP Rental Rate Function

Variable	Mean	SD	Min	Max
CRP rental rate, $ per acre	78.4	8.4	35.0	90.0
Land-use capability class	3.36	0.96	2	8

parameters are not reported here but are available from the authors on request.

ACKNOWLEDGMENTS Kling was a visiting researcher at INRA, LEERNA, and IDEI, University of Toulouse, France, while this research was undertaken. We are thankful to Bruce Babcock for stimulating discussions and to Phil Gassman and Todd Campbell for computational assistance. We appreciate the many insightful comments from participants of the Market-Based Incentives Workshop held at UC Santa Barbara, August 2003. The comments from discussant Kathleen Segerson were particularly cogent and thoughtful. All remaining errors and lack of clarity remain our responsibility.

NOTES

1. A few examples include Oates et al. (1989), Hahn (1989), and Kling (1994). Tietenberg (1985) provides an excellent table and summary of this literature.

2. Kolstad's (1986) work is an important early exception.

3. The political motivation for adopting a subsidy was likely due more to its voluntary nature than any efficiency property associated with its market-based price information.

4. This is an example of the more general case known in the literature as a closed class, see Holderness (1988).

5. Though not the stated goal of the program, analysts have concluded that the implementation was largely consistent with a maximum acreage objective.

6. As Kathleen Segerson noted when discussing this topic, an alternative approach to achieving least-cost land retirement would have been to issue land-use permits for farming on HEL and allow them to be traded. This would have retained the voluntary nature of the program with a much lower total program cost.

7. Specifically, the points associated with the three remaining factors are: enduring benefits up to fifty points, air quality up to thirty-five, and up to twenty-five for location in a Conservation Priority Area. Agricultural Outlook/October 1997 by Economic Research Service/USDA provides more information on the computation of the EBI.

8. As long as the budget is large enough, the constraint on total acreage described will not be binding; if the budget is not large enough, no solution is feasible.

9. The CRP also limited the number of acres that could be enrolled within any county, but this limit was very rarely reached and appears to have not affected the participation in the program.

10. Throughout the chapter, we use an asterisk to indicate optimized values.

11. As noted in the introduction, if the social cost of funds is greater than the private costs, the total program costs will underestimate the full social costs. Additionally, as a reviewer noted, if an efficient bid system is not used, as occurred in the pre-1990 CRP signups, the social and program costs will not coincide.

12. As with model (1)–(2), as long as the budget is large enough, the constraint on total acreage described will not be binding, and if the budget is not large enough, no solution is feasible.

13. Note that the budget constraint is used to identify how many parcels can be enrolled, that is, how far down the rank ordered list the authority can afford to go, but unlike the optimal environmental CRP, the cost of enrolling parcels is not used to rank the parcels.

14. For the same field, it is not straightforward whether the CRP payment should be higher or lower than the cash rental rate. On one hand, because the CRP payment is guaranteed for a long period of time, ten or fifteen years, it should be lower than cash rental rate. On the other hand, because of this long-term commitment, some option value may be required for a farmer to enroll into the CRP. Empirically, for 1987, the average CRP payment for Iowa is higher than the cash rental rate. However, for 1997, the reverse is true. This might be because, in the earlier days of the program, not much effort was made to minimize program cost. Of course, it may also be the case that with the implementation of EBI, more marginal land, which is associated with lower cash rental rate, is enrolled in the CRP.

15. EI is a number that indicates the potential of a soil to erode based on climatic factors and the physical and chemical properties of the soil. A higher index indicates a greater investment is needed to maintain the sustainability of the soil resource base if intensively cropped, thus a higher index for enrolled land indicates more program erosion benefits.

16. Note there is no inconsistency between discussion here and the message shown in figure 9.3, which shows the relation between EI and costs for parcels with top EIs (the selected parcels in the improved MBI–equal cost scenario). Even given the relatively flat trend of costs in the figure, it may still be true that the costs shown in the figure tend to be lower than parcels not shown.

REFERENCES

Arimura, Toshi. "An Empirical Study of the SO_2 Allowance Market: Effects of PUC Regulations," *Journal of Environmental Economics and Management* 44 (2002): 271–89.

Babcock, Bruce, P. G. Lakshminarayan, Junjie Wu, and David Zilberman. "The Economics of a Public Fund for Environmental Amenities: A Study of CRP Contracts," *American Journal of Agricultural Economics* 78 (1996): 961–71.

Babcock, Bruce, P. G. Lakshminarayan, Junjie Wu, and David Zilberman. "Targeting Tools for the Purchase of Environmental Amenities," *Land Economics* 73 (1997): 325–39.

Baumol, William, and Wallace Oates. *The Theory of Environmental Policy.* Englewood Cliffs, NJ: Prentice Hall, 1988.

Bramhall, D. E., and E. S. Mills. "A Note on the Asymmetry between Fees and Payments," *Water Resources Research* 3 (1966): 615–16.

Carlson, Curtis, Dallas Burtraw, Maureen Cropper, and Karen Palmer. "Sulfur Dioxide Control by Electric Utilities: What Are the Gains from Trade?" *Journal of Political Economy* 108 (2000): 1292–326.

Claassen, Roger, LeRoy Hansen, Mark Peters, Vince Breneman, Marca Weinberg, Andrea Cattaneo, Peter Feather, Dwight Gadsby, Daniel Hellerstein, Jeff Hopkins, Paul Johnston, Mitch Morehart, and Mark Smith. "Agri-Environmental Policy at the Crossroads: Guideposts on a Changing Landscape." Agricultural Economic Report No. 794, ERS, USDA, 2001.

Feather, Peter, Daniel Hellerstein, and LeRoy Hansen. "Economic Valuation of Environmental Benefits and the Targeting of Conservation Programs: The Case of the CRP." USDA, ERS, Agricultural Economics Report No. 778, April 1999.

Goodwin, B. K., and V. H. Smith. "An Ex Post Evaluation of the Conservation Reserve, Federal Crop Insurance, and Other Government Programs: Program Participation and Soil Erosion," *Journal of Agricultural and Resource Economics* 28:2 (2003): 201–16.

Hahn, R. W. "Economic Prescriptions for Environmental Problems: How the Patient Followed the Doctor's Orders," *Journal of Economic Perspectives* 3:2 (1989): 95–114.

Holderness, C. "The Assignment of Rights, Entry Effects and the Allocation of Resources," *Journal of Legal Studies* (1989): 181–89.

Kamien, M. I., N. L. Schwartz, and F. T. Dolbear. "Asymmetry between Bribes and Charges," *Water Resources Research* 1 (1966): 147–57.

Kling, Catherine. "Emission Trading vs. Rigid Regulations in the Control of Vehicle Emissions," *Land Economics* 70 (1994): 174–88.

Kolstad, Charles. "Empirical Properties of Economic Incentives and Command-and-Control Regulations for Air Pollution Control," *Land Economics* 62 (1986): 250–68.

Nusser, S. M., and J. J. Goebel. "The National Resources Inventory: A Long-Term Multi-Resource Monitoring Programme," *Environmental and Ecological Statistics* 4 (1997): 181–204.

Oates, Wallace, Paul Portney, and Albert McGartland. "The Net Benefits of Incentive-Based Regulation: A Case Study of Environmental Standard Setting," *American Economics Review* 79 (1989): 1233–42.

Osborne, Tim. "The Conservation Reserve Program: Status, Future, and Policy Options," *Journal of Soil and Water Conservation* 48 (July–August 1993): 271–78.

Reichelderfer, Katherine, and William Boggess. "Government Decision Making and Program Performance: The Case of the Conservation Reserve Program," *American Journal of Agricultural Economics* 70 (1988): 1–11.

Schmalensee, Richard, Paul L. Joskow, A. Denny Ellerman, Juan Pablo Montero, and Elizabeth M. Bailey. "An Interim Evaluation of Sulfur Dioxide Emissions Trading," *Journal of Economic Perspective* 12 (summer 1998): 53–68.

Smith, Rodney B. W. "The Conservation Reserve Program as a Least-Cost Land Retirement Mechanism," *American Journal of Agricultural Economics* 77 (February 1995): 93–105.

Tietenberg, Tom. *Emissions Trading: An Exercise in Reforming Pollution Policy.* Washington, DC: Resources for the Future, 1985.

Troeh, F. R., and L. M. Thompson. *Soils and Soil Fertility,* 5th edition. New York: Oxford University Press, 1993.

USDA/Farm Service Agency (USDA/FSA). CRP Contract Data. Unofficial USDA data files. USDA, Kansas City, MO. Accessed May 2003.

Wu, Junjie. "Slippage Effects of the Conservation Reserve Program," *American Journal of Agricultural Economics* 82:4 (2000): 979–92.

Wu, Junjie, and Bruce Babcock. "The Relative Efficiency of Voluntary versus Mandatory Environmental Regulations," *Journal of Environmental Economics and Management* 38 (1999): 158–75.

10

An Assessment of Legal Liability
as a Market-Based Instrument

Kathleen Segerson

INTRODUCTION

Early environmental policies relied primarily on command-and-control approaches to changing polluter behavior. However, recognition of the potentially high costs associated with these policies, due in large part to their inflexibility, prompted scholars and policy makers to search for alternatives that were more flexible and less costly. Environmental economists have advocated policies that rely on the pricing of environmental services, such as taxes and marketable permits. Such policies make polluters pay for consumption of environmental services or, equivalently, deterioration of environmental quality, in the same way that they pay for other inputs, such as labor, land, and capital.

Market-based instruments have been advocated primarily as means to control environmental contaminants that are emitted continuously as a known and anticipated by-product of some production process. Examples include sulfur dioxide (SO_2) emissions and continuous waste discharges into water bodies. However, pricing policies can also be used for environmental concerns that stem from the unintentional and unanticipated release of hazardous substances, or environmental accidents. Examples include oil spills, unanticipated chemical releases, leaking underground storage tanks, and the leaching of pesticides or landfill wastes into soil and surface water or groundwater. In this context, polluters can be made to pay for consumption of environmental services through the imposition of legal liability for the damages associated with environmental contamination. The rule of strict liability requires polluters to pay for damages whenever they occur, regardless of whether the polluter took reasonable steps to avoid them. It is thus equivalent to a pricing rule under which a user must pay for a good or service whenever it is used. It is a contingent price, however, in the sense that rather than paying ex ante for expected damages, polluters are required to pay for damages only if (and when) they occur.

In contrast to strict liability, under negligence-based liability polluters pay only if they did not take sufficient care to avoid contamination. If an accident occurs despite this care, the polluter is not required to pay for the damages. Payment under a negligence rule acts like a fine on failure to comply with a due standard of care. It parallels a regulatory approach rather than a tax approach and hence is effectively a quantity-based instrument (Cooter 1984). Thus, although use of a negligence rule can create incentives for compliance with the due standard, it differs from the usual notion of a market-based approach, which relies on the pricing of environmental goods and services.

Liability for certain types of environmental damages has always been available under common law. Under common law, actions against polluters can be brought under a number of rules or doctrines, including private or public nuisance law, property law, trespass, riparian rights, negligence, and product liability (Baram 1982; Dewees et al. 1996). More recently, however, liability for environmental damages has been imposed statutorily. At the federal level, the most notable examples of statutes imposing liability for environmental damages are the Comprehensive Environmental Response, Compensation, and Liability Act (CERCLA, or Superfund), the Clean Water Act, the Outer Continental Shelf Act, and the Oil Pollution Act. Of these, CERCLA has been the most controversial. In addition to these federal laws, many states now have statutes that impose liability for environmental contamination, such as the many state-level versions of CERCLA (mini-Superfund laws) that exist.[1]

The imposition of legal liability for environmental damages can serve a number of purposes, and it can be evaluated according to each of these goals (see Dewees et al. 1996). The first, and the one of primary interest here, is deterrence. Holding polluters liable for environmental damages can create an incentive for them to undertake actions to reduce the potential for or the extent of environmental damages resulting from their activities. A second, and in some contexts an equally important goal, is victim compensation. Liability payments provide a source of revenue that can be used to compensate the victims of pollution either directly (as under common law) or possibly indirectly (as when statutorily imposed liability payments finance activities that indirectly benefit victims). Finally, liability can provide a form of corrective justice under which wrongful conduct is punished.

In this chapter, I focus solely on the deterrence effect of liability, recognizing that the motivation for imposition of liability (particularly retroactive imposition) may instead be victim compensation or corrective justice.[2] I evaluate what we know to date about whether liability creates an effective market for environmental goods and services. Because strict

liability most closely parallels a pricing or market-based approach, I focus
on the deterrence effect of strict liability (rather than negligence). There is
an extensive theoretical literature on the incentive effects of strict liability,
which shows that in theory it can (under some conditions) provide incentives for polluters to reduce the likelihood or magnitude of environmental accidents. In contrast, there has been relatively little empirical
analysis to determine if this potential has been realized in practice.

   This chapter is not intended to be an exhaustive review of the literature
on environmental liability and the specific results that emerge from it.[3]
Rather, I provide an overview of the issues regarding the impact of liability that have been addressed in the theoretical literature in an effort to
identify key conditions or factors that can be expected to influence the
effectiveness of liability as a policy tool. I then turn to a well-known and
controversial example of the imposition of liability—liability under
CERCLA, to demonstrate the role of some of these factors in a specific
policy context. Finally, I look more generally at the empirical literature
that exists to see what, if anything, it suggests about the effectiveness of
pricing environmental services through the use of liability. I focus on
statistical rather than anecdotal evidence regarding the impact of liability.

BENCHMARKS FOR EVALUATION

To evaluate the deterrence effect of strict liability either theoretically or
empirically, it is essential to identify clearly the benchmark that is being
used for comparison, because different benchmarks can lead to different
conclusions. Two types of benchmarks are possible: (1) absolute efficiency, and (2) relative efficiency or effectiveness. Under the first benchmark, the question is whether strict liability can achieve the first-best
outcome, whereas under the second benchmark the question is whether
strict liability yields a better outcome than an alternative policy (possibly
the status quo). Because of the importance of the benchmark, I discuss
these alternatives briefly before turning to the theoretical literature on
strict liability.

Absolute Efficiency

The benchmark most commonly used in the theoretical economic literature
on strict liability is economic efficiency, that is, whether a strict liability rule
will lead to efficient behavior, where efficiency is defined in terms of maximizing social welfare or net benefits. If not, one can ask whether it leads to
under- or overdeterrence, that is, too much or too little deterrence relative
to the efficient level. Although deterrence is often treated as a single variable, in fact it comprises any of the behaviors that can influence the likelihood or magnitude of environmental contamination, including (1) the
amount of care exercised by the polluter in conducting the pollution-
generating activity, (2) the amount of that activity that the polluter con-
ducts, (3) the amount of mitigation or care exercised by the potential

victim(s) to avoid or reduce damages through reduced exposure, and (4) the amount of the exposure-reducing activity undertaken by the victim. For example, the damages from contamination of groundwater from the use of agricultural chemicals depend on (1) the care used in the application of pesticides, (2) the amount of the pesticide used, (3) the extent to which the victim invests in filtration to reduce the contamination level of the water, and (4) the extent to which the victim reduces exposure by reducing the amount of contaminated water consumed (e.g., by switching to an alternative water source). Efficient deterrence requires that each of these components of deterrence be chosen efficiently.

In addition to the direct impact on deterrence, the efficiency of strict liability can also be evaluated based on its impact on other, related activities. For example, when applied to contamination of land, the imposition of strict liability on the buyer or seller can affect incentives for the purchase or sale of contaminated properties (Segerson 1993, 1997). In this context, one can ask whether strict liability will lead to efficient buy/sell incentives. Similarly, if strict liability is extended to lenders or capital owners, it can affect the cost of capital and hence a firm's capital structure (Heyes 1996; Pitchford 1995; Garber and Hammitt 1998; Ulph and Valentini 2000). In this context, one can evaluate whether strict liability yields efficiency regarding the use of capital. When liability is applied retroactively to finance the cleanup of contaminated sites, one can examine whether strict liability leads to efficient cleanup (Sigman 1998). In all of these cases, the liability is expected to have an indirect effect on a related activity, which could be an important determinant of the overall efficiency results.

Relative Efficiency or Effectiveness

Although absolute efficiency is the benchmark used most frequently when evaluating alternative liability rules in theoretical models, it is generally not a practical benchmark in empirical analyses because the benchmark is generally not observable. Instead of using the efficient level of deterrence as a benchmark, an alternative is to compare the level of deterrence under strict liability with the level that would have been attained otherwise. In this context, one can simply ask (1) whether strict liability leads to more or less deterrence than the alternative (a ranking based on total deterrence), or (2) whether strict liability leads to a level of deterrence that is more or less efficient than the alternative (a ranking based on social welfare). Of course, a ranking based on social welfare suffers from the same drawback as the absolute efficiency benchmark when doing empirical analysis, namely, the lack of observability of social welfare under the two alternatives. Thus, in practice, most empirical analyses use a ranking based on deterrence.

Whether based on deterrence or social welfare, the answer to the question of whether strict liability is preferred or not clearly depends on what the alternative policy is. Possible alternatives include (1) no policy, that is, the status quo; (2) a command-and-control policy (i.e., regulation);

and (3) a negligence-based liability rule. In the first case of no policy, the question is simply whether strict liability has any effect at all on deterrence or other polluter decisions, that is, is it better than nothing? The second case relates to the debate over whether it is better to use regulation or liability to control externality-generating activities, such as pollution (e.g., Shavell 1984a, 1984b; Segerson 1986, 1987; Kolstad et al. 1990). Finally, if liability is to be used, the third case asks whether strict liability or a negligence rule is preferred (e.g., Shavell 1980; Polinsky 1980).

ISSUES IN ASSESSING THE IMPACT OF LIABILITY:
THEORETICAL BACKGROUND

I now turn to the question of assessing strict liability as an incentive-based tool for environmental protection. I briefly review some of the theoretical literature evaluating the impact of strict liability, both in absolute and relative terms. The goal is to highlight the factors that emerge from the theoretical literature as important determinants of the likely effectiveness of liability in a specific context.

Absolute Efficiency

As already noted, because in theory strict liability imposes the full costs of any pollution that occurs on the polluter, it essentially makes polluters pay a price for pollution. Although under strict liability the payment is not determined until after damages occur (if they occur at all), at the time the polluter is making decisions about pollution-generating activities, he has some expectation about what those damages will be (based on the probability of a release and the likely damages that would result from a release) and hence some expectation about what the likely liability will be, given different decisions he might make. Thus, in making those decisions, he will consider the expected liability and presumably adjust his behavior accordingly. It is well known that if polluters expect to have to pay the full amount of damages regardless of their care level,[4] then in theory they will make efficient decisions regarding both care and activity levels. Victims, on the other hand, will not face efficient incentives for either care or activity level, because they will be fully compensated for damages and thus have no incentive to undertake costly actions to reduce those damages. It is important to note, however, that the deterrence incentives created by strict liability only exist if the liability is applied prospectively. When applied retroactively, the liability will not have a deterrence effect because the opportunity for deterrence will have already passed.[5]

Although in theory strict liability can provide efficient deterrence incentives, it is also well known that the ideal conditions under which this holds are not likely to exist in practice, and as a result polluters are not likely to pay the full amount of damages resulting from their activities (Menell 1991). There are a number of reasons why polluters might not be held fully responsible even under strict liability. These include

(1) insufficient polluter assets, (2) the difficulty in proving causation, (3) insufficient incentives for victims to bring costly suits, (4) restrictions on who is allowed to bring suit (standing), and (5) statutes of limitations. Although limited polluter assets can in theory lead to overdeterrence (Beard 1990), in general polluters who are not likely to be required to pay the full amount of damages for the reasons given can be expected to underdeter (e.g., Shavell 1984a).

In any particular context, the severity of these limitations will depend on the nature of the environmental accident. For example, with small to medium accidental spills or releases from a single facility, it is likely that it will be easy to ascertain quickly that the spill has occurred, identify the responsible party, and hold the responsible party liable for full damages. However, for contamination resulting from slow leaching of hazardous substances where many victims are exposed after (and possibly over) a long period of time, these factors are likely to be more limiting.

Rules have been developed to try to overcome these barriers. For example, class action suits can reduce litigation costs per victim and encourage groups of victims to seek redress when it would not be economically worthwhile for any individual victim to do so on their own. Likewise, market share or joint and several liability provide a means of assigning liability when the individual polluter responsible for the plaintiff's damages cannot be easily identified but the group of possible responsible parties can be, or when the assets of some are limited. Discovery rules delay the start of the clock for statutes of limitations until the time of discovery to allow victims ample time to seek redress once the discovery of damages has occurred. Despite these provisions, victims continue to face considerable barriers to recovery for environmental damages through the common law system of torts (Menell 1991; Dewees et al. 1996). Similarly, statutory liability is often incomplete. For example, liability under CERCLA covers damages to natural resources but not third-party damages.

Of course, if polluters are required to pay *more* than the damages generated by their activities, they might overdeter, that is, invest in too much precaution (relative to the efficient amount) or engage in the activity too little. When held jointly and severally liable for damages, a firm can be forced to pay an amount that exceeds its contribution to damages. However, the incentive effects of this depend on whether the firm is able to shift some of its liability onto other parties through price adjustments (see further discussion).[6] Thus, although in many contexts the concern is that the limitations of the legal system will lead to underdeterrence even under strict liability, it is certainly possible in theory for some forms of strict liability to create incentives for overdeterrence.

Relative Efficiency or Effectiveness

Even if strict liability does not fully internalize the damages resulting from pollution, one can still ask whether it is better than the alternative. Relative to no policy, economic theory would predict that in a simple world the imposition of strict liability would, ceteris paribus, provide incentives for increased deterrence by forcing polluters to pay for the use of environmental inputs. However, it is also possible that the imposition of strict liability could change the structure of the industry in a way that would actually lead to higher expected damages than would exist without it. For example, if in response to liability firms contract out risky operations to fly-by-night operators who are shielded from liability by their limited assets, then the risk of environmental damages may actually increase rather than decrease when liability is imposed (Ringleb and Wiggins 1990).

Likewise, it is also possible that the imposition of strict liability will have no effect on deterrence. This can occur when costs can be shifted from one party to another through a contractual relationship and price adjustment (e.g., Landes and Posner 1985; Shavell 1980; Segerson 1990). For example, imposing strict liability on an employer for damages due to exposure of workers to hazardous substances will not necessarily lead to greater precaution by the employer if, even in the absence of liability, the employer was effectively bearing the cost of the environmental dangers associated with the facility through higher wages necessary to induce workers to work in a more hazardous environment. Thus, even relative to the alternative of no liability, the effect of imposing strict liability will depend on whether opportunities for shifting liability through price adjustments exist.

If the benchmark for comparison is the level of deterrence under regulation rather than the level under no policy, the effect of strict liability is still ambiguous. In the absence of any imperfections in the legal system or asset limitations, strict liability induces efficient choices by polluters for both care and activity levels. In principle, regulations can also be designed to yield efficient care. However, because polluters do not pay for residual damages under regulations, they do not face the full social costs of their activities and hence can be expected to choose an activity level that is too high. Thus, even if both policies yield the same level of care, total damages are likely to be higher under regulation because activity levels would be expected to be higher. In addition, strict liability yields efficient care even when polluters are heterogeneous. For regulations to be efficient in this context, those regulations must be polluter-specific, that is, uniform regulations will be inefficient. This again tends to favor strict liability on efficiency grounds.

However, once imperfections in the legal system and polluter asset limitations are considered, the efficiency of strict liability is reduced and the relative ranking of the two policies becomes ambiguous.[7] The limitations inherent in both approaches have led some authors to advocate the combined use of liability and regulation (e.g., Shavell 1984a; Segerson 1986, 1987; Kolstad et al. 1990).

Because a negligence rule acts in many ways like a regulation, the comparison between strict liability and negligence is similar to the comparison between strict liability and regulation. For example, it is well known that in the absence of any legal imperfections or asset limits, either can lead to efficient care, although only strict liability also yields an efficient activity level (Shavell 1980, 1987). Likewise, if polluters are heterogeneous, then a uniform due standard of care (comparable to a uniform regulation) will not be efficient, whereas strict liability will continue to be efficient even in this case. There is, however, a key difference between negligence rules and regulations that can affect their relative efficiencies. Regulatory standards are known to the polluter at the time that deterrence decisions are made, but the exact standard of care that would be imposed by a court ex post is not. This uncertainty about the standard of care that would be imposed under a negligence rule can affect the polluter's deterrence incentives (e.g., Craswell and Calfee 1986; Kolstad et al. 1990). Depending on the nature of the uncertainty and the marginal cost of care, it can lead to either over- or underdeterrence. In addition, to the extent that it is more difficult to prove negligence, victim incentives to sue may be weaker under a negligence rule than under strict liability. Ceteris paribus, this would make strict liability more efficient.

Conclusions from the Theoretical Literature

The overview suggests the following general conclusions that emerge from the theoretical literature on strict liability:

- In theory, prospective application of strict liability can act like a pricing mechanism, which provides incentives for polluters to take efficient care to reduce the likelihood or magnitude of environmental accidents.
- In practice, there are several barriers to recovery that often prevent polluters from facing full liability for the damages they create and hence reduce the incentives for them to undertake care, although some of the attempts to overcome these barriers (e.g., the use of joint and several liability) can actually lead to overdeterrence.
- Because polluters can avoid liability in ways other than deterrence (e.g., changing firm structure, avoiding certain contracts), the imposition of liability can also have unintended indirect effects that can undermine deterrence or distort other markets.
- Polluters sometimes have the possibility of shifting liability to other parties through price adjustments, which can also affect the deterrence incentives created by the imposition of liability.

These conclusions suggest that except in the simplest context, the effects of strict liability are complicated and depend on the specific context. As a result, economic theory does not suggest unambiguous conclusions regarding the deterrence or social welfare effects of strict liability either in absolute terms or relative to other policies, including the status quo, regulation, and negligence-based rules. Nonetheless, it does suggest that the following issues or factors will be important determinants of the incentive effects of liability:

- Is the imposition of the liability retroactive or prospective?
- Is there a long latency period between the time of the contamination and the time when the resulting damages occur or become known?
- Can the responsible party or parties be easily identified, or is causation difficult to prove?
- Is the magnitude of the damages large relative to the assets of the polluter?
- Are the damages concentrated or dispersed across space and victims?
- Are there indirect ways in which the polluter can avoid liability other than through increased deterrence?
- Does the polluter have a contractual relationship with the victim or other responsible parties that allows liability to be shifted through price adjustments?

The answers to these questions will determine the likely effects of strict liability relative both to an overall efficiency standard and to alternative policy options.

AN EXAMPLE: CERCLA LIABILITY

In this section, I briefly illustrate the role of the factors just identified in a specific context, namely, liability under CERCLA. The purpose is not to provide a thorough analysis or evaluation of CERCLA liability but to see how the general principles and results can be applied.[8]

For many people the phrase "environmental liability" is associated primarily with CERCLA liability. The primary goal of CERCLA is to provide a mechanism for responding to and paying for cleanup of contamination from hazardous substances. The statute charges the U.S. Environmental Protection Agency (EPA) with identifying the parties responsible for the contamination. In identifying the potentially responsible parties (PRPs), the EPA is allowed to cast a wide net to include nearly anyone who was involved with the hazardous substance at some point between generation and final disposal. If responsible parties can be identified, the EPA can then either force those parties to undertake cleanup or undertake the cleanup itself and then seek reimbursement for its expenses through legal actions against those parties. In determining the responsible parties' liability, the courts have interpreted CERCLA as imposing strict, retroactive, and joint and several liability.

In evaluating the provisions of CERCLA and the criticisms that have been leveled against it, it is important to note that liability under this law applies to two distinct types of contamination from hazardous substances. The first type stems from sudden and accidental releases or spills. The second type results from gradual releases that may occur after an extended period of time, primarily from the disposal of hazardous wastes. Although the end result in both cases is contamination from hazardous substances, the policy issues that arise in the control of these two types of contamination can be very different. For this reason, I discuss the application of liability to these two types of contamination separately.

Waste Disposal Sites

Most of the concerns about CERCLA liability relate to its application to the cleanup of hazardous waste sites. In this context the potential for retroactive and joint and several liability primarily arises, and concerns about excessive cleanups have been voiced.

Retroactive Liability

As noted, CERCLA liability can be applied retroactively, that is, at sites that are contaminated as a result of activities that were undertaken long before the enactment of the statute in 1980. As already mentioned, in general, retroactive application of liability will have no effect on the likelihood or magnitude of contamination at a site, because it is not possible to change the way the past activities that led to the contamination were conducted. Thus, when applied retroactively, the use of liability will not have a deterrence effect, that is, an effect on the incentives to generate less waste or dispose of it more carefully (although it should provide an incentive for early detection and containment). Thus, in this context liability serves mainly to finance cleanup rather than deter contamination. The majority of CERCLA cases at waste disposal sites have involved retroactive application of liability.

Joint and Several Liability

A second controversial aspect of CERCLA is its imposition of joint and several liability, under which a party can be held liable for the full amount of cleanup even if its contribution to the contamination is very small. In considering the deterrence effect of joint and several liability, it is important to distinguish between cases where liability is extended horizontally and where it is extended vertically. I consider each of these in turn.

Horizontal joint and several liability extends to a group of parties that are otherwise unrelated, that is, that have no other interactions through market transactions. For example, although different waste generators may contribute waste to the same waste disposal site, these waste generators are otherwise independent of each other. Numerous authors have considered the deterrence effects of joint and several liability in this context.[9] In general, the results suggest that the deterrence effects are ambiguous. They depend on the costs and benefits associated with each party's activities, the solvency levels of each party, and the EPA's targeting strategy. Thus, in this context I cannot uniformly conclude that the use of joint and several liability will lead to either under- or over-deterrence or more or less deterrence than a several-only rule.

In contrast, joint and several liability can generally be expected to increase deterrence (relative to a several-only rule) when applied vertically. Under vertical liability, the parties who are jointly and severally liable have a contractual or market relationship, that is, they interact through the purchase/sale of a good or service. For example, waste generators have market relationships with their transporters, disposers, and the owners or operators of a site when they purchase transportation and disposal services. Similarly, buyers and sellers of land have a market relationship, as do lenders and borrowers. As noted, when parties have a market relationship, the purchase/sale price provides a mechanism for shifting the expected costs of liability between parties. Although such shifting may be imperfect, it can affect deterrence incentives. For example, if a property owner plans to sell his or her land in the future, the knowledge that he or she will be held jointly and severally liable for any contamination that is detected at the site in the future can create an increased incentive for the landowner to take precautions now. Similarly, holding both the generator and transporter of hazardous waste jointly and severally liable provides an incentive for generators not to contract with fly-by-night transporters who might cut prices but otherwise have little incentive to take care in the transportation of waste.

Excessive Cleanup Costs

Many have argued that cleanups at CERCLA sites are excessive (e.g., Hamilton and Viscusi 1999). Specifically, they claim that the cleanup that is required is inefficient because the costs exceed the benefits. If so, in addition to the inefficiency in the level of cleanup, other inefficiencies can result as well. For example, holding parties strictly liable for these costs will, ceteris paribus, result in excessive care and too little output because the total costs incurred by the firm would exceed the social costs of its activities. However, the increase in costs due to excessive cleanup can be offset somewhat by other factors that tend to reduce the firm's costs, such as limited assets (which limit the firm's exposure to liability) or insufficient incentives for individuals to bring suit for third-party damages.

Accidental Spills

Many of the concerns about CERCLA liability that have been voiced do not apply when the statute is applied to sudden spills. First, for most sudden spills, the application of CERCLA liability will be prospective rather than retroactive. This implies that at the time of the hazardous activity (such as transportation of the hazardous substance), the liability imposed is known and presumably considered when making decisions regarding that activity. Thus, the application of liability to spills can have a deterrence effect, because parties will be aware of the liability at the time they make deterrence-related decisions.

Second, the occurrence of the spill and the identity of the responsible party is generally known, so latency is not an issue, and causation and responsibility are relatively easy to establish. In addition, there is generally a single responsible party. This implies that the issues (and hence the concerns) regarding joint and several liability do not normally arise in the context of spills.

For these reasons, when applied to accidental spills, the imposition of liability more closely parallels the simple strict liability rule already discussed. This suggests that it will be more efficient in this context than when applied to waste disposal sites.

STATISTICAL EVIDENCE ON THE DETERRENCE EFFECT OF LIABILITY

I turn next to the limited statistical evidence that exists regarding the effect of strict liability. As already mentioned, rather than using an absolute efficiency benchmark, empirical evaluations by necessity use a relative benchmark, which is usually the status quo or a negligence-based liability rule.

There are two basic approaches to studying the empirical effects of liability. The first is to try to establish empirically a direct link between liability and some measure of (or proxy for) environmental performance. The second is to seek to establish the impact of liability indirectly by examining the link between liability and another variable (such as an input price) that in theory would provide an incentive for increased deterrence. I consider each of these in turn.

Direct Measures

Challenges

Estimating the incentive effects of any liability rule directly requires observations on both the liability rule that the polluter would expect to face if damages occurred and the behavior that directly affects the probability or level of damages. Unfortunately, in many cases neither of these will be readily observable. For this reason, empirical studies of the direct effect of liability generally employ imperfect proxies for one or both of these variables.

One possible proxy for polluter care or activity level is a measure of environmental damages (or, alternatively, improvements in environmental quality).[10] Although this approach provides information on the net effect of liability on damages, it does not necessarily provide information about the impact of liability on polluter incentives. For example, when damages depend not only on polluter behavior but also on the behavior of victims, then observations on damages will reflect the combined effect of liability on both polluters and victims. Because the imposition of strict liability shifts costs from victims to polluters, it could lead to an increase in polluter care but a decrease in victim care, with little impact on overall damages. Thus, the policy might be very effective in changing behavior without any significant change in damages. An empirical analysis that uses damages as a proxy for polluter care would then inappropriately conclude that the policy was not effective.

Even when damages are a suitable proxy for polluter decisions, it may be difficult to measure damages accurately. Two possible proxies for the actual damages are the number of accidents and the dollar amounts awarded for damages by courts. Using the number of accidents as the proxy captures behavioral changes linked to the frequency but not to the severity of accidents, although it may be possible to capture this somewhat by correcting for accident type. Likewise, actual damage awards often reflect a number of factors other than simply damages.

Empirical examination of the effect of liability is also made more difficult by the confounding effects of regulation. In many cases, changes in liability occurred at the same time as regulatory changes (Dewees et al. 1996). For example, the liability under CERCLA followed closely after the regulatory changes embodied in the Resource Conservation and Recovery Act (RCRA). Because both liability and regulation are generally designed to reduce environmental contamination, it can be difficult to isolate the effect of either individual policy change when the two are changed concurrently.

Existing Evidence

Some of the earliest empirical studies of liability examined accidents in the contexts of workplace safety and product safety. Overall, the evidence that emerges from this literature is mixed. The workplace safety studies examined the impact that increases in workers' compensation have had on safety. Early studies showed that observed accident rates and claims actually rose when worker's compensation was imposed, possibly due to reduced victim care (see the overview by Ehrenberg 1988). More recent evidence shows, however, that workers' compensation has been effective in reducing death risks (Moore and Viscusi 1989, 1990). It has been less effective, though, in addressing disease-related claims where there are long latency periods and causation is more difficult to prove (Viscusi 1991). This suggests that liability is more likely to be effective when the link between injurer behavior and damages is clear and immediate, so that causation and responsibility can be readily established.

Dewees et al. (1996) review direct evidence regarding the deterrence effect of environmental liability. Their conclusions are consistent with the results from the studies of workplace safety. They conclude that although there is little evidence of a general response to the potential for environmental liability under common law, there is anecdotal evidence that firms have responded to statutory liability imposed under CERCLA. Most CERCLA cases share the characteristics noted, namely, they involve large amounts of pollutants discharged from a single source that harm property (mainly land) or a small group of individuals, implying that causation and responsibility can be readily established.

Although anecdotal evidence is useful for establishing hypotheses, to test these hypotheses I would like to see whether a statistically significant link exists between liability and polluter behavior. Such studies have only recently begun to emerge because of the difficulties already identified. Recent studies by Alberini and Austin (1999, 2001, 2002) and Stafford (2003) exploit cross-sectional variability in state hazardous waste laws to examine the impact of the liability provisions in those laws. Although their results are mixed, Alberini and Austin (1999) and Stafford (2003) both find some evidence that strict liability may reduce rather than increase care relative to a negligence rule. Alberini and Austin (1999) use data on the number of accidents and spills involving hazardous substances to test whether their frequency is lower in states with strict liability. They find that for some chemicals, spills are in fact more numerous in states imposing strict liability. Similarly, Stafford (2003) uses facility-level data on inspection and compliance from the RCRA Information System to test whether the probability of inspection and the probability of detecting a violation are higher in states with strict liability hazardous waste laws than in those with negligence-based laws. Although the results on inspections support this hypothesis, the results for violations are mixed.

A possible explanation for the mixed results is the potential endogeneity of the choice of liability regime. It is possible that states that are likely to experience a higher number of accidents or violations are more likely to adopt strict liability rather than negligence. Alberini and Austin (2002) find empirical support for this conjecture. Correcting for this endogeneity, they then find that imposition of strict liability rather than negligence does reduce the number of spills.[11]

Recent evidence on Superfund cleanups suggests, however, that the imposition of liability can have unintended effects. Sigman (1998) hypothesizes that holding PRPs liable for cleanup of a given Superfund site may affect the extent of cleanup that the EPA decides to undertake there. Using data on the EPA's cleanup decisions on sites that are on the National Priorities List and proxies for the share of cleanup costs that the EPA expects PRPs to pay, she finds that the EPA chooses less extensive cleanup remedies when PRPs could be expected to bear a larger share of cleanup costs. Remedies are more extensive at orphan sites, which involve no PRP liability. These findings suggest that the existence of PRP liability leads to less environmental improvement than would have existed without liability. Similarly, studies have found that PRP liability can affect the pace of cleanup, that is, that cleanup is delayed at sites with greater PRP liability (Rausser et al. 1998; Sigman 2001b).

However, neither less extensive cleanup nor cleanup delays necessarily imply that PRP liability is inefficient (Sigman 2001a). Several studies of Superfund cleanups have suggested that the extent of cleanup at some sites exceeds the efficient level (e.g., Hamilton and Viscusi 1999). In this case, a reduction or delay in cleanup resulting from PRP liability could actually be welfare-improving.

Indirect Measures

The studies mentioned seek to determine the impact of liability by directly linking a measure of liability to a measure of environmental performance. It is also possible to examine the impact of liability indirectly by determining its effect on measures that polluters are likely to care about, such as stock or land prices. The implicit assumption underlying this indirect approach is that changes in these prices or related measures will induce polluters to take steps to mitigate those changes. However, whereas observing that liability affects prices provides information about the incidence of liability, it does not provide any direct evidence that those price changes lead to increased care or otherwise reduced environmental contamination.

Opaluch and Grigalunas (1984) conducted one of the earliest empirical studies of the impact of environmental liability, which relied on an indirect approach. They examined the impacts of the liability provisions of the Outer Continental Shelf Lands Act, which holds firms strictly liable for damages from offshore oil spills. More specifically, they considered whether the potential for greater liability in environmentally sensitive areas affected bids for Outer Continental Shelf leases in those areas. They found evidence supporting the hypothesis that potential liability is capitalized into bid prices.

Similarly, Garber and Hammitt (1998) examined the impact of Superfund liability on the cost of capital for firms. Using data on monthly stock returns for the chemical manufacturing industry and various measures of exposure to Superfund liability for contaminated sites, they find that increased Superfund exposure does increase the cost of capital for large chemical companies. However, they are unable to find a similar effect for small firms.

Although these studies do not focus on deterrence behavior directly, they presume that the effect of liability on prices will induce increased deterrence in an effort to reduce their liability exposure. However, as noted, firms can seek to limit their liability not through increased deterrence but rather through other means of avoiding liability. For example, there is evidence that liability affects the incentives to purchase property that is or might be contaminated.[12] A recent survey by Alberini et al. (2003) finds that developers view sites with contamination as less attractive than sites without, suggesting, ceteris paribus, that they would be less likely to purchase a contaminated site. Although this might be partially due to the negative effect that contamination could have on the intended use, it is likely that it also reflects concerns about the associated liability for cleanup. This is consistent with the results of an earlier survey by the Rand Corporation (Reuter 1988).

Alternatively, firms can avoid liability by changes in corporate structure. For example, in anticipation of potential liability, firms can spin off hazardous operations to small firms that can avoid liability through bankruptcy. Studies have found evidence of such an effect. Using cross-sectional data on firm structure across industries that differ in their degree of hazard, Ringleb and Wiggins (1990) and Merolla (1998) found evidence of corporate restructuring in response to potential liability. In particular, they find that more hazardous industries have more small, private independent firms and firms with shorter life spans. Both of these findings suggest that firms may seek to avoid liability by concentrating hazardous activities in firms that can easily hide behind the protection of bankruptcy. This conclusion is consistent with anecdotal evidence presented by Wiggins and Ringleb (1992).

The recent study by Alberini and Austin (2002) also examines the link between strict liability and firm size. Using variability across states in the liability provisions of mini-Superfund laws, they find no evidence that there are relatively more small firms in states with strict liability than in states with negligence. To the extent that liability is greater under strict liability than under negligence, this implies that increased liability has not resulted in relatively more small firms, in contrast to the Ringleb and Wiggins (1990) results. However, they did find that in strict-liability states smaller firms have a greater propensity to spill. This suggests that small firms may in fact be more likely to undertake hazardous operations. Thus, the effect of liability may be more through the types of operations that small firms choose to undertake rather than an increase in the number of small firms.

Conclusions from the Empirical Literature

Because the empirical literature is still very limited, it is difficult to draw firm conclusions regarding the impact of liability. Nonetheless, the work to date suggests some preliminary conclusions.

First, there is convincing evidence that prices respond to reflect increases in liability. One can hypothesize that this will in turn affect polluter behavior, but the mere existence of a price effect does not provide evidence of a behavioral response. Thus, the literature on price effects provides little evidence regarding the deterrence effect of liability.

Second, studies that examine the direct impact of liability on a measure of environmental performance (e.g., accident rates) provide some support for the hypothesis that strict liability has lead to increased deterrence relative both to no liability and to a negligence rule. However, interpretation of these results is complicated by the inability to control for victim responses and by the endogeneity of the policy choice. The evidence does suggest, however, that liability has been most effective when applied in contexts where causation and responsibility can be readily established and damages are concentrated on a small number of victims.

Finally, there is growing evidence that liability has triggered unanticipated responses that can run counter to its deterrence goals. Because firms can reduce their liability not only through deterrence but also by avoiding payment, they have an incentive to take steps to reduce their likelihood of paying, and they appear to be doing so. Examples include avoiding purchases of contaminated sites, restructuring or reorganizing the allocation of operations to minimize liability exposure, and getting involved in the decision-making process for National Priorities List sites in an effort to influence the extent or timing of cleanup.

CONCLUSION

Strict liability for environmental damages is an example of a pricing approach to environmental protection under which firms are forced to pay for the environmental goods and services that they consume. Although generally used for control of stochastic pollution events, such a policy is similar to the use of taxes or marketable permits for control of continuous emissions of air or water pollutants. The increased use of statutorily imposed liability over the past twenty years parallels the experimentation with these other market-based approaches to environmental protection during that same period.

This chapter has examined the impact of liability on polluter behavior in an effort to determine whether this policy approach has proven to be successful. To date, the literature has been primarily theoretical, although there is a limited body of empirical analysis. Taken together, the theoretical and empirical literatures suggest that strict liability can act like a market-based incentive mechanism and provide incentives for polluters to reduce the likelihood and magnitude of environmental accidents. The strength of these incentives is likely to be greatest under the following conditions: (1) Liability is applied prospectively rather than retroactively; (2) the damage is known shortly after it occurs, that is, there is no latency period; (3) the responsible party or parties can be easily identified, and, if there are multiple responsible parties, the allocation of responsibility is clear; (4) the responsible parties have sufficient assets to cover the liability; and (5) the damages are concentrated rather than dispersed across space and victims.

However, even when these conditions are met, in addition to its deterrence incentive, it is possible that strict liability will also create incentives for other types of behavior that can undermine deterrence or distort other markets. When comparing strict liability to other policy options, the potential for these indirect effects should be considered as well.

NOTES

1. *See* Pendergrass (2002) for an analysis of these programs.

2. In fact, much of the original motivation for CERCLA stemmed from the need to generate revenue to finance the cleanup of sites already contaminated by past activities. Retroactive liability of this type is designed primarily to provide funds for redress rather than to deter.

3. For a more thorough treatment, *see* Segerson (2002).

4. For a discussion of the deterrence effects of alternative liability rules, *see* Shavell (1980, 1987).

5. Strict liability would, however, provide an incentive to reduce the damages from contamination through early detection and containment or other mitigation strategies. For a discussion of retroactive application of liability, *see* Tilton (1995).

6. For discussions of joint and several liability, *see*, for example, Tietenberg (1989), Kornhauser and Revesz (1989, 1990), and Miceli and Segerson (1991).

7. The relative ranking of the two approaches can also depend on the transaction costs associated with each. *See*, for example, Shavell (1984b).

8. Detailed discussions of CERCLA liability can be found in Grigalunas and Opaluch (1988) and Strasser and Rodosevich (1993).

9. *See*, for example, Tietenberg (1989), Kornhauser and Revesz (1989, 1990), and Miceli and Segerson (1991).

10. Dewees et al. (1996) refer to this as an output analysis of the impact of liability.

11. However, even though strict liability was found to reduce the number of spills relative to what would have been expected if the strict liability state had imposed a negligence standard instead, the number of spills is greater in strict-liability states than in negligence states. This is attributable to the characteristics of states that adopt strict liability. Such states tend to have industry characteristics that lead to a greater propensity for spills. *See* Alberini and Austin (2002) for a detailed discussion.

12. *See* Segerson (1993, 1997) and Boyd et al. (1996) for discussions of the incentives to buy and sell property subject to CERCLA liability.

REFERENCES

Alberini, Anna, and David Austin (1999), "Strict Liability as a Deterrent in Toxic Waste Management: Empirical Evidence from Accident and Spill Data," *Journal of Environmental Economics and Management* 38:20–48.

Alberini, Anna, and David Austin (2001), "Liability Policy and Toxic Pollution Releases," in Anthony Heyes (ed.), *The Law and Economics of the Environment*, Cheltenham, UK: Edward Elgar.

Alberini, Anna, and David Austin (2002), "Accidents Waiting to Happen: Liability Policy and Toxic Pollution Releases," *Review of Economics and Statistics* 84(4): 729–41.

Alberini, Anna, Alberto Longo, Stefania Tonin, Francesco Trombetta, and Margherita Turvani (2003), "The Role of Liability, Regulation and Economic Incentives in Brownfield Remediation and Development: Evidence from Surveys of Developers," Fondazione Eni Enrico Mattei, Nota di Lavoro 7.2003.

Baram, Michael S. (1982), *Alternatives to Regulation: Managing Risks to Health, Safety, and the Environment*, Lexington, MA: Heath.

Beard, Randolph T. (1990), "Bankruptcy and Care Choice," *Rand Journal of Economics* 21(4): 626–34.

Boyd, James, Winston Harrington, and Molly K. Macauley (1996), "The Effects of Environmental Liability on Industrial Real Estate Development," *Journal of Real Estate Finance and Economics* 12: 37–58.

Cooter, Robert (1984), "Prices and Sanctions," *Columbia Law Review* 84: 1523–60.

Craswell, Richard, and John E. Calfee (1986), "Deterrence and Uncertain Legal Standards," *Journal of Law, Economics and Organization* 2:279–303.

Dewees, Don, David Duff, and Michael Trebilcock (1996), *Exploring the Domain of Accident Law: Taking the Facts Seriously*, New York: Oxford University Press.

Ehrenberg, Ronald G. (1988), "Workers' Compensation, Wages, and the Risk of Injury," in John F. Burton (ed.), *New Perspectives in Workers' Compensation*, Ithaca, NY: Cornell University ILR Press.

Garber, Steven, and James K. Hammitt (1998), "Risk Premiums for Environmental Liability: Does Superfund Increase the Cost of Capital?" *Journal of Environmental Economics and Management* 36(3): 267–94.

Grigalunas, Thomas A., and James J. Opaluch (1988), "Assessing Liability for Damages under CERCLA: A New Approach for Providing Incentives for Pollution Avoidance," *Natural Resources Journal* 28(3): 509–33.

Hamilton, James T., and W. Kip Viscusi (1999), "How Costly Is 'Clean'? An Analysis of the Benefits and Costs of Superfund Site Remediations," *Journal of Policy Analysis and Management* 18: 2–27.

Heyes, Anthony (1996), "Lender Penalty for Environmental Damage and the Equilibrium Cost of Capital," *Economica* 63: 311–23.

Kolstad, Charles D., Thomas S. Ulen, and Gary V. Johnson (1990), "Ex Post Liability for Harm vs. Ex Ante Safety Regulation: Substitutes or Complements?" *American Economic Review* 80: 888–901.

Kornhauser, Lewis A., and Richard L. Revesz (1989), "Sharing Damages among Multiple Tortfeasors," *Yale Law Journal* 98: 831–84.

Kornhauser, Lewis A., and Richard L. Revesz (1990), "Apportioning Damages among Potentially Insolvent Actors," *Journal of Legal Studies* 19(2): 617–51.

Landes, William, and Richard Posner (1985), "A Positive Economic Theory of Products Liability," *Journal of Legal Studies* 14: 535–67.

Menell, Peter S. (1991), "The Limitations of Legal Institutions for Addressing Environmental Risks," *Journal of Economic Perspectives* 5: 93–113.

Merolla, A. Todd (1998), "The Effect of Latent Hazards on Firm Exit in Manufacturing Industries," *International Review of Law and Economics* 18: 13–24.

Miceli, Thomas J., and Kathleen Segerson (1991), "Joint Liability in Torts: Marginal and Inframarginal Efficiency," *International Review of Law and Economics* 11: 235–49.

Moore, Michael J., and W. Kip Viscusi (1989), "Promoting Safety through Workers' Compensation: The Efficacy and Net Wage Costs of Injury Insurance," *RAND Journal of Economics* 20: 499–515.

Moore, Michael J., and W. Kip Viscusi (1990), *Compensation Mechanisms for Job Risks: Wages, Workers' Compensation, and Product Liability*, Princeton, NJ: Princeton University Press.

Opaluch, James J., and Thomas A. Grigalunas (1984), "Controlling Stochastic Pollution Events through Liability Rules: Some Evidence from OCS Leasing," *RAND Journal of Economics* 15: 142–51.

Pendergrass, John (2002), "An Analysis of State Superfund Programs: 50-State Study, 2001 Update," Environmental Law Institute, Washington, DC.

Pitchford, Rohan (1995), "How Liable Should a Lender Be? The Case of Judgment-Proof Firms and Environmental Risk," *American Economic Review* 85: 1171–86.

Polinsky, A. Mitchell (1980), "Strict Liability vs. Negligence in a Market Setting," *American Economic Review* 70: 363–67.

Rausser, Gordon C., Leo K. Simon, and Jinhua Zhao (1998), "Information Asymmetries, Uncertainties, and Cleanup Delays at Superfund Sites," *Journal of Environmental Economics and Management* 35(1): 48–68.

Reuter, Peter (1988), "The Economic Consequences of Expanded Corporate Liability: An Exploratory Study," N-2807-ICJ, Santa Monica, CA: RAND Corporation.

Ringleb, A. H., and S. N. Wiggins (1990), "Liability and Large-Scale, Long-Term Hazards," *Journal of Political Economy* 98: 574–95.

Segerson, Kathleen (1986), "Risk Sharing in the Design of Environmental Policy," *American Journal of Agricultural Economics* 68: 1261–65.

Segerson, Kathleen (1987), "Risk-Sharing and Liability in the Control of Stochastic Externalities," *Marine Resource Economics* 4: 175–92.

Segerson, Kathleen (1990), "Liability for Groundwater Contamination from Pesticides," *Journal of Environmental Economics and Management* 19(3): 227–43.

Segerson, Kathleen (1993), "Liability Transfers: An Economic Assessment of Buyer and Lender Liability," *Journal of Environmental Economics and Management* 25: S46–63.

Segerson, Kathleen (1997), "Legal Liability as an Environmental Policy Tool: Some Implications for Land Markets," *Journal of Real Estate Finance and Economics* 15: 143–59.

Segerson, Kathleen, ed., 2002, *Economics and Liability for Environmental Problems,* Aldershot, UK: Ashgate.

Shavell, Steven (1980), "Strict Liability versus Negligence," *Journal of Legal Studies* 9: 1–25.

Shavell, Steven (1984a), "A Model of the Optimal Use of Liability and Safety Regulation," *Rand Journal of Economics* 15: 271–80.

Shavell, Steven (1984b), "Liability for Harm vs. Regulation of Safety," *Journal of Legal Studies* 13: 357–74.

Shavell, Steven (1987), *Economic Analysis of Accident Law,* Cambridge, MA: Harvard University Press.

Sigman, Hilary (1998), "Liability Funding and Superfund Clean-up Remedies," *Journal of Environmental Economics and Management* 35: 205–24.

Sigman, Hilary (2001a), "Environmental Liability in Practice: Liability for Cleanup of Contaminated Sites under CERCLA," in Anthony Heyes (ed.), *The Law and Economics of the Environment,* Cheltenham, UK: Edward Elgar.

Sigman, Hilary (2001b), "The Pace of Progress at Superfund Sites: Policy Goals and Interest Group Influence," *Journal of Law and Economics* 44(1): 315–44.

Stafford, Sarah L. (2003), "Assessing the Effectiveness of State Regulation and Enforcement of Hazardous Waste," *Journal of Regulatory Economics* 23: 27–41.

Strasser, Kurt A., and Denise Rodosevich (1993), "Seeing the Forest for the Trees in CERCLA Liability," *Yale Journal on Regulation* 10(2): 493–560.

Tietenberg, Tom H. (1989), "Indivisible Toxic Torts: The Economics of Joint and Several Liability," *Land Economics* 65: 305–19.

Tilton, John E. (1995), "Assigning Liability for Past Pollution: Lessons from the U.S. Mining Industry," *Journal of Institutional and Theoretical Economics* 151(1): 139–54.

Ulph, Alistair, and Laura Valentini (2000), "Environmental Liability and the Capital Structure of Firms," University of Southampton, Discussion Paper in Economics and Econometrics.

Viscusi, W. Kip (1991), *Reforming Products Liability*, Cambridge, MA: Harvard University Press.

Wiggins, Steven N., and Al H. Ringleb (1992), "Adverse Selection and Long-term Hazards: The Choice between Contract and Mandatory Liability Rules," *Journal of Legal Studies* 21:189–215.

11

An Economic Assessment of Market-Based Approaches to Regulating the Municipal Solid Waste Stream

Peter S. Menell

In the late 1980s and early 1990s, it was not uncommon to read that a municipal solid waste crisis loomed in the United States.[1] These news reports warned that landfill space was soon to be exhausted and that new capacity would not become available in time due to regulatory constraints, "not in my back yard" (NIMBY) opposition, and not in my term of office politics. As a result, tipping fees, the per ton disposal fees at landfills, were rising at an unprecedented rate. Incineration, the other major disposal option, was seen as a threat to air quality,[2] and new capacity also faced NIMBYism. Recycling, the third waste management option, was unable to gain much traction. The United States trailed far behind Europe and Japan in recycling rates.[3] Environmental advocates chastised America as the "throwaway society." This was a moral issue, and Americans either did not care enough or were too lazy to protect the environment. This crisis was perhaps most poignantly symbolized in 1987 by the odyssey of the *Mobro*, a trash-laden barge that was unable to find any place to unload its fetid cargo.[4] The futility of this voyage, broadcast frequently on national news reports, brought attention to environmental problems surrounding the municipal solid waste (MSW) stream and awakened government officials at all levels to the need for action. But what action was called for?

In 1989, the Office of Technology Assessment (OTA) issued a detailed report calling for government intervention.[5] The OTA offered numerous recommendations, but relatively little in the form of coherence or clear priorities. Environmental groups and ultimately the public called for aggressive action to address what was often presented as a national problem. Many states adopted recycling goals and mandatory recycling laws, a few passed deposit-refund laws for beverage containers, and one even went so far as to ban drink boxes because they are difficult to recycle after consumer use.

Economists tended to react in a less alarmist and scattershot manner. In their view, the cause of the so-called crisis could be attributed to the failure to confront the relevant decision makers (consumers and households) with the social cost of their choices. The marginal cost to most households of disposing waste in landfill was effectively zero, whereas the cost of recycling or reducing waste generated was positive due to the inconvenience of separating recyclable materials and transporting them to a recycling depot.[6] In almost every municipality in the United States, households paid for waste disposal through their property taxes. The cost per household was the same regardless of how much or what they disposed and, in many cases, was not even reflected in a separate line item on the tax bill. Cities either operated their own waste pickup trucks or franchised out this work. There was typically no limit on the amount of trash that households could put out each week. Furthermore, recycling typically required time and effort to find suitable recycling facilities.

To economists, the solution to the various problems comprising the solid waste crisis lay in imposing the cost of waste disposal on consumers and households. How and where to impose this cost posed the challenges. It is not possible to determine the cost of disposal at the point of purchase because we cannot know what the consumer will ultimately do with the packaging and spent product. The cost will vary depending on whether the consumer litters the waste material, disposes of it in mixed refuse, separates the material for recycling, or reuses it. Setting up a disposal checkout stand at each of these points might work in theory, but is hardly feasible. A deposit-refund system accomplishes both of these pricing functions but applies to only a modest portion of the municipal solid waste (MSW) stream and imposes significant transaction cost burdens on households, retail businesses, and beverage manufacturers and distributors in dealing with the return of and payment for empty containers.

From an economic perspective, charging households based on the volume or weight of their mixed refuse while providing free curbside collection of recyclable and compostable materials offered a promising approach. Such fees could be implemented rather simply and inexpensively by charging households an annual fee based on the size of their trash receptacle. To economize on this cost, households could select a smaller can than traditionally used and devote greater energy to diverting waste into the free pickup containers for recyclable materials and yard waste. They could also seek to reduce their total waste production by purchasing products with less waste, reusing containers, and home composting.

In 1990, the idea of charging households based on the amount that they disposed (and picking up recyclables without charge) was largely untested. The past decade has witnessed a significant rise in the number of households facing such economic incentives to reduce their waste disposal and separate recyclable materials. A variety of programs using such incentive mechanisms—referred to as unit-based pricing, variable rate pricing, or pay-as-you-throw (PAYT)—have taken root throughout the United States. Since 1990, the number of communities using some form of variable pricing has grown fiftyfold from approximately 100 to more than 6,000 today.[7] Approximately 20 percent of Americans now reside in a variable rate pricing community, and the approach continues to spread both here and abroad.

The time is ripe to examine whether such programs have lived up to the promise that was anticipated and to assess the lessons of these experiments. The principal purpose of this chapter is to review the range of empirical studies that have examined unit pricing policies and MSW regulation strategies more generally since the early 1990s. Unlike other contributions to the volume, this chapter does not focus specifically on comparing a particular prescriptive (command-and-control) policy with a market-based instrument. Rather, it explains the theoretical basis for a particular class of market-based instruments (variable rate pricing) and then reviews empirical studies studying its effects. In so doing, it provides a partial basis for assessing the relative efficacy of variable rate pricing.

As the chapter explains, variable rate pricing has proven to be a successful strategy in many communities for increasing waste diversion from landfills, but its net economic impact, considering the operational costs and adverse impacts, are somewhat more ambiguous. Given the desire of many communities and states to substantially increase waste reduction and diversion, whether or not it produces a favorable cost-benefit ratio, there is good reason to believe that variable rate pricing in conjunction with curbside collection of recyclables represents the most cost-effective strategy for many communities. Many cities that have adopted variable rate approaches have seen their total cost of disposal decline. Initial concerns that charging for waste disposal would trigger increased levels of illegal disposal have largely proven to be modest and manageable. After some initial opposition or at least hesitancy toward what might appear like a new tax, most citizens of these communities have embraced this approach. Although the rollout has been most significant in suburban communities, where the prevalence of single-family homes makes curbside charges relatively easy to implement, there have been notable successes in larger cities such as Seattle, San Francisco, San Jose, and Austin. Although the overall benefit-cost ratio of market-based approaches is open to question, particularly in high-density communities, there is little question that this approach to MSW management is here to stay and can be expected to expand and become more sophisticated over time.

Although concern that the United States faced a MSW crisis largely abated by the mid-1990s, it would be an exaggeration to credit variable rate pricing and the growth of curbside recycling programs with averting a crisis.[8] The fear that America was rapidly approaching the limits of available landfills was more the product of media hype than a reflection of the realistic prospects for disposal capacity. As more systematic data on landfill capacity have revealed, federal solid waste disposal regulations put in place in the 1980s led to a significant reduction in the number of landfills but a substantial expansion in capacity as this industry shifted toward larger scale operations.[9] Nonetheless, due in part to variable rate pricing, MSW is seen as a manageable environmental problem. Since 1990, the average amount of solid waste generated per person in the United States has remained constant at 4.5 pounds per person per day despite a substantial rise in average incomes. The percentage of this amount going to landfills and incinerators has fallen from 84 percent to 70 percent, as the recycling rate (including yard waste composting) has doubled from 16.2 percent to over 30 percent nationally.[10] Reports of landfill shortages have faded from the headlines. Tipping fees have stabilized, and much more resilient recycling markets have emerged.

As background for understanding the management of municipal solid waste, this chapter begins by characterizing the MSW stream and the ways consumer and household behavior affect the size and composition of the waste stream and recycling activity. The second part presents an economic perspective on the MSW stream and examines ways pricing mechanisms can be instituted to internalize the costs and benefits associated with waste decisions. The next part surveys the landscape of MSW policy since 1990, reports on the diffusion of variable rate pricing approaches in the United States, discusses the implementation challenges that the Environmental Protection Agency (EPA) and communities faced supplanting conventional MSW systems with incentive-based alternatives, and explores the challenges of diffusing variable pricing approaches to large cities. The last section assesses the economic and environmental effects of variable rate pricing.

CHARACTERIZING THE MSW STREAM AND THE ROLE OF CONSUMER BEHAVIOR

To construct the policy matrix governing the MSW stream, it is necessary to understand the wide range of economic actors who contribute to its size and composition. The MSW stream reflects various levels of decisions made by product and packaging manufacturers, consumers, households, waste processors, and municipalities. The waste stream begins with product design and raw material choices made by manufacturers. These choices respond to consumer demand for products and packaging, as well as the availability and cost of materials. Consumers influence the MSW stream through their purchasing decisions and later through their reuse and disposal choices. To the extent that they seek to reduce solid waste, consumers will demand products or packaging that reduces the amount of residual material after the product is consumed or spent. Alternatively, they may opt for packaging that can be reused, such as sauces sold in reusable jars. In any event, competition among product manufacturers (and retailers) for households' consumption dollar will affect the types of products and packaging that are sold.[11]

After a product has been consumed, households play a critical role in diverting waste from landfills (or incineration) by separating waste materials into economically valuable waste streams. The economics of recycling turn critically on the availability of a steady, homogenous supply of waste—whether glass, metal, newsprint, paperboard, plastics, or yard waste—because it is costly to separate materials from mixed refuse streams. Hence, if wastes become intermingled at the household level, it is likely that they will remain so and ultimately be disposed in a landfill or incinerator. If a household separates wastes into discrete waste streams that can reach recycling enterprises, such materials can often be reprocessed for less cost than manufacturing from raw materials. In some cases, it is more economical to produce new products, such as plastic lumber made from recycled plastics used to produce decking, park benches, waste receptacles, signs, and play structures.

Waste separation occurs at mixed waste processing facilities in a growing number of communities.[12] Magnets have been used for quite some time to separate ferrous metals, which have a significant salvage value and can be removed at relatively low labor cost. Modern technology, such as customized fans for extracting light materials (plastics) and conveyor belts for sorting materials, have increased the use of centralized separation, but it remains a rather small piece of the overall recycling equation.[13]

Most recyclable materials pass through a materials recovery facility (MRF) prior to reentry into a manufacturing process. Even streams of recyclable materials must typically be further separated. Many curbside collection programs allow households to place all beverage containers— glass, metal, and plastic—into the same bin. The materials must be further segregated at an MRF. In addition, some materials are processed (e.g., shredded) and packaged prior to shipping. At low-technology MRFs, these activities are done by hand. The growing number of high-technology facilities use eddy currents, magnetic pulleys, optical scanners, and air classifiers to segregate wastes.[14]

Table 11.1 shows the composition of the MSW stream as of 1990 as well as the percentage of waste being recycled (or, in the case of yard and food wastes, being composted) at that time. With regard to glass and metal beverage containers, it should be noted that nine states enacted deposit-refund or container redemption laws during the 1970s and 1980s, predominantly for litter control purposes.[15] These laws significantly increased the number of beverage containers being recycled in these states.

Table 11.1 Composition of the MSW Stream: 1990

Materials	Tons (000s)	% of MSW	% Recovered
Paper and paperboard	72,730	35.4%	27.8%
Glass	13,100	6.4%	20.1%
Metals	15,550	8.1%	24.0%
Plastics	17,130	8.3%	2.2%
Rubber and leather	5,790	2.8%	6.4%
Textiles	5,810	2.8%	11.4%
Wood	12,210	6.0%	1.1%
Food wastes	20,800	10.1%	<.05%
Yard wastes	35,000	17.1%	12.0%
Other wastes	6,090	3.0%	11.2%
Total MSW generated	205,210	100%	16.2%

* Includes recovery of paper for composting.
Source: U.S. Environmental Protection Agency, Municipal Solid Waste in the United States: 2000 Facts and Figures 32–33 (June 2002).

AN ECONOMIC APPROACH TO CONSUMER-LEVEL MSW REGULATION

The MSW policy literature highlights a range of goals:

- reducing the amount of solid waste generated (reduce, reuse, recycle);
- diverting waste from landfill (50 percent is an oft-cited goal; and higher for beverage containers);
- reducing litter and other forms of illegal disposal;
- sharing the costs of solid waste management equitably (polluter pays principle);
- promoting eco-friendly product design (green design);
- reducing energy use and pollution from product and packaging manufacturing; and
- reducing extraction of raw materials.

Economic analysis generally seeks to promote efficient resource use. In some cases, that might entail source reduction or recycling, but economists are agnostic about the particular results. Rather, they focus on whether the decision-making processes and institutions internalize the full social benefits and costs of decisions.

The complex nature of the MSW stream creates opportunities and challenges for confronting consumers and households with the full benefits and costs of their choices. Take, for example, the decision to purchase a beverage packaged in a glass as opposed to plastic container.[16] The total economic cost of the container over its life cycle depends not just on its manufacturing cost but also on how the container is ultimately disposed. At the time of purchase, there is no way to know how that container will be disposed. Therefore, an advance disposal charge based on the average disposal cost will underprice social disposal cost if the consumer litters the container or throws it into a mixed refuse receptacle and overprice the social disposal cost if the consumer brings it to a recycling center or separates it for curbside collection.[17] A two-tier tax, such as a deposit-refund system, can control for both aspects of consumer decision making—which container to purchase and how it is ultimately disposed—but entails substantial transaction costs. Retail stores or redemption centers must be staffed to provide the refunds, and consumers must incur storage, transportation, and time costs in redeeming containers.[18] A curbside charge for pickup of mixed refuse with free collection of valuable recyclable materials (such as beverage containers, newsprint, and paperboard) creates a relative price differential between disposal options that can roughly approximate social cost possibly at a more modest transaction cost.

This section presents an economic approach to regulation of consumer decisions bearing on the size and composition of the MSW stream. It begins by assuming zero transaction costs to identify a first-best policy in a frictionless world—that is, how society could completely internalize the social costs and benefits associated with MSW stream. It then introduces transaction costs to focus on those policies best attuned to the reality of regulating the MSW stream. The next section examines a number of additional considerations—the problem of illegal disposal, achieving critical mass and coordination within recycling markets, and additional environmental externalities associated with materials use—bearing on the formulation of an economic approach to governing (MSW). The final section provides an overall qualitative comparison of the principal consumer-oriented MSW policies.

Pricing the MSW Stream in the Absence of Transaction Costs

In a world without transaction costs, the optimal policy would confront consumers with the full economic costs and benefits of their purchasing and disposal decisions. This hypothetical world can be represented by two checkout stands. The first actually exists at most retail stores. Consumers place the items they wish to purchase on a conveyor belt. The items are scanned, and consumers are charged the individualized retail cost for each item before it is placed in a bag at the end of the conveyor system.

The second checkout stand is hypothetical and can be characterized as a complex conveyor system at the curbside or wherever else the consumer ultimately disposes of waste material or packaging. Consumers would face a choice of how they wished to dispose of items. The easiest method would be to place items in the mixed refuse bin. This material would be weighed, and the consumer would be charged the cost per pound of landfilling or incinerating the waste, whichever was most competitive at that point in time.[19] Alternatively, the consumer could separate some of its waste material into different bins—glass (by color), plastic (by type), metal (by type), newsprint, paperboard, food waste, yard waste, and so on. A checkout clerk would weigh each of the bins and determine a total bill. Some items might have a negative price where the salvage value of the item exceeded the hauling cost. Waste haulers and recyclers would compete for the consumers' trash, thereby producing a competitive market in waste removal and reprocessing. Over time, consumers would factor these costs and net salvage values into not only their waste separation decisions but also their demand for products and packaging. Product and packaging manufacturers would receive these signals through the derived demand for their goods and would have appropriate incentives to design better products. As virgin resource availability and cost, recycled material salvage values, landfill and incineration tipping fees, and hauling costs changed over time, consumers would respond accordingly, and an efficient allocation of resources would be achieved.

Regulating the MSW Stream in the Presence of Transaction Costs

Despite technological advances in weighing and billing systems, the first best world of perfect curbside charges is unlikely to be attainable. The labor costs, time commitment, capital equipment, and physical space required to effectuate the perfect curbside charge outweigh the benefits under current circumstances.[20] The difference in net economic value between disposing of mixed refuse in a landfill and separating newsprint or even glass or aluminum beverage containers for recycling is not nearly great enough to justify such a complex and expensive system for diverting waste materials into distinct streams. Nonetheless, this simple exercise highlights the basic goal of trying to provide consumers with at least rough price signals relating to their purchasing and disposal decisions. The key for policy design is to balance these considerations with the very real costs of administering a system of charging for waste disposal that provides incentives for consumers to reuse waste components, separate the most valuable waste streams, and consider the waste end of the product life cycle in their product and packaging choices.

Principal Design Considerations

The design of the optimal waste disposal governance system must account for a variety of transaction costs. These costs in turn depend on a variety of factors, including the nature of trash hauling markets, technology, demographic, socioeconomic, geographic, and climactic variables and the state of recycling markets.

Waste Hauling Markets   In addition to households, waste hauling enterprises play a critical role in waste separation and disposal. In most markets, only a single company handles this activity because of economies of scale. Due to the labor and transportation costs and the relatively small amount of waste per household, it makes little sense for multiple haulers of the same type of refuse to travel the same route.[21] There are significant savings in regularized pickups and practices throughout residential communities. Therefore, most municipalities contract out this work to a single vendor through a competitive bidding process. With the rise in curbside collection of recyclable materials, it is now feasible to have one vendor handling mixed refuse, another responsible for separated recyclable materials, and possibly a third in charge of picking up yard waste. The role of municipalities in contracting and coordinating these services influences the cost structure of MSW policies.

Technology Technology affects the options for solid waste policy on various levels. The viability of source separation depends on the means for separating wastes at curbsides (e.g., design of trash bins, garbage bags), in multifamily dwellings (e.g., trash chutes, locked garbage bins), and at material recycling facilities. Charging households for their waste disposal and recycling depends on the effectiveness of weighing systems. The degree to which curbside pickup can cover multiple waste categories turns on the design of recycling truck bins and compactors. On-board computer systems for weighing waste and billing households make possible more precise and efficient charges. Labor-saving technologies, such as reverse vending machines, affect the economic viability of deposit-refund systems.

Demographic, Socioeconomic, Geographic, and Climactic Variables The viability of waste disposal charges and household-based separation varies significantly across communities based on a range of factors. Relatively affluent suburban communities have thus far proven to be the most promising setting for variable rate pricing because of the fact that most households have a distinct curbside at which trash is removed and generate substantial waste that can usefully be diverted from the mixed refuse stream (most notably, yard waste), and the risk of illegal disposal is relatively low. Many factors, however, affect the feasibility of curbside recycling and different market-oriented approaches. For example, high average annual precipitation undermines curbside pickup of paper and paperboard, although covered bins can address this problem. Large apartment buildings having only a single chute for waste make separation and individualized billing particularly difficult.

Recycling Markets The benefits of materials separation depends on the salvage value of separated materials as well as secondary effects on other markets (including employment).[22] Such markets depend on the larger infrastructure of industrial activity and the state of recycling technology. Many industries established their production processes and facilities based on the use of virgin materials. Therefore, when significant levels of separated waste material became available as a result of state and local policies favoring recycling, prices plummeted.[23] Over time, salvage values for making recycled content streams have stabilized as a result of further development of processes for using separated materials, the growth of transportation infrastructure and marketing organizations for making these materials more widely available, the relocation of industry to take advantage of these new sources of input material, and government and consumer preferences for products made from recycled content.

Policy Options

Drawing on these considerations, the principal options for influencing consumer decisions bearing on the size and composition of the MSW stream are:[24]

1. Advance Disposal Charges—charging consumers a surcharge at the retail level for products and packaging.
2. Curbside Pickup of Recyclable Materials—providing curbside pickup of designated categories of recyclable materials, such as newsprint, paperboard, bottles and cans, and yard waste, without direct charge. Communities can also offer annual or semi-annual pickup of odd-sized wastes (such as spent appliances) and household hazardous wastes.
3. Disposal Bans—typically done in conjunction with curbside pickup, banning disposal of certain categories of recyclable materials in mixed refuse. Some communities, for example, prohibit disposal of certain types of recyclable materials in mixed refuse. Many communities also ban disposal of yard waste in mixed refuse.
4. Variable Rate Disposal Charges or Unit Pricing—charging households for mixed refuse based on amount (volume or weight). This policy is typically done in conjunction with free curbside pickup of recyclable materials. It can be implemented in a variety of ways:
   a. Variable Can—Households select a particular sized mixed refuse receptacle (such as sixteen, thirty-two, or sixty-four gallons per week) and are charged an annual fee for regular (typically weekly) pickup.
   b. Bag, Tag, or Sticker Charges—Households purchase designated trash bags, tags, or stickers that they can place on generic trash bags or receptacles. Bags or other marking designations can be purchased at city hall, community centers, fire stations, or local grocery and convenience stores.
   c. Hybrid Systems—This system combines the variable can with a bag, tag, or sticker approach. Households register for regular weekly pickup of a particular sized receptacle and can augment that disposal with designated bags or tags.
   d. Weight-Based Systems—This approach uses specially equipped waste hauling trucks that can weigh each household's mixed refuse, record the relevant information in a database, and bill households by the pound on a regular basis. In more sophisticated versions, radio frequency tags are affixed to

waste receptacles to identify the household and automate data collection.
5. Recycling Centers—providing or subsidizing facilities for free or paid drop-off of recyclable materials.
6. Deposit-Refund Programs—combining a retail charge with a redemption refund for some classes of recyclable materials, typically beverage containers.

Transaction Costs

The transaction costs associated with these policies fall into the following principal categories: waste hauling; billing, administrative, and retail systems; consumer costs; and enforcement costs. Providing for the pickup of separate categories of waste significantly increases the cost of waste removal. It typically requires specialized bins, specialized trucks, greater direct fuel cost, and additional labor. It does, however, result in mixed refuse disposal fees because of the reduced tonnage delivered to landfills and incinerators and may produce significant salvage revenue. Many of these policies also involve the creation and maintenance of billing and administrative systems. Some of the policies also require the operation of retail enterprises for selling bags, tags, or stickers to households. A third class of transaction costs fall on consumers. In addition to the physical labor and time associated with separating wastes, there are storage costs and other forms of inconvenience. Some systems also impose transportation costs on consumers. These costs can affect some households much more significantly than others. For example, the elderly may find some of the requirements particularly onerous and inconvenient. Enforcement comprises a fourth category of transaction costs. Under some of these policies, local law enforcement, waste haulers, or regulatory officials must monitor consumer behavior and impose fines or other penalties on households. In addition, the availability of valuable separated wastes at the curbside can lead to a problem of waste theft—people who "cherry pick" wastes that can be redeemed at material recycling facilities. These activities can undermine the overall economic viability of waste collection activities.

The principal transaction costs associated with particular consumer-oriented MSW policies can be characterized as follows.

1. Advance Disposal Charges—This system entails substantial administrative costs in establishing fees, imposing these fees at the retail level, and collecting revenues. These costs are borne by the regulatory authority and most significantly by retail establishments. Bar coding and optical scanning technology reduce these costs to some extent, but there would be a significant additional layer of paperwork involved in administering this system.
2. Curbside Pickup of Recyclable Materials—As noted, curbside pickup of recyclable materials entails substantial hauling and

consumer costs, which increase proportionately with the number of separate categories designated. Climate, geography, and population density can influence these costs.

3. Disposal Bans—These policies add enforcement expenses to the costs of curbside pickup of recyclable materials.

4. Variable Rate Disposal Charges or Unit Pricing—These policies are also typically pursued in conjunction with curbside pickup of recyclables and therefore entail those additional transaction costs. In addition, the following versions have other transaction cost ramifications:
   a. Variable Can—This approach has relatively low administrative costs, because fees can be included in an annual property tax statement.
   b. Bag, Tag, or Sticker Charges—This approach requires systems to be established and administered for enabling households to obtain designated bags, tags, or stickers. Because households pay for disposal through the purchase of bags, tags, or stickers, there is no need for billing through annual or more frequent statements.
   c. Hybrid Systems—This approach requires both aspects of billing noted in (a) and (b), although the bag, tag, or sticker transactions will be less than under a pure system of that nature because most households will be able to make due with their variable can.
   d. Weight-Based Systems—This approach entails substantial additional labor, equipment, and administrative expense to track household mixed refuse disposal.

5. Recycling Centers—These facilities involve labor, storage, and processing costs. In addition, to the extent that they pay for materials, there is an administrative cost for weighing or otherwise measuring delivered material. Households choosing to use these centers incur substantial transportation and time costs.

6. Deposit-Refund Programs—These programs entail substantial administrative costs in providing those who redeem containers with refunds. Consumers may also bear substantial storage, transportation, and time costs in returning containers. In addition, retailers and distributors incur additional costs for storing and transporting empty containers.[25]

Additional Considerations

Illegal Disposal

The imposition of variable rate disposal charges aroused concern that some households might seek to save money on waste disposal by illegally disposing of their refuse.[26] Even modest increases in improper disposal of refuse could undermine the efficacy of variable rate policies because the social costs of such activity vastly exceed the costs of proper disposal. Improper disposal is much more likely to contaminate waterways, promote the spread of disease, and contribute to litter problems and associated aesthetic blight. There are various ways of addressing the illegal disposal problem, including education campaigns, careful design of variable rate policies, making available positive rewards for legal diversions (such as recycling centers providing refunds for separated wastes), enforcement efforts, and periodic free pickup of particularly problematic wastes (such as tires and large appliances). In addition, commercial enterprises can locks dumpsters to prevent others from using their disposal facilities. In many respects, the problem of illegal disposal represents an additional form of transaction costs borne by enforcement officials, regulatory officials, and commercial facilities.

Facilitating Recycling Markets

A well-functioning recycling market requires the availability of a steady and reasonably pure stream of input material—newsprint, paperboard, glass, metal, plastic, or organic material (yard and food waste).[27] As these streams form, recycling entrepreneurs, waste arbitragers, and entire industrial sectors have an incentive to take advantage of these sources of input material. Product manufacturers have incentives to redeploy their operations accordingly to take advantage of these input streams. Well-functioning high-volume curbside recycling programs as well as deposit-refund systems create such streams and provide the impetus for investment in new business models and industrial processes utilizing recycled materials. They also provide incentives to the development of entirely new product lines, such a plastic lumber. By hastening the formation of recycling markets and standardizing the type and quality of materials available, state and regional initiatives address a critical coordination problem in the formation and development of recycling markets.

Environmental Externalities and Nonmarket Values

Recycling has the potential to augment media-specific environmental protection efforts by reducing energy use, air pollution, water pollution, mining wastes, water use, and related ecological effects associated with manufacturing from virgin materials.[28] The extent to which these effects are external to existing regulatory activities is difficult to gauge. Furthermore, recycling can have adverse environmental effects as well. For example, by shifting the locus of manufacturing activities from more remote areas (closer to virgin resource sources) toward urban areas (where recycling stream can be found), recycling could in some circumstances increase stresses on critical waterways, air resources, and already compromised habitats. Nonetheless, there appear to be some benefits that can be derived from partially closing some loops in product life cycles.

A less tangible benefit associated with MSW policy can be characterized as the nonmarket value of recycling activities. Many consumers and households appear to derive positive utility from engaging in separating of recycling material. The fact that a significant number of consumers brought separated materials to recycling centers without any economic reward reflects some of this value. The significant participation in curbside recycling efforts even without variable rate pricing of mixed refuse reinforces this point. It seems reasonable to attribute some nonmarket value to making recycling opportunities widely available. Consumers derive personal satisfaction (or assuaged guilt) from taking responsibility for addressing a social cost to which they contribute. Moreover, as one of the most direct ways in which consumers and households affect the larger environmental system, waste disposal has some value in teaching and inculcating moral responsibility. It may also spillover into a better appreciation of environmental values. It is important to bear in mind, however, that consumer perception of environmental effects are often quite distorted and can be manipulated.[29] Nonetheless, there can be some benefit from harnessing this goodwill and channeling it in productive directions.

The MSW Policy Matrix

MSW policy should integrate the incentive effects of internalizing the costs and benefits of product choices and disposal decisions on consumer and household behavior, transaction costs, and various other effects. Table 11.2 provides a summary of the main effects of the range of consumer and household-oriented policies.

Based on this qualitative assessment, the most promising options are the relatively simple variable rate policies for areas where curbside pickup is feasible. Many residential communities already arrange for pickup of waste on a regular basis. Economies of scale in collecting recyclables at the curbside presents a plausible optimal solution to balancing the costs and benefits of alternative MSW policies. It should be noted, however, that collection of recyclables (without charge) could potentially achieve a high diversion rate without the imposition of a variable charge for curbside collection of mixed refuse. Thus, where the marginal effect of a curbside charge is modest (beyond the diversion achieved through dual (mixed and recyclable) curbside collection, and the transaction or illegal disposal costs of variable rate policies are high, then a policy of curbside collection will be preferred. It is important, therefore, to focus on the marginal impact (beyond curbside collection) of variable cost policies and compare them with the incremental costs (transaction and illegal disposal).

Advance disposal charges do nothing to promote separation activities by households, and therefore it is difficult to see how such an approach could be preferred. Such charges could, however, be used in conjunction with curbside collection and/or variable rate policies.

Table 11.2 MSW Policy Matrix

MSW Policy	Incentive Effects			Transaction Costs				Other Effects	
	Purchasing	Separation	Waste Hauling	Billing Systems	Consumer Costs	Enforcement Costs	Illegal Disposal	Promoting Recycling Markets	Reducing Environmental Externalities
(1) Advance disposal charge	low-medium*	none	none	high	none	none	none	none	low
(2) Curbside pickup	low	medium	medium	low	medium	low	low	+	+
(3) Disposal ban	low	high	medium	low	medium	high	?	+	+
(4) Variable rate disposal charge									
(a) Variable can	low	high	medium	low	medium	none	?	+	+
(b) Bag, tag, sticker	low	high	medium	medium	medium	low-medium	?	+	+
(c) Hybrid	low	high	medium	medium	medium	low-medium	?	+	+
(d) Weight	low	high	high	high	medium	none	medium	+	+
(5) Recycling centers	low	low	low	low	high	none	none	low	low
(6) Deposit-refund	low	high*	low	medium	medium	none	none	+*	+*

*Limited to specific products covered (typically beverage containers).

Deposit-refund systems entail relatively high transaction costs for addressing a relatively small portion of the waste stream.[30] As noted earlier, such policies were initially adopted in the United States to combat litter problems.[31] If this were the only benefit, increased fines and publicly funded sanitation might well be more cost-effective means of addressing this problem. More recent interest in such policies (particularly in Australia) sees container deposit legislation as a more general form of environmental management policy directed toward extended producer responsibility.[32] Where curbside collection of mixed refuse already takes place, encouraging consumers to make special trips to retail stores or recycling centers to redeem deposits and requiring these enterprises to administer a labor-intensive refund system would appear to create a needless (and redundant) cost. Deposit-refund programs can, however, produce an additional waste diversion benefit for those beverage containers that do find their way into consumers' homes. A significant percentage of beverages are consumed outside of the home—at work, at play, or while shopping—and hence are largely beyond the reach of curbside collection systems. In addition, deposit-refund laws motivate people other than the consumers of the container contents to collect discarded beverage containers. On the other hand, deposit-refund systems address a relatively small portion of the recyclable waste stream; they do not deal with paper, cardboard, or yard waste. Therefore, although there may well be some redundancy, deposit-refund policies potentially complement curbside collection and variable rate approaches.[33] In addition, curbside collection and variable rate policies may not be feasible in urban areas. Nonetheless, the full economic costs of deposit-refund systems must be considered.[34]

MSW POLICY DURING THE 1990S

As noted at the outset of this chapter, a series of events and media reports raised the salience of MSW policy in the mid- to late 1980s. All levels of government became involved in what had traditionally been a local environmental issue. This section first discusses the larger federalism landscape surrounding MSW policy. It then examines the most significant policy development affecting consumer MSW behavior during the past decade—the development and diffusion of variable rate policies throughout the nation. The following section will then examine the efficacy of this set of instruments.

MSW Federalism and Legislation

As its environmental profile has broadened and its salience increased, MSW policy has grown beyond city and local politics to involve federal and state legislation, regulation, and hortatory efforts. Municipalities and counties continue to play the principal role in determining how solid waste generated within their jurisdictions is disposed and setting policy directed at household behavior. This section summarizes the emerging landscape of MSW regulation.

Federal Role

The federal government has come to play a variety of roles in the MSW field. Pursuant to its authority under the Solid Waste Disposal Act of 1965 as amended by the Resource Conservation and Recovery Act of 1976 (RCRA) and the Hazardous and Solid Waste Amendments of 1984,[35] the EPA has responsibility for regulating the transportation, storage, and disposal of wastes.[36] Of most significance with regard to MSW policy, RCRA prohibited open dumping of waste and mandated strict requirements for treatment, storage, and disposal of wastes. In October 1991, the EPA promulgated new standards for MSW landfills, requiring installation of costly technological safeguards, such as liners, leachate collection systems, ground water monitoring equipment, and gas vents.

These requirements have significantly altered the environmental practices and business models for solid waste disposal. Prior to the mid-1970s, most MSW was disposed in open dumps owned and operated by municipalities and counties. As federal regulations imposed and tightened environmental controls on solid waste facilities, many municipalities were forced to close their dumps. Much of the uproar over an imminent shortage of landfill capacity grew out of this new regulatory environment. By the mid-1990s, private enterprises had taken over much of the disposal business, building vast new facilities that have greatly expanded landfill capacity.[37]

The EPA has played a comparable role in the regulation of incineration. Most of these facilities are designed to both reduce the amount of waste materials as well as generate energy—either directly through combustion in mass burn facilities or by shredding and screening wastes to produce highly combustible fuel pellets (refuse-derived fuel). These processes produce two types of pollutants—air emissions and ash residues. Under the Clean Air Act, the EPA sets standards for conventional and hazardous air pollutants that affect the design and siting of waste to energy incinerators. The disposal of incinerator ash falls within the scope of federal waste disposal regulation. Depending on the composition of the wastes burned and the design of the incineration facility, this ash can contain significant concentrations of toxic metals. In an important 1994 decision,[38] the U.S. Supreme Court ruled that RCRA does not exempt ash produced by municipal waste incinerators from stringent hazardous waste regulations. The EPA and one federal appeals court had previously interpreted RCRA as exempting the ash produced from incinerating municipal solid waste. Under the Supreme Court's decision, incinerator ash that contains hazardous constituents exceeding specified levels now must be managed, stored, treated, and disposed of as hazardous waste. This substantially raises the cost of incineration as a waste disposal method.

At the consumer level, the EPA has played largely an advisory role in advising states and municipalities to adopt particular MSW policies. In 1989, the EPA issued its Agenda for Action, in which it established a national goal for source reduction and recycling of 25 percent by 1992.[39] During the 1990s, the agency convened a series of roundtable policy fora to assess and develop guidance materials regarding MSW policies at the community and consumer level. In 1993, the EPA decided to take an active role in encouraging variable rate pricing of MSW.[40] EPA officials came to see variable rate pricing as a way of addressing three important principles: environmental sustainability, economic sustainability, and equity. Under its PAYT program, the agency developed an information clearinghouse and education materials to guide local decision makers. It also funded a series of studies and pilot projects designed to assess variable rate pricing.[41] As these studies confirmed both the efficacy of PAYT and illuminated design challenges, the EPA entered a tool-building phase in which it produced pamphlets, presentation materials, implementation guides, and summaries of success stories. Workshops on implementation of variable rate pricing were convened by the EPA, states, and solid waste organizations throughout the nation. Publications such as *Waste Age*, *Resource Recycling*, and *Biocycle* published numerous articles on variable rate pricing in the mid- to late 1990s.

As it completes the last phase of this project, the EPA is focusing on the more complex targets. Its American Big City Campaign aims to assist larger communities in adapting PAYT to reach higher density living patterns.[42] High-rise apartment buildings with common trash disposal chutes make it difficult to determine household-specific waste quantities, a critical aspect of any variable rate pricing approach. Variable rate policies might well encourage littering and illegal disposal problems in low-income and high-crime pockets within urban communities. Such communities are likely to be more sensitive to the introduction of a positive marginal cost for trash removal, and litter enforcement occupies a relatively low priority in high-crime areas.

The federal government has also played a role in fostering recycling markets. Pursuant to Section 6002 of RCRA, federal agencies must give preference in their procurement programs to products and practices that conserve and protect both natural resources and the environment. Under this provision, the EPA has developed guidelines to assist federal agencies with procuring products containing recovered or recycled materials.[43] Federal agencies that purchase more than $10,000 of an item listed by the EPA in its Comprehensive Procurement Guideline are required to establish an affirmative procurement program for that item "that assures that items composed of recovered/recycled materials are purchased to the maximum extent practicable."[44] As the largest consumer in the world, the federal government plays a substantial role in spurring demand for recycled content in many important product markets.

State Policies and Mandates

State governments also play a variety of roles in the regulation of MSW. Under RCRA, many states have assumed responsibility for implementing and enforcing federal requirements for the design and operation of disposal facilities. Many state environmental agencies also take on comparable responsibilities for overseeing air pollution regulations.

Of more direct significance for consumer-level MSW policies, most states have become involved in promoting recycling and encouraging localities to adopt specific solid waste regulatory approaches. Several states have funded studies of MSW policies, including variable rate pricing. Nearly all states have established recycling goals, typically ranging from 25 percent to 50 percent of MSW generated.[45] As of 1999, thirty-nine states had adopted policies promoting the adoption of variable rate approaches by municipalities.[46] Minnesota and Washington require that all municipalities adopt such programs, whereas Wisconsin and Iowa require adoption only if a community has not met a 25 percent recycling goal. Thirty-four states provide education and grants to municipalities to help finance recycling programs, with some states allocating funds specifically for use in the implementation of variable rate approaches. Twenty-three states ban disposal of yard waste in mixed refuse. Seven states require all municipalities to implement curbside recycling programs and to pass local ordinances prohibiting disposal of designated categories of recyclable materials in mixed refuse.[47] Eleven states have enacted some form of deposit-refund or redemption system for beverage containers. In addition, many states have sought to stimulate the demand side of recycling markets. Twenty-nine states require state government offices to purchase recycled materials.

Local Regulation

Local governments remain the principal decision makers in the setting of household-level MSW policies. Prior to 1990, most municipalities approached solid waste policy as a local government service funded out of property taxes. They perceived their role as arranging for hauling trash to town and county dumps. They typically had available land for such purposes. The principal administrative function was in operating or contracting out for trash hauling services.

With the rising level of MSW generated, imposition of strict federal environmental regulations on the operation of landfills, tightening budgets, concern about rising taxes, and growing public concern about waste issues, municipalities increasingly found themselves in a bind. State mandates to establish curbside recycling programs tended to increase their costs of service, adding to budgetary pressures. EPA and state encouragement of variable rate pricing, as well as a growing number of success stories showing that these policies could reduce waste generated while providing a direct and acceptable means of funding such programs, brought many communities to adopt this approach.

The Rise of Variable Rate Pricing

The adoption of variable rate disposal approaches greatly expanded from approximately 100 programs nationally in 1990 to more than 6,000 to-day.[48] More than 20 percent of Americans reside in communities using some form of variable rate pricing. Among these communities, variable can policies are most common (approximately one-third), followed by bag (one-quarter), and hybrid and sticker programs (one-sixth each).[49]

Over the past decade, numerous approaches to variable rate pricing have been tested across thousands of laboratories of local government. Despite early enthusiasm based on some promising pilot studies,[50] no weight-based programs have reached full-scale operation in the United States.[51] Relatively simple systems tend to be the norm, with variable can policies more common in larger communities and bag, tag, and sticker models more common in smaller communities.[52] The more recent trend has been toward hybrid approaches, which keep implementation costs relatively low while allowing for greater precision in pricing.[53]

Based on the range of experiences, the EPA and consultants have developed reliable tools for determining program design considering a wide range of community characteristics and goals.[54] Community acceptance has proven to be a critical factor in getting programs established. Whereas variable can programs involve relatively little change in the nature of household waste mechanics, bag, tag, and sticker programs entail significant changes in household practices. Education plays a central role in getting variable rate programs off the ground.

Communities tend to view variable rate pricing as part of a comprehensive set of policies addressing waste reduction, promoting recycling and diversion from landfills, control of improper disposal, and equity concerns. Essentially all communities using variable rate pricing have instituted some form of pickup of recyclables and yard waste at no additional charge. Many also offer periodic pickup of bulky items (such as appliances and odd-sized wastes). Some offer free pickup or drop-off of household hazardous waste (such as unused paints, pesticides, and cleaning solvents). Most variable rate communities have also deployed educational campaigns and enhanced enforcement to deal with illegal dumping of mixed refuse and theft of recyclable materials. Many communities have also instituted rebates and discounts for low-income residents.[55]

Multifamily residences pose particular challenges for variable rate programs due to the commingling of wastes in common trash receptacles. The lack of a one-to-one relationship between the curbside and each household makes it difficult to monitor individual household behavior. In addition, high-rise apartments buildings typically have a single trash chute, which makes separation of wastes complicated. Storing separated wastes on each floor of the building increases the incidence of pests and raises labor costs. Multiunit dwellings tend to have much lower recycling diversion rates and higher contamination of recycling streams than single-family communities.[56] Not surprisingly, the adoption of variable rate pricing has tended to be most rapid in suburban communities, although these approaches have achieved success in several large communities throughout the nation, including Los Angeles (nearly 4 million residents), San Jose (850,000), San Francisco (775,000), Austin (650,000), Oklahoma City (500,000), Minneapolis (380,000), and Norfolk (260,000).[57]

Variable rate programs have proven quite workable in smaller scale multifamily dwellings, such as garden apartments and townhouses. New technology is now available for high-rise apartments that allows tenants to direct a disposal chute electronically into six different bins. Pilot studies find that households consider this technology convenient. Such technology has increased recycling significantly and promises a payback period of three years.[58] Newer multistory buildings can be designed to facilitate variable rate programs and recycling. Companies are now selling air-lock waste containers that only tenants can access using personal access cards.[59]

Variable rate programs can be tailored to the particular waste profile of particular communities. Studies of San Francisco's waste stream revealed that food waste comprised a particularly large percentage of the city's mixed refuse after the implementation of variable rates in conjunction with curbside collection of recyclables and yard waste.[60] After experimenting with a variety of separation options for food scraps, the city developed the Fantastic Three program. Households received three carts (wheeled receptacles): a free blue thirty-two-gallon cart for recyclables (paper, bottle, and cans), a free thirty-two-gallon green cart for compostables (yard waste, food waste, and soiled paper), and a variable rate black cart (twenty, thirty-two, or sixty-four gallons) for all other refuse. In addition, the city provided households with a convenient two-gallon kitchen pail for collecting food scraps. After an extensive outreach and educational program through direct mail, the targeted neighborhoods achieved a 46 percent diversion rate (14 percent for organics and 32 percent for recyclables), representing a 90 percent increase over prior experience of recycling and trash collection in that neighborhood. Almost two-thirds of the increase was attributable to the new compostables collection effort. Nearly three-fourths of those surveyed preferred the new approach to recycling.

The success and rapid adoption of variable rate pricing in the United States has spurred interest in such approaches internationally.[61] The European Commission has in the past several years begun to play a role comparable to that served by the U.S. EPA in encouraging communities throughout Europe to adopt variable rate policies. With nearly 80 percent of its population residing in cities, Europe faces significant implementation challenges. PAYT builds on the polluter pays principle, which is widely accepted in Europe.[62] Germany, Austria, Sweden, and the Netherlands have begun to adopt this approach.

ECONOMIC AND ENVIRONMENTAL ANALYSIS OF VARIABLE RATE PRICING

The rapid and widespread adoption of variable rate pricing of MSW by municipalities suggests that it addressed many of the goals sought by these communities: source reduction, promotion of recycling, diversion of wastes from landfill and incineration, and equitable sharing of the costs of solid waste management. This section presents the available empirical research on the efficacy of these programs. There are two principal sources of such evidence—wide-scale census data and case studies collected by the EPA and private consultants working in the solid waste field[63] and a few academic econometric studies focused on relatively small-scale experiments.[64] This section begins by examining changes in the size and composition of the MSW stream over the past decade and empirical estimates of the role of variable rate pricing in these patterns. It then looks at direct economic benefits and costs of variable rate pricing. It concludes by examining additional factors bearing on the efficacy of variable rate pricing.

Effects on the Size and Composition of the MSW Stream

After rising steadily from 2.68 pounds per person per day in 1960 to 4.50 pounds per person per day in 1990, the generation of MSW per person remained constant throughout the 1990s, notwithstanding the fact that per capita income rose 17 percent in real terms during the decade.[65] The amount of discards to landfill and incineration declined during the 1990s from an average of 3.07 pounds per person per day to 2.50 pounds per person per day. This was due to a substantial rise in the amount of waste recycled (up from 0.64 to 1.04 pounds per person per day) and composted (up from 0.09 pounds to 0.32 pounds per person per day). Table 11.3 shows the change in the composition of the MSW stream over this period.

The increase in resource recovery over the course of the 1990s is striking, nearly doubling from 16.2 percent to 30.1 percent. The most dramatic changes can be seen in composting of yard wastes, which grew from 12 percent to nearly 57 percent. There were also notable increases in the recycling of paper and paperboard, metals, plastics, and rubber.

These data alone, however, do not establish the role of variable rate pricing in raising diversion rates. As noted earlier, even at the end of the period, only 20 percent of the national population resided in communities using variable rate pricing. Furthermore, it is necessary to separate out the effects of contemporaneously adopted policies, most significantly the adoption of curbside collection of various categories of recyclable materials (including yard wastes). In addition, eleven states have had some form of deposit-refund system in place for this period. Recycling rates of bottles and cans are quite high in these jurisdictions.[66]

Table 11.3 Composition of the MSW Stream: 1990–2000

Materials	1990			2000		
	Tons (000s)	% of MSW	% Recovered	Tons (000s)	% of MSW	% Recovered
Paper and paperboard	72,730	35.4	27.8	86,740	37.4	45.4
Glass	13,100	6.4	20.1	12,770	5.5	23.0
Metals	15,550	8.1	24.0	18,020	7.8	35.4
Plastics	17,130	8.3	2.2	24,710	10.7	5.4
Rubber and leather	5,790	2.8	6.4	6,370	2.7	12.2
Textiles	5,810	2.8	11.4	9,380	4.0	13.5
Wood	12,210	6.0	1.1	12,700	5.5	3.8
Food wastes	20,800	10.1	<.05	25,900	11.2	2.6*
Yard wastes	35,000	17.1	12.0	27,730	12.0	56.9
Other wastes	6,090	3.0	11.2	7,530	3.2	11.4
Total MSW generated	205,210	100	16.2	231,850	100	30.1

*Includes recovery of paper for composting.
Source: U.S. Environmental Protection Agency, Municipal Solid Waste in the United States: 2000 Facts and Figures 32–33 (June 2002).

Three types of empirical evidence are available to assist in establishing the effects of variable rate pricing on source reduction, recycling rates, and economic performance. A team of Duke University researchers gathered extensive data from a range of variable rate programs throughout the nation. Table 11.4 contains data from those cities in which waste disposal tonnage is available from the year preceding adoption of a variable rate policy through the first full year or two of the plan. These data strongly suggest that variable rate pricing significantly encourages waste diversion. These case studies also provide some basis for distinguishing between improvements in diversion rates attributable to variable rate pricing and those resulting from curbside pickup of recyclable and compostable wastes. San Jose began its curbside collection programs more than four years before the implementation of its hybrid PAYT system. Waste diversion rates increased dramatically following the introduction of the variable rate charge for mixed refuse. The data on total waste generated suggest that variable rate programs not only increase waste diversion but also promote source reduction. The magnitudes, however, are modest, and the sample size is small. It is notable that all of the programs experienced some reduction in total volume without accounting for population or economic growth. In a subsequent study of 212 communities across 30 states, the Duke researchers found that the annual amount of waste disposed per household decreased by 14 percent and that recyclable collections increased by 32 to 59 percent in the first year of the variable rate program.[67]

Table 11.5 contains data from a more recent series of case studies of programs adopting variable rate programs. These communities were selected for study because of their large diversion rates.[68] Nonetheless, they reflect diverse community characteristics. The results reinforce the strong results found in the Duke study. The increased diversion rates are quite striking—from 11 percent to 49 percent over the rates that had been achieved with curbside collection of recyclable materials. The last column—possible source reduction—represents the percentage change in total solid waste per household that was picked up at the curbside. It does not account for the effects of rising income or home composting.[69]

A second approach looks at actual per household waste disposal quantities immediately preceding and immediately following the introduction of unit pricing. Don Fullerton and Thomas Kinnaman collected data from seventy-five households in Charlottesville, Virginia, following the implementation of an eighty cents per thirty-two-gallon bag curbside charge on July 1, 1992.[70] Using regression analysis, they found that the implementation of unit pricing reduced the volume of waste disposed in mixed refuse by 37 percent, but much of this gain was attributable to greater trash compaction by residents. The data revealed that the weight of mixed refuse fell by only 14 percent. Fullerton and Kinnaman also found that the program increased the weight of recycled material by 16 percent.

Table 11.4 Variable Rate Case Studies: Effects on Volume and Diversion

	Community Characteristics				MSW Regulation			Performance			
City	Type	Population Density (pop/sq. mile)	Median Income	PAYT Year Type	Curbside Recycling Year Type	Yard Waste Collection Year Type	Landfill Volume Time	Recycling Volume Time	Yard Waste Diversion Time	Total Waste Volume
Downers Grove, Illinois	suburban	47,883 3,521	$48,266	1990 sticker	1990 free	1990 $1.50/sticker	−24% 1991–93	+43% 1991–93	+6.5% 1991–93	−3.4% 1991–93
Glendale, California	suburban	177,621 5,806	$34,372	1992 var. can	1988 free	1992 free	−36% 1990–92	+62% 1990–92	0→27%MSW 1991–92	−5.0% 1990–92
Hoffman Estates, Illinois	suburban	47,266 2,528	$49,475	1992 sticker	1990 free	1990 $0.75/bag	−38% 1991–93	+52 1991–93	+23% 1992–93	−5.6% 1991–93
San Jose, California	urban	782,225 4,678	$46,206	1993 hybrid	1987 free	1989 free	−37% 1993–95	+154% 1993–95	+45% 1993–95	−4.1% 1993–95
Santa Monica, California	suburban	87,064 10,490	$35,997	1992 hybrid	1989 free	none	−5.5% 1991–93	+30% 1991–93	not applicable	−2.9% 1991–93

Source: Marie Lynn Miranda and Joseph E. Aldy, Unit Pricing of Residential Municipal Solid Waste: Lessons from Nine Case Study Communities (Mar. 1996).

Table 11.5 Variable Rate Case Studies: Effects on Volume and Diversion

| | Community Characteristics | | | Waste/HH/Day before PAYT | | | | Waste/HH/Day after PAYT | | | | |
| | | | | | | Percent Diverted | | | | Percent Diverted | | Possible |
City	Type	Population Density (HH/sq. mile)	Median HH Income (1989)	Total (lbs)	Percent Discards	Recycle	Compost	Total	Percent Discards	Recycle	Compost	Source Reduction
Bellevue, Washington	suburban/ urban	103,700 2,875	$48,900	7.3	89	6	5	9.18	40	26	34	−26%
Chatham, New Jersey	suburban	8,289 1,363	$62,129	16.85	63	13	50	15.81	35	22	43	6%
Fitchburg, Wisconsin	rural	17,266 216	$35,550	6.16	65	24	11	5.89	50	29	21	4%
Portland, Oregon	urban	503,000 1,437	$25,592	6.14	71	24	5	7.10	60	23	17	−16%
San Jose, California	urban	873,300 1,539	$46,206	8.61	67	10	23	8.82	55	19	26	−2%
Seattle, Washington	urban	534,700 2,706	$29,353	5.61	81	19	0	6.34	51	29	20	−13%

Source: U.S. Environmental Protection Agency, Cutting the Waste Stream in Half: Community Record Setters Show How p. 22, table 10 (June 1999) (study conducted by the Institute for Local Self-Reliance).

A third set of empirical evidence comes from cross-sectional and time series modeling conducted by Lisa Skumatz on the basis of a vast database her firm (Skumatz Economics Research Associates) has collected since the late 1980s.[71] In a nationwide study based on data from more than 500 communities, cross-section regression analysis controlling for the influence of demographic, community, and program features found that variable rates provided a larger increment to recycling than any other single factor, adding 5.5 percent to a community's recycling rate and 4.5 percent to the yard waste diversion rate.[72]

In a further study using waste disposal data from more than 1,000 communities implementing a variety of MSW approaches, Skumatz computed "generation" per capita rates and found that communities using variable rates discarded (to landfills and incinerators) on average 16 percent less waste than communities without such programs.[73] Of this 16 percent, Skumatz was able to attribute 5–6 percent to increased recycling and 4–5 percent to increased yard waste diversion, leaving a residual of 5–7 percent attributable to source reduction. Skumatz corroborated these cross-section regression results with a time-series model. She first estimated waste generation as a function of population, households, gross domestic product, recycling prices, and a packaging index (to control for changes in packaging efficiency over time), among other variables. This model showed that total discards would be 17.3 percent higher in a given community without variable rate pricing. Skumatz then estimated the extent to which this effect is attributable to recycling and yard waste collection. She found that these effects are responsible for 11.5 percent of the reduction in discards, leaving a residual of 5.8 percent attributable to source reduction.[74]

Direct Economic Benefits and Costs of Variable Rate Policies

The principal economic benefits of variable rate policies lie in the reductions in landfill and incineration tipping fees attributable to diversion to recycling and composting and source reduction. The national average tipping fee in 2002 stood at $33.70, up from $19.12 in 1988, although it has remained relatively constant since 1995.[75] Nonetheless, rates vary widely across regions, with the low range throughout much of the South, West, and Midwest ($20–40 per ton), moderate to high range in the mid-Atlantic states ($45 per ton), and highest range in the Northeast ($60–90 per ton).[76]

Tipping fees represent just a portion of overall MSW costs. Based on a series of case studies in the early 1990s, the Solid Waste Management Association of North America found that approximately half of total MSW management system costs are attributable to collection activities, 19 percent go to facilities construction and maintenance, 15 percent for general and administration, 12 percent for tipping fees, and 4 percent for transfer activities.[77] These percentages, however, merely provide a rough guide. Actual costs and their allocation depend on a wide variety of local factors, including tipping fees, program design, community structure and geography, demographics, and climate.

In addition to these cost factors, municipalities can derive revenue from the sale of recycled waste streams, compost, and possibly from energy derived from incineration or sale of refuse-derived fuel. In September, 2004, the prices in table 11.6 could be obtained in the Midwest for suitably prepared recycled streams.

Variable rate policies may impose additional administrative costs on municipalities. During the early to mid-1990s, Wisconsin and Iowa conducted surveys of operating and administrative costs in communities adopting variable rate policies. In Wisconsin, 40 percent of communities adopting variable rates experienced a decline in program costs, 27 percent had level costs, and the remaining third had higher costs.[78] The Iowa survey produced similar results, with 60 percent of the communities adopting variable rates experiencing lower or stable program costs.[79] A more recent study of communities across California conducted by Skumatz corroborated these findings.[80] Her research found that the incremental administrative costs of variable rate policies tended to be small. In some cases, administrative costs declined. The higher diversion rates, however, produced significantly higher costs for collection and processing of diverted material. These costs offset tipping fees for mixed refuse and produced some income from the sale of recycled materials.

Table 11.7 presents two scenarios for assessing hypothetical net savings available from adoption of variable rate pricing: one with a national average tipping fee ($33.70 per ton) and the other with a tipping fee from the range encountered in the Northeast ($70 per ton). Apart from these differences in tipping fees, both communities are identical. They have 50,000 households with average daily per household discards prior to the implementation of variable cost pricing (PAYT) of eleven pounds of refuse per day prior to the introduction of PAYT. To simulate the effect of

Table 11.6 Recycled Materials Market Prices (Midwest, September 2004)

Material	Price Range
Cardboard (#11)	$100 per ton
Newsprint (#6)	$80 per ton
Newsprint (#8)	$95 per ton
Aluminum cans	$600 per ton
Steel cans	$90 per ton
Clear glass	$40 per ton
Amber glass	$30 per ton
Green glass	$20 per ton
PET plastic (soda bottles)	$300 per ton
HDPE plastic (milk jugs)	$440 per ton

Source: Associated Recyclers of the Midwest, Recycled Materials Market Trends (September 2004) www.recyclingcoop.org/ martket.htm (visited Sept. 5, 2004).

Table 11.7 Variable Rate Benefit Scenarios

	Pre-PAYT			Post-PAYT				
	Landfill	18% Recycling	5% Composting	Landfill	Recycling	Composting	Source Reduction	Net Savings
Scenario 1: National Ave Tipping Fee 50,000 households 11 lbs/HH/day								
Volume (tons)	80,300	15,056.25	5,018.75	67,452	19,874.25	8,230.75	4,818	
Tipping fee/revenue	$33.70	($15)	($5)	$33.70	($15)	($5)		
Disposal cost	2,706,110	(225,843.75)	(25,093.75)	2,273,132.4	(298,113.75)	(41,153.75)		
Net disposal cost		$2,455,172.50			$1,933,864.90			
PAYT transaction cost				50,000 HH * $6/HH/year = $300,000				
Total cost		$2,455,172.50			$2,233,864.90			$221,307.6
Scenario 2: Northeastern State 50,000 households 11 lbs/HH/day								
Volume	80,300	15,056.25	5,018.75	67,452	19,874.25	8,230.75	4,818	
Tipping fee/revenue	$70	($15)	($5)	$70	($15)	($5)		
Disposal cost	5,621,000	(225,843.75)	(25,093.75)	4,721,640	(298,11.75)	(41,153.75)		
Net disposal cost		$5,370,062.5			$4,382,372.50			
PAYT transaction cost				50,000 HH * $6/HH/year = $300,000				
Total cost		$5,370,062.5			$4,682,372.5			$687,690

variable cost pricing, the table incorporates Skumatz's estimates of variable rate diversion and source reduction: 6 percent increased recycling, 4 percent increased yard waste diversion, and 6 percent source reduction. The table assumes a relatively conservative additional per household transaction cost of $6 per household for the year,[81] average materials revenue of $15 per ton for recyclables, and average materials revenue of $5 per ton for yard waste. These assumptions produce a $221,000 annual cost saving in a community facing the national average tipping fee and nearly a $688,000 cost saving in a Northeastern community paying $70 per ton.

Due to the wide range of variables affecting MSW costs and revenue opportunities for particular communities, determining the overall direct economic costs of variable rate pricing and whether it improves on traditional mixed refuse pickup and curbside collection systems can be complex. The efficacy of variable rate programs are quite sensitive to administrative costs. For example, if additional transaction costs for implementing a variable rate system were doubled to $12 per household annually, then adopting PAYT would result in a net loss of nearly $80,000 in a community paying the national average tipping fee. PAYT would still yield a net savings of approximately $390,000 in a community paying $70 per ton for landfill disposal.

Waste collection involves various nonlinear (or lumpy) cost factors. For example, reducing the frequency of collection from once per week to every other week, altering the number and types of vehicles used, and changing the number of workers per vehicle significantly affect overall cost. The waste reductions possible as a result of variable pricing can possibly open up significant opportunities for reorganizing collection services.[82] In addition, transaction costs of variable rate policies may require an additional staff member to be hired. Furthermore, transaction costs, diversion rates, and source reduction may change over time. It seems likely that these effects would favor the cost-effectiveness of variable rate pricing. As communities become better acquainted with PAYT and as households adapt their consumption choices and recycling behavior, it can be expected that transaction costs would fall and diversion rates rise. Therefore, it is important to consider evidence from actual programs.

The most direct data bearing on program cost effects of variable rate policies comes from the detailed case studies assembled by the Institute for Local Self-Reliance in the late 1990s. Table 11.8 presents a comparison of program costs for five cities prior to and following implementation of variable rates.[83] Due to changes in landfill tipping fees and possibly materials revenue for recycling before and after implementation, these numbers do not provide direct comparison of overall program costs. Nevertheless, they are supportive of the cost-effectiveness of variable rate policies in these communities. Fitchburg, Wisconsin, experienced a significant drop in overall program costs notwithstanding a rise in landfill

Table 11.8 Variable Rate Case Studies: Net Costs

| | Net Program Costs/HH/year | | | | | | | Cost/Ton Post-PAYT | | |
| | Pre-PAYT | | | Post-PAYT | | | | | | |
City	Disposal (Tip Fee)	Diversion	Total	Disposal (Tip Fee)	Diversion	Total	Percent Change in Cost/HH	Disposal (Tipping Fee)	Recycling (Materials Revenue)	Compost (Materials Revenue)
Chatham, New Jersey	$393 ($141)	$64	$457	$158 ($101)	$70	$228	−50	$157 ($101)	$39 ($8*)	$48 ($8*)
Fitchburg, Wisconsin	$72 ($31)	$54	$126	$52 ($36)	$55	$108	−14	$100 ($36)	$117 (0**)	$78 (0**)
Portland, Oregon	$187 ($72)	$54	$241	$144 ($63)	$67	$211	−12	$188 ($63)	$196 ($15*)	$132 ($15*)
San Jose, California	$143 ($29)	$64	$207	$82 ($28)	$105	$187	−10	$95 ($28)	$206 ($0**)	$96 ($0**)
Seattle, Washington	$155 ($60)	$0***	$155	$101 ($45)	$54	$155	0	$173 ($45)	$121 ($0**)	$142 ($0**)

* Averaged over recycled materials and compost.
** No direct materials revenue received by municipality; reflected implicitly in agreement with hauling contractor.
** No recycling costs borne by city.

Source: U.S. Environmental Protection Agency, Cutting the Waste Stream in Half: Community Record Setters Show How p. 22, table 10 (June 1999) (study conducted by the Institute for Local Self-Reliance).

tipping fees. The numbers for Chatham, New Jersey, reflect a substantial drop in tipping fees, although this explains only a portion of the 50 percent drop in program costs. The high cost of recycling per ton in Portland and San Jose suggest that curbside recycling in these cities is not cost-effective. Nonetheless, implementation of variable rate pricing reduced total cost per household in these cities due to efficiencies in mixed refuse collection, source reduction, and yard waste diversion.

Other Effects

Various additional factors bear on the environmental and economic performance of variable rate policies. On the negative side, placing a positive price on mixed refuse may encourage avoidance behavior in the form of illegal or improper disposal. On the positive side, variable rate policies may promote the smooth functioning of recycling markets, address environmental externalities, and alleviate landfill capacity concerns. More ambiguously, such policies may produce nonmarket benefits and costs for households and consumers.

Illegal Disposal

In addition to creating incentives for source reduction and diversion of waste to recycling and composting, variable rate pricing also creates an incentive to dispose of waste illegally—such as by dumping it in the back woods or depositing it in someone else's dumpster. Such activities contribute to harm, pollution, and aesthetic blight. They also raise the costs of MSW regulation by requiring additional expenditures on public education about and enforcement of prohibitions on illegal disposal. Furthermore, they impose additional costs on the private sector, such as added monitoring of property, installation of security fences, and placing locks on dumpsters.

Notwithstanding some early expressions of concern about illegal disposal rising as a result of variable rate policies,[84] the problem has proven to be modest in size and manageable in the communities in which variable rate pricing has been implemented. A 1996 survey by Duke researchers of 212 communities adopting variable rate policies found that 48 percent experienced no change in illegal diversion following implementation of a unit pricing program, 19 percent reported an increase, 6 percent reported a decrease, and 27 percent reported that they did not know whether there had been any change.[85] In surveys of over 1,000 variable rate communities, Skumatz found that much of the illegally dumped material is not residential in origin. The largest categories are construction and demolition waste (more than 25 percent), yard wastes (approximately 40 percent), and white goods (such as bulky appliances, sofas, and mattresses).[86] Her research finds that illegal dumping was initially a problem in less than a third of the communities adopting variable rates, but it has largely abated and no program managers consider it a barrier to adoption of variable rates.[87] Other studies also find relatively little increase in illegal disposal following implementation of variable rate pricing.[88]

Experience in implementing variable rate policies has revealed relatively inexpensive and effective ways to address the problem.[89] Convenient or annual free curbside pick-up of white goods and hazardous household wastes, which pose the largest pollution problems, substantially reduce disincentives for improper disposal.[90] Education and outreach programs have also proven to be effective at relatively modest cost. The problem can also be addressed in the design of the rate structure (keeping the marginal cost of legal mixed refuse disposal reasonable), by offering discounts and rebates for lower income households to ease their income constraints and providing convenient means for disposing of recyclable and compostable wastes. The problem of illegal disposal can also be stemmed by securing public disposal areas, increased site maintenance, and targeted monitoring and enforcement. These policies in many cases will be worth pursuing for environmental protection, crime, and public health reasons regardless of implementation of variable rate pricing.[91]

Risk of illegal disposal is a factor in considering further diffusion of variable rate pricing, particularly in urban areas with poverty-stricken neighborhoods. Communities with high crime, gang and drug activity, and abandoned properties are particularly prone to illegal disposals and may be less appropriate for a full-scale variable rate program. Illegal disposal might also be more of a concern with a weight-based program because households would face a positive marginal cost for each ounce of mixed refuse. Under variable can systems, households have zero marginal cost up to the volume of their trash receptacle. That provides some leeway for avoiding additional charges through compaction and storage of waste until there is more room available.

Recycling Markets

As curbside recycling programs blossomed in the early 1990s, recycling markets struggled to absorb the rise of input material. The prices available for many forms of recycled materials—most notably paper—plummeted as supply greatly outstripped industrial capacity and demand for recycled products.[92] Reports of separated paper (which already increased the costs of MSW collection) being stored in warehouses and tossed into landfills,[93] led some observers to conclude that recycling was nothing more than a palliative that in reality wasted resources.[94] New York City's troubled recycling program[95] became a poster child for a dark side of recycling.[96] An inability for recycling markets to make productive use of separated materials would certainly dampen the economic and environmental benefits from diverting solid waste from landfills and incinerators. Economic markets rely on not just the availability of materials but also coordination of time and place. As the OTA's 1989 report noted, "most [paper] mills are located close to sources of wood pulp, so it is unlikely that it would be cost-effective to transport large amounts of [old news-print] to be used as [secondary fiber] instead."[97]

One of the great virtues of markets is their ability to adapt over time to economic opportunity. A glut of potentially valuable material encourages entrepreneurs to enter the market to take advantage of the inexpensive supply.[98] The transition from economic markets built predominately on virgin input materials toward those than can take advantage of both virgin and recycled input streams has gradually taken place during the past decade in many regional and product markets. The growth of re-cycling streams has spurred tremendous growth in recycling enterprises. Traditional industries—such as paper, paperboard, and metals—have shifted manufacturing operations toward the utilization of recycled con-tent. Industry and a growing proportion of the public have come to realize that the pure closed loop vision of recycling is not a practical reality because of the costs of collecting and reprocessing materials. It is not currently economically efficient to recycle a used polystyrene cup into a new polystyrene cup,[99] but it may make sense to burn it for energy or use it as input to some other production process.[100] Thus, new products in-corporating recycled materials—such as plastic lumber, regrinding of construction and demolition waste to use a road base materials, and the use of organic wastes to produce renewable fuels—have opened up new business and manufacturing opportunities.[101] On the demand side of the market, government programs favoring procurement of products made from recycled content as well as higher quality standards for recycled products and growing consumer purchasing of recycled products have accelerated this transition to some extent.

These developments have stabilized recycling markets. Whereas early recycled material programs were subject to erratic salvage prices for paper and other separated materials in the early to mid-1990s, salvage prices have become much more stable as these markets have matured. As of 2001, recovered paper represented more than 36 percent of the total fiber supply in the paper industry and was expected to grow by an average of 2.2 percent.[102] The infrastructure for plastics recycling is now well-established, with one industry expert noting that "demand is strong and prices are sustainable."[103] Compost industry experts now believe that the market for compost is beginning to mature on a national level. According to one consultant, "concerns about oversupply of compost are unfounded, except in limited locations and instances of poor quality."[104] Growth in recycling industries has spurred exchange infrastructures to develop, which have reduced market volatility.[105] The Internet has begun to play a role in stabilizing and expanding recycling marketing channels.[106] Vola-tile postconsumer commodity markets of the early to mid-1990s settled down significantly by 2000.[107] The principal industries in the United States now rely on both virgin and recovered materials in their manu-facturing processes, and conditions exist for continued evolution toward use of the growing recycled material stream.[108] This promises to improve the outlook for variable rate programs.

Environmental Externalities

A well-functioning recycling marketplace also offers benefits in reducing adverse environmental impacts from virgin resource extraction, transportation, and energy-intensive manufacturing processes associated with raw material inputs.[109] The extent to which these benefits are not forthcoming in the marketplace depends on whether existing regulatory institutions adequately internalize adverse environmental effects. The principal virgin material industries—mining, timber, and oil extraction— each have long legacies of ecosystem damage and pollution.[110] Although they have each come under greater regulatory and legal constraints over the past few decades, there remain significant ecological and pollution concerns with their activities. Fully analyzing these regulatory regimes extends beyond the scope of this chapter, but it is worth noting some of the most significant effects and the comparison between virgin sources and recovered materials. Tables 11.9 and 11.10 present in summary fashion energy and climate change benefits flowing from the substitution of recovered materials for their virgin counterparts in manufacturing processes.[111]

It should be noted, however, that recycling is not always an environmentally benign activity.[112] By shifting more manufacturing activity closer to urban populations, there can be greater human exposure, increased congestion, and more effluents and emissions into surrounding ecosystems with less absorptive capacity. So long as environmental regulatory controls are reasonably effective and markets have adequate time to adjust, the diversion of waste into recycling streams offers far-reaching environmental and ecological benefits by reducing raw material extraction and energy-intensive manufacturing processes.

Landfill Disposal Capacity

As noted at the outset of this chapter, widespread public perception of a looming shortage of landfill capacity of crisis proportions mobilized interest in MSW policy at the federal, state, and local levels during the late 1980s. The experience of the 1990s has revealed the perceived crisis to have been driven more by mass media hype than by economic or environmental reality. Though restrictive federal solid waste disposal regulations and constraints on siting did bring about a dramatic decline in the number of operating landfills from 7,924 in 1988 to just 1,967 in 2000,[113] total landfill capacity grew significantly during this time period. RCRA regulations shifted the nation away from relatively small town dumps toward massive regional landfills. These technology-based requirements created enormous operating economies-of-scale for landfills

Table 11.9 Energy and Climate Change Effects of Substituting Recovered Materials for Virgin Raw Materials

Materials	Grade	Energy Savings vis-à-vis Virgin Production	Million BTUs per Ton	Oil Barrel Equivalents per Ton	CO_2 Tons Avoided
Aluminum		95%	196	37.2	13.8
Paper*	Newsprint	45%	20.9	3.97	(0.03)
	Boxboard	26%	12.8	2.43	0.04
Glass	Recycle	31%	4.74	.9	0.39
	Reuse	328%	50.18	9.54	3.46
Steel		61%	14.3	2.71	1.52
Plastic	Polyethylene terephthalate (PET)	57%	57.9	11	0.985
	Polyethylene (PE)	75%	56.7	10.8	0.346
	Polypropylene (PP)	74%	53.6	10.2	1.32

*Energy calculations for paper recycling count unused wood as fuel.

Source: Adapted from Natural Resources Defense Council, Too Good to Throw Away: Recycling's Proven Record table 1 (Feb. 1997), www.nrdc.org/cities/recycling/recyc/recyinx.asp, compiled from data derived supplied by Argonne National Labs (1980, 1981), U.S. Department of Energy (1982), Franklin Associates (1990), AL Associates, AISI, Phillips 66, Wellman (1991).

Table 11.10 Environmental Benefits from Substituting Recycled Inputs

Reduction Of	Paper	Glass	Steel	Aluminum
Energy use	23–74%	4–32%	47–74%	90–97%
Air pollution	74%	20%	85%	95%
Water pollution	35%	—	76%	97%
Mining wastes	—	80%	97%	—
Water use	58%	50%	40%	—

Source: C. Pollak, Mining Urban Wastes: The Potential for Recycling 22 (Worldwatch Paper No. 76, 1987).

that for example make it half as expensive (on a per ton basis) to operate a 300 thousand ton per year landfill than a 60 thousand ton per year operation. The required pollution control equipment is more a function of footprint than of volume. Private firms had an edge in that they are generally not restricted by political boundaries, can command larger service areas from which to draw volume, and have greater access to capital markets. Enormous financial wherewithal is necessary to permit and construct new capacity.[114]

As a result, the numerous landfill closures of the late 1980s and 1990s represented only 8 percent of national capacity, whereas new landfills established during the 1990s were on average twenty-five times larger than those they were replacing.[115] The average size of landfills increased from 1 million tons of capacity to 3.5 million tons.[116] The significant rise in diversion of waste to recycling and composting has helped extend the life of landfills, although the total quantity of waste destined for disposal has declined by only 8.5 percent during the 1990s due to population and income growth.[117]

The net effect of these developments has been to expand national excess landfill capacity from under ten years in 1988 to approximately twenty years today.[118] It has also increased the average distance that discarded waste travels from approximately fifteen miles in 1990 to fifty miles today.[119] Due to the cost of transporting waste long distances and public resistance in some states to serving as waste repositories, there remain some regional problems. The densely populated Northeastern states face the most severe capacity concerns. Pennsylvania and Virginia have eased this pressure significantly through accepting interstate transfers, but public resistance to importing waste and expanding landfill capacity has increased in recent years.

For these reasons, incineration has continued to play a significant role in MSW management in the Northeastern states. Approximately one-third of solid waste in this region is burned in waste-to-energy incineration facilities.[120] Connecticut incinerates approximately 65 percent of its municipal solid waste.[121]

The perception that the United States faces a national MSW crisis has passed. Few in the industry or the environmental community speak in such terms any longer. The discussion has shifted to the means for managing waste and debate centers on new technology. Perhaps the most controversial issue in waste treatment today is the concept of bioreaction. Whereas modern landfill technology is based on the principle of long-term storage and management of waste to reduce environmental effects from leachate and air emissions, the waste management industry has begun implementing landfill designs and operating procedures intended to promote bioreaction. Such reactivity hastens the generation of biofuel waste energy and increases the rate of compaction to free up more space for additional wastes. This approach transforms landfills from slowly decomposing tombs to active biological vessels, which arguably creates greater environmental exposure. The organics/composting industry fears that this new approach threatens to divert its growing waste stream and exacerbates the severe regulatory disadvantage of allowing the landfill industry to defer costs of inevitable environmental contamination to future generations.[122] The EPA is currently considering whether to develop additional regulatory controls on this disposal technology.[123]

Nonmarket Effects

Recycling poses an interesting paradox from the standpoint of households, consumers, and citizens. On the one hand, the public generally exhibits strong support for recycling through its actions and political support as reflected in surveys and the passage of lofty recycling goals in most states in the late 1980s and early 1990s.[124] On the other hand, recycling itself imposes significant costs on households, and many did not fully participate until it came to them along with financial incentives.[125]

From a policy standpoint, this paradox can be approached in a number of ways. It can be taken at face value, and recycling could be treated as a goal that should be pursued, regardless of its economic or environmental merits. It can be justified on the grounds that what matters most is what people perceive. It can also be justified as involving consumers and households in an activity that directly affects the environment and in-culcates affinity for environmental concerns. Just as economists seek to measure and give significance to existence value of natural resources using contingent valuation studies, it is certainly possible to consider policies promoting recycling as creating value not commodified in traditional markets. Thus, the benefits to variable rate policies should include not just reduced tipping fees and recycled materials revenues but also an estimated dollar amount per household or citizen.[126] In fact, people may derive utility not merely from their own activities but also from those of their neighbors or complete strangers. Meeting specific diversion goals or even beating the Europeans or Japanese in Olympics-like national competitions could be seen as socially valuable.

Alternatively, the strong support for recycling can be viewed as a proxy for strong support for a clean environment. From this perspective, the policy maker should look behind the stated preference and determine the best approach to pursue the electorate's implicit goal. This perspective would not place recycling on a pedestal but approach the policy matrix with a cost-benefit scale (with no attention paid to soft preferences). This approach could be rationalized on the grounds that citizens have fallen victim to distorted media accounts of the underlying issues surrounding MSW and recycling and that policy matters in this area should be left to the experts.[127]

A poignant vignette from Steven Soderbergh's 1989 film *Sex, Lies, and Videotape* captures the misperception that may underlie the almost religious quality surrounding recycling for some. The film opens with a woman explaining to her psychiatrist what has been troubling her lately: "All I've been thinking about all week is garbage. I mean, I just can't stop thinking about it.... I've just gotten real concerned over what's gonna happen.... I started feeling this way ... when that barge was stranded." As the film develops, it is clear that the character's real problems lie in sexual and marital unhappiness and not MSW policy. Though rather extreme, the notion that consumers latch onto symbolic environmental issues arises frequently. Consumer guilt over drink boxes, disposable diapers, polystyrene clamshell packaging (after Chlorofluorocarbons were no longer used as blowing agents), and plastic grocery bags all likely reflect misapprehension of the complexities of the MSW stream and the economic and environmental effects of recycling. Yet these distorted views can have real effects. As one waste industry reporter astutely observed:

> The misadventures of the 1987 garbage barge, *Mobro*, did more to increase recycling in America than all of the combined efforts of legislative delegations and environmental groups. With the nation focused on and fearing an apparent lack of disposal space, an emphasis to recycle and reduce waste soared.[128]

Under this view, it can be argued that policy makers should seek to measure the inconvenience associated with recycling directly and factor it into policy decisions. Thus, the cost of variable rate (and curbside recycling) policies should be adjusted upward to reflect the actual time spent and space devoted to separating recyclable materials. John Tierney, the author of a controversial *New York Times Magazine* piece titled "Recycling Is Garbage," attempted this calculation:

> I tried to estimate the value of New Yorkers' garbage-sorting by financing an experiment by a neutral observer (a Columbia University student with no feelings about recycling). He kept a record of the work he did during one week complying with New York's recycling laws. It took him eight minutes during the week to sort, rinse and deliver four pounds of cans and bottles to the basement of his building. If the city paid for that work at a typical janitorial wage ($12 per hour), it would pay $792 in home labor costs for each ton of cans

and bottles collected. And what about the extra space occupied by that re-cycling receptacle in the kitchen? It must take up at least a square foot, which in New York costs at least $4 a week to rent. If the city had to pay for this space, the cost per ton of recyclables would be about $4,000. That figure plus the home labor costs, added to what the city already spends on its collection program, totals more than $3,000 for a ton of scrap metal, glass and plastic.[129]

This approach, however, overrides a central premise of traditional eco-nomic analysis—that consumer preferences should be taken as given.[130] Even if one were open to overriding consumer choice in some cases, this hardly seems like a compelling situation. Respecting households' joy in (or at least willingness to undertake) separating recyclables does not pose any harm to others or oneself.

Variable rate pricing strikes a sensible balance between these two ap-proaches. By imposing at least a partial measure of the social costs of disposal on households and allowing them the opportunity to separate recyclables in some reasonably convenient manner, this policy encourages household sovereignty, promotes a relatively high diversion rate, and imposes costs more equitably on those responsible for social costs. Some cities have considered equity effects to be an important selling point for adopting variable rate pricing. For example, elderly households, many of which are on fixed incomes and tend to produce relatively small levels of solid waste, have been able to reduce their waste disposal costs by choosing the smallest container size.[131]

Even though on net it may not be worth the administrative costs in all circumstances, the nonmarket benefits would appear to weigh in favor of adopting such an approach. Corroborating this conclusion, Skumatz finds that more than 90 percent of customers are pleased with variable rate policies and perceive them to be more fair than alternatives after they are implemented.[132] Of the 6,000 communities to have adopted this policy, none have reversed course.

CONCLUSIONS

Pulling all of these considerations together, variable rate policies have been modestly successful as a means of regulating MSW efficiently and quite effective as a means of boosting diversion rates beyond the levels that can be achieved through curbside collection of recyclables alone. In so doing, this approach has fostered the development of recycling markets that may yield even larger environmental benefits over the long run in terms of reduced adverse impacts from virgin resource extraction and more efficient resource use and reprocessing within the broader economy. Municipal governments and households throughout thousands of com-munities of varying sizes and demographic characteristics have embraced variable rate pricing of MSW, as have both environmental organizations and conservative think tanks.

The experience with variable rate policies represents a promising example of noncoercive, information-oriented government intervention. With a relatively small budget and no authority to impose household solid waste policy on local governments, the EPA has been remarkably successful at developing and diffusing effective solid waste management policies. The EPA approached this area without a particular policy result in mind. Based on a broad review of policy options, it used a series of pilot studies to assess a theoretically appealing but not fully tested policy initiative. Through pilot studies and follow-up research, the agency was able to glean valuable lessons, develop effective evaluation and education materials, and disseminate this knowledge widely.

The economic theory underlying variable rate pricing has proven, after some tinkering at the implementation stage, to be quite workable in practice. In fact, the practical realities of implementing charges have shown that theoretical perfection in terms of getting the prices right is less important in the grand scheme than keeping the transaction costs manageable. Over time, variable rate pricing can be expected to become even more economically advantageous as recycling markets continue to mature, landfill tipping fees rise, and improved technologies for curbside collection, monitoring, billing, and measuring waste develop.

ACKNOWLEDGMENTS I am grateful to Janice Canterbury (U.S. EPA, Office of Solid Waste) and Lisa A. Skumatz (Skumatz Economic Research Associates) for providing data and background information about variable rate pricing policy. Thanks to the participants at the Conference on Market Based Incentives held at the Donald Bren School of Environmental Science and Management (at the University of California at Santa Barbara), and especially the conference organizers, Jody Freeman and Charles Kolstad, for comments on an earlier draft.

NOTES

1. *See* e.g., Church, *Garbage, Garbage, Everywhere*, Time, Sept. 5, 1988, at 81; Beck, *Buried Alive—The Garbage Glut: An Environmental Crisis Reaches Our Doorstep*, Newsweek, Nov. 27, 1989, at 66. *See generally* Natural Resources Defense Council, Cities & Green Living: Recycling, ch. 4 (Feb. 1997) ("In 1986, more than two hundred articles appeared in major newspapers and magazines throughout the United States quoting local public works officials throughout the country who found that polluting landfills, rising waste disposal costs, and fights over dangerous waste incinerators were among the two or three greatest public-policy problems they had to deal with"), www.nrdc.org/cities/recycling/recyc/recyinx.asp. *See also* Solid Waste: Public Concern about Garbage Tops Police, Fire, Affordable Housing, Poll Shows, 19 Env't Rep (BNA) 1247 (Oct. 28, 1988); MSW Disposal Crisis: Hearings Before the Subcomm. on Transportation and Hazardous Materials of the House Comm. on Energy and Commerce, 101st Cong., 1st Sess. (1989); Office of Solid Waste, Environmental Protection Agency, The Solid Waste Dilemma: An Agenda for Action (1989) (final report of the Municipal Solid Waste Task Force); Office of Technology Assessment, U.S. Congress, Facing America's Trash: What Next for Municipal Solid Waste? (1989) (hereinafter cited as OTA Report).

2. Incinerators emit carbon monoxide, sulfur dioxide, and particular matter, as well as heavy metal compounds and other hazardous air pollutants. Various pollution control technologies—such as stack scrubbing and filtering—can reduce these emissions significantly. *See generally* C. Brunner, Hazardous Air Emissions from Incineration (1985). In addition, solid waste incineration produces large quantities of ash comprising a sufficiently high concentration of toxic metals and other hazardous materials to subject the residual waste stream to stringent transport, storage, and disposal regulation.

3. *See* J. E. McCarthy, Recycling and Reducing Packaging Waste: How the United States Compares to Other Countries, 2 (Washington, DC: Congressional Research Service, Library of Congress, 1991); National Solid Waste Management Association, Resource Recovery and the Environment 1 (1990); Keep America Beautiful, Overview: Solid Waste Disposal Alternatives (1989).

4. The *Mobro* owes its fifteen minutes (or more precisely, two months) of fame in part to Salvatore Avellino, a reputed Mob boss who thought he could find a lower disposal fee than Islip, Long Island's prevailing tipping fee of $86 per ton. *See* Jane Katz, *What a Waste*, Regional Quarterly Q1 2002 (Federal Reserve Bank of Boston) 22, 30. He identified a landfill in Louisiana that would charge only $5 per ton. Problems arose when it turned out that his partner had not closed the deal after the barge set off down the coast. The partner then decided to cut a deal with a landfill in North Carolina, but state regulators vetoed the transaction out of concern that the trash aboard the barge might be concealing hazardous waste, a ruse associated with organized crime. Once this story hit the news wires, no jurisdiction wanted to do business with Avellino. After being rejected by six states, Mexico, and Belize, the barge eventually returned to New York, where the trash was incinerated in Brooklyn and the ash disposed in a landfill near Islip. *See* U.S. EPA Web site, Milestones in Garbage: A Historical Timeline of Municipal Solid Waste Management, www.epa.gov/epaoswer/non-hw/muncpl/timeline_alt.htm. Later that year, Avellino went to prison after pleading guilty for conspiring to kill two trash haulers, although neither appeared to be connected to the *Mobro*. *See* Katz, *supra*.

5. *See* U.S. Congress, Office of Technology Assessment, Facing America's Trash: What Next for Municipal Solid Waste? (Oct. 1989).

6. *See* Peter S. Menell, *Beyond the Throwaway Society: An Incentive Approach to Regulating Municipal Solid Waste*, 17 Ecology Law Quarterly 655 (1990); Lisa A. Skumatz, Variable Rates for Municipal Solid Waste: Implementation Experience, Economics, and Legislation, Reason Foundation Policy Study 160 (Jun. 1993); Robin R. Jenkins, The Economics of Solid Waste Reduction: The Impact of User Fees (1993).

7. *See* U.S. EPA, EPA and PAYT Celebrate 10 Years of Growth and Success, PAYT Bulletin: Fall 2003, www.epa.gov/epaoswer/non-hw/payt/tools/bulletin/fall03 .htm; Lisa A. Skumatz, Maximizing Variable Rate/Pay as You Throw Impacts— Policies, Rate Designs, and Progress, Resource Recycling (June 2001, August 2001).

8. Such programs have grown from approximately 1,500 in 1989 to nearly 10,000 today, serving approximately half of all Americans *See* California Integrated Waste Management Board, Curbside Recycling, the Next Generation: A Model for Local Recycling and Waste Reduction (July 2002) www.ciwmb.ca.gov/LGLibrary/Innovations/Curbside.

9. *See* Frank Ackerman, *Why Do We Recycle*? Markets, Values, and Public Policy 19 (1997).

10. *See* U.S. Environmental Protection Agency, Municipal Solid Waste in the United States: 2000 Facts and Figures 1–3 (June 2002) (hereinafter cited as EPA 2000 Report). With a relatively stable proportion of discarded material being incinerated (approximately 15 percent of total solid waste), the percentage of MSW going to landfills declined from nearly 70 percent to 55 percent during the 1990s. *Id.* at 125.

11. Data from Procter and Gamble, a large consumer product manufacturer, indicates that grocery packaging as a percentage of MSW decreased from 15.3 percent to 12.1 percent between 1980 and 1993 notwithstanding substantial economic growth. *See* Lisa A. Skumatz, Measuring Source Reduction: Pay as You Throw/Variable Rates as an Example 4 (Slumatz Economic Research Associates) (May 2000) (hereinafter cited as Measuring Source Reduction). Landfill archeology data compiled by William Rathje similarly reveals a decline in the percentage of packaging in landfills over this time period. *See The Archaeology of Plastic Packaging and Source Reduction*, prepared for the ULS report by the Garbage Project, Tucson, Arizona (Jul. 1997) (cited in *id.*).

12. The number of mixed waste processing facilities has grown from approximately 100 in 1990 to nearly 500 by 1999. *See* Eileen Brettler Berenyi, *Whither MRF-Based Recycling?* Resource Recycling 12 (Apr. 1999).

13. *See* Katz, *supra* n. 4, at 27.

14. *See* EPA 2000 Report, *supra* n. 10, at 116.

15. *See* Facing America's Trash, *supra* n. 1, at 35. Eleven states container deposit or redemption laws today. *See* www.bottlebill.org/USA/States-ALL.htm; John K. Stutz and Susan M. Williams, *Economics of Expanding Bottle Bills*, Resource Recycling 20 (Apr. 1999).

16. *See generally* Menell, *supra* n. 6.

17. Uniform taxes cannot reflect material-specific differences in packaging. Advance disposal fees cannot reflect the actual social cost of disposal because it is not known at the point of purchase how the consumer will dispose of any waste materials. *See* Menell, *supra* n. 6.

18. Reverse vending machines, which allow consumers to obtain refunds of deposits through an automated device, reduce some of these costs. Such machines identify the container and brand owner by optically scanning bar codes, sort containers by material type, compact or shred containers, and provide refunds to consumers. Such machines, which are typically located in stores, shopping centers, and recycling centers, account for approximately 30 percent of redemptions. *See* Businesses and Environmentalists Allied for Recycling, Understanding Beverage Container Recycling: A Value Chain Assessment 3–11 (Jan 2002) (hereinafter cited as BEAR Report), www.globalgreen.org/bear/Projects/FinalReport.pdf.

19. *See* e.g., Lisa A. Skumatz, Garbage by the Pound, Resource Recycling (November 1989) (proposing such a system; hereinafter cited as Skumatz 1989); *see also* Menell, *supra* n. 6.

20. It should be noted that larger scale commercial hauling companies have increasingly implemented weight-based systems that distinguish among waste stream components.

21. In many communities, commercial waste hauling is handled on a contract basis. The quantities of refuse from commercial enterprises are sufficiently large per pickup for ongoing competition, as opposed to periodic competition for exclusive waste collection contracts, to make economic sense.

22. *See* George Goldman and Aya Ogishi, The Economic Impact of Waste Disposal and Diversion in California (A Report to the California Integrated Waste Management Board) (Apr. 2001), www.are.berkeley.edu/extension/EconImp Waste.pdf.

23. *See* Luoma, *Trash Can Realities*, Audubon, Mar. 1990, at 86, 90 (noting virtual collapse of recycled materials prices as a result of sudden increase in supply).

24. Some communities have at times considered bans of specific products and packaging for purposes of managing MSW. For example, Maine banned the sale of asceptic packaging (multimaterial drink boxes) in 1990, but later lifted the ban after environmental studies showed that this packaging was relatively benign, had distinct environmental advantages, and could be recycled (although not easily). *See* Ackerman, *supra* n. 9, at 87–94. Vermont considered but ultimately dropped a proposal to ban disposable diapers. *See* Peter S. Menell, Eco-Information Policy: A Comparative Institutional Perspective, Stanford Law and Economics, Working Paper Series, April 1993. Product bans of otherwise nonhazardous products no longer appear to be a serious consideration in MSW policy circles.

25. The magnitude of these costs has been the subject of heated debate between a multistakeholder coalition seeking to promote recycling and a trade organization for the soft drink manufacturers. *See* BEAR Report, *supra* n. 18 (estimating costs associated with deposit-refund systems); Northbridge Environmental Management Consultants, Review of BEAR Report (prepared for the National Soft Drink Association) (Jan. 2002) (questioning findings of the BEAR Report), www.globalgreen .org/bear/Projects/NorthbridgeStudy.doc; Response to Northbridge Environmental Management's Analysis of the MSRP Report (Feb 2002), www.globalgreen .org/bear/Projects/response%201-7.pdf.

26. *See* Don Fullerton and Thomas C. Kinnaman, *Garbage, Recycling, and Illicit Burning or Dumping*, 29 Journal of Environmental Economics and Management 78 (1995); Don Fullerton and Thomas C. Kinnaman, *Household Responses to Pricing Garbage by the Bag*, 86 American Economic Review 88 (1996).

27. Goldman and Ogishi, *supra* n. 22, find that waste diversion has significant economic benefits through multiplier effects—impacts from increased employment and secondary economic effects.

28. *See* BEAR Report, *supra* n. 18, at chapter 4; Lester Brown, Eco-Economy: Building an Economy for the Earth (2001); C. Pollack, Mining Urban Wastes: The Potential for Recycling 22 (Worldwatch Paper No. 76, 1987).

29. *See* Menell, *Structuring a Federal Market-Oriented Eco-Information Policy*, 54 Maryland Law Review 1435 (1995); Menell, *The Uneasy Case for Ecolabelling*, 4 Review of European Community and International Environmental Law (RECIEL) 304 (1995).

30. Economic analysis of such policies depend significantly on the value attributed to inconvenience of container redemption. *See* Ackerman, *supra* n. 9, at 133–34. The early economic studies struggle with this issue. *See* Richard C. Porter, *A Social Benefit-Cost Analysis of Mandatory Deposits on Beverage Containers*, 5 Journal of Environmental Economics and Management 351 (1978); Richard C. Porter, *Michigan's Experience with Mandatory Deposits on Beverage Containers*, 59 Land Economics 177 (1983); D. W. Pearce and R. K. Turner, *Market-Based Approaches to Solid Waste Management*, 8 Resources, Conservation and Recycling 63 (1993); Ingor Brisson, *Packaging Waste and the Environment: Economics and Policy*, 8 Resources, Conservation and Recycling 183 (1993). One recent study of container deposit legislation chose to ignore costs to consumers and households on the ground that "many consumers are

willing to pay (by donating time)." *See* Stuart White, Final Report, Independent Review of Container Deposit Legislation in New South Wales, vol. II, p. 9 (Institute for Sustainable Futures, University of Technology, Sydney, Australia) (3 vols.) (Nov. 2001) (hereinafter cited as New South Wales CDL Study), www.isf.uts.edu.au/ CDL_Report; *see also* F. Ackerman et al. (1995), Preliminary Analysis: The Costs and Benefits of Bottle Bills, Tellus Institute, Draft Report to the U.S. Environmental Protection Agency 24 (Boston, MA, 1995) (stating that "we do not consider it appropriate to calculate household costs beyond the value of unclaimed deposits"); *cf.* Access Economics, Critical Assessment of Independent Review of Container Deposit Legislation in New South Wales 13 (Apr. 2002) (criticizing omission of inconvenience costs), www.accesseconomics.com.au/reports/cdlreport.pdf; *but see* Stuart White, Response to Critical Assessment of Independent Review of Container Deposit Legislation in New South Wales 4–5 (May 2002), www.isf.uts.edu.au/CDL_Report/ C4ES_response_130502%20doc.pdf.

31. The most recent state to adopt such a system, Hawaii, also considers litter control to be a prime virtue. *See* "So What's the Deal with the Bottle Bill?" (Web site for www.bottlebillhawaii.org) (citing litter control as top reason for adopting bottle bill), www.bottlebillhawaii.org/lowdown.htm. Given the importance of the tourist trade in Hawaii, this may well make aesthetic and economic sense. *See* Container Research Institute, Beverage Containers Maintain Position as Second Most Littered Item on America's Beaches (News Release, Jul. 2, 1997), www .container-recycling.org/mediafold/newsrelease/pr7-97lit.htm.

32. *See* New South Wales CDL Study, *supra* n. 30.

33. *See id.* (recommending the use of a deposit-refund system in conjunction with a curbside recycling program); *but see* Access Economics, *supra* n. 30, at 17 (contending that a deposit-refund system will decrease curbside collection yields, undermining the economic efficiency of this waste management policy); *but see* White, *supra* n. 30, at 3–4 (responding that reducing the collection of high-volume low-mass containers improves financial performance of curbside collection of recyclables).

34. This chapter seeks to assess whether variable rate pricing has provided an effective *and* efficient means of diverting waste from disposal to recovery. It is beyond the scope of this chapter to make a full assessment of deposit-refund systems, which result in relatively high costs for administration. Two recent sets of studies and responses—*see* BEAR Report and responses, *supra* n. 18, and New South Wales CDL Study and responses, *supra* n. 30—explore this terrain, although both of the principal studies focus foremost on achieving high diversion rates. *See also* Ackerman, *supra* n. 9, at 123–41 (offering a provocative account of the economics of refillable bottles).

35. *See* U.S. Environmental Protection Agency, Office of Solid Waste, 25 Years of RCRA: Building on Our Past to Protect Our Future (2001).

36. *See* 42 U.S.C. §§ 6901–6992.

37. *See Demand Is Finally Catching up with Excess Capacity; Critical in the Northeast*, Solid Waste Digest: National Edition, October, 2002, at p. 1.

38. *City of Chicago v. Environmental Defense Fund*, 511 U.S. 328 (1994).

39. In 2000, the EPA raised this goal to 35 percent by 2005.

40. *See* EPA, *supra* n. 7.

41. *See* Evaluating Unit-Based Pricing of Residential Municipal Solid Waste as a Pollution Prevention Mechanism (U.S. EPA Cooperative Agreement #CR822-927–010); Marie Lynn Miranda, Scott D. Bauer, and Joseph E. Aldy, Unit Pricing

Programs for Residential Municipal Solid Waste: An Assessment of the Literature (Mar. 1996); Marie Lynn Miranda and Joseph E. Aldy, Unit Pricing of Residential Municipal Solid Waste: Lessons from Nine Case Study Communities (Mar. 1996); Scott D. Bauer and Marie Lynn Miranda, The Urban Performance of Unit Pricing: An Analysis of Variable Rates for Residential Garbage Collection in Urban Areas (Apr. 1996); Marie Lynn Miranda and Sharon LaPalme, Unit Pricing of Residential Solid Waste: A Preliminary Analysis of 212 Communities (1997) (hereinafter cited as Study of 212 PAYT Communities); Marie Lynn Miranda, Unit-Based Pricing in the United States: A Tally of Communities, www.epa.gov/epaoswer/non-hw/ payt/comminfo.htm. The Institute for Local Self-Reliance has also conducted a series of important case studies for the EPA. *See* U.S. Environmental Protection Agency, Cutting the Waste Stream in Half: Community Record Setters Show How (Jun. 1999) (hereinafter cited as Cutting the Waste Stream in Half).

42. *See* U.S. EPA, *Large Cities Use PAYT to Overcome Unique Challenges*, PAYT Bulletin: Winter 2002, www.epa.gov/epaoswer/non-hw/payt/tools/bulletin/ winter02.htm; U.S. EPA, *Could PAYT Offer Hope for New York City's Recycling Program?* PAYT Bulletin: Winter 2003, www.epa.gov/epaoswer/non-hw/payt/ tools/bulletin/winter03.htm.

43. *See* U.S. EPA, Comprehensive Procurement Guidelines, www.epa.gov/ cpg/products.htm.

44. *See* U.S. EPA, Fact Sheet: Affirmative Procurement (August 1994), es.epa.gov/techinfo/facts/pro-act9.html. *See also* Executive Order 13101, Greening the Government through Waste Prevention, Recycling, and Federal Acquisition (Sept. 14, 1998) (expanding on prior such order establishing guidelines and oversight bodies to promote recycling through federal procurement activities).

45. *See* Jim Glenn, *The State of Garbage in America*, Biocycle 32–43 (April 1998).

46. *See* Lisa A. Skumatz, Variable-Rate or "Pay-as-You-Throw" Waste Management: Answers to Frequently Asked Question, 10–11 (Reason Foundation Policy Study 295, Los Angeles, California 2000) (hereinafter cited as Skumatz 2000).

47. *See* Glenn, *supra* n. 45.

48. *See* U.S. EPA, *supra* n. 7; Skumatz, *supra* n. 7, at 5.

49. *See* Skumatz 2000, *supra* n. 46, at 6.

50. *See,* e.g., Skumatz 1989, *supra* n. 19. Lisa A. Skumatz, Hans Van Dusen, and Jennie Carton, *Garbage by the Pound: Ready to Roll with Weight-Based Fees*, Biocycle (Nov. 1994).

51. *See* Skumatz, *supra* n. 7, at 6. A weight-based program that was slated to be implemented in Iowa was scuttled prior to full-scale operation as a result of the sale of the hauling company that was to run the service. Several hauling firms have used weight-based technology in commercial applications. There are numerous full-scale residential weight-based programs currently operating in Europe. *See* Lisa A Skumatz, "Factoids" on Variable and Weight-Based Rates in Solid Waste (Skumatz Economic Research Associates) (June 2001) (hereinafter cited as Variable Rate Factiods).

52. *See* Skumatz, *supra* n. 7, at 7–9.

53. *See* Variable Rate Factoids, *supra* n. 51.

54. *See* e.g., U.S. EPA, Rate Structure Design: Setting Rates for a Pay-as-You-Throw Program (Jan. 1999); U.S. EPA, Pay-as-You-Throw Success Stories (Apr. 1997); U.S. EPA, Pay-as-You-Throw: Lessons Learned about Unit Pricing (Apr. 1994); Skumatz, *supra* n. 7.

55. *See* Lisa A. Skumatz, Hans Van Dusen, and Jennie Carton, Illegal Dumping: Incidence, Drivers, and Strategies, Research Report 9431–1 (Skumatz Economic Research Associates) (Nov. 1994, updated 2000) (hereinafter cited as Illegal Dumping).

56. *See* e.g., Scott D. Bauer and Marie Lynn Miranda, The Urban Performance of Unit Pricing: An Analysis of Variable Rates for Residential Garbage Collection in Urban Areas 23 (Apr. 1996) (finding recycling rates for single-family dwellings of 35 percent and multiunit buildings of 10 percent in San Jose, California).

57. *See* U.S. EPA, *supra* n. 7. In July 2003, Fort Worth, Texas, with a population of more than half a million residents, adopted a variable rate policy. *See* U.S. EPA, *Big City, Big State, Big Results: Fort Worth, Texas, Adopts PAYT*, PAYT Bulletin: Spring 2004, www.epa.gov/epaoswer/non-hw/payt/tools/bulletin/spring-04.htm.

58. *See* Lisa A. Skumatz and John Green, Reaching for Recycling in Multi-Family Housing, Resource Recycling (Skumatz Economic Research Associates) (Oct. 1999).

59. *See* U.S. EPA, *European Union Promotes PAYT Using Innovative Technology*, PAYT Bulletin: Winter 2003, www.epa.gov/epaoswer/non-hw/payt/tools/bulletin/winter03.htm.

60. *See* California Integrated Waste Management Board, Curbside Recycling, the Next Generation: A Model for Local Government Recycling and Waste Reduction 7–10 (Jul. 2002) (hereinafter cited as Next Generation); Jack Macy, *San Francisco Takes Residential Collection Full-Scale*, Biocycle 51 (Feb. 2000).

61. *See* Tonia Horton, *Environomic$: Can the Marriage of Economics and the Environment End Happily Ever After?* MSW Management Elements 50 (1999) (noting that PAYT programs have taken root in Japan, China, Germany, Canada, Italy, and the Netherlands).

62. Christian Patermann, director of the Environment and Sustainable Development Research Programme, notes that: "The polluter pays principle is one of the main pillars of the PAYT project which addresses the critical issue of waste management in cities. The principal objective is to design a variable rate pricing system as a policy option for reducing household discards. Flat rate taxes are not effective in reducing the generation of wastes at the source, hence the idea to develop and test a 'pay-as-you-throw' (PAYT) scheme in several European cities. The project will assess if such a scheme can effectively incite households to divert an increased portion of their domestic waste away from traditional disposal, for example through a higher recourse to recycling or the purchasing of goods with less bulky packages. This project could contribute to a substantial modification of household behaviour towards increased responsibility." Christian Patermann, Sustainable Development in European Cities: How Research Can Contribute, www.ekt.gr/ncpfp5/eesd/info/material/developement.doc. *See also* Variable Rate Pricing Based on Pay-As-You-Throw as a Tool of Urban Waste Management: A Joint Research Project funded by the European Commission under the environmental component "Energy, Environment and Sustainable Development" (describing a 30-month project exploring PAYT approaches for European communities), web.tu-dresden.de/intecuspay.

63. Lisa Skumatz is the most prominent of these researchers. In addition, researchers at Duke University conducted a series of studies pursuant to an EPA grant. Evaluating Unit-Based Pricing of Residential Municipal Solid Waste as a Pollution Prevention Mechanism (U.S. EPA Cooperative Agreement #CR822-927–010). *Supra* n. 41.

64. Don Fullerton of the University of Texas at Austin and Thomas C. Kinnamon at Bucknell University have been the most active scholars in the academic empirical solid waste field. They have collected their principal papers in the volume The Economics of Household Garbage and Recycling Behavior (2002). Robin Jenkins, now with the EPA's National Center for Environmental Economics, carried out one of the first major empirical assessments of variable rate programs, The Economics of Solid Waste Reduction: The Impact of User Fees (1993); see also Robin Jenkins, Salvador A. Martinez, Karen Palmer, and Michael J. Podolsky, The Determinants of Household Recycling: A Material Specific Analysis of Recycling Program Features and Unit Pricing, 45 Journal of Environmental Economics and Management 294 (2003).

65. See U.S. Department of Commerce, Bureau of Economic Affairs, Table 2.1 Personal Income and Its Disposition, www.bea.doc.gov/bea/dn/nipaweb/TableViewFixed.asp?SelectedTable=27&FirstYear=2002&LastYear=2003&Freq=Qtr.

66. See BEAR Report, supra n. 18, at ES-7 (average recovery rate of 61.6 percent in states with deposit-refund laws in place); Container Recycling Institute, Solid Waste (documenting recovery rates for beverage containers in bottle bill states), bottlebill.org/impacts/solid_waste.htm.

67. See Study of 212 PAYT Communities, supra n. 41.

68. See Cutting the Waste Stream in Half, supra n. 41.

69. Eleven of the eighteen communities profiled in this study used variable rates as a central part of their overall MSW policy. Table 11.5 omits three of the cities studied because they implemented curbside recycling at the same time as variable rate pricing or have incomplete data, making it impossible to distinguish the incremental effect of variable rate pricing from the introduction of curbside collection of recyclables. (Not surprisingly, these communities experienced greatly increased diversion following implementation of their new MSW regimes.) The same study identified seven other cities that achieved high diversion rates through curbside collection and education programs (without introducing variable rates). See Cutting the Waste Stream in Half, supra n. 41. Each of the cities that used variable rates considered this element of their program to be key to its success. The authors of the study conclude that variable rate policies can be a particularly effective strategy for diverting waste toward recycling and composting and source reduction. See id., at 20–21.

70. See Don Fullerton and Thomas C. Kinnaman, Household Responses to Pricing Garbage by the Bag, 86 American Economic Review 88 (1996).

71. See Measuring Source Reduction, supra n. 11.

72. See Lisa A. Skumatz, Nationwide Diversion Rate Study—Quantitative Effects of Program Choices on Recycling and Green Waste Diversion: Beyond Case Studies (Skumatz Economic Research Associates, Superior, Colorado) (July 1996); Lisa A. Skumatz, Beyond Case Studies: Quantitative Effects of Recycling and Variable Rates Programs, Resource Recycling (Sept. 1996).

73. See Measuring Source Reduction, supra n. 11; Lisa A. Skumatz, Source Reduction Can Be Measured, Resource Recycling (August 2000).

74. Skumatz has also examined the relative effects of different variable rate policies. This research finds that bag and hybrid programs produced higher diversion rates that variable can programs, controlling for community and other program factors. See Lisa A. Skumatz, Maximizing VR/PAYT Impacts: Policies, Rate Designs, and Progress, Resource Recycling (Jun. 2001).

75. *See* Ed Repa, *Tipping through Time*, Waste Age (Nov. 1, 2002); Nora Goldstein, *The State of Garbage in America*, Biocycle 42 (Dec. 2001).

76. *See id.*

77. *See* Solid Waste Management Association of North America, Integrated Municipal Solid Waste Management: Six Case Studies of System Costs and Energy Use: Summary Report (GR-G 2700 1995); *see also* Peter Kemper and John M. Quigley, The Economics of Refuse Collection (1976).

78. *See* Gruder, Wisconsin Volume Based Rate Collection Guide (University of Wisconsin Extension, Madison, 1993).

79. *See* Frable and Berkshire, Pay as you Waste: State of Iowa Implementation Guide for Unit-Based Pricing (Iowa DNR, Des Moines, Iowa 1997).

80. *See* Lisa A. Skumatz, Achieving 50% in California: Analysis of Recycling, Diversion, and Cost-Effectiveness (conducted for the California chapters of the Solid Waste Association of North America [SWANA], Sacramento, CA) (April 1999); Lisa A. Skumatz, Resource Recycling (Sept. 1999).

81. Skumatz considers the high end of the range for additional transaction costs to be $0.56 per capita (less than $1.50 per household) per year. *See* Source Reduction, *supra* n. 11.

82. Households generally put out fewer receptacles after implementation of variable rate charges. Following adoption of variable rates in Seattle, the number of thirty-two-gallon equivalent cans put out declined from 3.5 per week to 1. Households have strong incentives to reduce volume by reducing, diverting, and compacting waste. The latter phenomenon came to be known in PAYT circles as the Seattle Stomp. Although such compaction does not reduce landfill costs, which are based on weight, it can reduce collection costs by reducing the time per household loading trucks and the number of truck runs. *See* Lisa A. Skumatz, Variable Rates for Municipal Solid Waste: Implementation, Experience, Economics, and Legislation, Reason Foundation Policy Study 160 (Jun. 1993).

83. These were the only cities of the eleven variable rate communities profiled for which adequate comparative cost data was available. As noted earlier (see *supra* n. 69), two of the cities implemented PAYT at the same time that they commenced curbside collection of recyclables and yard waste, and therefore they do not provide a clear basis for distinguishing the effects of these elements of the change in MSW regime. *See* Cutting the Waste Stream in Half, *supra* n. 41.

84. An early 1990s series of interviews with local solid waste officials from fourteen variable rate communities found no problems in six communities, minor problems in four, and significant problems in four. *See* Daniel R. Blume, Under What Conditions Should Cities Adopt Volume-Based Pricing for Residential Solid Waste Collection?, Office of Management and Budget, Office of Information and Regulatory Affairs, Natural Resources Branch (May 1991); *see also* Don Fullerton and Thomas C. Kinnaman, *Garbage, Recycling, and Illicit Burning or Dumping*, 29 Journal of Environmental Economics and Management 78 (1995).

85. *See* Study of 212 PAYT Communities, *supra* n. 41.

86. *See* Lisa A. Skumatz, The State of Variable Rates: Economic Signals Move into the Mainstream, Resource Recycling (Aug. 1997) (hereinafter cited as The State of Variable Rates), Illegal Dumping, *supra* n. 55; *see also* U.S. Environmental Protection Agency, Region 5, Illegal Dumping Prevention Guide (Mar. 1998) (targeting construction, demolition, remodeling, roofing and landscaping contractors, waste management and general hauling companies, automobile repair and tire shops, and scrap collectors as among the major contributors to the problem of illegal disposal).

87. *See* The State of Variable Rates, *supra* n. 86; Illegal Dumping, *supra* n. 55; Variable Rates for Municipal Solid Waste: Implementation Experience, Economics, and Legislation, Reason Foundation Policy Study 160 (Jun. 1993).

88. *See* Michael J. Podolsky and Menahem Speigel, *Municipal Solid Waste: Unit-Pricing and Recycling Opportunities*, 3 Public Works Management and Policy 27 (1998); James G. Strathman, Anthony M. Rufolo, and Gerald C. S. Mildner, *The Demand for Solid Waste Disposal*, 71 Land Economics 57 (1995).

89. *See* Jill Slovin, *Communities Form Strategies against Illegal Dumping*, World Wastes, (Jan. 1995); Illegal Dumping, *supra* n. 55.

90. *See* Illegal Dumping, *supra* n. 55.

91. *See* U.S. Environmental Protection Agency, Region 5, Illegal Dumping Prevention Guide (Mar. 1998).

92. *See* Ackerman, *supra* n. 9, at 71–76; Philip Burgert, *Slow Recovery Reported for Recycling Markets*, Waste Age (Dec. 1, 1993).

93. *See* Luoma, *supra* n. 23; *Success Hits Paper Recycling*, Chicago Tribune, Sep. 10, 1989, at D14, col. 1 (noting a drop in recycled newsprint prices in some cities from $25 per ton to less than zero, meaning that municipalities were having to pay for removal of separated newspapers).

94. *See* Jeff Bailey, *Waste of a Sort: Curbside Recycling Comforts the Soul, But Benefits Are Scant*, Wall Street Journal A1 (Jan. 19, 1995); John Tierney, *Recycling Is Garbage*, New York Times Magazine, June 30, 1996, at 24 (hereinafter cited as Recycling Is Garbage).

95. *See* Recycling Is Garbage, *supra* n. 94 (reporting that in 1996 New York City was spending an extra $200 per ton to collect recyclables and an additional $40 per ton to persuade salvage companies to accept it). The problem in part related to volatility of recycling prices and the high cost of collecting recyclable materials in New York City. Tierney notes that a brief surge in the price of old newspapers to $150 per ton brought New York's recycling program to solvency, but the program suffered as prices ebbed. *See id.*

96. *See* Kivi Leroux, *Recycling's War of Words*, Waste Age (Apr. 1, 2000).

97. *See* OTA Report, *supra* n. 1, at 145.

98. *See* Sharla Paul, *Reaching Equilibrium in Recyclables Markets*, Waste Age (Aug. 1, 1995) (noting large investments by various industries to develop the capacity to utilize recycled input streams).

99. *See* Martin B. Hocking, *Paper versus Polystyrene, A Complex Choice*, 251 Science 504 (1991); *see also Letters*, 252 Science 1361 (1991).

100. Plastics have the highest energy content of the major components of the MSW stream, producing 15,000–20,00 BTUs per pound, twice the heating content of Wyoming coal and nearly as much as residual fuel oil. *See* Office of Solid Waste, U.S. Environmental Protection Agency, The Solid Waste Dilemma: An Agenda for Action, Background Document, 1–36 (1988).

101. *See* Cheryl L. Dunson, *Constructing the Future*, Waste Age (Jan 1, 2000).

102. *See* Kivi Leroux, *An Eye on the Economy*, Waste Age (Apr. 1, 2001).

103. *See id.*

104. *See id.*

105. *See* Sharla Paul, *Reaching Equilibrium in Recyclables Markets*, Waste Age (Aug. 1, 1995).

106. *See* William Moore, *The Recovered Paper Industry Dots the Internet*, Waste Age (Sep. 1, 2000).

107. *See* Kivi Leroux, *Boring Is Good*, Waste Age (May 1, 2000). Commenting on the relationship between recycling market prices and curbside collection programs, Steve Edelson, director of materials marketing for Recycle America, the recycling subsidiary of Waste Management, observed that "the most advantageous scenario is a good market basket, not where you have lots of high and lots of lows. . . . I don't want high prices. That just leads to scalping from the curbside and fly-by-night traders who capitalize on the scene."

108. *See* Cheryl L. Dunson, *Constructing the Future*, Waste Age (Jan. 1, 2000), quoting Will Ferretti, executive director of the National Recycling Coalition, a Alexandria-based nonprofit organization dedicated to the advancement of recycling, source reduction, composting and reuse, commenting that "the fact that basic industries in the United States now utilize, to a significant degree, recovered materials as part of their feed stock indicates that recycling development and innovations have transformed an industrial economy from a virgin base to a recovered industrial economy."

109. *See* U.S. Environmental Protection Agency, Puzzled about Recycling's Value? Look beyond the Bin 8 (Jan. 1998).

110. *See* generally Natural Resources Defense Council, Too Good to Throw Away: Recycling's Proven Record (Feb. 1997), www.nrdc.org/cities/recycling/recyc/recyinx.asp.

111. The BEAR Report, *supra* n. 18, at 4-1–4-6, presents related information on environmental benefits of recycling beverage containers.

112. *See generally* OTA Report, *supra* n. 1, at 190–94.

113. *See* EPA 2000 Report, *supra* n. 10, at 15.

114. *See Demand Is Finally Catching up with Excess Capacity; Critical in the Northeast*, Solid Waste Digest: National Edition, October, 2002, p. 1.

115. *See id.*

116. *See id.*

117. *See* EPA 2000 Report, *supra* n. 10, at 125.

118. *See id.*; Jim Glenn, *The State of Garbage in America*, Biocycle 32–43 (Jul. 1998).

119. *See id.*

120. *See* Nora Goldstein, *The State of Garbage in America*, Biocycle 42, 43, 45 (Dec. 2001)

121. *See id.*

122. For a spirited debate about bioreaction, see *Bill* Sheehan and Jim McNelly, *Bioreactors and EPA Proposal to Deregulate Landfills*, 44 BioCycle 60 (Jan. 2003); Nora Goldstein, *Composting and Organics Recycling vs. Bioreactors: Another Perspective*, Biocycle 44 (May 2003); Ed Skernolis and Gary Hater, *Letter to the Editor*, Biocycle (May 2003); Ed Skernolis and Gary Hater, *Waste Management, Inc. Response*, Biocycle 38 (May 2003); Bill Sheehan and Jim McNelly, *Authors Respond to Waste Management, Inc.*, Biocycle 39 (May 2003).

123. *See generally* U.S. EPA Workshop on Bioreactor Landfills, Feb. 27–28, 2003, www.epa.gov/epaoswer/non-hw/muncpl/landfill/bio-work/index.htm #plenary.

124. Seven out of ten Americans view recycling as an important solution to environmental problems. *See*, e.g., National Solid Waste Management Association, Public Attitudes towards Garbage Disposal (Washington, DC, 1988); *Shades of Green: Eight of 10 Americans are Environmentalists*, Wall Street Journal, Aug. 2, 1991

at 1. *See generally* Frank Ackerman, *supra* n. 9, at 7–13, 55–59, 133–34; *cf.* Anne E. Carlson, *Recycling Norms*, 89 California Law Review 1231 (2001).

125. *See* Thomas C. Kinnaman, *Explaining the Growth in Municipal Recycling Programs: The Role of Market and Nonmarket Factors*, 5 Public Works Management and Policy 37 (2000); G. W. Schaumberg Jr. and K. T. Doyle, Wasting Resources to Reduce Waste: Recycling in New Jersey (Policy Analysis No. 202) (Cato Insitute) (1995); but *cf.* Don Fullerton and Thomas C. Kinnaman, *Household Responses to Pricing Garbage by the Bag*, 86 American Economic Review 971, 975 (1996) (finding that nearly three-fourths of the Charlottesville population participated in recycling without any legal or financial incentive).

126. Using survey responses to hypothetical questions about how much individuals would pay to retain a curbside recycling program, Kinnaman found that Lewisburg, Pennsylvania, residents would be willing to $92.48 per year (net of any household resource costs). *See* Thomas C. Kinnaman, *Explaining the Growth in Municipal Recycling Programs: The Role of Market and Nonmarket Factors*, 5 Public Works Management and Policy 37 (2000). *Cf.* R. DeYoung, *Some Psychological Aspects of Reduced Consumer Behavior, the Role of Intrinsic Satisfaction and Competence Motivation*, 38 Environment and Behavior 358 (1996) (finding that individuals derive intangible satisfaction from engaging in frugal or conservation activities).

127. *Cf.* Stephen Breyer, Breaking the Vicious Circle (1993).

128. *See* Cheryl L. Dunson, *Constructing the Future*, Waste Age (Jan. 1, 2000).

129. *See* Recycling Is Garbage, *supra* n. 94. *See also* Schaumberg and Doyle, *supra* n. 125 (estimating the costs of household separation of wastes at $60 per ton based on assumptions that households devote five minutes per week to this activity and value their labor cost at $7.50 per hour).

130. *See* George J. Stigler and Gary S. Becker, *De Gustibus Non Est Disputandum*, 67 American Economic Review 76 (1977); *see also* Ackerman, *supra* n. 9, at 14.

131. *See* U.S. EPA, *supra* n. 57.

132. *See* Variable Rates, *supra* n. 86.

12

"No Net Loss": Instrument Choice
in Wetlands Protection

James Salzman & J. B. Ruhl

INTRODUCTION

Since European settlement, the continental United States has lost roughly half of its wetlands through drainage, conversion, and erosion.[1] Much of this destruction has occurred over the past five decades, with annual losses of almost 60,000 acres of wetlands occurring just six years ago.[2] Beyond the aesthetic loss, this has resulted in real economic loss. Wetlands provide a range of ecosystem services, from trapping nutrients and sediments, water purification, and groundwater recharge, to flood control and support of bird, fish, and mammal populations. Although not sold in markets, all of these services have real value. Often, however, their value is only realized after the wetlands have been destroyed—when property owners survey their flooded homes or face a large tax increase to pay for a new water plant to treat polluted drinking water. Opinions may differ over the value of a wetland's scenic vista, but they are in universal accord over the contributions of clean water and flood control to social welfare.

Though it is not a high-priority issue for most people, the public has long recognized the general importance of wetlands. During President George H. W. Bush's campaign in 1988, he pledged to ensure there would be "no net loss" of wetlands. President Clinton reiterated this commitment in his own campaign four years later. In its National Wetlands Mitigation Action Plan issued in December 2002, President George W. Bush's administration stated its commitment to no net loss of wetlands.[3]

Despite these continuous presidential pledges to protect wetlands, in recent decades, as more people have moved to coastal and waterside properties, the economic benefits from developing wetlands (and political pressures on obstacles to development) have significantly increased.

Seeking to mediate the conflict between no net loss of wetlands and development pressures, the U.S. Environmental Protection Agency (EPA) and U.S. Army Corps of Engineers (the Corps) have employed a range of policy instruments to slow and reverse wetlands conversion. Through the 1970s and 1980s, the EPA and the Corps relied on prescriptive regulation that discouraged development of wetlands and, even if a permit for wetland filling were granted, required on-site mitigation of destroyed wetlands to ensure no net loss. To defuse the growing political pressure for substantial change to this 404 permit process for developing wetlands, however, since the 1990s the agencies and state governments have favored a market mechanism that seeks to ensure wetlands conservation at minimum economic and political cost.

This instrument is known as wetlands mitigation banking (WMB). In WMB, a "bank" of wetlands habitat is created, restored, or preserved and then made available to developers of wetlands habitat who must "buy" habitat mitigation as a condition of government approval for development. This mechanism has also provided a model for endangered species protection and is in the process of being extended to other settings, including watershed protection.

Given the shift in emphasis from prescriptive regulation to trading, the government's long-standing pursuit of no net loss of wetlands provides a particularly useful case study for this volume. First, WMB provides a rare example of robust trading outside the air pollution context. As we shall see, trading habitat-based goods raises very different concerns than seen in trading mobile pollutants. Moreover, the history of wetlands protection shows an evolution from on-site mitigation to banking and offsite mitigation. In many respects, on-site mitigation represented a form of prescriptive regulation, whereas banking introduces a market mechanism. Thus one can compare the application of different types of policy instruments in the same setting.

Second, examining WMB forces us to think carefully over how to assess the success of a trading program. The traditional measure would likely be efficiency. But one must also consider effectiveness. In this regard, WMB poses two different types of failures—failure of instrument design (a front-end problem) and failure of implementation through monitoring and enforcement (a back-end problem). As many of the case studies in this book illustrate, performance of WMB depends critically both on institutional design and implementation. Another important measure of success concerns distributional equity. Who wins and who loses from banking? Such concerns are far more difficult to assess as good or bad policy in habitat trading than the traditional hot spots of pollutant trading programs.

The first part of the chapter describes the legal and historical background to wetlands mitigation banking, identifying the expected advantages and highlighting the practical difficulties. The discussion then focuses on the three main limitations of WMB design: ensuring meaningful compliance monitoring, currency adequacy, and exchange adequacy.

These theoretical concerns are then tested by looking at experiences to date in the field. The chapter ends by drawing out key lessons for market-based approaches to watershed protection.

WETLANDS COMPENSATORY MITIGATION

The primary law conserving wetlands in the United States is the Clean Water Act (CWA), passed in 1972. Section 311 of the CWA broadly prohibits "the discharge of any pollutant by any person" into navigable waters, where a pollutant is defined as a discrete unit of pollution (e.g., an emission of sulfur dioxide or discharge of toxic waste). On its face, this would seem to prevent the filling of most wetlands.[4] The CWA provides a limited exception to this prohibition in Section 404, which authorizes the Secretary of the Army to "issue permits, after notice and opportunity for public hearings for the discharge of dredged or fill material into navigable waters at specified disposal sites."[5] These permits, administered principally through the Corps and known as 404 permits, wetland permits, or Corps permits, are the cornerstone of federal efforts to encourage protection of wetland resources through market-based means. The permitting program, however, suffers many exceptions and nuances. For the purposes of this discussion, we note that many routine land development activities require and receive 404 permits before they can proceed. Our focus is on how market mechanisms have been developed within this framework to promote the conservation of wetlands.

In granting 404 permits, the Corps guidelines call for a sequencing approach, which essentially lists wetland protection actions in the following order of desirability: (1) avoid filling wetland resources, (2) minimize adverse impacts to those wetlands that cannot reasonably be avoided, and (3) provide compensatory mitigation for those unavoidable adverse impacts that remain after all minimization measures have been exercised.[6] Thus, when applying for a 404 permit, a developer must convince the Corps that no reasonable alternatives exist to the development of the wetlands, that the design of the development minimizes harm to the wetlands, and, if these two conditions have been satisfied, that other wetlands have been restored to compensate for the wetlands destroyed (known as compensatory mitigation).[7]

The EPA and the Corps have traditionally preferred on-site to off-site locations for compensatory mitigation activities and have preferred in-kind mitigation to mitigation that uses a substantially different type of wetland.[8] As an example, if a mall is built on a salt marsh, on-site mitigation would require restoring a wetland on immediately adjacent land (versus a distant site) and in-kind mitigation would require restoring a salt marsh (versus a freshwater cattail marsh). Finally, regardless of location, the EPA and the Corps favor measures that restore prior wetland areas, followed by enhancement of low-quality wetlands and creation of new wetlands. Least favored of all is the preservation of existing wetlands.

Notwithstanding its official status as the least favored alternative in the agencies' sequence of preferences, compensatory mitigation proved popular because it freed at least some highly valued wetlands for development. Building a shopping center around an avoided wetlands site, on choice commercial development land, can present costly design constraints. Compensatory mitigation freed up highly valued wetlands for more comprehensive and flexible development. The developer is in the best position to evaluate these economic efficiencies and knows when the compensatory land swap is superior in comparison to the avoidance strategy. Compensatory mitigation thus took some of the sting out of 404 permits and reduced the frequency of incidents when 404 permitting could be portrayed as unreasonably obstructive.[9]

Nonetheless, the on-site and in-kind mitigation requirements remained unpopular with developers, who started exerting significant political pressure in the 1980s to loosen up or even gut the 404 permitting process. Though compensatory mitigation does share some features of an offsets program, if closely following the Corps guidelines there are few opportunities for market transactions to arise for the simple reason that mitigation should take place *on site.* Calls for reform of the 404 program came from environmentalists as well, who decried the practical performance of mitigation projects.

Indeed, though attractive in theory and providing some political shelter, the project-by-project compensatory mitigation approach soon became widely regarded as having failed miserably in terms of environmental protection. Whether on-site or near-site, the piecemeal approach complicated the Corps' ability to articulate mitigation performance standards, monitor success, and enforce conditions.[10] Many developers went through the motions of so-called landscape mitigation—planting what was required or regrading where required to meet the minimum letter of the permit—then moved on, leaving the restored wetland to revert back to its original habitat, usually a wetland in name only, if even that. For reasons that are still not entirely clear, there was remarkably little compliance monitoring of the mitigated sites by the EPA, the Corps, or relevant state agencies. Without the threat of being found out, a wetlands restoration expert bluntly noted, it was "easier and cheaper to hire, say, a landscaper who will design and build something that looks green and wet . . . than hire a restoration expert."[11] The net result of this institutional failure, as Royal Gardner observed, was that "the failure of compensatory mitigation is wetland regulation's dirty little secret."[12]

ENTER THE MARKET MECHANISM

In light of these problems, the Corps and the EPA (supported by many commentators) started shifting compensatory activities from on-site to off-site mitigation, thus opening the door for greater use of market instruments, in particular, the WMB technique. This approach, its proponents argued, would prove advantageous both in terms of efficiency and eco-logical benefits, aggregating small wetlands threatened by development into larger restored wetlands in a different location. Defined generally as "a system in which the creation, enhancement, restoration, or preservation of wetlands is recognized by a regulatory agency as generating compensation credits allowing the future development of other wetland sites,"[13] WMB allows a developer who has mitigated elsewhere in advance of development to draw from the resulting bank of mitigation credits as the development is implemented and wetlands are filled.

When contrasted with the compensatory mitigation experience, the arguments presented by the EPA and the Corps for WMB in 1990 seemed compelling.[14]

- It may be more advantageous for maintaining the integrity of the aquatic ecosystem to consolidate compensatory mitigation into a single large parcel of contiguous parcels when ecologically appropriate.
- Establishment of a mitigation bank can bring together financial resources, planning, and scientific expertise not practicable for many project-specific compensatory mitigation proposals. This consolidation of resources can increase the potential for the establishment and long-term management of successful mitigation that maximizes opportunities for contributing to biodiversity or watershed function.
- Use of mitigation banks may reduce the time spent on permit processing and provide more cost-effective compensatory mitigation opportunities for projects that qualify.
- Compensatory mitigation is typically implemented and functioning in advance of project impacts, thereby reducing temporal losses of aquatic functions and uncertainty over whether the mitigation will be successful in offsetting project impacts.
- Consolidation of compensatory mitigation within a mitigation bank increases the efficiency of limited agency resources in the review and compliance monitoring of mitigation projects, and thus improves the reliability of efforts to restore, create, or enhance wetlands for mitigation purposes.
- The existence of mitigation banks can contribute toward attainment of the goal of no overall net loss of the nation's wetlands by providing opportunities to compensate for authorized impacts when mitigation might not otherwise be appropriate or practicable.

To help describe how wetland banking works in practice, a pictorial representation is given in figure 12.1. The developer obtains a permit from the Corps to fill twenty-five hectares of wetlands and negotiates the permit conditions—in this case, to restore fifty hectares elsewhere. Rather than undertaking this restoration work itself, however, the developer negotiates to acquire credits for the required fifty hectares from a wetland

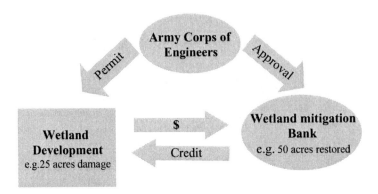

Figure 12.1. Wetland Mitigation Banking in Practice

mitigation bank that has been approved by the Corps. The bank (not the developer) has the legal and financial responsibility to maintain the restored wetlands. In simple terms, WMB can be described as a transaction where in exchange for a payment from the developer, the wetlands mitigation banker informs the regulatory agency that a certain number of mitigation acres have been purchased by the developer (and presumably are sufficient for the agency to grant the 404 permit to the developer).

The establishment of wetlands mitigation banks must follow clear federal (and increasingly state) guidelines. The *Federal Guidance for the Establishment, Use and Operation of Mitigation Banks* (*Federal Guidance*) articulates a standard review procedure for establishing and using wetlands banks in the 404 permit process.[15] A prospective bank must submit a prospectus to the Corps. This prospectus is reviewed by a Mitigation Bank Review Team, which takes account of its compliance with the sequencing approach and other preferences applicable to compensatory wetlands mitigation. The review team and bank then negotiate all the details of bank objectives, ownership, operation, and enforcement before the proposed bank is submitted for public notice and comment. In addition to these federal guidelines, a number of states have provided statutory or regulatory frameworks for using wetlands mitigation banks to ensure compliance with state wetlands protection laws.

Although there is no uniform bank model, most banks fit either a "single client" or "entrepreneur" approach. Under single client models, one developer, whether public (e.g., a state roads department) or private (e.g., a utility company), establishes a bank for personal use. The entrepreneur model involves a bank developer who intends to sell credits to a number of land developers from those building a mall or a housing complex to state highway departments building roads. In both cases, the banking entity must gain the approval of federal and state regulators.

With the support of federal agencies, as well as many environmental advocacy groups,[16] land development interests,[17] and academics,[18] the

WMB program has blossomed since the early 1990s.[19] A decade later, wetland mitigation banking resembles a commodity market, with free-wheeling, entrepreneurial wetlands banks offering for sale (and profit) finished off-site wetlands as credits to anyone who is in need of mitigation for 404 permits.[20] It is precisely this technique that the Corps and the EPA officially endorsed in their 1995 *Federal Guidance*.

In a wide range of fora, its advocates have contended that off-site mitigation banking should be preferred over on-site or near-site compensatory mitigation because of greater efficiency, scale effects, and environmental protection.[21] If these arguments seem similar to those advanced on behalf of mainstream environmental trading markets over the prescriptive model of regulation, it is no coincidence. Notwithstanding the substantial expense and procedural rigor associated with establishing a commercial wetlands mitigation bank, the program, both conceptually and by official endorsement, has all the makings of a trading market. One commentator describes it as "akin to a commercial paper transaction: Party A (the credit producer) informs Party B (the regulatory agency) that the credits should be released to Party C (the entity with mitigation requirements)."[22] The Corps succinctly describes this feature of commercial wetlands banks as "an implicit move away from a rigid, onsite, in-kind preference for piece-meal compensatory mitigation towards a broader-based trading system that takes advantage of qualitative differences among wetlands and that can use the potential economic profits from the development of some low-valued wetlands (that may be doomed in any event)."[23]

What do such exchanges look like? The town of Libertyville, Illinois, for example, converted eighty acres of former corn fields into a wetland bank. A private company converted the fields into wetlands for $1.2 million. For every acre sold to developers as a mitigation credit, developers pay about $65,000 and the town gets $6,000.[24] Nationally, the cost of credits can run from as low as $7,500 in rural areas to $100,000 per acre in urban or suburban regions. In theory, the price covers the costs of maintaining and monitoring the site to ensure that it maintains conditions conducive to wetland plant and animal life.[25]

The Corps tracks the national acreage of permitted wetlands fill and mitigation required. From 1993 to 2000, 9,500 hectares of wetlands were filled in exchange for 16,500 hectares restored or created in mitigation.[26] Despite the rapid growth of mitigation banks and their use, though, a number of questions remain. Most important, we need to ask whether performance has matched expectations. Has wetlands mitigation banking led to the conservation of wetlands and no net loss of wetlands? In what follows, we disentangle the experience of wetlands mitigation banking by focusing on whether the trades have exchanged wetlands of equivalent value (an issue we call currency adequacy) and how the exchanges have been restricted to ensure equivalent value (an issue we call exchange adequacy).

CURRENCY ADEQUACY

In any environmental trading market, whether exchanging sulfur dioxide, halibut, chlorofluorocarbons, or wetlands, a fundamental issue is determining the trading metric—the currency. The currency establishes what is being traded and therefore protected. Currencies drive the structure of environmental trading markets, directly influencing their construction, rules of exchange, and provision for public participation. Whether we can confidently trade x for y depends on what we are trying to maximize and our standard of measurement, both of which turn on the currency of exchange. Put simply, unless the currency captures what we care about, we can end up trading the wrong things.

To ensure equivalent trades of wetlands, the currency must incorporate important values provided by both the wetlands to be lost and the wetlands used for mitigation. Of course, this begs the questions of what the relevant values are, how we measure them, and how we reflect them in a conveniently traded currency. Put another way, since 1988 successive presidential administrations have solemnly pledged to ensure no net loss of wetlands, but what does that mean? No net loss of *what*? If all that concerns us about wetlands protection is acreage, then the job is simple— identify acres of wetlands lost and restored and count up the net gain or loss in area. But is that really why we care about wetlands? Isn't it more likely that we care about wetlands, at least in large part, because of their functional value to the environment and the economy? If so, then counting acres may make for easy accounting but poor policy. Not all wetlands are created equal. Context matters. Wetlands differ by type, location, and the services they deliver. If one cares about the ability of wetlands to provide flood control, safeguard water quality, and act as a nursery for fish and wildlife, then acres are a terrible currency because they cannot capture these service values. They necessarily remain outside of the transaction and become uncaptured externalities. In other words, unless currencies can capture some meaningful measure of service provision, wetlands become increasingly nonfungible commodities when their ecosystem values are considered.

To express this in a simple example, let's consider the ideal case of trading, where the objects exchanged are completely fungible and all variance across space, type, and time is eliminated. Here, trades of homogenous commodities simultaneously take place in a small, discrete location—small blue marbles traded at the same time across a kitchen table. If we are trading identical blue marbles, the number of marbles may serve as a perfectly adequate metric (five marbles for five marbles). If we are trading blue and yellow marbles, the number and color of marbles are adequate currencies (three yellow marbles for four blue marbles). If, however, some marbles are highly radioactive and others are not, the simple currency metrics of color and quantity fail to capture an important variable.[27] If the currency cannot incorporate the environmental values we care about, these become external to the exchange and, as a result, trades may actually worsen the environment or natural services delivered. Inadequate currencies allow externalities to bleed out of the trading market. We may end up with a nice pile of marbles that glow in the dark.[28] In the extreme case, the currency can actually encourage environmentally harmful behavior.[29]

This problem is not unique to WMB. Indeed, the problem of currency adequacy is present in all environmental trading markets. As the table sets out, nonfungibilities can arise across three dimensions—space, type, and time—and in a number of settings, and depending on the market, an effective currency may need to capture all three.

As table 12.1 demonstrates, one can easily see how mitigation banking would encompass trades between nonfungible wetlands. Different types of wetlands may be exchanged for one another; wetlands in different watersheds might be exchanged; wetlands might be lost and restored in different time frames. As the potential range of variables we care about increases, the need for a refined currency becomes acute. More particularly, when the currency cannot accurately capture the important values (e.g., the habitat service, the flood control service, the water filtration service), we have less reason to be confident in the equivalency of trades. Thus, assessing the success of WMB must start with an examination of the wetland assessment methodology used by banks and the government.[30]

To be meaningful, we argue, wetland assessment methodologies must be able to capture the provision of valuable services for both the wetlands to be lost and the wetlands used for mitigation. One might try to compensate for margins of error in estimating service provision values through using simple trading ratios. Thus, for instance, where the Corps is uncertain over the true range of functions, it might require that two or three times as much wetlands area be restored as destroyed. This approach works well if the goal is no net loss of wetlands acreage, but it fails to address meaningfully the conservation of wetlands services. Thus, for example, the loss from filling a wetlands that provides a valuable service of flood control upstream of a community cannot be meaningfully compensated by restoring twice as much wetlands that provides little flood control or, taking into account landscape context, provides flood control downstream of the town.

To the extent that reliable measurements of function value can be made within a landscape, WMB offers a flexible mechanism for achieving wetland protection goals at minimum cost. In practice, however, reviews of assessment methodology suggest that explicit measures of service values remain beyond the reach of virtually all assessment methods in use.

The Corps has granted broad discretion to state and local authorities to select currencies.[31] Roughly forty different wetlands assessment methods have been developed, varying in terms of the type of habitats in which the method is used, the basic targets of assessment, and the functional and social values encompassed in the assessment.[32] Over half of the

Table 12.1

Environmental Trading Market	Nonfungibility of Space	Nonfungibility of Type	Nonfungibility of Time
California Rule 1610: Program allows trading of reduced vehicle volatile organic emissions for increased refinery volatile organic emissions emissions	Vehicle emissions are geographically diffused versus hot spot of concentrated refinery emissions	Vehicle emissions may be less carcinogenic than refinery emissions	Vehicle emissions fluctuate in regular patterns over twenty-four-hour periods whereas refinery emissions experience irregular peaks
Wetlands Mitigation Banking: Corps of Engineers permit allows destruction of wetlands in return for contributing to wetlands restoration project located elsewhere	The lost ecosystem services may have been delivered to many people, whereas the services of the restored wetlands may be delivered to few	The destroyed wetlands may have had a higher capacity of service provision compared to the restored wetlands	The permit may allow destruction of the wetlands before the quality of the restoration of other wetlands is known
Habitat Conservation Plans: Fish and Wildlife Service permit allows destruction of endangered species habitat in return for securing preservation of another parcel of the habitat located elsewhere	The lost habitat may have been part of a contiguous habitat system for the species, whereas the preserved habitat may be isolated and thus of less overall value	The lost and preserved habitats may have provided functional values to different populations of the species, and we do not know which population is more important to the overall viability of the species	The lost habitat may have been of ideal vegetative maturity for the species, while the preserved habitat may require time to achieve that state

Acid Rain Program: Market for SO_2 emissions allows power plant to exceed allowed emissions by purchasing credits from other power plants that emit less than their allowance	Emissions from the plant purchasing credits may be blowing over Eastern states, whereas emissions from the plant selling credits may have been blowing over the ocean	Negligible potential for differences	The two plants may have different peak emissions periods if, for example, one is located in a cold climate (winter peak) and the other in a hot climate (summer peak)
Alaska Halibut Individual Transferable Quotas: Permits to catch Alaska Halibut are traded among fishers to avoid derby pressures in fishery	One fisher may catch in halibut breeding area, while other may catch fish in nonbreeding zones	Tons of halibut does not account for bycatch, highgrading or size of fish (juvenile instead of mature)	One fisher may catch halibut during breeding season, while other catches out of breeding season

methods go beyond assessment of habitat suitability to encompass some
assessment of wetland function, but many of these function-based
methods are bounded by limitations on type of habitat for which the
method can be used (e.g., coastal wetlands only) and limited in terms of
the functions assessed (e.g., limited to avian species functions).[33] Moreover, the data requirements for these advanced methods are significant.[34]

Reviews of wetland assessment methodology theory and practice conducted since banking sprang onto the scene have categorized assessment
methods into three major types.

- *Simple indices* are derived from quickly and easily observed characteristics of a wetland and usually serve as surrogate indicators of
  one or more ecological functions (e.g., percent cover of aquatic
  vegetation).
- *Narrowly tailored systems* attempt to measure directly a limited
  range of wetland services, such as wildlife habitat, through a detailed procedure focusing on that particular wetland service (e.g.,
  percent duck habitat).
- *Broadly tailored systems* examine a range of wetland functions
  covering a number of observable characteristics.[35]

Simple index methods, such as counting acres, make mitigation
banking easier and less costly, but "are often the least sensitive to
wetlands values and functions. Also, most simple indices do not take into
account scale effects."[36] As many of the preceding examples have made
clear, it would be difficult to integrate ecosystem service valuation into
WMB programs relying on simple index methods. Narrowly tailored
methods, such as those attempting to evaluate habitat values, are generally focused on specific habitat types or species and represent an improvement over counting acreage, but they still do not directly measure
service provision. Moreover, they can result in "mitigating to the test"—
that is, driving the banking process toward the favored habitat type or
species. "Comparing cumulative [habitat units] for different sets of species involves risks inherent in comparing apples and oranges."[37] In other
words, the narrowly tailored methods fail to produce a currency that can
be reliably used across nonfungible features of assessment, suggesting
that these methods will not successfully integrate all the value measurements needed if the goal is to produce a currency applicable across
nonfungible biological, economic, and social factors. Thus, the Environmental Law Institute concludes, "for wetland managers concerned about
the spectrum of functions provided by a wetland, there is no substitute for
a carefully considered, broadly tailored analysis."[38]

In practice, however, these broader assessment methods tend to be
expensive and produce reams of qualitative results, which, for ease of
comparison, wetlands managers tend to reduce to quantitative value
scores that often mask the ecological rationales.[39] Indeed, comprehensive
reviews in 1992 and 1993 of wetlands mitigation banks in operation

concluded that only a small number employed a broadly tailored method (a complex currency), whereas among the rest "debiting and crediting transactions are based on two basic currencies—acreage and functional replacement."[40] To determine whether banks established after these studies have adopted more complex currencies, we contacted new banks by telephone and email.[41] We identified and were able to describe in detail thirty-six banks established after 1994.[42]

Overall, we found that wetlands assessment methods used by wetlands mitigation banks have advanced very little from the beginning of the banking program and simple currency methods continue to dominate.[43] WMB entities seem focused on using the simplest and most expedient assessment method that the relevant regulatory bodies will approve, and to date, most regulatory bodies do not appear to require or even encourage a more sophisticated approach. A comprehensive currency seems too expensive to mint and too arduous to use. Thus instead of developing and refining valuation approaches for assessment and trades, WMB assessment methods have largely stagnated in the acre-based and narrow function-based approaches, resulting in the use of relatively crude currencies for wetlands habitat trading purposes.

EXCHANGE ADEQUACY

The analytical framework we have proposed in earlier research predicts that crude currencies, such as those derived from the simple index measures of wetland qualities that prevail in WMB programs, will result in tightly constrained trading schemes if the market maker desires to control for environmental externalities.[44] By contrast, sophisticated wetland assessment methods, such as ones that fully reflect wetland function values, can be converted to currencies that limit externalities sufficiently to allow the market maker to permit trades to be made regardless of type, space, and time differences. The comprehensive currency, reflecting function and service value, would make differences in type irrelevant, allow comparison of impact to different locations, and permit discounting for purposes of timing differentials.[45] The WMB program, hamstrung as it is by its crude currency forms, bears out this postulated inverse relationship between currency sophistication and intensity of market constraint. The following paragraphs briefly set out how WMB trading rules have sought to squeeze out the nonfungibilities of type, space, and time.

Nonfungibility of Type

The preference the Corps and the EPA demonstrate for in-kind compensatory wetland mitigation reflects the substantial differences in rarity, time to maturity, and functions that different wetland types exhibit. Because crude currencies such as acres and habitat function fail to capture these complex differences in wetlands, WMB programs also are reluctant to stray far from a strict in-kind policy. For example, the *Federal Guidance* allows, at least in principle, out-of-kind mitigation in banking only "if it is determined to be practicable and environmentally preferable."[46] Even when out-of-kind trading is allowed, however, banks typically impose fixed trading ratios between acres of the wetland types as a surrogate for more precise measurements of comparative function value.[47] In short, as compared to open or fixed ratio out-of-kind trading, "in-kind mitigation requires less understanding of tradeoffs because it is based on the assumption that certain wetland functions . . . will follow the wetland form."[48] The cost of this in-kind requirement, however, is a thinning of the wetlands trading market from all wetlands to only the defined in-kind type.

Nonfungibility of Space

The value of wetlands' services depends fundamentally on their landscape context.[49] Even controlling for type, a bog wetland in Maine may not provide the same function values as one in Oregon, or even one in the next county. And even if it does, it certainly will not deliver the services of nutrient trapping, flood control, or nursery habitat to the same parties. Obviously, however, the preference for on-site mitigation the Corps and the EPA have adopted for compensatory mitigation in general cannot apply strictly to WMB. Instead, the concept of a geographically defined service area is imposed on wetlands banks to define the area "wherein a bank can reasonably be expected to provide appropriate compensation for impacts to wetlands and/or other aquatic resources."[50] In general, service areas should be no larger than the watershed within which the bank is located, unless reaching beyond that market is "practicable and environmentally desirable."[51] Coupled with an in-kind constraint, this service area constraint should further narrow the potential supply of wetlands in the trading market.[52]

Nonfungibility of Time

One of the purported advantages of WMB programs is that the bank has created the wetlands before the credits are drawn, so that the mitigation is secured before the wetlands are filled. In general, therefore, the *Federal Guidance* provides that "the number of credits available for withdrawal (i.e., debiting) should generally be commensurate with the level of aquatic functions attained at a bank at the time of debiting."[53] With large commercial banks, however, the expense and time involved with establishing functional wetlands, particularly those of types that require long maturation periods, could make the banking cost prohibitive if credits could not be drawn before the bank's wetland values are fully in place. The *Federal Guidance* thus allows some leeway in the timing requirement, allowing credit withdrawal before equal wetland values are established, if the bank possesses adequate financial assurance and has exhibited a high probability of success.[54] In some cases this policy results in lags of up to six years between the times of wetland destruction and wetland replacement.[55]

HOW WELL DOES MITIGATION BANKING WORK?

The Process

Our findings and those of others suggest that practical constraints on the implementation of more sophisticated assessment methods designed to produce a refined currency for trades—in terms of costs, time demands, and complexity—have prevented WMB from ensuring currency adequacy. Thus, WMB has been forced into the next best alternative—designing market constraints to plug the holes that the crude currency otherwise leaves open to externalities. Assessment methodology has become the proverbial tail that wags the dog, keeping the wetlands program from tapping the full benefit of market trading efficiency as the market makers (the EPA and the Corps) attempt to shore up the weak currency with market constraints.

There is good reason to believe this problem will be endemic to *habitat* trading programs in general until ecologists can deliver a cheaply calculated, refined currency for habitat values.[56] The cost of valuing the currency in the sulfur dioxide program is low—a ton is a ton. But the cost of creating habitat currencies is either very cheap—an acre is an acre—or, if we demand reliable measures of environmental and social service values, very expensive.

It is important to recognize that WMB trading programs differ in another fundamental way from typical markets as well. Assume, for example, that Charlie sells a bike to Jody. Jody has every reason to ensure that the bike works well and will hold up for her rides around town. This transaction has a built-in quality check. Jody does not want to buy a lousy bike. The WMB program, however, does not work in a similar manner, for quality is not valued. Indeed, the developer has virtually no interest in the quality of the wetlands being restored. He simply wants a permit from the Corps. Similarly, the banker doesn't care about the quality of the wetlands, either. She simply wants the Corps to sign off so she can sell credits. She is supposed to maintain restored wetlands after the credits have been sold, of course, but will likely only do so if compliance monitoring and enforcement by the Corps are probable. Thus in all key respects, the central player in all this is the Corps. There is no invisible hand at work here. It falls on this agency, *which is not a market participant*, to ensure the quality of the restored wetlands because neither the buyer nor seller have incentive to do so.

Developers and bankers have an obvious profit incentive to use the least expensive currency the government will allow. But the government needs to be careful in demanding wetlands quality and equivalence of trades. It has an incentive not to make the currency too expensive to mint, or no one will use it and the trading program will expire of its own accord. Because of these agency and participant incentives, the net result has been Gresham's law in practice—simple currencies have driven out complex ones.

Despite policies mandating that habitat trading ensure equivalent value and function,[57] the experience is that most programs are not administered this way. In practice, most habitat trades to date in wetlands programs have been approved on the basis of acres, in many instances ensuring equivalence in neither value nor function. If parties have a choice between a complex (and expensive) currency that measures equivalent function or a simple metric, and both deliver a 404 permit, simplicity will always prevail. Thus, given the choice in the habitat context of acres or complicated measures of value, acreage has won.

Moreover, now that the Corps has committed to the WMB program as the ideal of compensatory mitigation, many believe that there is pressure within the Corps to facilitate the program by easing the official avoid-minimize-compensate sequencing policy that has already eroded substantially.[58] Avoiding wetlands and minimizing wetland impacts reduce the demand for mitigation bank credits and thus thin the market. Predictably, the pressures to adopt crude currencies and keep markets thick combine to allow the seepage of externalities from the WMB market.[59]

One way to ground this problem might be to subcontract the oversight role to a party that has an institutional concern over wetlands quality—perhaps a group such as Ducks Unlimited or The Nature Conservancy. These organizations could play the role of approving wetlands banks and determining the ratio of filled to restored wetlands. Beyond public accountability, the obvious downside to such an approach is that conservation organizations can have their own narrow interests (most notable in the case of Ducks Unlimited and protecting wetlands for waterfowl hunting).

Given this state of affairs, the aggressive integration of open trading models into wetlands and other habitat contexts poses concerns for environmental protection. Even the most developed habitat assessment methods presently in use are ill-prepared to produce reliable, inexpensive, and ready measurements of a habitat's environmental and service values. Such measurements require far more money and time to produce on a site-specific basis than developers, habitat bankers, and the government seem prepared to allocate. In the absence of such measurements, the government and environmental groups will likely require at a minimum constraints on habitat trading markets (e.g., stronger exchange adequacy).

But even the current trading constraints are seen by many as too restrictive. Observers have criticized the *Federal Guidance* for adhering too strictly to the sequencing approach and other conditions applied generally to compensatory mitigation, arguing that "this policy could prevent a banking market from ever emerging."[60] This is the inevitable pressure any regulated market faces when externalities must be controlled through market constrictions rather than through a refined currency—at some point the constraints threaten to swallow the market. Surely a loosening of type, space, and time constraints would make banking more flexible and economically attractive to entrepreneurs, but at what price to the environment?

Indeed, the *Federal Guidance* invites further pressure to restrict the market with its "practicable and environmentally desirable" standard for exceptions to the set of trading constraints. As commercial banking becomes more widespread, it is likely that the criticisms bank sponsors have already lodged against the *Federal Guidance* will intensify if the market for credits does not swell. Moreover, to the extent that mitigation banking is intended to replace the project-by-project approach to compensatory mitigation in the regime of 404 permits, the Corps already feels pressure to ensure that the market does not become too thin. And make no mistake, the Corps *is* feeling pressure to loosen the timing restrictions of the *Federal Guidance* and other exchange adequacy safeguards and has openly discussed relaxation of its restrictions.

At the extreme, of course, land developers and bank sponsors most prefer a nationwide bank of freely transferable credits and have been pushing for this and relaxation of other restraints.[61] Such relaxation of space, type, and time restraints may seem reasonable if the Corps believes the existing crude wetlands currencies are sufficient. If so, though, it will be banking on sheer serendipity to believe that WMB and other habitat trading programs will produce consistently positive results for the environment.

How to Measure Success?

The preceding analysis has focused on the problems inherent in creating a wetlands market for nonfungible goods and services. But have these theoretical concerns been borne out in practice? There are three useful ways to measure success—efficiency, distributional equity, and effectiveness.

Despite all its potential shortcomings, WMB certainly remains popular. Credits in Florida are now trading anywhere from $30,000 to $80,000 per acre. There clearly is demand, and banks are still being created to supply it. The program seems efficient, in that calls for gutting the 404 program have fallen off the political landscape while wetlands protection and development both continue at costs that appear acceptable to the parties. But this is only one measure of success, and it is arguably deceptive.

If one looks at distributional equity—market-driven migration of wetlands across the urban–rural landscape—the case is less clear. As noted earlier, landscape context matters. Even if a restored wetlands provides the same biophysical level of services as the filled wetland, the services may have little or no value if they are not delivered to a population that needs them. This is an issue of *distributional equity*—who is winning and who is losing through WMB trades? A study of wetland banking in Florida, for example, found that trades, even in the same watershed, have produced "a transfer of wetlands from highly urbanized, high-population density areas to more rural low-population density areas."[62] The same problem has plagued mitigation banking in Virginia, where a study found that most mitigation banks are located in rural areas but most wetland losses take place in urban and suburban areas.[63] In other words, as can be expected from a market efficiency perspective, developers want to develop wetlands where land is dear (urban) and wetland banks want to locate where land is cheap (rural). The result is trades that move wetlands out of areas where they may provide valuable services to urban populations and into sparsely populated areas, where most likely their service provision is either redundant or less valuable. The existing WMB framework lets this happen, or at least fails to scrutinize the externality effects of the practice.

Should we be concerned about this market-driven shift of wetlands from urban to rural areas, even if it simply reflects the efficiency of trading? If we care about the equity of who receives wetland services and their value, then the answer is yes, and we should closely examine the redistribution of wetland service values within the environment and between human populations.[64] Are there identifiable groups that would be harmed by conversion in one area and not compensated by mitigation in another? And if so, how severe is that damage, and what mechanisms might be put in place to compensate these losers? If we care primarily about keeping the wetland banking market thick or no net loss of wetland acreage, however, then maybe we shouldn't be overly concerned, because to add another location restriction based on keeping trades within the same population shed would surely thin the market.

And what can we say about whether WMB is effectively meeting the overarching goal of no net loss? Despite its role as the central justification for wetlands policy, there are surprisingly few detailed data available on WMB trades. Although a number of case studies in the literature provide trade-specific data on the size of mitigated areas, few disclose price or functional details. Indeed, we have come across no studies that closely track trends in regional or local volume of trading over time (either number of trades or land area), the prices of mitigation credits, or the costs of establishing and operating banks. Reflecting this dearth of data, the most comprehensive study on mitigation banking to date, a 2001 report by the National Academy of Sciences, recommended the creation of a national database to track the loss and restoration of wetlands function over time.[65] Any overall conclusions on the WMB experience are hampered by this lack of data and the Bush administration has responded in its National Wetlands Action Plan of 2002 by pledging to establish a comprehensive mitigation database and annual public report card on wetlands programs by 2005. As of 2006, no comprehensive database has been produced. But the Council on Environmental Quality did issue a report on progress toward the president's goal.[66]

If one looks at acreage, the overall results of the nation's wetlands protection programs appear positive. According to the National Wetlands Inventory, conducted every ten years by the U.S. Fish and Wildlife Service, the rate of wetlands loss from 1985 to 1995 was 0.11 percent per year.[67] The National Resources Inventory, conducted by the U.S.

Department of Agriculture and employing a different sampling method, reached a roughly similar conclusion, finding a net wetlands loss of 0.07 percent per year from 1982 to 1992.[68] These are almost a quarter lower than rates of loss from the preceding decade.[69] WMB has contributed to this trend. The Corps estimates that from 1993 to 2000, roughly 24,000 acres of wetlands were permitted to be filled and 42,000 were required as compensatory mitigation, a *gain* of 1.8 acres for every acre developed.[70]

If one looks at service provision, though, the data suggest that WMB has not performed well. For example, despite claims by the Maryland Department of the Environment that the state had gained 122 acres of wetlands between 1991 and 1996, a Chesapeake Bay Foundation study found that there had been a net *loss* of 51 acres of wetlands functions.[71] In the most comprehensive study to date on this issue, in 2001 the National Academy of Sciences examined the practice of wetlands compensatory mitigation. The very first of the committee's principal findings was that "the goal of no net loss of wetlands is not being met for wetland functions by the mitigation program."[72] In response to this report, the Bush administration has gone even further, acknowledging in its recent Wetlands Mitigation Action Plan that

> As a general matter, compensatory mitigation decisions are made on a case-by-case basis and often do not consider the proper placement of mitigation projects within the landscape context, the ecological needs of the watershed, and the cumulative effects of past impacts.... EPA has identified improving wetlands ecological performance and results of compensatory mitigation as a priority.[73]

Given the reliance on crude currencies and loose exchange restrictions, such a conclusion is hardly surprising. To its credit, the Bush administration has pledged in its action plan to implement most of the committee's recommendations. Given the trade-offs between thick markets, on one hand, and refined currencies and tight trading restrictions, on the other, however, we remain cautious over whether the promised reforms (assuming they are implemented) will produce significantly different results on the ground.

CONCLUSION: LESSONS FOR HABITAT MARKET-BASED INSTRUMENTS

Environmental trading markets remain popular and are growing. Mature environmental trading markets are active in reducing air pollution and regulating land development, and they are under serious consideration for endangered species habitat. It is easy to imagine the use of such a mechanism in forestry, where a particular land use is valued for its watershed protection services.

In asking whether mitigation banking has been successful, one must look beyond market volume and consider what success means and in comparison to what alternative. As described, focusing on the identification of trading currencies forces policy makers to articulate what the goal of the market-based mechanism should be. If the goal is no net loss of wetland acreage, then acres are a fine currency. If the goal is no net loss of wetlands function and delivery of services, then the current reliance on acreage metrics will likely to continue to fail.

In comparing on-site versus off-site mitigation (which in this context serve as rough proxies for prescriptive regulation versus a market-based approach), one must assess whether the gains from the mitigation areas are sufficient to offset the losses in the conversion area. This must be done from the view of distributional equity, overall loss of service provision, and overall value of service provision.

To be sure, creating an environmental market by no means ensures environmental protection. Beyond design issues such as creation of stable property rights lies the equally critical issue of implementation. In retrospect, the greatest failing of on-site mitigation may well not have been its prescriptive approach but rather the virtually nonexistent monitoring and enforcement of the mitigation projects. This was an institutional (not an instrument design) failure. As a result, one cannot draw a conclusion from the wetlands case over whether prescriptive regulation or market instruments was more effective. Had on-site mitigation actually been monitored and enforced, perhaps services would not only have been conserved but continue to be delivered to the same populations as before. We just don't know.

More generally, as this chapter has pointed out, WMB programs are particularly vulnerable to implementation failures because the government, not the market actors, must ensure the quality and equivalence of the exchange. This inherent challenge is no different than with the other important habitat trading instrument—habitat conservation plans (HCPs) under the Endangered Species Act. In exchange for taking endangered species and adversely modifying part of the species habitat, development interests agree to manage (and often restore) other parts of the landscape. This does not produce credits that can be traded, but the similarities to WMB are striking because in both schemes the government decides on the equivalency of the exchanges. In both cases, there is an inherent tendency that will lead to a net loss of prime habitat/wetlands over time. In the case of HCPs, this occurs because there is an overall reduction in habitat as a result of the permitted development. In the case of WMB, the reduction occurs not in the form of total acreage but rather in a likely decrease of valuable service provision.

At a basic level, if the currency is unable to capture accurately the value sought to be measured (the ecosystem service values), then confidence in the procedural and substantive adequacy of the trading system will erode. Developing an assessment methodology that measures the ecosystem service value, or some reliable indicator of the valued product (e.g., water quality, floodwater retention, etc.), will be the critical first step in developing a framework for any trading-based mechanism. The actual shape of the trading mechanism for habitat protection will, of course, depend on the particular setting and management goals. If the currency can be easily set, measures of value determined cost-effectively, and trading restrictions established that still provide a market thick with participants, then trading mechanisms will work well. If any of these are lacking (as most are in the case of wetlands), then one will have less confidence that the trading ensures and promotes environmental protection.

ACKNOWLEDGMENTS This chapter draws from our prior publications in the area, including James Salzman and J. B. Ruhl, *Currencies and the Commodification of Environmental Law*, 53 Stanford Law Review 607 (2001) [hereinafter Currencies]; J. B. Ruhl and J. Gregg, *Integrating Ecosystem Services into Environmental Law: A Case Study of Wetlands Mitigation Banking*, 20 Stanford Environmental Law Journal 365 (2001); and James Salzman and J. B. Ruhl, *Paying for the Protection of Watershed Services—Lessons from Wetland Banking in the USA*, in S. Pagiola et al., Selling Forest Environmental Services: Market-based Mechanisms for Conservation (2002). We are particularly grateful for the comments of Michael Bean, Jim Boyd, Dan Cole, Dick Craswell, Alyson Flournoy, Jody Freeman, Royal Gardner, Larry Goulder, Bob Hahn, Oliver Houck, Jason Johnston, Charlie Kolstad, Carol Rose, Mark Seidenfeld, Dick Stewart, Dan Tarlock, Buzz Thompson, and Tom Tietenberg. The empirical research for this article was supported by the U.S. Environmental Protection Agency's Science to Achieve Results (STAR) program grant R82612-01. Because this chapter was not subjected to any EPA review and does not necessarily reflect the views of the agency, no official endorsement should be inferred.

NOTES

1. *See* www.epa.gov/OWOW/wetlands/vital/status.html.

2. Information on the current status of U.S. wetlands can be found at www .epa.gov/owow/wetlands.

3. *See* www.epa.gov/owow/wetlands/NWMAP122402signed.pdf.

4. Although the CWA makes no reference to wetlands with respect to the 404 program, early in the program's history judicial interpretation required the Corps to extend its reach to tidal wetland areas. *See Natural Resources Defense Counsel v. Callaway*, 392 F. Supp. 685, 686 (D.D.C. 1975).

5. The EPA has the power to veto Corps permits if it finds the discharge would have an unacceptably adverse effect on environmental resources, but it has exercised this power infrequently. *See* S. Burkhalter, *Oversimplification: Value and Function: Wetland Mitigation Banking*, 2 Chapman Law Review 1 (1999).

6. *See* Memorandum of Agreement between Department of the Army and the Environmental Protection Agency Concerning the Clean Water Act Section 404(b)(1) Guidelines, 55 Federal Register 9210, 9211–12 (1990) [hereinafter Memorandum of Agreement].

7. Section 404 does not mention a mitigation requirement for permit issuance. Rather, this provision of the statute directs the EPA, in conjunction with the Corps, to develop guidelines that the Corps must apply in deciding whether to authorize the fill disposal at a wetlands site.

8. Ecologists generally divide wetlands into seven major types, within which there is tremendous variation from region to region in terms of physical characteristics and functions. *See* Environmental Law Institute, Wetland Mitigation Banking 77 [hereinafter ELI-Wetland] (1993).

9. *See* Royal C. Gardner, *Banking on Entrepreneurs: Wetlands, Mitigation Banking, and Takings*, 81 Iowa Law Review 527, 586 (1996) ("The federal retreat from strict sequencing is an attempt to provide regulatory relief to small landowners and small businesses") [hereinafter Gardner]. One study of commercial wetlands mitigation banks concluded that "it is the practice of regulators to relax the first two sequencing requirements—avoidance and minimization of wetland impacts—if the wetland that will be impacted is of low to mid quality," thus creating a market for mitigation. Shirley Jeanne Whitsitt, *Wetlands Mitigation Banking*, 3 Environmental Law 441, 463–64 (1997).

10. *See* Michael S. Rolband, Antoinette L. Pepin, Chris Athanas, and Ineke Dickman, *Wetlands Banking for Sound Mitigation? Yes, Virginia*, National Wetlands Newsletter, May–June 1999, at 4.

11. Keith Bowers, *What Is Wetlands Mitigation?*, Land Development, Winter 1993, at 28, 33. Lawrence R. Liebesman and David M. Plott, *The Emergence of Private Wetlands Mitigation Banking*, 13 Natural Resources and Environment 341 (1998) [hereinafter Liebesman and Plott] (discussing a Florida state agency study finding a 27 percent success rate of such projects); Gardner, *supra* note 9, at 540–42 (discussing the Florida study); *see also* ELI-Wetland, *supra* note 8, at 31 (discussing the dismal record of piecemeal on-site mitigation projects); Chesapeake Bay Foundation, Maryland Nontidal Wetland Mitigation: A Progress Report 30–39 (1999) [hereinafter Chesapeake Bay Foundation] (discussing independent study finding poor record of compensatory mitigation). It is also worth noting that although compensatory wetland mitigation policies relying primarily on wetland creation can result in no net loss of wetlands, they are likely to result in overall loss of habitat because the land being converted to wetlands usually is already open space. That is, the net result is less undeveloped land than before. Compensatory mitigation that relies on enhancement or preservation of existing wetlands is likely to produce a net loss of wetlands. *See* Alyson C. Flournoy, *Preserving Dynamic Systems: Wetlands, Ecology, and Law*, 7 Duke Environmental Law and Policy Forum 105, 128–29 (1996). Under any compensatory approach, of course, there is no guarantee that the mitigated site would have remained undeveloped indefinitely, but even in this sense the compensatory mitigation approach can present a baseline problem. Wetlands are dynamic systems. By considering only existing wetlands in deciding what should be protected, compensatory mitigation stifles the process of wetlands creation (e.g., the hardening of coastal shorelines). The result is an "invisible loss of wetlands" that are not naturally created and will never have the chance to become so. Interview with Alyson Flournoy, University of Florida School of Law (April 28, 2000).

12. Gardner, *supra* note 9, at 540; *see also* Michael J. Bean and Lynn E. Dwyer, *Mitigation Banking as an Endangered Species Conservation Tool*, 30 Environmental Law Report (Environmental Law Institute) 10537, 10538–39 (2000) [hereinafter Bean and Dwyer] ("The track record of traditional, project-by-project wetland mitigation is dismal"); Virginia C. Veltman, *Banking on the Future of Wetlands Using Federal Law*, 89 Northwestern University Law Review 654, 670 (1995) [hereinafter Veltman] ("The California State Coastal Conservancy sponsored a review of fifty-eight permits issued for creation and restoration projects in the San Francisco Bay Area between 1978 and 1983. The report found that only two of the fifty-eight projects could be deemed successful").

13. *See* ELI-Wetland, *supra* note 8, at 3.

14. *Federal Guidance for the Establishment, Use, and Operation of Mitigation Banks*, 60 Federal Register 58605 (Nov. 28, 1995). Veltman similarly summarizes the ra-

tionales cited for shifting from on-site to off-site mitigation locations and from small to large scales of mitigation sites: "Offsite mitigation provides a greater selection of hydrologically and ecologically favorable locations, thus increasing the opportunity for a well-functioning replacement. Additionally, offsite projects can be joined into one large mitigation, which is beneficial because 'larger wetland systems are generally more self-sustaining. They can provide habitat for more types of species, a longer and more self-sustaining food chain, more habitat niches, and a wider variety of habitat types—which, in turn, can better accommodate ecosystem succession, migration, and change.' Thus, the presumption in favor of onsite versus offsite mitigation often encourages, rather than prevents, poorly designed wetlands that will either fail or, if viable, provide a nonequivalent replacement." Veltman, *supra* note 12, at 673 (citations omitted); *see also* Michael Rolland, *The Systemic Assumptions of Wetland Mitigation: A Look at Louisiana's Proposed Wetland Mitigation and Mitigation Banking Regulations*, 7 Tulane Environmental Law Journal 497, 510–11 (1994) (noting also that on-site mitigation "puts the mitigation for wetlands loss in the hands of a sometimes hostile developer"). Notwithstanding these often cited benefits, replacing many small "postage stamp" wetlands with large contiguous mitigation projects is not necessarily always a desirable approach, as research indicates that some systems of small isolated wetlands provide more biodiversity value than a large contiguous wetland of the same type. In sufficient abundance and proximity, small isolated wetlands provide greater variability of conditions, insurance against natural perturbations, and source-sink population dynamics than can a contiguous wetland of equal total size. Moreover, the desirability of either kind of wetland habitat will depend on the particular species in mind, thus a policy favoring large contiguous wetlands necessarily disadvantages species that depend on systems of small isolated wetlands. *See* Raymond D. Semlitsch, *Size Does Matter: The Value of Small Isolated Wetlands*, National Wetlands Newsletter, Jan.–Feb. 2000, at 5.

15. *See generally* Gardner, *supra* note 9, at 563–77.

16. *See* ELI-Wetland, *supra* note 8, at 153 (concluding that wetlands mitigation banking can offer ecological advantages to on-site mitigation in some instances and "can also provide economies of scale and greater regulatory certainty").

17. *See* Liebesman and Plott, *supra* note 11, at 371 (touting wetlands mitigation banking as "an innovative, market-based solution for many of the problems with the existing wetlands regulatory system").

18. *See* Gardner, *supra* note 9, at 557–62 (advocating the ecological and efficiency benefits of wetlands mitigation banking).

19. Robert Brumbaugh, manager of the Corps of Engineers' Institute for Water Research National Wetlands Mitigation Banking Study, reports that there were 5 banks in operation in 1985, 40 in 1992, and more than 100 in 1995 with hundreds more in development at that time. *See* Robert W. Brumbaugh, *Wetland Mitigation Banking: Entering a New Era*, Wetlands Research Program Bulletin, Oct.–Dec. 1995, at 3 and fig. 1 (available at www.wes.army.mil/el/wrtc/wrp/bulletins/v5n3/brum.html) [hereinafter Brumbaugh]. An annual national conference on wetlands mitigation banking, now in its third year of production, has sponsors including the Corps, the EPA, and a wide variety of private and public entities and pitches itself to mitigation bankers, landowners, developers, regulators, local government, suppliers, nurseries, engineers, and a host of others interested in banking policy and methods. *See 3rd National Mitigation Banking Conference: Learn about Wetlands, Habitat & Conservation Banking* (brochure for May 17–19 conference, Denver, Colorado).

20. There are over seventy such commercial mitigation banks operating in the United States today. *See* Liebesman and Plott, *supra* note 11.

21. *See* Federal Guidance, *supra* note 15, at 58,607. Banking also avoids the threat of takings claims that may arise from exercising the avoid and minimize requirements of sequencing.

22. *See* Royal C. Gardner, *Federal Wetland Mitigation Banking Guidance: Missed Opportunities,* 26 Environmental Law Report (Environmental Law Institute) 10075, 10075 (1996) [hereinafter Gardner II].

23. *See* Brumbaugh, *supra* note 19, at 4.

24. Madhu Krishnamurthy, *Wetlands Restoration Pays off for Libertyville,* Chicago Daily Herald, Aug. 14, 2001, at 4.

25. *See* Anika Myers, *Progress Report; As Wetlandsbank Enters Ninth Year, Jury of Environmentalists Still Out on Mitigation Efforts,* Broward Daily Business Review, April 19, 2001, at A1.

26. National Research Council, Compensating for Wetland Losses under the Clean Water Act (2001, National Academy Press) [hereinafter NAS report].

27. To take another example, knowing that one car costs $20,000 and another costs $80,000 tells me a great deal about the cars and that consumers value one more than the other; but if I need to buy a car that can haul a trailer the currency of dollars is inadequate. It fails to capture an important value and express it. Or, to introduce a market dynamic, assume that apple trees in an orchard produce two types of apples, pretty and ugly, but that both taste the same. Farmers currently sell apples by the bushel. A supermarket will pay a higher price per bushel than a canning factory but only wants to buy pretty apples. In this case, there is a market incentive to develop a grading system (a more sophisticated currency) so the values important to the supermarket are meaningfully captured and communicated.

28. In the example, the currency must capture color, number, and, hopefully, radioactivity. Note, however, that a similar result may occur even if the currency *does* capture radioactivity. This will happen if the parties are indifferent to this value. In such a case the disjunction between private and public interests in trading can result in a loss of social welfare. Choosing the wrong currency increases the chances that environmental protection will suffer, but one might argue that serendipity can work both ways on a case-by-case basis and may on occasion lead to environmental improvements.

29. "With respect to fishing allowances, a [tradable environmental allowance] may employ a relatively simple measure, as would be the case where an individual fishing quota is measured in pounds or tons of a particular target fish. But fishermen know that bigger fish bring more at the market than smaller ones, and this can induce them to 'high-grade,' keeping the bigger fish and simply discarding the smaller (and now dead) specimens, with potentially disastrous effects on the fish population as a whole.... The quest for simplicity in [tradable environmental allowances] has feedback effects on what actually gets preserved." Carol Rose, *Expanding the Choices for the Global Commons: Comparing Newfangled Tradable Allowance Schemes to Old-Fashioned Common Property Regimes,* 10 Duke Environmental Law and Policy Forum 45, 60 (1999).

30. Wetland function assessment methods "attempt to establish, in either a qualitative or quantitative fashion, the nature and extent of different services which a wetland may provide. Once those services are known, they may be translated into a 'currency' which can serve as the medium of trade for a wetland mitigation bank." ELI-Wetland, *supra* note 8, at 77.

31. "Because wetlands are complex and incompletely understood, it is difficult to assign a quantitative number to their value. Instead of confronting this difficulty head-on, the Corps-EPA Mitigation MOA provides broad guidelines for valuing wetlands, leaving local permitting authorities with virtually unfettered discretion in determining whether a just compensation for destroyed wetlands has been achieved." Veltman, *supra* note 12, at 673–74.

32. *See* Candy C. Bartoldus, A Comprehensive Review of Wetland Assessment Procedures: A Guide for Wetland Practitioners (1999).

33. *Id.* at tables 1–3.

34. *Id.* at table 3.

35. ELI-Wetland, *supra* note 8, at 78.

36. *Id.* at 89.

37. *Id.* at 90. For example, if we measure habitat value based on what makes good habitat for ducks, which for a variety of institutional reasons many of the habitat-based indices use as the benchmark, we will wind up with more duck habitat and less habitat for species that do not thrive in duck habitat. *See id.* at 36.

38. *Id.* at 90.

39. *Id.* at 91.

40. Writing in 1994, ELI found four banks used the Wetland Evaluation Technique (WET), a broadly tailored method, and the rest were split between using acre counts (a simple index) and the Habitat Evaluation Procedure (HEP) (a narrowly tailored method). *See* ELI-Wetland, *supra* note 8, at app. B. Similarly, in its 1994 First Phase Report of the National Wetland Mitigation Study, the Corps' Institute for Water Resources (IWR) reviewed forty-four banks existing in 1992. The IWR's conclusions were consistent with those of the ELI, finding twelve banks used an inventory method (acres) exclusively, eight used a function evaluation method (usually habitat units) exclusively, and the other banks used other methods and combinations of methods. The IWR counted none using what the ELI would call a broadly tailored index method. Institute for Water Resources, U.S. Army Corps of Engineers, National Wetlands Mitigation Study: First Phase Report 31–32 (1994) [hereinafter First Phase Report].

41. This work was conducted under an EPA STAR grant with Jim Salzman as principal investigator. *See* Ruhl and Gregg in acknowledgment note.

42. Nineteen of these banks use an acre-based index, fifteen use one of the function-based methods, and two use a "best professional judgment" approach. This split between acre-based and function-based methods is consistent with the ELI's and the IWR's earlier findings. *See* First Phase Report, *supra* note 40, at 31–32 (providing pre-1994 data).

43. Indeed, the Corps has been criticized for being unwilling to engage in broad functional measurement in other aspects of the 404 permit program as well, including wetland delineation and permit approval and denial. *See* Michael J. Mortimer, *Irregular Regulation under Section 404 of the Clean Water Act: Is the Congress or the Army Corps of Engineers to Blame?*, 13 J. Environmental Law and Litigation 445, 460–73 (1998) (providing an empirical study of Corps actions). Many state wetland protection programs are accused of suffering from the same shortcoming. For example, Maryland has one of the most sophisticated regulatory programs in place for wetlands protection, yet it, too, relies on a simple currency. As a Chesapeake Bay Foundation report described, the Maryland Department of the Environment's method "to calculate the amount of mitigation required to compensate for wetland impacts is replacement ratios. While this method considers acreage,

vegetation, and to a limited extent, uniqueness, it does not specifically consider wetlands functions gained or lost." Chesapeake Bay Foundation, *supra* note 11, at 10.

44. *See* Currencies, listed in the acknowledgments, at 638.

45. For example, when Florida recently enacted legislation requiring all state and local agencies engaged in wetland mitigation banking to devise and adopt a uniform functional assessment method, it anticipated the type, space, and time nonfungibilities inherent in the process. The assessment method thus must (1) "account for different ecological communities in different areas of the state"; (2) "determine the value of functions provided by wetlands...considering... location"; and (3) "account for the expected time-lag associated with offsetting impacts." Fla. H.B. 2365, § 4 (2000) (amending Fla. Stat. § 373.414(18)). The Florida Department of Environmental Protection had until January 2002 to devise this all-encompassing currency for mitigation banking.

46. Federal Guidance, *supra* note 15, at 58,611.

47. *See* ELI-Wetland, *supra* note 8, at 92. Trading ratios also are often imposed to adjust for different mitigation forms (e.g., restoration versus preservation) and for the general uncertainty that the bank wetlands will exhibit as much acre-for-acre integrity as the filled wetlands. *See id.*

48. *Id.* at 30.

49. *See* James Salzman, *Valuing Nature's Services,* 24 Ecology Law Quarterly 887, 896 (1997) ("The value of a wetland's nutrient trapping services, for instance, depends on the location of its out-flow. Does it flow to shellfish beds (high value) or a fast-flowing ocean current (low value)?"). In our EPA grant, we studied a trade in Florida of inland wetlands for wetlands located on a small island in a river. Even if the two wetlands have the same biophysical capacity, the delivery, and therefore value, of their services will differ significantly. *See also* ELI-Wetland, *supra* note 8, at 30 ("Most wetland functions have value because of where they exist in the landscape").

50. Federal Guidance, *supra* note 15, at 58,611.

51. *Id.*

52. The spatial fungibility issue is even more complicated in the endangered species context, where strategic siting of bank service areas must account for species movement, habitat succession, and discontinuities in suitable habitat locations. *See* Bean and Dwyer, *supra* note 12, at 10,537.

53. Federal Guidance, *supra* note 15, at 58,611. Studies of wetland restorations have found a remarkably low rate of success. The Florida Department of Environmental Regulation found a success rate of 45 percent for tidal wetlands creation, 12 percent for freshwater wetlands creation. Veltman, *supra* note 12, at 669.

54. *See* Federal Guidance, *supra* note 15, at 58,611. Explaining the pressure to relax time restraints, a Corps official has written: "Among the most critical issues that affect the financial success of commercial banks, and thus the willingness on the part of the private sector to get involved in commercial banking, is the timing of debiting versus accrual of credits in the bank. Ideally, mitigation banks are constructed in advance of development projects that result in wetland losses and are seen as a way of reducing uncertainty in the wetlands replacement process. However, virtually all private commercial bank entrepreneurs argue that for their banking ventures to be economically viable, they need to be allowed to sell credits before replacement wetlands are fully functioning or self-maintaining. Allowing a bank to be debited before it achieves a fully functioning stage involves a trade-off

between ecologic and economic risks. The later the bank may be debited (along a time continuum from planning through design, construction, and operation), the lower the ecologic risk. However, delays in allowing debiting increase the financial risk to the investor. The private sector generally needs some level of immediate return to justify the financial risk or to supplement initial funding. . . . Private commercial banks implemented to date reflect the value of time. Regulators have allowed debiting (generally to a limited extent) shortly after bank construction, during construction, or even shortly before construction, if there was an approved site plan and appropriate real estate arrangements and financial assurances (such as funds for remedial work, if needed, and for long-term management)." Brumbaugh, *supra* note 19, at 4–5.

55. *See* Michael G. Le Desma, *A Sound of Thunder: Problems and Prospects in Wetland Mitigation Banking*, 19 Columbia Journal of Environmental Law 497, 506 (1994).

56. One of these authors, Salzman, recently returned from a year in Australia studying ecosystem service markets for biodiversity, water quality, and salinity. In every single market, the assessment methodology for use in the field to score specific land parcels was absolutely critical to the success of the market mechanism.

57. *See* Memorandum of Agreement, *supra* note 6, at 9212 (wetland values shall be determined "by applying aquatic site assessment techniques generally recognized by experts in the field and/or the best professional judgment of Federal and State agency representatives, *provided such assessments fully consider ecological functions included in the Guidelines*.") (emphasis added).

58. *See* Bean and Dwyer, *supra* note 12, at 10,550 ("Conservation interests worry that the practical effect of the mitigation banks is to tempt regulators to skip rather lightly past avoidance and minimization and proceed instead directly to compensation in the form of purchasing credits from a bank").

59. In another article (Currencies), we argue that this state of affairs suggests the need for a third layer of analysis—"review adequacy" to ensure that trades really do promote the public welfare. Such an approach, however, will surely raise transaction costs, undercutting the efficiency benefits of environmental markets. At the workshop for this volume, Johnston suggested a way around this problem by having expert third parties take over the role of the Corps. Thus the Nature Conservancy or some other land trust might decide whether trades ensure no net loss of services. Whether such parties would be regarded by developers as neutral or acceptable, however, is an open question.

60. Liebesman and Plott, *supra* note 11, at 342; *see also* Gardner II, *supra* note 22, at 10,075 (stating that the Federal Guidance "does not go far enough to encourage private-sector investment in the process of wetland mitigation"); William W. Sapp, *The Supply-Side and Demand-Side of Wetlands Mitigation Banking*, 74 Oregon Law Review 951, 981–90 (1995) (arguing for relaxation of strict sequencing, on-site mitigation preference, and in-kind mitigation preference to increase the demand for mitigation banking credits—i.e., to thicken the market).

61. *See* ELI-Wetland, *supra* note 8, at 58.

62. Dennis King and L. W. Herbert, *The Fungibility of Wetlands*, 19 National Wetlands Newsletter 10, 11 (1997).

63. *See* Ann Jennings, Roy Hoagland, and Eric Rudolph, *Down Sides to Virginia Mitigation Banking*, National Wetlands Newsletter, Jan.–Feb. 1999, at 9, 10. The Virginia study also found an increasing trend toward the use of banks in one watershed to compensate for losses in a different watershed. *See id.* at 9–10.

64. We are not suggesting that the shift from urban to rural wetlands is necessarily an unwise policy in all cases. In some settings, the urban wetlands to be developed may consist of many small, isolated wetlands of poor quality, whereas the rural mitigation bank may produce a large, contiguous, high-quality habitat. We are suggesting, however, that the shift between the human populations serviced may be significant and thus should be considered in the evaluation of the mitigation banking policy, whereas the Florida and Virginia studies show that it has not been. Moreover, research has revealed the importance of small, isolated wetlands to maintaining biodiversity and habitat for some species, thus the ideal of large, contiguous rural wetlands will not always provide superior environmental value.

65. *See* NAS Report, *supra* note 26.

66. *See* Council on Environmental Quality, Conserving America's Wetlands 2006: Two Years of Progress Implementing the President's Goal, available at pubs.bna.com/ip/BNA/DEN.NSF/is/PF04252006/$FILE/den60425.pdf.

67. David Sounding and David Zilberman, *The Economics of Environmental Regulation by Licensing: An Assessment of Recent Changes to the Wetland Permitting Process*, 42 Natural Resources Journal 59, 71 (2002).

68. *Ibid.*

69. The largest single category of wetland loss is that of agricultural and silvicultural activities, neither of which are subject to the compensatory mitigation procedures described.

70. It is worth noting that the National Academy of Sciences study did not trust the mitigation data, saying they were inadequate to determine the status of compensated wetlands. NAS Report, *supra* note 26, at 3. It is also worth noting that when compared to the overall estimate of 58,545 acres lost *per year*, then the contribution of WMB is minor.

71. *See* Chesapeake Bay Foundation, *supra* note 11, at i.

72. NAS Report, *supra* note 26, at 2.

73. EPA, National Wetlands Action Plan 4 (Dec. 24, 2002).

Part III

POLITICAL AND LEGAL DYNAMICS

13

Tradable Pollution Permits
and the Regulatory Game

Jason Scott Johnston

INTRODUCTION

For over three decades, federal, state, and local environmental regulators and the polluting industries that they regulate have been bargaining to reduce the amount of pollution put into America's air, water, and groundwater. They have done so pursuant to a set of federal statutes that by and large tell regulators to base pollution standards on what is technologically and economically achievable within various industry categories and subcategories. For decades, this regime—which is known as command-and-control (CAC) environmental regulation—has been widely decried as inefficient.[1] For an equally long time, economists have been advocating an alternative regulatory regime, one based on tradable pollution permits (what I shall refer to as a TPP regime). TPP regimes set an overall aggregate cap on the emissions of a particular pollutant and then allocate that aggregate cap among individual sources of the pollutant in the form of tradable pollution permits. There is now a vast theoretical, empirical, and experimental economics literature examining both positive issues regarding the actual operation of such markets and normative questions involving when and whether such market mechanisms may improve social welfare relative to various benchmarks.[2] Indeed, so powerful is the standard economic argument for TPP regimes that their relative scarcity in American environmental regulation now stands as something of an unexplained paradox.[3] However, as shown by the relative success of sulfur dioxide permit trading under Title IV of the 1990 Clean Air Act,[4] TPP regimes are more than just a theoretical possibility. TPP regimes have moreover been proposed recently as an instrument for limiting mercury, NO_X and greenhouse gas emissions, as well as for controlling nutrient-laden wastewaters in various watersheds.[5]

Economists have exhaustively analyzed the efficiency of incentives created by theoretical TPP regimes and, as other contributions to this volume show, they have also mounted sophisticated and illuminating ex post empirical analyses of the performance of the one large-scale existing TPP regime in the United States (the Title IV acid rain trading program). Left underexplored, however, has been a very basic question of positive political economy, a question that is fundamental to explaining when TPP regimes are actually likely to move from theory to reality: Among polluting firms, who are the winners and losers in the move from CAC to a TPP regime? When will the majority of polluting firms support such a move, and when will they not?

This chapter contributes toward an answer to these questions. In my view, a major reason why these questions have been neglected in the economic literature on TPP regimes is because analysts have generally worked with a highly oversimplified and unrealistic notion of what CAC regulation actually means for polluting firms.[6] To understand this, one must understand not only a bit of the stylized history of late-twentieth-century American environmentalism but also the relatively arcane and complex world of the regulatory system that environmentalism created. Both the legislative birth and regulatory elaboration of CAC pollution laws have clear and powerful political-economic explanations. I begin therefore with some general positive observations regarding the evolution of CAC environmental regulation in the United States and a brief but relatively detailed look at how laws and regulation have in fact shaped the CAC regulatory bargaining process.

I then develop a more formal analysis of the CAC regulatory bargaining process. Though highly simplified, the model captures an important feature of regulatory bargaining: Whether through the initial (federal level) regulatory categorization process or in bargaining with state and local permitting authorities, the higher a firm's regulatory compliance cost, the more the firm has at stake in the regulatory game, and therefore the greater the resources that the firm will devote to fighting regulation and the lower the actual regulatory burden imposed. The model predicts the widely observed but otherwise paradoxical phenomenon that under CAC regulation, it is usually those firms that have the highest compliance costs (firms with the oldest and dirtiest plants) who are regulated the least.

To discern winners and losers in a hypothetical transition from CAC to a TPP regime, I compare the equilibrium distribution of firm costs under alternative versions of CAC to firm net costs under a TPP regime. Net costs under a TPP regime depend on whether a particular firm is a buyer or seller of tradable permits. Using a simple model of equilibrium in a TPP market, I show that for a given pollution reduction standard (permitted level of pollution) implementing that standard via a TPP regime will make both low and high compliance cost firms in an industry better off relative to idealized CAC (where every firm complies with the stated pollution reduction standard). Relative to equilibrium, firm-specific pollution reduction levels under bargained CAC, however, moving to a TPP regime is likely to make high compliance cost firms (permit buyers under TPP) worse off. With this result and others (such as that firm support for a move to a TPP regime depends on such factors as permit demand elasticity and the stringency of the aggregate cap), the analysis helps explain why polluters sometimes do not support TPP regimes as well as why they sometimes do. It also suggests that the normative evaluation of TPP reform proposals should be based on realistic rather than idealized descriptions of the CAC system being reformed.

THE EVOLUTION OF FEDERAL CAC REGULATION

The social problem underlying modern (that is, late-twentieth-century) American pollution control regulation was that publicly owned resources such as air and water were traditionally treated as free public goods, used as waste receptacles on a first-come, first-served basis. By the late 1960s, the post–World War II boom in American manufacturing had accomplished two things that together created a national demand for environmental cleanup and control: The boom brought mass affluence and dramatic increases in leisure time, thus generating a new mass demand for outdoor recreation; on the other hand, so much waste had been put into American airsheds and waterways that those resources had been pushed to the point where they were either affirmatively dangerous to health or at the very least unsuitable for precisely the kinds of outdoor recreation that Americans demanded. On this view, which I elaborate in considerable detail elsewhere,[7] the environmental problems that modern federal environmental legislation and regulation were designed to fix were decidedly local. Federal environmental regulation was designed to improve and protect air, surface water (and later, through the Resource Conservation and Recovery Act (RCRA)[8] and the Comprehensive, Response, Compensation and Liability Act (CERCLA)[9]) groundwater quality so as to benefit people who resided near and therefore would be benefited most by such improvement and protection.

In other words, federal environmental regulation was designed to provide local environmental goods. The fact that American industrial polluters had no common law property right to pollute is absolutely crucial in understanding why American environmental regulation took the form of technology-based CAC requirements rather than either TPPs or emission taxes. From the point of view of beneficiaries from pollution control, the fact that polluters did not have a common law property right to use public resources meant that polluters could (legally if not as a matter of equilibrium cost distribution) be made to bear the entire cost of cutting pollution by installing costly pollution abatement technologies.

From the point of view of pollution abatement beneficiaries, such a system seemed clearly preferable to one in which they paid polluters to abate their pollution. Of course, giving polluters a limited statutory right to pollute and making that right tradable would not have necessarily entailed a payment to polluters. A system of tradable rights is, however, based on statutorily defined rights. Given that the status quo regime in a typical American industrial city as of, say, 1965, was a de facto if not a formal right to pollute, moving from the status quo to a regime with very limited rights to pollute would have entailed enormous costs to American industry, American workers, and the industrial heartland communities where such industries were located. Because the American government had actively encouraged and even subsidized the creation of the status quo regime, to drastically switch regimes would not only have been economically destructive but in a very real sense unfair.

Rather than a dramatic switch in property rights regimes, the first generation of American federal environmental statutes attempt a relatively modest adjustment in rights. Today, the CAC regime created pursuant to these statutes is much decried. Such criticism exemplifies hindsight bias. Much to the contrary, given the level of sunk investments in plant and production processes and the existing technology that prevailed in the early 1970s, the first-generation federal environmental laws approximate a market-mimicking, value-maximizing solution to the problem of pollution reduction. Although it is true that federal environmental statutes contain language suggesting a goal of zero pollution,[10] those statutes are enormously (deliberately) complex. Read carefully and correctly, statutes such as the Clean Air and Clean Water Acts tell federal environmental regulators to reduce what had been an unlimited right to pollute, but to do so subject to the constraint that the economic and social cost of such reduction not rise to politically unacceptable levels.[11] Unsurprisingly, such a mandate has been translated into a set of pollution control standards that look at what can be done to reduce pollution given existing technological and economic realities. No one ever thought that these were clear and precise statutory mandates. Indeed, as I have argued elsewhere, the congressional interest in environmental as in other similar regulatory legislation is to clearly endorse consensus goals while providing substantial discretion to regulators in how to realize those goals, thus enabling ad hoc congressional intervention to prevent the regulatory imposition of politically unacceptable costs.[12] Still, as of the early 1970s, with large and as yet unrealized investments in sunk industrial facilities and very little known pollution abatement technology available, the CAC edict approximates what an informed observer might well have understood by a "reasonable" or net value maximizing approach to the problem of pollution reduction.

By cutting polluters' entitlements—from free and uncontrolled use of the air and waterways for waste disposal, to only those levels of disposal consistent with a reasonable investment in abatement technology—

modern environmental laws adjusted an analytically inevitable and historically ever-present bargaining game between polluters and government. Readjusting entitlements in this way is certainly no less a "market" response than would be the imposition of a tax on pollution. Indeed, a CAC regulatory regime may be understood merely as shifting the focus of bargaining between polluters and government—away from the magnitude of harm caused by pollution, which idealized pollution taxes capture—and toward how it is that polluters must seek to reduce that harm. Indeed, from a traditional law and economics perspective, the difference between pollution taxes and a readjustment in pollution entitlements through CAC may be usefully understood as the difference between a property rights approach under CAC versus a liability rule approach under pollution taxes.[13] The property rights approach taken by CAC regulation cut back on what had been a relatively clear entitlement to pollute, limiting polluters' rights to that level of pollution consistent with statutorily required abatement efforts. By giving polluters the right to pollute as much as they wish but charging them a tax equal to the harm caused by their pollution, taxes give the public a right to be free of pollution but do not allow them to demand reductions in pollution below the levels induced by pollution taxes. They may thus be understood as recognizing a public right to be free of pollution but allowing polluters to infringe that right so long as they pay the required price.

As a positive matter, it is relatively easy to see why first-generation federal environmental regulation eschewed pollution taxes in favor of CAC. Pollution taxes might well have seemed attractive to beneficiaries from pollution reduction. Like CAC requirements, pollution taxes induce a reduction in pollution. Unlike CAC requirements, they compensate beneficiaries from pollution reduction for the continuing harm from reduced levels of pollution. Taxes would therefore seem preferable from a beneficiary point of view. By the same token, however, pollution taxes increase the cost of pollution control to polluters: In addition to the cost of reducing pollution that they would incur under a command and control regime, they also must pay for the harm caused by pollution that remains after compliance with the standard.[14] Moreover, pollution taxes can work only if pollution is effectively monitored. As Stavins observes in his chapter in this volume, such monitoring is now possible for some pollutants and some industries but was generally nonexistent when modern environmental laws were enacted. Monitoring pollution is, moreover, a minor problem compared with the problem of determining the magnitude of the tax. Pollution taxes anticipate the pollution will continue, albeit at reduced levels relative to a no-tax world. The economic ideal is to set pollution taxes equal to the level of actual harm caused by pollution. Monetizing the actual harm caused by pollution remains a highly imperfect and controversial process. Finally, and perhaps most important, although it is theoretically possible to understand pollution taxes as recognizing a public entitlement to be free of pollution but then allowing polluters to take that entitlement provided they pay compensation, it is equally possible to view pollution taxes as giving polluters a conditional entitlement to pollute. A fundamental political goal of late-twentieth-century American environmentalism was to change the status quo allocation of property rights, to declare that polluters did not have a right to pollute but rather the public had a right to be free of pollution, to move from one property rights regime to another. Inasmuch as pollution taxes can be interpreted as granting a conditional right to pollute, they were and remain inconsistent with this structural goal.

WHAT IS CAC? SOME EXAMPLES OF THE TECHNOLOGY-BASED ENVIRONMENTAL REGULATORY REGIME

To develop a sensible economic model of the regulatory bargaining game under CAC environmental regulation, it is necessary to describe, albeit briefly, what CAC regulation actually looks like. It is important to begin with a clear understanding of the precise sense in which uniform CAC regulation is uniform. Federal environmental laws (such as the Clean Air Act and Clean Water Act [CWA]) that mandate technology-based regulatory standards do require uniform emissions reductions, but only for plants or facilities that are in the same industry category and are of the same approximate age. Under the Clean Water Act (CWA), for instance, the Environmental Protection Agency (EPA) promulgates five different kinds of technology-based standards for each of several hundred industry subcategories.[15] Each effluent standard (or effluent guideline, as they are called under the CWA) sets a ceiling on a particular sort of source of pollution (or class of pollutants). The ceiling is the EPA's belief—obtained from sampling existing facilities that have such sources, or independently through modeling or from abatement industry consultants—about the level of emissions reduction that a particular source category can achieve if they install a particular pollution control technology. New facilities (those constructed after the promulgation of the first set of CWA regulations) were required to meet the toughest standard, one based on the "best available demonstrated control technology."[16] Facilities in existence at the time that the CWA was passed were required to install the "best practicable control technology currently available by 1977" (BPT) which in the case of "conventional pollutants" (such as organic, biological oxygen demanding, and fecal coliform) meant "best conventional pollutant technology" (BCT)[17] and for other pollutants meant the "best available technology economically achievable" (BAT).[18] The CWA instructs the EPA to determine BPT limitations by considering "the total cost of application of technology in relation to the effluent reduction benefits to be achieved from such application," taking into account a variety of factors relating to production and effluent control technologies, nonwater quality environmental impacts, and other factors deemed appropriate by the EPA.[19]

In setting BPT- and BCT-based emissions limits,[20] the EPA first determines for each industry category or subcategory the level of control associated with the average of the best pollution control performance by exemplary plants of varying ages, sizes, and production processes. It then does what may be called a loose categorical (versus facility or source-specific) cost-benefit analysis.[21] Under such an analysis—which is common to statutes mandating technology-based standards—the agency inquires into the significance of compliance costs as a share of industry total costs and into whether those costs could be imposed without causing substantial economic dislocation, meaning firm closures. On the benefits side, the question for the agency was whether compliance with the standards would produce substantial progress toward the CWA's statutory goal of eliminating pollution discharges.[22] Thus although both the BPT and BCT standards require the EPA to take compliance costs into account, this is only an industry category basis.[23] Even within a given industry category, however, no two facilities are exactly alike, not only in their physical layout but also in the actual efficacy of any given pollution abatement technology.[24] Early in the history of the CWA, industry argued that the statute obligated or at least permitted the EPA to take individual, facility-specific costs and benefits into account in setting effluent guidelines. The Supreme Court rejected that argument,[25] making it quite clear that the EPA is to set technology-based standards that are indeed uniform within facilities of a given age and industrial category.

A very similar regulatory structure pertains under the Clean Air Act (CAA). The CAA amendments of 1970 gave the EPA the job of establishing National Ambient Air Quality Standards (NAAQS) for specific criteria pollutants in ambient air, but delegated to the states the task of coming up with state implementation plans (SIPs) that would achieve these standards by specific deadlines. The original 1970 CAA generally eschewed resort to technology-based standards, except for new sources of air pollution, for which the EPA was required to establish emissions standards for different categories of pollution sources based on the

> degree of emission limitation and the percentage reduction achievable through application of the best technological system of continuous emission reduction which (taking into consideration the cost of achieving such emission reduction, any nonair quality health and environmental impact and energy requirements) the Administrator determines has been adequately demonstrated.[26]

Although the courts interpreted this provision to approve the EPA's use of a variable standard for reducing sulfur dioxide emissions from coal-burning power plants of between 70 and 90 percent, depending on the sulfur content of the fuel being used,[27] they also declared that fuel switching alone was insufficient to satisfy the "best technological system" language of the new source performance standard (NSPS).[28] Thus although the EPA has the statutory authority to subcategorize sources,[29] the courts have upheld the EPA's discretion to instead issue uniform standards for broad source categories.[30] Thus in practical effect, the EPA has often interpreted NSPS to require some plants to adopt costly but unnecessary control technologies.

The federally determined technology-based standards governing new sources were an exception to the general approach taken by the 1970 CAA amendments, which was to set NAAQS and then let the states figure out how to achieve those standards. Over the period 1970–90, however, states consistently failed to achieve the NAAQS by statutory deadlines, and in many areas of the country, air quality actually worsened. In reaction, Congress in 1977 and 1990 substantially amended the CAA so that it is now, like the CWA, a statute that relies primarily on uniform federal technology-based standards. In 1977, Congress specified that SIPs could allow new major sources of air pollution in nonattainment areas only if the new polluter met the lowest achievable emissions rate (LAER).[31] LAER, which is generally determined on a case-by-case basis during preconstruction permit review, is defined by the CAA as the most stringent emission limitation contained in regulations applicable to that source, or the most stringent limitation that is achieved in practice for such source.[32] For existing major sources, the 1977 amendments require that SIPs "provide for the implementation of all reasonably available control measures as expeditiously as is practicable"[33] and must in the meantime accomplish "such reductions in emissions from existing sources in the area as may be obtained through the adoption, at a minimum, or reasonably available control technology (RACT)."[34] In practice, both LAER and RACT have amounted to uniform technology-based standards determined by the EPA from which SIPs cannot generally deviate.[35] The 1990 amendments retained these technology-based standards and added some new ones, such as "generally achievable control technology,"[36] and "best available control measures."[37] Moreover, the 1990 amendments clearly moved the CAA toward the CWA model by explicitly requiring permits for air pollution sources covered by the statute.[38]

For present purposes, the most important thing to see about technology-based emissions standards that are uniform within industry subcategories is that the standards are themselves the outcome of an intense bargaining process between environmental regulators and industry. Under both the CWA and CAA, the EPA determines best practicable, best available, and reasonably available technologies by securing technical analyses from engineering and economic consultants who sample actual industry practices and pilot projects. The EPA's studies are then critiqued by industry during (and even before) the notice and comment period. The process of promulgating technology-based standards is a long, costly battle between industry and the EPA over issues regarding the cost and effectiveness of a particular technology, how these vary with facility type, and how these variations go into the initial decision of how to draw industry categories and subcategories.[39] Time and time again, industry has persuaded the EPA to withdraw proposed standards by arguing that the standards are either technologically infeasible or much less effective than the EPA at first thought, so that compliance with emissions reductions standards predicated on those technologies could only be achieved at much greater cost than estimated, so costly that their adoption would force an unacceptably large number of firms in the industry into bankruptcy.[40]

As discussed, technology-based standards apply to general categories of sources of regulated pollutants. Examples of regulatory targets under such a system include things such as nitrous oxide emissions from fossil fuel–burning industrial boilers and electric utility generating units, volatile organic compounds (VOCs) emissions from the industrial coating or painting of metals and other surfaces, and organic pollutant discharges from pulp and paper mills. That is to say that the sources of pollution that are actually targeted by a technology-based CAC system are the exhausts or waste streams from particular sorts of industrial production processes. Because these production processes are common to industries or industry sectors, bargaining over initial standard setting takes place between the EPA and the industrial categories it seeks to regulate.

The end result of this bargaining game is not, however, regulation of a particular firm. Technology-based standards are not actually binding on individual firms until they are implemented by state regulators, who write those standards into source-specific permits under the CWA, and into SIPs (and, more recently, source-specific permits) under the CAA.[41] At this stage, firms have an incentive again to argue against the application of the general standard to their particular facility. As mentioned above, the courts held early on in the history of both the CAA and CWA that uniform technology-based standards are precisely that, and neither the EPA nor state regulators are to consider the particular costs and benefits from having one firm versus another comply with the uniform standards. There is, however, considerable evidence that suggests that firms actively contest the terms of source-specific permits, as well as the enforcement of those permits against them. In one EPA region, for example, 37 percent of initial CWA permits were contested, with over half the challenges resulting in permit modifications that went in favor of the polluting firm.[42]

Both the CAA and CWA, moreover, tend to encourage such source-specific contests by including specific provisions allowing source-specific variances from the otherwise uniform emissions standards. The CWA specifies that where meeting the BAT standard poses severe economic consequences for an individual facility, a §301(c) variance can be granted.[43] Although the 1970 CWA did not explicitly authorize variances from BPT standards, the EPA allowed them for existing sources who are able to persuade permitting authorities that the industrial process, control technology, costs, or energy considerations applicable to a specific plant are "fundamentally different" from those used in setting the uniform limitations.[44] After the Supreme Court upheld such variances (as well as the

EPA's view that the mere fact a particular plant has above average costs of complying with BPT standards does not make it "fundamentally different"),[45] Congress specifically approved this practice in amending the CWA.[46] Although current academic wisdom has it that such variances are of little practical significance,[47] such wisdom is based on the fact that only about sixty variance requests had been submitted to EPA headquarters as of 1985.[48] Not only does the number understate the total number of variance requests submitted to states and EPA regions,[49] it also fails to recognize that the availability of a potential variance will often affect the decisions made by a state permitting authority even when no formal variance request is filed.

More generally, the history of the CWA's technology-based standards was not one of successive tightening to keep up with new technology, but rather one of a series of successful efforts by particular polluters and particular industries to persuade the agency or Congress that their situation was atypical and justified relaxing rather than tightening the technology-based standard.[50]

As a legal matter, source-specific variances under the CAA are more complex than under the CWA. The EPA defines a variance under the CAA as a "temporary deferral of a final compliance date for an individual source subject to an approved regulation, or a temporary change to an approved regulation as it applies to an individual source."[51] The language of the statute itself, however, allows the EPA to approve exemptions of sources from compliance with SIPs only under very limited circumstances.[52] As interpreted by the Supreme Court and the EPA, a source-specific variance granted by a state can only be recognized by the EPA if it is submitted to the agency as revision of the state's SIP.[53] The EPA, moreover, has traditionally required states to produce very costly and time-consuming emissions modeling data before it would approve such revisions.[54] The 1990 amendments to the CAA did nothing to upset such rules, requiring any SIP revision submitted as a revision to a RACT-based control requirement achieve the same overall level of emissions reductions as would be achieved under the RACT standard.[55] As before 1990, it seems that the EPA will only approve source-specific variances if the state seeking such a variance produces costly modeling data showing that the variance will not produce a net increase in emissions.[56] Because such an increase is the point of granting a variance, it is generally pointless for states to make such an attempt to get the EPA to approve source-specific variances as SIP revisions.

Does this mean that firms facing very high costs of complying with the CAA's technology-based standards (or for whom compliance is simply not technically feasible) have given up and simply incurred the costs or closed down? Perhaps some have, but local air quality regulators and the EPA have generally found ways to get around the legal impediments to SIP revisions and succeed in granting variances. In at least one instance, the EPA has approved a SIP that gives the discretion to local regulators to approve alternate compliance methods proposed by companies (so that approving such methods does not require revising the SIP).[57] In California, which has thirty-four air quality districts, hearing boards in each district decide variance requests under a set of rules established by state statute.[58] Given a showing that the company requesting the variance is a good actor and is attempting to minimize the pollution, such hearing boards routinely grant variances on the grounds that the cost to the company of meeting a local RACT-based standard is large or would even cause the company to shut down, while the emissions increase involved in granting the variance is relatively minor.[59] Even though they would generally not meet with EPA approval if submitted as SIP revisions,[60] around 1,200 such variances (mostly for VOC emissions) were granted in California each year during the late 1980s and early 1990s.[61] Individual case studies of the variance process would be of great interest but are rare. Those that do exist indicate suggest that although variances are sometimes granted to firms that have made every effort to comply with the existing standard but face insuperable technological obstacles to so doing (so great that they would shut down rather than comply), in other cases they have been granted to firms that are important local employers but have made little or no effort to comply.[62]

Even if facility-specific compliance costs are not grounds for granting a variance, such costs can be considered at the regulatory enforcement stage. Indeed, early in the judicial interpretation of the CAA, the Supreme Court held that while assertions of technological or economic infeasibility were irrelevant in the EPA's determination of NAAQS, it was appropriate for regulators to consider them in fashioning compliance orders for noncomplying firms.[63]

ALTERNATIVE MODELS OF CAC REGULATORY STANDARDS

The Regulatory Contest Summarized

The bargaining game generated by the system of technology-based standards described in the previous section has the following key features.

1. Because emissions standards apply to categories of point sources of pollution that are typically within the same industry group or subgroup, bargaining over such standards involves EPA bargaining with both individual firms within such categories and trade groups that represent such industries.

2. Entitlements in bargaining over emissions standards are blurry, uncertain, and categorical, versus individual. Thus EPA is allowed to consider, and firms to argue, that the economic costs and dislocations to local economies will be high, and the corresponding reduction in pollution low, but only relative to the regulatory category as whole. Typical of the issues that arise in

this persuasion game are: What proportion of firms in the industry will go out of business if they are required to meet the proposed standards? How much will firm costs increase on average across the industry or source category if the proposed standards are implemented? What will be the average emission reduction achieved by firms if they install the technology that provides the basis for the standard? Are better alternative approaches available, and if so, at what cost?

3. Industry- or source-wide standards are not actually effective until implemented and enforced by state and local regulators. At the implementation and enforcement stage, bargaining is primarily between state and local regulators and individual firms. Although the law does not generally allow regulators to take the uniform, categorical standards and craft them into particularized requirements that are designed to reflect the costs and benefits from the standard at a particular plant or facility, state and local regulators are sensitive to such costs and benefits and will exercise their discretion by allowing varying amounts of time for firms to comply with the uniform standards and, even more important, by generally eschewing rigid enforcement in favor of negotiation toward compliance.

Under uniform, categorical, technology-based emissions standards, such bargaining affects not only the emissions standard that is set for a given industrial category but the categorization scheme. Although facilities performing a particular industrial operation may seem very similar to a layperson, they often are quite different from a technical or engineering point of view, and these differences can cause large differences in their actual cost of achieving a given emissions reduction standard. Two metal finishing shops, for example, may both anodize aluminum for surface coating. Wastewater from such anodizing shops contains aluminum and sulfate, and both can be precipitated out by using a lime slurry. However, if other metals are present in the wastewater—introduced, for example, in electrolytic coloring baths—then there will often be a trade-off between precipitating out these metals and aluminum: To get the other metals out, less aluminum can be eliminated.[64] Thus if one of the metal finishing shops is coloring its anodized aluminum and the other is not, then the shop doing the coloring will have a higher cost of meeting any given aluminum effluent reduction requirement. Variations in plant size and operating levels also generate variations in compliance costs. There are a number of different ways for plants to remove particulate air pollutants from their airborne waste streams, including mechanical collectors, fabric filters, wet scrubbers, and electrostatic precipitators.[65] The efficiency of these various methods of removing particulates depends on the level at which they are operated (the flow of particulates), with efficiency falling off for many types of equipment when operations fall above or below design capacity.[66] Somewhat more simply, a coal-burning electric utility generating plant's cost of reducing its sulfur dioxide emissions depends on its location relative to sources of low-sulfur coal.[67] Plants that have cheap access to low-sulfur coal can reduce sulfur dioxide emissions more cheaply than can plants for whom such coal is more expensive and for whom scrubbers are actually cost-minimizing.

In virtually any industry, production facilities vary so much in age, design, operation rates, raw material composition, and transportation and other costs that few if any have precisely the same cost of achieving a given level of reduction in pollution. For this reason, when the EPA bargains with industry over uniform, categorical emission standards, it typically faces arguments to the effect that certain kinds of plants are in fact so dissimilar that they should be categorized differently. More precisely, because any given pollution reduction technology achieves different levels of pollution reduction in different plants, it will often (perhaps usually) be true that lots of plants will not be able to achieve the average level of emissions reduction that the EPA finds from its sample of facilities employing the technology. For these plants, the actual cost of achieving the targeted emissions reduction will be much higher than for the average, sampled facility. Companies owning such high-cost plants have every incentive to argue to the EPA that their plants should actually be recategorized in a different (regulatory if not product market) industry. As indicated by the large number of categories and subcategories created by the EPA under statutes such as the CAA and CWA, those arguments often meet with success.

However the categories are ultimately drawn, categorical standards are not actually effective until implemented and enforced in facility-specific permits written by state and local regulators. At the implementation and enforcement stage, bargaining is primarily between state and local regulators and individual firms. Though the law does not generally allow regulators to take the uniform, categorical standards and craft them into particularized requirements that are designed to reflect the costs and benefits from the standard at a particular plant or facility, state and local regulators are sensitive to such costs and benefits and will exercise their discretion by allowing varying amounts of time for firms to comply with the uniform standards and, even more important, by generally eschewing rigid enforcement in favor of negotiation toward compliance.

Formalizing Alternative Versions of CAC

With so many stages—beginning with lobbying over the initial promulgation and finalization of a regulation, continuing through challenges to the regulation in court, and ending with bargaining over the actual implementation and enforcement of a regulation—it is perhaps unsurprising that environmental economists have failed to develop formal models of how CAC regulation actually works. That is, they have been quick to argue that because environmental regulators lack the information to craft

emissions standards accurately reflecting facility-specific costs and benefits, incentive-based alternatives to CAC such as TPP regimes are likely to
be more efficient than CAC.[68] But they have not attempted a formal
specification of CAC that would allow more realistic comparison with
outcomes under such incentive-based regimes.[69]

In the absence of any existing, canonical formal specification, I consider
instead two contrasting versions of CAC: *idealized* and *bargained*.

Idealized CAC

Under what I call idealized CAC, the regulation requires all firms to abate
their pollution from a status quo of one unit down a level $x \in (0, 1)$. Hence
the cost to the ith firm of complying with such a pollution reduction
standard is given by $(1 - x)c_i$. Under idealized CAC, the regulatory standard is costlessly and perfectly enforced, and with such a high sanction
for noncompliance, F, that every firm finds it cheaper to comply than to
incur the sanction.

Bargained CAC

To formalize bargained CAC, I adapt a simplified version of a model
developed by Montero.[70] In this model, there is a continuum of firms, of
mass equal to 1, each of which emits one unit of a uniform pollutant.
Firms vary according to their (constant) marginal cost of abating this one
unit of pollution, and the distribution of firm (constant marginal) abatement cost c is given by the continuous density function $g(c)$ defined on
$[\underline{c}, \bar{c}]$, with cumulative distribution function $G(c)$. Given its knowledge of
this distribution function, the regulator can infer the aggregate industry
abatement cost curve $C(q)$ for $0 \leq q \leq 1$.[71]

Under bargained CAC, firms do not automatically comply with a regulation requiring pollution to be reduced in the amount $(1 - x)$. Rather,
assuming still that the fine for noncompliance, F, is so high that firms would
never simply fail to comply and acquiesce in paying the fine, they choose
instead between complying and fighting the regulation. That is, in bargained CAC there is a chance that by fighting the regulation—playing the
regulatory game—the firm will either get its plant recategorized into a
different (and less stringently regulated) category or else obtain a variance
or some other plant-specific relief. Now the regulatory game obviously has
several stages, and a complete analysis of outcomes in that game can only
be done within the context of a sequential bargaining model.[72] There are,
however, a number of very general features of equilibria in such games
that can be seen even within a very simple, reduced-form model.

The following is a fairly general version of such a model. To simplify
the regulatory game, I assume that it is a complete information game
played by a risk-neutral regulator and firm, and I restrict attention to
subgame-perfect equilibria. In the regulatory game, the firm chooses

whether to comply or contest the regulation. If it contests the regulation, then the firm and the government simultaneously choose how much to invest in the contest—their effort levels—and these effort levels are the sole determinant of the outcome of the contest. (Thus the restriction to subgame-perfect equilibria means that a firm will engage in the regulatory contest only if its expected total cost from the contest is less than the cost of compliance.) To sharpen the basic result, I assume that if the firm wins the regulatory game, it is not regulated at all. Let the probability that the firm wins the regulatory contest (and is not regulated) be given by $q(e_i, e_g)$ where e_i is the firm's effort level in the conflict and e_g is the government's effort level in the conflict. Assume that effort has unit cost, and assume further that $q_1 < 0, q_{11} > 0, q_2 < 0, q_{22} > 0$; that is, both the firm and government have declining marginal productivity of effort. I assume also that the regulatory contest function is perfectly symmetric, in that $q(e_i, e_g) = 1 - q(e_g, e_i)$.[73]

Now taking the government's effort level as fixed (the Cournot assumption), a firm with compliance cost c_i chooses its effort level e_i to solve

(1) $$\min_{e_i} q(e_i, e_g)e_i + [1 - q(e_i, e_g)](e_i + c_i + F).$$

The first-order condition to this problem (which exists, by the assumptions just made), e_i is defined by

(2) $$q_1(e_{i*}, e_g) = \frac{1}{c_i + F}.$$

From equation (2), it follows immediately that (provided the firm's reservation profit constraint is satisfied) the higher c_i, the firm's marginal cost of compliance, the higher will be optimal effort level in the regulatory game, e_{i*}.

Now consider the government regulator. Suppose that the regulator perceives a benefit $B(1 - x)$ from eliminating an amount x of pollution, with $dB/d(1 - x) > 0$, so that $dB/dx < 0$.[74] That is, the regulator's benefit increases as the required level of pollution reduction increases (the permitted level of pollution falls.)

The government's objective in the regulatory game is to choose e_g so as to

(3) $$\max_{e_g} [1 - q(e_{i*}, e_g)](B(1 - x) - e_g) - q(e_{i*}, e_g)e_g.$$

The first-order condition defining the interior solution e_{g*} to this problem is given by

(4) $$q_2(e_i, e_{g*}) = \frac{-1}{B(1 - x)}.$$

As $q_{22} > 0$ by assumption, $\partial e_{g*}/\partial B > 0$; that is, the government's optimal effort level increases with its benefit.

For a given pollution standard x_s, let the net expected payoffs to the government regulator and to the firm (net, that is, of effort cost) from the regulatory game be denoted respectively by:

(5) $$R_g(x_s) = [1 - q(e_{i*}, e_{g*})]B(1 - x_s) - e_{g*}, \quad \text{and}$$

(6) $$R_i(x_s) = [1 - q(e_{i*}, e_{g*})](c_i(1 - x_s)) + F) + e_{i*}.$$

Several observations may now be made regarding the regulatory contest.

1. As a general matter, as in any complete information game of conflict, the firm and the government are both better off negotiating and settling rather than actually fighting the regulatory contest. The reason is that by settling, they both save the expenditure on contest effort that they would have made were the contest not averted. From the government's point of view, the continuity of the benefit function $B(1 - x)$ means that there is always some level of negotiated pollution reduction, x_i such that $B(1 - x_i) = R_g(x_s)$. The analogous result holds for the firm. Provided that $R_g(x_s) < R_i(x_s)$, that is, provided that the government's net expected benefit from the regulatory game is less than the firm's expected total cost from the regulatory game, there will always be a negotiated firm-specific pollution reduction x_i that makes both the firm and the government better off relative to their expected payoffs from a regulatory contest.
2. However, unlike private litigation—where the defendant's loss at trial equals the plaintiff's gain—the stakes in the regulatory contest are generally unequal. For this reason, one cannot be sure unambiguously that there is room for settlement in the regulatory contest. Indeed, there are two general cases.
   a. When the government has much more at stake in the contest than does the firm (the regulatory benefit of winning, $B[1 - x]$, is much greater than the private cost of losing, $c_i + F$), then there will be no agreed level of compliance that makes both parties better off than they are (in expected value terms) contesting over the standard x_s. If the contest ensues, then by the first-order conditions (2) and (4), the government will expend much more effort than will the firm, leading to a low probability of firm success q. Thus when the firm has a low compliance cost c_i, it will probably lose the regulatory contest and will probably be better off simply complying than contesting the regulation. Quite differently, a low fine, F, can be seen to have a somewhat paradoxical effect: ceteris paribus, a low fine induces a lower level of firm effort in the regulatory contest, increasing the expected regulatory payoff from such a contest.

By keeping fines low, the government lessens firm incentives to fight regulation.

b. As the firm's cost of compliance c_i increases (holding $B[1 - x]$ constant), it will eventually be the case that $R_g(x_s) < R_i(x_s)$, so that a negotiated, firm-specific pollution reduction will typically make both parties better off than they would be (in expected value terms) if they proceed with the contest. Moreover, because of my symmetry assumption on $q()$ and on effort costs, when $c_i + F \gg B(1 - x)$, it will also be the case that $e_{g*} \ll e_{i*}$ and that $\partial e_{g*}/\partial e_{i*} < 0.$[75] When the firm has a lot more at stake than the government, it puts a lot more effort into the regulatory contest, and when this is true of relative effort levels, the government's optimal effort level is actually falling in the firm's optimal effort level.[76]

3. Another way to put the last fact is that the higher is the firm's compliance cost, the bigger is the firm's expected cost in the regulatory contest—$(R_i(x_s)$—but also the lower is the government's expected payoff from the contest—$R_g(x_s)$. Though the precise bargaining solution varies, of course, with the relative bargaining power of the firm and the regulator, it is likely that as the firm's compliance cost increases, its impact in driving down the government's expected payoff from the contest will be the dominant effect on settlement.[77] If this is so, then the negotiated firm-specific pollution reduction that the government will demand in lieu of fighting the regulatory contest will be lower, the higher the firm's compliance cost.

4. It follows directly that for sufficiently high firm compliance cost c_i, the government's expected return from the regulatory contest will be negative for all $e_{g*}(c_i) > 0$. So the government no longer has a credible threat to regulate, and firms with such high compliance cost are not required to reduce their pollution.

5. The rational regulator's expected benefit—either from the regulatory contest or via a regulatory settlement—does not necessarily increase monotonically with $(1 - x_s)$, the pollution reduction standard. As can be seen by totally differentiating (3) with respect to x, the indirect effect of increasing $(1 - x_s)$ in inducing more firm effort in the regulatory contest can actually cause the government's expected payoff to begin to fall with such increases.

6. It may seem unreasonable to suppose that the regulator and firm engage in the bargaining game with complete information about each other's payoffs (that is, with the firm knowing $B[1 - x]$ and the regulator knowing c_i). Though a full analysis of the incomplete information case is beyond the scope of the present chapter, the usual effect of incomplete information about payoffs in making settlement less likely may not be a severe problem in the regulatory contest context. For instance, if the regulator knows

only the average firm compliance cost $\mu = E[c_i]$, then provided that fighting the contest is credible for the average firm and for the regulator given the average firm's effort investment, it might seem that even firms with above average costs (and optimal contest effort levels) may end up engaging in the contest because they cannot find a way to credibly persuade the regulator that their investment will be so high that the regulator is better off settling for a lower, firm-specific pollution reduction. But in such a case, firms actually have an incentive to reveal information to the regulator, in that both will be better off if the conflict is avoided. Of course, incentives are not perfectly aligned, because firms have an incentive to overstate their costs to get as small a bargained, firm-specific pollution reduction as possible. Still, the shared interest in avoiding a costly regulatory conflict does create an incentive to share at least some information.

This foregoing relatively formal analysis of bargained CAC may be summarized in the following proposition:

Proposition 1. For a given formal regulatory pollution standard x_s, when firms can contest regulation, and both the firm and the regulator optimally choose efforts levels in the contest with full information regarding each other's payoffs and settlement is possible, the likely regulatory outcome is one in which (a) firms with compliance cost c_i below a cutoff value c_l comply and do not contest the regulation; (b) firms with compliance costs c_i such that $c_l \leq c_i \leq c_h$ settle with the regulator for a firm-specific pollution level $x_i > x_s$; and (c) firms with compliance costs $c_i > c_h$ are not regulated and do not reduce pollution, where c_h is defined by $R_g(x_s; c_h) = 0$.

TPP PROGRAMS AS BOTH A RESULT AND INCREASINGLY IMPORTANT SOLUTION TO THE PATHOLOGIES OF CATEGORICAL, TECHNOLOGY-BASED FEDERAL ENVIRONMENTAL STANDARDS

Why Are There Any TPP Programs?

That TPP programs were not included in first-generation American environmental regulation is hardly surprising. Before creating markets in entitlements to pollute, those entitlements had to be created in the first place. Given that the status quo was a right to pollute and that reductions in pollution typically involved large sunk investments (in secondary wastewater treatment, end-of-stack scrubbers, and similar equipment), new entitlements were worked out only through a long and costly negotiation process involving literally thousands of lawsuits. To the extent that new entitlements were actually negotiated, they took the form of the technology-based standards that I have already described in some detail. A regulatory regime based on such technology-based standards is inherently inconsistent with a TPP regime. TPP regimes, after all, operate by setting aggregate pollution caps for a particular pollutant, allocating that aggregate amount of pollution across identified sources of such pollutant, and then allowing firms to comply either by reducing the pollution sources they own down to the level of their allocation, or by buying allocations from other firms. As even their most committed advocates concede, the effectiveness of a TPP regime, as with any regulatory regime, hinges on effective enforcement—enforcement that makes it cheaper for firms to comply either by buying permits or by reducing pollution than to fail to comply. Because TPP regimes are output-oriented—they do not regulate *how* firms get into compliance but whether they are in compliance—the effectiveness of TPP regimes hinges on accurate monitoring of firms' emissions and permit purchases and on the assessment of an adequately severe penalty on those firms found not to be in compliance.

The existing technology-based CAC system does not possess the preconditions for successful pollution permit trading. The first problem is that technology-based standards do not, by their very definition, require source-specific monitoring. Hence cap-and-trade regimes that are simply grafted on existing technology-based regulations (such as the Regional Clean Air Incentives Market (RECLAIM) program set up for the L.A. basin) require firms to self-report their emissions. Given that regulators have limited budgets and can only audit and (imperfectly) verify a small fraction of the emissions self-reports, there is an obvious incentive for firms to underreport their actual emissions. Critics of existing cap and trade schemes such as RECLAIM that rely on self-reporting[78] argue that such underreporting is pervasive.[79]

There is another much more basic obstacle to grafting emissions trading on the existing technology-based regulatory framework. Even with limited enforcement resources, the existing CAC regulatory system has generally been effective in creating an incentive for the largest and most visible firms to come into compliance with existing technology-based standards. As argued, however, even if most firms are in compliance with such standards, there is little if any incentive for them to go beyond compliance when operating in such a regulatory environment. Hence, although there may well be firms that are not in compliance—and that might be willing buyers of pollution permits—there will not be many firms that have gone so far beyond existing regulatory requirements that they would have unused pollution permits to sell. That is, if firms are minimizing their compliance costs under an existing technology-based regulatory regime that they expect to be relatively stable in the future, then the aggregate level of emissions will be slightly above what the technology-based standard would imply (because some firms are out of compliance in equilibrium). A cap-and-trade regime that sets the aggregate cap at or below the emissions level that should be obtaining under the status quo regulatory regime will therefore generate lots of firms that would like to buy—because they were not really in compliance, and hence need to buy permits—but very few if any that are willing to sell. Simple economics might seem to teach that lots of buyers versus only a few sellers means that the price of pollution permits will be very high. But this is simplistic rather than simple economics. When transaction costs are high, markets may fail to exist in the first place. Moreover, unlike most goods, the supply of pollution permits is fixed (by regulators). With a fixed supply that falls far short of the number of permits demanded, market equilibrium will involve lots of willing buyers who simply were unable to find a permit to buy.

This story helps explain the relative failure of the EPA's oldest experiment with TPPs, the requirement under the CAA that new major air pollution sources in nonattainment areas offset new source emissions with decreases from an existing source or sources.[80] There were thousands of offsets during the first ten years of this program (1977–86), but the vast majority of these were internal offsets—offsets obtained because a firm that constructed a new source of air pollution found a way to reduce pollution at an existing source that it owned. There were few if any external offsets, exchanges where the firm building a new source contracted for a reduction of emissions at some other firm.[81] The failure to observe very many offset trades was due to a number of factors. Notably, without a scheme that first gives firms credit for extra emissions reductions relative to status quo regulatory requirements—as by allowing them to bank such excess emissions reductions—offset trades across firms are possible only when there is a lucky coincidence of one firm reducing emissions at the same time another is building a new source. Given that few states had implemented banking and that the status of banked emissions was at best uncertain, the transaction costs obstacles to the formation of offset markets were even higher than dictated by the incentives created by the status quo CAC regulatory regime.[82]

The difficulty of grafting trading schemes on existing CAC regimes also explains why TPP programs have sometimes worked. There are two examples of relatively successful TPP regimes in federal environmental law and regulation—the Title IV acid rain trading scheme, and the EPA's lead phasedown program. These programs are discussed in some considerable detail in other chapters (see chapters 7 and 8). For present purposes, what is most notable about each of these programs is that they did not simply involve grafting a tradable permits regime on an existing technology-based system. Initiated in 1982, the EPA's lead phasedown program allowed gasoline refiners to trade lead content allowances under an overall cap on lead gasoline additives that declined to zero over the life of the program.[83] The program allowed unused allowances to be banked for up to three years and succeeded in encouraging an active market in lead allowances. Although there were a number of factors accounting for the program's success as a trading regime—such as its simplicity, relatively small number of participants and the certainty that banked allowances could indeed be sold[84]—perhaps the key factor in explaining the program's success was that the overall goal of the program (the steady decline in and eventual elimination of lead additives) was clear. Given that this goal was relatively inexpensive for some firms to meet but completely infeasible for others (who went out of business), perhaps the clearest lesson of the lead phasedown program is that by lowering the cost of achieving an ambitious overall emissions reduction goal, trading can make such a goal politically feasible when it otherwise would not be.

A similar but more extensive illustration of this phenomenon is provided by the Acid Rain Program. Enacted as Title IV of the 1990 amendments to the CAA,[85] this program set up a stand-alone sulfur dioxide cap-and-trade program applying (over two phases) to some 800 electricity-generating units. That program sought to achieve a steady reduction in aggregate, nationwide sulfur dioxide emissions. The accumulating evidence indicates not only that the program has succeeded but that it has succeeded both because it allows firms the flexibility to find the lowest cost way of reducing emissions (installing scrubbers, buying low-sulfur eastern or western coal) but also because some high cost of compliance firms have complied by buying emissions permits from low compliance cost firms (see chapter 8). That the Title IV program happened at all was due to perceived breakdown of technology-based regulation as applied to the electric utility generating industry. Under the differential treatment of old versus new sources, which is typical of such regimes, the CAA's acid rain regulations had focused on new power plants while grandfathering older plants, producing a situation where by 1985, 83 percent of power plant sulfur dioxide emissions came from generating units that did not meet that 1971 standards required of new sources.[86] Environmentalists and political representatives from Eastern states perceived as bearing the costs of acid rain wanted faster and greater reductions in aggregate emissions, and in particular wanted emissions reductions at the dirtiest facilities. Given the cost to such facilities of meeting such tough emissions targets, the cap-and-trade system emerged as a compromise: the least cost method of achieving overall emissions standards that were significantly tougher than under the existing law.[87] Thus, the Title IV program did not represent a situation where tradable permits were grafted on an existing technology-based system, but rather a movement from such a system to a relatively pure TPP system in which firms were given source-specific permits. "Given" is indeed a misnomer, in that the statutory allocation of initial Title IV permits reflected a costly legislative lobbying game.[88]

How TPPs Change the Regulatory Bargaining Game

The previous section's discussion of existing TPP programs in American federal environmental law suggests that while attempts to graft TPP regimes on existing technology-standards-based systems have often failed for lack of support from industry and others, there are circumstances when such programs can succeed. The case studies just discussed indeed suggest that TPP regimes may make it much easier for regulators to impose tougher emissions standards, relative to technology-based standards. This section formalizes this intuition. I show that unlike proposals to base emissions standards on particularized, source-specific, cost-benefit determinations—which often threaten firms with big changes in equilibrium compliance costs that have big consequences for their relative profitability and competitiveness—most and sometimes even all firms in an industry sector can be better off under a TPP regime than they would be if regulators attempted to achieve the same level of aggregate emissions using technology-based standards.

Underlying this demonstration is a basic intuition that trading itself may significantly alter the dynamics of the regulatory bargaining game. The reason is that whenever firms differ in their costs of meeting a given regulatory standard—by which I mean an emissions target—trading will unambiguously lower the regulatory compliance costs of those firms with the highest such costs, firms that spend the most in opposing tougher CAC standards.

Firm Costs under a TPP Regime of Varying Ambition: Formal Analysis

To see these points formally, consider again the formal model already developed. Consider first a tradable permits regime under which each firm is given a permit to emit x amount of pollution. Under such a regime, firms can comply either by incurring the marginal cost c of compliance or by buying permits at market price p. I shall assume that a tradable permits regime is one in which firms are required to install an emissions monitoring system that perfectly informs the regulator as to their emissions level and that regulators have perfect knowledge of each firm's permit buy and sell history. Hence under the tradable permits regime, the regulator costlessly obtains perfect information as to whether each firm is in compliance. As under idealized regulation, firms that are not in compliance are made to pay a very large fine F.

The question of interest is how firms' equilibrium costs differ under the CAC versus the tradable permits regimes. To answer this question, I must solve for the equilibrium under a tradable permits regime. And as discussed, equilibrium cost distribution under a tradable permits regime depends on the market equilibrium, on which firms will buy permits and which will sell. To solve for this equilibrium, I simplify by considering a closed system: one in which only the regulated firms may buy or sell permits.[89] Let p be the equilibrium price of permits. Consider first those firms with $c < p$. Because for such firms $c < p$, they will always be better off abating fully (the entire one unit of pollution) and selling the excess allowance than abating just down to the allowed level (that is, $c(1 - x) > c - xp$ when $p > c$). Such firms are better off fully abating and selling excess permits than not complying provided that $c - xp < F$, which must be true for a sufficiently high fine.

Now consider firms with $c \geq p$. It is cheaper for such firms to buy permits than to abate and sell (that is, for these firms, $c - xp > c(1 - x)$). Such firms are better off buying permits than failing to comply provided that $(1 - x)p < F$, which once again must hold for sufficiently large fine F.

The market price p is determined by the market equilibrium condition that supply equals demand

(7)
$$x \int_{\underline{c}}^{p} dG = (1 - x) \int_{p}^{\overline{c}} dG, \quad \text{or}$$

$$xG(p) = (1 - x)(G(\overline{c}) - G(p)), \text{ which becomes}$$

$$(1 - x) = G(p), \text{ so that}$$

(8)
$$p(x) = G^{-1}(1 - x).$$

Using expression (5) for $p(x)$, I have that

$$p'(x) = \frac{-1}{g(1 - x)} < 0 \quad \text{and}$$

$$d/dx[xp(x)] = p(x) - \frac{x}{g(1 - x)} = G^{-1}(1 - x) - xg(1 - x) > 0 \Leftrightarrow$$

(9)
$$\frac{G^{-1}(1 - x)}{xg(1 - x)} = \eta_d > 1,$$

where η_d is the elasticity of demand for permits.

Expressions (8) and (9) have a number of implications for how changes in the stringency of the cap-and-trade program affect buyers versus sellers of permits. Most directly, by (8) a change in x, the initial number of permits given to each polluter, obviously changes the identity of the marginal buyer and seller of permits. For nonmarginal buyers and sellers, I have the following.

Result 1. As the number of permits given to polluters, x, increases—as the cap-and-trade program becomes relatively less ambitious in its pollution reduction goal—the price of permits falls and so the net cost of the cap and trade program to high compliance cost permit buyers falls;

Result 2. For permit sellers, an increase in the number of permits initially given to each polluter may increase or reduce their net expected cost under the permit program. Only if the elasticity of permit demand $\eta_d > 1$ will an increase in the number of permits actually reduce the net cost of the cap-and-trade program to permit sellers. That is, if demand is elastic, then an increase in the number of permits for sale has only a small effect in depressing the permit price, so net seller revenue increases for nonmarginal sellers.

Comparison with CAC

Letting the CAC pollution standard be denoted simply by x (rather than x_s as earlier), the two stylized versions of CAC developed earlier generate the following equilibrium outcomes. Under idealized CAC, all firms reduce by one unit, at cost c_i. Under bargained CAC, firms with cost $c_i < c_l$ comply by reducing pollution down to the standard level x_s, and those with c_i such that $c_l < c_i \leq c_h$ reduce pollution down to a negotiated level $x_i > x$, and those with $c_i > c_h$ do not reduce at all.

1. Under idealized CAC, firms that would be buyers in a cap-and-trade program would have costs equal to $c(1 - x)$, which must exceed their actual net cost under cap-and-trade, given by $p(1 - x)$, because these firms are such that $c > p$. Likewise, firms with $c \leq p$ sell permits under cap-and-trade have a net cost under that regime of $c - xp$ but would have a net cost of $c(1 - x)$ under the CAC regime, but for $c \leq p, c - xp \leq c - xc = c(1 - x)$ and so have lower net costs under cap-and-trade than under CAC.
2. Under bargained CAC, only firms with $c_i \leq c_h$ actually incur compliance costs and reduce pollution. Moreover, under bargained CAC, firms with c_i such that $c_l \leq c_i \leq c_h$ reduce pollution not by the full amount $(1 - x)$, but rather by some amount $(1 - x_i)$ with $x_i > x$. Under the cap-and-trade regime, only firms with $c_i < p(x)$ actually comply by reducing pollution, but firms with $c_i > p$ incur costs of $(1 - x)p$ to comply by buying permits. Depending on the structure of the regulatory conflict-bargaining game under CAC, it is clearly possible that the negotiated firm-specific reductions x_i and the threshold for no reduction c_h are such that the majority of firms would actually have higher costs under the cap-and-trade regime than they do in the status quo bargained CAC regime. Especially when firm costs increase more rapidly with a toughening emissions standard (decreasing x_s) than do regulatory benefits, the actual bargained CAC regime may be one in which fewer firms incur compliance costs than would incur such costs under the (perfectly enforced) TPP regime. If something like bargained CAC is the status quo against which the TPP regime is compared, then the majority of firms might well oppose a move to TPP.

A POSITIVE IMPLICATION: EXPLAINING TITLE IV ALLOCATIONS

The general predictions of my model are confirmed by the pattern of congressional allocations of sulfur dioxide pollution allowances under Title IV of the 1990 CAA. As observed earlier, this sulfur dioxide allowance trading program is the most well known and most successful TPP program to date. One of the great contributions of Ellerman et al. is their detailed explication of the complex congressional bargaining process that culminated in the passage of Title IV.[90] Congressional bargaining focused on the number of allowances that different coal-fired generating units would be given. That is, Title IV not only set an aggregate emissions reduction goal but set the number of allowances both for Phase I, which applied beginning in 1996 to 225 large, dirty generating units with sulfur dioxide emissions rates above 2.5 pounds of sulfur dioxide per million Btu, and for Phase II, which began in 2001 and applied to all generating units with emissions rates above 1.2 and capacity above 75 MW (as of 1985).[91] As Ellerman et al. show, congressional allocation of both Phase I and Phase II allowances departed significantly from the basic apolitical statutory formula for allocations (which multiplied a unit's average 1985–87 energy input by a statutory emissions rate of 2.5 for Phase I units and 1.2 for Phase II units). Old, high-emission plants in high-emission states which facilities burned local high-sulfur coal used their political influence to get extra Phase I allowances.[92] For Phase II, over thirty special allocation rules written into the statute generated deviations from the base allocations.[93] These allocation rules effectively made the actual level of allocations received by a generating unit much more sensitive to variations among types of units than the baseline allocation formula countenanced. To the surprise of Ellerman et al., the actual pattern was the opposite, with the oldest, dirtiest units penalized and newer, cleaner units given extra allowances (relative to the base formula).[94] Ellerman et al. came up with decidedly noneconomic ad hoc explanations for this pattern, attributing it to a congressional sense of fairness—that it would be unfair to require even more of plants that already relatively clean—or conversely, to the desire of congressional representatives from clean coal (or natural) gas-burning Western states to get revenge for the costs the dirty coal state representatives had imposed on clean states in prior versions of the CAA.[95]

By a very direct extension,[96] my model provides a relatively simple economic explanation for the pattern of Phase II allowances under Title IV: differing marginal control costs under the existing, pre–Title IV status quo regulatory regime. Under the pre-1990 regime, the oldest, dirtiest plants had been grandfathered out of federal emission rate standards and were subject only to widely varying and often lax state regulation under state implementation plans. New plants were conversely subject to tough federal emission rate standards, plus the politically motivated, redundant scrubber requirement that was the subject of clean state ire. Under the rather bizarre pre-1990 status quo CAC regime,[97] the newest, cleanest plants were subject to the toughest emission rate regulations. Unsurprisingly, as found by Ellerman et al., because they had done little if anything to reduce their sulfur dioxide emissions, marginal sulfur dioxide control costs were lowest in old, dirty plants,[98] whereas they were higher in the cleaner, newer plants. This status quo regime is precisely what I have called the regime of bargained CAC, a regime under which the dirtiest plants have such large costs of meeting the target emissions reductions that they actually end up being unregulated. Newer, more efficient plants are regulated and required to achieve substantial reductions in emission rates. Such a regulatory regime generates a bargained equilibrium in which the cleanest plants have already been forced to reduce their emissions and hence have higher marginal costs of further reductions than to do the dirtiest plants, who have been left unregulated. My model explains the otherwise paradoxical pattern of Title IV Phase II allowances as reflecting opposition to a simple Title IV regime by owners of clean plants—those who relative to an equal baseline would have the lowest marginal control costs, but whose actual CAC-induced marginal control costs are quite high. That clean units demanded special additional allowances before their representatives would sign on to Title IV reflects that fact that they were the ones being most stringently regulated under the status quo CAC regime.

A NORMATIVE IMPLICATION: THE IDEAL VERSUS THE REAL IN AIR POLLUTION REGULATION

Another contribution of the analysis here is to show the significance of taking the correct baseline in evaluating a move from a CAC regime to a TPP regime. The significance of baselines is well illustrated by the recent debate over the Bush administration's Clear Skies inititative. According to the administration, Clear Skies would have generated "dramatic" reductions in power plant emissions of sulfur dioxide, nitrogen oxides, and mercury. According to many prominent environmental groups, however, the plan's goal of a 70 percent reduction in these emissions by 2018 was too little, and too late in coming. These groups argued that if existing CAA regulations were fully enforced, there would be bigger and quicker reductions in these pollutants from power plants.[99] Such claims are true. But my analysis suggests that the relevant comparison is very likely not between the administration's proposed TPP regime and an idealized CAC regulatory regime, for that regime clearly does not and has never existed. Rather the relevant normative question is whether the administration's (or any other) proposed TPP regime is likely to generate lower levels of emissions than the current, real-world CAC regime generates. If what I have called bargained CAC roughly describes the current CAC status quo, then it is one in which the oldest and dirtiest facilities will not actually have to reduce their emissions by very much, if at all. Compared to such a bargained regime, the administration's proposals tend to look far better than they do when compared with an idealized but nonexistent CAC regime.

ACKNOWLEDGMENTS I am grateful to the editors for helpful comments and suggestions, and to all of the participants in the August 2003 UC Santa Barbara workshop for stimulating discussion after presentation of the initial draft of these ideas, and especially to Juan Pablo Montero and Nathaniel Keohane for suggestions on the more formal analysis. I received helpful comments on later versions of this paper from participants in the Law and Economics Workshop at the University of Chicago and the Agricultural and Resource Economics Department Colloquium at the University of Arizona. Doug Lichtman and Dean Lueck had especially helpful written comments and suggestions. I of course remain responsible for remaining errors.

NOTES

1. In the legal literature, the classic critique and proposal for a move to auctioned, tradable permits, is Bruce A. Ackerman and Richard B. Stewart, *Reforming Environmental Law*, 37 Stanford Law Review 1333 (1985).

2. For a comprehensive (if now dated) discussion of many of the main theoretical and empirical results, *see* T. H. Tietenberg, Emissions Trading: An Exercise in Reforming Pollution Policy (1985); for a lucid and more recent introduction to the theory, *see* Charles D. Kolstad, Environmental Economics 155–77 (2000). For especially elegant recent contributions to the empirical analysis of tradable permit markets, *see* Juan-Pablo Montero, Testing the Efficiency of a Tradeable Permits, Testing the Efficiency of a Tradeable Permits Market (draft, Sept. 6, 2002) and Paul Joskow, Richard Schmalensee, and Elizabeth Bailey, *The Market for Sulfur Dioxide Emissions*, 88 American Economic Review 669 (1998).

3. For a summary of the American experience with permit markets, *see* Gert Tinggaard Svendsen, Public Choice and Environmental Regulation: Tradable Permit Systems in the United States and CO_2 Taxation in Europe 71–132 (1998). For a discussion of the failure to implement more TPP regimes, *see* Robert W. Hahn and Gordon L. Hester, *Where Did All the Markets Go? An Analysis of EPA's Emissions Trading Program*, 6 Yale Journal of Regulation 109 (1989).

4. *See* Keohane (this volume); A. Denny Ellerman et al., Markets for Clean Air: The U.S. Acid Rain Program (2000).

5. In 2002, the Bush administration introduced its Clear Skies bill, a cap-and-trade program designed to reduce power plant emissions of sulfur dioxide, nitrogen oxides, and mercury by 46 percent by 2010 and by 70 percent when fully implemented in 2018. The Clear Skies bill died in Senate Committee on Environment and Public Works. However, by regulation, the EPA has proposed very similar cap-and-trade schemes for the same pollutants, *see* 69 Federal Register 4, 566 (Jan. 30, 2004)(power plant sulfur dioxide and nitrogen oxide trading program) and 69 Federal Register 12398 (March 16, 2004)(mercury cap-and-trade program). Regardless of the fate of these regulations, the so-called $NO_x SIP$ Call, which uses market based emissions trading to reduce NO_x emissions from power plants and other large industrial sources in twenty-two states, has begun to be implemented. Finally, the EPA has issued a policy and guidance document on how water quality trading between point and nonpoint sources may be used to meet new water quality–based effluent limits generated by the development of Total Maximum Daily Loads under the Clean Water Act. *See Water Quality Trading Policy: Issuance of Final Policy*, 68 Federal Register 1608 (Jan. 13, 2003).

6. In the environmental economics literature, even the most thorough analysis of alternative CAC regimes, such as Gloria E. Hellfand, *Standards versus Standards: The Effects of Different Pollution Restrictions*, 81 American Economic Review 622

(1991) and other works reviewed there consider only what I call idealized CAC regimes, those that do not allow firms to contest and bargain over actual regulatory implementation, and which therefore do not approximate any real-world CAC regime.

7. Jason Scott Johnston, Federal Regulation and the Provision of Local Public Goods (draft, November, 2003).

8. Resource Conservation and Recovery Act, 42 U.S.C. §§ 9601–6992k.

9. Comprehensive Environmental Response, Compensation and Liability Act of 1980, 42 U.S.C. §§9601–9675.

10. *See,* for example, Section 101(a)(1) of the Clean Water Act, 33 U.S.C. §1251(a)(1), setting forth a statutory goal of eliminating the discharge of pollutants into the navigable waters by 1985.

11. For instance, in Section 301(a)(2)(A), 33 U.S.C. §1311(a)(2)(A), the Water Pollution Control Act instructs the EPA to base effluent limitations for various categories of point sources of water pollution on the "best available technology economically achievable"—otherwise known as "best practicable technology"—and then explains, in Section 304 of the Act, 33 U.S.C. §1314(b)(1)(B), that in determining what constitutes best practicable technology, the agency is to consider "the total cost of application of such technology in relation to the effluent reduction benefits to be achieved from such application, and shall also take into account the age of equipment and facilities involved, the process employed, the engineering aspects of the application of various types of control techniques . . . and such other factors as the Administrator deems appropriate."

12. *See* Jason Scott Johnston, *A Game-Theoretic Analysis of Alternative Institutions for Regulatory Cost-Benefit Analysis,* 150 University of Pennsylvania Law Review 1343, 1395–1401 (2002).

13. A point made by Louis Kaplow and Steven Shavell, *Property Rules versus Liability Rules,* 109 Harvard Law Review 713, 751–752 (1996).

14. On this point, *see* Clifford S. Russell, *Achieving Air Pollution Goals in Three Different Settings,* in To Breathe Freely: Risk, Consent and Air 233, 254 (Mary Gibson, ed., 1985).

15. *See* Howard Latin, *Ideal versus Real Regulatory Efficiency: Implementation of Uniform Standards and "Fine-Tuning" Regulatory Reforms,* 37 Stanford Law Review 1267, 1314 (1985 here in after cited as Latin, Ideal versus Real).

16. According to the statute, the new source standards are based on "the greatest degree of effluent reduction which the Administrator determines to be achievable through application of the best available demonstrated control technology, processes, operating methods, or other alternatives, including, where practicable, a standard permitting no discharge of pollutants." 33 U.S.C. §1316(a)(1).

17. 33 U.S.C. §1311(b)(2)(E).

18. 33 U.S.C. §1311(b)(1)(A).

19. 33 U.S.C. §1314(b)(1)(B).

20. This description is taken from P. D. Reed, *Industry Effluent Limitations Program in Dissarray as Congress Prepares for Debate on Water Act Amendments,* 12 Environmental Law Reporter (1982).

21. As the Supreme Court summarized the process, "every BPT limitation represents a conclusion by the Administrator that the costs imposed on the industry are worth the benefits in pollution reduction." *EPA v. National Crushed Stone Ass'n,* 449 U.S. 64 at 76 (1980).

22. This has been EPA practice for the past three decades. Compare, for instance, EPA, Final Development Document for Effluent Limitations Guidelines and New Source Performance Standards for the Phosphorus Derived Chemical Segment of the Phosphate Manufacturing Point Source Category §VIII (Jan. 1974), with the EPA's proposed but canceled new water pollution regulations for the metal finishing industry, described in Jason Scott Johnston, *The Promise and Limits of Voluntary Management-Based Regulatory Reform: An Analysis of EPA's Strategic Goals Program, in Leveraging the Private Sector (Cary Coglianese and Jennifer Nash, eds., 2005).*

23. *See* 33 U.S.C. §§1314(b)(1)(B) and (4)(B) and *EPA v. National Crushed Stone Ass'n.*, 449 U.S. 64, 71 n. 10, 76–77 and n.16 (1980), both discussed in Latin, Ideal versus Real, *supra* n. 15 at 1314.

24. *See* Latin, Ideal versus Real *supra* n. 15, Howard Latin, *The Feasibility of Occupational Health Standards: An Essay on Legal Decisionmaking under Uncertainty,* 78 Northwestern University Law Review 583, 588, 600–602, 611–17 (1983).

25. In *EPA v. National Crushed Stone Ass'n.*, 449 U.S. 64 (1980).

26. 42 U.S.C. §7411(a)(1).

27. *See Sierra Club v. Costle,* 657 F.2d 298 (D.C. Cir. 1981).

28. *Wisconsin Electric Power v. Reilly,* 893 F.2d 901, 918–919 (7th Cir. 1990).

29. Under 42 U.S.C.d'7411(b)(2). For an example of such subcategorization, see 44 Federal Register 33,580 (1979)(varying NO_X emissions standard for utility boilers based on boiler and fuel type).

30. *See Lignite Energy Council v. U.S. E.P.A.,* 198 F.3d 930, 933 (D.C. Cir. 1999)(upholding a uniform flue gas treatment technology for NO_X emissions from fossil-fired industrial and utility boilers).

31. 42 U.S.C. §7503(a)(2).

32. 42 U.S.C. §7501(3).

33. 42 U.S.C. §7502(b)(2).

34. 42 U.S.C. §7502(b)(3).

35. For illuminating discussions of the way the EPA guidance documents regarding RACT for particular source categories have in fact become uniform standards that SIPs must follow, *see State of Michigan v. Thomas,* 805 F.2d 176 (6th Cir. 1986); *National Steel Corporation v. Gorsuch,* 700 F.2d 314 (6th Cir. 1983); *Navistar International Transportation Corp. v. EPA,* 941 F.2d 1339 (6th Cir. 1991).

36. Which applies to area sources subject to the hazardous air pollutants program under 42 U.S.C. §7412(d).

37. Which applies under 42 U.S.C. §7513(a)(b)(1)(B) to sources of particulates in areas classified as "serious" for the nonattainment of the NAAQS for that pollutant.

38. 42 U.S.C. §7661a(a).

39. A former EPA general counsel's description of the effluent guidelines for textile mills gives a flavor of this process: "The regulation contains limitations for seven subcategories: wool scouring, wool finishing, dry processing, woven fabric finishing, knit fabric finishing, carpet mills, and stock and yarn dyeing and finishing. For each subcategory, there are limitations specified on the discharge of several pollutants . . . separate limitations are set forth for 'best practicable control technology currently available,' 'best available technology economically achievable,' and [new source performance standards]." Robert V. Zener, Guide to Environmental Law 90–91 (1981). For a case illustrating virtually the entire range of challenges that an industry may bring to technology-based standards, *see Chemical Manufacturers Assoc. v. EPA,* 870 F.2d 177 (5th Cir. 1989).

40. Striking recent examples include the metal finishing industry's recent success in persuading the EPA that it had far overestimated the effectiveness of its assumed technology, and so vastly underestimated the actual cost to industry of meeting proposed new effluent guidelines that compliance with those guidelines would have put 40 percent of the industy out of business, see Johnston, The Promise and Limits, supra note 22, and the natural gas distribution industry's success in persuading the EPA that the technology it had assumed would be used to reduce NO_X emissions in natural gas–fired internal combustion engines was technologically infeasible for certain types (lean burning, variable load) of these engines. *See* EPA, *Interstate Ozone Transport: Response to Court Decisions on the NO_X SIP Call, NO_X SIP Call Technical Amendments, and Section 126 Rules*, 67 Federal Register 8396, 8411–8413 (Feb. 22, 2002).

41. Under the CWA, for example, industry groups not only attacked the EPA's standards (the effluent guidelines) but at the same time tried to persuade the courts that the EPA's effluent guidelines were not binding on state permit writers. Until finally rejected by the Supreme Court in *E.I. DuPont de Nemours v. Train*, 430 U.S. 112, 126–136 (1977), this line of attack generated generated twenty federal court of appeals published decisions and no fewer than three Supreme Court opinions.

42. Zamanky and Zerbe, *Adjudicatory Hearings as Part of the NPDES Permit Process*, 9 Ecology Law Quarterly 1, 13, 17 (1980); Implementation of the Federal Water Pollution Control Act: Hearings before the Subcommittee on Investigation and Review of the House Comm. on Public Works and Transportation, 94th Cong., 2d Sess. 123 (176) (Report by the Comptroller of the United States).

43. FWPCA § 301(c), 33 U.S.C. § 1311(c).

44. *See*, e.g., 40 C.F.R. §§ 434.22, 434.32, 436.22. In *E.I. DuPont Nemours v. Train*, 430 U.S 112, at 128 (1977), the Court held that the structure of the CWA in fact required the EPA to allow source-specific variances.

45. *EPA v. National Crushed Stone Assn.*, 449 U.S. 64 (1980). One commentator has summarized the Court's holding in this case as follows: "The Court held that the statute requires consideration of whether the costs of BPT are reasonable for the industry category as a whole, but contemplates, as the legislative history clearly indicates, that the uniform standards would apply to all plants in the category, regardless of their economic effect on individual plants. The BPT variance is properly limited to cases where an individual plant so differs from others in the category, in terms of the technology and cost considerations, that it would be irrational to apply the category-wide standards to that plant." Reed, *supra* n. 20.

46. 33 U.S.C. §1311(n)(1).

47. *See* Farber, Taking Regulatory Slippage Seriously (citing William F. Pedersen, *Turning the Tide on Water Quality*, 15 Ecology Law Quarterly 69, 85.

48. Pedersen, *supra* n. 47 at 86, n. 81.

49. The source of the widely cited irrelevance of FDF variances, Pedersen, *supra* n. 86 at 85, 69, 85 was also careful to add these qualifications, *id.* at 86 n. 81, which have unfortunately been ignored in the subsequent literature.

50. Thus as Pedersen, *supra* n. 86 at 87, 87 observes, by 1983, Congress had been persuaded to amend the law to relax the technology-based control requirements for certain conventional pollutants, codified at 33 U.S.C. Section 1314(a)(4), to exempt municipal sewage treatment plants from the toughest technology-based requirements, *see* Municipal Wastewater Treatment Construction Grant Amendments of 1981, Pub. L. No. 97–117, Section 21(b), 95 Stat. 1623, 1632 (repealing

section 301(b)(2)(B) of the CWA), and even relaxing effluent standards for two particular pulp mills that had failed to persuade the EPA to grant them a variance. See Pub. L. No. 97–440, 96 Stat. 2289, codified as amended at 33 U.S.C. Section 1311(m), reversing the result in Crown Simpson Pulp Co. v. Costle, 642 F.2d 323, 326 (9th Cir. 1981).

51. EPA, Requirements for Preparation, Adoption, and Submittal of Implementation Plans, 40 C.F.R. §51.100(y).

52. See the discussion in George Hays and Nadia Wetzler, Federal Recognition of Variances: A Window into the Turbulent Relationship between Science and Law under the Clean Air Act, 13 Journal of Environmental Law and Litigation 115, 127–141 (1998).

53. Id., see also Marc Melnick and Elizabeth Willes, Watching the Candy Store: EPA Overfiling of Local Air Pollution Variances, 20 Ecology Law Quarterly 207 (1993).

54. See Hays and Wetzler supra n. 52. at 137.

55. 42 U.S.C. §7410(e).

56. Constraints set out in Train v. Natural Resources Defense Council, 421 U.S. 60 (1975).

57. Because such discretion is part of a SIP, when it is exercised to allow a company to depart from BACT, there is no change in the state's SIP and hence no need for EPA approval. For a case upholding such a SIP provision, see United States v. Ford Motor Co., 736 F.Supp. 1539 (W.D. Mo. 1990).

58. See the discussion in Melnick and Willes, supra n. 53 at 216–23.

59. Id.

60. For many years, the practice of the California Air Resources Board was to simply not submit variance orders to the EPA as SIP revisions. See Melnick and Willes, supra n. 53 at 227. The largest air quality district in California, the South Coast Air Quality Management District (which covers the Los Angeles basin) now operates under a rule worked out with the EPA under which variances are treated as Title V permit modifications rather than SIP revisions. Hays and Wetzler, supra n. 52 at 140–41.

61. Melnick and Willes, supra n. 53 at 223.

62. Melnick and Willes, supra n. 53 at 236–43.

63. Union Electric Co. v. EPA, 427 U.S. 246, 268 (1976).

64. See Ludwig Hartinger, Handbook of Effluent Treatment and Recycling for the Metal Finishing Industry 706 (2d ed. 1994)

65. See generally Kenneth Wark and Cecil F. Warner, Air Pollution: Its Origin and Control 143–254 (1981).

66. Wark and Warner, Air Pollution, supra n. 65 at 234-35.

67. See Ellerman et al., 221–96.

68. See, for example, Scott R. Milliman and Raymond Prince, Firm Incentives to Adopt Technological Change in Pollution Control, 17 Journal of Environmental Economics and Management 247 (1989); David A. Malueg, Emission Credit Trading and the Incentive to Adopt New Pollution Abatement Technology, 16 Journal of Environmental Economics and Management 52 (1989).

69. Often simply comparing an idealized command control regime—with optimal facility-specific performance standards—with trading regimes, as in Chulho Jung, Kerry Krutilla, and Roy Boyd, Incentives for Advanced Pollution Abatement Technology at the Industry Level: An Evaluation of Policy Alternatives, 30 Journal of Environmental Economics and Management 95 (1996).

70. That model is set forth in Juan-Pablo Montero, Prices vs. Quantities with Incomplete Enforcement, 85 Journal of Public Economics 435 (2002). For present

purposes, the simpler one-period model found in Juan-Pablo Montero, Prices versus Quantities with Incomplete Enforcement, Working Paper 99-009, Center for Energy and Environmental Policy Research, MIT (1999) suffices.

71. Where $y = G^{-1}(q)$, we have that $C(q) = \int_{\underline{c}}^{y} c\, dG$. By Leibnitz's rule, it follows that $C'(q) = y, C'(0) = \underline{c}$, and (using the inverse function theorem) that $C''(q) = 1/g(y)$.

72. For two such attempts, see Johnston, A Game Theoretic Analysis, supra, and John M. de Figueiredo and Rui J. de Figueiredo, *The Allocation of Resources by Interest Groups: Lobbying, Litigation, and Administrative Regulation*, 4 Business and Politics 161 (2002).

73. The symmetric case is considered in some detail by Avinash Dixit, *Strategic Behavior in Contests*, 77 American Economic Review 891 (1987), who also makes the other standard assumptions regarding the shape of this function that are made here. A particular, simple functional form for such a contest function is the logit, $e_i/(e_i + e_g)$.

74. For simplicity, this benefit is assumed to be constant across firms.

75. The latter assertion can be verified by differentiating the regulatory first-order condition with respect to e_{i*}.

76. This is what Dixit (1987) refers to as a case where the firm is the overdog or favorite, but here this arises not because the regulatory contest is biased toward the firm but because the firm has more at stake and so invests more in it.

77. The reason is that while the firm can offset its compliance cost increase in part by increasing effort in the contest, all the government sees is increased firm effort, which it will not offset but actually exacerbate by lowering its own effort level in these circumstances.

78. The RECLAIM program in the Los Angeles basin, which allows firms to trade NO_x and SO_x emissions, relies on such self-reporting. See South Coast Air Quality Management District, RECLAIM Program Three-Year Audit and Progress Report (1998); Scott L. Johnson and David M. Pekelney, *Economic Assessment of the Regional Clean Air Incentives Market: A New Emissions Trading Program for Los Angeles*, 72 Land Economics 277 (1996).

79. Richard Toshiyuki Drury, Michael E. Belliveau, J. Scott Kuhn, and Shipra Bansal, *Pollution Trading and Environmental Injustice: Los Angeles' failed Experiment in Air Quality Policy*, 9 Duke Environmental Law and Policy Forum 231, 259–60 (1999).

80. For a description of the statutory basis and regulatory implementation of this program, see Hahn and Hester, supra n. 3 at 109, 113–18; Richard A. Liroff, Reforming Air Pollution Regulation: The Toil and Trouble of EPA's Bubble (1986).

81. See Hahn and Hester, supra n. 3 at 120–23.

82. For more on the obstacles to offset trading, see Daniel J. Dudek and John Palmisano, *Emissions Trading: Why Is this Thoroughbred Hobbled?*, 13 Columbia Journal of Environmental Law 217 (1988).

83. See chapter 7; Robert W. Hahn and Robert N. Stavins, *Incentive-Based Environmental Regulation: A New Era from an Old Idea*, 18 Ecology Law Quarterly 1, 17 (1991).

84. See Robert W. Hahn, *Economic Prescriptions for Environmental Problems: How the Patient Followed the Doctor's Orders*, 3 Journal of Economic Perspectives 95, 101–3 (1989)

85. Codified as Clean Air Act §403; 42 U.S.C. §7651b.

86. A. Denny Ellerman et al., supra n. 4.

87. Ellerman et al., *supra* n. 4 at 20–30.

88. A game described in great detail by Ellerman et al., *supra* n. 4 at 31–76.

89. Title IV is roughly a closed system, in that most of the demand for permits has come from regulated firms themselves or permit brokers, rather than, say, environmentalists interested in reducing pollution

90. A. Denny Ellerman et al., *supra* n. 4 at 31–76.

91. *Id., supra* n. 4 at 23.

92. *Id., supra* n. 4 at 43.

93. *Ibid., supra* n. 4 at 43.

94. *Id., supra* n. 4 at 53–54.

95. *Id., supra* n. 4 at 54. They also explore, and find wanting, other potential explanatory variables, such as whether the state was an electoral swing state. *Id.* at 64–75.

96. The extension is from the world of the model—which assumes constant marginal cost of compliance for each facility (assumed to be a firm) but differences in this cost across facilities—to a world where each facility has increasing marginal abatement cost. In a model where each facility has increasing marginal abatement cost, the equilibrium under bargained CAC may be thought of as one in which the low-cost firms are those that have a lower cost of achieving a given discrete pollution reduction, but after achieving that reduction have been pushed so far out their marginal cost curves that the marginal cost of any further discrete reduction is higher to them than to the previously unregulated, formerly high cost firms.

97. For a discussion of the many perverse incentives created by this regime, *see* Byron Swift, *How Environmental Laws Work: An Analysis of the Utility Sector's Response to Regulation of Nitrogen Oxides and Sulfur Dioxide under the Clean Air Act*, 14 Tulane Environmental Law Journal 309 (2001).

98. Ellerman et al., *supra* n. 4 at 53.

99. *See,* for example, Sierra Club, Facts about the Bush Administration's Plan to Weaken the Clean Air Act, available at www.sierraclub.org/cleanair/clear_ skies.asp.

14

Environmental Trading Schemes and the Constitutional Leverage Effect

Daniel A. Farber

INTRODUCTION

For the past several decades, environmental economists have urged the replacement of conventional regulatory schemes with market-based systems.[1] This book seeks to evaluate how these proposals have worked in practice. Not surprisingly, many of the contributors focus on the economists' central claim that these systems produce equal environmental benefits at lower cost than conventional regulation.[2] Over the past thirty years, we have amassed sufficient experience with market systems to begin to evaluate those claims.

This chapter, however, examines that experience from a different perspective. Quite apart from the efficiency benefits claimed by economists, market systems may also have unexpected legal benefits—benefits that were not contemplated by their economist advocates and that in fact were less significant thirty years ago. In particular, environmental trading systems may mitigate the effects of recent Supreme Court decisions that call into question the use of conventional regulation in some situations.[3]

This beneficial effect is a counter to legal difficulties that have intensified since the beginning of the modern environmental era about thirty years ago. When the major federal environmental statutes were passed, federal regulatory authority was at its peak. Federalism concerns were at their lowest ebb in the twentieth century. Property rights received little attention from the Supreme Court, and there was some reason to hope that the lower courts might become receptive to environmental restrictions on property. Today, as we will see, these constitutional problems have grown in their prominence (and the recent appointment to the

Supreme Court of Chief Justice Roberts and Associate Justice Alito might expand them dramatically).

During the same period, another development has taken place, as command-and-control regulations have been supplemented with environmental trading systems.[4] These two developments seem quite unrelated, but there are some intriguing connections. In particular, the second change (the emergence of environmental trading systems) may offer a partial antidote to the first change (the intensification of constitutional restrictions). Market mechanisms expand the possibilities for accommodating federalism and property rights with strong environmental protection, thereby allowing the government to leverage its constitutional authority. As with most constitutional issues, the validity of leveraging is not crystal clear, but the Court has responded favorably in at least some contexts.

This is not to say that the constitutional difficulties are themselves entirely new, or that leverage is completely without precedent in earlier periods. Takings claims and federalism issues were not unheard of in the 1970s, and some mechanisms like transferable development rights (TDRs) were already in use as forms of leverage. Nevertheless, despite sporadic past use of leveraging, the concept has not yet received a systematic examination. Now is an especially appropriate time for an assessment of the leveraging concept. Market mechanisms are increasing the likelihood of leveraging at a time when the constitutional issues are themselves threatening to mushroom.

An example of how leveraging might work is provided by wetlands mitigation banking discussed at length in chapter 12 of this volume.[5] Under the Clean Water Act (CWA), passed in 1972, filling of wetlands requires a federal permit.[6] When the statute was passed, there seemed to be little question about federal regulatory jurisdiction. Taking claims were known to be a possibility, but were not yet receiving significant attention from the Supreme Court. Today, the Court has made it clear that some permit denials may amount to takings of private property requiring compensation and has also held that some wetlands may not be sufficiently closely connected with navigable waters to be subject to federal regulation, and this issue continues to be litigated in the Supreme Court. Mitigation banking could potentially offer solutions to these problems. Permit denials that would so sharply interfere with property rights as to constitute a taking may be avoided by approving the project in return for a contribution to the mitigation bank, or the land might be banked as a credit against other future projects. Either approach might prevent a court from finding a taking, as explained in the next section.

Similarly, some wetlands may provide important ecosystem services but be outside of direct federal control. By allowing such wetlands to be sold to the mitigation bank and used as mitigation for federally regulated projects, the federal government could indirectly inhibit development of those lands, as explained in the third section. This is not to suggest that wetlands mitigation banking be adopted as a ruse to avoid constitutional limitations. Ameliorating some of the limits on direct federal regulation is simply an incidental benefit of a market-based environmental program like mitigation banking.

Mitigation banking is not the only possible application of this concept. Other examples may involve noncommercial sources of air and water pollution (arguably beyond direct federal jurisdiction under the Commerce Clause), and restrictions on private land development to protect endangered species (which could sometimes be considered property takings and might in some instances exceed the Commerce power). If the Supreme Court becomes more aggressive in its campaigns to limit federal power and protect private property rights, the ability of market-based programs to counteract these limits may become even more important.

Although they involve a variety of constitutional and statutory provisions, the situations discussed in this chapter have a common structure. In each situation, the government's regulatory power extends to domain X but not domain Y. Y may be off-limits in terms of regulation for various reasons—for example, because it would be an unconstitutional taking of private property or because it would invade states' rights. How can the government leverage its ability to mandate X to accomplish Y?[7] As it turns out, the answer often involves some kind of exchange scheme, in which the government allows some kind of environmental harm that it could otherwise prevent in domain X in exchange for environmental benefits in domain Y. In such a scheme, the exchange can either be made directly with the affected party or via intermediate transactions with third parties.

The second part of this chapter explains how the taking clause may impact environmental regulation and shows how market-based systems such as wetlands banking may mitigate these constitutional impacts. The third section discusses recent judicial limitations on federal regulatory power based on federalism and explores the possible use of market-based systems as a remedy. The final section offers some concluding thoughts about the significance and legitimacy of this use of market-based environmental systems.

A note on terminology may be in order before I begin. This chapter will use the terms *environmental exchange, environmental trading,* and *market systems* more or less interchangeably to refer to any scheme that allows one environmental harm to be offset by the provision of some environmental benefit. The environmental benefit may take the form of a reduction in some other environmental harm, possibly by the same actor or at the same time and place, but possibly not. Thus, the exchange may or may not take place in an organized, multiparty market—the spectrum includes everything from pollution rights traded on the Chicago Board of Trade to barter transactions between a firm or landowner and the government.

For these purposes, intrasource netting of air pollutants or the use of bubbles count as market mechanisms, and so do the similar use of mitigation credits or on-site mitigation requirements for wetlands development.

For some reason, it is more common to thinking of air pollution bubbles as a kind of market mechanism than wetlands mitigation. But where an owner is allowed to develop some wetlands in return for an agreement to preserve or improve others, one really has just another form of bubble, this time for ecological impacts rather than pollution levels.

Thus, for my purposes, a market transaction includes any contracting, whether with private parties or the government, in which the medium of exchange is environmental impact, resulting in an agreement to allow increased impact of one kind in exchange for an otherwise nonmandatory reduction of another kind. In all these instances, the regulated party is trading something—whether the trade is with another regulated party (tradable permits or mitigation banking) or whether the trade is with the government (intra-site netting, bubbles, or owner-specific wetland mitigation).

It is important to avoid the implication that exchange schemes are merely some kind of clever ruse for avoiding constitutional limitations. On the contrary, the main benefit of exchange schemes is efficiency, and the constitutional advantages are serendipitous. The varying constitutional implications of command-and-control and exchange schemes flow naturally from their different structures. The essence of command-and-control regulation is that it provides a direct mandate to each individual source. This feature makes it vulnerable to source-specific constitutional limitations, based on the nature of the individual source (Commerce Clause restrictions) or regulatory impact on that source (takings restrictions). In contrast, exchange schemes are inherently more system-oriented—the goal is to provide some systemwide result (air or water quality, biodiversity, ecosystem services), and the scheme flexibly adjusts to allocate burdens among affected entities. By providing additional options for compliance, market schemes are also less coercive, thereby making it harder for a court to find government overreaching. So it is not surprising that these schemes are less likely to encounter constitutional barriers.

LEVERAGING THE POLICE POWER: ENVIRONMENTAL TRADES AND THE TAKING CLAUSE

In the early 1970s, when the Clean Air Act (CAA) and the CWA were passed, there were good grounds for optimism about whether private property rights would prove a constitutional barrier to environmental regulation. Taking claims (claims that overregulation amounts to a taking of property without just compensation) were far from unknown. There were signs, however, that courts might be moving toward a sympathetic view of environmental restrictions. For example, in 1972, the Wisconsin Supreme Court decided *Just v. Marinette County*,[8] in which a landowner claimed that his wetland property was "taken" because he was not allowed to fill and develop it. The court not only rejected his claim but spoke out broadly in favor of environmental preservation. It stressed that an "owner of land has no absolute and unlimited right to change the essential natural character of his land so as to use it for a purpose for which it was unsuited in its natural state and which injures the rights of others."[9] The court also proclaimed that "too much stress is laid on the right of an owner to change commercially valueless land when that change does damage to the rights of the public."[10]

Just was exceptional even at the time in its sensitivity to environmental concerns, yet it could have been a harbinger of things to come in the new age of environmentalism. But as it turned out, an increasingly conservative Supreme Court took quite a different doctrinal path. As a result, some significant environmental restrictions have become subject to more sustained constitutional attacks.[11]

In this section, I review the evolution of constitutional doctrine and examine how environmental exchange regimes may be used to overcome such constitutional problems. Two different kinds of exchanges are involved. In the first category, involving TDRs, the state prohibits a proposed use of the owner's land but in exchange awards additional rights to develop other land. In the other category, the state allows use of the land owner's land but in exchange requires the landowner to relinquish other rights.

An Introduction to Takings Law

The Taking Clause prohibits the government from taking "private property for public use without just compensation." As its language suggests, the clause's primary focus is on condemnation of private property for government use. For at least the past eight decades, however, the Court has also applied the clause to government regulations that "go too far" in regulating private property.[12] No one on the Court has ever seemed much worried by the awkward fit of this "regulatory taking" doctrine with the constitutional text or its fairly dubious connection with the original understanding.[13] In the early 1970s, when Congress passed the major federal environmental statutes, the Supreme Court seemed quite uninterested in takings law. It had devoted little attention to regulatory takings since the New Deal, when it had largely abandoned any effort to limit economic regulation. But the Court's apathy disappeared by the middle of that decade, and the Court has been very active in deciding takings cases in the past three decades. Some of the significant holdings are summarized in table 14.1.[14]

As table 14.1 indicates, the modern Court employs three separate tests in takings cases. First, the Court finds a taking when the government mandates an ongoing physical intrusion on private property. This intrusion is a taking even if it does not cause any damage, either in economic terms or as an invasion of privacy. The classic example is *Loretto*, in which the cable boxes occupied small amounts of roof space that were not used for any other purpose by the building owner. (Of course, if there is no financial harm, the compensation to the owner may turn out to be minimal.) The physical intrusion rule seems to be the easiest form of regulatory

Table 14.1 Selected Modern Takings Holdings

Case	Theory	Holding
Penn Central Transportation Co. v. City of New York[1]	Reasonable expectations	Upholds landmark preservation law
Kaiser Aetna v. United States[2]	Physical invasion	Marina owner cannot be required to allow public access
Loretto v. Teleprompter Manhattan CATV Corp.[3]	Physical invasion	Taking exists where landlords are required to give tenants cable access, because of cable box on building roof
Lucas v. South Carolina Coastal Commission[4]	Total taking	Prohibition of construction on fragile beach land is per se taking
Keystone Bituminous Coal Ass'n v. DeBendictis[5]	Reasonable expectations	Upholds law that required 50 percent of coal below any building to be kept in place to provide surface support
Andrus v. Allard[6]	Reasonable expectations	Upholds ban on sale of eagle feathers
Tahoe-Sierra Preservation Council, Inc. v. Tahoe Regional Planning Agency[7]	Reasonable expectations	Upholds multiyear moratorium on construction in environmentally sensitive area

1. 438 U.S. 104 (1978).
2. 444 U.S. 164 (1987).
3. 458 U.S. 419 (1982).
4. 505 U.S. 1003 (1992).
5. 480 U.S. 470 (1987).
6. 444 U.S. 51 (1979).
7. 535 U.S. 302 (2002).

taking law to justify, because at common law, it is necessary to acquire a specific property interest (typically an easement) to make physical use of the property of another. Applying this rule to minimal intrusions may seem overly zealous but avoids the need to engage in any line-drawing.

The second category, established in *Lucas*, applies to so-called total takings. The crux of these cases is that the government has in effect engaged in an appropriation by completely depriving the owner of any economically beneficial use of "the property."[15] The reason for using scare quotes is that it is often difficult to define the relevant property. For instance, in *Penn Central*, the owner was completely deprived of any use of the airspace over an existing building, which in Manhattan is a valuable asset. The majority of the Court, however, viewed the airspace as only one part of the unified parcel of property, rather than as a separate item of property that was totally taken. Total takings are further from classic government appropriations than physical intrusions, but this category can be considered to be a loophole closer, preventing the government from engaging in the functional equivalent of acquiring open space simply by depriving the owner of the right to use it for any purpose.

The third (default) category is governed by the *Penn Central* test, which requires a determination of whether the government regulation interferes with reasonable, investment-backed expectations. The *Penn Central* case is considered in more detail in the next subsection. The basic thrust of the test is to prevent destruction of investment through retroactive rule changes, except where such changes should have been anticipated by the investor.[16] It seems to be much less common for the courts to find a taking under this test.

Why does any of this matter to environmental regulators? Classic pollution statutes rarely if ever implicate takings concerns. They almost never have the economic effect of prohibiting all economically viable uses of land, and they do not require that the general public have access to polluter's land. Thus, they are generally covered by the *Penn Central* test, and potential investors cannot claim much in the way of a reasonable expectation of being able to cause harm to the downwind or downstream public. Indeed, even in a total takings case, the government could probably defend on the ground that the activity was a common law nuisance and hence not included within the owner's property rights. Thus, in the typical air or water pollution case, the takings issue does not arise.

But takings doctrine is a more serious problem for preservation laws, such as those designed to prevent the destruction of ecosystems or biodiversity.[17] Such regulations may prevent the development of all or part of an owner's land or may require use of the land for the public to access waterways or other public areas. Thus, physical invasion or total takings claims are quite possible. Indeed, the Federal Circuit has responded favorably to taking claims in a number of wetlands cases.[18] In theory, the government could always condemn the land, but this may be impractical in an era of fiscal austerity and may also sometimes provide an unjustified windfall to the owner. The next two subsections consider ways environmental exchanges can be used to avoid takings claims.[19]

TDRs and Takings Law

Penn Central Transportation Co. v. City of New York was a noteworthy ruling for several reasons.[20] It provided Justice Brennan with the opportunity to synthesize existing takings doctrine in a way that has proved helpful to later courts. As mentioned earlier, *Penn Central* has also provided the default test for takings, applicable in the absence of a physical intrusion or a total taking. The case is also significant, however, because it marks the Court's first encounter with an environmental trading system. The system combined a limited right to make transfer to third parties with a kind of bubble, allowing the owner to transfer development rights between nearby parcels.[21]

Because *Penn Central* was the Court's main encounter with TDRs, it is worth examining the specific system involved in the case in some detail. As Justice Brennan explained:

> Although the designation of a landmark and landmark site restricts the owner's control over the parcel, designation also enhances the economic position of the landmark owner in one significant respect. Under New York City's zoning laws, owners of real property who have not developed their property to the full extent permitted by the applicable zoning laws are allowed to transfer development right to contiguous parcels on the same city block. . . . In 1969, the law governing the conditions under which transfers from landmark parcels could occur was liberalized. . . . The class of recipient lots was expanded to include lots "across a street and opposite to another lot or lots which except for the intervention of streets or street intersections form a series extending to the lot occupied by the landmark building, [provided that] all lots [are] in the same ownership." In addition, the 1969 amendment permits, in highly commercialized areas like midtown Manhattan, the transfer of all unused development rights to a single parcel.[22]

The owner's ability to make use of the bubble or transfer to a third party was hemmed in by various restrictions:

> To obtain approval for a proposed transfer, the landmark owner must follow the following procedure. First, he must obtain the permission of the Commission which will examine the plans for the development of the transferee lot to determine whether the planned construction would be compatible with the landmark. Second, he must obtain the approval of New York City's Planning Commission which will focus on the effects of the transfer on occupants of the buildings in the vicinity of the transferee lot and whether the landmark owner will preserve the landmark. Finally, the matter goes to the Board of Estimate, which has final authority to grant or deny the application.[23]

In upholding the application of the ordinance to prevent the construction of a large office building perched above Grand Central Terminal, the New York court had relied in part on the existence of the TDRs. It found that "the development rights above the Terminal, which had been made transferable to numerous sites in the vicinity of the Terminal, one or two of which were suitable for the construction of office buildings, were valuable to appellants and provided 'significant,' perhaps 'fair,' compensation for the loss of rights above the terminal itself."[24] The Supreme Court also found the existence of the TDRs significant:

> To the extent appellants have been denied the right to build above the Terminal, it is not literally accurate to say that they had been denied *all* use of those pre-existing air rights. Their ability to use these rights has not been abrogated; they are made transferable to at least eight parcels in the vicinity of the Terminal, one or two of which have been found suitable for the construction of new office buildings. Although appellants and others have argued that New York City's transferable development-rights program is far from ideal, the New York courts here supportably found that, at least in the case of the Terminal, the

rights afforded are valuable. While those rights may well not have constituted "just compensation" if a "taking" had occurred, the rights nevertheless undoubtedly mitigate whatever financial burdens the law has imposed on appellants, and, for that reason, are to be taken into account in considering the impact of regulation.[25]

In dissent, then Justice Rehnquist argued that the building restriction was a taking but wanted a remand to determine whether the TDRs constituted "just compensation."[26]

TDRs have been used not only in urban areas but also by many state and local governments to preserve agricultural lands and natural areas.[27] The significance of *Penn Central*'s treatment of TDRs has not been lost on property rights advocates. In a later case in which the majority failed to reach the issue, Justice Scalia called for overruling this aspect of *Penn Central* or limiting it to its facts (involving the owner of contiguous parcels). Otherwise, he feared, the existence of TDRs could have a drastic effect on takings law:

> Putting TDRs on the taking rather than the just compensation side of the equation . . . is a clever, albeit transparent, device that seeks to take advantage of a peculiarity of our Takings Clause jurisprudence: Whereas once there *is* a taking, the Constitution requires just (i.e. full) compensation, a regulatory taking generally does not *occur* so long as the land retains substantial (albeit not its full) value. If money that the government-regulator gives to the landowner can be counted on the question of whether there *is* a taking (causing the courts to say that the land retains substantial value, and has thus not been taken), rather than on the question of whether the compensation for the taking is adequate, the government can get away with paying much less. That is all that is going on here.[28]

Justice Scalia concluded that "the relevance of TDRs is limited to the compensation side of the takings analysis, and that taking them into account in determining whether a taking has occurred will render much of our regulatory takings jurisprudence a nullity."[29]

Despite Justice Scalia's suggestion to the contrary, neither the language of the *Penn Central* decision nor its facts were limited to transfers of rights to a landowner's contiguous plot. Nor has *Penn Central* been overruled, as he would have liked. But he is correct in asserting that TDRs do blunt the effects of current takings rules.

Justice Scalia's critique of *Penn Central* seems misguided. TDRs cannot be considered merely a form of takings compensation because their issuance does not depend on a prior finding that a taking has occurred. Indeed, landowners receive TDRs even when it is clear that no takings liability exists. Moreover, Justice Scalia views development rights on a specific parcel as having some intrinsic value beyond their financial return,[30] but it seems inconsistent to then describe the ability to transfer such rights and exercise them elsewhere as merely being a financial gain.[31] In any event, the Scalia critique does not seem to have been successful. As a disgruntled commentator concedes, most courts today have "considered TDRs as an economic use existing with the land, thus mitigating the effects of regulation."[32]

Regulatory Tie-Ins

Rather than granting rights in exchange for development limitations, the government may demand rights in exchange for allowing development. For example, under a habitat conservation plan (HCP), a landowner may be required to preserve some land for an endangered species in return for being allowed to develop other areas.[33] Sometimes, the government's demand for preservation would be a taking if it took place independently, requiring just compensation. The question is whether the government can obtain such property rights without compensation, in return for a discretionary decision to allow development. The answer is a resounding "sometimes."

Nollan v. California Coastal Commission was the first of two Supreme Court decisions dealing with this issue.[34] The owners of beachfront property in California sought a permit to demolish a dilapidated bungalow and replace it with a three-bedroom house.[35] The permit was granted subject to the condition that the owners record an easement allowing the public to cross their property to reach the beach. (The public already had the right to reach the ocean by walking along the beach from other access points.) The government's theory was that the new construction would increase blockage of the view of the ocean, creating a psychological barrier to beach access.[36] Justice Scalia's opinion for the Court first concluded that obtaining the easement outright would be a taking and then asked "whether requiring it to be conveyed as a condition for issuing a land-use permit alters the outcome."[37]

In analyzing this question, Justice Scalia explicitly assumed that the government could have denied the permit altogether based on the visual impact of the house. He also agreed that the government's "power to forbid construction of the house in order to protect the public's view of the beach must surely include the power to condition construction upon some concession by the owner, even a concession of property rights, that serves the same end."[38] Without such a "nexus," however, a permit condition would not be a "valid regulation of land use but 'an out-and-out plan of extortion.' "[39] Indeed, he argued, allowing such unrelated conditions on permits would actually undermine the accomplishment of legitimate land use goals:

> One would expect that a regime in which this kind of leveraging of the police power is allowed would produce stringent land-use regulation which the State then waives to accomplish other purposes, leading to lesser realization of the land-use goals purportedly sought to be served than would result from more lenient (but non tradeable) development restrictions. Thus, the importance of the purpose underlying the prohibition not only does not *justify* the imposition of unrelated conditions for eliminating the prohibition, but positively militates against the practice.[40]

In *Nollan*, the Court found no plausible connection between the alleged impact on ocean viewing and the requirement of an access easement.[41] Such a connection must be a "substantial" one where an actual conveyance of property is involved, "since in that context there is a heightened risk that the purpose is avoidance of the compensation requirement, rather than the stated police-power objective."[42]

In a second case, *Dolan v. City of Tigard*, decided seven years later, the Court embellished on *Nollan's* nexus requirement.[43] Here, the land was used for a plumbing and electric supply store next to a creek. The owner wanted to double the size of the store and add a paved parking lot. As conditions on the development, the city required the owner to dedicate open land for a public greenway adjoining the creek's floodplain and agreed to the construction of a pedestrian/bicycle pathway within the floodplain.[44] The Court found both requirements to have the requisite nexus with the impacts of the project. The Court found it obvious that "a nexus exists between preventing flooding along Fanno Creek and limiting development within the creek's 100-year floodplain," for the proposed development would expand the "impervious surface on the property" thereby "increasing the amount of storm water runoff into Fanno Creek."[45] Similarly, the Court found that a bike path would help relieve traffic congestion in the area that otherwise would be worsened by the development.[46]

Finding the nexus requirement satisfied, the Court went on to add an additional requirement of "rough proportionality," saying that "no precise mathematical calculation is required, but the city must make some sort of individualized determination that the required dedication is related both in nature and extent to the impact of the proposed development."[47] The Court found this new requirement had not been satisfied— the government could not demonstrate any relationship between flood prevention and the requirement of public access to the greenway, and there was no showing that the bike path would actually be likely to offset the increased traffic demand.[48] Note that the Court's objections all went to the public access requirements; apparently, the requirement that green space be preserved was otherwise unobjectionable.

In environmental exchange programs, the nexus requirement is unlikely to be a serious issue. The government is typically requiring an environmental benefit of the same genus as the environmental harm caused by the project. A more difficult problem may be posed by the "rough proportionality" requirement, given the difficulty of devising a suitable metric for measuring environmental benefits. In the case of wetlands, one possibility would be to use the concept of ecosystem services as such a measuring rod, but there are inevitable trade-offs between the complexity of the metric and the transaction costs of exchange, as explained in chapter 12 of this volume.[49] A similar issue of proportionality might arise with respect to HCPs under the Endangered Species Act (ESA), given the difficulty of measuring the value of specific habitat.[50] But since the *Dolan* Court did not demand mathematical precision, the measurement problems may not be a serious obstacle. Thus, subject to some possible constraints, an environmental exchange program may allow the government to obtain development restrictions that would otherwise constitute takings.[51]

The analysis becomes more complex when a ban on development would otherwise constitute a taking: Can the government avoid the taking by allowing some of the development in return for mitigation measures? This seems fairly unproblematic when the mitigation measures do not involve a transfer of property interests that might be considered a taking in their own right. If the defendant is required to preserve or restore part of the parcel as a condition of developing the rest of the parcel, this should not be considered a taking (so long as the appropriate nexus is present), even if a flat ban on development (which is the alternative to providing mitigation) would have been a taking.

Such restrictions on development activities are routine in land use regulation, as illustrated by the bikeway easement and green space requirements in *Dolan*. For example, building regulations generally require setbacks, leaving part of the land unused for construction. Yet no one seriously contends that these setback requirements are takings, even though the alternative to complying is a prohibition on construction, which might well be a taking if it were unconditional. It makes little sense to think of a setback requirement as a way of extorting owners into leaving part of their land undeveloped; rather, they are a way of regulating the impacts of the development. The same is true of other mitigation measures, provided they have the necessary nexus to the development.

The situation is more complex when banning development would itself constitute a taking, and the mitigation measures would *also* be considered a taking if they were directly mandated by the government. Examples would be a requirement that the owner dedicate a conservation easement for part of the land as a condition of making any economic use of the rest of the land, or that the owner purchase mitigation credits from third parties to make any use of land. A property rights advocate might argue that the government is only offering the owner a choice between having property (in the form of an easement or cash) taken via the development ban and having it taken via the mitigation. Arguably, giving the owner a choice between two uncompensated takings is no better than imposing either one of them would be separately.

Superficially, this might seem like the kind of extortion that the Court found objectionable in *Nollan*. But a less formalistic response would be that the owner is not in fact being completely denied the right to develop its property under *Lucas* or losing any reasonable investment-backed expectation under *Penn Central*, and hence there is no taking.[52] As discussed below, the latter approach seems preferable. So long as the mitigation measures satisfy *Nollan* and *Dolan*, the exchange of development permission for mitigation measures seems like an entirely reasonable accommodation of the interests of both parties.

Recall that in *Dolan* the Court accepted the appropriateness of the green-way and bike path requirements as counters to environmental problems created by the store (provided, of course, that the city could sufficiently document the linkage). In *Dolan*, the plan was to expand an existing store. But suppose the land was undeveloped and the only economically feasible use was for a store. Under *Lucas*, flatly denying permission to develop would be a taking. Nevertheless, it should still be legitimate for the government to demand the bike path and green space, assuming it can appropriate the necessary linkages. It would make little sense to say that the city can constitutionally demand these features as a condition of expanding an existing store, but not when the same facility is being built from scratch. The fact that a flat denial of development would be a taking should have no relevance to determining the validity of conditions on development.

To see why exchanging mitigation for development permission is acceptable, it may be helpful to assess the problem that troubled the Court in *Nollan*. Whether we think that the government's action was objectionable or even harmful to *Nollan* depends to a large extent on what we think about the government's motivation and how it would have acted if obtaining an easement were not a possibility. Suppose the government strongly objected to Nollan's building plan, enough to deny him permission to build. Then it would be to Nollan's advantage to be able to offer the option of dedicating an access easement as a way of sweetening the deal. In such a scenario, it is hard to see how he would be harmed or how the government would gain anything illicit in such a transaction. But in fact that there was reason to doubt that the government did object strongly to the building—for example, it was unrealistic to suppose that after the easement requirement was struck down in *Nollan*, the Coastal Commission would begin denying building permits on a widespread basis. Instead, permission to build at least arguably functioned mostly as a pretext for securing the easements. If these concerns about the government's motivation were valid, then the threat to deny permission to build was made only to obtain something the government is not otherwise entitled to—the access easement. The purpose of the nexus requirement is to reduce the government's temptation to use its powers in bad faith to accomplish unrelated goals. The *Nollan* and *Dolan* tests are designed precisely to screen out these pretextual mitigation demands, where what is supposedly being mitigated is not reasonably tied to the mitigation being demanded.

The kind of leverage considered in this section is far removed, however, from the pretextual mitigation requirements that concerned the Court in *Nollan* and *Dolan*. In the exchange mechanisms proposed here, the permit denial is not a ruse to get the owner to buy mitigation credits. Rather mitigation credits are simply a way of reducing the harm that the permit would otherwise cause, by offsetting the loss of wetlands. Like the bike path or the green space in *Dolan*, these credits are merely a way of lessening the harmful impacts of the development itself. As the *Dolan*

Court made clear, such forms of mitigation are acceptable provided the government can establish their proportionality to the harm caused.

LEVERAGING REGULATORY JURISDICTION: TRADING AROUND FEDERALISM

Background on the Commerce Clause

The Commerce Clause gives Congress the power to regulate interstate and foreign commerce. Until the late nineteenth century, this provision did not cause much legal perplexity simply because Congress rarely attempted to use this power. With the rise of the modern regulatory state, all that changed. The cases over the past century can be divided into three periods.

The first began around 1890 and ended abruptly during the New Deal. As table 14.2 shows, the Court vigorously policed federal legislation to ensure that laws were limited to interstate transactions rather than regulating local matters. Agriculture, manufacture, and mining were not considered to be commerce, nor were local retail transactions. Thus, much of what the federal government now regulates was considered off-limits during this period.

As table 14.3 shows, however, the Court was not absolutist even during this time. Rather, under some circumstances, it was willing to allow federal regulations that were directed at noncommercial goals or reached intrastate transactions. An understanding of these doctrines is needed to comprehend later developments. Three major exceptions existed to the

Table 14.2 Commerce Clause, Period I: Unfavorable Rulings

Case	Federal Regulation	Ruling
United States v. E.C. Knight[1]	Antitrust Law	National sugar monopoly involves only manufacturing, not commerce
Hammer v. Dagenhart[2]	Child labor ban	Child labor involves manufacturing, not commerce
Railroad Retirement Bd. v. Alton Rd.[3]	Railroad pensions	Unconstitutional: labor regulation, not truly commerce
A.L.A. Schechter Poultry Corp. v. United States[4]	National Industry Recovery Act	Retail sales are beyond congressional control
Carter v. Carter Coal Co.[5]	Coal Conservation Act	Regulation of mining is beyond congressional power

1. 156 U.S. 1 (1895).
2. 347 U.S. 251 (1918).
3. 295 U.S. 330 (1935).
4. 295 U.S. 495 (1935).
5. 298 U.S. 238 (1936).

Table 14.3 Commerce Clause, Period I: Favorable Rulings

Case	Theory	Ruling
Champion v. Ames[1]	"Outlaws of commerce": Congress can ban undesirable items from interstate commerce	Upholds ban on interstate shipment of lottery tickets
Swift & Co. v. United States[2]	Stream of commerce: Congress can regulate local activities before goods have "come to rest"	Upholds regulation of animal stockyards
Hipolite Egg Co. v. United States[3]	"Outlaws of commerce"	Congress can ban unsafe or adulterated food and drugs from interstate commerce
Hoke v. United States[4]	"Outlaws of commerce"	Upholding prohibition on transportation of women in interstate commerce for "immoral purposes" (primarily prostitution)
Shreveport Rate Case[5]	Effect on commerce: Congress can regulate local activities that threaten or harm commerce	Congress can regulate rates for intrastate railroad shipments, because indirect effect on interstate rates

1. 188 U.S. 321 (1903).
2. 196 U.S. 375 (1905).
3. 220 U.S. 45 (1911).
4. 227 U.S. 308 (1913).
5. *Houston, East & West Texas Railway v. United States*, 234 U.S. 342 (1914).

general requirement that the object of regulation be some essentially interstate aspect of the transaction. First, Congress could close interstate commerce to noxious items or persons, even if they caused no harm while actually in transit. For instance, it could ban the interstate sale of lottery tickets even though the actual transportation of the pieces of paper across state lines was harmless. Second, Congress could regulate local actors or events if they were part of the "stream of commerce." Thus, when cattle were shipped into a state to be slaughtered, with the meat being almost immediately shipped out to other states, the local operations of slaughterhouse could be regulated. Third, Congress could regulate local transactions that had a sufficient impact on interstate commerce, such as by preventing state regulators from shifting costs from local rail shipments to interstate shippers. But, as a glance back at the later cases in table 14.2 confirms, these exceptions were not construed broadly enough to save much of the early New Deal legislation from the constitutional ax.

The collision between the Court and the New Deal resulted in the famous "switch in time that saved nine" of 1937, when the Court reversed itself under fierce political pressure and began to uphold New Deal legislation. Whether the political pressure was the direct cause of the switch is debated among modern constitutional historians,[53] but within a few years President Roosevelt's appointments had transformed the composition of the Court. From 1937 to 1995, the Supreme Court rejected every Commerce Clause challenge to federal regulation of the private sector without exception. A sense of the change in the Court's approach can be gleaned by comparing table 14.2 with table 14.4, which summarizes some of the leading Commerce Clause decisions from this second period. When Congress passed most of the modern federal environmental law statutes from the late 1960s to the early 1980s, it had little reason to be concerned about any limits on its regulatory powers. But as the comparison of the tables also indicates, there is no guarantee that

Table 14.4 Commerce Clause: Period II

Case	Regulation	Ruling
NLRB v. Jones & Laughlin Steel Corp.[1]	Collective bargaining rules	Upheld because disruption of steel manufacturing would disrupt the stream of commerce
United States v. Darby[2]	Minimum wage law	Rejects the manufacturing/commerce distinction
Wickard v. Filburn[3]	Agricultural production quotas	Quotas constitutional as applied to wheat grown for use on farm rather than sale, because such uses cumulatively affects commerce
Heart of Atlanta Motel v. United States[4]	Ban on racial discrimination by public accommodations	Upheld because segregation affects interstate commerce and travel
Perez v. United States[5]	Ban on loansharking	Upheld because loansharking generates funds for organized crime, an interstate problem
Hodel v. Virginia Surface Mining and Reclamation Bd.[6]	Federal strip mining regulation (prime farmland restoration requirement)	Upheld because of cumulative effect of destruction of farm land on interstate commerce

1. 301 U.S. 1 (1937).
2. 312 U.S. 100 (1941).
3. 317 U.S. 111 (1942).
4. 379 U.S. 241 (1964).
5. 402 U.S. 146 (1971).
6. 404 U.S. 336 (1971).

long-established federalism doctrines will remain intact when placed under political stress. More changes were yet to come in the Supreme Court's federalism doctrines.

Looking backward, one can see signs of a federalism revival before the most dramatic changes occurred. Hindsight, however, can be misleading. What now seems an inevitable trend was much less foreseeable at the time. For example, in the mid-1970s the Court reinforced the Tenth Amendment as a limit on the federal government's power to regulate the activities of state government in *National League of Cities v. Usery*.[54] Yet this was hardly an inevitable development: To reach that result, the Court had to overruled one of its own recent precedents. In a series of later cases, the Court consistently rejected efforts to apply *National League of Cities* to other federal statutes.[55] It also emphasized that *National League of Cities* merely restricted Congress's ability to regulate the states, not its ability to regulate private parties.[56] Then, in the mid-1980s, the Court overruled itself again, holding that states have no special protection from federal regulation.[57] Thus, as of 1990 or so, there did not seem to be any accelerating trend toward limiting congressional regulatory power.

To the surprise of many constitutional scholars, in 1995 the Court signaled a change of direction in *United States v. Lopez*,[58] opening what seems to be a third period in Commerce Clause jurisprudence. In *Lopez*, a sharply divided Court struck down a federal ban on possession of guns near schools. Chief Justice Rehnquist's opinion for the Court interpreted previous decisions as establishing three rules. First, Congress may regulate the use of the channels of interstate commerce, either by eliminating obstructions or banning certain users (such as sellers of lottery tickets). Second, Congress can regulate the instrumentalities of interstate commerce and protect them from threats, whether those threats are local or interstate. Third, Congress can regulate activities having substantial effects on interstate commerce. The ban on gun possession in or near schools did not focus on the channels or instrumentalities of commerce, and the Court maintained that such possession "is in no sense an economic activity that might, through repetition elsewhere, substantially affect any sort of interstate commerce."[59] The Court was unswayed by the argument that school violence impaired education, which in turn affected the economy by limiting the formation of human capital.[60]

Five years later, the same majority ruled in *United States v. Morrison* that Congress lacked the power to legislate against violence to women.[61] Viewing domestic violence as a local concern, the Court pointedly set aside evidence of substantial economic effects in the form of health costs and lost productivity. "If accepted," Rehnquist wrote, this rationale "would allow Congress to regulate any crime as long as the nationwide, aggregated impact of that crime has substantial effects on employment, production, transit, or consumption."[62] Thus, the Court rejected "the argument that Congress may regulate noneconomic, violent criminal conduct based solely on that conduct's aggregate effect on interstate commerce."[63]

The results in these particular cases may not themselves have been earthshaking. But they were sharply at odds with existing precedent—recall that when the *Lopez* was decided the Court had not struck down a statute under the Commerce Clause during the lifetime of most Americans. The Court had previously been willing to uphold regulation on what seemed to be far weaker evidence of interstate effects. For example, in one case it held that racial discrimination against a restaurant's customers was within federal jurisdiction, even though the restaurant was far from any major highway, on the theory that the restaurant bought barbecue meat from out-of-state sources.[64] An earlier classic case upheld federal regulation of grain grown by a farmer for his own use.[65] Given such precedents, federal regulation of nationwide problems like guns at schools or violence against women did not seem particularly problematic.

Thus, when the Court ended six decades of support for federal regulation of the private sector, scholars began to talk about a possible "federalism revolution."[66] This may well be an overstatement, but it does reflect how the Court's recent decisions have reshaped the legal landscape. The open question at this point is what effect these decisions will have on environmental law.

The Extent of Federalism Constraints on Environmental Law

There are several areas in which the new federalism decisions may threaten federal environmental regulation. The most vulnerable regulations are those that do not directly address interstate effects or specifically target commercial activities. The following areas are illustrative,

The Safe Drinking Water Act imposes drinking water standards on public water supplies,[67] which are often provided by local government. To the extent that these are considered noncommercial, *Lopez* might limit federal regulation.[68]

The ESA regulates the "taking" of endangered species,[69] which includes some forms of habitat modification.[70] Whether a particular species has any actual effect on commerce may be debatable, and the activity in question may not be commercial.[71]

The CAA mandates reductions in air pollution levels,[72] which may require controls on sources such as leaf burning, residential fireplaces, personal driving, and barbecues, as well as pollution from government-owned vehicles and buildings. Such pollution may or may not have any measurable interstate effects.

Besides regulating water pollution, the CWA also restricts the filling of wetlands.[73] Some of these wetlands may be physically removed from any "channel of interstate commerce" (a navigable stream), and the filling may or may not have a commercial purposes. Congressional jurisdiction over these activities may raise Commerce Clause questions. Federalism concerns may also lead to a narrow reading of the statute.[74]

Only the last of these issues has been decided by the Supreme Court, although the Court failed to provide a definitive answer to the question of constitutionality. In *Solid Waste Agency of Northern Cook County v. United States Army Corps of Engineers (SWANCC)*,[75] the Court limited regulatory jurisdiction over wetlands, relying primarily on statutory grounds but with a strong constitutional overlay. The government had claimed jurisdiction over a former sand and gravel pit, on the theory that the ponds remaining on the site were used by migratory birds.[76] In a previous case, the Court had upheld the exercise of federal jurisdiction under the same provision of the CWA to wetlands adjacent to open waters.[77] But in *SWANCC*, the Court rejected the argument that "isolated ponds, some only seasonal, wholly located within two Illinois counties, fall under [the statute's] definition of 'navigable waters' because they serve as habitat for migratory birds."[78]

This holding was based partly on the view that the statute's use of the phrase "navigable waters" must mean *something*,[79] but the Court also indicated that a contrary interpretation of the statute would raise constitutional doubts. Unfortunately, the Court's discussion of the constitutional issues makes up in obscurity for what it lacks in length:

> Twice in the past six years we have reaffirmed the proposition that the grant of authority to Congress under the Commerce Clause, though broad, is not unlimited. Respondents argue that the "Migratory Bird Rule" falls within Congress' power to regulate intrastate activities that "substantially affect" interstate commerce. They note that the protection of migratory birds is a "national interest of very nearly the first magnitude," and that, as the Court of Appeals found, millions of people spend over a billion dollars annually on recreational pursuits relating to migratory birds. These arguments raise significant constitutional questions. For example, we would have to evaluate the precise object or activity that in the aggregate, substantially affects interstate commerce. This is not clear, for although the Corps has claimed jurisdiction over petitioner's land because it contains water areas used as habitat by migratory birds, respondents now, *post litem motam*, focus upon the fact that the regulated activity is petitioner's municipal landfill, which is "plainly of a commercial nature." But this is a far cry, indeed, from the "navigable waters" and "waters of the United States" to which the statute by its terms extends.[80]

Recognizing federal jurisdiction over "ponds and mudflats falling within the 'Migratory Bird Rule' would result in a significant impingement of the States' traditional and primary power over land and water use," and the Court found "nothing approaching a clear statement from Congress" that it intended the statute to reach so far.[81]

Thus, *SWANCC* clearly indicates some doubt about whether Congress has the constitutional power to regulate isolated wetlands, though the basis for those doubts is much less clear. *SWANCC* also holds that administrative agencies may not extend ambiguous statutes into constitutional gray zones of this kind. Just how significant this ruling will be remains to be seen. Potentially, it could signal future constitutional restrictions on the federal government's power to pursue environmental regulations. Less speculatively, it could also affect the interpretation of other federal environmental statutes, especially as they apply to non-commercial actors or activities lacking obvious interstate effects.[82]

Is Federalism Leverage Permissible?

Before considering how leveraging might work in the specific context of environmental law, it is important to address a preliminary question. It may seem suspicious for Congress to use its regulatory authority over one category of activities to get authority over another class of activities that it could not regulate directly. Can Congress use this kind of leverage to regulate otherwise immune activities? The answer is clearly "yes," as illustrated by three cases.

The first case was part of the post–New Deal reconceptualization of the Commerce Clause. At the time, Congress had authority over interstate shipments of goods, and the Court held that Congress could prohibit interstate shipment of goods produced in violation of minimum wage laws. Earlier cases had held that the wages paid to workers producing goods were not themselves subject to direct federal control. But the Court held that Congress could regulate those wages as a way of effectuating the ban on interstate shipment—the most effective way to ensure that the goods in question were not shipped in interstate commerce was to prevent them from being manufactured in the first place.[83]

A second case involved Congress's power under a different clause of the Constitution, the Property Clause, which authorizes Congress to regulate federal lands. Activities on nonfederal lands are not directly within the coverage of the clause. Yet the Court unanimously held that the federal government could regulate activities on adjoining nonfederal lands to ensure that federal lands could be used for their designated purposes.[84]

A recent example of federalism leverage is provided by *Sabri v. United States*.[85] When Congress directs funds to a state program, it is not much of a stretch to say that it can criminalize misuse of those funds or the acceptance of bribes by officials in that program. But the Supreme Court has held that Congress could leverage its authority over that particular program to get jurisdiction over the entire state agency.[86] As the Court explained:

> Money is fungible, bribed officials are untrustworthy stewards of federal funds, and corrupt contractors do not deliver dollar-for-dollar value. Liquidity is not a financial term for nothing; money can be drained off here because a federal grant is pouring in there. And officials are not any the less threatening to the objects behind federal spending just because they may accept general retainers. See *Westfall v. United States*, 274 U.S. 256, 259, 47 S.Ct. 629, 71 L.Ed. 1036 (1927) (majority opinion by Holmes, J.) (upholding federal law criminalizing fraud on a state bank member of federal system, even where federal funds not directly implicated).[87]

Thus Congress can criminalize activity by one state official, who is *not* within its direct constitutional jurisdiction, to effectuate its authority over another official who *is* within its direct jurisdiction. Note that there are two examples of leverage here: First, a power to spend money is leveraged into a power to impose criminal penalties for misconduct by the direct recipients, and then the authority over direct recipients is leveraged into authority over persons who might be indirect recipients.

Sabri is an especially apt example because environmental problems share some of the hydraulic quality that the Court attributed to money: What is "pouring in there" can "be drained off here," given that air basins, watersheds, and ecosystems are tightly interconnected. There is something artificial about saying that the federal government can regulate some aspects but not others, when all are part of the same integrated system. In *Sabri,* where the Court rejected such artificial distinctions, the system involved in the case was financial, but the principle is just the same, where the setting is ecological.

Examples of leveraging such as *Sabri* have a firm constitutional basis. The Constitution does not just give Congress power over specific matters such as interstate commerce or federal lands or payment of federal funds. It also gives Congress the power to make any laws "necessary and proper" for implementing the specific powers. The Necessary and Proper Clause— or the "sweeping" clause, as it is sometimes called—explicitly authorizes Congress to take actions that are not directly covered by its specific powers when necessary to effectuate the use of these specific powers. Constitutional leverage is simply a new application for a venerable doctrine.

Leverage and Environmental Federalism

As we have seen, the Supreme Court's view of the Commerce Clause changed radically about sixty years ago and now shows some signs of shifting back in the direction of that period. No one really expects a complete reversion to pre-1937 doctrine, but no one really knows how far the new federalism trend will go—not even the Justices themselves, because the answer depends to an important extent on the choices of recent and future appointments to the Court. Clearly, the more aggressive the Court becomes in limiting federal power, the more important will be the possible ameliorative effect of market-based systems.

For example, as part of the federal response to *SWANCC,* the government might allow banking of wetlands over which it does not have jurisdiction to be used for mitigation by developers of other wetlands over which it does have jurisdiction.[88] Such use of isolated wetlands for mitigation would not exceed the commerce power, for the only actual regulation that takes place involves the wetlands over which the government *does* have jurisdiction. That the owners of such covered wetlands choose to meet their mitigation obligations through restoration or preservation of other wetlands is their voluntary choice, not the government's regulatory mandate.

One especially modest form of leverage would be for the federal government to bargain for state implementation of such mitigation systems, or even more simply, to bargain with states to regulate non-covered wetlands to obtain federal funding of some kind or to obtain approval to take over part of the federal permitting system for covered wetlands. As part of such arrangements, states could be required to impose legally enforceable restrictions on those wetlands used for mitigation purposes and to monitor compliance. To the extent that the new federalism cases are motivated by concerns about state autonomy, this kind of bargain should be unobjectionable. The Court has been quite receptive, for example, to conditional funding requirements, which give states the choice between participating and losing funding. To uphold such funding, the Court requires only a nexus between the funding condition and the purposes of the funding. Similarly, the courts have never been troubled by the many hoops through which states must jump through to obtain approved state implementation plans under the Clean Air Act, because the state has the option of refusing and letting the federal government develop and enforce a federal plan. Similarly, through bargaining with states, the federal government can clearly use its control over covered wetlands to encourage states to adopt mitigation markets that include isolated wetlands or for states to regulate those wetlands directly.[89]

A bolder use of leverage would be for the federal government to leverage its control over covered wetlands by creating a federal mitigation system that includes non-covered wetlands. Although the government would not be directly regulating the non-covered wetlands, it would obtain enforceable restrictions on them by putting pressure on owners of covered wetlands who in turn would bargain with the owners of the isolated wetlands. Once the credits were used by the owner of covered wetlands, development restrictions on the non-covered wetlands would become federally enforceable. Such a system might significantly expand the effective ability of the federal government to protected wetlands that it lacks the direct power to regulate itself.

A fuller description of such a system might be helpful. The federal government clearly has jurisdiction over some waterways and wetlands under the Commerce Clause. As a condition of allowing use of those wetlands, it can require owners to mitigate environmental impacts. It might limit their ability to mitigate to actions that would be independently within federal jurisdiction, that is, mitigation measures that independently affect interstate commerce. But federalism surely does not prohibit Congress from adopting a more lenient attitude and allowing mitigation measures to qualify even if those measures themselves would not be subject to regulation. This is not an expansion of federal regulatory authority over the wetland owners. Indeed, it is actually a relaxation of authority, allowing owners to save money by adopting cheaper mitigation measures and thereby making it easier for them to comply with federal law. To ensure the integrity of the trading system, however, the federal government could then reasonably police the trades to ensure that the non-covered wetlands were in fact adequately preserved.

For instance, part of the trading system could include the purchase of credits from a wetlands mitigation bank. Now the question is whether the bank needs to be limited to lands that are within direct federal jurisdictional authority. But why should this be? Allowing owners of non-covered wetlands to enter into transactions with the bank benefits rather than restricts them. Clearly, Congress could directly buy mitigation credits itself from the bank, using its power to spend money in pursuit of the general welfare. It is hard to see any great intrusion on federalism if Congress allows regulated entities to meet their federal obligations by buying such credits. Why would federalism require restricting the compliance options of regulated firms?

If those firms can comply by voluntarily entering into agreements with third parties, why shouldn't these agreements be federally enforceable? Indeed, once a banking system is established, the banking system itself becomes a form of interstate commerce. Whatever else one might say about a wetlands mitigation bank, it is engaged in commercial transactions, entering into agreements with landowners and buying and selling credits. Just as it may regulate the local business transactions of firms that are also engaged in interstate commerce, Congress should have the power to regulate all of the transactions of mitigation banks.

This may seem like a form of bootstrapping, but the federal government's power over commerce should not depend on whether the market in question is natural or created by government intervention. For example, the markets in government bonds and postage stamps are surely a form of interstate commerce subject to federal regulation. So is the market for student loans, even though the market exists primarily because of federal subsidy programs. For exactly the same reasons, the market in mitigation credits should also be subject to regulation. Even if Congress has played a role in prompting the creation of the market, it nevertheless should have authority to regulate trading or banking transactions. Such regulation could well include providing federal enforcement and monitoring of credited mitigation to ensure that the market was not impaired by unreliable mitigation credits. Because unmerited credits from non-covered wetlands could undermine the integrity of the market just as much as credits from federal wetlands, Congress could also have authority over lands that are actually used to generate mitigation credits.

One can imagine a more aggressive application of leverage. Assume that a lively market for mitigation credits already exists. Such a market could have several connections with interstate commerce: Some of the mitigation trades might actually be interstate, the availability of credits might significantly impact land development decisions that themselves have interstate commerce, and the cumulative environmental benefits of mitigation might impact commerce. Once such a market exists, as argued earlier, it is likely to be subject to federal regulation. The next step could be to extend federal regulation beyond the mitigation market itself to place federal limits on development of non-covered wetlands. State regulation of non-covered wetlands affects the supply of possible mitigation credits, affecting the price for the remaining credits in the system. Thus, Congress could arguably regulate isolated wetlands on the theory that the supply of mitigation credits is intimately related with the operation of the already regulated market for credits. An analogy would be to the *Hodel* cases, where the Court upheld a requirement of restoring prime farmland from strip mining to make that land available to support the interstate market in food. Here, the argument would be to the contrary: that the interstate market was now flooded by cheap mitigation credits because of excessive supply, requiring restrictions on supply. It would not be im-plausible to argue that states were artificially expanding the supply of credits from isolated wetlands by restricting their own wetlands regula-tions, creating a race to the bottom among the states. Thus, to maintain an orderly interstate trading system, the federal government might step in and restrict the use of isolated wetlands.

Would the Court be willing to accept this form of leverage? No doubt the Court would be skeptical if it appeared that the trading system was established solely to establish a foothold for the commerce power. But the longer the trading system is in place, the more natural the argument for expanding jurisdiction becomes. The scale of the market for wetland mitigation would also make a difference. It would also be easier to make the argument for federal jurisdiction if the effects on the interstate miti-gation market were not the sole basis of federal jurisdiction over non-covered wetlands but instead could be added to other connections with interstate commerce (even if those other connections would not them-selves be sufficient).

And of course, in considering all of these constitutional issues, much might depend on the composition of the Court. A Court that was more sympathetic to federal regulation than the Rehnquist Court was, but that did not want to directly confront *SWANCC*, might be happy to accept leverage as a convenient way of resolving the dilemma. In contrast, a Court that was dedicated to rolling back federal power to its pre–New Deal dimensions would probably run roughshod over any leverage scheme.

The Court in recent years has been somewhere between these extremes, and correspondingly harder to predict. Much would depend on how in-dividual cases were litigated. And the recent appointments make pre-dictions even harder to make. Much also depends on whether the Court ultimately decides that *SWANCC* was merely a statutory interpretation decision with some constitutional dictum or was truly expressive of constitutional limits on congressional authority. The use of leverage to expand statutory jurisdiction seems less likely to raise judicial hackles than its use to expand constitutional jurisdiction.

Another example of federalism leverage might be the use of effluent allowance trading between regulated point sources of water pollution and unregulated nonpoint sources.[90] The program could be established by states, under federal auspices, or perhaps directly by the Environmental Protection Agency (EPA). Such a trading system is useful to fill a statutory gap, because the CWA does not regulate nonpoint sources effectively even when those sources are clearly covered by the Commerce Clause (such as agricultural operations causing pollution of interstate water bodies). But given *SWANCC,* it is also possible that at least some nonpoint sources—especially government or residential sources of runoff—may be outside the scope of the Commerce Clause, and a trading system would be one way of trying to bring their activities under control.[91]

The simplest way to create such a system would be to impose stringent limitations on point sources via the Total Maximum Daily Load setting process (required by the CWA for water bodies that do not meet state water quality standards), but then give point sources credit against these limitations for obtaining enforceable reductions from nonfederally regulated nonpoint sources. More ambitiously, a formal market for nonpoint source credits could be established.

Other Possible Applications

Although probably not as significant as the issues already discussed, there are two other situations where a market-based system could mitigate federalism problems. One relates to federal commandeering of state and local governments; the other relates to territorial limits on state regulatory power.

Even where an activity might otherwise be subject to federal jurisdiction, certain types of regulation may violate principles of federalism. In the 1970s, as mentioned earlier, the Court held that certain activities of state governments are immune from federal regulation even if the same activities by private actors would be covered by the Commerce Clause.[92] A decade later, the Court overruled that decision, holding that states must seek protection from such legislation through the political process.[93] Somewhat surprisingly, the Rehnquist Court's revival of federal limitations did not lead it to revisit this issue, although the Roberts Court certainly may.

The Rehnquist Court has, however, recognized another form of regulatory immunity for states. In *New York v. United States,*[94] Congress acted at the request of the states to deal with the problem of low-level nuclear waste. The statute provided a variety of incentives for states to pass legislation establishing disposal sites. The incentives included authorization for states with disposal sites to impose a surcharge on waste received from other states and ultimately to deny access altogether to waste generated in states lacking disposal sites. The Court also stressed that Congress could make federal funding conditional on a state's willingness to establish local disposal sites. But what the federal government could not do (even though the states themselves had designed the statute) was to impose a direct mandate on states requiring them to pass legislation. In a later case, the Court extended this ruling to state administrative agencies, which are also now exempt from being commandeered to enforce federal rules.[95]

As *New York* made clear, the federal government may use a variety of incentives when it wants to enlist the states as active participants in federal programs. One possible incentive could be to give private firms (or states when they are engaged in activities subject to federal regulation) credit for the environmental benefits that a state produces by voluntarily implementing a federal program. In other words, by engaging in the program, the state can produce credits that can be banked and then drawn on by private firms. For example, if states agree to expand their regulation of nonpoint source pollution in certain ways, they might create credits that could be used by point sources to obtain more relaxed effluent limitations. From the state's point of view, the incentive is to reduce federally regulatory burdens on itself or on private firms, when doing so produces a net benefit to the state. But the result is that the state enacts the legislation or administrative program desired by Congress, yet without a direct federal mandate or direct financial incentive. The EPA has a history of getting states to take initiatives without directly mandating them, which can sometimes allow the EPA to promote programs that it lacks the legal authority to adopt directly.

This discussion assumes that states must comply with federal regulation of their own environmentally harmful activities. (The commandeering doctrine applies only when the federal government is enlisting the states to police private parties, not when the federal government is policing the state's own activities.) If the Roberts Court revisits the general issue of federal regulation of state activities, resurrecting some or all of *League of Cities,* the doctrinal shift might call into question at least some applications of federal pollution laws to states. The federal government might not be able to directly regulate at least some polluting or environmentally destructive activities of state governments. If so, the leveraging effects of trading systems might become even more significant. States could be induced to limit their own environmentally destructive activities to provide credits for the use of local firms, the activities of which are subject to federal regulation. In essence, the use of state implementation plans under the CAA already provides such an incentive: The more air pollution a state government produces, the more private sources must reduce their pollution to meet the national air quality standards. A trading system would be another way of generalizing this kind of trade-off by states, if the federal government loses the authority to directly regulate pollution by state government agencies.

In contrast to these uses of leverage against the states, another use of trading systems might assist states in reaching their own environmental goals. In general, state regulatory authority is limited to its own boundaries. A business in Minnesota does not need a permit from the state of Wisconsin. Indeed, the Supreme Court has held that states may not even use their own nuisance laws against polluters in other states.[96] But a state may find that its own air or water, or a common resource shared with other states, is harmed by pollution from other states. Federal law provides some limited remedies dealing with this situation,[97] but a state may wish to take some independent initiative. Although this approach has some obvious limits, one possibility is to offer in-state firms (which are subject to state jurisdiction) credits if they obtain pollution reductions by the relevant out-of-state sources. One problem with this approach is that it transfers money out of state; another is that it may encourage the other state to drag its feet in imposing regulations of its own. But where the state government cares sufficiently about the local environmental impacts of out-of-state activities, this mechanism could be worth exploring.

THE LEGITIMACY AND SIGNIFICANCE OF THE CONSTITUTIONAL LEVERAGE EFFECT

As we have seen, environmental trading programs offer significant opportunities for constitutional leverage. Under current law, by using TDRs, the government can lower its exposure to takings liability. It can also trade with permit applicants, allowing some forms of environmental degradation in return for mitigation measures. It also seems likely that the federal government can reach beyond its direct regulatory power under the Commerce Clause by making local activities eligible for participation in a trading program with interstate activities.

There may seem to be something a little suspect about leveraging, for it seemingly allows the government to bootstrap its limited regulatory powers to surpass those limits. Doesn't every first-year law student learn that "you can't do indirectly what you can't do directly?" Actually, the process should not be considered troublesome. For, as law students also soon learn, quite often you *can* do indirectly what you would not be allowed to do directly. Indeed, a good deal of lawyers' work can be described as assisting people to do so.

Whether this is something that society should applaud or condemn depends partly on whether the legal rule in question is based on an objection to the goal or simply on a particular choice of means. (It also depends partly on whether the ban on the direct method is itself desirable. The Court's current constitutional doctrines regarding takings and federalism are quite controversial, but considering these critiques is outside of the scope of this chapter.) It is also worth noting that the form over substance argument is essentially pragmatic, and hence should have less appeal for legal formalists like Justice Scalia.

In any event, the form over substance argument is unpersuasive with respect to constitutional leveraging of the kind discussed in this chapter. It is important to keep in mind the nature of the constitutional limitations involved in these environmental cases. Consider, in contrast, the use of leverage to allow some form of discrimination against racial minorities or to limit political dissent. We would frown on the government using an indirect method to achieve these goals as much as we would reject a direct method, for the goals themselves are illegitimate. But the goals involved in environmental cases are public health and welfare, preserving nature, and ecosystem integrity—all of them perfectly legitimate.

The legitimacy of these goals is evident from the fact that there is no constitutional objection to accomplishing them through government spending programs. This is most obvious in the taking case, where the whole point of the litigation is to make the government condemn and pay for the property to achieve its goals rather than achieving its result through regulation. But the same is also true in the federalism cases. Unlike the federal government's regulatory powers, which are limited to specific areas like interstate commerce, the spending power is sweepingly defined. As Chief Justice Rehnquist made clear in his opinion for the Court in *South Dakota v. Dole*,[98] Congress may spend money in pursuit of any general public purpose and may place conditions on the recipients so long as the conditions are germane to the purposes of the expenditure. Thus, under current law, there would be no federalism objection if the government chose to protect isolated wetlands or endangered species by purchasing the land or paying the owner for a conservation easement. There also would be no objection if the government chose to pay individuals to refrain from socially destructive activities, even if those activities did not themselves affect interstate commerce.

Thus, the federal government's concern with environmental preservation is beyond reproach. The only constitutional question, in both takings and federalism cases, is whether the government has the power to achieve these results through a direct regulatory mandate. But leverage does not involve a direct mandate. It is clear that the government may buy environmental quality, and the only question is whether it must use cash or whether environmental exchanges are an acceptable currency.

One might possibly fear that this currency would be abused. Recall Justice Scalia's concern that the government would overregulate in the first place to generate the currency to exchange. But as Justice Scalia recognized, these exchange systems are too valuable to ban entirely. Rather, his solution in *Nollan*, as elaborated by the Court in *Dolan*, was to add a qualitative requirement of nexus and a quantitative requirement of "rough proportionality." To put it another way, the government can use leverage, but only to achieve goals related to the source of the leverage, and not where the leverage would be grossly disproportionate.

A similar requirement could be established as a safeguard in the federalism cases. Under such an approach, local activities that would not be subject to direct federal regulatory jurisdiction, could be made part of the trading system only where doing so advances the same environmental goal as the interstate portion of the program, and only where the local part of the trading system is not disproportionate compared with the portion subject to federal regulatory jurisdiction. In practice, federal trading systems will generally meet these requirements anyway, whether or not the requirements themselves are constitutionally mandated. Subject to these safeguards, using trading programs for constitutional leverage seems no more objectionable than the kinds of conditions that the government is already allowed to place on spending or on permit issuance.

In a world with fewer restrictions on federal regulatory power, constitutional leverage would have less significance. In a world with drastic restrictions on direct federal regulation, constitutional leverage would become extremely important. Our world—that of constitutional doctrine at the beginning of the twenty-first century—is somewhere in between. Restrictions on regulatory power have sprouted in fields long thought to be dead, but whether these will remain small bushes or become large trees is not yet clear. In the meantime, constitutional leverage will be a significant benefit of environmental trading schemes.

Regardless of legal doctrines, regulatory leverage of some sort is likely always to be with us. An agency's regulatory tools may fail to match its goals because of constitutional barriers, statutory gaps, or procedural obstacles. Whenever this occurs, the regulated party and the agency can both benefit by making a deal, whereby the agency forbears to exercise some of its authority in return for concessions from the other side, concessions that it would not obtain directly. In the end, regulators and regulated are likely to bargain their way to results both sides prefer, regardless of the formal legal rules. Whether Coase would be pleased or not is unclear, but the process is a striking example of the Coase Theorem in action.

ACKNOWLEDGMENTS Ann Burkhart, Jody Freeman, and an anonymous referee contributed useful comments on drafts of this chapter.

NOTES

1. *See*, e.g., Charles Schultze et al., Setting National Priorities: The 1973 Budget 368–73 (1972).

2. For a sampling of some of the previous debates on this question, *see* Robert Shapiro and Thomas McGarity, *Not So Paradoxical: The Rationale for Technology-Based Regulation*, 1991 Duke Law Journal 729; Howard Latin, *Ideal versus Real Regulatory Efficiency: Implementation of Uniform Standards and "Fine-Tuning" Regulatory Reforms*, 37 Stanford Law Review 1267 (1985); Bruce Ackerman and Richard Stewart, *Reforming Environmental Law*, 37 Stanford Law Review 1333 (1985).

3. Although the focus will be on constitutional restrictions, trading systems may be even more helpful in dealing with statutory limits on direct regulation. *See* following discussion in the text and notes.

4. For a good overview, *see* Jeremy Hockenstein, Robert Stavins, and Bradley Whitebread, *Crafting the Next Generation of Market-Based Environmental Tools*, Environment 13 (May 1997).

5. For an extensive discussion of wetlands mitigation and banking, *see* Royal Gardner, *Banking on Entrepreneurs: Wetlands, Mitigation Banking, and Takings*, 81 Iowa Law Review 527 (1996).

6. For an overview of federal wetlands regulations, *see* Margaret Strand, *Federal Wetlands Law: Part I*, 23 Environmental Law Reporter 10185 (1993); Margaret Strand, *Federal Wetlands Law: Part II*, 23 Environmental Law Reporter 10284 (1993).

7. The term *leveraging* was used by the Supreme Court to describe this kind of arrangement in *Nollan v. California Coastal Comm'n*, 483 U.S. 825, 837 n. 5 (1987).

8. Wis. 2d 7, 201 N.W.2d 761 (1972).

9. N.W.2d at 768.

10. *Id.* at 770.

11. Similar attacks might be made under anti-expropriation provisions of certain international agreements, though such attacks will not be specifically discussed here. *See* Jenny Harbine, *NAFTA Chapter 11 Arbitration: Deciding the Price of Free Trade,* 29 Ecology Law Quarterly 371 (2002) (discussing the decision in the *Metalclad* case under NAFTA).

12. William Treanor, *Jam for Justice Holmes: Reassessing the Significance of* Mahon, 86 Georgia Law Journal 813 (1998). The foundational case is *Pennsylvania Coal v. Mahon,* 260 U.S. 393 (1922). The precise significance of that case is still a matter of debate among scholars. See Robert Brauneis, *"The Foundation of Our 'Regulatory Takings' Jurisprudence": The Myth and Meaning of Justice Holmes's Opinion in* Pennsylvania Coal Co. v. Mahon, 106 Yale Law Journal 613–702 (1996).

13. On the original understanding, *see* David A. Dana and Thomas W. Merrill, Property: Takings 8–25 (2002) (Takings Clause intended to codify existing legal practices); John Hart, *Takings and Compensation in Early America: The Colonial Highway Acts in Social Context,* 40 American Journal of Legal History 253 (1996) (diverse practices of colonies in compensating for land taken for highway use); Kris W. Koben, 1996 Utah Law Review 1211 (early nineteenth-century origins of regulatory takings concept); William Treanor, *The Original Understanding of the Takings Clause and the Political Process,* 95 Columbia Law Review 782 (1995) (Takings Clause directed at government appropriation, not regulation). *But see* Kris Kobach, *The Origins of Regulatory Takings: Setting the Record Straight,* 1996 Utah Law Review 1211 (early courts found takings when government interfered with water rights of downstream landowners or destroyed access by closing streets or highways).

14. A good overview of current doctrine can be found in Dana and Merrill, *supra* note 13.

15. The Court recognized an important exception, allowing an activity to be completely banned when it constitutes a common law nuisance. For discussion of this exception, *see* Richard Lazarus, *Putting the Correct "Spin" on Lucas,* 45 Stanford Law Review 1411 (1993).

16. The Court has also recently extended takings protections to some situations where retroactivity is not involved, causing some confusion in the process. *See Palazzolo v. Rhode Island,* 533 U.S. 606 (2001).

17. For a recent discussion, *see* John Echeverria and Julie Lurman, *Perfectly Astounding Public Rights: Wildlife Protection and the Taking Clause,* 16 Tulane Environmental Law Journal 333 (2003).

18. *See,* e.g., *Loveladies Harbor, Inc. v. United States,* 28 F.3d 1171 (Fed. Cir. 1994). For discussion of the Federal Circuit's approach, *see* Margaret Strand, *Recent Developments in Federal Wetlands Law: Part III,* 26 Environmental Law Report 10399, 10402–403 (1996); Michael Blumm, *The End of Environmental Law: Libertarian Property, Natural Law, and the Just Compensation Clause in the Federal Circuit,* 25 Environmental Law 171 (1995).

19. Other exchange possibilities may also exist. For example, a recent article proposes that coastal landowners be required to exchange reduced takings compensation in the future for subsidized flood insurance in the present. *See* Daniel D.

Barnhizer, *Givings Recapture: Funding Public Acquisition of Private Property Interests on the Coasts,* 27 Harvard Environmental Law Review 297, 368–69 (2003).

20. U.S. 104 (1978).

21. More sophisticated versions include the use of banking to increase the liquidity of the market. *See* Sarah J. Stevenson, *Banking on TDRs: The Government's Role as Banker of Transferable Development Rights,* 73 New York University Law Review 1329 (1998) (student comment).

22. *Id.* at 113–15.

23. *Id.* at 114 n.14.

24. *Id.* at 121.

25. *Id.* at 137.

26. *Id.* at 152.

27. *See* Dwight H. Merriam, *Reengineering Regulation to Avoid Takings,* 33 Urban Law 1, 29–32 (2001). A recent overview of the use of TDRs and their legal implications can be found in James E. Holloway and Donald C. Guy, *The Utility and Validity of TDRs under the Takings Clause and the Role of TDRs in the Takings Equation under Legal Theory,* 11 Pennsylvania State Environmental Law Review 1 (2002).

28. *Suitum v. Tahoe Regional Planning Agency,* 520 U.S. 725, 748 (1997) (Scalia, J., concurring in part and concurring in the judgment).

29. *Id.* at 750.

30. Here, I am thinking particularly of his dissent in *Brown v. Legal Found.,* 122 U.S. 1406, 1421 (2003), where he argued that the owner of a bank account was entitled to compensation when the government received interest on the account, even though the interest could not have been lawfully paid to the owner anyway. Thus, the owner had suffered no financial injury.

31. For further discussion of Justice Scalia's position, *see* Paul Merwin, *Caught between Scalia and the Deep Blue Lake: The Takings Clause and Transferable Development Rights Programs,* 83 Minnesota Law Review 815 (1999) (student note).

32. Arthur J. Miller, *Transferable Development Rights in the Constitutional Landscape: Has* Penn Central *Failed to Weather the Storm?,* 39 Natural Resources Journal 459, 491 (1999).

33. *See* Blaine I. Green, *The Endangered Species Act and Fifth Amendment Takings: Constitutional Limits of Species Protection,* 15 Yale Journal on Reglations 329 (1998)

34. U.S. 825 (1987).

35. *Id.* at 827.

36. *Id.* at 828–29.

37. *Id.* at 834.

38. *Id.* at 837.

39. *Id.*

40. *Id.* at 837 n.5.

41. *Id.* at 838–39.

42. *Id.* at 841.

43. *Dolan v. City of Tigard,* 512 U.S. 374 (1994).

44. *Id.* at 378–79.

45. *Id.* at 387.

46. *Id.* at 387–88.

47. *Id.* at 391.

48. Id. at 395.

49. *See* James Salzman and J. B. Ruhl, *Currencies and the Commodification of Environmental Law,* 53 Stanford Law Review 607 (2000). On the significance of

transaction costs in trading systems, *see* Robert N. Stavins, *Transaction Costs and Tradeable Permits,* 29 Journal of Environmental Economics and Management 133 (1995).

50. *See* Green, *supra* note 33, at 382–83 (finding, however, no evidence that current government demands have suffered from disproportionality).

51. *See* J. B. Ruhl, *Biodiversity Conservation and the Ever-Expanding Web of Federal Laws—Regulating Non Federal Lands: Time for Something Completely Different,* 66 University of Colorado Law Review 555, 633–34 (1995).

52. *See* Holloway and Guy, *supra* note 27, at 92 n. 365 ("In short, the provision of TDRs could mitigate the denial of all economically viable use by permitting the transfer of the right to develop as an alternative use. *Palazzolo* makes the equation more feasible by finding that *Lucas* may not apply where economic value indicates some economic use"); William F. Pedersen, *Using Federal Environmental Regulations to Bargain for Private Land Use Control,* 21 Yale Journal on Regulations 1, 45–46 (2004) (mitigation options would mitigate takings claim, where development restriction would otherwise be a taking under *Penn Central*).

53. *See* Daniel A. Farber, *Who Killed Lochner?,* 90 Georgia Law Journal 985 (2002) (discussing the scholarly disputes and attempting to sort out the historical evidence.)

54. 426 U.S. 833 (1976). In some cases under the CAA, lower courts had anticipated *League of Cities* by striking down direct federal mandates that states establish regulatory programs. *See District of Columbia v. Train,* 521 F.2d 971 (1975); *Brown v. EPA,* 521 827 (9th Cir. 1975) (construing the CAA narrowly to avoid constitutional doubts). In light of the government's concession that the EPA regulations were invalid to the extent they required the states to adopt specific regulations, the Supreme Court vacated and remanded these decisions in *EPA v. Brown,* 431 U.S. 99 (1977).

55. *See,* e.g., *FERC v. Mississippi,* 456 U.S. 742 (1982); *Hodel v. Indiana,* 452 U.S. 314 (1981).

56. *Hodel* makes this point most clearly. It is only when the states themselves were regulated that the doctrine applied.

57. *See Garcia v. San Antonio Metropolitan Transit Authority,* 469 U.S. 528 (1985). This holding itself was slightly qualified in *New York v. United States,* 505 U.S. 144 (1992), which held that Congress could not use its authority under the Commerce Clause to impose direct mandates on state legislators. In *Printz v. United States,* 521 U.S. 98 (1997), the Court extended this rule to federal commandeering of state administrative officers. Both cases, however, make it clear that Congress remains free to place negative restrictions on state officials; what it is not free to do is place direct obligations on state officials to enforce federal programs. As *New York* makes clear, even this rule is subject to leverage: What the federal government cannot do by imposing a direct mandate on state officials, it can do indirectly by demanding active state cooperation as a condition for related federal funding.

58. U.S. 549 (1995).

59. *Id.* at 566.

60. For a sampling of the voluminous commentary on *Lopez,* mostly critical, *see* Herbert Hovenkamp, *Judicial Restraint and Constitutional Federalism: The Supreme Court's* Lopez *and* Seminole Tribe *Decisions,* 96 Columbia Law Review 2213 (1996); Philip Frickey, *The Fool on the Hill,* 46 Case Western Law Review 695 (1996); Lawrence Lessig, *Translating Federalism:* United States v. Lopez, 1996 Supreme Court Review 125; Daniel A. Farber, *The Constitution's Forgotten Cover Letter: An*

Essay on the New Federalism and the Original Understanding, 94 Michigan Law Review. 615 (1995).

61. U.S. 598 (2000).

62. *Id.* at 615.

63. *Id.* at 618.

64. *Katzenbach v. McClung,* 379 U.S. 294 (1964).

65. *Wickard v. Filburn,* 317 U.S. 111 (1942).

66. For a thoughtful overview of the recent decisions, *see* Richard Fallon, *The "Conservative" Path of the Rehnquist Court's Federalism Decisions,* 69 University of Chicago Law Review 429 (2002).

67. Safe Drinking Water Act, 42 U.S.C. §§ 300f to 300j-26.

68. John Dwyer, *The Commerce Clause and the Limits of Congressional Authority to Regulate the Environment,* 25 Environmental Law Report 10421, 10427–28 (1995). The DC Circuit recently rejected a facial attack on the statute on the ground that the SDWA is at a minimum constitutional as applied to utilities that sell drinking water across state lines. *See Nebraska v. EPA,* 331 F.3d 995 (D.C. Cir. 2003).

69. ESA § 9, 16 U.S.C. § 1538.

70. *See Babbitt v. Sweet Home Chapter of Communities for a Greater Oregon,* 515 U.S. 687 (1995) (upholding regulation limiting habitat modifications affecting endangered species).

71. Thus far, the ESA has withstood such constitutional attacks. *See,* e.g., *GDF Realty Investments, Ltd. v. Norton,*362 F.3d 286 (5th Cir. 2004) (denying rehearing en banc to a panel decision upholding application of the act to a small invertebrate that lives in caves); *Rancho Viejo v. Norton,* 323 F.3d 1062 (D.C. Cir. 2003); *Gibbs v. Babbitt,* 214 F.3d 483 (4th Cir. 2000) (Wilkinson, J.) (upholding a regulation that prohibited the taking of red wolves on private lands). For discussion of the constitutional issues, *see* John Nagle, *The Commerce Clause Meets the Delhi-Sands Flower-Loving Fly,* 97 Michigan Law Review 174 (1998).

72. U.S.C. §§ 7401 to 7671q.

73. CWA § 404, 33 U.S.C. § 1344.

74. The lower courts grappled with this issue in cases such as *Hoffman Homes, Inc. v. EPA,* 999 F.2d 256 (7th Cir. 1993), and *United States v. Wilson,* 133 F.3d 251 (4th Cir. 1997).

75. U.S. 159 (2001).

76. *Id.* at 164.

77. *United States v. Riverside Bayview Homes, Inc.,* 474 U.S. 121 (1985).

78. *Id.* at 171–72.

79. *Id.* at 172.

80. *Id.* at 173.

81. *Id.* at 174. Considerable confusion existed over the interpretation of *SWANCC. See* Robin Craig, *Beyond SWANCC: The New Federalism and Clean Water Act Jurisprudence,* 23 Environmental Law 113, 129–36 (2003).

82. The lower courts had difficulties in applying *SWANCC.* Some notable decisions have interpreted federal jurisdiction broadly. While this book was in press, the Supreme Court ruled that wetlands ajacent to nonnavigable tributaries are subject to federal jurisdiction only if they significantly affect downstream navigable waters. *Rapanos v. United States,* 126 S.Ct. 2208 (2006).

83. *United States v. Darby,* 312 U.S. 100 (1941).

84. *Kleppe v. New Mexico,* 426 U.S. 529 (1976).

85. S.Ct. 1941 (2004).

86. *Id.* at 1946.

87. Another example is provided by *Minnesota v. Block*, 660 F.2d 1240 (8th Cir. 1981), cert. denied 455 U.S. 1007 (1982), which upheld a federal ban on the use of snowmobiles on private land to prevent noise from disturbing federal lands. See also *Stupak-Thrall v. United States*, 70 F.3d 881 (6th Cir. 1995)(upholding a federal prohibition on the use of houseboats and sailboats on portions of a lake that were not within an adjoining federal wilderness area).

88. Some difficult design questions might be posed by such a system, to prevent credits for lands that would not have been developed in any event.

89. *See* Pedersen, *supra* note 52, at 41–46.

90. *See* Richard Ayres, *Expanding the Use of Environmental Trading Programs into New Areas of Environmental Regulation,* 18 Pace Environmental Law Review 87, 104–13 (2000); Kurt Stephenson, Leonard Shabman, and L. Leon Geyera, *Toward an Effective Watershed-Based Effluent Allowance Trading System: Identifying the Statutory and Regulatory Barriers to Implementation,* 5 Environmental Lawyer 775 (1999).

91. The EPA could also protect some isolated wetlands by making them the subject of supplemental environmental project agreements with violators of other regulatory requirements. For a discussion of these agreements, *see* Kathleen Boergers, *The EPA's Supplemental Environmental Projects Policy,* 26 Ecological Law Quarterly 777 (1999).

92. *National League of Cities v. Usery, supra,* n. 54 (striking down a law that extended the federal minimum wage to cover state employees).

93. *Garcia v. San Antonio Metropolitan Transit Authority, supra,* n. 57.

94. 505 U.S. 144 (1992).

95. *Printz v. United States,* 521 U.S. 98 (1997) (striking down provisions of a federal gun control statute requiring state law enforcement officials to perform background checks on gun purchasers).

96. *See International Paper Co. v. Ouellette,* 479 U.S. 481 (1987) (nuisance suit may be brought in state or federal court in the "recipient" state, but the court must apply the "emitting" state's nuisance rules).

97. *See Arkansas v. Oklahoma,* 503 U.S. 91 (1992) (CWA mechanism); *Air Pollution Control Dist. v. United States EPA,* 739 F.2d 1071 (6th Cir. 1984) (CAA mechanism).

98. 438 U.S. 203 (1987).

15

A Proposal to Use Transactions to Leverage Environmental Disclosure and Compliance

Michael B. Gerrard

The transfer of property is the occasion—often the only occasion—for a searching examination of the debts and obligations that adhere to the property and of the validity of the title. In a handful of states it is also the time for a study of contamination. When the property is very valuable, as in a large manufacturing facility, the usual transaction costs may be so high that additional studies can be funded without adding a large percentage to the costs. This is especially so when what is being transferred is not just a single facility but a company or a business unit that owns many facilities and other assets.

For these reasons, the transfer of property provides the opportunity for government to require, or at least offer incentives for, a close look at a facility's compliance with a range of environmental laws. The experience to date with the incentives for site investigation provided by the liability scheme for hazardous substances suggests that this mechanism could become a powerful tool for identifying noncompliance with environmental laws and, in many cases, correcting it.

This would be a market-based instrument in the sense that it takes the characteristics of the property market into account in adjusting incentives. Unlike a command-and-control mechanism, which would impose a set of more or less fixed mandates, requiring environmental studies when property is transferred would induce those selling or acquiring property to move toward compliance because—and to the extent that—it would become in their own economic self-interest to do so.

The laws that create liability on the transfer of property have a pervasive impact on the daily practice of environmental law and perhaps inadvertently create greater economic incentives for reducing hazardous wastes than the combination of all the laws that have that as their explicit purpose. My thesis in this chapter is that under current environmental law the transfer of property is the occasion for many important economic incentives, some with positive environmental effects and some with negative ones; with certain adjustments, the positive can be made much more important than the negative. In short, the sound regulation of the transfer of property can address many environmental problems.

CERCLA

The central law in this context is the Comprehensive Environmental Response, Compensation, and Liability Act (CERCLA). The most descriptive words in its name are *comprehensive* and *liability*. CERCLA imposes liability that is more comprehensive than anything else in environmental law and arguably that is more comprehensive than anything else in Anglo-American jurisprudence. Liability is strict, retroactive, and joint and several. Masses of companies and individuals can be classified as potentially responsible parties (PRPs), which sounds like perpetrators, and the punitive connotations have carried over into much of the enforcement stance of the U.S. Environmental Protection Agency (EPA) and the U.S. Department of Justice. CERCLA is much feared and despised by big companies, which resent being held liable for massive expenditures for which they do not feel contractually or morally responsible.

In the world of CERCLA, the early and mid-1980s was an age when lawyers like me would explain to incredulous and infuriated corporate executives why their companies are liable in the tens or hundreds of millions of dollars for the actions of companies they had acquired prior to CERCLA, actions that were perfectly legal at the time they were performed, such as dumping mine tailings in a stream or solvents in a municipal landfill. The late 1980s and early 1990s was an age of lawyers telling incredulous and infuriated bankers that they could be liable for the pollution of their borrowers.[1]

These unpleasant conversations had a lasting impact. They made corporations and banks quite wary of having anything to do with hazardous waste. Because there seemed to be no limits to the zeal of federal government lawyers in expanding the bounds of CERCLA liability and the willingness of federal judges to go along, there was a remarkable overinclusiveness to the deterrent effect.

This deterrent effect operated chiefly in the context of transactions. Before buying a piece of real property, buying a business, or giving a loan or mortgage to someone who wanted to make such a purchase, a corporation or a bank would ask its lawyers to perform due diligence about what liabilities might ensue. If the investigation found a history of hazardous waste, whether actual or strongly suspected, the lawyers were unable to give a clean opinion that the transaction was safe. Thus many deals fell through.

This in turn made companies wary of generating, treating, storing, or disposing of hazardous wastes if they could avoid it, because a history of such activities could impede their ability to attract buyers or financing. This is an economic incentive of enormous magnitude.

The consequences were similarly great. Between 1991 and 1995— probably the years of greatest concern over CERCLA liability in the financial community—the generation of hazardous waste in the United States by large-quantity generators dropped from 306 million tons to 214 million tons, or 30 percent.[2] The Resource Conservation and Recovery Act (RCRA), the principal law regulating the generation, handling, treatment, and disposal of hazardous waste, has no requirement limiting or requiring a reduction in waste generation, in stark contrast to the mandates for pollution reduction in the Clean Air Act (CAA) and the Clean Water Act (CWA). RCRA's 1984 amendments did impose restrictions on land disposal of hazardous waste, but that basically made disposal more costly and required predisposal treatment, without explicitly limiting waste generation.[3] The toxic release reporting requirements of the Emergency Planning and Community Right-to-Know Act (EPCRA) also created an incentive to generate less reportable waste. Thus the remarkable reduction in hazardous waste generation was not dictated by a command-and-control statute; it stemmed in no small part from the costly liability scheme of CERCLA, the costly land disposal restrictions of RCRA, and the publicity penalties of EPCRA. This decrease in hazardous waste generation compares favorably to the percentage reduction during the period 1970–98 of U.S. emissions of several major pollutants heavily regulated by the CAA.[4]

CERCLA also helped to create the environmental site assessment industry—the legions of consultants who investigate the hazardous waste history of a property or a company. Performing a site assessment became a prerequisite to obtaining the innocent purchaser defense under the 1986 amendments to CERCLA and to obtaining the bona fide prospective purchaser defense and other defenses under the 2002 Brownfields amendments to CERCLA. A site assessment is a precondition for obtaining financing for many transactions (especially those involving industrial property) and for obtaining any kind of environmental insurance. Roughly 250,000 Phase I environmental site assessments are now performed in the United States annually; most of them are a direct response to CERCLA liability concerns. The average cost of these is $2,100 each.[5] This comes to about $525 million per year—a massive program of environmental study.

Several consequences have flowed from all the resulting site assessments. Many contaminated areas have been discovered, and as a result many of them have been cleaned up; many of the others were at least managed in a way that avoided human exposure. For those companies that could not avoid hazardous waste in their operations, CERCLA created additional incentives to handle these materials properly because reported spills would show up as a black mark on site assessments and possibly lead to the performance of invasive Phase II assessments instead of the simpler, faster, and cheaper Phase I assessments.

Thus the CERCLA liability scheme has led to tremendously improved practices for the generation, handling, and cleanup of hazardous substances. Only a tiny fraction of contaminated sites are subject to government enforcement; the principal mechanism of this impact is through property, corporate, and financial transactions.

But this liability scheme has also had negative effects. The best-known is the brownfields phenomenon—the situation where slightly contaminated properties remain as blighting influences in their communities because potential purchasers and lenders do not want to touch them for fear of inheriting CERCLA liability. Many contaminated properties are simply kept off the market, not only because no one will buy or finance them (see chapter 10 in this volume) but also because attempting to sell them will expose them to testing and possibly governmental cleanup orders.

Where a site has received governmental attention, CERCLA liability will often lead the largest PRPs to try to draw out the study and cleanup process, so as to postpone the date when they may need to write very large checks.[6] The EPA requires less thorough cleanups when there are financially stable PRPs.[7] Fear of CERCLA liability has also inhibited the development of cleanup technologies, as the firms providing these new technologies fear that they will themselves be drawn into the liability web.[8]

The focus on CERCLA liability has also narrowly shaped the subject matter of environmental site assessments. A facility's greatest environmental and health impacts are likely to come from its ongoing operation— its current emissions into the air and the water, and the exposure of its workers to toxic chemicals. However, site assessments instead concentrate on the presence of contamination on and below the surface, because that is the primary subject of CERCLA liability. The 2002 Brownfields amendments to CERCLA endorse American Society for Testing and Materials (ASTM) Standard no. E1527–97 as the approved protocol for site assessments until the EPA devises its own.[9] That standard centers on finding historical contamination. It does not look at the facility's compliance with the CWA, the CAA, or the other command-and-control statutes (other than RCRA, the hazardous waste management law), and it does not examine occupational safety and health issues.[10] The EPA adopted its own Standards and Practices for All Appropriate Inquiries in November 2005; they have these same characteristics as the ASTM standard.[11]

Some corporations with strong environmental policies order assessments that do consider a broad array of compliance issues. It is entirely feasible to do compliance reviews, but they are the exception rather than the rule because the law generally does not require them or provide incentives for preparing them.

The site assessments that stem from CERCLA's liability scheme, and the associated efforts to reduce and apportion liability under that statute, are at the center of what many if not most environmental lawyers in the private sector do every day. This is not a law at the periphery; it is at the red hot core of how environmental law is practiced today by tens of thousands of lawyers throughout the country. In contrast, I estimate that environmental trading systems seriously engage no more than a few hundred lawyers (though that may change in coming years as greenhouse gas regulation through cap-and-trade regimes begins in earnest).[12]

OTHER IMPACTS OF CERCLA ON PROPERTY TRANSFER

The liability scheme of CERCLA secs. 107 and 113 as originally enacted in 1980 and 1986 had the effect of leading to liability in the transactional context, and the 1986 and 2002 amendments codified that site assessments on transfer are necessary to utilize certain defenses. Several other aspects of CERCLA also impose environmental consequences at the time of property transfer.

One of them is CERCLA sec. 120(h),[13] which provides that before a federal agency may transfer property on which hazardous substances had been stored for a year or more or had been released or disposed of, the agency must give notice to the purchaser, record the notice in the deed, and (subject to certain exceptions) warrant that it has undertaken any necessary remediation.[14]

In the implementation of CERCLA cleanups, one important technique to limit cleanup costs is to perform only a partial cleanup, and then impose "institutional controls" to ensure that the property is not later put to a use (typically residential) that would have required a greater degree of cleanup.[15] A common type of institutional control is the deed restriction that passes on a use limitation to subsequent owners. These restrictions, imposed as part of the property trading process, may not do much good for the environment, but they have a public health benefit because they reduce human exposure to contamination.

Liens are often used to recover, at the time of property transfer, the costs of governmental site investigation and cleanup. Such liens are imposed under CERCLA[16] and under many state cleanup programs.[17] The 2002 amendments to CERCLA specify that the EPA may recover "windfall liens" on property to the extent that the EPA's cleanup actions have increased its fair market value.[18]

OTHER FEDERAL LAWS

A few other federal environmental programs impose obligations or make recommendations at the time of transactions. For example, regulations pursuant to the Residential Lead-Based Paint Hazard Reduction Act of 1992 require disclosure of lead hazards at the time of the purchase, sale, or lease of certain residential dwellings,[19] and the EPA recommends testing for radon at or before the sale of certain kinds of residential properties.[20]

STATE LAWS

Several states have adopted laws that require site investigations, disclosures, and sometimes even cleanups before property can be transferred. The best known and most demanding of these laws is the New Jersey Industrial Site Recovery Act (ISRA). The owner or operator of an industrial establishment in New Jersey may not transfer or close its operation until it has determined whether the site is contaminated and, if it is, until the state environmental agency has found that provisions are in place to assure its cleanup.[21] In Connecticut, the owner of an establishment where hazardous substances were generated or spilled must make disclosure to potential purchasers and either clean it up or made provisions to do so.[22] Numerous other states have laws that require study and disclosure on transfer.[23]

Beginning with California in 1985, many states have adopted legislation requiring sellers of residential real property and participating brokers to disclose to prospective purchasers specified information about the condition of the property, often including environmental conditions.[24] Moreover, state common law typically provides that if a property owner has knowledge of latent defects, he or she is liable on failure to disclose that defect to a purchaser.[25]

A few local governments have passed laws imposing other restrictions at the time of property transfer. Two Michigan counties require that on-site water and sewage disposal systems be inspected when property is transferred.[26] Marin County, California, requires the installation of ultra-low-flow toilets when a home is sold.[27] In some states the transfer of property by or to a governmental agency also triggers environmental review under the state little NEPA laws.[28]

OTHER COMPLIANCE AUDITING REQUIREMENTS

As noted, site assessments performed under CERCLA focus on a site's current practices and prior history with respect to hazardous waste, with little attention to other aspects of environmental compliance. Some corporations have set up elaborate internal monitoring systems concerning compliance with all manner of laws, though there is substantial question in the academic literature (though not focused specifically on environmental compliance) about whether the benefits of such systems in improving compliance exceed the considerable costs of such systems, or "largely serve a window-dressing function that provides both market legitimacy and reduced legal liability."[29]

The Delaware Chancery Court, one of the most important tribunals in U.S. corporate law, has suggested that corporations should set up information-gathering and monitoring mechanisms designed to ensure legal compliance.[30] It does not appear that this conclusion has been translated into a standard practice at most corporations for systematic monitoring of environmental compliance.

Various rules of the Securities and Exchange Commission (SEC), especially those under the SEC's Regulation S-K, mandate environmental disclosures. Item 101 of this regulation requires a company to disclose any material effects that compliance with federal, state, or local environmental laws may have on the company's financial situation.[31] Item 103 requires disclosure of any pending legal proceedings against the issuer other than ordinary, routine litigation. An environmental proceeding must be disclosed if it is material to the business or financial condition of the company, or if it involves primarily a claim for damages, or involves potential monetary sanctions or capital expenditures exceeding 10 percent of the current assets of the company; or a government authority is a party to such a proceeding and there are potential monetary sanctions of at least $100,000.[32] Item 303 requires a statement of "Management's Discussion and Analysis" that must include disclosure of events that could have a material impact on net sales, revenues, or income.[33] Along similar lines, the SEC's Staff Accounting Bulletin no. 92 requires the disclosure of certain environmental contingencies if they are "reasonably estimable."[34]

The materiality threshold means that a liability must be very large before it must be disclosed by a large corporation, and the reasonably estimable requirement creates a very large exception from the disclosure rule. Moreover, the U.S. Government Accountability Office has found that there is very little monitoring by the SEC of compliance with these rules.[35] The Sarbanes Oxley Act requires top corporate executives to certify their companies' SEC filings, and it mandates the implementation of an internal management system, but it does not require more environmental disclosure than is already mandated. Standards from the Financial Accounting Standards Board and the American Institute of Certified Public Accountants also require certain environmental disclosures, but here, too, only a very limited amount of environmental disclosure actually takes place as a result.

All in all, several recent studies find that existing disclosures fall far short of revealing corporations' environmental compliance situation in any depth at all.[36] Lawyers performing environmental due diligence know that a company's SEC filings are unlikely to reveal anything but perhaps a few extremely large environmental liabilities; these filings merely skim the surface of what an environmental compliance assessment would explore.

OPTIMIZING THE USE OF PROPERTY TRANSFER RESTRICTIONS

CERCLA, ISRA, and other laws have shown that the imposition of restrictions or liabilities at the time of property transfer and other transactions is extremely powerful. Unfortunately this powerful tool has been directed to a relatively minor problem.[37] It is very difficult to find estimates of the number of lives saved by CERCLA cleanups in the aggregate; in fact using the only study I have found that attempts to calculate this number, and if realistic exposure assumptions are used, the total number of lives saved nationwide by all CERCLA cleanups combined seems to be somewhere between one and ten.[38] Perhaps a few more were saved by restrictions on entry to or use of contaminated sites as a result of the statute. In contrast, according to some estimates tens of thousands of people in the United States die annually of air pollution,[39] and more than 17,000 die from inhalation of cancer-causing agents in the workplace.[40] One can only imagine the number of lives that could have been saved had it become almost impossible in the 1980s and the 1990s to buy or sell a business that emitted substantial air pollution or where any workers were exposed to dangerous levels of chemicals on the job. But there are no laws that create a compelling economic incentive to avoid such transfers.

Now that we know that property transfer restrictions are such a powerful tool, we should consider how to make the most of it. A solution could draw on CERCLA and ISRA but expand their scope: Provide incentives to perform an environmental compliance assessment whenever control over a permit is transferred. This would increase the kinds of transactions that trigger assessments and broaden the scope of those assessments.

Environmental assessments prior to property transfer have a powerful economic logic. The absence of information about site and facility conditions, or the existence of asymmetric information, creates poor (inefficient) outcomes. Generating and disclosing this information at the time of property or permit transfer brings market pressures to bear. Potential buyers may offer lower prices for properties with lingering environmental problems if they know about them. This lower price gives sellers an incentive to take action to resolve the problems or to accept a lower price when the buyer may be in a better position than the seller to resolve them.

Governmental intervention is unnecessary if all buyers—or at least those making competitive bids—insist on full information. But that is often not the case. In certain sectors of the economy, all market participants know that particular environmental problems are likely to exist, but they also know that the government is unlikely to learn of or take action against those problems unless someone makes affirmative disclosure. Thus the buyers may simply not want to know of the problems if their knowledge imposes an obligation to disclose and possibly to correct. Indeed, sellers often impose and buyers often accept conditions in purchase agreements that the buyers *may not* conduct certain kinds of site investigations before closing. This phenomenon may not appear in the literature, and there appear to be no statistics about it, but I have often observed it myself in the course of representing parties in transactions. Even more common, in my experience, is the conversation between the client and the lawyer about the degree of scrutiny desired in the environmental due diligence; some purchasers only want to know about $100 million liabilities, because anything smaller is immaterial to the transaction, whereas others have a much lower threshold. Practitioners also often advise each other not to tell the government more about environmental conditions than they have to.[41] Government inspection resources are so limited that only a fraction of environmental conditions will ever be discovered—and even if they are, only a fraction of those will ever become the subject of enforcement action, given the limitations on enforcement personnel and also the pervasive ambiguities in regulations that make their actual application to specific facilities an exercise in discerning shades of gray.[42] Thus the prospect that a vaguely suspected (but not searched for) noncompliance will lead to governmental discovery, and then to an expensive corrective action, involves multiple layers of speculation: Is there really noncompliance? If so, will the government learn about it? If so, will the government attempt to require that it be corrected? If so, will the government prevail in this attempt? If so, what will it cost to correct the problem, when will that expenditure be incurred, and who (shareholders, customers, taxpayers) will bear that expense? When all these uncertainties are multiplied out, it may be difficult for a purchaser to argue effectively that suspected noncompliance should lead to a real price reduction. If the price were discounted to reflect presumed noncompliance, the seller would have an incentive to achieve and demonstrate compliance; but the uncertainties are typically so great that possible environmental noncompliance will ultimately burden the buyer that this factor is often lost in the already complex process of setting the price of a transaction.

During a large corporate or real estate deal, however, often so much money is at stake that the added cost of an environmental investigation is minor and readily absorbed within the context of transaction costs that are already enormous. Thus if the law required that such an assessment be performed, it could certainly be done. If the requirement for and approximate magnitude of a compliance cost were anticipated before the transaction closed, the cost could be reflected in the deal, and after the closing the buyer would be less likely to resist it as an unanticipated or unfunded expenditure.

The assessments should look not only for indicia of subsurface contamination but also at the facility's current compliance with the CAA, the CWA, the Occupational Safety and Health Act, and the other important command-and-control laws. Knowledge of a past unpermitted release of air or water pollution may be of little relevance, for the effluent will likely have irretrievably drifted away; however, it may ultimately cause damage downwind or downstream through airborne deposition, bioaccumulation, or some other mechanism. Pinning harmful chemicals to a particular source with enough certainty to impose liability is only possible in those unusual cases where chemical fingerprinting or the like is possible. But an ongoing violation can be remedied and thus is worth knowing about. Ultimately a uniform kind of compliance/contamination assessment might be required for both the kinds of transactions that can lead to CERCLA liability and the permit transfers that trigger a compliance inspection; often they are the same transactions.

ISRA was drafted to capture transfers of the control of property—not only when title changes but also when the ownership of the title-owning entity changes, when ninety-nine-year or longer leases are executed, or when other triggering events occur. A permit is a kind of property; conceptually there is no reason why a law could not be enacted providing that the transfer of ownership or control of a permit triggers an environmental compliance assessment. There might be an initial instinct to set a dollar threshold below which a transaction does not trigger an assessment, but in practice many extremely contaminated properties may be sold for a nominal amount—below any likely threshold level—precisely because they are in such bad condition. Those are among the transactions for which an environmental assessment is most important. But one could devise a safe harbor provision that would exempt certain kinds of otherwise covered properties from the assessment requirement, where for example there is already sufficient information to establish that there are no environmental problems. Similarly, the incentives to perform site assessments might proceed in steps, with more thorough assessments called for at properties that pose more serious environmental risks; that would increase the proportionality between the costs and benefits of these studies.

If a statute explicitly and unambiguously requires pretransaction compliance assessments, there should be little doubt that such assessments will be performed. And if there are clear protocols about what must be included in such assessments (along the lines of the EPA's All Appropriate Inquiry regulations), the adequacy of the assessments can be reasonably ensured. The statute could make a certificate from a licensed professional that an assessment was performed in accordance with set standards a condition of the closing of the transaction. That way the participants in the transaction who make it their business to be sure that all closing conditions are met (typically the title company and the bank) will insist that the assessment has been done, and the professionals who certified that the assessment met the standards will not want to jeopardize their licenses by doing an inadequate job. Moreover, these professionals could also be subject to malpractice actions and other civil liabilities if their assessments were later shown to have missed an important instance of noncompliance that should have been caught under the standard procedures. Thus even if the sellers and the buyers have their own incentives not to do so, there is nonetheless a ready mechanism to ensure that an adequate assessment is performed. That is not to say that environmental assessments will always be done when they should, or that they will be perfect, but the statute proposed here should lead to a reasonably high level of performance.

On the other hand, requiring the completion of the assessment before a transaction can close would collide with the fast pace of many corporate and real estate deals. The predecessor statute of ISRA was met with tremendous outcries from the business community, in no small measure because it imperiled or impeded many transactions.[43] This led to amendments in 1993 that reduced the barriers, sped up the process, and clarified many ambiguities.[44] Some of the lessons of this cautionary tale can be followed by providing incentives to increase the number of assessments that are performed but not making the assessments mandatory, at least prior to closing. For example, for companies that perform these assessments, the expiration date of the permits could be extended, penalty relief could be granted for pretransaction violations (comparable to CERCLA's new bona fide prospective purchaser defense), and environmental liens could be waived. The costs and benefits of these incentives would have to be assessed, of course. Additionally, performance of these assessments could be made an element of certification that environmental management systems are in place (already an element of some governmental incentive programs)[45] or that a company or building is "green" (and thus, in some states, entitled to certain tax benefits). Insurance companies might well require these assessments before providing environmental coverage. As a more extreme measure, but still short of always requiring an environmental assessment, a statute could require that some portion of the closing cost must be deposited in governmental escrow until a certified environmental assessment is performed. An incentive for speedy performance of the assessment would be provided if the government kept the interest earned on the escrow.

I do not recommend that full environmental compliance (as opposed to completion of the assessment) be made a precondition of closing. Often the buyers are in a better position than the sellers to achieve compliance, and the buyers will have the future responsibility of remaining in compliance. If both parties to the transaction have full information, they can make appropriate adjustments in the price and other terms of the deal to reflect their agreement about which costs are to be borne by which party. Requiring preclosing compliance could be counterproductive because it could inhibit the sale of many properties or businesses to entities that are better equipped to achieve and maintain compliance. Moreover, if a company acquires a facility that it knows is violating environmental laws and does not quickly move to correct the violation, the company may be subject to criminal penalties and (if the noncompliance is causing injury to others) punitive damages in toxic tort litigation.

The question arises whether the government should mandate public disclosure of the results of the environmental assessments. A number of federal and state statutes and regulations already require that the government be informed—sometimes within the hour—on the occurrence or discovery of certain kinds of spills and other hazards.[46] The SEC also requires disclosure of certain conditions, especially those that would materially affect the balance sheets of public companies.[47] Public disclosure of information about emissions and violations has been found to have a significant effect on corporate behavior.[48] Whether, beyond those requirements, privately conducted site assessments had to be disclosed to the government was the subject of great debate in the late 1990s, in the context of demands by some environmental enforcement agencies for copies of environmental audit reports, and resistance by some states that sought to shield those reports from discovery. The ultimate result was an EPA policy that shielded these reports but with important exceptions, such as when criminal activity or imminent and substantial endangerment to public health or the environment is involved.[49] This debate led to a general understanding that requiring the routine disclosure of voluntarily performed environmental audit reports would powerfully inhibit their preparation. This argument applies with much less force if there is a legal mandate to require their preparation, though mandatory public disclosure might make sellers less candid in sharing information with site assessors.

There would, of course, be transition issues in implementing a system that required the preparation of site assessments. The transferability terms of existing environmental permits vary widely; some permits may be freely transferred,[50] and other transfers can be fully effectuated only on an exhaustive demonstration of the transferee's suitability and financial capacity.[51] The government may modify permits if certain administrative procedures are followed and subject to certain conditions.[52] It has been held as a general proposition that a permit holder has no property right to renewal of that permit,[53] but when a permit by its own terms can be renewed or transferred as of right, a legitimate expectation can be formed on which investments may be based. Thus, depending on the particular permits involved, a substantial phase-in period may be required for a new system under which an environmental compliance audit (especially one that looks at compliance with requirements other than those embodied in the subject permit) can be required before a permit transfer may be effected.

Limitations on permit transfers can address an important environmental justice issue. Environmental and land use statutes—whether at the federal, state, or local level—typically have grandfather provisions that allow facilities to continue operating under old regulations even after new rules are put into place. A consequence is that manufacturing units may continue to cause pollution in excess of current standards. Given historical patterns of plant siting, many of these old facilities are located in what are now minority and low-income communities. Today's procedural and substantive requirements for the siting of new facilities (especially in the waste management sector) are so stringent that the net effect is that old facilities continue to operate in minority communities because new ones cannot be sited anywhere.[54] One partial way to address this problem would be to limit the transferability of grandfathered permits. The subject facilities are typically so old that the investment in their construction was fully amortized years earlier. Some states and municipalities have used amortization periods as a way to achieve the closure of prior nonconforming uses.[55] Proposals to limit transferability might be met with arguments that it is an impermissible restraint on alienation as well as a taking, but if it were coupled with showings that, for example, the facility posed public health or environmental risks and that the investment had been amortized, it might well survive, and this technique might help reduce the disproportionate exposure of minority communities to environmental insults. If this technique is deemed to be too bold, at least requiring an environmental compliance assessment when facility ownership is transferred would reduce the chances that facilities in minority communities will continue their excessive pollution.

In recent years environmental advocacy organizations have exerted increasing pressure on financial institutions to make environmental impacts a major factor in their lending decisions; one manifestation of this pressure was the issuance of the Collevecchio Declaration in January 2003 by over 100 nongovernmental organizations.[56] Several months later, ten leading banks from seven countries announced the adoption of the Equator Principles, a voluntary set of guidelines for managing social and environmental issues in the financing of development projects. The guidelines apply to projects with a total capital cost of $50 million or more. They require the preparation of environmental assessments and, in some cases, environmental management plans. These assessments will look not only at historical hazardous waste practices but also at a much broader range of current environmental and social impacts.[57]

The experience of CERCLA has shown that when lending institutions take an environmental hazard seriously, the practices of their borrowers can be profoundly affected. The Equator Principles and similar voluntary measures attempt to use the market mechanism of lender oversight as a force for environmental improvement. A statute that compels preclosing environmental compliance assessments could be an even greater force. It would depend very little on governmental oversight if, as proposed, the private enforcers of closing obligations—lenders and title companies— were required to make sure that assessments were performed, and those performing the assessments had to certify that the assessments met set standards, at peril of losing their licenses or being subject to civil liabilities.

ACKNOWLEDGMENTS The author is indebted to Tom Tietenberg, Jody Freeman, Charles Kolstad, Michael Vandenbergh, and the participants in the Santa Barbara conference for their constructive comments on this chapter.

NOTES

1. In view of the very limited number of cases in which banks and other lenders have been held liable for the hazardous waste activities of their borrowers, it is entirely possible that these cautions were overstated. However, they indisputably had an impact on the behavior of lenders. For a theoretical treatment of how some lawyers overstate risks to their clients, see Donald C. Langevoort and Robert K. Rasmussen, *Skewing the Results: The Role of Lawyers in Transmitting Legal Rules*, 5 Southern California Interdisciplinary Law Journal 375 (1996–97).

2. U.S. Environmental Protection Agency, Office of Solid Waste and Emergency Response, *National Biennial RCRA Hazardous Waste Report*, 1991 and 1995, www.epa.gov/epaoswer/hazwaste/data. After 1995 the EPA changed reporting definitions in a way that makes it very difficult to derive comparable numbers for the post-1995 period.

3. 42 U.S.C. § 6924.

4. Robert W. Hahn, Sheila M. Olmstead, and Robert N. Stavins, *Environmental Regulation in the 1990s: A Retrospective Analysis*, 27 Harvard Environmental Law Review 377, 411 (2003).

5. ICF Consulting, *Economic Impact Analysis for the Proposed All Appropriate Inquiries Regulation* (Office of Brownfields Cleanup and Redevelopment, U.S. Environmental Protection Agency, August 3, 2004).

6. *See* Gordon C. Rausser et al., *Information Asymmetries, Uncertainties, and Cleanup Delays at Superfund Sites*, 35 Journal of Environmental Economics and Management 48 (1998) (cleanup takes longer at sites with larger PRP liability).

7. Hillary Sigman, *Liability Funding and Superfund Clean-Up Remedies*, 35 Journal of Environmental Economics and Management 205 (1998).

8. Daniel Mazmanian and David Morell, Beyond Superfailure: America's Toxics Policy for the 1990s 107 (1992).

9. 42 U.S.C. § 9601(35)(B)(iv)(II).

10. ASTM, E1527–97, Standard Practice for Environmental Assessments: Phase I Environmental Site Assessment Process (1997).

11. 40 C.F.R. pt. 312.

12. One may ask whether the environmental consequences of trading systems (such as acid rain reduction) exceed the environmental consequences of the work undertaken by the far larger number of lawyers involved in managing CERCLA liabilities and the like, such that the lawyers involved in the former are much more important for the environment than the lawyers involved in the latter. There are so many incommensurables in that question that I do not know how to address it.

13. 42 U.S.C. § 9620(h); 40 C.F.R. pt. 373.

14. *See* Susan L. Smith, *Remediation and Redevelopment of Contaminated Federal Facilities*, in Brownfields Law and Practice: The Cleanup and Redevelopment of Contaminated Land (Michael B. Gerrard, ed., 2006 supp.) § 14.07.

15. See Amy L. Edwards, ed., Implementing Institutional Controls at Brownfields and Other Contaminated Sites (2003); Lawrence P. Schnapf, *Institutional Controls*, in Brownfields Law and Practice: The Cleanup and Redevelopment of Contaminated Land (Michael B. Gerrard, ed., 2006 supp.), ch. 24; John Pendergrass, *Sustainable Redevelopment of Brownfields: Using Institutional Controls to Protect Public Health*, 29 Environmental Law Report 10,243 (1999).

16. 42 U.S.C. § 9607(1); *see also Reardon v. United States*, 947 F.2d 1509 (1st Cir. 1991) (holding aspects of EPA enforcement of CERCLA liens to violate due process clause of Constitution).

17. *See* Cheryl Kessler Clark, *Due Process and the Environmental Lien: The Need for Legislative Reform*, 20 Boston CollegeEnvironmental Affairs LawReview 203 (1993).

18. 42 U.S.C. § 9607(r).

19. 24 C.F.R. § 35.84, 40 C.F.R. pt. 745.

20. EPA, EPA's Strategy to Reduce Risk of Radon 18 (June 1993).

21. N.J. Stat. Ann. § 13:1K-9, N.J. Admin. Code Tit. 7, §§ 26B et seq.

22. Conn. Gen. Stat. § 22a-134.

23. David B. Farer, *Transaction-Triggered Environmental Laws*, in Environmental Aspects of Real Estate Transactions 70 (James B. Witkin, ed., 2d ed., 1999).

24. *See* Robert M. Washburn, *Residential Real Estate Condition Disclosure Legislation*, 44 DePaul Law Review 381 (1995); Judith G. Tracy, *Beyond Caveat Emptor: Disclosure to Buyers of Contaminated Land*, 10 Stanford Environmental Law Journal 169 (1991).

25. Restatement (Second) of Torts § 353 (1965).

26. Washtenaw County (*see* www.ewashtenaw.org/government/departments/environmental_health/wells_septic); Macomb County (*see* www.co.macomb.mi.us/publichealth/Env%20Health/Onsite%20sewage).

27. *See* www.marinwater.org/TOS.html.

28. *Devitt v. Heimbach*, 58 N.Y.2d 925, 460 N.Y.S.2d 512 (1983) (transfer of real property by government agency is subject to review under the New York State Environmental Quality Review Act). But *see* *Sierra Club v. City of Industry*, No. B160270 (Cal. App. Ct. June 26, 2003) (city purchase of wilderness land from the Boy Scouts of America not subject to review under California Environmental Quality Review Act when there are no plans to alter it).

29. Kimberly D. Krawiec, *Cosmetic Compliance and the Failure of Negotiated Governance*, 81 Washington University Law Quarterly 487, 491 (2003); similarly, Donald C. Langevoort, *Monitoring: The Behavioral Economics of Corporate Compliance with Law*, 2002 Columbia Business Law Review 71.

30. *In re Caremark International Inc. Derivative Litigation*, 698 A.2d 959 (Del. Ch. 1996).

31. 17 C.F.R. § 229.101(c)(xii).

32. 17 C.F.R. § 229.103.

33. 17 C.F.R. § 229.303.

34. 58 Federal Register 32843, 32851 (June 8, 1993).

35. U.S. Government Accountability Office, Rep. GAO-04–808, Environmental Disclosure: SEC Should Explore Ways to Improve Tracking and Transparency of Information (July 2004).

36. *See* Robert Repetto, *Are Companies Coming Clean?* Environmental Forum, September/October 2004, p. 19.

37. The relatively minor health and environmental impacts of hazardous waste contamination in comparison to air pollution and certain other environmental insults is extensively discussed in the literature on comparative risk assessment. *See* Daniel T. Hornstein, *Reclaiming Environmental Law: A Normative Critique of Comparative Risk Analysis*, 92 Columbia Law Review 562 (1992).

38. James T. Hamilton and W. Kip Viscusi, Calculating Risks? The Spatial and Economic Dimensions of Hazardous Waste Policy 15–16, 91–108 (1999). These figures focus on long-term cleanups rather than short-term removal actions, such as removing leaking barrels or evacuating residents; removal actions probably save more lives at far lower cost than long-term cleanups, but no estimates of the lives saved appear to be available.

39. D. W. Dockery and C. A. Pope III, *Acute Respiratory Effects of Particulate Air Pollution*, 15 Annual Review of Public Health 107 (1994).

40. American Lung Association, *Occupational Health*, www.lungusa.org/occupational.

41. *See* e.g., Gordon C. Duus and Douglas I. Eilender, *Reporting Historical Contamination: Report Only When Required, Because Doing So May Create an Obligation to Investigate and Clean up the Property*, New Jersey Law Journal, February 16, 2004.

42. *See* David L. Markell, *The Role of Deterrence-Based Enforcement in a "Re-invented" State/Federal Relationship: The Divide between Theory and Reality,* 24 Harvard Environmental Law Review 1 (2000).

43. David B. Farer, *ECRA Verdict: The Successes and Failures of the Premiere Transaction-Triggered Environmental Law,* 5 Pace Environmental Law Review 113 (1987).

44. David B. Farer, *Industrial Site Recovery Act: New Jersey's Chosen Road to ECRA Reform,* 8 Toxics Law Report 147 (BNA) (July 7, 1993); Mark K. Dowd, *New Jersey's Reform of Contaminated Site Remediation,* 18 Seton Hall Legislative Journal 207 (1993).

45. *See* Michael B. Gerrard, *EPA, DEC Expand Roles of Environmental Management Systems,* New YorkLaw Journal 3, July 23, 2004.

46. The most important of these requirements is section 103(a) of CERCLA, 42 U.S.C. § 9603(a). Others are found, e.g., in the CWA, 33 U.S.C. § 1321(b)(3), (5), RCRA, 40 C.F.R. § 280.12, 280.61, the EPCRA, 42 U.S.C. §§ 11001 et seq., the Hazardous Materials Transportation Act, 49 C.F.R. § 5103(a), the Toxic Substances Control Act, 40 C.F.R. § 761.120, and elsewhere.

47. 17 C.F.R. pt. 229.

48. *See* David Case, *The Law and Economics of Environmental Information as Regulation,* 31 Environmental Law Report 10773 (2001); Bradley C. Karkkainen, *Information as Environmental Regulation: TRI and Performance Benchmarking, Precursor to a New Paradigm,* 89 Georgia Law Journal 257 (2001).

49. EPA, *Final Policy Statement on Incentives for Self-Policing: Discovery, Disclosure, Correction and Prevention of Violations,* 65 Federal Register 19618 (Apr. 11, 2000), www.epa.gov/compliance/resources/policies/incentives/auditing/finalpolstate.pdf.

50. *See* National Pollutant Discharge Elimination System (water pollution) permits, 40 C.F.R. § 122.61.

51. *See* RCRA permits, 40 C.F.R. § 270.40.

52. For the general EPA regulations on the procedures for permit transfers, *see* 40 C.F.R. § 124.5.

53. *United States v. 42.13 Acres of Land,* 73 F.3d 953 (9th Cir.), cert. denied sub. nom. *Pacific Gas & Electric Co. v. U.S.,* 518 U.S. 1017 (1996).

54. *See* Heidi Gorovitz Robertson, *If Your Grandfather Could Pollute, So Can You: Environmental "Grandfather Clauses" and Their Role in Environmental Inequity,* 45 Catholic University Law Review 131 (1995); Michael B. Gerrard, *The Victims of NIMBY?,* 21 Fordham Urban Law Journal 495 (1994).

55. Robertson, *supra* note 54, at 173–76; *see also Harbison v. City of Buffalo,* 152 N.E.2d 42 (1958).

56. *See* Rainforest Action Network, Collective NGO Analysis of the Equator Principles (2003), available at www.ran.org/news/equator_ngo.html.

57. *The 'Equator Principles,'* available at www.equator-principles.com/princi ples.shtml.

16

Design, Trading, and Innovation

David M. Driesen

Proponents of economic incentives frequently state that emissions trading promotes technological innovation.[1] This chapter examines the claim that this trading of compliance obligations fosters innovation. Although I use the term *emissions trading* throughout for the sake of concreteness, the claims made here apply fully to other kinds of environmental benefit trading.

This chapter makes two theoretical claims and two empirical claims. The first theoretical claim is that emissions trading does a poorer job, in theory, of encouraging expensive innovation than traditional regulation. I will also argue that expensive innovation has special value that justifies the expense in some important cases. The second theoretical claim is that emissions trading may perform worse than traditional regulation in encouraging inexpensive innovation as well, at least in theory.[2]

My first empirical claim is that both emissions trading and traditional regulation have sometimes encouraged innovation and sometimes failed to do so. My second claim is that we do not have convincing empirical evidence that trading fosters innovation better than a comparably designed traditional regulation.

A casual review of the literature might lead one to assume that emissions trading's advantages in encouraging innovation are well established both in theory and empirically.[3] The theory many academics mention most often, I will argue, focuses too much attention on the incentives trading creates for sellers of credits and pays too little attention to the incentives created for buyers. It also relies on a skewed picture of traditional regulation created by academic lawyers. In light of these problems with the basis for the trading encouraging innovation argument, it is not surprising that some economists have recently questioned the premise that emissions trading always provides superior incentives for innovation.[4]

The empirical case, I argue, is much more difficult than generally assumed. The choice between authorizing and not authorizing trading is not the only variable in a regulation that influences innovation. Decisions about the form and stringency of limits are also important.[5] It is difficult to tell whether innovation observed in conjunction with a trading program would have occurred with a performance standard providing identical emission limits but not authorizing trading. The empirical literature has not always rigorously considered counterfactuals in assessing a trading program's capacity to encourage innovation.

I limit these claims to grandfathered trading programs in which allowances are given away rather than sold. Whether or not polluters can trade allowances, a requirement that all polluters purchase allowances for each ton of pollution can create incentives to innovate and reduce pollution. This chapter, however, focuses on emissions trading programs that give away limited allowances for free and then authorize trades to redistribute them. I choose this approach because all existing U.S. pollution trading programs give away (rather than sell) the overwhelming majority of allowances, and because this focus sharpens analysis of trading's effect on innovation.

The first part of this chapter will establish some background concepts. It will define innovation, explain its value, and establish an analytical framework that will inform the rest of the chapter. This analytical framework posits that to compare a trading program to a traditional regulation, one needs to compare programs with identical underlying emission limits. More widespread use of this framework will improve the rigor of both theoretical and empirical analysis.

The next two parts defend the theoretical and then the empirical claims. The fourth part explains the analysis's implications. I argue that we need to consider more imaginative use of economic incentives with an explicit goal of encouraging innovation, rather than short-term efficiency. I also spell out a research agenda suggested by the analytical framework and subsequent analysis.

INNOVATION AND TRADING: A FRAMEWORK

Defining Innovation

Most of the literature claiming that emissions trading fosters innovation does not define innovation. Economists frequently define innovation as the commercialization of an invention.[6] They distinguish this from diffusion— the adoption of a successful innovation by firms or individuals.

This definition of *innovation* as commercialization separate from invention jibes less well with common understandings of what innovation connotes in the environmental area than it does in the production of goods. For most people, innovation involves some nonobvious change. But a definition of innovation as commercialization might accept uses of very well understood but not yet widely deployed pollution reducing technique as innovation. If this were the case, then a lot of command-and-control regulation would be seen as innovation-inducing, because it has frequently spurred use of well-understood but little used technological options. But the policy literature usually treats adoption of techniques well understood by regulators or polluting firms as diffusion, not innovation.

For this reason, I define *innovation* as involving both the invention and use of something new. Newness, however, means something more than "it has not been done" before by a particular company or even industry. A company with no environmental controls may adopt standard, well-established techniques used in the past by their competitors or by another industry. This normally involves technological diffusion, not technological innovation.

Innovation implies a nonobvious departure from prior practice, to borrow a concept found in patent law. Innovation in this sense advances the state of the art. As we shall see, innovation defined in this manner has special value. I refer to this as the "newness" definition. This definition implies that a regulatory program induces innovation when a polluter or vendor develops a new technique in response to that program and then a polluter uses the technique to reduce pollution but does not generally accept diffusion of techniques invented before the program's onset as innovations.

A second concept will also prove useful here, that of radical innovation. Radical innovation in the environmental area addresses multiple pollution problems simultaneously and changes fundamental technologies at the base of the economy, not just end-of-the-pipe controls. Examples might include switches from fossil fuels to renewable energy and from pesticide-based agriculture to organic agriculture or genetically modified crops.

The need to distinguish innovation from diffusion to analyze instrument choice influence on innovation makes empirical research difficult no matter what definition is employed.[7] The newness definition implies a need to assess the novelty of a technological changes. This chapter's references to innovation will apply the newness definition unless otherwise stated. It will assume that radical innovation is a subset of innovations found under the newness rubric.

The Importance of Innovation

Innovation can perform one of two basic functions. It can lower the cost of a product or increase its quality.[8] Computers with word processing programs, for example, cost much more than pen and paper or a typewriter, but they offer a much higher quality writing aid, making revision relatively easy.

So too with environmental innovation.[9] Innovation can reduce the cost of pollution control or make it possible to perform basic economic functions with less pollution than existing approaches. In other words, environmental innovation can either offer qualitatively better environmental results or reduce the cost of achieving a particular result.

I have argued elsewhere that this former qualitative function has immense importance.[10] We suffer from continued air pollution problems and worsening climate change largely because we remain addicted to very old basic technologies, such as coal-fired power plants and gasoline-burning car engines.[11] Pollution from cars and power plants bears a major portion of the responsibility for tens of thousands of annual deaths from air pollution, millions of cases of asthma, cancer risks, reproductive toxicity risk, widespread destruction of ecosystems, and global climate change (which may produce rising seas, a spread of infectious diseases, ecosystem harms, and, in places, drought and starvation).

Because of this we may need radical innovation to address these problems comprehensively in the economically dynamic world we live in—a dynamic world of growing population, increased consumption, and fierce lobbying fueled by the proceeds of increased consumption. This economic dynamic tends to make environmental problems grow over time. This dynamic almost always undermines some of the progress environmental regulation would otherwise bring about and at times leads to absolute declines in environmental quality.

Technological innovation generally (not just radical innovation) also performs an important political function—making progress possible where it otherwise could not occur.[12] The climate change regime, for example, assumes that the richer countries will develop and share the technologies that will make it possible for relatively poor countries to enjoy a good quality of life and contribute to efforts to address climate change. Absent this sort of developed country leadership, developed countries may have great difficulty persuading tomorrow's greatest greenhouse gas emitters, such as China and India, to reduce emissions to tolerable levels.

We need to reframe the environmental policy debate around the question of addressing the economic dynamics of environmental law. This involves, among other things, asking how we can design environmental law that stimulates environmental innovation as effectively as we currently stimulate material innovation (some of which is environmentally destructive). In any case, environmental policy analysts generally agree on the desirability of stimulating technological innovation to improve the environment.[13] But the emphasis on dynamic efficiency in the trading literature tends to emphasize the cost saving advantages of innovation, while drawing attention away from the qualitative advantages.

Emissions trading has been widely implemented.[14] Hence, the question of whether it encourages innovation matters a great deal.

An Analytical Framework for Comparing Trading and Nontrading Programs

When not analyzing emissions trading, economists commonly employ the induced innovation hypothesis—an assumption that high cost will tend to encourage innovation. This hypothesis would suggest that more stringent regulation would induce more innovation than less stringent regulation. Stringent regulation (with or without trading) raises the cost of routine compliance and creates an incentive to innovate to escape the high cost.

This observation has implications for the analysis of emissions trading programs, because all trading programs involve government decisions about stringency. Although policy makers sometimes act as if trading programs offer an alternative to regulation, experts in the area understand that trading is a variant on an ordinary performance standard. To establish a trading program, government officials must establish a set of performance standards for regulated pollution sources, just as they would if they were establishing a traditional regulation. When a regulator permits a regulated polluter to forgo local compliance with the performance standard if she purchases equivalent reductions from elsewhere, she has created a trading program. The trading program still contains pollution limits reflecting a policy choice about the amount of reductions to demand, but it introduces flexibility about the location of the reductions.

Because stringency decisions can influence the amount of innovation, isolating the effect of permission to trade on innovation requires comparison of programs with equivalent stringency.

Let's assume that one state demands a 70 percent reduction from power plants through an emissions trading program and another demands a 50 percent reduction from power plants through a set of source-specific performance standards. Assume that the power plants were identical in all respects prior to regulation and that the emissions trading program induced more innovation than the performance standard program. One could not assume that the trading produced the innovation. One would have to at least consider the possibility that the difference in stringency accounted for the difference in innovation rates.

Another important variable involves the form of standards. The acid rain program, the phaseout of ozone-depleting chemicals (which I treat as a traditional regulation, because nobody seems to have used the trading provisions), and the most recent new source performance standard for power plants (which do not allow trading) feature mass-based limits. Most emissions trading programs (e.g., the open market trading programs in the states, the bubbles, and mobile source emissions trading programs) and traditional regulations, however, use rate-based limits. Mass-based limits will tend to induce more innovation than rate-based limits, because they do not allow pollution levels to rise when production increases. Hence, the form of standards provides another potentially significant variable.[15]

A valid comparison between a trading program and a nontrading program should compare programs having emission limits of identical stringency and form. To isolate trading's effect on innovation, one has to ask whether an emissions trading program induces more innovation than a comparably designed traditional performance standard.

THE THEORETICAL CLAIMS

The induced innovation hypothesis suggests that emissions trading discourages innovation. Because it lowers the cost of routine compliance, it would seem to reduce the impetus to innovate. High costs encourage innovation, low costs discourage it. So a trading program should produce less innovation than a comparably designed traditional regulation.

Oddly, though, the economics literature on trading generally does not analyze the implications of the induced innovation hypothesis. I first discuss the theory supporting the claim in the literature that emissions trading encourages innovation. I then support my claim that trading discourages high cost innovation. Finally, I discuss the more difficult claim—that traditional regulation might induce more low-cost innovation than a comparably designed trading program.

The Existing Theory

It is common for the selection of the unit of analysis to influence results in economic theory and in other realms. This is certainly true of emissions trading.

Imagine an argument against emissions trading's capacity to stimulate innovation that went like this: In an emissions trading program, some polluters emit more than their allowable emissions; therefore, these polluters have less of an incentive to innovate than they would have under a traditional program, and emissions trading decreases incentives to innovate. Let's assess this argument.

Well, emissions trading does provide an incentive for some polluters to emit more than they would under a traditional regulation.[16] But those polluters must pay other polluters to make extra emission reductions to make up the gap. Resting a model of emissions trading on the experience of only half the polluters (the buyers of credits) in the market skews the results. This model leaves the sellers of emission credits, who make extra reductions to sell to the buyers, out of the picture. It is obviously incomplete.

If we change the unit of analysis, we can flip this result. The argument would go like this: Polluters have an incentive to make extra emission reductions under emissions trading so that they can sell credits;[17] therefore, emissions trading stimulates innovation.

This model accurately explains the situation of sellers of credits. But it is also obviously incomplete. It leaves the buyers of credits out of the picture. Whereas emissions trading encourages sellers to decrease emissions below the levels of a comparable traditional regulation, trading encourages buyers to increase their emissions above what a traditional regulation allows.

The seller-based model, incomplete as it is, actually forms the theoretical predicate for the standard argument that emissions trading encourages innovation.[18] Basing an economic model only on the seller's decrease of emissions amounts to treating emissions trading as a program that generates extra net emission reductions. If emissions trading did that, obviously it would create a greater net incentive for innovation. For stricter regulation demands more than laxer regulation and therefore heightens incentives for innovation. But an emissions trading program does not generate more net emissions reductions than a comparable traditional regulation.

If the market functions perfectly, then an emissions trading program produces precisely the same amount of reductions that a traditional regulation with the same emission limits would produce, no more and no less.[19] Emissions trading shifts emission reductions, concentrating the same number of reductions among the facilities with the lowest pollution reduction costs.[20] The right question is whether this shift of reductions from high-cost to low-cost facilities encourages innovation.

I am not the first scholar to point out the incompleteness of a seller-based analysis. In 1987, David Malueg, now of Tulane University's economics department, wrote an article discussing the incompleteness of the seller-based model.[21] He argued that an economic model of emissions trading must recognize that some polluters make more reductions under a trading regime than they would under a traditional regulation, and some polluters make less.[22] This argument seems irrefutable. Indeed, the desire of some polluters to avoid otherwise required reductions generates the demand for extra emission decreases that drives emissions trading. In a real sense, emission increases (above otherwise required levels) finance emission decreases in an emissions trading program.[23] The savings realized by not making expensive reductions at buyers' own facilities finance the purchase of credits that drives the market.[24]

It is not clear why a measure that reduces innovation incentives for some facilities and increases them for others will lead to an increase in overall levels of innovation among facilities subject to a regulation. The relevant question for public policy, of course, must address overall levels of innovation, not just of a chosen subset of facilities.

Economists have recently have begun to use Malueg's model to analyze emissions trading's influence on technological change; they acknowledge that Malueg's model casts doubt on the thesis that emissions trading without auctioned allowances encourages innovation.[25] The selection of a seller-based model would be systematically biased toward the position that emissions trading encourages innovation, just as the selection of a buyer-based model would be systematically biased toward the conclusion that emissions trading discourages innovation. Hence, economists are right to be giving increased attention to the Malueg framework.

Why Trading Discourages Costly Innovation

Emissions trading disfavors costly innovation. Emissions trading creates an incentive for a polluter facing high control costs to purchase credits that cost less than the cost of control at the buyer's facility.[26] Furthermore, the buyer has an incentive to purchase the cheapest credits possible. Knowing this, rational sellers will only generate credits that cost less to produce than (1) the control cost of prospective buyers and (2) credits with which the seller must compete. Emissions trading by lowering the cost of compliance restricts the price range of innovations that are economically rational.

Thus trading rules out the purchase of credits generated by relatively expensive innovation (i.e., higher than the equilibrium price created in a trading regime). But that raises the question of whether expensive innovation is desirable. In answering that question, we should bear in mind that useful innovations often follow a path where they cost a lot at the outset, but the costs of using innovations fall as producers learn better production techniques and realize savings through economies of scale.[27] Thus, an expensive innovation might function as an investment in future cheap reductions. The emissions trading market does not encourage such investments because the buyer of credits chooses the cheapest current reductions, not considering societal cost savings in the future. Because today's luxury goods often become tomorrow's important technological advance (e.g., computers), this failure to stimulate advanced technologies may be detrimental in the long run.

Furthermore, radical innovations, which might be expensive, offer a qualitative improvement that makes them quite worthwhile, even if they do cost more. Thus, for example, a technology that produces a whole raft of environmental benefits may prove valuable even if it does not offer the cheapest current method of obtaining the benefit sought by a targeted emissions trading program.

Innovations that decrease reliance on fossil fuels offer both this qualitative superiority and the possibility of future cost savings. Renewable energy technologies have experienced rapid declines in prices as production has increased, even though they have never achieved the scale that might facilitate really enormous reductions in price.[28] And renewable technologies promise relief not just from a particular air pollutant, but from a host of pollutants, associated destruction of land from drilling and mining, water pollution, and much else besides.[29] Yet emissions trading tends to favor low-cost solutions, like better scrubbers and catalysts, to environmentally and economically superior solutions for the long haul.

Trading and Low-Cost Innovation

Though the case against emissions trading as a method to stimulate expensive but potentially invaluable environmental innovation seems simple, irrefutable, and very strong, the question of whether it provides superior incentives for cost reducing innovation is more complex.[30] I now turn to that question.

The Theory of Trading

In theory, emissions trading may weaken net incentives for innovation. If a regulation allows facilities to use trading to meet standards, then the low-cost facilities will tend to provide more of the total reductions than they would provide under a comparable traditional regulation. Conversely, the high-cost facilities will tend to provide less of the total required reductions than they would under a comparable traditional regulation. One would expect the low-cost facilities to have a greater ability to provide reductions without substantial innovation than the high-cost facility. A high-cost facility may need to innovate to escape the high costs of routine compliance; the low-cost facility may have less of a need for this. The induced innovation hypothesis, widely employed by economists, suggests that high costs will spur, not deter, innovation.[31] So lowering the cost of routine compliance, through trading or otherwise, does not encourage innovation. Trading, by shifting reductions from high-cost to low-cost facilities, may lessen the net incentives for innovation.

High local control costs often serve as the catalyst for innovation. Companies do not routinely pursue all innovations.[32] Investigation of innovation often involves substantial investment without certainty about pay-off.[33] Many companies' management structures further discourage environmental innovation because environmental projects must compete with other more favored projects for company resources needed to investigate and implement the innovation. When companies face either the impossibility of compliance without innovation or very high control costs, however, the environmental compliance division acquires some bargaining power to secure resources to investigate innovation. Absent such incentives, companies will tend to comply or overcomply through application of routine technology.

Some analysis of the low emission vehicle (LEV) program, a regulatory program that several states have enacted to stimulate innovation and secure emission reductions from automobiles, illustrates the way emissions trading may decrease incentives for innovation. The program requires introduction of a fairly large number of vehicles that must meet emission standards that car manufacturers can realize with fairly modest technological improvements, such as introduction of very efficient catalysts. But the program also requires introduction of a small number of zero emission vehicles (ZEVs), most likely electric cars.[34] The automobile industry claims that the ZEVs will prove expensive to produce. One could, in theory, design a program that provides the same net emission reductions as the LEV program by requiring more widespread implementation of the emission reduction requirements other than the zero emissions mandate as the basis for a trading program. In the short run at least, this would produce (in theory) the same emission reductions for less cost. But the zero emissions mandate provides the incentive to develop new technologies that may revolutionize the environmental performance of automobiles over time and even lower long-term costs.[35] Hence, there is a trade-off between the short-term efficiency that emissions trading promotes and the desire to promote environmentally superior techno-logical innovation.

Another example comes the use of international emissions trading programs to meet climate change goals. The European Union is adopting trading programs that may make it possible for electric utilities, signifi-cant sources of greenhouse gases, to claim credits undertaken abroad as a substitute for making reductions below current levels at home. If Euro-pean states imposed strict reduction requirements on electric utilities, they might have to switch fuels to meet the requirements. They might need to switch from coal to natural gas to meet fairly stringent reduction targets and very strict standards might drive them toward innovative technolo-gies, such as almost-zero polluting fuel cells and solar energy.[36] But trading may allow them to avoid significant changes. Utility operators may eschew expensive innovation to meet a strict reduction target at home in favor of upgrading a very dirty plant abroad with off-the-shelf technology at very modest cost, or better yet, claim credits for tree planting projects of uncertain benefit.

Some writers have suggested that emissions trading provides a con-tinuing incentive to reduce "because the number of permits remain limited."[37] Hence, economic growth will increase the demand for permits, raise the price, and provide a greater incentive for polluters to reduce their emissions.

Limiting the number of permits does not create an incentive for con-tinuous net emission reductions below the equilibrium level required by the program. Limiting the number of total permits without decreasing the amount of emissions the permits allow would involve tolerating increases in emissions attributable to economic growth to the extent that existing polluters generate compensating pollution reductions (credits). Net emis-sions would remain consistent with those authorized by the promulgated emission limits, but would not decrease below that level.[38]

A legal rule limiting the number of permits creates incentives to avoid increases above the mandated level, whether or not the permits can be traded. The premise that a trading program limits the number of permits tacitly assumes that a legal rule prohibits the sources of additional pol-lution caused by economic growth from operating without purchased emission allowances. An argument that a trading program restrains growth in emissions from economic growth also requires an assumption that the trading regime imposes a cap on the mass of emissions of the sources within a trading program (as in the Acid Rain Program). A pro-gram authorizing trading to meet rate-based emission limitations or al-lowing any pollution source to operate without purchased allowances would tolerate increases in emissions associated with economic growth without demanding compensating credits.[39] So even the modest argument that trading can restrain growth in emissions applies only to a particular idealized trading program, not emissions trading in general.

A traditional regulatory program that prohibits economic growth from creating additional emissions would in theory also provide a continuing incentive to avoid net emission increases in response to economic growth.[40] Of course, traditional regulations can limit pollution by mass rather than by rate and sometimes has.[41] Hence, traditional regulation and emissions trading based on rates fail to constrain emissions in the face of growth in production, but limits on mass, whether expressed in performance standards or tradable allowances, may constrain emissions in the face of growth. A legal rule prohibiting all nonpermitted emissions would improve the environmental performance of either an emissions trading scheme or traditional regulation. But even an idealized emissions trading program does not provide a more continuous incentive for pollution reduction than a comparable traditional regulation.

One might support the idea that trading provides superior incentives for innovation by pointing out that once a planned reduction goal is met, the government can always set another more ambitious reduction goal. If the government could be counted on to continuously revise standards, then a continuous incentive to reduce would exist. But notice that this would be true whether or not the government authorized trading as the means of meeting the continuously revised goal. Even without trading, a government program that could be reliably counted on to makes its requirements more stringent would provide an incentive for continuous reductions.

But a major critique of traditional regulation holds that it fails to provide an incentive for continuous environmental improvement, precisely because the government cannot be depended on to strengthen standards in a predictable manner. Problems of complexity, uncertainty, and delay prevent regulators from predictably tightening limits. These problems limit traditional regulation's ability to stimulate innovation. Does emissions trading overcome this problem?

The answer seems to be no. If an administrative body sets the limits underlying a trading program, then the problems of the complexity of administrative environmental decision making and the attendant delay may infect these decisions, just as they infect decision making in traditional programs. A good example comes from Environmental Protection Agency (EPA) efforts to foster a regional market for nitrogen oxides across a broad region of ozone transport, which has been plagued by delays and uncertainty.[42] The resulting uncertainty can lessen incentives to innovate, just as uncertainty about future emission limitations reduces such incentives in traditional regulation.[43] Also, private parties have significant incentives to litigate disliked stringency determinations and allocation decisions.[44]

Congressional mandates of specific emission reductions may circumvent some of the problems with administrative decision making, including hard look judicial review.[45] Congress has in fact circumvented administrative problems by mandating specific cuts of named pollutants both through emissions trading[46] and through standard setting.[47] The scarcity of congressional time may limit the frequency of congressional mandates.[48] However, congressionally set limits have often fared relatively well and should be pursued.[49] Yet the advantages of specific quantitative congressional decision making occur whether or not pollution sources may use trading as a means to comply with the limits.

Hence, the intuition that trading programs are easier to establish and change than traditional programs rests on confusion of institutional choice with instrumental choice. Administrators establishing trading programs face many of the same problems that have interfered with efforts to make nontrading programs predictable stimulants of continuous innovation. And Congress, to the extent it avoids political paralysis, can overcome these problems with either trading or nontrading programs.

Some analysts believe that trading programs may prove easier to establish, because lowered cost will translate into lowered polluter resistance. But polluters with high local pollution control costs may not have information about lower cost options at other facilities and may therefore fight just as hard as ever. Much will depend, however, on political circumstances. Polluters will lobby if the potential gains from doing so make it worthwhile, regardless of whether the potential maximum loss has diminished. Often, even if polluters anticipate fully the reduced cost from trading, potential gains from avoiding limits or weakening them may often provide sufficient incentives for vigorous advocacy sufficient to stall progress.[50] Certainly, no rule exists that trading automatically leads to tightened limits.

In any case, most claims that trading encourages innovation have not relied on political economy arguments hypothesizing tighter limits. Rather, they have rested on inherent characteristics of trading that apply even when they aim at identical limits to those used in a traditional regulation. Hence, this identical limits framework, putting political economy questions aside for the time being, is the framework employed here.

The Theory of Traditional Regulation: The Command-and-Control/ Economic Incentive Dichotomy and the Law

Most analysts employ a simplistic command-and-control/economic incentive dichotomy as a substitute for cogent analysis. They claim that traditional regulation discourages innovation.[51] Indeed, some of the less careful writing states that standard regulation prohibits innovation.[52] If this were true, emissions trading obviously would encourage innovation better than traditional regulation.

Although the claim that traditional regulation often does not stimulate innovation has great merit, the view that it prohibits or blocks innovation altogether involves gross exaggeration and some significant misunderstandings.[53] These misunderstandings interfere with sound comparison of traditional regulation with emissions trading.

Environmental statutes usually encourage performance standards—a form of a standard that specifies a level of environmental performance[54] rather than the use of a particular technique.[55] Performance standards may encourage innovation by allowing polluters to choose how to comply.[56]

Many statutory provisions severely restrict the EPA's authority to specify mandatory compliance methods, often by requiring a performance standard unless the EPA finds that one cannot measure emissions directly to determine compliance.[57] Even when the statutes permit work practice standards or other types of standards that *do* command specific control techniques, the statutes often require the EPA to approve adequately demonstrated alternatives.[58]

This predominance of performance-based standards over command-and-control regulation exists regardless of the criteria used to determine the standards' stringency. Statutory provisions requiring technology-based standards, for example, instruct implementing agencies to set standards that are achievable with either existing or, in some cases, future technology.[59] Hence, agency views concerning technological capability help determine the standards' stringency.[60] Owners of pollution sources may generally use any adequate technology they choose to comply with the performance standards that an agency has developed through the evaluation of a reference technology.[61]

Ackerman's detailed study of a particularly controversial New Source Performance Standard (NSPS) under the 1977 Clean Air Act (CAA) amendments may have indirectly contributed to frequent characterization of technology-based standards as command-and-control regulation.[62] Economists accustomed to a static framework of analysis read Ackerman's statements that this NSPS involved "forced scrubbing" as indicating that "technology-based standards identify particular equipment that must be used to comply with the regulation."[63] This NSPS, however, allowed utilities to meet their emission limitations through innovative means, although it precluded complete reliance on techniques that could not meet the emission limitations.

This NSPS limited sulfur dioxide emissions to 1.2 pounds per million British thermal units (MBtu).[64] It also required a 90 percent reduction from uncontrolled levels except for plants emitting less than 0.6 lbs/MBtu. These cleaner plants needed only to meet a 70 percent reduction requirement. Nothing in the regulation specifically required any particular technology, such as wet scrubbing. Indeed, the EPA specifically designed the regulation to leave open opportunities for plants to meet the standards through dry scrubbing and other alternatives that the EPA regarded as somewhat experimental.[65] Hence, if a plant operator developed some completely new approach that met these standards, the utility could use it.

Operators probably could not meet this standard solely through the use of coal washing, because coal washing, which was not a new innovation at the time, probably could not produce a 70 percent reduction by itself.[66] If reading Ackerman's reference to the NSPS as a standard based on full scrubbing to indicate that the NSPS precluded subsequent innovations, meeting the numerical standards would involve technical misunderstanding of the regulation. The U.S. Court of Appeals for the District of Columbia explained in reviewing this NSPS that *"given the present state of pollution control technology,* utilities will have to employ some form of . . . scrubbing."[67] This necessarily implies that if utilities can develop a new technology that meets the required emission limit, nothing in the regulation precludes its use, a conclusion that necessarily flows from the numerical limits stated in the standard in any case.

This error reflects a habit of thinking in static terms. Thinking in more dynamic terms about the possibility of new technology makes it impossible to equate the NSPS Ackerman studies with specification of a technology.

A static frame of reference has frequently led to characterization of technology-based regulation as command-and-control regulation. This term is misleading, except as applied to the relatively rare standards that actually specify techniques rather than just performance levels.

Moreover, emissions trading cannot substitute for true command-and-control regulation, regulation that requires specific techniques.[68] The law only authorizes command-and-control regulation when measurement of emissions is impossible. Trading, however, relies on good monitoring.[69] When good measurement proves impossible, trading will not succeed.

The incorrect suggestion that traditional regulation generally requires government-chosen technology would lead to a conclusion that traditional regulation legally forbids innovation. But some have made more subtle incentive-based arguments for characterizing traditional regulation as discouraging innovation.

The fundamental notion that economic incentives are powerful would suggest that polluters have substantial economic incentives to use the flexibility that performance standards offer to employ innovative means of meeting emission limitations that are less costly than traditional compliance methods. Such use of innovations saves polluters money. This incentive exists even for technology-based performance standards that did not contemplate the innovative compliance mechanism a polluter discovers.

Richard Stewart, however, has stated that polluters have "strong incentives to adopt the particular technology underlying" a technology-based performance standard because "its use will readily persuade regulators of compliance."[70] He does not explain why this countervailing persuasion incentive would overcome the economic incentive to realize savings through an effective and cheaper innovation, even if the persuasiveness incentive were powerful. Polluters, after all, have a number of means of persuading regulators that their innovations perform adequately if they in fact do so. First, polluters may monitor their pollution directly to demonstrate compliance. Second, in some cases polluters may eliminate regulated chemicals, which certainly demonstrates compliance. Traditional regulation offers ample incentives for pollution prevention by eliminating chemicals or reducing them below regulatory thresholds, because of the substantial savings involved. Although the uncertainty of innovation's outcome may discourage innovation under traditional regulation in spite of opportunities for cost savings, it may do the same thing with respect to emissions trading, in spite of the opportunity for some profits from extra reductions.

In any case, neither Stewart nor anybody else has come forward with empirical evidence that polluters with compliant and cheap innovations have failed to employ them because of fears of permitting difficulties under a performance standard.[71] Indeed, as we shall see, the empirical record shows that at least on some occasions, this negative incentive, if it exists, has been overcome.

EMPIRICAL EVIDENCE

The literature, however, gives the impression that solid empirical proof supports emissions trading's superiority in stimulating innovation. The literature discusses two types of evidence, both surprisingly thin:[72] Evidence that traditional regulation does not simulate innovation and evidence that emissions trading does. In fact, what the literature shows is something much less dramatic—that both trading and traditional regulation sometimes stimulate innovation and sometimes do not.

Traditional Regulation

The empirical literature on traditional regulation shows that industry sometimes chooses techniques different from those an agency relies on in standard setting.[73] Because so many studies claim that traditional regulation, usually described as command-and-control regulation, thwarts innovation, a brief review of some of the cases where this simply has not proven true seems worthwhile. Most industry responded to the Occupational Safety and Health Administration's (OSHA's) and the EPA's regulation of vinyl chloride in ways that the agencies anticipated. But a proprietary stripping process, commercialized within a year of promulgation, significantly improved polyvinyl chloride resin production while lowering vinyl chloride exposure, and the industry adopted a number of other innovations as well.[74] Textile manufacturers met OSHA's cotton dust standard to a significant extent through modernization of equipment unanticipated by the government, which was needed anyway to compete with foreign companies.[75] Though a few metal foundries responded to standards for formaldehyde in the workplace through ventilation and enclosure (as expected by OSHA), most developed low-formaldehyde resins.[76] Similarly, though most established smelters responded to sulfur dioxide limits by using available technologies, copper mining firms developed a new, cleaner process to assist their entry into the smelting business.[77] These examples show that traditional regulation can encourage pollution prevention.

Industry responded to a ban on ozone-depleting chemicals with a variety of innovations.[78] The makers of ozone-depleting substances developed new chemicals that damaged the ozone layer less severely.[79] And many former users of ozone depleters simply substituted soap and water for chemical solvents.[80] Operators of chloralkali plants responded to EPA regulation of mercury with some process innovations.[81] When the EPA began phasing out mirex (a pesticide that controlled fire ants), the agency had registered no acceptable substitutes. But during a two-year phaseout period, four companies sought registration of substitutes.[82] Clearly the claim that traditional regulation always discourages innovation is simply wrong.

These examples do not, however, show that traditional regulation regularly stimulates innovation. Whereas evidence on this subject is actually thin because of the scarcity of postcompliance studies, most traditional regulation probably does little to stimulate innovation. Most of this regulation allows polluters to meet the standard through relatively cheap existing technology.[83] This mediocre regulation does not require stringent pollution reductions that would make conventional techniques either insufficient or very expensive.[84] By contrast, when the government imposes very stringent regulation, companies tend to innovate because the conventional approaches become either inadequate or expensive.[85]

Emissions Trading

The evidence regarding emissions trading establishes that it, like traditional regulation, sometimes encourages innovation, but sometimes does not. A brief review of some of the principal programs follow.

Bubbles: Inadequate Environmental Performance

Bubble programs allow plant operators to trade emission reductions among polluting units within a plant. The empirical literature raises especially serious questions about whether bubbles have spurred adequate environmental performance.[86] The few studies of bubble implementation reveal that polluters often could not document claims that they had made required emission reductions.[87] Where polluters could verify claimed reductions, they often involved using credits from activities that would have occurred anyway to justify escape from pollution reduction obligations that would have otherwise generated additional pollution reductions.[88] Hence, gaming has been a problem.

The EPA introduced bubbles primarily as deregulatory mechanisms,[89] and they have often stimulated neither innovation nor adequate environmental performance at a cheaper price.[90] Rather, they have generated cost savings for industry, often by allowing unverifiable claims of compliance and paper credits to substitute for actual emission reductions and by reducing pollution reduction demands.[91]

Lead Phasedown: A Stringent Limitation Driving Substantial Change

The EPA allowed gasoline producers to trade lead allowances during a phasedown of lead from gasoline.[92] The lead phasedown did create a substantial change—the reformulation and then virtual elimination of leaded gasoline. But the driver for this achievement seems to be the underlying requirement of a phasedown of lead. Faithful implementation of a traditional phasedown without trading would probably have produced the same change more quickly.[93]

Indeed, in a very sophisticated empirical analysis of the lead trading program employing the Malueg model, economists Suzi Kerr and Richard Newell conclude that *"increased stringency . . . encouraged adoption of lead-reducing technology."*[94] They credit the trading with providing flexibility in the timing and distribution of reductions, which lowered the cost of the technological transition the stringency of a phaseout brought about.[95]

Acid Rain: Little Initial Trading or Innovation

Phase one of the acid rain trading program has produced some changes in scrubber technology, operational methods, and the use of cleaner coal, which some analysts described as innovations.[96] But at the time that scholars began citing the acid rain program's stimulation of these methods as evidence that trading stimulates innovation, only three of fifty-one firms used interfacility trading to meet their reduction obligations (although thirty of the fifty-one did use some intrafacility averaging).[97] So analysts should have to ascribe those results to trading. Byron Swift of the Environmental Law Institute has claimed that the EPA's old rate-based standards would not have permitted some of the innovations he identified, but he admits that a mass-based program without trading would have allowed most of the technologies he identifies as innovations.[98]

As a general matter, it's hard to consider coal scrubbing, use of low-sulfur coal, or dispatch orders favoring cleaner units as innovations, because all of these techniques have been well understood options for many years.[99] Nevertheless, some of the improvements in scrubbing have received patents, which suggests that they might qualify as genuine innovations.[100]

But the most detailed study available comparing innovation in sulfur dioxide control technology before and after the Acid Rain Program has concluded that "the history of innovation in SO_2 control technology does not support" trading's superiority in inducing innovation.[101] Similarly, David Popp finds that both the Acid Rain Program and prior traditional regulation encouraged the patenting of new technology.[102] Indeed, he shows that there was more patenting of new environmental technologies prior to the introduction of the program. He states, however, that the two programs created different types of technological incentives: The traditional program led to innovations reducing the cost of scrubbing, whereas the trading program produced patents improving pollution control characteristics. Yet this very useful research stops short of proving even the limited proposition that trading changes the type of innovation, because the nontrading programs that limited sulfur dioxide emissions prior to 1990 have much laxer limits and a different form of limits than the trading program enacted in the 1990 amendments to the CAA. These differences, rather than the trading, may account for the observed difference.

In any case, so far the Acid Rain Program has not produced significant diffusion or creation of much cleaner technologies, such as natural gas power plants or renewable energy, nor has it resulted in really ground-breaking radical innovation (such as new designs for fuel cells).[103] This suggests that something other than the mere existence of a trading program may be important to stimulating meaningful innovation.

State Programs after 1990

Since 1990, states have implemented a variety of emissions trading programs. These programs have performed unevenly in a number of respects. For example, New Jersey suspended a trading program for poor performance and California's RECLAIM program came under heavy fire for reasons of environmental justice and poor environmental performance.[104]

Facilities have primarily relied on tried-and-true control technologies in many of these programs. For example, the regional trading program for nitrogen oxide emission reductions, organized by the EPA to aid state attainment of the old ozone standard, produced a large number of orders for selective catalytic reduction technologies.[105] But some sources have relied on less conventional techniques, such as ThermaloNO$_x$, rotating overfired air, and reburn technology. And many RECLAIM sources have relied on junking of old cars, which seems imaginative, but hardly constitutes an advanced innovative technology and creates fraud problems.[106] The EPA's evaluation of RECLAIM states that most sources relied on conventional off-the-shelf technology, but a few used innovative compliance methods.[107] Because very few sources generated credits through overcompliance to sell into the market, we do not know whether it is correct to ascribe the innovation that did occur under the RECLAIM program to the program's authorization of emissions trading.[108]

A Summary of the Empirical Record

I provide all of this evidence to support a very modest assertion: Both traditional regulation and trading have often failed to produce innovation but sometimes succeeded. I do not claim that traditional regulation is free from design flaws or gaming. Nor do I claim that all trading programs are bad. I have offered extensive treatment of a variety of trading programs only to cure a tendency to compare the best trading program we have ever had, the Acid Rain Program, to negative stereotypes about traditional regulation. The proper analysis compares a trading program to a traditional regulation with equivalent emission limits.

IMPLICATIONS

Emissions trading obviously does nothing to encourage expensive innovation—even innovation that would produce long-term efficiency and enormous environmental improvement. Nor does either the empirical record or sound economic theory strongly support a milder conclusion, that emissions trading does a better job of encouraging relatively cheap innovation. Under traditional regulation, the high-cost sources have an incentive to adopt any innovation promising compliance for less cost than its relatively high cost of control. Under emissions trading, only innovations costing less than the marginal cost of additional reductions at facilities with relatively low control costs can find a market. Thus, trading discourages innovation by lowering the price at which innovation will become economically viable.

A Research Agenda

I argue that we need more research on the topic. Malueg's model and Popp's empirical work suggest a milder hypothesis than a generic assertion of trading's superiority in encouraging innovation: The hypothesis is that trading may change the type of innovation rather than the amount. The low-cost sources under trading have an incentive to generate extra emission reductions. High-cost sources under comparable traditional regulation face incentives to adopt innovations that save them money, but not necessarily innovations that increase control efficiency. So polluters may have better incentives to innovate to increase control efficiency under a trading regime than under traditional regulation, even if overall incentives for maximizing the number of innovations have declined.

A recent empirical analysis, however, concludes that more innovation in improving environmental performance occurred prior to the Acid Rain Program.[109] Several reasons exist to doubt even Popp's milder thesis. First, emissions trading creates enormous opportunities to use a very wide variety of traditional technologies to generate credits while avoiding the uncertainty involved in innovation. These opportunities may weaken incentives for innovations with greater control efficiencies. Traditional technologies typically provide excess reductions under traditional regulation because sources need to make sure that they remain in continuous compliance. Under trading, polluters using conventional techniques will sell some of this surplus, thus lessening any demand for innovation. Furthermore, trading provides opportunities to engage in minor noninnovative tweaking of operating conditions to generate excess emission reductions. An example involves using dispatch orders from electric utilities to use cleaner units more extensively. This is hardly innovative, but it does realize some extra emission reductions. Trading might well provide good incentives to seize noninnovative (i.e., obvious) pollution prevention opportunities that provide a small quantity of emission reductions. Finally, the flexibility for trading may invite the use of traditional technologies with relatively weak environmental performance because every increment has some value. An example involves the use of low-sulfur coal in the Acid Rain Program. Second, by weakening incentives for cost-reducing innovation at high-cost facilities, trading may indirectly limit innovations that will produce higher control efficiencies. Facilities whose high costs come from exceptionally dirty processes may adopt new technologies just to meet (not exceed) emission limits at their own facilities, but these same technologies may provide superior environmental performance at cleaner facilities. And new ideas pursued to lower costs may lead to ideas for greater pollution control. For a variety of reasons, the hypothesis that emissions trading may systematically change the type of innovation induced in a desirable manner might not stand.

This much milder claim about the nature of innovation, however, stands on firmer ground than the traditional claim that emissions trading spurs more innovation than traditional regulation. It certainly merits further research and exploration. Even if trading turns out to have some innovation-stimulating advantages, trading's clear inferiority in spurring initially expensive but environmentally excellent innovation stands as a significant problem.

The framework for analysis that I have offered points the way toward a research agenda to explore both Popp's claims about the nature of innovation under trading and more general claims about low-cost trading. I have pointed out that when innovation occurs in conjunction with the trading program, it is very hard to figure out whether the trading or some other feature of the program explains the observed increase in innovation. Because empirical analysis shows that stringent traditional regulation has encouraged innovation, it is possible that when we see innovation in a trading program, stringent underlying emission limits, not the trading itself, explain the observed results. The proper way to test this involves comparing trading programs based on a set of limits to a nontrading performance standard based on the same limits. Some of the analysis of the Acid Rain Program applies this approach to the program, relying primarily on Swift's analysis. It may appear, however, that this poses an impossible challenge for empirical research, because two identical programs may not exist in the real world.

It is possible, however, to find this situation in real life. Existing analyses reach conclusions about innovation by examining compliance choices of pollution sources subject to trading programs, *whether or not they actually trade*. But a pollution source that does not buy or sell credits has innovated or failed to innovate because of the underlying requirement for reductions, not because of the incentives provided by trading. Researchers might compare the compliance strategies of facilities earning extra credits or buying credits that they eventually sell in a trading program to the strategies of firms subject to the same program rules that opt for local compliance without trading. The trading sources (both buyers and sellers of credits) should reflect the incentives trading provides, whereas the nontraders' choices should provide some information about how a performance standard without trading would influence compliance choices. In this way, we might be able to reach more convincing conclusions about innovation and trading than we have to date.

The Importance of Design

Framing the question of whether trading improves innovation as requiring a comparison with an identical performance standard without trading yields important insights. Because both trading and traditional regulation sometimes stimulated innovation and sometimes did not, some factors besides instrument choice must influence the degree of innovation. This chapter has already suggested that the stringency of limits has a large influence.[110] Elsewhere, I explain that the form of emission limits matters as well (building on work by Swift on mass-based limits).[111] One would expect that a program with mass-based limits and relatively stringent targets would produce more innovation than a rate-based program with lax limits, whether or not trading was used. In spite of widespread recognition that good monitoring is essential to trading, the EPA has allowed states to continue programs that do not feature continuous monitoring. Such programs tend to produce no innovation and usually fail to produce contemplated environmental improvements. The literature's preoccupation with a simplistic and misleading command-and-control/economic incentive dichotomy has led to a failure to adequately address crucial design issues. Design considerations such as stringency and the existence of adequate monitoring may matter even more than the choice between trading and nontrading programs.

Broader Theoretical Implications

The significance of emissions trading's inferiority in stimulating innovation (especially expensive innovation) depends on the value of innovation relative to other factors. Emissions trading retains significant cost saving advantages over traditional regulation, something that regulators will take into account. In an earlier book, I explain why innovation deserves more emphasis than it has received, especially with respect to environmental problems difficult to reverse.[112] Leading economists agree that the development and spread of new technologies may in the long run play a major role in determining the "success or failure of environmental protection efforts."[113]

Although this chapter has focused primarily on a comparison between traditional regulation and emissions trading, a more interesting point may be that both have significant shortcomings in stimulating innovations, especially radical innovation. Neither mediocre regulation nor most emissions trading programs do very well in stimulating radical innovation. They both depend on government standard setting, which tends toward demands unlikely to disrupt the status quo. Pollution taxes would suffer from the same problem.[114] Recognizing the weaknesses of trading and other often discussed approaches in stimulating innovation should make us eager to explore more imaginatively the possibilities for more creative use of economic incentives.

We can design more dynamic economic incentives that encourage competition to reduce pollution, much as the free market creates competition to provide better amenities. This requires creation of mechanisms that circumvent the need for repeated government decisions and allow private actions, rather than government decisions, to stimulate reductions in pollution.

The law can apply either positive economic incentives (revenue increases or cost decreases) or negative economic incentives (revenue decreases or cost increases) to polluters. This reveals a possibility that has received too little attention.[115] Negative economic incentives can fund positive economic incentives.

Governments have designed programs that use negative economic incentives to fund positive economic incentives. New Zealand addressed the depletion of its fishery by imposing fees on fishing (a negative economic incentive) and using revenue from these fees to pay some fishermen to retire (a positive economic incentive). This may reduce pressure on the fish if fees are high enough.[116] The California legislature has considered a program (called Drive ++) that involves imposing a fee on consumers purchasing an energy-inefficient or high-pollution vehicle and using the proceeds to fund a rebate on the purchase of an energy-efficient vehicle or low-polluting vehicle.[117] Similarly, New Hampshire officials have proposed an Industry Average Performance System that redistributes pollution taxes to the polluting industry in ways that favor lower emissions.[118]

One can build on this principle to craft laws that mimic the free market's dynamic competitive character far better than taxes or subsidies. In a competitive free market, a firm that innovates to reduce its cost or increase its revenues not only increases its profits but also often reduces its competitors' profits. Hence, firms in a very competitive market face strong incentives to innovate and improve.[119] Failing to do so can threaten their survival. Doing so can make them prosper.

One could craft an environmental competition statute that requires polluters to pay any costs that competitors incur in reducing pollution plus a substantial premium, thereby creating a significant incentive to be among the first to reduce pollution.[120] An environmental competition statute would directly attack a fundamental problem with existing free market incentives: The polluting firm must bear any cleanup costs itself. Because the firm does not experience all of the costs of pollution itself (most are externalized and felt by the general public), it rarely pays to clean up.[121] If firms could systematically externalize the costs of cleanup without substantial administrative intervention, just as they externalize the cost of pollution, then even a fairly modest premium might create adequate incentives to control pollution.

An environmental competition statute would create a private environmental law with a few public decisions setting up the law, but with substantial enforcement by low-polluting businesses against competitors. The statute could create a private right of action to allow a business that realized environmental improvements through investment in pollution-reducing (or low-pollution) processes, control devices, products, or services to secure reimbursement for expenses, plus some premium, from more polluting competitors. Hence, the scheme could create economic incentives for some companies to become enforcers of the law, rather than creating incentives for all companies to resist enforcement.

Such a proposal overcomes the fundamental problem with traditional regulation, emissions trading, and taxes. These mechanisms rely on government decisions as the driver for pollution reductions. An environmental competition statute makes private initiative, motivated by the prospect of gain and the fear of loss, the driver of environmental improvement, thus replicating free market dynamics.[122] The magnitude of the incentive may depend on the extent of industry fears about competitors' achievements rather than the fixed cost directly imposed by government.

Moreover, such a scheme provides a continuous incentive to reduce pollution. Any company can profit by making an environmental improvement or lose money by failing to make one.[123] The government does need to establish the premium to be paid to first movers. But once it established this, repeated government decisions are not necessary. Securing maximum incentives for innovation may require legal structures that induce competition to produce environmental improvement and lessen the need for repeated government decisions.

I do not mean to suggest that the environmental competition statute sketched here offers the only possible approach to inducing innovation. For example, government research and subsidies may have a legitimate and important role to play or may be ineffective because of special interest capture. But I do wish to suggest that a recognition of trading's limits in stimulating innovation should encourage a more imaginative exploration of potential alternatives.

CONCLUSION

Emissions trading certainly does a poor job of stimulating radical innovation and other relatively expensive (but potentially valuable) innovation. It may stimulate less innovation than a comparably designed traditional regulation. As a result, we should think more critically about the automatic preference for emissions trading. Though policy makers will continue to rely on emissions trading in the near future,[124] we need more attention to design issues and, in the long run, creative alternatives to emissions trading.

ACKNOWLEDGMENTS The author thanks Charles Kolstad, David Popp, and an anonymous reviewer for helpful comments and Rodney Richardson, Peter Rolph, and Melissa Pennington for research assistance. The author takes responsibility for any errors and the chapter reflects only his views.

NOTES

1. *See, e.g.*, Bruce A. Ackerman and Richard B. Stewart, *Reforming Environmental Law: The Democratic Case for Market Incentives*, 13 Columbia Journal of Environmental Law 171, 183 (1988); Daniel J. Dudek and John Palmisano, *Emissions Trading: Why Is this Thoroughbred Hobbled?*, 13 Columbia Journal of Environmental Law 217, 234–35 (1988); Robert W. Hahn and Robert N. Stavins, *Incentive-Based Environmental Regulation: A New Era from an Old Idea*, 18 Ecology Law Quarterly 1, 13 (1991); Richard B. Stewart, *Controlling Environmental Risks through Economic Incentives*, 13 Columbia Journal of Environmental Law 153, 160 (1988); Robert N. Stavins, *Policy Instruments for Global Climate Change: How Can Governments Address a Global Problem?*, 1997 University of Chicago Legal Forum 293, 302–3. *See also* Adam B. Jaffe et al., *Environmental Policy and Technological Change*, 22 Environmental and Resource Economics 41, 51 (2002) (economic incentives stimulate innovation by paying firms to clean up "a bit more").

2. I have advanced both of the claims previously. *See* David M. Driesen, *Is Emissions Trading an Economic Incentive Program?: Replacing the Command and Control/Economic Incentive Dichotomy*, 55 Washington and Lee Law Review 289, 313–22, 325–38 (1998) [hereinafter Driesen, *Dichotomy*]; David M. Driesen, *Free Lunch or Cheap Fix?: The Emissions Trading Idea and the Climate Change Convention*, 26 Boston College Environmental Affairs Law Review 1 (1998) [hereinafter Driesen, *Cheap Fix*].

3. *See*, e.g., Byron Swift, *The Acid Rain Test*, 14 Environmental Forum, May/June 1997, at 17 (describing fuel switching and use of scrubbers as innovations from the Acid Rain Program).

4. *See*, e.g., Joel F. Bruneau, *A Note on Permits, Standards, and Technological Innovation*, 48 Journal of Environmental Economics and Management 1192 (2004); Juan-Pablo Montero, *Permits, Standards, and Technology Innovation*, 44 Journal of Environmental Economics and Management 23 (2002); Juan-Pablo Montero, *Market Structure and Environmental Innovation*, 5 Journal of Applied Economics 293 (2002) (trading, taxes, or traditional regulation can best encourage research and development when firms' products are strategic substitutes). *See also* David A. Malueg, *Emissions Credit Trading and the Incentive to Adopt New Pollution Abatement Technology*, 16 Journal of Environmental Economics and Management 52 (1987)

(pointing out the error and offering a correction); W. A. Magat, *Pollution Control and Technological Advance: A Dynamic Model of the Firm*, 5 Journal of Environmental Economics and Management 95 (1978).

5. *See*, e.g., Suzi Kerr and Richard Newell, *Policy-Induced Technology Adoption: Evidence from the U.S. Lead Phasedown*, 51 Journal of Industrial Economics 317, 320 (2003) ("We find that increased stringency ... encouraged greater adoption of lead reducing technology").

6. *See*, e.g., Adam B. Jaffe et al., *Technological Change and the Environment, in*The Handbook of Environmental Economics 464–65 (Jeffrey Vincent ed., 2003).

7. *See id.* at 467 (finding it difficult to distinguish innovation from diffusion using a "commercialization" definition).

8. David M. Driesen, The Economic Dynamics of Environmental Law 78–80 (MIT Press 2003).

9. For a definition of environmental innovation, *see id.* at 77–78. Cf. Richard B. Stewart, *Regulation, Innovation, and Administrative Law: A Conceptual Framework*, 69 California Law Review 1256, 1279 (1981) (distinguishing between market and social innovation).

10. *See* Driesen, Economic Dynamics, *supra* note 8.

11. David M. Driesen, *Sustainable Development and Air Quality: The Need to Replace Basic Technologies with Cleaner Alternatives*, 32 Environmental Law Review 10277, 10280, 10284 (Mar. 2002) (detailing contributions to air pollution from vehicles and power plants and the persistence of outmoded technologies); Environmental Law Institute (ELI), Cleaner Power: The Benefits and Costs of Moving from Coal Generation to Modern Power Technologies (2001).

12. Timothy F. Malloy, *Regulation by Incentives: Myths, Models, and Micromarkets*, 80 Texas Law Review 531, 541 (2002) (innovation can ease "the way for broader environmental improvements."). *Cf.* Jaffe et al., *supra* note 1, at 54–55 (noting that cost-saving innovation may make optimal environmental policy more stringent).

13. *See*, e.g., Jaffe et al., *supra* note 1, at 49.

14. *See* Driesen, *Dichotomy, supra* note 2, at 291–92. *See*, e.g., Royal C. Gardner, *Banking on Entrepreneurs: Wetlands, Mitigation Banking, and Takings*, 81 Iowa Law Review 527 (1996) (reviewing an intertemporal trading program for wetlands conservation); David M. Driesen, *Choosing Environmental Instruments in a Transnational Context*, 27 Ecology Law Quarterly 263 (2000) (discussing international application of emissions trading); Ann Powers, *Reducing Nitrogen Pollution on Long Island Sound: Is There a Place for Pollutant Trading?*, 23 Columbia Journal of Environmental Law 137 (1998) (discussing proposal to use nitrogen trading regionally to control water pollution).

15. The economics literature sometimes uses the phrase "emissions standard" to refer to a rate-based standard and the phrase "performance standard" to refer to a mass-based standard. *See* Bruneau, *supra* note 4 at 1193 n. 1. The Clean Air Act, however, defines both these terms much more broadly. *See* 42 U.S.C. § 7602(k) (defining an "emission standard" as any standard that limits air pollution, including both numerical standards and instructions about what techniques to use); 42 U.S.C. §§ 7411(h), 7602(1) (defining a performance standard as either a rate-based or mass-based numerical limit on air pollution, as opposed to a work practice standard that dictates technological choice).

16. *See* Driesen, *Dichotomy, supra* note 2, at 334; Kerr and Newell, *supra* note 5, at 319 (relatively high-cost plants will have decreased incentives to adopt technology under a trading system).

17. *See* Malueg, *supra* note 4, at 8–9 and n. 33.

18. *See id.;* Jaffe et al., *supra* note 1, at 51 ("market-based instruments can provide powerful incentives for companies to adopt cheaper and better pollution-control technologies . . . because . . . with market-based instruments, it pays firms to clean up a bit more").

19. *See* Hahn and Stavins, *supra* note 1, at 8–9 and n. 33 (describing trading's tendency to seek equilibrium). *See generally* J. H. Dales, Pollution, Property, and Prices 92–100 (1968).

20. *See* Driesen, *Dichotomy, supra* note 2, at 334; Driesen, *Cheap Fix, supra* note 2, at 43.

21. *See* Malueg, *supra* note 4.

22. *Id.* at 54–56.

23. *See* Driesen, *Dichotomy, supra* note 2, at 337.

24. *Id.*

25. *Id.* at 334 (employing the Malueg model); David Wallace, Environmental Policy and Industrial Innovation: Strategies in Europe, the U.S.A., and Japan 20 (1995) (explaining that Malueg's "more sophisticated model" casts doubt on the claim that emissions trading necessarily spurs innovation); Malloy, *supra* note 12, at 543 n. 33 (discussing Malueg as suggesting that emissions trading may cause a decrease in research and development in pollution reducing technology); Kerr and Newell, *supra* note 5, at 319 (employing the Malueg model as part of a very sophisticated analysis of the lead trading program); Hahn and Stavins, *supra* note 1, at 8–9 n. 33 (pointing out, consistent with Malueg, that trading encourages abatement by some sources, while encouraging high cost sources to increase emissions); Robert P. Anex, *Stimulating Innovation in Green Technology: Policy Alternatives and Opportunities,* 44 American Behavioral Scientist 188, 201 (2002) (market incentives do not necessarily improve incentives for innovation); Chuhlo Jung et al., *Incentives for Advanced Pollution Abatement Technology at the Industry Level: An Evaluation of Policy Alternatives,* 30 Journal of Environmental Economics and Management 95, 95 (1996) ("marketable permits may not provide greater incentives than standards, because the incentive effects of marketable permits depend on whether firms are buyers and sellers."); V. Kerry Smith and Randy Walsh, *Do Painless Environmental Policies Exist?,* 21 Journal of Risk and Uncertainty 73, 75–76 (2000) (addressing the Malueg model); Michael Grubb and David Ulph, *Energy, the Environment, and Innovation,* 18 Oxford Review of Economic Policy 92, 104 (2002) (expressing lack of confidence in environmental policy's ability to encourage innovation without a technology policy). *See also* Jean-Jacques Laffont and Jean Tirole, *Pollution Permits and Environmental Innovation,* 62 Journal of Public Economics 127, 128 (1996) (permits can create "inefficiencies with regard to innovation").

26. *See* Malloy, *supra* note 12, at 542–43; Driesen, *Cheap Fix, supra* note 2, at 42 (buyers will purchase cheap credits).

27. *See, e.g.,* Julie Edelson Halpert, *Harnessing the Sun and Selling it Abroad: U.S. Solar Industry in Export Boom,* New York Times, June 5, 1996, at D1; Jaffe et al., *supra* note 6, at 490 (discussing economic models predicated on falling abatement costs from learning by doing); Commission on Sustainable Development (CSD), *Acting as the Preparatory Committee for the World Summit on Sustainable Development, Energy, and Transport: Report of the Secretary General,* at 4, U.N. Doc. E/CN.17/2001/PC/20 (2000) (price of solar photovoltaic modules has come down about 25 percent).

28. *See,* e.g., CSD, *supra* note 27, at 4 (discussing declines in prices of solar photovoltaic modules); James McVeigh et al., Winner, Lower, or Innocent Victim?: Has Renewable Energy Performed as Expected (Resources for the Future Discussion Paper 99–28, 1999).

29. *See* Driesen, *supra* note 5, at 34–35.

30. In fact, the case is not completely ironclad. The lead trading case may demonstrate that notwithstanding the drag trading may place on innovation, sufficiently stringent limits will force innovation if they cannot be met without it. If one reduces pollution to zero, innovation often must take place. Though trading can retard the pace of innovation, as it did in the lead case, it will not prevent it. *See* Driesen, *Dichotomy, supra* note 2, at 317 n. 131.

31. *See* Richard G. Newell et al., *The Induced Innovation Hypothesis and Energy-Saving Technological Change,* 114 Quarterly Journal of Economics 941 (1999). *Cf.* Malloy, *supra* note 12, at 546 (linking the induced innovation idea to the idea that traditional regulation may induce innovation)

32. *See* Malloy, *supra* note 12, at 537–38, 556.

33. *See id.* at 557; Jaffe et al., *supra* note 1, at 44 (discussing how uncertainties can lead to insufficient investment in innovation).

34. *See Motor Vehicle Mfrs. Ass'n of the United States v. New York State Dep't of Envtl. Conservation,* 17 F.3d 521, 528 (2nd Cir. 1994). For a discussion of some of the technological issues, see James J. Mackenzie, The Keys to the Car: Electric and Hydrogen Vehicles for the 21st Century (1994).

35. *See* generally Michael Shnayerson, The Car that Could: The Inside Story of GM's Revolutionary Electric Vehicle (1996) (detailing innovations and the role of the ZEV mandate in stimulating them).

36. *See* generally, *At Last, The Fuel Cell,* Economist, Oct. 25, 1997, at 89; Andrew C. Revkin, *Under Solar Bill, Homeowners Could Cut Electricity Cost to Zero,* New York Times, July 25, 1996, at B1.

37. *See,* e.g., James T. B. Tripp and Daniel J. Dudek, *Institutional Guidelines for Developing a Successful Transferable Rights Program,* 6 Yale Journal of Regulations 369, 374 (1989).

38. *See* Richard B. Stewart, *Economics, Environment, and the Limits of Legal Control,* 9 Harvard Environmental Law Review 1, 13 (1985) ("Given a fixed supply of permits . . . the system will ensure that we . . . keep in place").

39. *See* Swift, *supra* note 3, at 18 (explaining that emission rates do not necessarily prevent increases in the mass of emissions).

40. The traditional program would simply duplicate the assumptions implicit in the trading model Tripp and Dudek tacitly advance. The government would set mass-based emission limitations for pollution sources, something that must occur in the trading program as well. The same background legal rule would apply prohibiting the government from granting permits to new sources of emissions.

41. *See,* e.g., *Reynolds Metal Co. v. EPA,* 760 F.2d 549, 559 n.14 (4th Cir. 1985) (discussing the EPA's promulgation of mass-based standards for total toxic organics for the can-making industry); *Citizens for a Better Environment-California v. Union Oil Co. of California,* 861 F.Supp. 889, 895 (N.D. Cal. 1994) (discussing mass-based limits on the amount of selenium that refineries could discharge).

42. *See Appalachian Power Co. v. EPA,* 249 F.3d 1032, 1036–1040 (D.C. Cir. 2001) (reciting some of litigious history of this emissions trading program, prior to remanding the EPA's rule calling on states to adopt an emissions trading program). In fact, the EPA's rule making in this case does not create the emissions trading

program directly, but relies on subsequent state implementing rules. In addition, a long effort to negotiate this program precedes the event recited in the opinion.

43. Jeanne M. Dennis, *Smoke for Sale: Paradoxes and Problems of the Emissions Trading Program of the Clean Air Act Amendments of 1990*, 40 University of California at Los Angeles Law Review 1101, 1105 (1993) (if the need for reduction in acid rain becomes more urgent, allowances might be confiscated, thus upsetting the market); Suzi Clare Kerr, Contracts and Tradeable Permit Markets in International and Domestic Environmental Protection 6 (unpublished Ph.D. dissertation, Harvard University) (because of high levels of scientific uncertainty and changing preferences regulatory systems must periodically readjust targets). Stewart envisions "depreciating permits" over time according to a predetermined schedule. *See* Stewart, *supra* note 9, at 1333. He suggests that this proposal would obviate the need for "constant administrative or legislative tightening." *Id.* at 1332–33. Emissions trading schemes that do not have a fixed long-term depreciation schedule still may require periodic tightening. A long-term depreciation schedule can be applied to either marketable or unmarketable permits. Hence, whatever certainty this idea might create would exist with or without emissions trading. Stewart's proposal may make sense. But it's not really an argument about emissions trading.

44. *See Texas Mun. Power Agency v. EPA*, 89 F.3d 858, 861 (D.C. Cir. 1996) (involving claim seeking additional emission allowances); *Indianapolis Power & Light Co. v. EPA*, 58 F.3d 643, 647 (D.C. Cir. 1995) (same); *Madison Gas & Elec. Co. v. EPA*, 25 F.3d 526, 526 (7th Cir. 1994) (same); *Monongahela Power Co. v. Reilly*, 980 F.2d 272, 272–74 (4th Cir. 1992) (same).

45. *See* David Schoenbrod, *Goals Statutes or Rules Statutes: The Case of the Clean Air Act*, 30 University of California at Los Angeles Law Review 740, 808, 815 (1983). Stewart and Ackerman seem to have assumed that Congress would always set the limits associated with emissions trading. *See* Ackerman and Stewart, *supra* note 1, at 190.

46. *See* 42 U.S.C. §7651(b) (setting goal of acid rain trading program at a cut of 10 million tons of sulfur dioxide).

47. *See* 42 U.S.C. §§7521(g) (setting numerical standards for vehicle emissions) 7511a(b)(1) (generally requiring states to cut volatile organic compounds by 15 percent from 1990 levels).

48. *See* David M. Driesen, *Loose Canons: Statutory Construction and the "New" Nondelegation Doctrine*, 66 Pittsburgh Law Review 1, 65–67 (2002) (describing constraints on congressional time as a barrier to specific legislation).

49. *See* David M. Driesen, *Five Lessons from Clean Air Act Implementation*, 14 Pace Environmental Law Review 51, 53–55 (1997).

50. *See, e.g.*, Brian Doherty, *Selling Air Pollution*, 28 Reason 32 (1996) (discussing vigorous industry efforts to influences baselines for California's RECLAIM program, a leading emissions trading effort).

51. *See* Dudek and Palmisano, *supra* note 1, at 220; Robert W. Hahn and Gordon L. Hester, *Where Did All the Markets Go? An Analysis of EPA's Emissions Trading Program*, 6 Yale Journal on Regulations 109, 109 (1989).

52. *See, e.g.*, Hahn and Hester, *supra* note 51, at 109 ("command and control regulations . . . specify the methods and technologies that firms must use to control pollution"). *See also* Dudek and Palmisano, *supra* note 1, at 220.

53. *See* Driesen, *supra* note 8, at 183–87 (discussing error of treating regulations not encouraging innovation well as "barriers to innovation").

54. *See United States v. Ethyl Corp.,* 761 F.2d 1153, 1157 (5th Cir. 1985); 42 U.S.C. §§ 7521(g); 7502(c)(1); *Michigan v. Thomas,* 805 F.2d 176, 184–85 (6th Cir. 1986).

55. *See* Hahn and Stavins, *supra* note 1, at 5–6 ("A performance standard typically identifies a specific goal . . . and gives firms some latitude in meeting this target. These standards do not specify the means, and therefore, provide greater flexibility"); Stewart, *supra* note 9, at 1268 ("Performance standards allow regulated firms flexibility to select the least costly or least burdensome means of achieving compliance"). *Cf.* Stewart, *supra* note 1, at 158 ("Regulatory commands dictate specific behavior by each plant, facility, or product manufacturer").

56. Louis Tornatzky and Mitchell Fleischer, The Processes of Technological Innovation 101 (1990); Malloy, *supra* note 11, at 546–47 and n. 52 (performance standards have the express purpose of "encouraging innovation").

57. *See* 42 U.S.C. §§ 7411(h)(1); 7412(d)(2)(D), (h)(1)–(2), (h)(4).

58. *See* 42 U.S.C. §§7412(h)(3); 7411(h)(3).

59. *See, e.g.,* 42 U.S.C. §7412(d)(2); *Michigan v. Thomas,* 805 F.2d 176, 180 (6th Cir. 1986); *International Harvester Co. v. Ruckelshaus,* 478 F.2d 615, 628–29 (D.C. Cir. 1973).

60. *See, e.g., Sierra Club v. Costle,* 657 F.2d 298, 360–69 (D.C. Cir. 1981). Usually statutory provisions do allow the EPA to take cost and some other factors into consideration. *See, e.g., id.* at 319–36.

61. *See, e.g.,* 33 U.S.C. §1314(b)(1)(A), (b)(2)(A); *E.I. du Pont de Nemours v. Train,* 430 U.S. 112, 122 and n. 9 (1977); *American Petroleum Inst. v. EPA,* 787 F.2d 965, 972 (5th Cir. 1986); *Association of Pac. Fisheries v. EPA,* 615 F.2d 794, 802 (9th Cir. 1980); *American Paper Inst. v. Train,* 543 F.2d 328, 340–42 (D.C. Cir. 1976); *American Iron & Steel Inst. v. EPA,* 526 F.2d 1027, 1045 (3d. Cir. 1975), modified, 560 F.2d 589 (3d. Cir. 1977).

62. *See* Bruce A. Ackerman and William T. Hassler, Clean Coal/Dirty Air 15–21 (1981).

63. Compare Hahn and Stavins, *supra* note 1, at 5 with Bruce A. Ackerman and William T. Hassler, *Beyond the New Deal: Coal and the Clean Air Act,* 89 Yale Law Journal 1466, 1481–88 (1980) (discussing NSPS that allegedly mandated flue gas scrubbing); Ackerman and Hassler, *supra* note 62, at 15–21 (same).

64. *Sierra Club v. Costle,* 657 F.2d 298, 312 (D.C. Cir. 1981).

65. *Id.* at 324, 327–28, 340–43, 346–47.

66. *See id.* at 368–73; Ackerman and Hassler, *supra* note 63, at 1481; Bruce A. Ackerman and William T. Hassler, *Beyond the New Deal: Reply,* 90 Yale Law Journal 1412, 1421–22 n. 43 (1981). *Cf.* Howard Latin, *Ideal versus Real Regulatory Efficiency: Implementation of Uniform Standards and "Fine-Tuning" Regulatory Reforms,* 37 Stanford Law Review 1267, 1277 n. 41 (1985) (noting that standard allows using coal washing as offset, decreasing the percentage reduction needed from scrubbing); Ackerman and Hassler, *supra* note 52, at 15, 66–68 (noting that coal washing reduces any given emissions base by only 20–40 percent, but replacing new source standards with less stringent reduction requirement that also applies to existing sources would produce better results)

67. *Sierra Club,* 657 F.2d at 316 (emphasis added).

68. *See* Kerr, *supra* note 43, at 66.

69. Hahn and Hester, *supra* note 51, at 111 (monitoring and enforcement issues play critical role in efficient design of emissions trading); Sidney A. Shapiro and Thomas O. McGarity, *Not so Paradoxical: The Rationale for Technology-Based Regulation,* 1991 Duke Law Journal 729, 748–49 (1991) ("emissions trading and

pollution taxes require inspectors to monitor constantly the amount of pollution that a plant emits"); Stewart, *supra* note 1, at 161, 166.

70. Stewart, *supra* note 9, at 1269.

71. Driesen, *Dichotomy, supra* note 2, at 302 n. 65; Nicholas A. Ashford and George R. Heaton Jr., *Regulation and Technological Innovation in the Chemical Industry*, 46 Law and Comtemporary Problems, 109, 139–40 (1983).

72. *See* Jaffe et al., *supra* note 1, at 55 (because of a "paucity of available data," there has been "exceptionally little empirical analysis" of instrument choice's effect on innovation); Malloy, *supra* note 12, at 547 (empirical evidence provides "inconclusive evidence of significant environmental innovation under existing trading programs.")

73. *See* Kurt Strasser, *Cleaner Technology, Pollution Prevention, and Environmental Regulation*, 9 Fordham Environmental Law Journal 1, 32 (1997) (innovation sometimes results from emission and discharge limits). *See, e.g.,* U.S. Congress, Office of Technology Assessment, Gauging Control Technology and Regulatory Impacts in Occupational Safety and Health—An Appraisal of OSHA's Analytical Approach, OTA-ENV-635, at 64 (U.S. Government Printing Office 1995) [hereinafter OTA Study]; Ashford and Heaton, *supra* note 71, at 109, 139–40.

74. OTA Study, *supra* note 73, at 89. Nicholas A. Ashford et al., *Using Regulation to Change the Market for Innovation*, 9 Harvard Environmental Law Review 419, 440–41 (1985).

75. OTA Study, *supra* note 73, at 90.

76. *Id.* at 95. OSHA anticipated this possibility, but not the extent to which it dominated compliance strategies.

77. *See* Strasser, *supra* note 73, at 28–29.

78. *See* Ozone Depletion in the United States: Elements of Success (Elizabeth Cook, ed. 1996).

79. *See id.* at 14–15, 23–26, 58–60, 90–94, 98–104, 109.

80. *See* U.S. EPA, *Benefits of the CFC Phaseout, at* www.epa.gov/ozone/geninfo/benefits.html (last visited Jan. 24, 2001) (citing "aqueous cleaning" as an example of a cleaning process that reduced cost in phasing out CFCs); ICOLP Technical Committee, Eliminating CFC-113 and Methyl Chloroform in Precision Cleaning Operations 114 (1994) (defining "aqueous cleaning" as cleaning parts with water to which suitable detergents, sapnifers, or other additives may be added).

81. *See* Ashford et al., *supra* note 74, at 437 (describing separation of process from cooling water to reduce contact with mercury as a "significant process innovation").

82. Thomas O. McGarity, *Radical Technology-Forcing in Environmental Regulation*, 27 Loyola of Los Angeles Law Review 943, 947 (1994) (discussing experience with lead and pesticide bans).

83. *See generally* Adam B. Jaffe et al., Environmental Regulation and International Competitiveness: What Does the Evidence Tell Us? (1993) (regulation's economic impact to minor to have great impact on competitiveness). *See also* Stephen M. Meyer, Environmentalism and Economic Prosperity: Testing the Environmental Impact Hypothesis (Oct. 5, 1992) (unpublished manuscript).

84. *See, e.g.,* Environmental Law Institute, Barriers to Environmental Technology Innovation and Use (1998).

85. *See* Malloy, *supra* note 12, at 549–50; Ashford et al., *supra* note 74, at 432–44 (discussing examples); McGarity, *supra* note 82, at 945–52 (discussing experience with lead and pesticide bans).

86. *See* Richard A. Liroff, Air Pollution Offsets: Trading Selling and Banking 28–29 (1980) (noting the need to avoid "paper offsets," reductions in emissions that exist only on paper). *See* generally Dudek and Palmisano, *supra* note 1, at 236–37 (noting that emissions trading has been the "harbinger of bad news").

87. For example, when the EPA and its California counterpart inspected plants to verify compliance with bubble regulations for the aerospace industry in the late 1980s, they found that "almost all large sources operating under... bubbles... are not achieving the emission reductions or levels of control that are required." *See* California Air Resources Board and U.S. EPA, Phase III Rule Effectiveness Study of the Aerospace Coating Industry 4 (1990) (unpublished report); *see also* David Doniger, *The Dark Side of the Bubble,* 4 Environmental Law Forum 33, 34–35 (1985); Richard A. Liroff, Reforming Air Pollution Regulation: The Toil and Trouble of EPA's Bubble 80–89 (1986) (examples of bubbles that avoided requirements to reduce actual emission levels). Hahn and Hester have concluded that emissions trading (defined to include bubbling and netting) has had "a negligible effect on environmental quality." Hahn and Hester, *supra* note 51, at 137. They do not, however, base this assertion on empirical data. Rather, they rely "on the fact that the rules governing the various trading programs contain prohibitions against trades that would result in significant increases in emissions." *Id.* at 137 n. 146. They do not explain the basis for their belief that these rules are adequate and the implicit assumption that they have been regularly and correctly enforced. In any case, subsequent experience suggests they have not prevented abuse.

88. Liroff provides many examples of these bubbles. *See* Liroff, *supra* note 87, at 62–67, 89–91.

89. *See id.* at 37–38 (describing genesis of the bubble idea in the steel industry).

90. *Id.* at 100 (most "innovations" under bubbles are merely rearrangements of conventional technologies).

91. *See id.* at 99 ("cost saving approaches are not necessarily more cost-effective ways of meeting a goal, instead, they may be ways to avoid costs that may be necessary to meet the goal"); Richard A. Liroff, *Point and Counterpoint: The Bubble: Will it Float Free or Deflate* 4 Environmental Forum 28, 30 (Mar. 1986) (stating that a compliance method that relaxes regulatory requirements at some points without compensating reductions may be more prevalent than bubbles that reduce actual emissions); David D. Doniger, *Point... and Counterpoint,* 4 Environmental Forum 29, 34 ("In practice... there has been far more innovation in shell games and sharp accounting practices than in pollution control technology"); *Proposed Open Market Trading Rule for Ozone Smog Precursors,* 60 Federal Register 39668, 39670 (Aug. 3, 1995) ("Bubbles, netting and offsets have reduced source's overall compliance costs. However, there have been significant problems of quality control, reducing the environmental effectiveness of the programs").

92. For accounts of the program, *see* Suzi Kerr and David Mare, *Market Efficiency in Tradeable Permit Markets with Transaction Costs: Empirical Evidence from the United States Lead Phasedown* in Kerr, *supra* note 43; Robert W. Hahn and Gordon L. Hester, *Marketable Permits: Lessons for Theory and Practice,* 16 Ecology Law Quarterly 361, 380–91 (1989); Kerr and Newell, *supra* note 5.

93. The introduction of interrefinery trading into the lead phasedown program probably slowed the pace of environmental improvement. The EPA's 1985 trading rule actually led to increased production of leaded gasoline in 1985 (rather than purely unleaded) because the rule allowed increased production of low-lead gasoline to generate credits. *See Regulation of Fuels and Fuel Additives; Banking of*

Lead Rights, 50 Federal Register 13116, 13119 (Apr. 2, 1985); Hahn and Hester, *supra* note 92, at 382 n. 125; U.S. General Accounting Office, Vehicle Emissions: EPA Program to Assist Leaded Gasoline Producers 20 (1986) [hereinafter GAO, Vehicle Emissions]. The EPA's 1985 lead trading rule supplanted a rule that required refiners to meet a standard of 1.1 grams of lead per leaded gallon, effective January 1, 1986. 50 Federal Register at 13116. The 1985 trading rule allowed refiners that banked purchased credits to continue exceeding these limits through the end of 1987. 50 Federal Register at 13177, 13127 (codified at 40 C.F.R. §80.20(e)(2)). Furthermore, in actual implementation inadequate reporting, compliance verification, and enforcement may have marred environmental performance. *See* GAO, Vehicle Emissions at 3–4, 18–19, 23–24 (citing failure to enforce against twenty-five potential violators, forty-nine cases of claimed credits not matching claimed sales of credits, error rates in reporting between 14 percent and 49.2 percent and no verification of compliance). *Cf.* Hahn and Hester, *supra* note 92, at 388, n. 146.

94. *See* Kerr and Newell, *supra* note 5, at 320 (emphasis added).

95. *Id.* at 320.

96. *See,* e.g., Byron Swift, *Command without Control: Why Cap-and-Trade Should Replace Rate Standards for Regional Pollutants,* 31 Environmental Law Review 10330 (Mar. 2001).

97. *Id.* at 10331.

98. Swift does claim that trading was essential to two technologies. *Id.* at 10338. One of those technologies, trading, is a transaction, not a technology. He does not claim that the other technology, power shifting, is an innovation. Indeed, the shifting of dispatch orders to use cleaner units more intensively than dirty units is a well-understood operational option.

99. *See* generally Malloy, *supra* note 12, at 548–49 (discussing debate about innovation under the Acid Rain Program).

100. Other publications also employ very broad definitions of innovation and stop short of attributing the observed innovations to trading alone. For example, Dallas Burtraw describes various kinds of nonpatentable practices as innovations. Dallas Burtraw, Innovation under the Tradable Sulfur Dioxide Emission Permits Program in the U.S. Electricity Sector 17 (Resources for the Future Discussion Paper 00–38, 2000). These include rather routine adaptations to the opportunity to sell abatement technologies, which one would expect with a comparably designed performance standard. For example, he describes laying track and changing the size of trains (to deliver low-sulfur coal) as innovations. *See id.* at 19. He makes no effort to determine whether the minority of firms engaged in trading employed these innovations more vigorously than firms that simply complied as if this were a standard technology-based performance standard expressed as a mass-based limit. The paper's conclusion, consistent with the limitations of this mode of study, does not claim that emissions trading induced innovation. Instead, he claims that the Acid Rain Program contributes to the employment of innovation. *See id.* at 18. But this simply begs the question of whether a mass-based program with the same limits and no trading would induce as much or more innovation.

101. *See* Margaret R. Taylor, Edward S. Rubin, and David A. Hounshell, *Regulation as the Mother of Innovation: The Case of SO$_2$ Control,* 27 Law and Policy 348, 370 (2005).

102. *See* David Popp, *Pollution Control Innovations and the Clean Air Act of 1990,* 22 Journal of Policy Analysis and Management 641 (2003).

103. *See* A. Denny Ellerman et al., Markets for Clean Air: The U.S. Acid Rain Program 130 (2000).

104. *See* Curtis Moore, RECLAIM: Southern California's Failed Experiment with Air Pollution Trading 2 (2003) (describing RECLAIM as a failure in reducing emissions); Richard Toshiyuki Drury et al., *Pollution Trading and Environmental Injustice: Los Angeles' Failed Experiment in Air Quality Policy*, 9 Duke Environmental Law and Policy Forum 231 (1999); *Approval and Promulgation of Air Quality Implementation Plans; New Jersey; Open Market Emissions Trading Program*, 67 Federal Register 64347 (October 18, 2002) (announcing the EPA decision not to proceed with processing New Jersey SIP revisions, because New Jersey had found such serious problems in its emissions trading program that it was planning to abandon it).

105. *See* Nescaum, Power Companies' Efforts to Comply with the NO_X SIP CA; and Section 126, 4 (2003) (61 of 100 units with announced commitments have chose selective catalytic reduction).

106. *See* Drury et al., *supra* note 104, at 258–63 (discussing fraud in the estimation of credits and debits that systematically undermines environmental performance).

107. *See* EPA, An Evaluation of South Cost Air Quality Management District's Clean Air Incentives Market—Lessons in Environmental Markets and Innovation 26–27 (2002).

108. *See id.* at 21, 27 (relying on design variables other than the trading possibility to explain the innovation).

109. *See* Taylor, Rubin, and Hounshell, *supra* note 101, at 369 (most improvement in sulfur dioxide control efficiency occurred before the 1990 amendments).

110. *Cf.* Kerr and Newell, *supra* note 5, at 320 (explaining that stringency induced innovation in the lead program).

111. *See* Swift, *supra* note 3; Driesen, *supra* note 8, at 193–97.

112. *See* Driesen, *supra* note 8.

113. *See, e.g.,* Jaffe et al., *supra* note 1, at 49.

114. *Cf.* Nathaniel O. Keohane et al., *The Choice of Regulatory Instruments in Environmental Policy*, 22 Harvard Environmental Law Review, 313, 348 (1998) (explaining that polluters' preferences have generally prevented enactment of pollution taxes); James M. Buchanan and Gordon M. Tullock, *Polluters' Profits and Political Response: Direct Control Versus Taxes*, 65 American Economic Review 139, 141–42 (1975) (explaining why polluters oppose pollution taxes); Driesen, *Dichotomy, supra* note 2, at 340–43 (describing various impediments to setting tax rates for pollution).

115. It has received some attention. *See, e.g.,* Stewart, *supra* note 38, at 12 n. 31 (fees from a pollution tax could be used to subsidize pollution reduction); Robert W. Hahn, *Economic Prescriptions for Environmental Problems: How the Patient Followed the Doctor's Orders*, 3 Journal of Economic Perspectives 95, 104–7 (describing effluent taxes dedicated to funding environmental improvement); Mikael Skou Andersen, Governancy by Green Taxes: Making Pollution Prevention Pay (1994) (advocating earmarking of green taxes to fund pollution reduction).

116. T. H. Tietenburg, *Using Economic Incentives to Maintain our Environment*, Challenge, Mar./Apr. 1990, at 42, 43.

117. *See* Nathanael Greene and Vanessa Ward, *Getting the Sticker Price Right: Incentives for Cleaner, More Efficient Vehicles*, 12 Pace Environmental Law Review 91, 94–97 (1994).

118. *See* New Hampshire Representative Jeffrey C. MacGillivray and Kenneth Colburn, Director, New Hampshire Department of Environmental Services, A New Approach to Air Pollution Regulation, Industry-Average Performance Systems (IAPS) (1997).

119. *See* Tornatzky and Fleischer, *supra* note 56, at 168 (intense competition tends to stimulate spread of innovation).

120. I have sketched this idea previously in Driesen, *Dichotomy, supra* note 2, at 344–47 and Driesen, *supra* note 11, at 10288–10290. The idea receives a fuller defense in Driesen, *supra* note 8, at 151–61, 163, 213. An EPA economist has recently offered a "feebate" proposal for electric utility that bears some resemblance to my proposal. *See* Andrew M. Ballard, *Fee/Rebate System May Offer Flexibility in Reducing Emissions, EPA Economist Tells Conference,* 33 Environmental Report (BNA) 1437 (June 28, 2002).

121. *See* Anderson et al., Environmental Improvement through Economic Incentives 3–4 (1977).

122. An environmental competition statute might seem to only create incentives to reduce first and do nothing to motivate reductions from slow movers. But the dynamic such a program creates, like the dynamic of a free market, works more broadly than that. Nobody would know a priori who the first movers would be. This means that anybody who didn't actively seek emission reductions would risk financial loss of uncertain dimension, precisely the risk companies face when they fail to innovate in making new products (or improving old ones) in a competitive market.

123. Companies might conclude that they would rather collude to avoid such a scheme than compete to earn money from it. All of the companies subject to the statute could defeat it by deciding to do nothing. To prevent this collusion, lawmakers might restrict communication between companies regarding their plans under the law.

124. *See, e.g., "Clear Skies" Legislation to Cut Emissions from Power Plants Introduced in Congress,* 33 Environmental Report (BNA) 1693, 1694 (Aug. 2, 2002) (both Jefford's bill and the Bush administration's Clear Skies proposal rely on a cap-and-trade approach, says Holmstead).

Index